I0824258

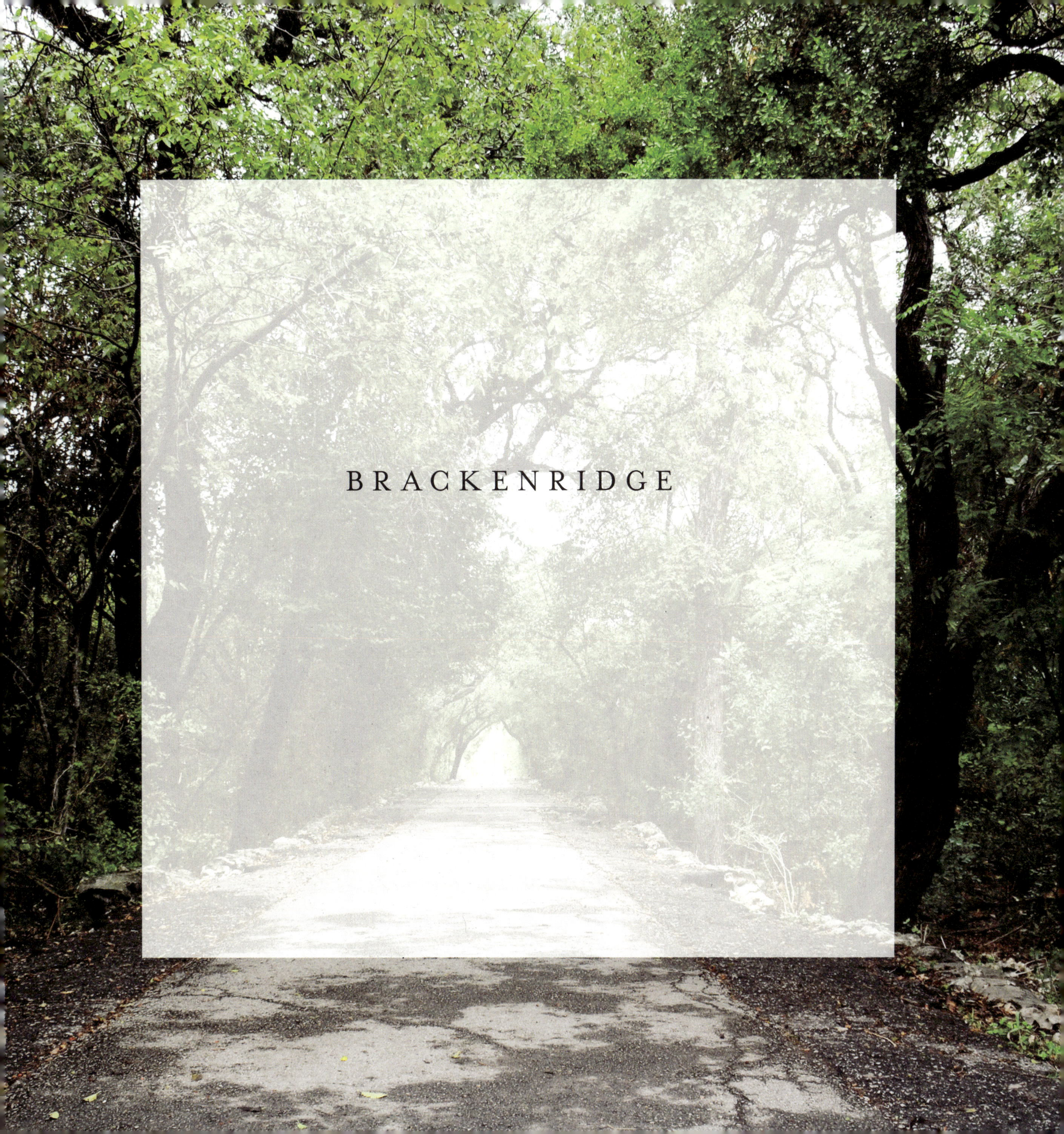

BRACKENRIDGE

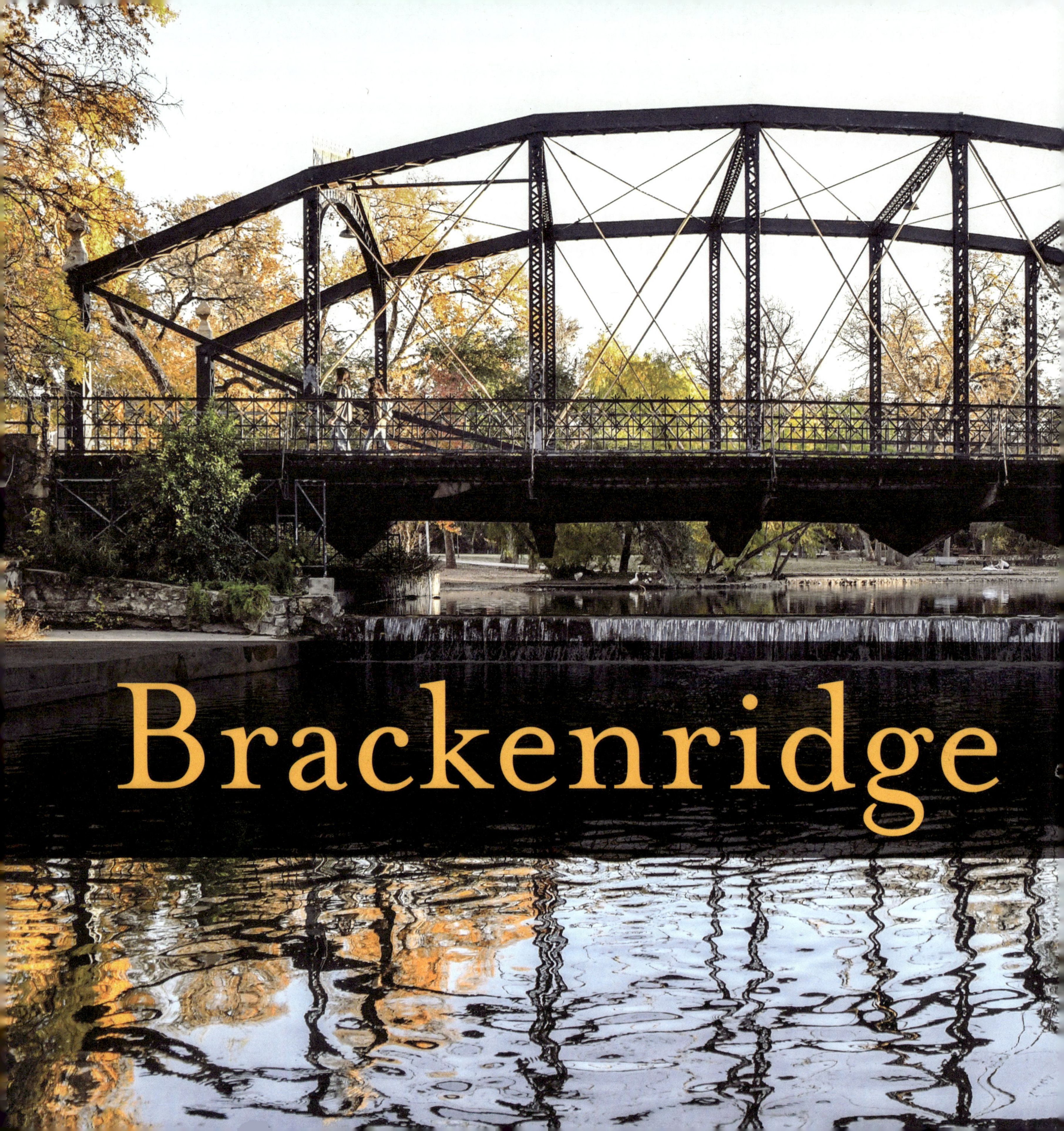
Brackenridge

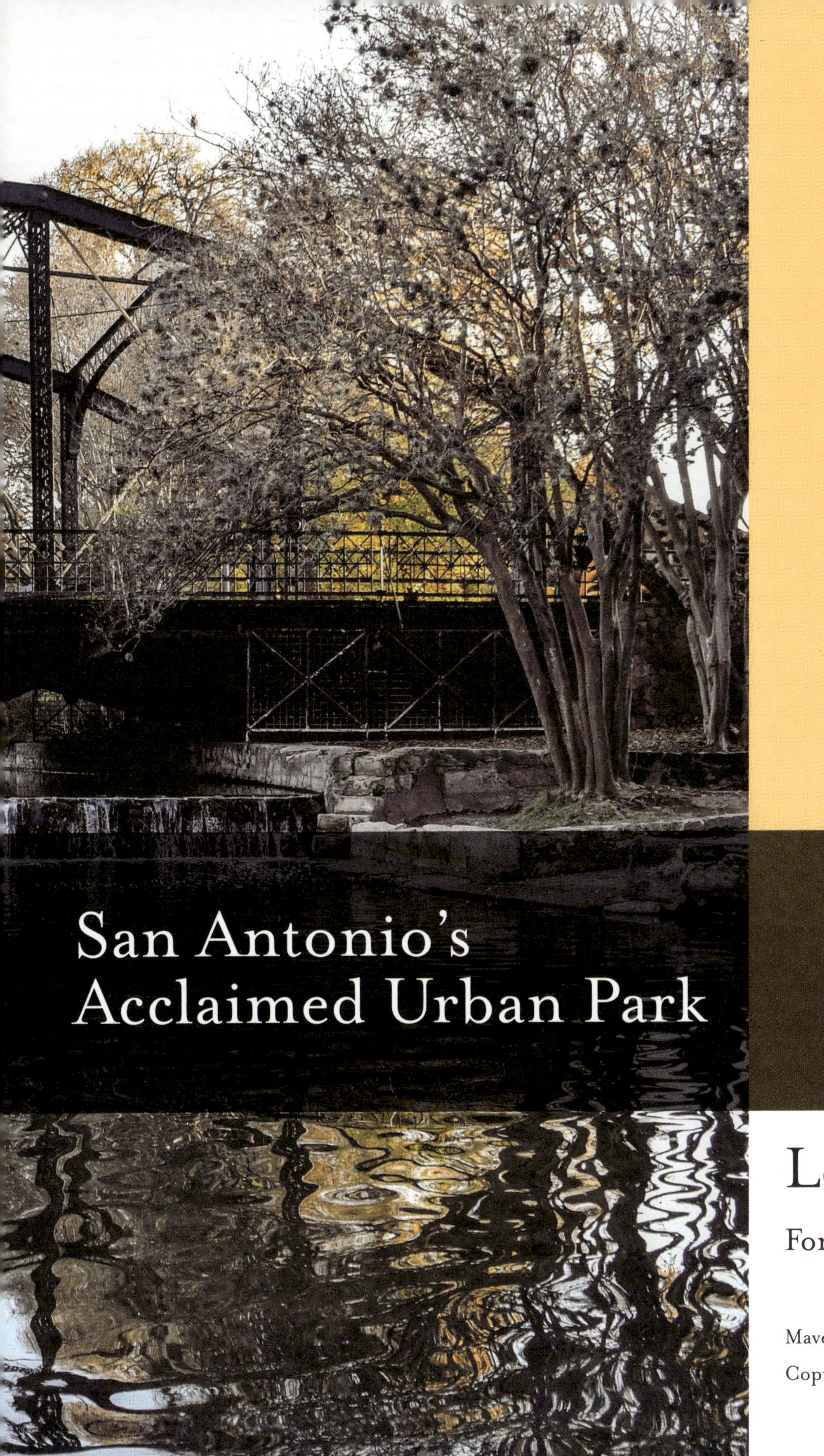

San Antonio's Acclaimed Urban Park

Lewis F. Fisher

Foreword by Charles A. Birnbaum

Maverick Books / Trinity University Press
Copublished with the Brackenridge Park Conservancy

Published by
Maverick Books, an imprint of
Trinity University Press
San Antonio, Texas 78212
and the Brackenridge Park Conservancy

Book design by Anne Richmond Boston
Cover: "San Antonio's Gem," by Daira Austin. San Antonio River in Brackenridge Park
Frontis: Photograph by Charlotte Mitchell. An iron bridge built across the San Antonio River at Saint Mary's Street downtown in 1890 was moved to Brackenridge Park in 1925

ISBN 978-1-59534-966-8 hardcover
ISBN 978-1-59534-967-5 ebook

Trinity University Press strives to produce its books using methods and materials in an environmentally sensitive manner. We favor working with manufacturers that practice sustainable management of all natural resources, produce paper using recycled stock, and manage forests with the best possible practices for people, biodiversity, and sustainability. The press is a member of the Green Press Initiative, a nonprofit program dedicated to supporting publishers in their efforts to reduce their impacts on endangered forests, climate change, and forest-dependent communities.

The paper used in this publication meets the minimum requirements of the American National Standard for Information Sciences—Permanence of Paper for Printed Library Materials, ansi 39.48–1992.

Printed in Canada

CIP data on file at the Library of Congress
26 25 24 23 22 | 5 4 3 2 1

Publication of this book was made possible by the generous support of the Semmes Foundation

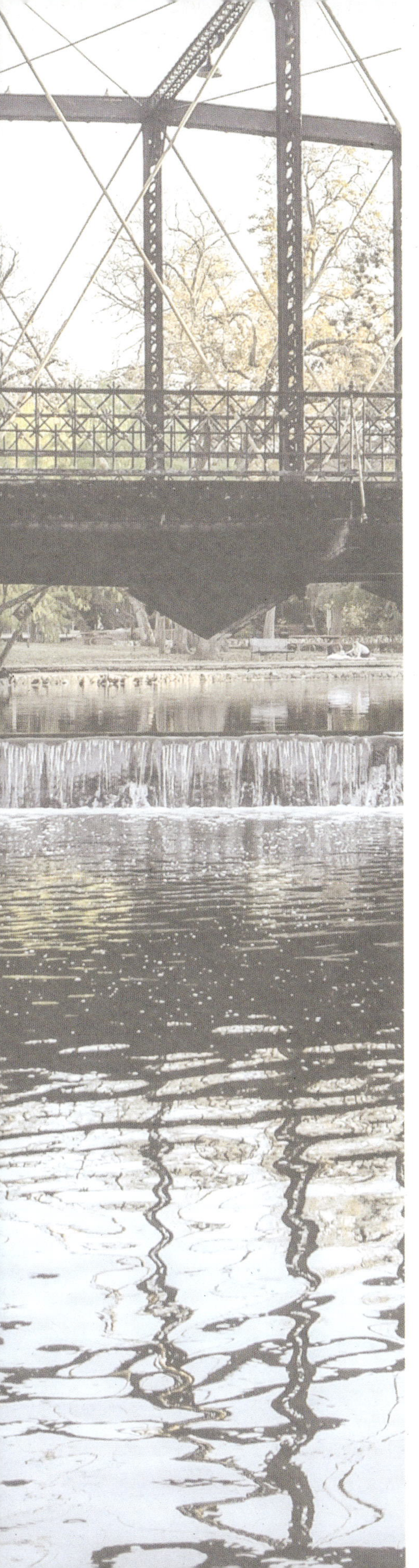

Contents

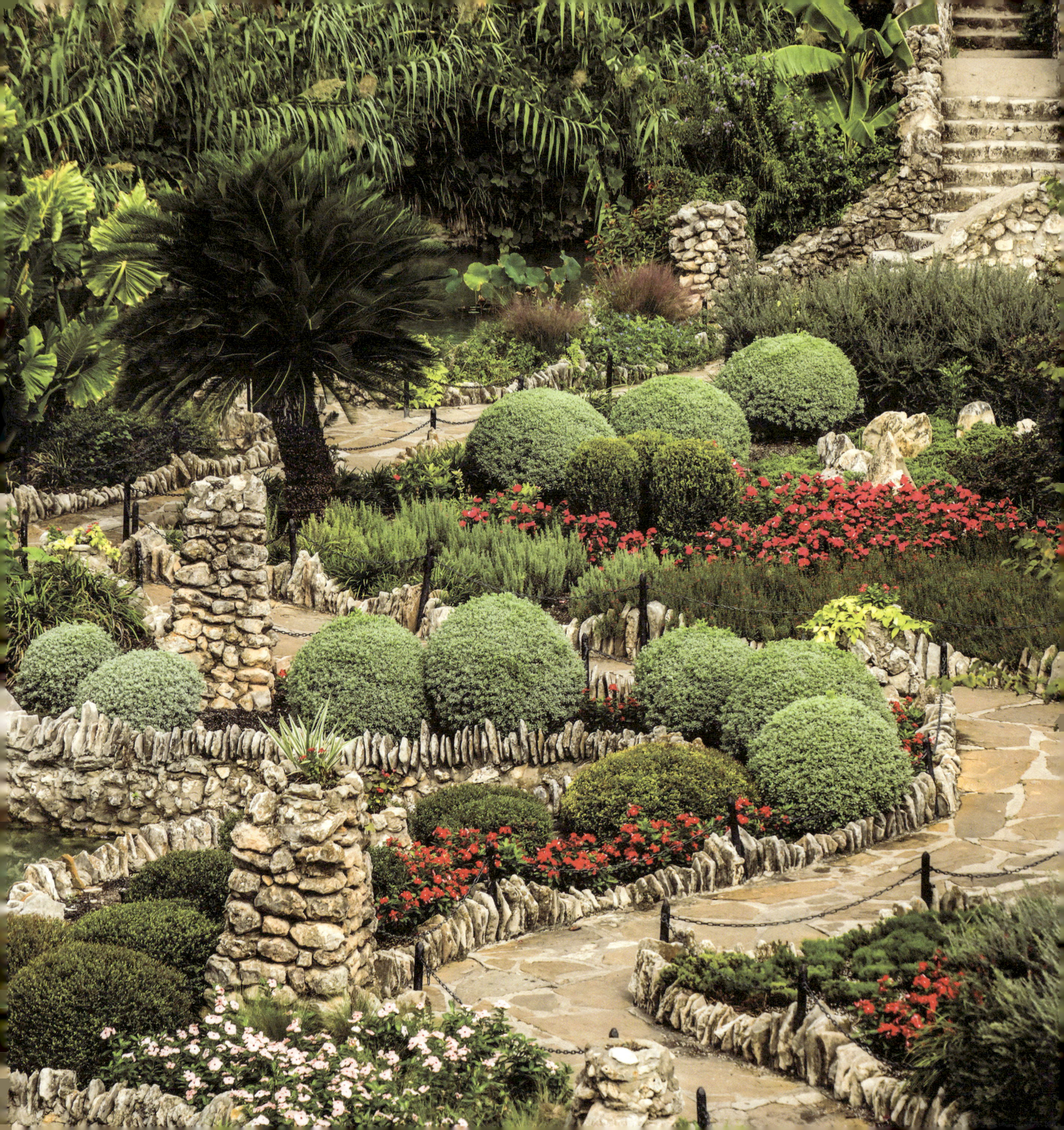

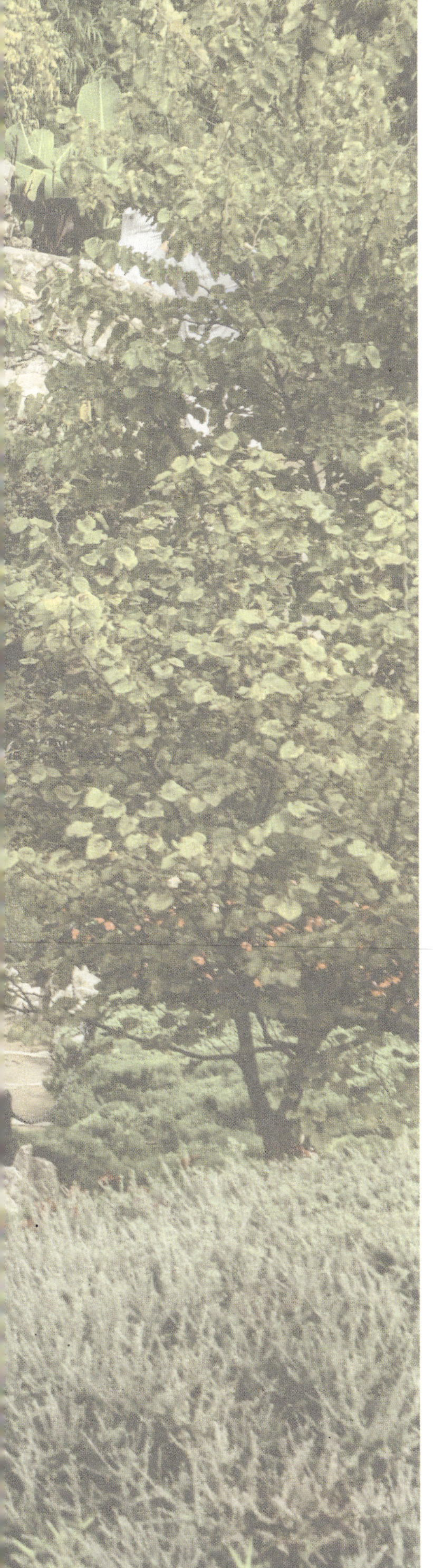

Foreword

Charles A. Birnbaum

When the great park maker Frederick Law Olmsted Sr. visited San Antonio in 1854 he noted: "We have no city, except, perhaps New Orleans, that can vie, in point of the picturesque interest that attaches to odd and antiquated foreignness, with San Antonio. Its jumble of races, costumes, languages and buildings; its religious ruins, holding to an antiquity, for us, indistinct enough to breed an unaccustomed solemnity; its remote, isolated, outposted situation, and the vague conviction that it is the first of a new class of conquered cities into whose decaying streets our rattling life is to be infused, combine with the heroic touches in its history to enliven and satisfy your traveler's curiosity."

Five years before his life changed with his competition-winning Greensward plan for Central Park in New York City, the thirty-one-year-old Olmsted experienced firsthand a young San Antonio—a relatively inaccessible city whose diverse residents had affected, influenced, and literally shaped its built and natural environment.

This is what a cultural landscape looks like.

In 1850, a few years before Olmsted's visit, the city's first census was undertaken. It documented 716 families with 3,168 people living in San Antonio. Demographically, the population was mixed: 53 percent Hispanic (including 24 percent Tejanos and 29 percent native Mexican), 23 percent "natives of Europe," and 23 percent "natives of the United States." By 1850, slaveholding had increased; 8 percent of heads of households were slaveholders, and 220 people, representing about 6 percent of the population, were enslaved. (It's worth comparing this statistic with the state during the same period; 27.4 percent of the state's population was documented as enslaved at the time.)

Today San Antonio's population of more than 1.58 million is Texas's second largest after Houston when suburban areas are excluded from the count. According to the recent census, San Antonio's demographics are as mixed as in the 1850 census: 64.2 percent Hispanic, 24.7 percent White, 6.95 percent Black, and 2.83 percent Asian. For this reason, the city is a cultural landscape steeped in a continuity of ethnographic associations that go beyond material artifacts.

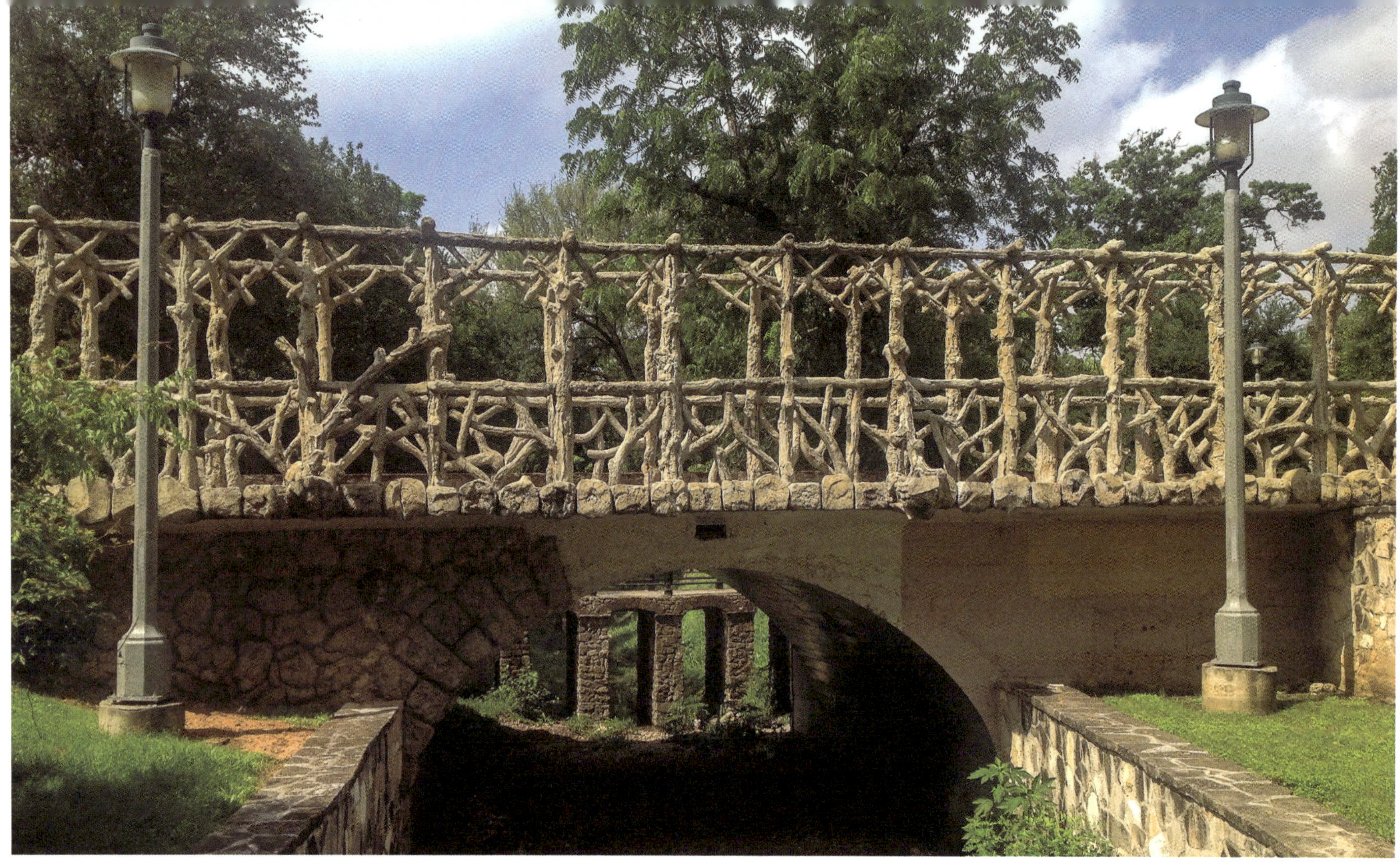

At least four layers of Brackenridge Park's past are visible in this image, overlooking the dry 1878 raceway from the river to the upper pump house. The iconic *trabajo rústico* arbor top center was designed by Dionicio Rodríguez as a pedestrian bridge. It is next to the 1878 Water Works vehicular bridge, with part of its original rock arch showing center left. Visible through the arch is a 1920s stone span that took the donkey trail over the raceway. Retaining walls and lights were added during park renovations in 2003.

I believe the definition of a city includes cultural lifeways and their associated significant historic resources. For example, the five missions in San Antonio were listed as World Heritage Sites in 2015 because of their geographical and functional relationship with the San Antonio River Basin and their unique and deep natural and cultural histories. The four-hundred-acre Brackenridge Park has a similar relationship as chronicled in Lewis F. Fisher's *Brackenridge*, which recognizes that the park's cultural landscape displays a remarkable twelve thousand years of documented prehistoric and human engagement with the upper course of the San Antonio River.

"The San Antonio Spring," Olmsted wrote, "may be classed as of the first water among the gems of the natural world. The whole river gushes up in one sparkling burst from the earth. . . . The effect is overpowering. It is beyond your possible conceptions of a spring."

Olmsted's cultural observations were penned four decades before Yosemite became a national park in 1890 and half a century before Brackenridge became a municipal park. What Olmsted described, and Fisher illuminates, is central to the work that the Brackenridge Park Conservancy is today advancing through a holistic way of seeing the park—a way of seeing that recognizes that nature and culture are inextricably intertwined and that present-day stewardship (from interpretation to how we assign significance and value) must recognize and support this.

Brackenridge Park's place in American landscape history is not only little understood, but also largely absent from most textbooks. The same can be said of San Pedro Springs Park, which Olmsted described as a "wooded spot of great beauty" following his 1854 visit, four years before Central Park opened to the public. Furthermore, San Pedro Springs, like Brackenridge Park, is not the creation of a nationally recognized designer like Olmsted and Vaux (Central Park). In fact, if we were to ask the general public or students of landscape architecture to name three iconic American parks they would likely cite Central and Prospect Parks (New York City), Fairmount Park (Philadelphia), or Golden Gate Park (San Francisco). People from the heartland might mention Jackson Park (Chicago), Swope Park (Kansas City), or Forest Park (Saint Louis). All of those parks can be attributed to pioneering landscape architects, and each reflects its respective practitioner's design intent.

This book, when coupled with the recent Cultural Landscape Report for Brackenridge Park prepared by Reed Hilderbrand and Suzanne Turner Associates, represents an interdisciplinary systems-based approach that is foundational to reconsidering Brackenridge Park today. It is the most significant urban cultural park owned by a local municipality, as opposed to the state or federal government. Thanks to this book and the purposeful efforts of the Brackenridge Park Conservancy, we can gain a deeper understanding of how this cultural landscape has long served as a gathering place, from the time Native peoples first inhabited the area through the sixteenth century when Spanish settlers established a sophisticated water system, traces of which remain today.

Fisher's rich narrative also reveals George W. Brackenridge's extraordinary act of patronage in 1899 when he donated two hundred acres to the city for recreational use. While similar contemporaneous civic gestures can be documented in Dallas, Houston, and other cities, that work involved the creation of new parks by landscape architects like George Kessler and Hare and Hare, not the retention of built historic fabric.

In addition to the pre-park history, Fisher lays out the park's twentieth-century evolution, which began with city park commissioner Ludwig Mahncke, a friend of Brackenridge who had encouraged the land donation. Mahncke established the park's wild game preserve and developed curvilinear paths and drives that meandered through the trees along the river. He was followed in 1915 by Commissioner Ray Lambert, who used local rough-cut stone for walls and structures throughout the park, conveying its distinctly rustic character. Lambert also in 1915 transformed rocky lands nearby into the thirty-five-acre San Antonio Zoo; established in 1916 what is now the state's oldest municipal golf course, designed by A. W. Tillinghast and largely restored by John Colligan; and in 1917 converted a former limestone quarry into the Japanese Tea Garden, with assistance from local artist Kimi Eizo Jingu.

Lambert's other contributions include the Joske Pavilion in 1926, and the beginnings of the Sunken Garden Theater, carved out of another abandoned quarry, in the 1930s. The park retains its rustic charm, with tree-lined paths, places for picnicking, playgrounds and athletic fields, and a two-mile miniature railway, as well as the Japanese Tea Garden, an elongated arbor designed by the celebrated *faux bois* artist Dionicio Rodríguez, and two Water Works Company pump houses, individually listed in the National Register of Historic Places.

For a city that is passionate about its history, Brackenridge Park has until recently been under the radar. Fortunately, Lewis Fisher's evocative narrative brings the park's rich palimpsest to life. The chapters that follow enhance the conservancy's mission as "a steward of and an advocate for the park." They invite park users, advocates, and first-time visitors to understand how the park connected to its physical and historical context over time, how the park was shaped, and how it has shaped us.

This is a cultural landscape. This is Brackenridge Park.

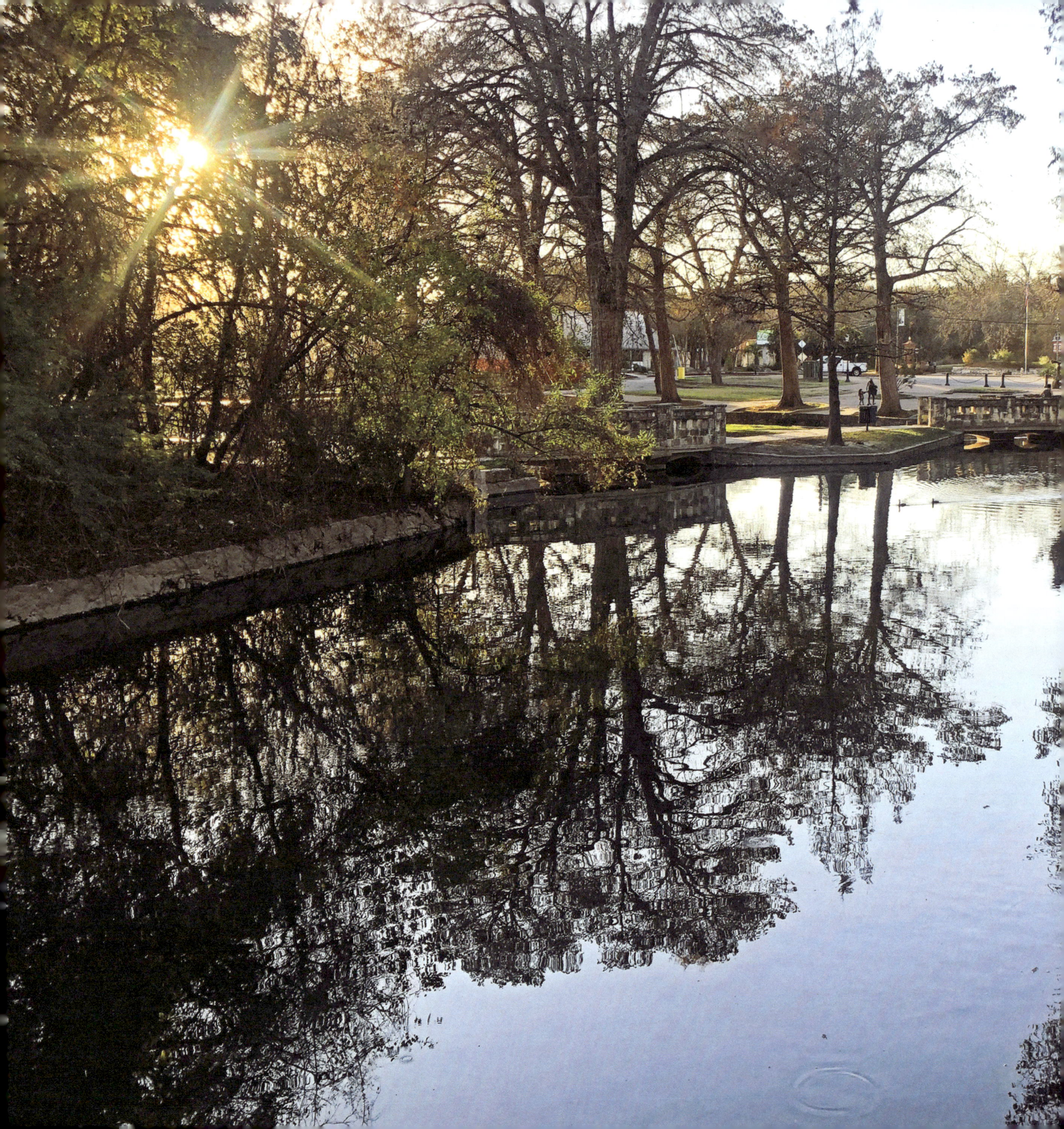

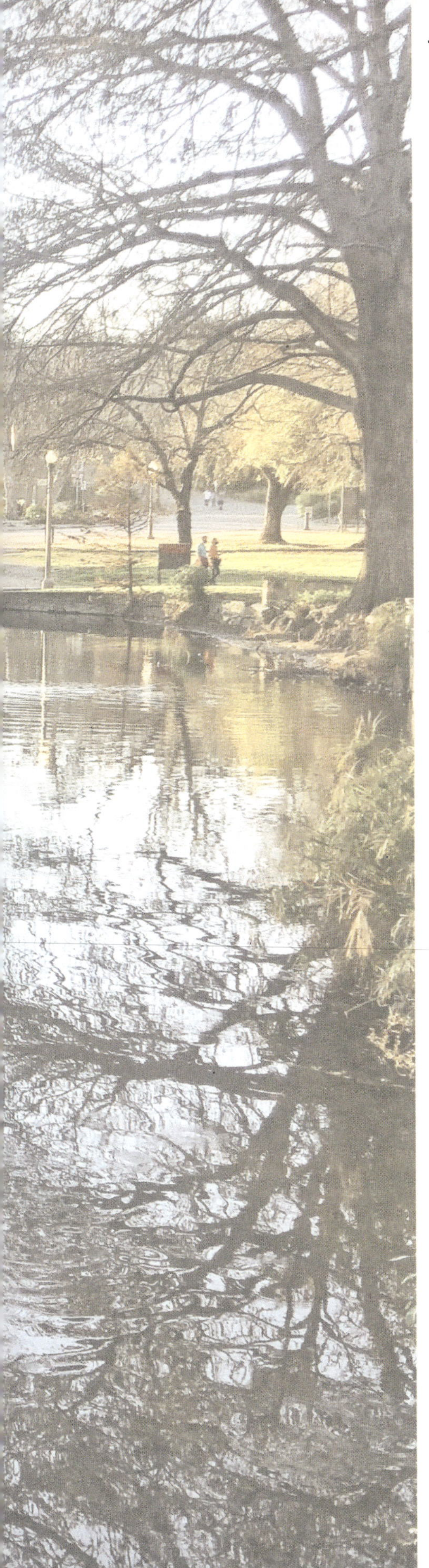

Introduction

"Palimpsest" is an uncommon word, one not often associated with public parks. Many of us have to look it up, a challenge since it's hard to spell.

Palimpsest is usually defined as parchment bearing layers of writing of ages past, when writing material was so costly that someone would take a sheet that had been written on, scrape off the old text, and inscribe something new in its place. That could happen again and again. Inevitably, traces were left of what was underneath.

Brackenridge Park was created in 1899. But on the park's surface it's not uncommon to find fragments of what remains from Native Americans—stone tools and projectile points left as long ago as twelve thousand years. As some scholars specialize in scientifically analyzing ancient manuscripts to learn what lies beneath the surface, so are archeologists, historians, planners, and environmental scientists now thorough as they probe the layered history of Brackenridge Park.

Brackenridge Park is newly ranked among the nation's foremost cultural parks. It is one of very few urban parks in the country whose evolution so closely reflects, layer by layer, the history and development of the city around it.

This distinction stems from Brackenridge Park's location near the headwaters springs of the San Antonio River. From the time the first Native Americans ventured across what became South Texas, the life-giving springs and river drew ongoing generations of passers-through and inhabitants. Shortly after San Antonio was founded in 1718, acequias dug south from two river diversion dams within the future park carried water to the Alamo mission and the town.

More than a century and a half later, San Antonio's first modern water system was powered by water-driven pumps near one of those dams. Other commercial enterprises within what would become Brackenridge Park—an ice factory, a cement plant, and one of the state's largest nurseries—also counted on the water. So did military installations—a Confederate army tannery during the Civil War plus two Spanish-American War–era regimental camps that needed to set up where ample water was available. Once the park was formed, the river's waters filled lily ponds and golf hazards, sustained animals in the zoo, and encouraged fishing, swimming, boating, and even baptisms.

National recognition was slow in coming to Brackenridge Park, long dismissed by leading authorities as of little significance for not having had the sort of distinguished master planner whose design flourishes gained renown for urban parks elsewhere. Instead, frugal San Antonio made do with city officials, whose uneven efforts produced the park's beloved crazy-quilt design.

First to try his hand in designing the park was alderman Ludwig Mahncke, a hotelier and onetime beer garden proprietor, with assistance from his friend and park donor George Washington Brackenridge. Both loved nature, but neither had background for the job. Brackenridge was a financier, and the closest Mahncke had to a landscaping credential was prior chairmanship of a city park committee.

Next came Ray Lambert, a stonecutter-turned-saloonkeeper who happened to be holding elective office when a change in city government gave oversight of municipal departments to specific aldermen/commissioners. Lambert took charge of city parks. Unpromising though his bona fides may have been, Ray Lambert met the moment.

Lambert dove into his new duties as parks commissioner with gusto; drawing from his enjoyment of natural landscapes while hunting and fishing. A series of innovative homegrown designs included his signature accomplishment—the "Japanese" Tea Garden, its focus a lily pond in an abandoned quarry pit. Lambert's low-budget projects, some built with the aid of prisoners from the city jail, added a touch of magic to the park.

Such a scattershot approach has caused Brackenridge Park to embody the sort of idiosyncrasies San Antonio has long been noted for, sometimes to the envy of more stodgy neighbors. The city grew in isolation on the frontier from 1718 until a railroad finally connected San Antonio with the rest of the world in 1877. That year a newspaper in the up-to-date city of Houston explained away San Antonio's sudden flood of tourists by tartly commenting that "many came on pleasure only for a day to peep at the old town, and then go away to tell how queer it looked."[1]

While cities elsewhere thrived with booming economies and industries that could fund great institutions and lavish civic amenities, San Antonio struggled with an economic base so thin that only one of its nineteenth-century citizens—banker George Brackenridge—approached the level of tycoon, though his wealth paled in comparison with the industrial fortunes of the Northeast.

Progressive residents worked toward a time when a no longer antiquated San Antonio would gain respect as a modern city. But more citizens than not were averse to being taxed to build for the future. And rather than keeping precise records they turned to tall tales and oral tradition, leaving later generations with mare's nests to sort out in determining what had actually gone on.

One victim of the long-term imprecision has been Brackenridge Park. It seems less a clearly drawn entity than a state of mind, with a patchwork recorded story and ill-defined boundaries. Its presence is glimpsed along heavily traveled Broadway between gaps in a built-up fringe long dominated by second-hand shops, motels, and fast-food restaurants. Of eight park entrances only three have signs identifying entry—one on a low wall near the Witte Museum, one for the golf course alone, and the third, on Broadway across from Mahncke Park, at an entrance so inconvenient that hardly anyone uses it. If you try a former entrance on Broadway oddly marked "George W. Brackenridge," you discover that it dead-ends at a side road.

You think you're finally in the middle of Brackenridge Park when an impressive red sandstone gate suddenly announces the presence instead of Otto Koehler Park. Since there's no

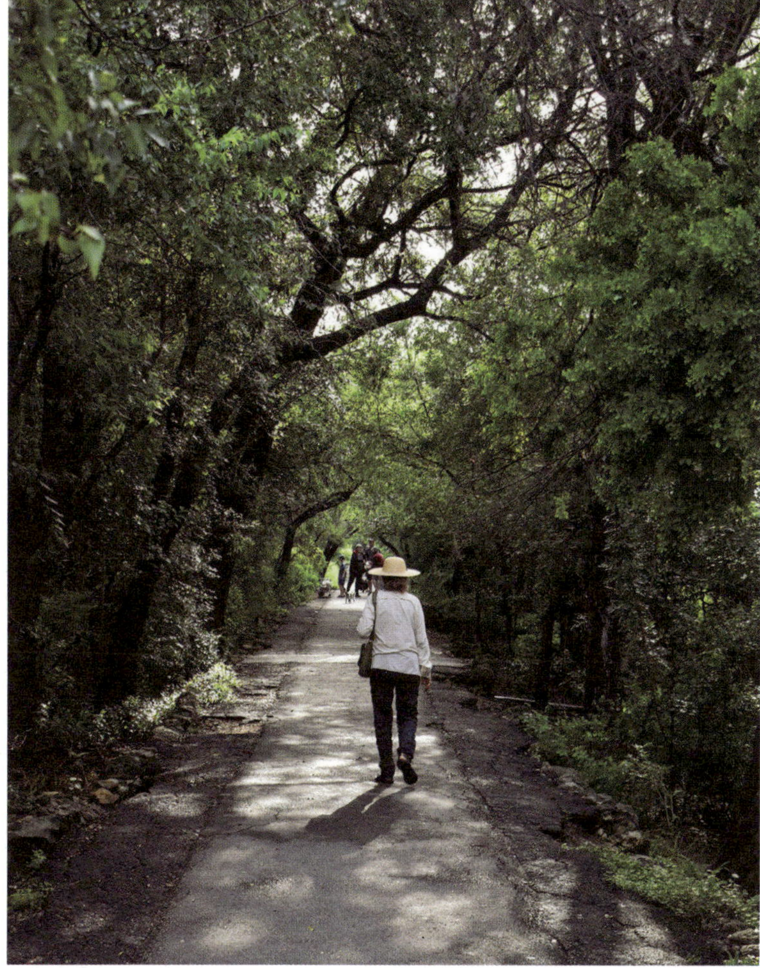

This sylvan arrow-straight path at the edge of the Japanese Tea Garden predates Brackenridge Park's formation. The walkway was laid in the 1880s as a tramway route for rail cars hauling rocks from a cement quarry.

companion gate beyond, you can't be sure whether you're coming or going, much less where you've already been.

For decades authorities have reported Brackenridge Park's size as 343 acres. But there is no park survey to back up the claim. It turns out the park's area depends upon which acres one counts or does not. It's very hard to end up at 343.

In 1974 the *San Antonio Express* wondered of Brackenridge Park, "Where is the city's 248.73 acre park?" The response reported from parks department officials was that "they don't know just what the boundaries of the park are." Instead, "arbitrary boundaries" were being used because, officials said, "the staff has never been directed to establish the actual, legal boundaries of the park." Nearly fifty years later the answer is the same, with no explanation of how the park expanded from 248.73 acres to 343.[2]

Given the confusion, for this book Jay Louden, an architect involved in several recent park projects, studied conflicting city maps and determined acreage using computer mapping programs.

It turns out that the formally designated boundaries of Brackenridge Park—including the separately defined but adjacent Koehler Park—surround 317 acres, with a margin of error of 5 acres. Not legally part of any park are 86 additional acres that include the Japanese Tea Garden, the Sunken Garden Theater, the Tuesday Musical Club, and most of the San Antonio Zoo. These are on a larger tract of city-owned property, though all are commonly regarded, maintained, and promoted as being part of a "343-acre" Brackenridge Park. Devising an "approximate understood park boundary," Louden found Brackenridge Park to encompass 403 acres—nearly 20 percent more than official statistics report.

Fortunately, an intervention is already addressing the park's deep-rooted issues, spurred on by the Brackenridge Park Conservancy, active since 2009, and most recently aided by nationally recognized landscape design and planning professionals. Like the early train visitors from Houston transfixed by the oddity of San Antonio, these newcomers were intrigued by the park's unique history, resources, and potential. An extensive cultural landscape report completed in 2020 forms a blueprint for reversing Brackenridge Park's decline, with recommendations ranging from restoring ecological health to improving traffic patterns and access.

Muddled awareness of the history of the park is also improving. This helps avoid situations like one as recent as 2012, when unknowing archeologists approved a site in Koehler Park for construction of a water treatment plant for the San Antonio Zoo. Five feet down excavators encountered massive hewn limestone blocks that seemed to form a sluiceway. Having been told nothing significant was down there, baffled workers guessed the blocks remained from a forgotten eighteenth-century acequia.

In fact, the blocks were found to be not from the eighteenth century but from the nineteenth, laid in 1863 by the Confederate army for a sluiceway during construction of a tannery, the first facility in what was to have been an industrial complex serving the entire Confederate army west of the Mississippi. Remains of the tannery's main building, with its network of vats and sunken conduits, are buried in Koehler Park beside the present-day zoo's children's education building. An account of the operation and fortunes of the tannery, organized and commanded by a great-grandnephew of George Washington, is published for the first time in this book.

Like working a palimpsest, scraping beneath one part of Koehler Park would first reach the level of Madarasz Family Park, opened in 1901 by brewer Otto Koehler. Next would appear traces of one of the largest nurseries in nineteenth-century Texas, then remains of the tannery, and, finally, layers of Native American campsites dating back thousands of years.

Below one green on Brackenridge Park's golf course lies whatever remains of its first clubhouse. The next level holds residue of two Spanish-American War–era military camps, followed by remnants of world heavyweight champion Jim Corbett's training center, then relics of an 1890s grandstand and racetrack. Below that would be reminders of Native American occupation.

Less visible layers of political, social, and economic impacts also reflect the park's evolution. Odd boundaries can be tied to political discord, beverage restrictions to the temperance movement, and maintenance deficiencies to chronic long-term financial shortages caused by the city's poor tax base. The vagaries of prejudice can be traced through the changing names of the Japanese Tea Garden, managed when it opened by members of a Japanese family. When they were evicted in reaction to World War II it was renamed the Chinese Tea Garden. As the Cold War followed and the United States fell out with China it became the Sunken Gardens, until repentant San Antonians took it back to the Japanese Tea Garden.

And so it goes in this first comprehensive look at the story of Brackenridge Park and of how its diverse landscapes evolved to reflect what the 2020 cultural landscape report saw as Brackenridge Park's "defining spirit—whimsical, romantic, and uniquely San Antonian."[3]

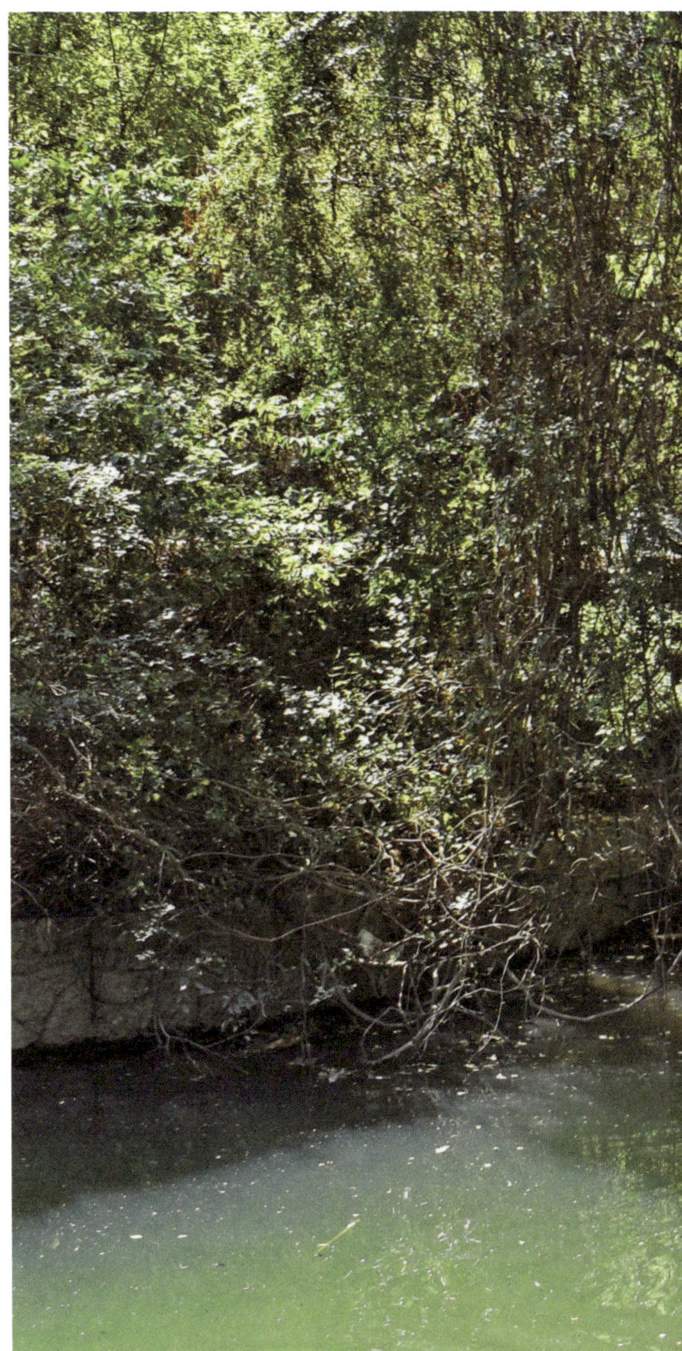

A cross-section of the riverbank across from the Koehler Pavilion reveals curving walls that once opened to a mile-long raceway canal, dug in 1885 to the pump house now known as the Borglum Studio. This section of the canal beyond the river was filled circa 1920 to become Red Oak Road.

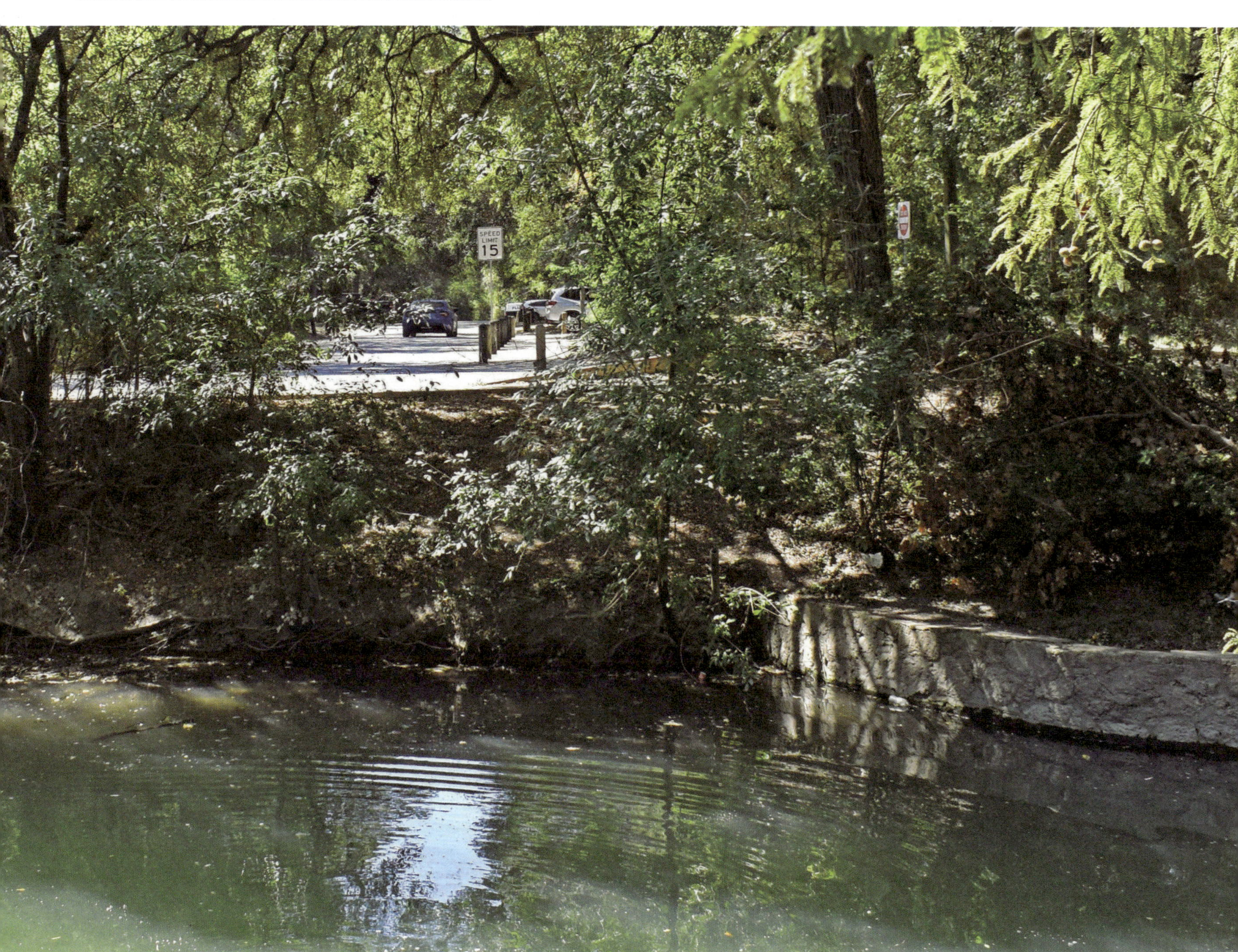

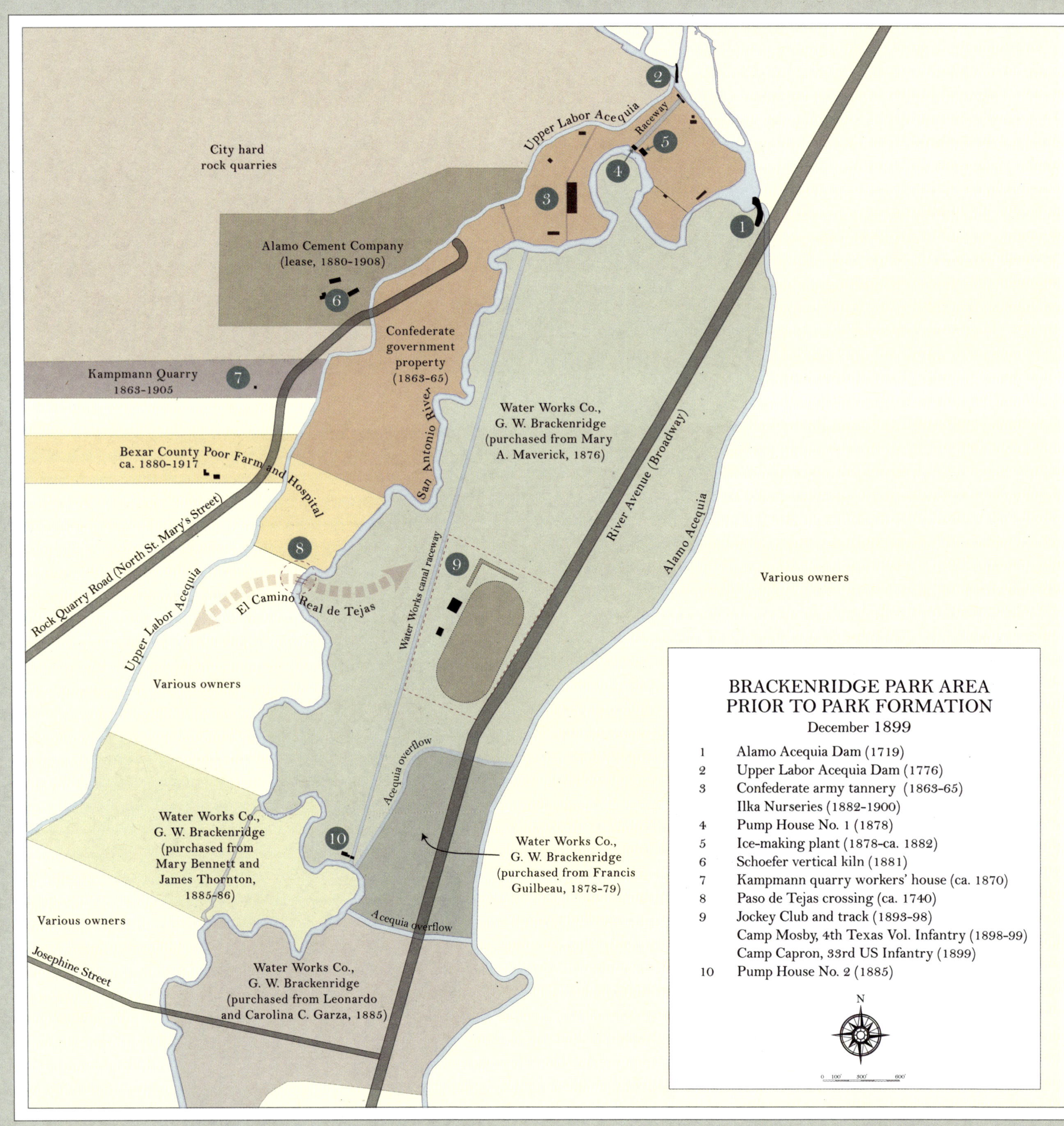
City hard
rock quarries
Upper Labor Acequia
Raceway
Alamo Cement Company
(lease, 1880-1908)
Confederate
government
property
(1863-65)
Kampmann Quarry
1863-1905
Bexar County Poor Farm and Hospital
ca. 1880-1917
San Antonio River
Water Works Co.,
G. W. Brackenridge
(purchased from Mary
A. Maverick, 1876)
River Avenue (Broadway)
Alamo Acequia
Rock Quarry Road (North St. Mary's Street)
Upper Labor Acequia
El Camino Real de Tejas
Water Works canal raceway
Various owners
Various owners
Acequia overflow
Water Works Co.,
G. W. Brackenridge
(purchased from
Mary Bennett and
James Thornton,
1885-86)
Water Works Co.,
G. W. Brackenridge
(purchased from Francis
Guilbeau, 1878-79)
Various owners
Acequia overflow
Josephine Street
Water Works Co.,
G. W. Brackenridge
(purchased from Leonardo
and Carolina C. Garza, 1885)
BRACKENRIDGE PARK AREA
PRIOR TO PARK FORMATION
December 1899
1 Alamo Acequia Dam (1719)
2 Upper Labor Acequia Dam (1776)
3 Confederate army tannery (1863-65)
Ilka Nurseries (1882-1900)
4 Pump House No. 1 (1878)
5 Ice-making plant (1878-ca. 1882)
6 Schoefer vertical kiln (1881)
7 Kampmann quarry workers' house (ca. 1870)
8 Paso de Tejas crossing (ca. 1740)
9 Jockey Club and track (1893-98)
Camp Mosby, 4th Texas Vol. Infantry (1898-99)
Camp Capron, 33rd US Infantry (1899)
10 Pump House No. 2 (1885)
N

PART 1

The First Twelve Thousand Years

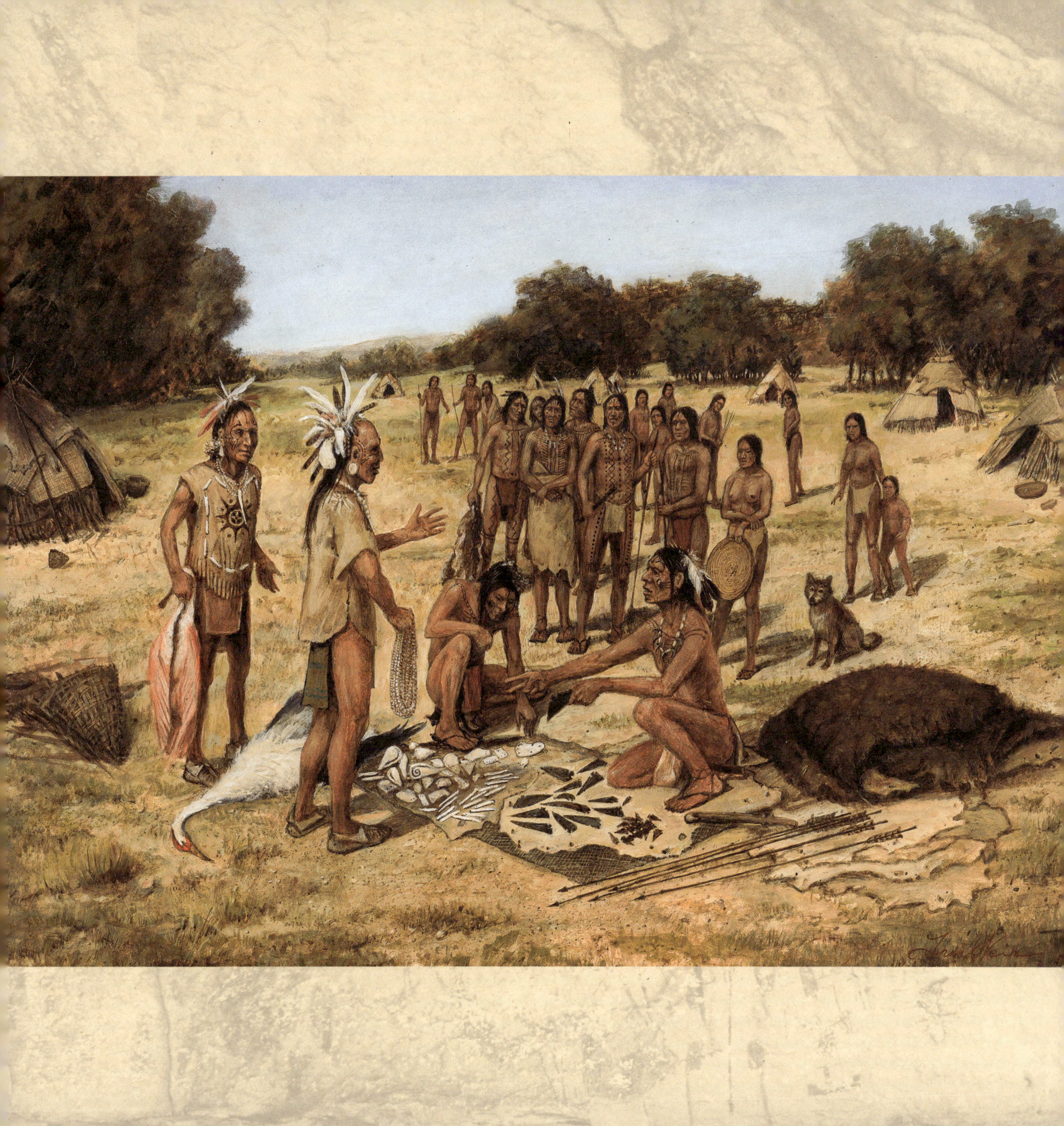

Riverside Haven

At least twelve thousand years ago hunter-gatherers began ranging through the upper reaches of the San Antonio River. Their story and the stories of those who followed mixed on a several-hundred-acre palette that became San Antonio's Brackenridge Park.

The park lies within three ecological zones, uncommon for an urban park. Rock cliffs of the Balcones Escarpment cut through the northwestern corner of the park, home to stands of live oak typical of the uplands. High on the park's western border come prickly pear and agave common to the Chihuahuan Desert of southwestern Texas. The South Texas Coastal Plain with its red oaks and grasses enters the park at the southeast.

Diversity of the zones' plants and animals along with ample water attracted indigenous people for thousands of years. At the time the Spanish arrived in 1690 there were a hundred or more seminomadic groups or bands collectively termed Coahuiltecans who passed through the area, camped within what would become the park, and utilized its many resources. These indigenous people roamed through the present Mexican state of Coahuila into the Lower Pecos region of southwestern Texas and beyond, each group usually having fewer than a hundred members and its own name, territory, and language.[4]

A twenty-six-foot collection of pictographs drawn by generations of these Native Americans beginning as early as four thousand years ago highlights a rock shelter above the Pecos River two hundred miles west of San Antonio. Protected in a preserve owned since 2017 by Brackenridge Park's Witte Museum, the imagery is variously interpreted as a ceremonial record, an astronomical guide, or a combination of both.

Members of two of the seminomadic tribes that camped along the river in the present-day park trade goods in this painting by Frank Weir.

Over the millennia, indigenous people left layers of artifacts throughout what is now Brackenridge Park, though precise identification of site use and dates has been hindered by erosion, construction, and loss to generations of relic hunters. By as early as 6500 BC Native Americans were not just passing through but settling in the future Brackenridge Park, where two major sites indicate seasonal villages. A cluster of hearths from one, discovered beneath the sod of the park's former polo field, revealed evidence of intermittent occupations. Two other sites may have been small camps or specialized activity areas.

Eleven more areas are designated "collecting localities," identified by concentrations of chert flakes left from making stone tools, by scattered scraping and cutting tools, and by burned limestone, indicating hearths.[5]

A special attraction of the Brackenridge Park area was the presence of the San Antonio River's headwaters, one of four major groups of springs at the foot of the southeastern arc of the Balcones Escarpment, a rocky rampart uplifted across south-central Texas a hundred million years ago. Waters once shot upward as high as twenty feet at the San Antonio River headwaters springs as well as at the other three—the Comal Springs in New Braunfels, San Marcos Springs in San Marcos, and Barton Springs in Austin.

The headwaters area abounded with elements to sustain Native Americans. Softshell turtles, large freshwater mussels, fish, and waterfowl thrived in the narrow, rushing San Antonio River. Stands of pecans, oaks, black walnuts, and anaquas held nests of edible birds and produced bountiful harvests. Hunter-gatherers carrying a curved stick could club a hapless rabbit darting from the underbrush. Close by were lush grasslands, where slow-moving mammoths and a now extinct species of bison made easy targets for a well-aimed spear hurled from an atlatl.

Eventually the huge animals were hunted out and the climate became hotter and drier. Much of Texas emptied of game and human inhabitants in the face of a searing, three-thousand-year mega-drought. Banks of the spring-fed river through Brackenridge Park and beyond became, however, an oasis, still sustaining human habitation.

By 500 BC the climate was shifting from arid to semiarid, and nomadic hunter-gatherers again flourished, along with their prey—bison, deer, mice, snakes, and other creatures. Nets were crafted for hunting and fishing, though, for some, eating fish was taboo. Food was stored in baskets and processed on stone grinding slabs—metates—and in wooden vessels.[6]

Recorded history began in South Texas with the arrival of the Spanish explorer Álvar Núñez Cabeza de Vaca, shipwrecked off the Texas coast in 1528. Cabeza de Vaca and three other survivors were captives of coastal Native Americans for six years until they made their escape; they crossed the San Antonio River somewhere south of Bexar County in 1534.

By the early eighteenth century the Spanish encountered Coahuiltecan tribes throughout South Texas and as far north as the Colorado River. These tribes were often found together with other non-Coahuiltecan groups in rancherias, areas where they gathered for mutual aid and protection from the Apache. Spanish missionaries brought many potential Catholics into mission complexes, five of which were built between 1718 and 1731 along nine miles of the San Antonio River south of San Antonio.

Brackenridge Park and the uppermost reaches of the San Antonio River remain distinct in Bexar County for their unique concentration of archeological sites spanning the entire range of the region's prehistory; elsewhere in the county sites are usually specific to certain periods and are widely scattered. South of the park, most sites along the river have been obliterated by development.

Upstream from the park, most of the largest archaeological site in Olmos Basin was destroyed in 1923 during construction of the Olmos Dam. Charles David Orchard, an amateur archeologist and civil engineer who worked on the dam, observed the destruction of several hundred prehistoric hearths. His large collection of artifacts has helped interpret the rich prehistoric story of Olmos Basin and Brackenridge Park.[7]

Hunter-gatherers like those staying in the future Brackenridge Park drew this mural some four thousand years ago in a shelter west of San Antonio.

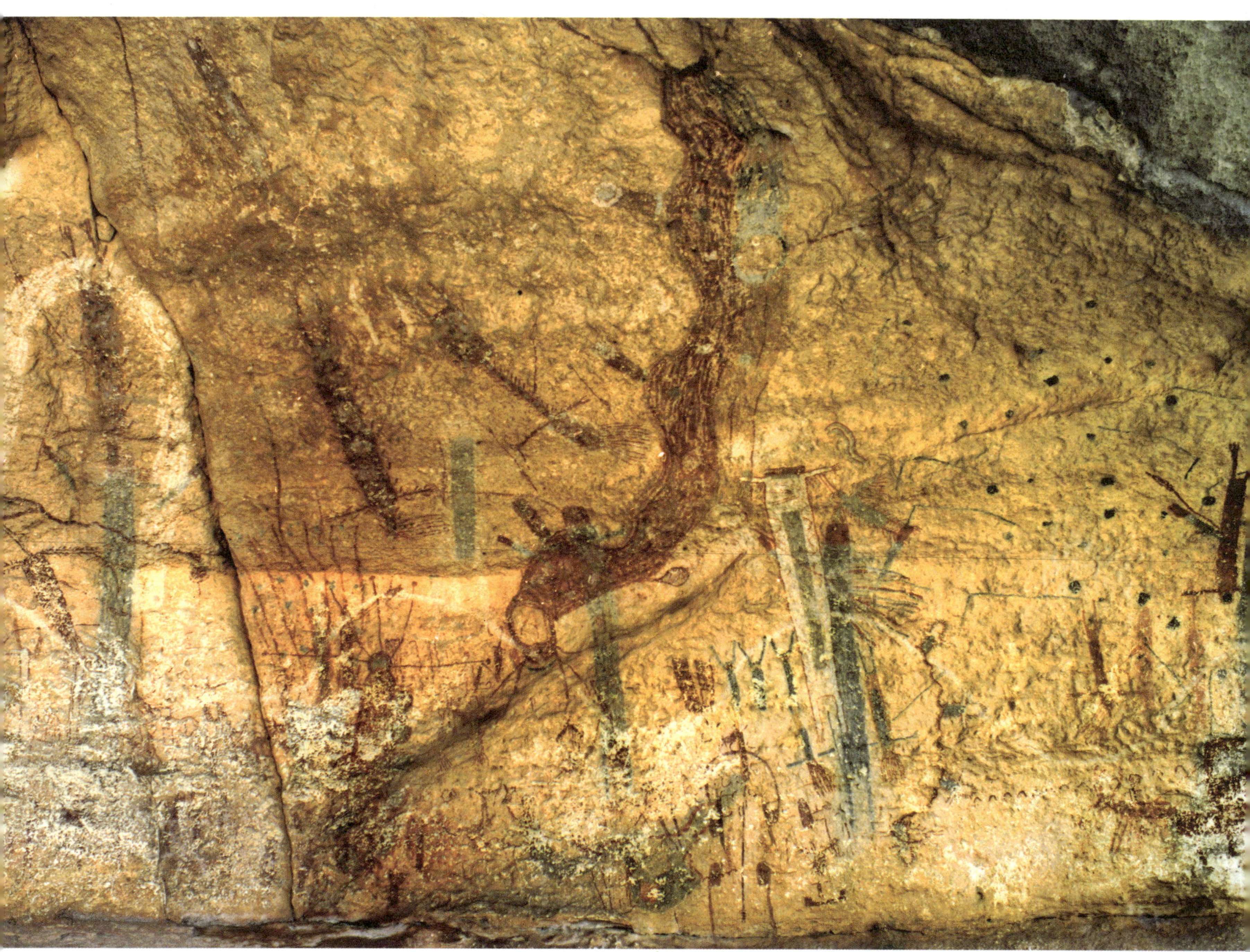

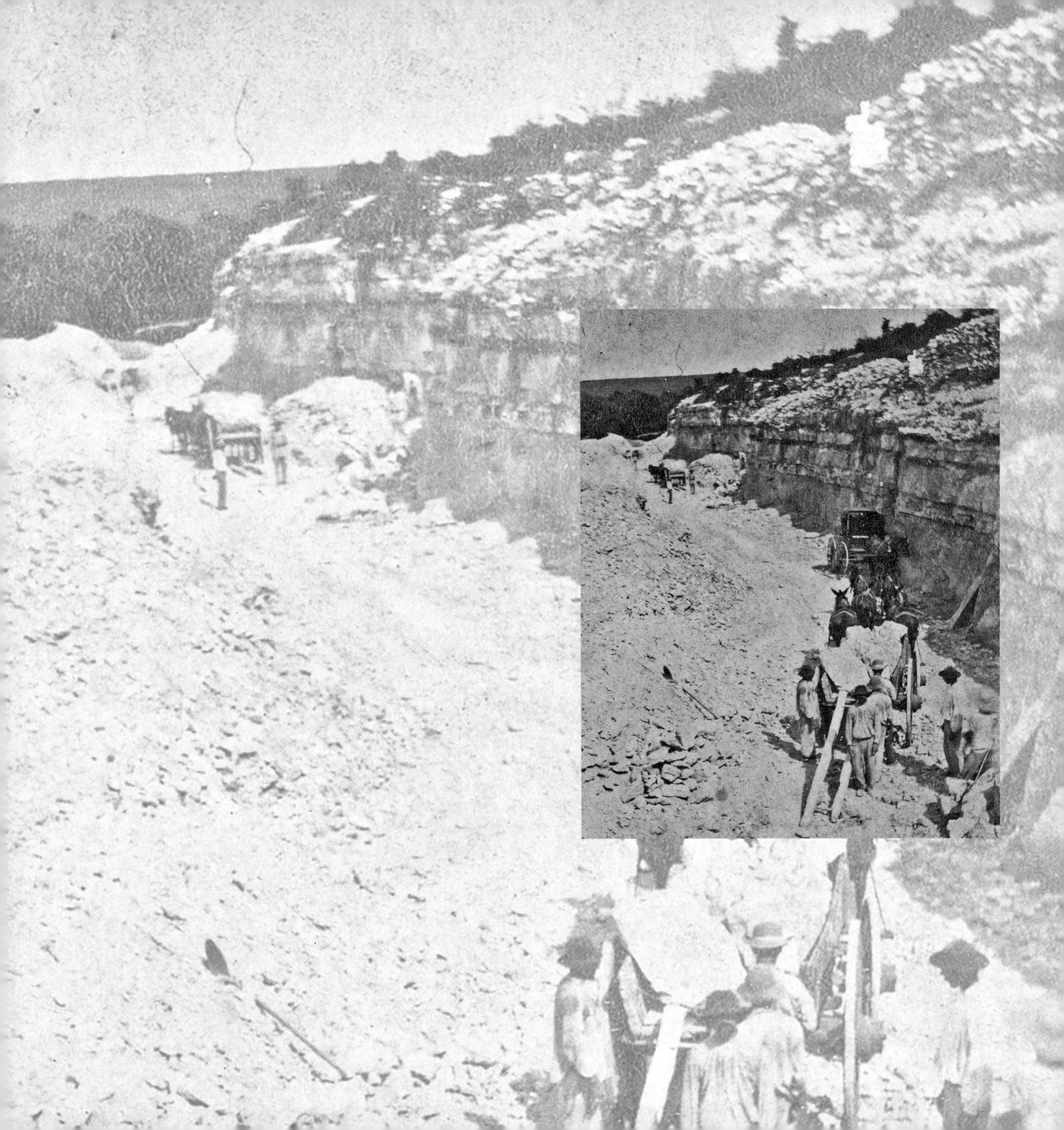

Water and Stone for a Spanish Outpost

Texas proved a challenge for Spain as European empires were solidifying their claims in the New World. France had a lock on Louisiana and was casting longing eyes past its Sabine River border with New Spain down to the rich Spanish silver mines beyond the Rio Grande in northern Mexico.

The link between settlements along the Rio Grande and faraway Spanish missions and presidios near the Sabine was El Camino Real (the "royal road"), which crossed the San Antonio River at the Paso de Tejas, today's low-water crossing near River Road in Brackenridge Park.[8]

In 1691 members of a Spanish expedition crossing Texas happened upon a spring-fed river they named for Saint Anthony, on whose feast day it was discovered. Eighteen years later, in 1709, another Spanish expedition camped at the river's headwaters, where they found plentiful fish and "beautiful shade trees and good pasturage," plus "hemp nine feet high and flax two feet high." Their reports led to the founding of San Antonio on May 1, 1718, as a way station between the Rio Grande and the French frontier. The community formed around the new Mission San Antonio de Valero near the headwaters of San Pedro Creek.

Limestone bluffs were quarried as far back as Spanish colonial times for stone to build the city.

A year later land grants to the fledgling municipality from the King of Spain included an area around present-day northern Brackenridge Park. There, sediment compressed at the bottom of the inland sea that had covered much of Texas for millions of years had uplifted to form the Balcones Escarpment. The escarpment's limestone bluffs were soft enough for early settlers to quarry for building materials. Holes were drilled into the rock to insert thin poles of cedar or cypress. Doused with water, the poles expanded and cracked the rock, which was broken off and randomly pieced together into lime-washed walls to help build the Presidio de Béxar and the growing civilian community. Small kilns near the quarry burned rocks into lime, which was mixed with sand, pebbles, and other ingredients to make mortar.

The San Antonio River valley was several miles wide, that of its tributary San Pedro Creek narrower. But the steady flow of both their springs allowed a system of acequias to expand the water supply to homes and fields. Residents drew from their

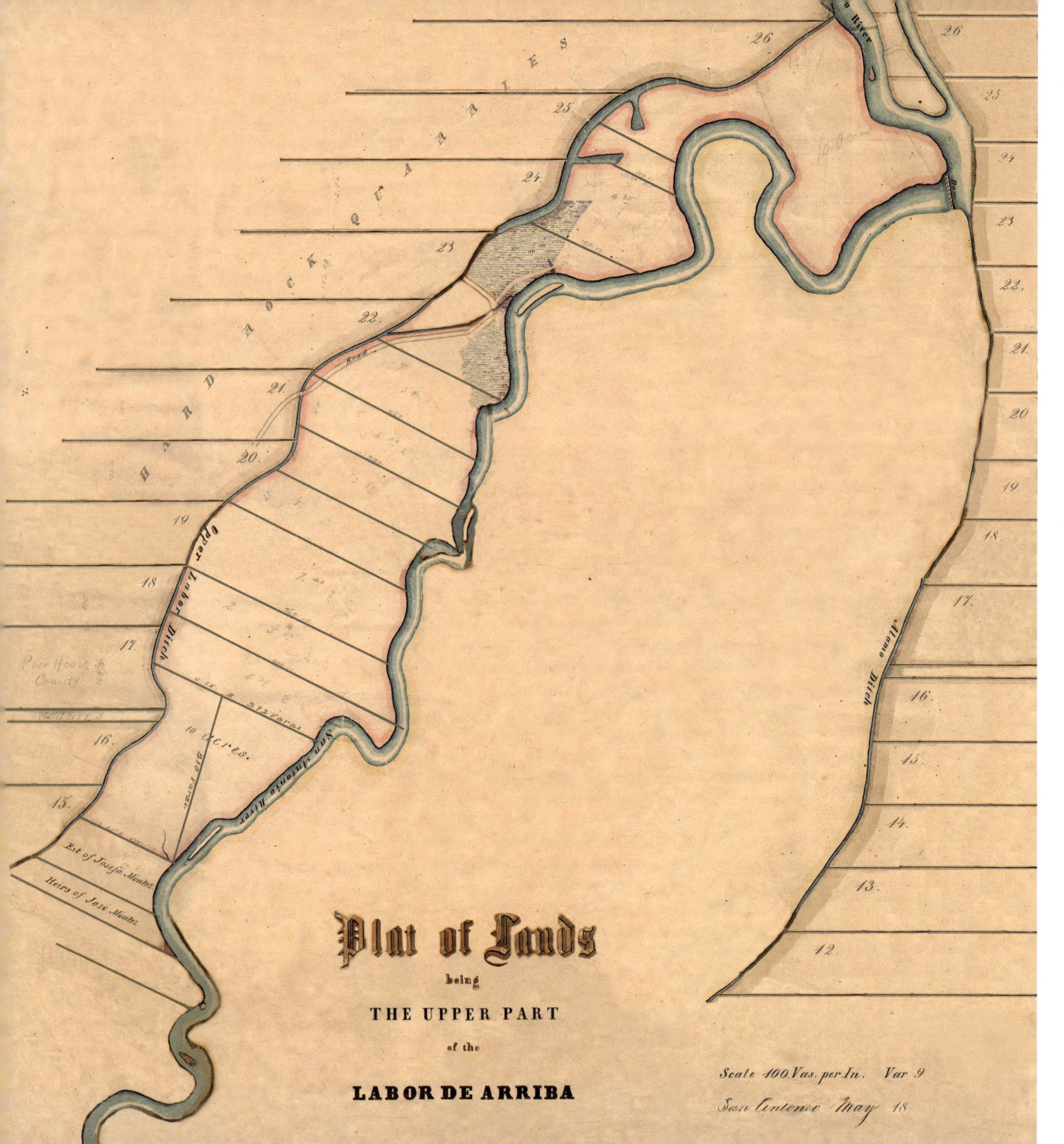
Plat of Lands
being
THE UPPER PART
of the
LABOR DE ARRIBA
Scale 100 Vas. per In. Var 9
San Antonio May 18
HARDROCK QUARRIES
Upper Labor Ditch
San Antonio River
Alamo Ditch
Road
Est of Josefa Montez
Heirs of Jose Montez
10 acres
Poor House
County
12.
13.
14.
15.
16.
17.
18
19.
20.
21.
22.
23
24.
25.
26.

Dams now at the park's northern edge diverted water into two acequias. This 1870s map shows how the Upper Labor Acequia, *left*, and Alamo Acequia, *right*, furnished water to adjacent properties south toward San Antonio.

experience in semiarid regions of Spain, where canal makers known as *acequiadores* were expert in engineering the flow of water down barely perceptible grades. The term "acequia," or canal, for an irrigation ditch is derived from the Arabic *al-saqiya*, indicating the system's ancient North African origins, imported to the Iberian peninsula during the Moorish occupation.

Spanish San Antonio ended up with at least ten acequias, the most extensive system in the present-day United States. Six primarily served the civilian community, with four originating at or near San Pedro Springs or along San Pedro Creek and two originating in what is now Brackenridge Park. Four more branched off the river to the south to serve four of the five Spanish missions.

Each acequia system began with a stone diversion dam that raised water behind it high enough to flow into a cut in the bank above. From there, gravity maintained a gradual flow down the acequia until excess waters returned to a creek or river a few miles downstream. Acequias crossed small depressions through *canoas*—hollowed sections of logs—and crossed deeper depressions on stone aqueducts. Mission Espada's acequia aqueduct, built in 1745, is still in use. Channels averaging three feet wide were unlined by stone during Spanish colonial rule. Raising or lowering wooden gates controlled water entering adjacent channels or fields.

Capt. Álvarez Barreiro, a member of the Royal Corps of Engineers, started San Antonio's first acequia system in January 1719 to serve the original San Antonio community near San Pedro Springs. Its replacement, the longer San Pedro Acequia, which flowed through central San Antonio, was begun in 1722 on the orders of the Marquis Aguayo, who funded its construction.[9]

A second acequia was begun soon after as the Mission San Antonio de Valero, later known as the Alamo, prepared to move to its third and final location at the eastern edge of San Antonio. The Spanish determined that the best place to tap the river for a gravity-driven channel to that location was inside the northern border of present-day Brackenridge Park. Workers put up a stone diversion dam forty feet long by fifteen feet wide to divert the flow from the eastern cluster of the San Antonio River's headwaters springs half a mile north. Known as the Acequia de Valero and then as the Alamo Acequia, it channeled water across present-day Broadway and down a ditch three and a half miles to the south and east before emptying into the river, along the way providing water to the mission and some three hundred acres of farmland.[10]

Vital though the headwaters springs were in forming the narrow San Antonio River and supplying acequias, water power downstream was nowhere near that of rivers powering the industrial might of cities elsewhere. But creative use of side channels could tease out strength for small industrial operations.

Sixty families abandoned the Spanish presidio of Los Adaes on the old French frontier and resettled in San Antonio in 1773. Known as Adaesaños, some of these people later settled between the San Antonio River and San Pedro Creek on the Upper Farms of Our Lady of Sorrows. The area was called the Labores de Arriba de Nuestra Señora de los Dolores, a "labor"—pronounced laBOR—being a block of farmland. One refugee, José Antonio de la Garza, in 1856 sold part of his grant within present-day southern Brackenridge Park to French consul and horticulturist François Guilbeau Jr., who added it to his agricultural properties. In the 1870s Guilbeau shipped several hundred tons of mustang grapevine cuttings to Europe to be grafted onto diseased vines, collaborating with others in saving the European wine industry.[11]

An acequia finally reached the Upper Farms after the Upper Labor Dam was begun in 1776, fourteen years after its construction was authorized. Each family had rights to tap into

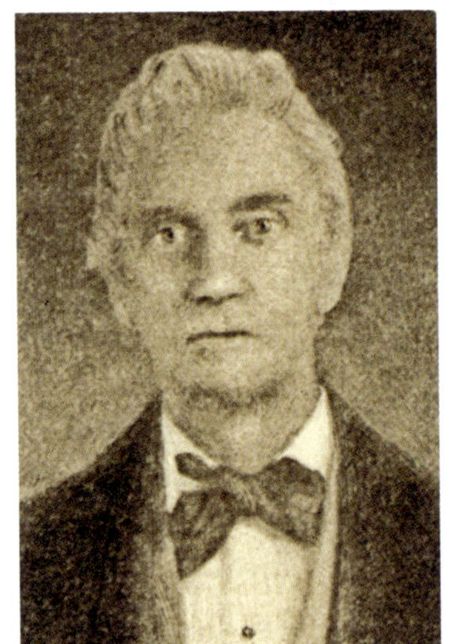

Samuel A. Maverick in 1843 bought what became the eastern half of the park, which his widow sold thirty-three years later to George W. Brackenridge.

the acequia for a total of one day's worth of water every twenty-six days.[12]

The Upper Labor Acequia's stone dam, within today's Brackenridge Park just south of Hildebrand Avenue, diverted water from a branch of the river flowing from the western cluster of headwaters springs. Its acequia went west, then meandered south not far from the river's western bank. Its winding path was responsible for part of the irregular western border of Brackenridge Park.[13]

Little was recorded of the Brackenridge Park area during the Mexican revolt from Spain that began in 1810 and ended in 1821. Nor was much written during the Mexican period from 1821 until the successful Texas revolt from Mexico, concluded at the Battle of San Jacinto in April 1836. Reports pick up with one of a cool and bright November day in 1839 when a dozen San Antonians and guests rode swiftly up to the head of the river, along the edges of what is now Brackenridge Park. The visitors were a woman from Boston, a judge and his daughter, and the secretary of war of the Republic of Texas, Col. J. W. Dancey. "They were, ladies and all, armed with pistols and bowie knives," hostess Mary Adams Maverick recalled in her memoirs, for the group "doubted not that Indians watched us from the heavy timber of the river bottom."[14]

This rare eyewitness account shows that the party risked little time in any one place. "We galloped up the west side and paused at and above the head of the river long enough to view and admire the lovely valley of the San Antonio," Maverick wrote. "The leaves had mostly fallen from the trees and left the view open to the missions below." After spotting three of the old Spanish missions, as far as San Juan Capistrano, seven miles below town, the group "galloped home down the east side."

The foray upstream was from a town struggling after years of warfare and political unrest had caused its population to shrink from two thousand to eight hundred. San Antonio was hard pressed to defend its territory from raids from still hostile Mexico or from Comanches raiders lurking along riverbanks. Many farms were abandoned, and acequias began falling into disrepair.

One of those who saw better times ahead was Mary Maverick's husband, Samuel A. Maverick. A signer of the Texas Declaration of Independence who was about to be elected to the Congress of the Republic of Texas, he had just returned from seven months' captivity in Mexico after being seized with four dozen San Antonians by a raiding Mexican army. With that behind him, in June 1843 Maverick added to his fast-growing inventory of Texas land by buying the eastern half of what would become Brackenridge Park. He placed it in his wife's name. The wooded land stretched from the San Antonio River east to the Alamo Acequia, beyond what is now Broadway, and from the head gates of the two acequia dams south to the southern area of the present park. The land was leased to others for farming. Crops included sugarcane.[15]

Following annexation of Texas by the United States in 1845 and the end of the Mexican-American War three years later, fear of military strikes from the south ended. Prosperity returned quickly to San Antonio. Aided by a flood of European immigrants, many of them Germans, the town swelled by ten times, to a population of eight thousand, in ten years. In the 1850s German was the most-spoken language.

Far from forests providing plentiful lumber for frame buildings and from major sources of clay for brick construction, San

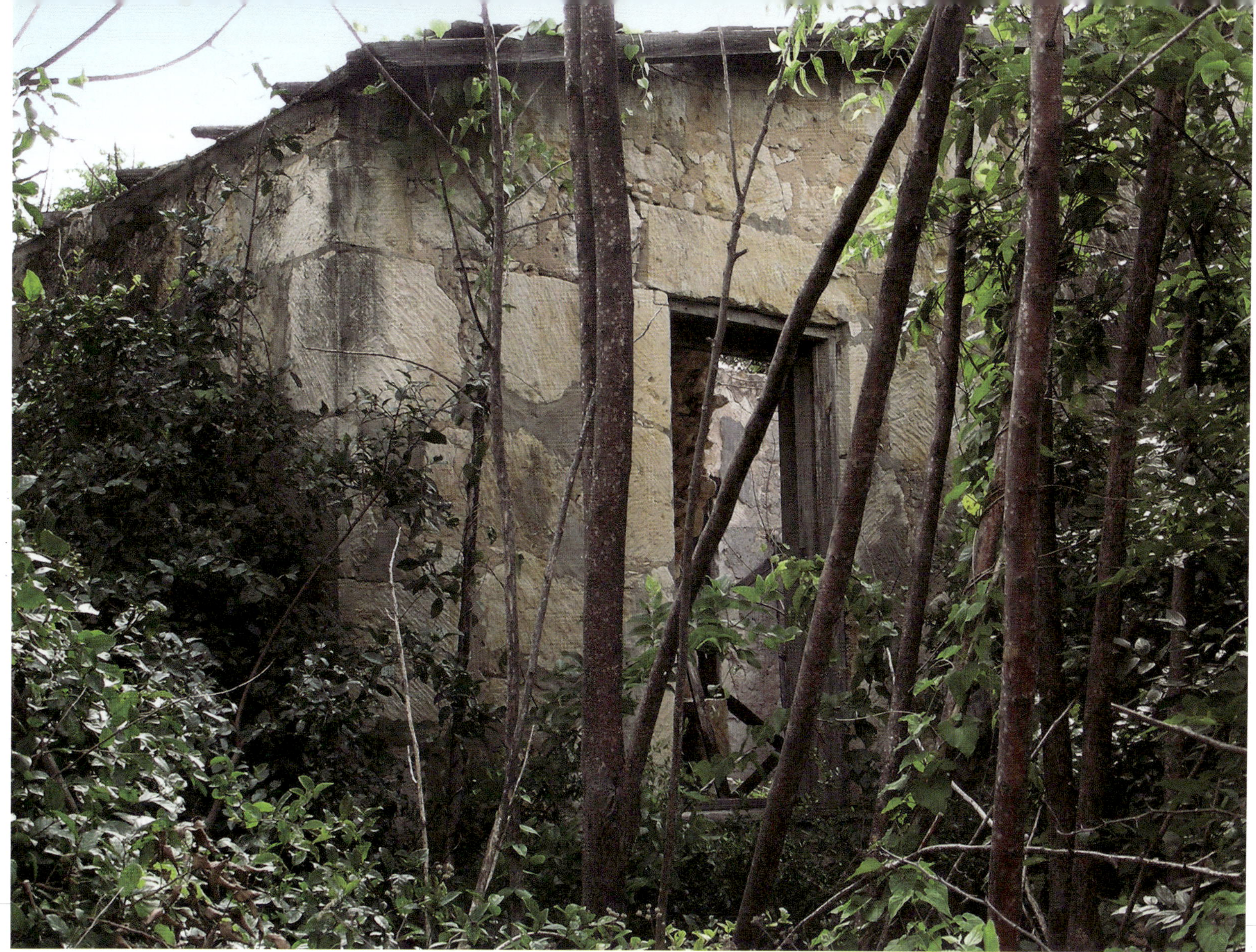

Walls of the circa 1870 home built by John H. Kampmann for his quarry workers survive in an overgrown corner of the park.

Antonio developed a distinctive built environment largely of stone. Bluffs of the Balcones Escarpment chipped away by the Spanish were quarried more extensively, this time to the point that in 1844 the city council passed an ordinance requiring a license to use the quarries.

The city retained ownership of most of its several hundred acres of quarries, extending from what is now the northwestern corner of Brackenridge Park west through the Trinity University campus, but it did sell some parcels outright. In 1863 leading contractor and builder John H. Kampmann purchased nineteen acres and began quarrying stone for many of San Antonio's Victorian landmarks. The road along the Upper Labor Acequia, now known as North Saint Mary's Street, was called Rock Quarry Road.[16]

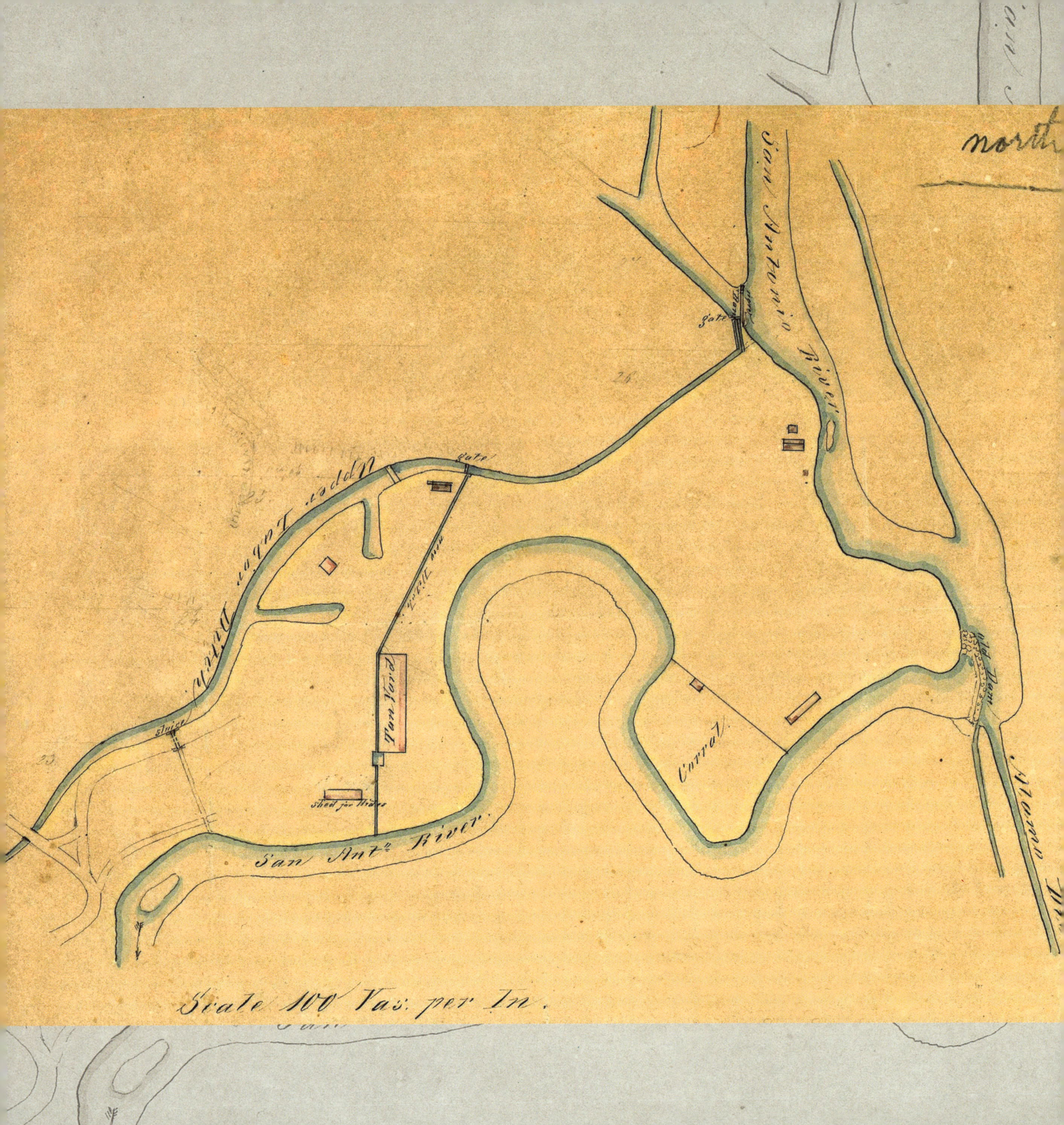
north
San Antonio River
Gate
Gate
Upper Labor Ditch
Sluice
Tan Yard
Shed for Hides
San Antº River
Corral
Old Dam
Scale 100 Vas: per In.

A Confederate Industrial Zone

Midway through the Civil War, the Confederate army planned a seventy-eight-acre industrial complex within present-day Brackenridge Park. The open area between the San Antonio River and the Upper Labor Acequia, below the acequia's dam, promised ample water to operate a state-of-the-art tannery and power a woolen factory, clothing factory, cotton mill, and shoe factory that could serve the needs of the entire Confederate army west of the Mississippi River.[17]

The tannery was completed, while plans for the others fell victim to the Confederacy's decreasing fortunes, and they were never built. But the tannery was an engineering triumph. Its carefully constructed stone-channeled water system of sluiceways, conduits, and drains enhanced operational efficiency in the main building. Though plagued by a lack of workers and mostly run at only half capacity, the tannery still managed to produce a major supply of leather for shipment elsewhere to make shoes, harnesses, and saddles for Confederate forces. Production was done in a short time and at half the cost of civilian leather.

The fall of Vicksburg in July 1863 put Union forces in control of the Mississippi River, splitting the Confederacy east and west. The major population and manufacturing centers were to the east, where most of the combat was occurring. The sparsely settled agrarian region to the west had few railways and little industry, and was now blocked from sending beef, wheat, wool, and cotton east and getting manufactured goods back in return. Commerce through Gulf ports was risky, for they were blockaded by Union ships.

Also cut off were the fifty thousand Confederate soldiers west of the river. Word went to Lt. Gen. Kirby Smith, commander of the Trans-Mississippi Department, headquartered in Shreveport, Louisiana, that he was on his own to find supplies for his men. Quartermaster depots and shops were already scattered through the settled parts of Texas, the most productive a clothing manufacturing plant run by prisoners at the Texas State Penitentiary at Huntsville. Now all production output had to increase sharply.

An 1867 city map pinpoints key features of the former Confederate army tannery.

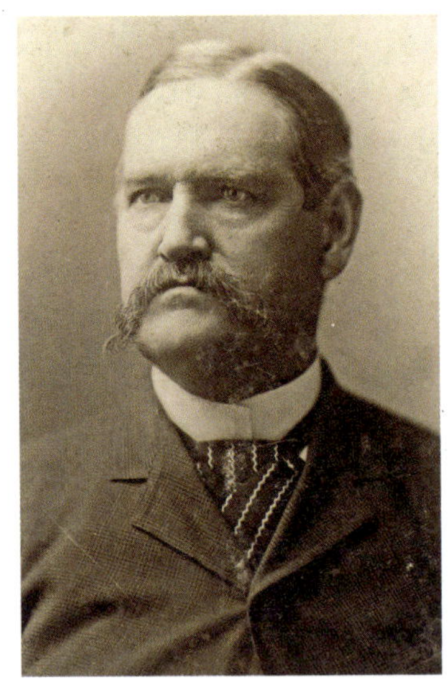

As a Confederate army major, Thornton A. Washington commanded a tannery in what is now Brackenridge Park.

If no local industries could be found that met military production requirements, army quartermasters were instructed to build new plants themselves, like the large tannery already under construction near San Antonio. General Smith wrote to headquarters of the San Antonio tannery's potential, and of the shoe factory planned near it: "I hope to be able to supply the entire army west of the Mississippi with shoes."[18]

An officer with both impeccable military credentials and firsthand knowledge of San Antonio was placed in charge of selecting the site, building the tannery, and overseeing its operation. Maj. Thornton Augustine Washington, thirty-seven, born in Virginia and an 1849 graduate of West Point, was a great-grandnephew of George Washington. At the outset of the war he was serving as aide to Maj. Gen. David E. Twiggs, commander of the US Army's Department of Texas, headquartered in San Antonio, where Washington had married a local girl, Olive Ann Jones.[19]

Once Twiggs surrendered his command in February 1861, both men resigned their commissions and became officers in the Confederate army. Major Washington was sent to Virginia, where he served on the staff of Gen. Robert E. Lee until mid-1862, when he was assigned to special service in Texas. He was first to set up "an extensive tannery and shoe manufactory" at Jefferson and then a clothing factory at Marshall. After that he was free to set up operations wherever he thought best. Frontier San Antonio was the crossroads of Texas, and Washington saw its potential for a major manufacturing operation. He moved to San Antonio to start out with a tannery. He also prepared to order machinery from Europe for a shoe factory and to buy equipment from Mexico to manufacture blankets in a woolen factory.[20]

Due to the noxious odors they produce, tanneries are usually located at the outskirts of towns. Fortuitously, one site two miles from San Antonio happened to offer an excellent source of water, one that a government inspector thought was "inexhaustible" due to the many nearby springs. That was a seventy-eight-acre tract between the San Antonio River and the Upper Labor Acequia below the acequia dam. Farther downstream, a meander brought the river to within a few hundred feet of the acequia, offering the opportunity for a short channel to connect the two. The channel could provide the tannery with a steady flow of water from the acequia into the tannery and then send the tannery's effluent on into the river to flow off downstream.[21]

Title to the property, however, was not clear. Part of the land was owned outright by the city, which was in litigation with a farmer, Pedro Flores, over his claim to the remainder. The dispute was settled in January 1863, when each party accepted $5,000 from the Confederacy for clear title to the entire tract.[22]

High on Washington's list was increasing the flow from the river into the acequia by improving the Upper Labor Dam. The city granted the Confederate army the right to take rock from the nearby quarry at no charge if Confederate engineers would make repairs to the dam; the city had not gotten around to fixing it since planning ten months before to assess property holders along the acequia for the cost. The army was also permitted to increase the dam's height to divert more water from the west branch of the upper river into the acequia.

Washington was well qualified to oversee the task. During his years as a West Point cadet the curriculum emphasized

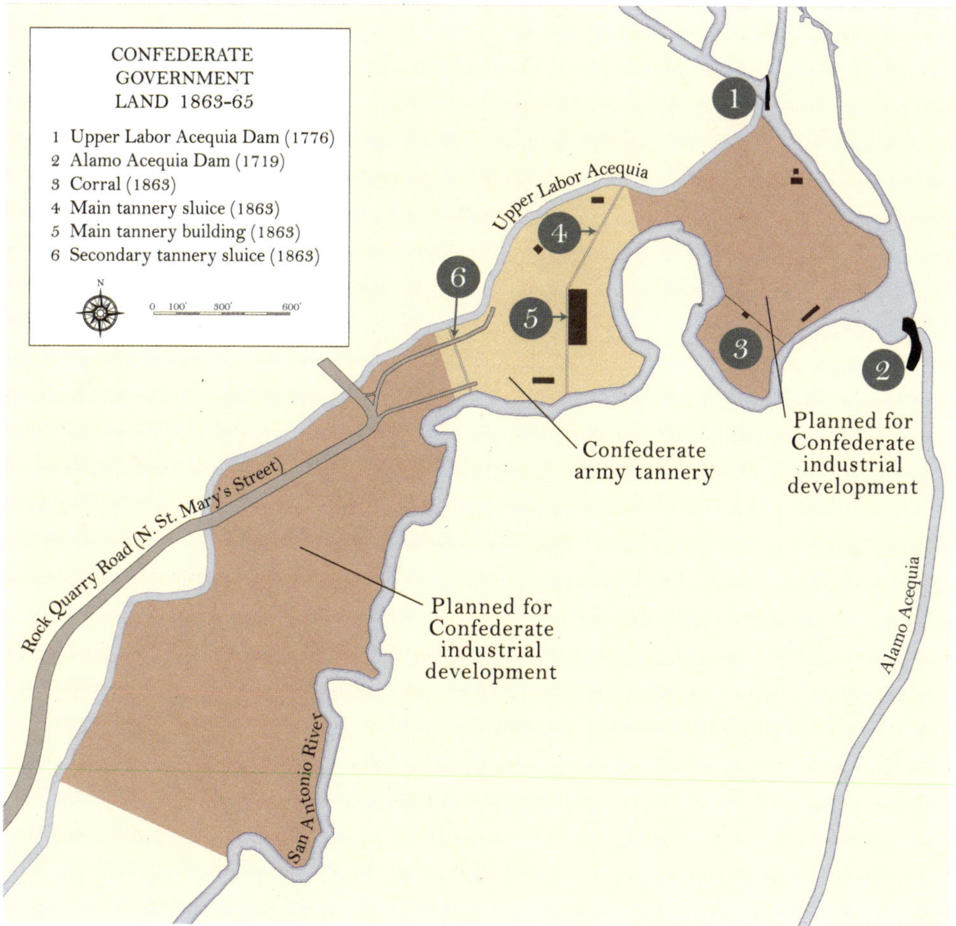

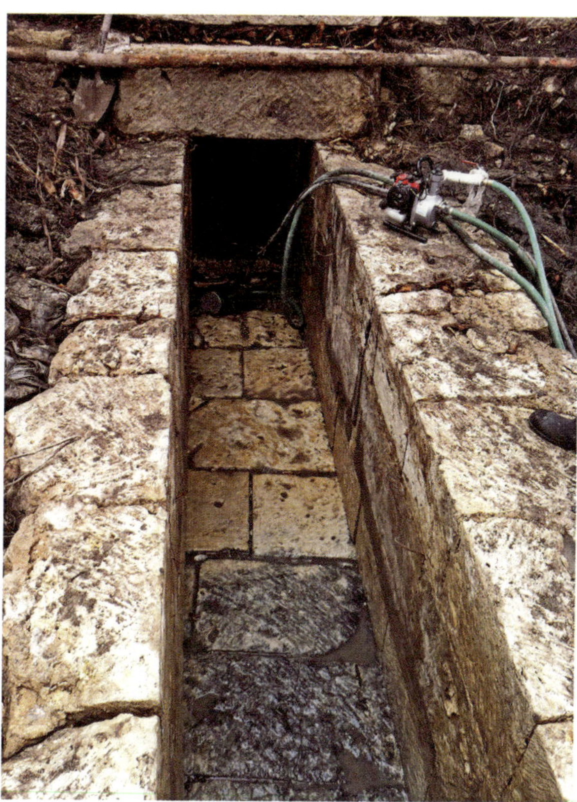

A sluiceway built by the Confederate army was uncovered in 2012.

training in engineering, intended to address the young nation's need for defensive military fortifications and facilities. Thus, under Washington, the Confederate army's tannery at San Antonio was designed with military precision. He heightened the Spanish-built dam of rough limestone rocks and mortar with rows of neatly dressed limestone blocks, which also lined a nearby water reserve that much later became a lily pond. Down the acequia, similar blocks created two underground sluiceways three feet wide by two feet deep running from the acequia to tannery buildings and beyond to empty into the river.[23]

The tannery was concentrated on ten of the seventy-eight acres, with the rest set aside for the other industries. Its design and operation followed Washington's orders to build "a new rapid system of tanning," drawing on advanced European techniques. The age-old method of turning

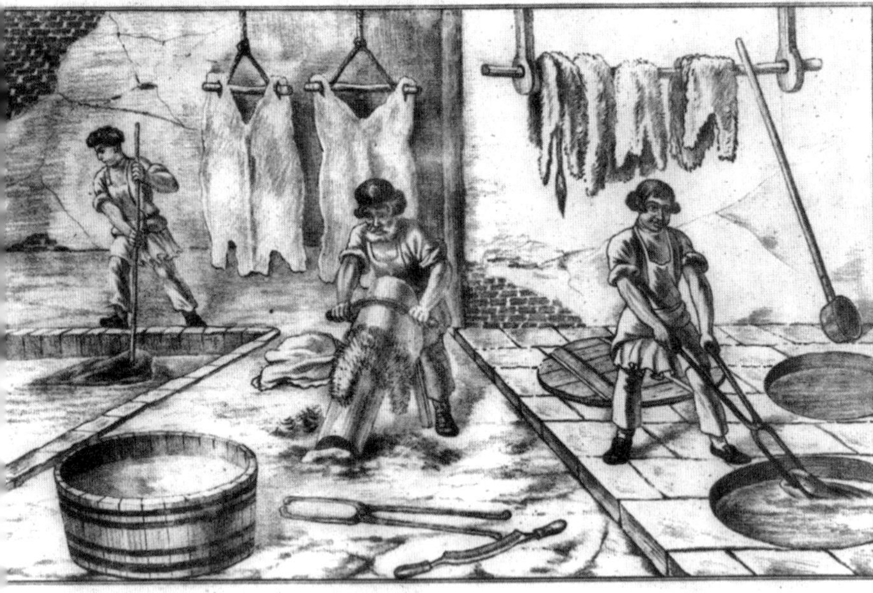

In a mid-nineteenth-century German depiction of *der gerber*—the tanner—hides were softened in a stone-lined vat, *left*; skinned of hair, *center*; and mixed with tanning agents in floor vats, *right*.

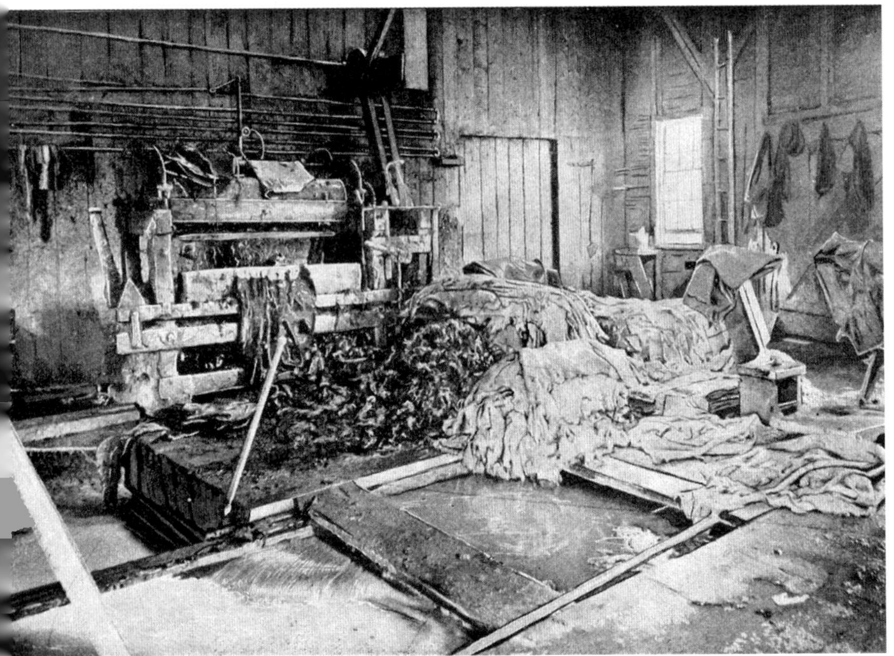

In a frame building similar to the one in the future park, hides were soaked at the end of the tanning process in a cistern filled with tallow.

animal hides into pliable, durable leather once took as long as a year and a half. This process would take less than three months.[24]

The center of operations was an 80-by-265-foot frame structure built along the eastern side of the main sluiceway. Channels along with pipes of gutta-percha—tough latex from a Malaysian tree—linked six eight-by-twelve-foot reservoirs of cut stone, and several stone and wooden vats. Embedded in the main building's flagstone floor were one hundred tanning vats eight feet long, four feet wide, and four feet deep. Outside the far end of the building was a reservoir twenty-five feet square and four and a half feet deep. Two underground cisterns were lined with cement.[25]

Reservoirs, vats, and cisterns had waste gates that could be raised independently to drain into an underground network of stone channels emptying into the river. A force pump kept an elevated wooden tank supplied with water for general purposes.[26]

First tanners had to soften the animal hides, readily available from local brokers, by soaking them in the outdoor reservoir for four or five days. The hides spent the next two weeks in a stone-lined vat so a lime mixture could loosen the hair, which was then removed by hand with knives. After being hung to dry the hides spent two days in a wooden vat, mixed with a salty brew to neutralize the caustic lime. Then they went into one of the hundred tanning vats, where they received periodic dumpings of the boiled essence of the tanning agent japonica, an extract of acacia leaves with a high level of tannin, sometimes replaced by sumac. A preservative made with Mexican huisache beans was added to keep the hides from decomposing in the summer heat.[27]

After six weeks the hides were taken out, dried, and moved to the first cistern, filled with tallow. That ended the process for leather for shoes and saddles, but hides intended for more pliable harness leather went into a second cistern filled with oil. Once the hides had dried, residue was scraped off them with sharp knives, and the leather was ready for use.[28]

Cost of the main building and equipment was 250,000 Confederate dollars, the equivalent by one measure of $3.1 million today. That apparently included 20,000 Confederate dollars spent for a twenty-five-horsepower steam engine that could power a saw to produce up to two hundred linear feet of lumber per hour. Except for the steam engine, imported from Europe, materials were purchased locally. That was a boost for local businesses suffering through the downturn caused by the loss of San Antonio's main economic generator, the US Army headquarters, which had closed two years earlier.[29]

The Confederate army's Trans-Mississippi Department, unable to garrison the frontier forts previously managed from San Antonio, established its district headquarters instead in Houston, closer to most combat areas. San Antonio was downgraded to headquarters of the Western Subdistrict.[30]

The tannery site also included more than half a dozen smaller buildings. A workers' dormitory was combined with a dining hall. By 1864 meals were prepared by a weekly rotation of two soldiers, other cooks having included a mother-daughter pair of enslaved workers, Emaline Miller and Eliza Walton. A shoe shop and a tailor shop made shoes and clothing for workers at the tannery and at the arsenal in town. A stable and corral in 1864 held two horses and fifteen mules, not enough to haul all of the eight six-mule wagons on hand, by then "old and worn." There was a blacksmith shop with two forges, each with bellows.[31]

The assistant superintendent, a captain required to live on the premises, resided in a stone house. The superintendent,

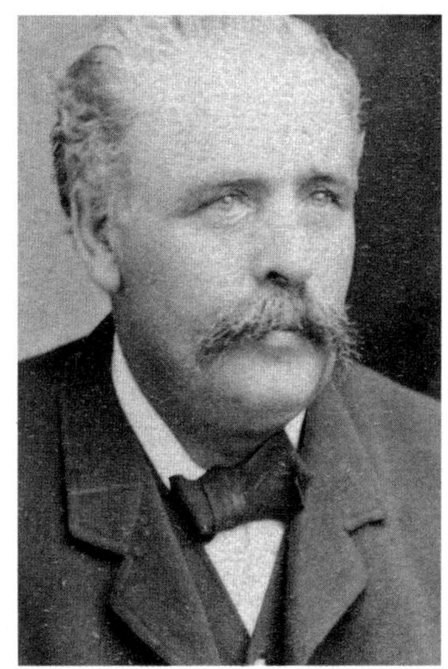

As a Confederate army captain, William Lyons, who later became San Antonio's city marshal, was superintendent of the tannery.

Capt. William Lyons, who had worked in a tannery in Illinois for four years before moving to San Antonio in 1857, lived with his wife in a small rock house nearby. Major Washington, the tannery commander, lived with his growing family in one of San Antonio's finest homes, the chandelier-hung Guilbeau house downtown.[32]

Construction of the tannery was among the least of Washington's problems. He was also beset by the difficulty of importing equipment and supplies while avoiding the Union blockade of coastal ports. In March 1863 he reported to General Smith that he expected to be in operation by summer but hedged by noting logistical uncertainties. A Confederate government purchasing agent was sending him nearly eight thousand bales of cotton that month to cover cost of purchases in England, where use of Confederate dollars was difficult. But "no transportation could be had except by mere chance," and the cotton did not arrive for another two months. After that Washington had to negotiate what he described as the "so complicated" export procedures to get the cotton across the Rio Grande to Matamoros, then have it shipped off to England. By November the tannery was still not completely finished.[33]

Raw cotton was as good as gold in the English milling port of Liverpool. It was quickly exchanged for machinery like the steam engine, bales of japonica, and bales of sumac shipped to Liverpool from Sicily. To avoid having to build large warehouses at the San Antonio tannery, Washington paid for storage in Matamoros for the japonica and sumac once they arrived there. Also warehoused in Matamoros were huisache beans obtained in Mexico by exchanging two pounds of cotton for each pound of beans. Inventories were drawn down as needed.[34]

The extent of Confederate commerce across the Mexican border annoyed Union officials to the point that in November 1863 seven thousand Union troops landed in the lower Rio Grande Valley in a short-lived attempt to shut it off. Fear of a Union invasion farther into Texas brought orders to Washington to use his tanners to defend the tannery by building a fort strong enough to resist an attack by light artillery and cavalry. Soldiers were sent to scour the countryside for enslaved workers to take over building the fortifications so tanners could go back to their jobs.[35]

At the same time the local depot commander conscripted several of Washington's key personnel and tanners. That prompted Washington to send a strong protest to General Smith requesting that the order be countermanded so he did not have to close the tannery. His conscripted workers did not need to be taken away, he asserted: "The men, being immediately at hand, could be sent to their companies in an hour in case of necessity."[36]

The tannery's site along the river was, however, quickly deemed "comparatively indefensible." The contingency plan became instead "to remove everything valuable from the tan-yard into the city," where defenses were hastily being constructed.[37]

The threat of an imminent invasion and the need for soldiers to repel it laid bare Washington's greatest difficulty: the Confederacy's manpower shortage. In August 1864 Maj. Joseph E. Dwyer, a former assistant inspector general recently assigned to subdistrict headquarters in his hometown of San Antonio, went out to perform a general inspection of the tannery for Texas Department headquarters in Houston. He held out hope that the San Antonio operation could furnish all the leather, if not all the finished shoes, for the Confederate army's entire Trans-Mississippi Department, but he recognized that it could not happen while the tannery was operating at half capacity. Only forty-three of its vats were in use. The other fifty-seven, with no one to work them, sat empty.[38]

About a hundred men were running the tannery, including seventy-two conscripts and soldiers who received additional pay for their work as tanners. Every Saturday evening they fell into company formation and were drilled by the assistant superintendent, Captain McAllister; roll calls were taken during the day to verify the workers' presence. In addition to a few men above age for military service were two enslaved men who worked at the stable and at the storeroom. That left "a deficiency of 25 or 30 tanners and about the same number of Negroes." This "great want of labor" left few to care for basic cleaning and pick-up tasks in the dangerous environment of cluttered workspaces and toxic brews, a need the inspector recognized as "of the utmost importance for the health of the employees."[39]

At the outset, Washington could afford to rent forty enslaved workers from Haywood Brahan, a Confederate army major who owned a plantation near Seguin. But by September 1864 they were gone from the tannery, and Washington complained to the quartermaster in Galveston: "I cannot hire Negroes except for specie [silver or gold coinage] & have at present *not one* at work in the tannery." He begged for help in getting "the service of 25 or 30 Negroes, as with them I could at least double the amount of leather production monthly."[40]

As it was, the San Antonio tannery was furnishing the Confederate army with as many as sixty hides each day, averaging fifteen hundred a month. Major Dwyer found the quality of regular production "not quite as good as Yankee leather," but the leather being made for harnesses "approximates it."

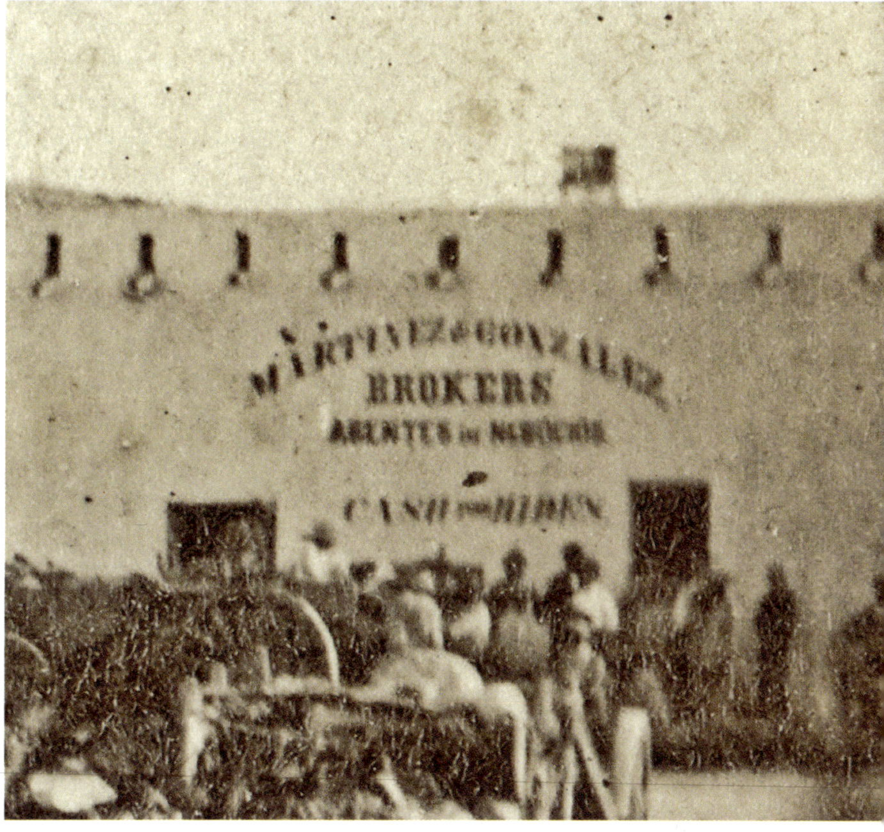

"Cash for Hides" is painted on this brokerage building at the site of the Bexar County Courthouse on Main Plaza.

The tannery's cost of production was half the price of leather on the open market, a bargain, the inspector noted, that would be even more beneficial if the tannery could get its full complement of workers.[41]

With no response to his longstanding request for additional workers to build up a backlog of inventory, Washington filled requisitions as best he could in the order they arrived. In January 1865 he got a second order for harness leather from the Texas District commander in Houston, Maj. Gen. John B. Magruder, before he had been able to fill the first order. Without having the additional tanners "for which I have long ago applied," Washington wrote Magruder's quartermaster in exasperation, "I much fear that it will be a long time before I will be able to comply with his wishes."[42]

Things did not get better as the war worsened for the Confederacy. A month after Washington last complained to headquarters about not having more workers, he was having trouble feeding those he did have. In early February 1865 he could not obtain any of the month's rations of meal and flour from the commissary in town, which risked having to close the tannery for want of food. A depot commissary officer hastened to explain that he was receiving and sending supplies "as fast as the limited transportation at my disposal can haul them," while a colonel remarked that such problems had been occurring elsewhere for months. Whether or not rations ever arrived to keep the tannery open is moot. Four months later news reached Texas that the war was over.[43]

As the former Confederate army's tannery personnel scattered to new lives, Thornton Washington, the tannery commander, stayed in San Antonio with his wife and six children, working as a civil engineer. He ended up in Washington, DC, with the US General Land Office. Capt. William Lyons, the superintendent, was made state commissioner of cotton and then became San Antonio's city marshal. Four of his assistants put their experience to good use by establishing their own tanneries in San Antonio. Formerly enslaved workers were aided in their transitions by the Freedmen's Bureau, begun early in 1865 as a branch of the US Army and officially named Bureau of Refugees, Freedmen, and Abandoned Lands.[44]

The bureau took over properties previously owned by "the late, so-called Confederate Government," including the San Antonio tannery. It financed bureau operations with funds from renting or selling the properties. In 1866 the bureau

One of the state's largest nurseries opened in 1882 at the site of the tannery, where some of the tanning vats were enclosed with glass to serve as hothouses.

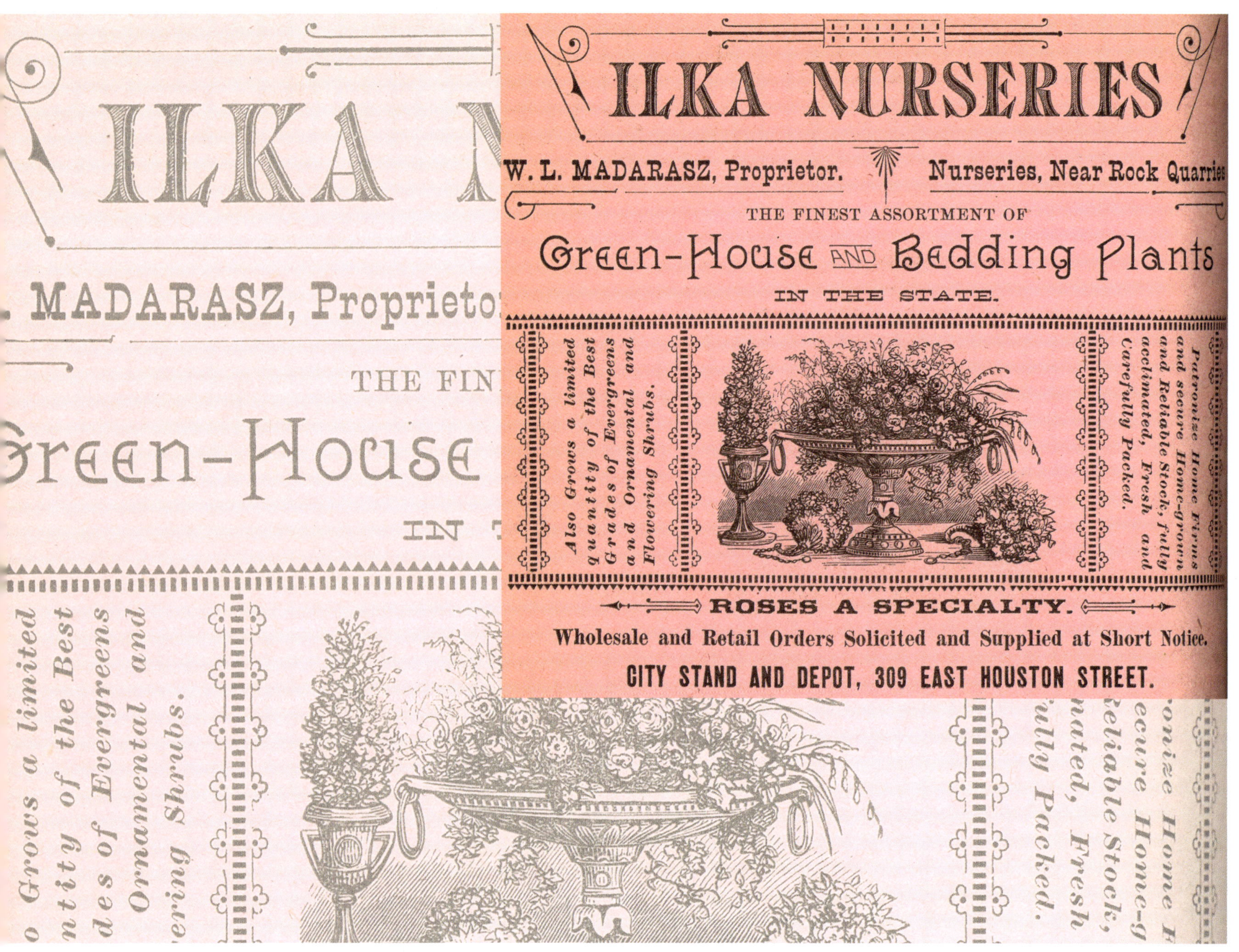

leased out the tannery, including its steam-powered sawmill, for apparently one year. In January 1867 Maj. Gen. Joseph B. Kiddoo, head of the Freedmen's Bureau in Texas, headquartered in Galveston, put the tannery and sawmill up for sale.[45]

San Antonio officials took a dim view of the tannery property being sold to a private buyer rather than being returned to city ownership. The city threatened a lawsuit, discouraging potential purchasers. In May the city offered the Freedmen's Bureau $25,000, the current equivalent of about $500,000, less than 20 percent of the original cost of improvements alone. Negotiations were still under way a year later when nature intervened. In May 1868 a storm struck San Antonio with unparalleled fury. A half-hour blast of wind, rain, and hailstones, often weighing two pounds or more, left the city, as the *New York Times* described on its front page, "a perfect wreck." Its appearance "could not have been worse under a severe bombardment." The tannery's frame buildings were flattened, their remaining equipment damaged beyond repair. The Freedmen's Bureau had been planning to sell the tannery's movable property, but now none of it was in any condition to be sold.[46]

After continued negotiations, the city offered the Freedmen's Bureau $22,500 in five installments. In July 1870 the bureau accepted. Most funds went to the bureau's teachers' school in Galveston, but a San Antonio Freedmen's Bureau board member, James P. Newcomb, was able to get $6,000 from the sale applied to construction of San Antonio's first school for Black children, at the corner of Convent Street and Rincon Street, now North Saint Mary's Street. Much of it was built with stone salvaged from the tannery, as was a new school for White children on South Flores Street. When the Freedmen's Bureau closed in 1870, it turned the Rincon School over to the city.[47]

The cash-needy city council held on to the northernmost fourteen acres of former Confederate-owned riverfront land but divided the remaining sixty-four acres into ten lots and auctioned them in 1875 to private bidders. The purchaser of four of the lots was a newcomer named George Washington Brackenridge.[48]

Eight years later, in 1883, George Brackenridge sold two of his lots—but kept the water rights—to Hungarian-born Helen Újházi Madarasz and her son, Ladislaùs. Helen was the youngest daughter of László Újházi, a nobleman and one of the most prominent exiles of the 1848–49 Hungarian Revolution to settle in the United States. Újházi lived nearby on a 550-acre estate on the site of the present-day suburb of Olmos Park. Helen Madarasz had already purchased an adjoining third lot, in 1882, from another seller, and opened Ilka Nurseries. It became San Antonio's largest nursery and one of a handful in Texas large enough to offer a combination of flowers, nursery stock, and seed. She left management to her son.[49]

Six greenhouses enclosed six thousand square feet with a wide variety of roses, Ilka Nurseries' specialty. There was a carnation house and rows of bedding plants and pot plants, from heliotrope to plumbago. Frames over former tannery vats were enclosed with glass to become hothouses. Flowering shrubs on sale ranged from crape myrtles to lilacs and yuccas, along with fruit trees, mulberries, weeping willows, magnolias, and more. Madarasz omitted "everything that is liable to suffer from extreme heat," offering only "such as can stand the periodical dry seasons that visit Southwest Texas."[50]

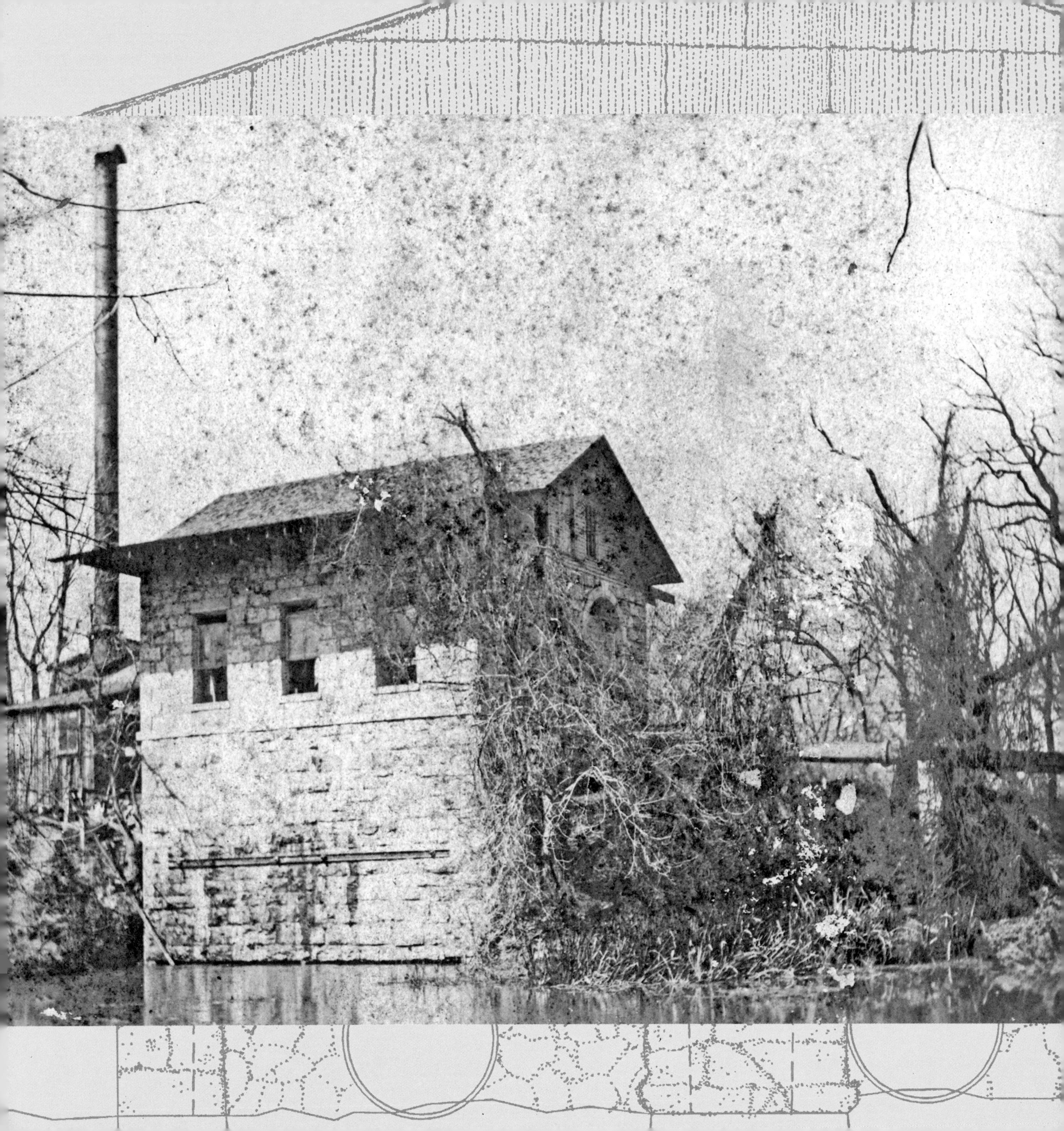

Turbines and Kilns

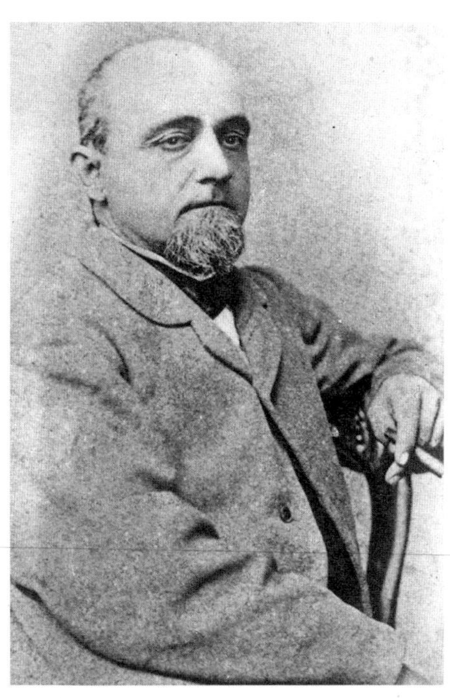

Jean Batiste LaCoste won the bid in 1877 to establish San Antonio's modern water system.

Until the last quarter of the nineteenth century, San Antonio's Spanish-era water system of acequias supplied perhaps the largest city in the nation lacking a modern water system. Civic leaders were increasingly bothered about the unhealthy and generally inadequate ditches, used for drinking, bathing, garbage disposal, and who knew what else. Since they flowed by gravity, acequias could not be extended if the city grew onto higher ground. In 1858 one short-lived group incorporated as the San Antonio Water Company to build a reservoir between the headwaters of the river and San Pedro Springs and to pump the water throughout the city. Two years later other investors with a similar plan formed the Hydraulic Company of San Antonio, also unsuccessful. Finally, in the early 1870s, with San Antonio's recovery from Civil War hardships well along, the city began to get serious about its water.[51]

Under threat of losing US Army headquarters, in 1873 San Antonio voters approved bonds to help subsidize a railroad, which would, at last, shorten access from the Texas coast to the city from days to hours and launch unprecedented growth. The city council asked Mayor François Giraud to come up with a general plan for public improvements, including a new water supply. Giraud, a civil engineer named in 1848 as the first city surveyor, had been the only participant in both prewar companies that proposed a new water system. But the job of getting the system set up fell to his successor as mayor, James H. French, whose efficient reform of city government made him, thought one historian, San Antonio's "most remarkable politician of his generation."[52]

Several bidders came forward to establish the water system, including the National Water Works Company of New York. But in April 1877 the council chose a low bidder, the San Antonio Water Works Company, headed by Jean Batiste LaCoste. A native Frenchman in the mercantile business, LaCoste had made a fortune in the cotton trade through Mexico during the Civil War and four years later acquired the city's first ice-making plant, beside the river on Losoya Street.

A second pump house was built in 1885 of rough-faced ashlar limestone blocks featuring limestone window sills, lintels, and entry door arches, shown in 1901.

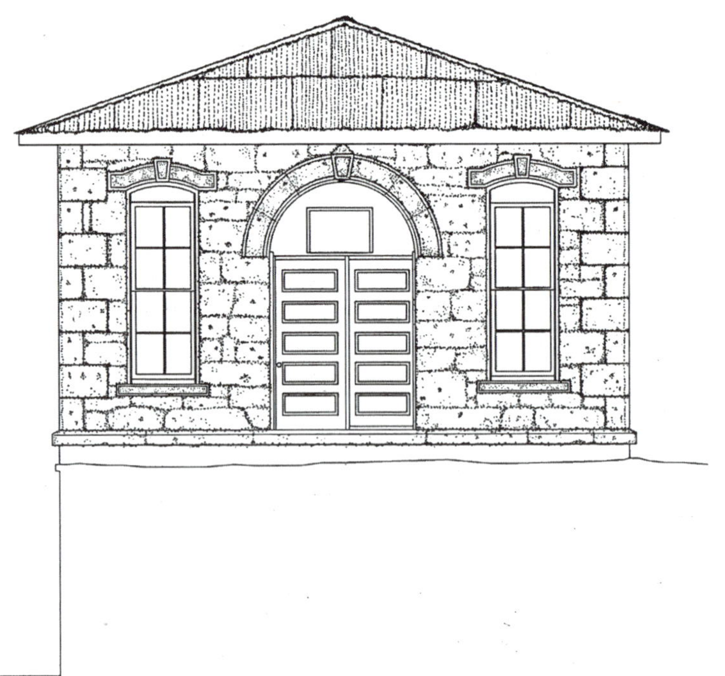

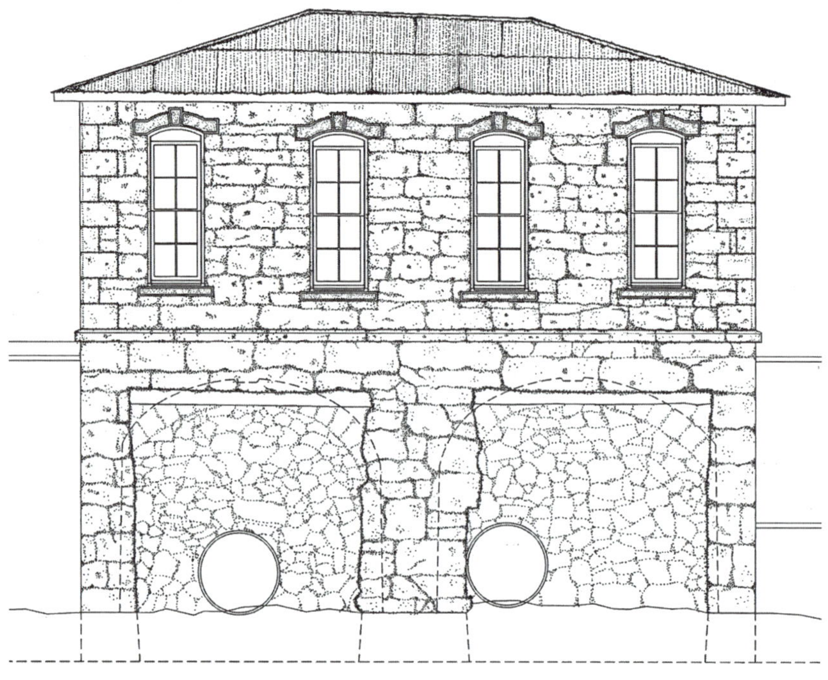

The 1878 water system featured a stone pump house, which survives. Horizontal wheels of two turbines forced water to the pump house's upper level to run two Worthington pumps, piping river water to a hilltop reservoir more than a mile away.

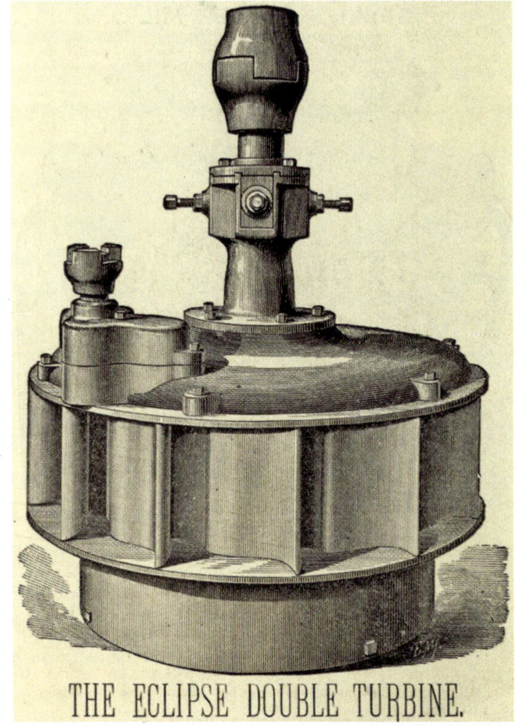

THE ECLIPSE DOUBLE TURBINE.

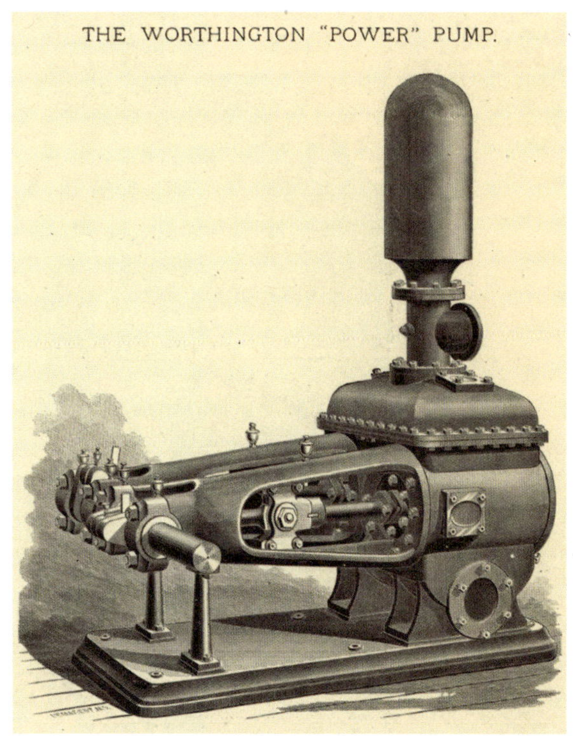

THE WORTHINGTON "POWER" PUMP.

LaCoste's San Antonio Ice Company could produce two tons of ice a day, giving LaCoste an understanding of water machinery and the importance of a water source purer than the San Antonio River and the acequias.[53]

The Water Works pumping operation would be in the Upper Labor Acequia dam area on the fourteen acres of former Confederate government property the city still owned. The city leased the site to LaCoste, and for building materials granted him use of the city rock quarry nearby. LaCoste picked William R. Freeman, a local civil and hydraulic engineer who had designed water systems in Kansas City and Austin, to design and supervise construction. Freeman also became secretary and construction contractor of the Water Works company. Treasurer was S. A. Oliver, local representative of King Iron Bridge and Manufacturing Company of Cleveland, Ohio, builder of several iron bridges in San Antonio. Oliver's company was the low bidder, at $94,000, for equipping a pump house and constructing the water system.[54]

A straight 40-foot-wide raceway was dug from the dam 650 feet to a river switchback, 9 feet lower. The incline created a flow strong enough to power pumps and force water through cast iron and wooden pipes a foot in diameter to a reservoir on the highest point nearby, a hilltop a mile east in what became Mahncke Park.[55]

Freeman built a stylish two-level limestone block pump house straddling the raceway where it met the river. The landmark building had large quoins, decorative second-level entry arches, and angled, raised window lintels with keystones. Two iron pumps from New York's Henry R. Worthington Hydraulic Works on the main floor could run at forty strokes a minute. They were powered by water from two horizontal waterwheels—Eclipse double turbines—directly below.[56]

The turbines' blades caught raceway water as it rushed through arched open bays in the lower level of the pump house. Turning thirty times a minute, the turbines spun the water upward through pipes to power the pumps. The turbines' horizontal wheels, six feet in diameter, were the pride of Stillwell & Bierce Manufacturing in Dayton, Ohio. By running an average of fourteen hours a day, the pumps could keep the reservoir full.[57]

The Water Works began operation on July 3, 1878. But the reservoir, delayed by a change in location, was not ready, and water had to be pumped directly into a twelve-mile pipe network throughout the city. Contractor Thomas Cavanaugh kept his "full force of men and mules with plows, scrapers, picks, and shovels" at work digging and finishing out the reservoir pit, twenty feet deep and able to hold more than five million gallons within stone walls 164 feet wide and 194 feet long.[58]

Seven months later the reservoir was finished. When city officials arrived to inspect the completed reservoir in April 1879 the water level was at seven feet and it was still being filled. The reservoir was expected to be full in three more days, when gravity would take over the flow to consumers. Much of the reservoir survives, long empty and half-filled with dirt, as an amphitheater in the San Antonio Botanical Garden.[59]

Ever the entrepreneur, Jean LaCoste did not stop with a waterworks. The strong flow down the raceway would produce more than enough water power for his turbines, and LaCoste saw the opportunity to use expertise from his ice-making operation on the river downtown for an ice plant. Adjoining the pump house's east wall, he put up a frame building sixty-five feet long and twenty-five feet wide and installed a machine from Chicago's Boyle Ice Machine Company. A belt through the eastern doorway of the pump house turned a shaft that likely powered the ice-making machine. An even flow of ammonia-based freezing fluids was maintained around a system of steel boxes holding water to manufacture four-hundred-pound blocks

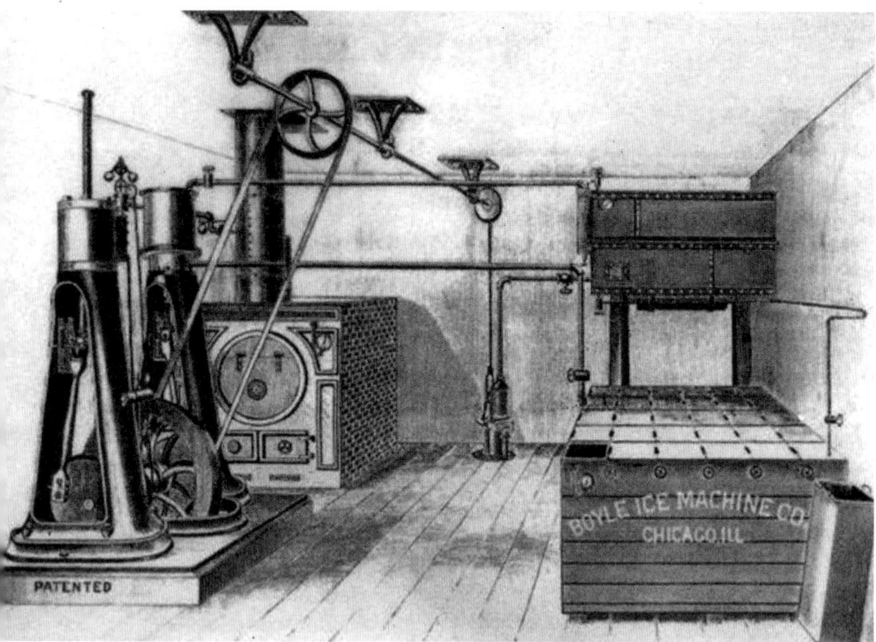

In an ice-making plant similar to the one beside the 1878 pump house, a pump piped ammonia-based freezing fluids around steel boxes holding water.

of ice. The ice plant went into production when pump house operations started in July 1878.[60]

There were few major customers for ice close by, but LaCoste was thinking large. Newly developed railroad refrigerator cars had revolutionized the shipment of meat. LaCoste gathered potential investors, including George Brackenridge and Thomas W. Peirce, head of the company that had built the railroad from Houston to San Antonio, who expressed interest in building a meatpacking plant near the pump house. A rail spur from downtown would bring cars to be cooled with fresh blocks of ice, unencumbered by the cost of being transported from elsewhere. The refrigerated cars would carry beef and mutton to Saint Louis and Chicago or to Galveston for loading on ships headed to markets in France.[61]

A year later, a city committee studying a water shortage in the acequias, still the source of water for more users than the waterworks, inspected the headwaters springs, many of which had dried up during a drought. The committee concluded that too much water diverted into the pump house raceway was being used for the ice factory. Whether or not that ominous finding dampened investors' optimism, LaCoste's financial grip on the Water Works company was slipping. He had already used the ice plant as collateral for a loan. Neither rail spur nor meatpacking plant materialized, and mention of the ice factory's existence eventually vanished.[62]

To build the waterworks, Jean LaCoste raised $100,000 from investors, some $2.5 million today. That barely paid for construction. Operations were to be covered by fees from the several hundred users expected to sign up at once. But only some businesses and a few dozen residents did. Change came slowly in San Antonio. Acequia water was still free, and drinking water from mobile vendors—who began pirating water from the new fire hydrants—was cheap. Even before the Water Works opened, LaCoste needed a loan. He got it from George Brackenridge's San Antonio National Bank.[63]

Brackenridge had been little involved in efforts to establish the waterworks. LaCoste laid water pipes to Brackenridge's home nearby, and Brackenridge let LaCoste use his telegraph poles to carry lines from the pump house to LaCoste's office downtown. But soon Brackenridge became fascinated with the engineering and began to sense opportunity. He traded his first and subsequent loans for new stock in the company, which he could see was ill positioned to expand in time to meet the needs of the fast-growing city. By 1879 Brackenridge owned a majority of the stock and was president of the company.[64]

By then San Antonians were catching on to the advantages of a modern water system, and the number of paid users had risen to more than five hundred. But the company still needed more cash, and by 1883 Brackenridge, with a few friends and relatives, owned all the stock. They reorganized as the Water Works Company with stock capitalization at $500,000 plus another $500,000 in bonds. LaCoste was out, but he still ranked among the city's ten wealthiest men.[65]

Meanwhile Brackenridge's fraught relationship with the city was souring further, provoked by resentment over his powerful financial position and his refusal to let the city renege on its

[DUPLICATE.]

San Antonio, Texas, ______ 187

To the San Antonio Water Works Co.

The Undersigned Hereby applies for water 1 year to be used upon the premises, located as follows: Menger Hotel

and for the following purposes: ~~Two~~ Twelve Water Closets two Bath Tubs and inside Hotel purposes

agreeing hereby to pay for said water privilege ~~monthly~~ Quarterly, in advance, the sum of Thirty dollars in U. S. currency, and hereby orders you or your authorized agent to tap the main ~~in front of~~ said premises and lay a 1½ inch Enameled service pipe with corporation and service stops from said main to Connect with Pipes at Curb Stone on Blum St also ½ in Pipe from St Sprinkler to Connect with Pipe already laid for a wash stand

and furnish in place, complete and ready for use, the following pipes and fixtures inside said premises:

for which pipes and fixtures I promise to pay the sum of Sixty Nine 25/100 in U. S. currency on the completion of said work, and agree hereby to observe and abide by the Rules and Regulations of the SAN ANTONIO WATER WORKS COMPANY.

[SIGNED.] Mary Menger.

Accepted – W. R. Freeman – Sect S.A.W.W.Co.

An early customer for running water was the Menger Hotel, which applied to use it for twelve bathrooms, two bathtubs, and "inside hotel purposes."

contractual obligations to the Water Works and on the loans his bank often made to the city to sustain municipal operations until tax revenues came in. He was derided as a "monopolizer," "rich banker," even "war profiteer." But in the case of the Water Works, he controlled both the land and the water rights needed to expand, and he had no need to negotiate with anyone.[66]

The reservoir soon needed more water to maintain a steady supply for the city, whose population had nearly doubled since the waterworks opened. Brackenridge was sufficiently concerned to train a telescope on the top floor of his home on the water level gauge at the hilltop reservoir a mile away so he could monitor the water level. The original water-powered pumps were operating at capacity. More powerful steam-powered pumps were an option for expanding service but cost more to run. A stronger water-powered pump needed more force than that provided by the existing raceway, and the narrow San Antonio River in the immediate vicinity dropped too slightly to provide sufficient force for a second pump house nearby.

Meanwhile, Brackenridge had been increasing his holdings in the area. He had already bought from Samuel Maverick's widow, in 1876, two hundred acres between the east bank of the river and the Alamo Acequia. During the next ten years, as his control of the waterworks grew, Brackenridge bought ninety acres of riverfront tracts to the south from the Guilbeau and de la Garza families and forty-five acres foreclosed on by the banking firm of Bennett and Thornton.[67]

The additional holdings were useful when a second pump house was needed. There was no place to gain enough new water power near the pump house already operating, but the winding river offered an opportunity a mile south on Brackenridge's new land. A raceway canal begun slightly downstream of the original pump house would encounter a bend in the river a mile straight south. Over the distance the river dropped twelve feet—three feet more than in the short raceway to the first pump house—and could run stronger pumps.

In 1885 a new pump house was built straddling the end of the new raceway canal, a structure that later gained fame as the Borglum Studio. Its two stories of rough-faced ashlar limestone blocks featured detailed limestone window sills, lintels, and entry door arches. Two turbines ran a single Worthington Duplex Double-Acting Power Pump that sent three million gallons daily up to the reservoir, more than doubling the capacity of the first pump house. Ten years later a pump run by steam was in place.[68]

Yet the waterworks was still challenged by San Antonio's unrelenting growth, and the reservoir needed even more water

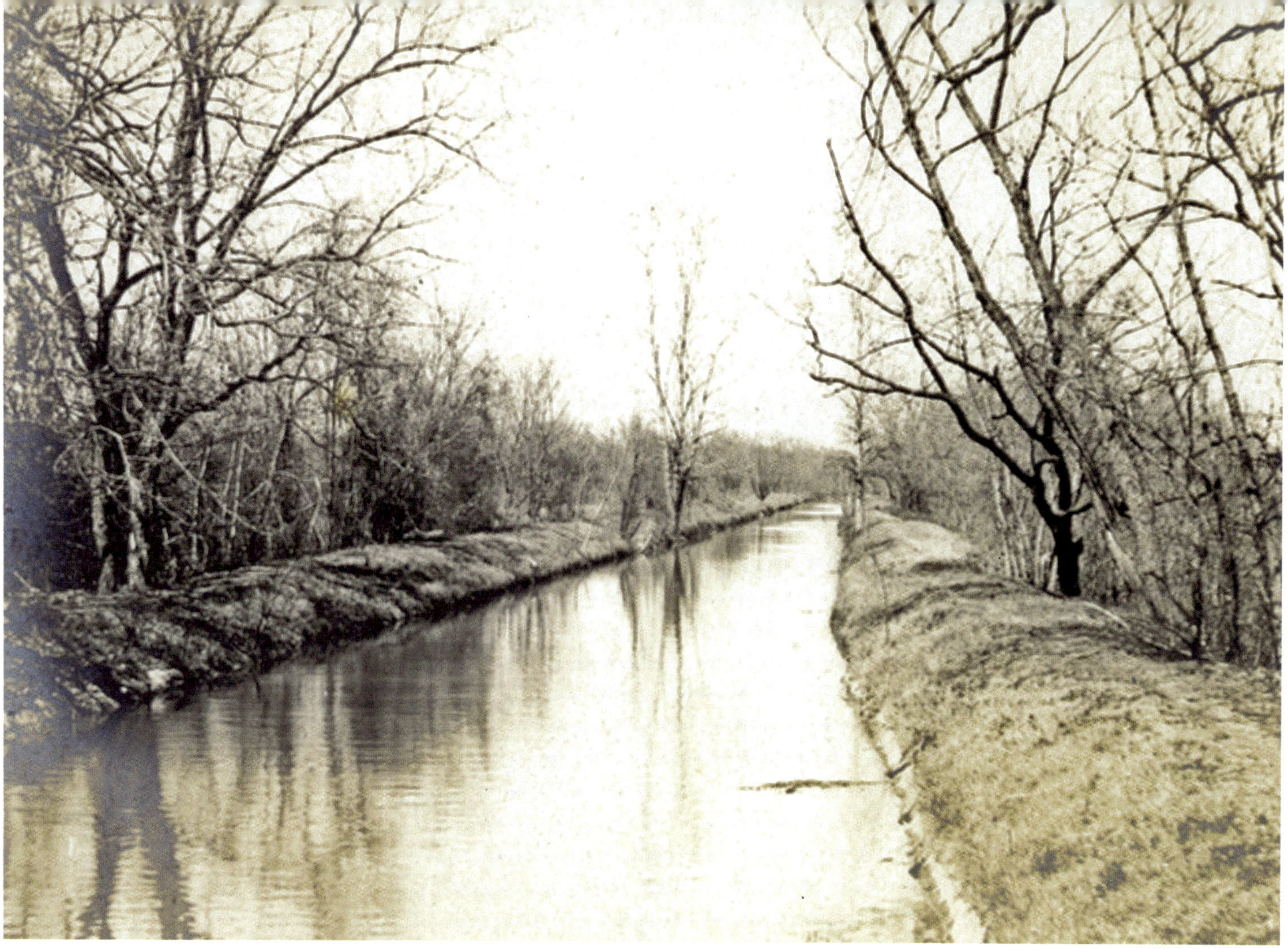

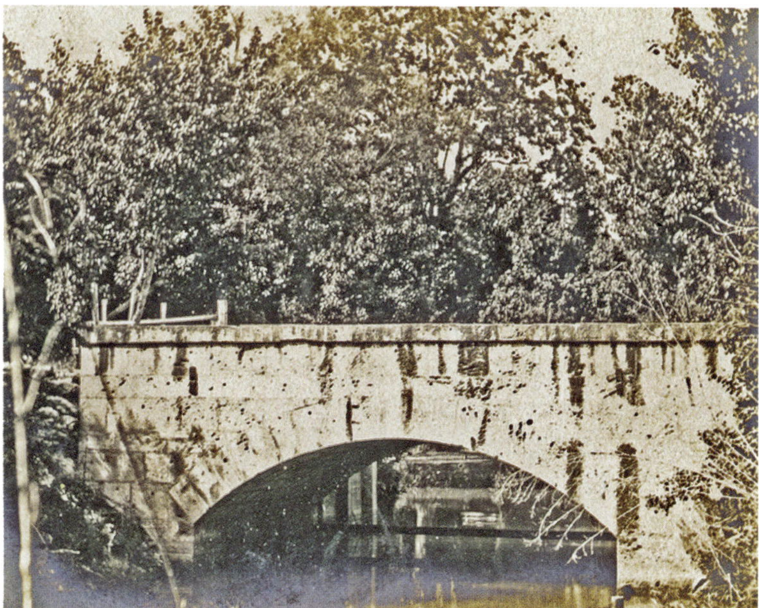

This canal was dug in 1885 from the river across from today's Koehler Pavilion to a second pump house, near the present-day golf course clubhouse. The bridge is believed to have been near the main low water crossing at the head of the canal, with water controlled by a gate below.

By the late 1880s, drilling into the Edwards Aquifer was producing gushers of water. An artesian well drilled unsuccessfully by Brackenridge in 1889 is beside the left wall of the Water Works reservoir, now half-filled with soil and shown adapted as an amphitheater in the San Antonio Botanical Garden. Some of the columns intended to support a stone covering, apparently never built, help form an arbor.

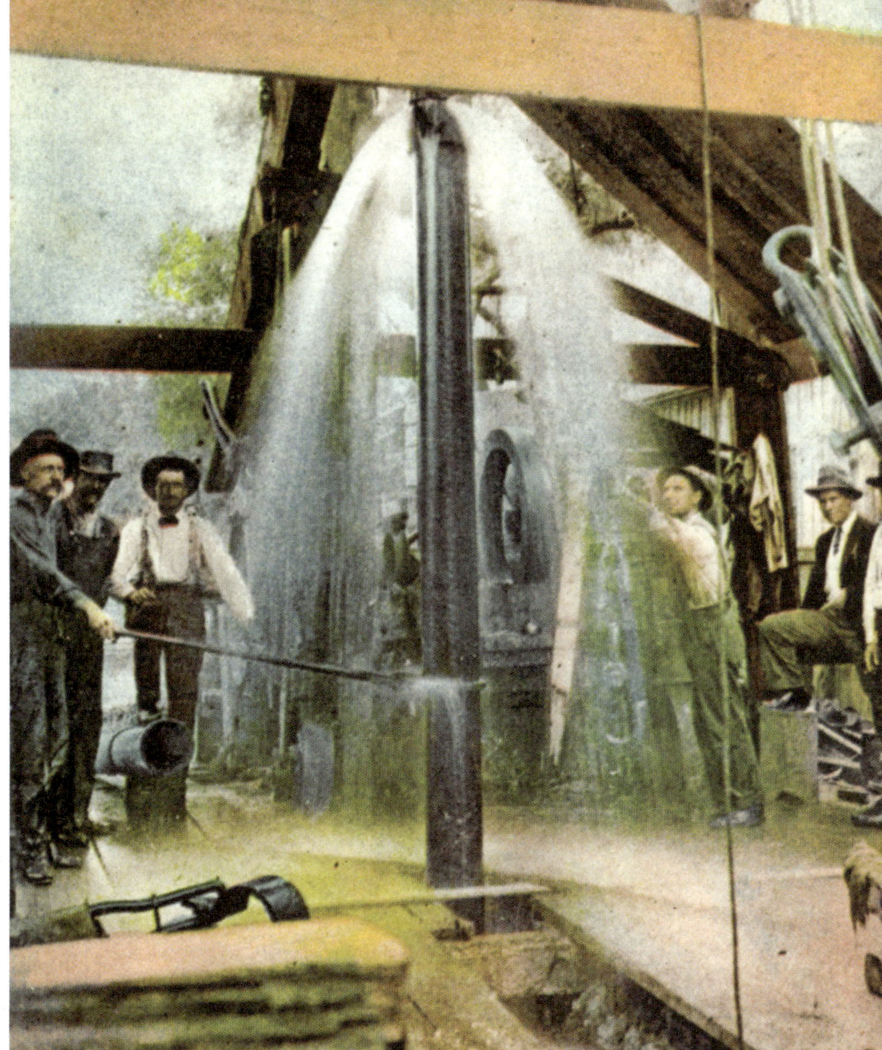

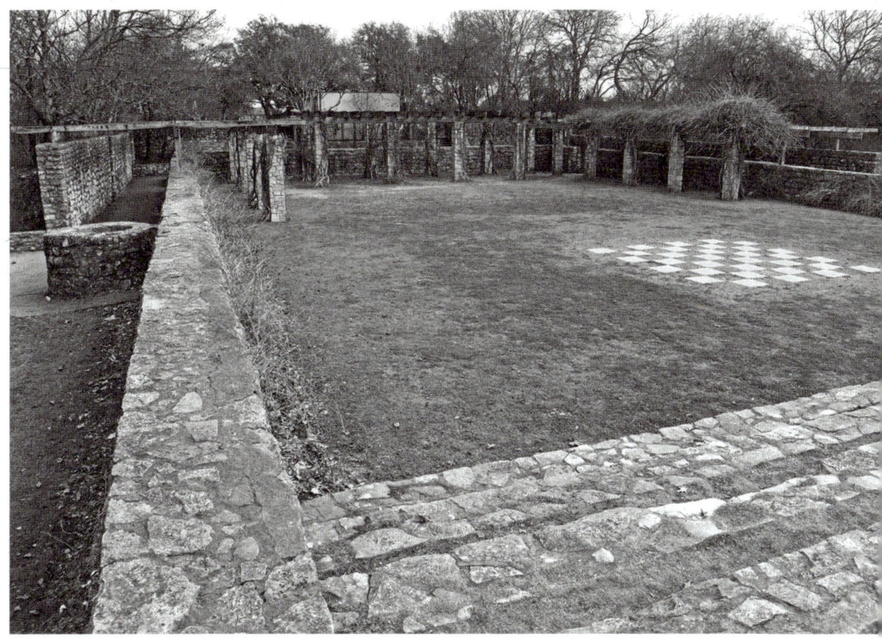

to maintain a steady supply. The water table was dropping and the lowering river level made it difficult to provide sufficient power for the existing pumps. In 1887 the river nearly dried up altogether, causing the waterworks to plead for limits on water use, especially for watering lawns.[69]

To the rescue came deep artesian wells. The wells had first been drilled in California, and the concept spread to Texas. Thanks to underground pressure the best artesian wells required no pumping; water "just flowed over the top." In 1889, beside the San Antonio River at the northern edge of downtown, the Crystal Ice Company completed the first artesian well into the Edwards Aquifer and began three more. Brackenridge took note.[70]

An artesian well beside the reservoir could pour water directly in, eliminating the need to pump water from the river. Brackenridge drilled next to the reservoir's north wall in 1889. "I remember as well as if it were yesterday our disappointment over the first well," H. E. Ellsworth, Water Works secretary at the time, recalled years later. "It cost the company, which meant Mr. Brackenridge, $10,000 to prove that it was a duster. The well was a miserable failure and the money was entirely lost."[71]

In 1891 Brackenridge drilled downtown at the corner of Market Street and the river. When it struck, rocks blew out "as large as a man's head." Water spouted twenty feet high over the pipe's rim. More wells were drilled nearby. Brackenridge built a pumping station on Market Street, where wells are still active.[72]

While Jean LaCoste and George Brackenridge were getting a modern municipal water system established, a chance discovery half a mile away, also within what is now northern Brackenridge Park, sparked a major industrial development.

In 1879 Englishman William Loyd was hunting game near the city-owned quarries when he noticed some blue argillaceous limestone. Familiar with cement production in England, he

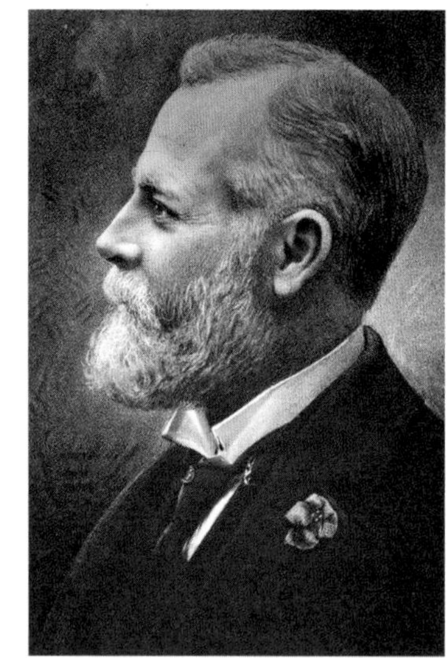

George Kalteyer established and headed a cement company within today's Brackenridge Park.

knew it to be a rock that cement was made from and took it to George H. Kalteyer, a druggist at his father's store on Military Plaza, for confirmation. Kalteyer, who was also the state chemist, had assisted in a government study of cement as a university student in Germany, which along with England dominated the industry.[73]

Kalteyer's analysis showed that the rock contained the right mixture of lime and clay to make high-grade Portland cement, noted for its ability to harden more quickly than the more common Roman cement and thus speed construction projects. Loyd and Kalteyer checked with William R. Freeman, the hydraulic engineer who supervised the initial waterworks construction. He confirmed that the local rock could be burned into the quality of Portland cement used for hydraulic cement, which could harden and endure underwater.[74]

Portland cement was being made in the United States only at a plant in eastern Pennsylvania, which could not keep up with demand. Most had to be imported at premium prices. Loyd and Kalteyer wasted no time in getting investors and forming the Alamo Portland and Roman Cement Company, chartered in January 1880 with offices upstairs from the Kalteyer drugstore. They got a renewable five-year lease from the city for a site on Quarry Road along the west bank of the Upper Labor Acequia that included water rights to the acequia. Remains of an old Spanish lime kiln were nearby.[75]

A tramway carried rock from the quarry to a brick-lined pot kiln, inefficient but easy to construct, standing thirty-two feet high and nine feet wide with openings at the base for refueling and a central opening for removing the product. It also produced lime. A second pot kiln was added the next year. Fires fueled by coke—charcoal produced by burning coal—heated the rock in a weeklong process to temperatures exceeding 2,000 degrees Fahrenheit.[76]

After burning removed the limestone's impurities, what would become Portland cement formed lumps known as clinkers. The rest was separated to make the lower quality Roman cement. Rocks were fed into a chillingly named Blake Jaw Crusher to be ground into smaller lumps and sent through a pair of rollers and into an elevator to the top floor of the three-story frame mill building. There lumps were ground into powder by a French burr mill powered by a small steam engine.

The powdery cement was spread six to nine inches thick across the two upper floors, where it was turned with shovels to aerate and season for a week. Then it was moved to wooden bins on the ground floor and hand-packed into barrels or heavy cotton bags. As orders came in, the containers were hauled three miles to a train station; the wagons returned with fuel. The initial capacity was ten barrels a day.[77]

By fall 1881 the company had fourteen workers and thirteen wagon drivers, and sales had reached a thousand barrels a year. The company shortened its name to Alamo Cement Company and upgraded to a Schoefer vertical kiln. Its design, originating in Germany, allowed for continuous production with chambers for heating, burning, and cooling the raw material. Average production rose to fifty barrels a day. Remains of the Schoefer kiln and chimney are a landmark in Brackenridge Park.[78]

Armed with glowing test results from a noted civil engineer in New York, George Kalteyer two years later persuaded the state to revise specifications for the capitol under construction in Austin and give preference to native Texas cement. Use of the Kentucky cement originally chosen went no further than the foundations and basement walls, and from 1884 to 1887 Alamo Cement delivered the remaining cement for the capitol. The number of company employees rose above forty, and production reached two hundred barrels a day.[79]

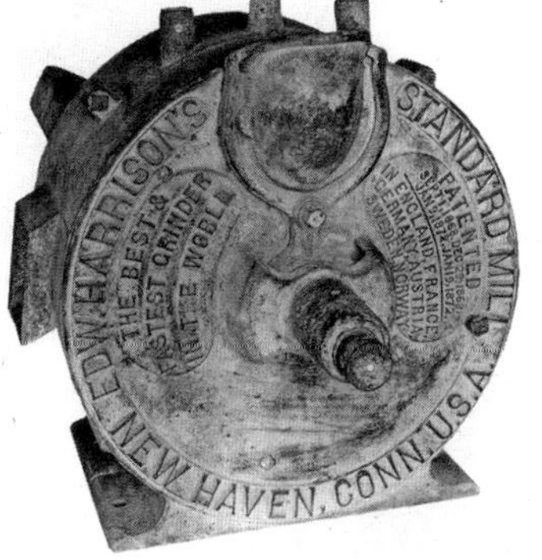

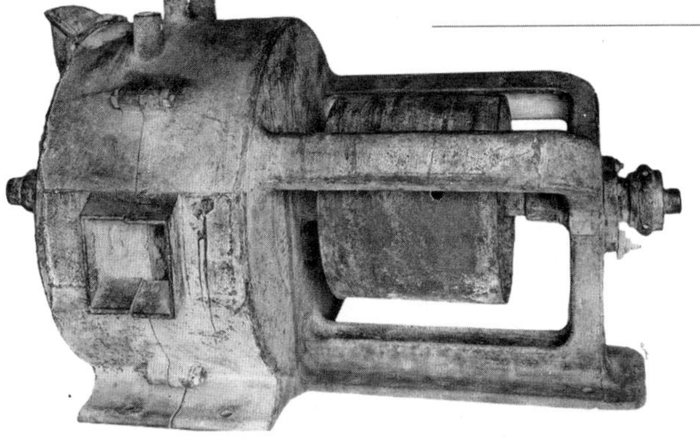

The Alamo Portland and Roman Cement Company saved one of its first pieces of equipment, this French burr mill, "the best & fastest grinder in the world." Rocks shoveled into its top were ground fine by two stone wheels powered by a small steam engine and discharged through the chute at left center.

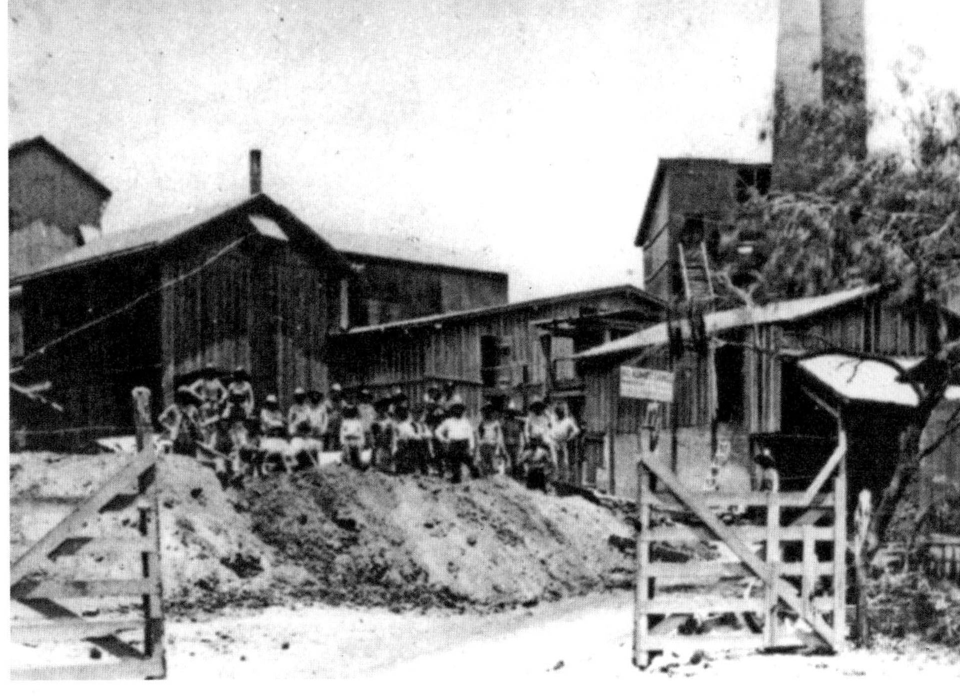

The cement company included a three-story building for grinding and processing cement.

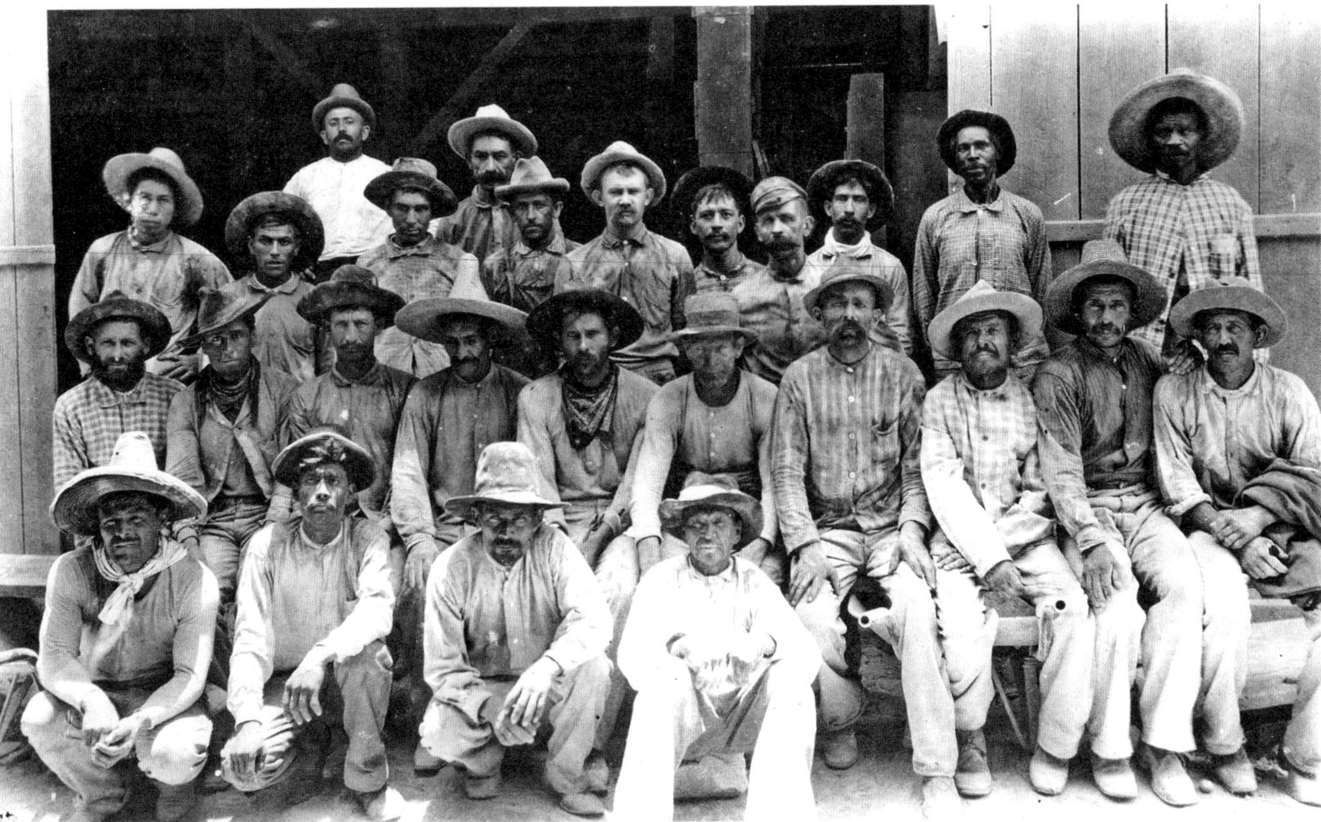

More than two dozen cement company workers gathered in about 1890.

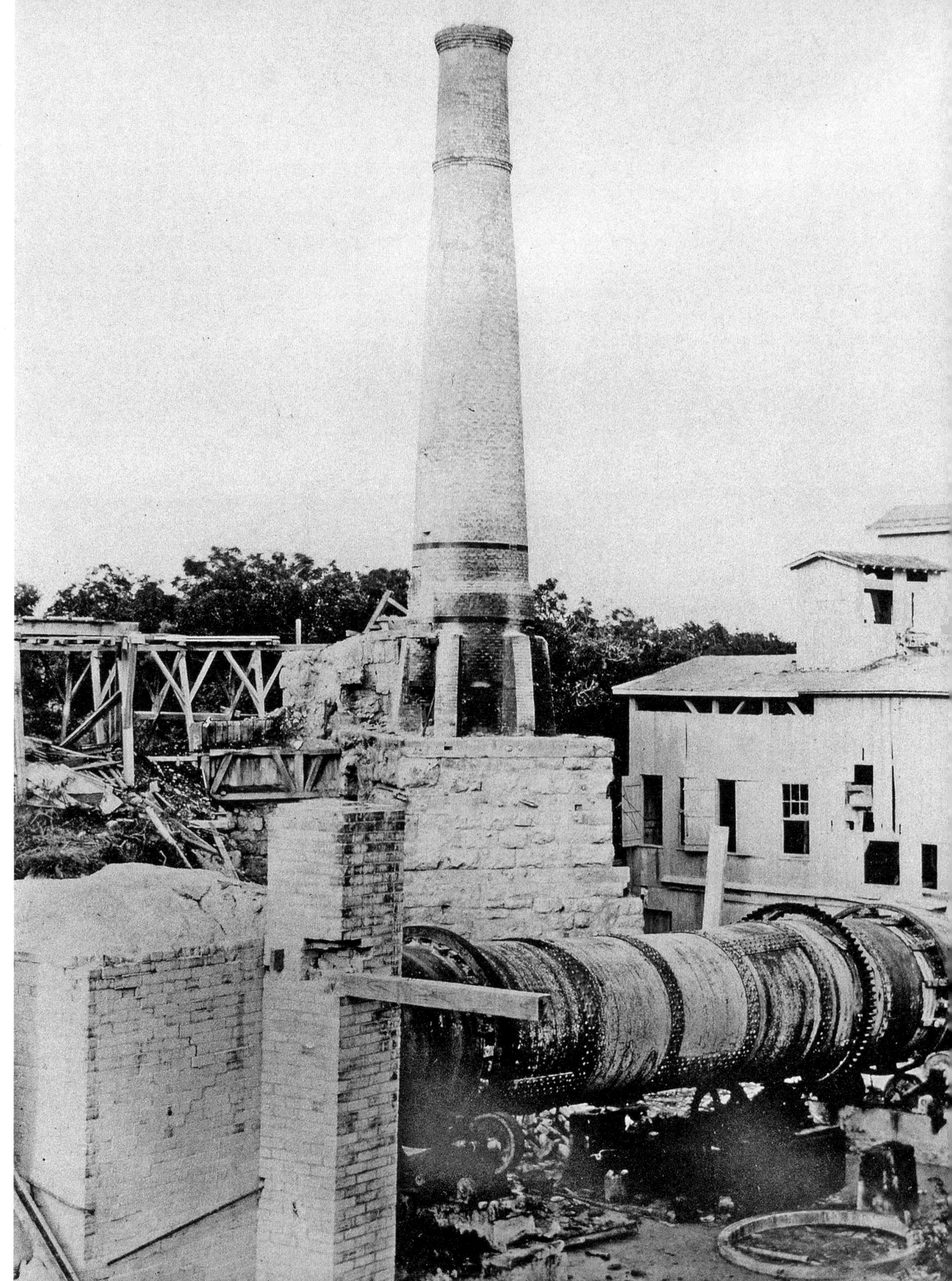

Alamo Cement installed an innovative rotary kiln, foreground, in the late 1890s. The Schoefer vertical kiln and chimney, background, were built in 1881.

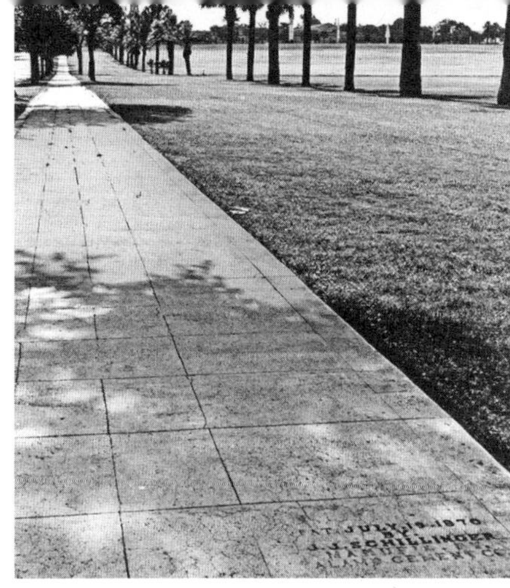

Sidewalks laid in the 1880s by Alamo Cement using a patented formula were still in use at Fort Sam Houston nearly a century later.

Seated at the right is German-born Nic Behles, plant superintendent from 1890 to 1910.

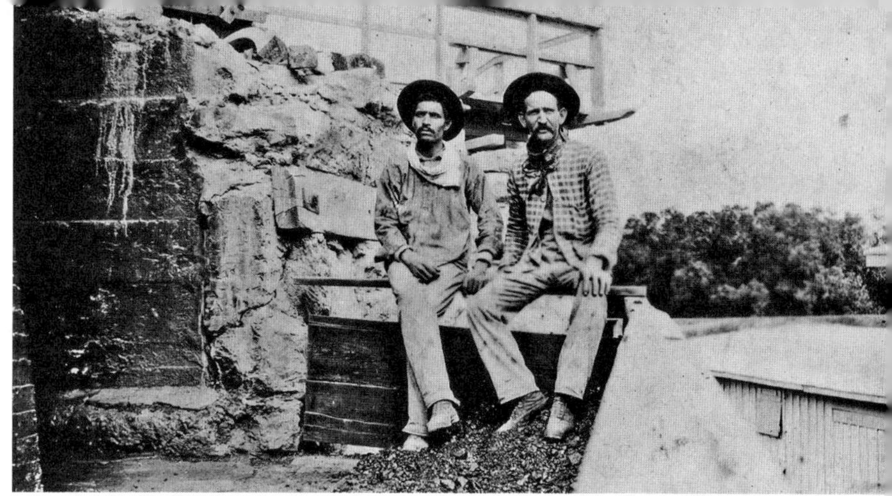

Like Brackenridge, Kalteyer benefited from access to sufficient funding to see his company through its difficult early days. He supplemented low cement sales with sidelines like providing quarried stone for construction and making lime for mortar. Unable to convince local contractors to build sidewalks not with lumber but with more durable if expensive concrete—then known as "artificial stone"—Kalteyer went into the sidewalk business himself. He paid $1,000, today's equivalent of $25,000, for Texas rights to New York manufacturer John J. Schillinger's patented technique and formula for making sidewalks of Portland cement. Alamo Cement put in sidewalks, laid in sections to allow for expansion and contraction, for the city of San Antonio and Fort Sam Houston.[80]

By the mid-1890s Portland cement companies were increasingly shifting from upright Schoefer kilns to horizontal rotary kilns, which turned slowly as they mixed and cooked the cement with hot gases. Their boilers, however, had to be fueled with oil as yet commercially unavailable in Texas. That was merely a small obstacle for Kalteyer, who had also transformed his family drugstore into the retail and wholesale San Antonio Drug Company and cofounded a Portland cement company in Ohio.

To solve the matter of boiler fuel, Kalteyer learned of modified equipment developed in Germany. He sailed there and obtained patent rights and equipment for using powdered coal instead of oil. But he returned seriously ill and died in a Philadelphia hospital in 1897 at age forty-eight.[81]

Purchasing and installing the fifty-foot-long rotary kiln fell to Kalteyer's successor as president, Charles Baumberger, who at seventeen began clerking at the Kalteyer drugstore and took on part-time bookkeeping at the Alamo Cement office upstairs. He soon went full-time. By 1890 he was Alamo Cement's secretary and manager.[82]

Alamo Cement continued to grow under Baumberger's management. But moving heavy barrels of cement by wagon to the nearest rail yard three miles away became an increasing burden. Officials also tired of being "continuously annoyed by the political factions" that trifled over lease terms with the city. In addition, with a park on one side and growing neighborhoods on another, there was no room for expansion. The company purchased a three-hundred-acre quarry site three miles north, just past Alamo Heights city limits, and moved there in 1908. Production increased from two hundred barrels to fifteen hundred barrels a day, and workers could live in Cementville, a tidy company town that was a far cry from the scattered small stone homes they had lived in around the first quarries.[83]

One of Baumberger's memories of Alamo Cement's earliest years was of the county poor farm south down Rock Quarry Road at East Mulberry Avenue that led his skeptical friends to josh investors that when the cement company failed they wouldn't have far to go.[84]

His quip is among the few references found to the Bexar County Poor Farm and Hospital, whose fields were within the western side of Brackenridge Park and its buildings farther west, beyond the present-day park. In 1886 residents included forty-one males and thirteen females who farmed the more than twenty acres as they were able. Also living there were the superintendent, Joseph A. Smith, and a druggist, Albert Huppertz, who served as steward.[85]

San An
LIDAY HOL

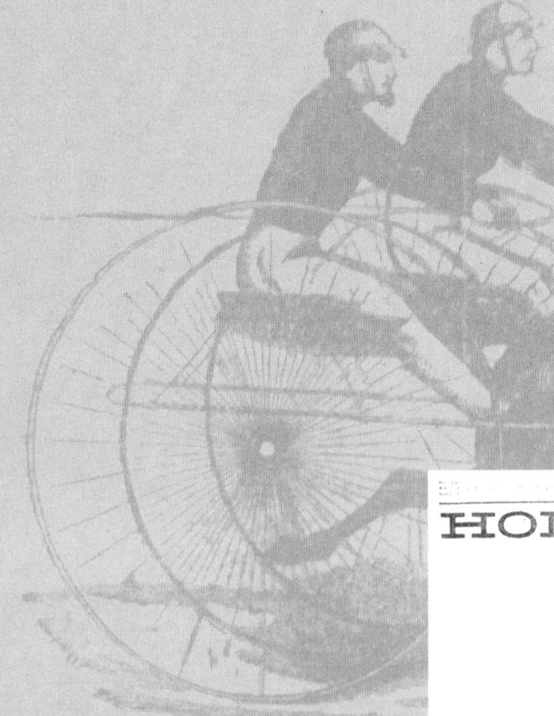

San Antonio, Texas.

HOLIDAY HOLIDAY

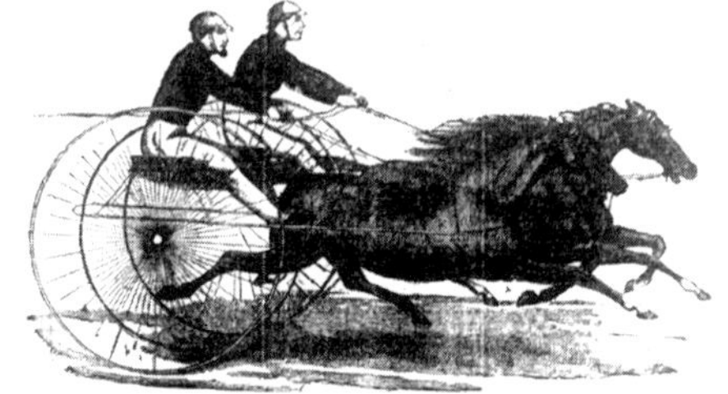

RACES! RACES! RACES!

Under the Auspices of the

SAN ANTONIO JOCKEY CLUB.

2 DAYS--TUESDAY AND WEDNESDAY

DECEMBER 26-27.

$1,000 IN CASH and SPECIAL PREMIUMS

H. D. KAMPMANN, President. J. R. HOOPER, Secretary.

CES! R R
Unde
ANTONI
DAYS--TUESDAY AND WEDNES
DECEMBER 26-2
IN CASH and SPECIAL PR
D. KAMPMANN, President. J. R. HOOPER, S

The Jockey Club and the International Fair

A group of racehorse owners met at Hermann D. Kampmann's Menger Hotel in May 1893 to organize the San Antonio Jockey Club. Its purpose was to sponsor two days of races on July 4 at Riverside Park, later renamed Roosevelt Park, home each fall to the International Fair. The races were a success, but club members were disenchanted with the general inconvenience of the indirect route to Riverside Park, three miles south of downtown.[86]

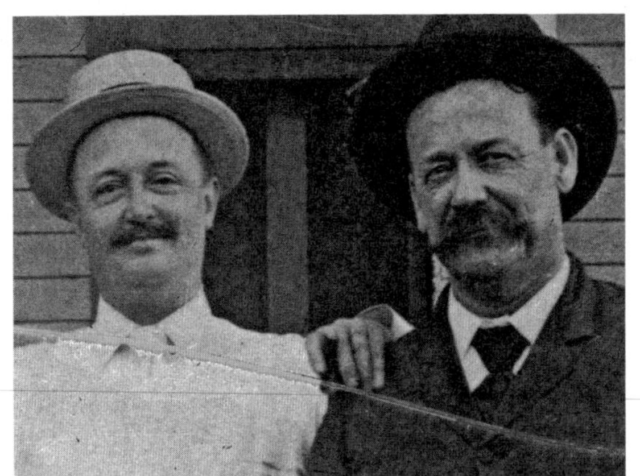

Hermann Kampmann, *left*, with Bryan Callaghan at a celebration of Callaghan's election as mayor.

Hermann Kampmann was the son of the late building contractor and quarry operator John H. Kampmann. His ownership of the Menger and of gas and electric companies helped rank him a distant second in local wealth to George Brackenridge, who also belonged to the Jockey Club. With Kampmann's encouragement, club members, soon numbering 130, thought they could find a place easier to reach than the privately owned Riverside Park and snag the International Fair. The fair, cosponsored by the city and the Mexican government, was in its fifth year and drawing tens of thousands of visitors annually to its grand exhibition hall, racetrack, stock show, and amusement area.[87]

In summer 1893 Jockey Club members formed the independent San Antonio Park Association to purchase from George Brackenridge twenty-six acres two miles north of downtown on a section of today's Brackenridge Park Golf Course. The site extended from River Avenue west to Brackenridge's Water Works raceway canal, still flowing but no longer needed for the city's water supply. The park association in turn leased the tract to the club in hopes of inspiring the International Fair to relocate there as soon as "the wisdom of the city embraces the splendid opportunity."[88]

In November 1893 the Jockey Club launched a fall racing season. Its half-mile oval track, rolled and fenced, was wide enough for seven sulkies to race abreast. Through an ornate triple-arched entrance on River Avenue, a gravel road and cinder paths led to the ticket office and turnstiles and to the grandstand beyond. Designed by noted architect and club member James Riely Gordon, whose credits would soon include the Bexar County Courthouse, the grandstand rose on the far side of the track and faced River Avenue. Ninety feet long, with twenty tiered rows of seating for 1,500, it included private boxes and refreshment rooms. On a floor

The track featured horse racing from 1893 to 1898.

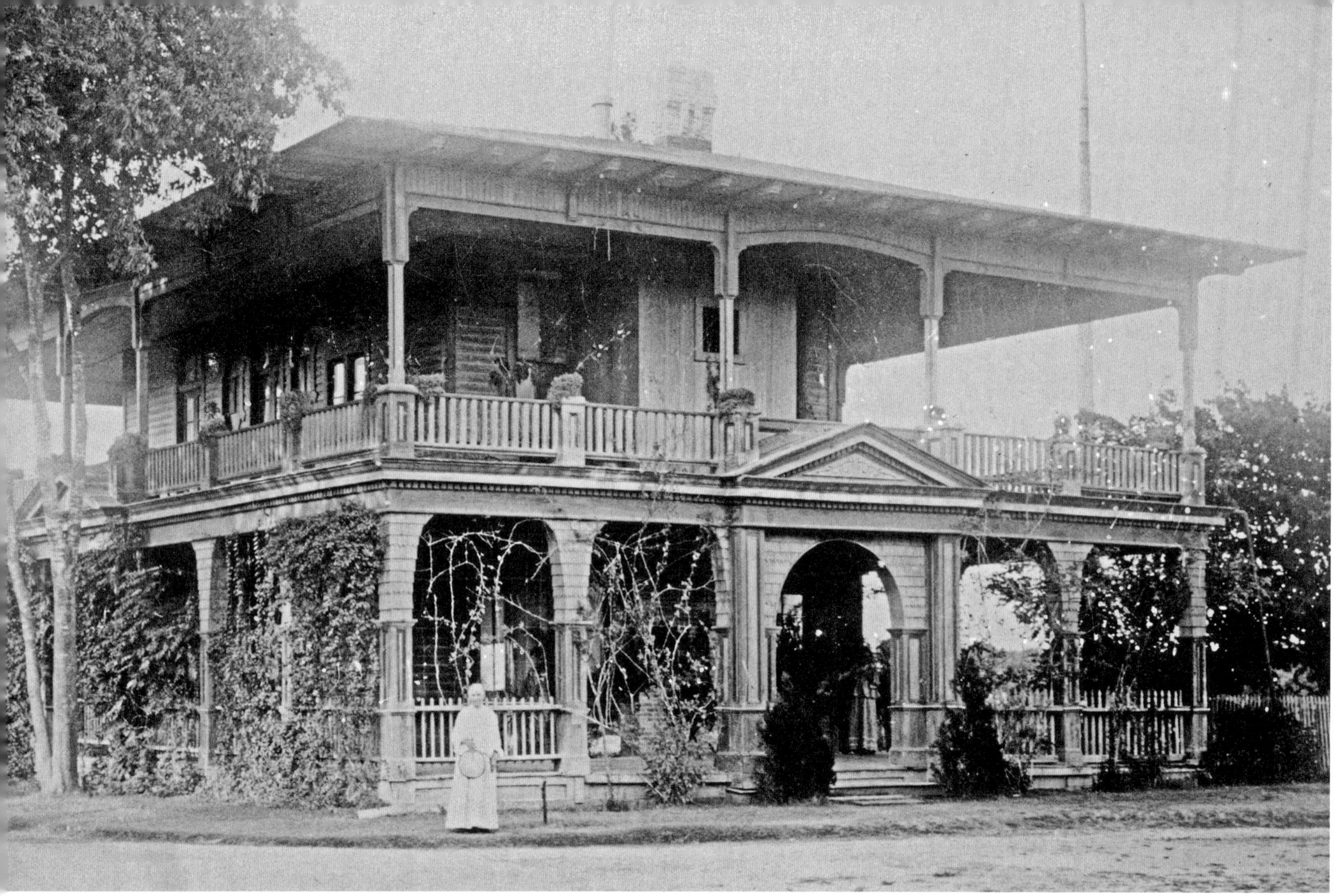

Jockey Club members could watch races from the clubhouse galleries.

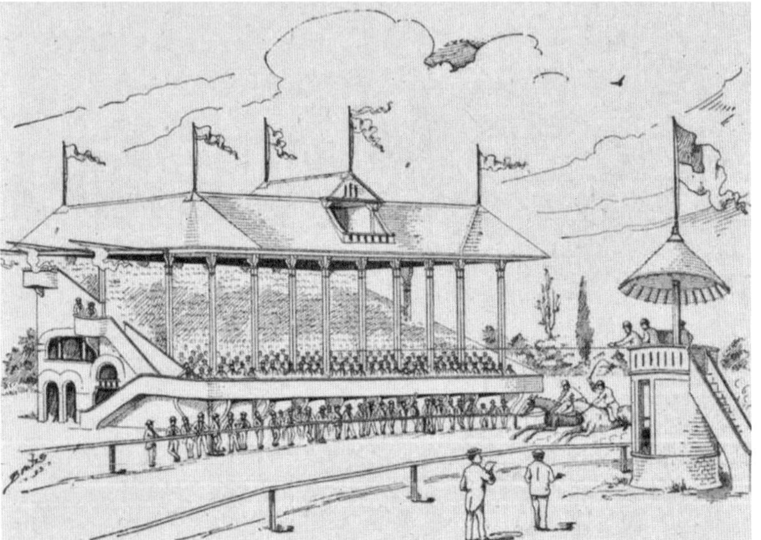

The Jockey Club's grandstand had twenty tiered rows of seating and a bandstand set into the roof.

Bicyclists competed on a track of wooden boards banked around the outer rim of the horse track.

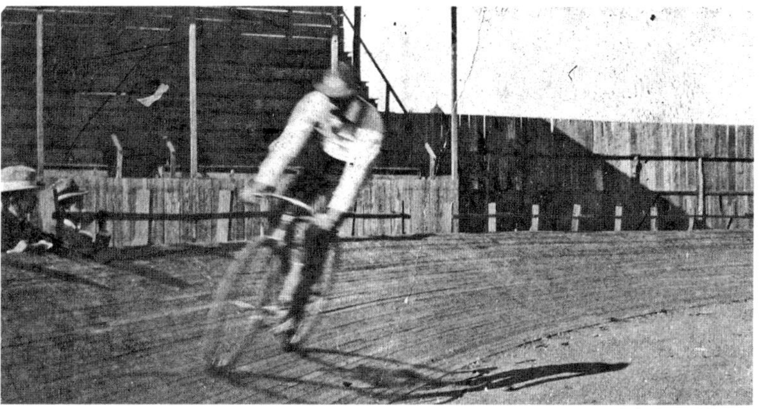

above the spectators and tucked into the roof, a bandstand was positioned so that "the blare of trumpets, the thunder of drums, and the clash of cymbals" would not reverberate too loudly in the seats below. Stables for two hundred horses lined the site's north end and continued around the western property boundary.[89]

Five days of racing began on November 7. Prizes totaled $5,000. Several dozen horses owned by San Antonians were supplemented by others brought in by stable owners elsewhere in Texas and beyond. Two more days of races were held after Christmas. During the spring 1894 season, newspapers reported brightly that even though "there was much to discourage the club in advance" the races went "far beyond the expectations." Reports did allow that due to a "scarcity of entries" club owners "may still fall a little short of complete financial success." Things picked up in the fall, when two thousand spectators "yelled themselves hoarse" on the season's first day. Betting was "not very heavy," but "merriment reigned supreme."[90]

Ready in time for the spring season was the two-story clubhouse, southeast of the grandstand and destined for a remarkable variety of uses in the three decades ahead. Apparently designed by the grandstand architect, James Riely Gordon, it was in the shape of a parallelogram, the longest side facing the track so Jockey Club members could watch from the wide galleries on both floors. A general reception room, bar, office, and men's restroom were on the first floor, and a large assembly room, ladies' reception room, and ladies' restroom occupied the second.[91]

Setting aside the open land south of the main entrance for future fair grounds, the club planned a stock show for fall 1894 like the International Fair's but on Water Works land across the canal from the grandstand. There were plans for agricultural and textile display buildings, but backers were unable to raise even the $4,000 needed to put on the stock show. Less ambitious projects succeeded. In June 1894 the club added seating and a stage at the grandstand's north end for a summer theater, opened with evening performances by the visiting Spanish Opera Company. Local clubs played baseball on the grounds. A showman named Col. Buck Hice put on a Wild West show.[92]

The Jockey Club's most famous guest was world heavyweight champion Jim Corbett, who trained there for a few weeks in October 1895 before an exhibition match with Bob Fitzsimmons at the Grand Opera House downtown. Corbett took over the clubhouse and worked out on a handball court built for him and on equipment in the new gymnasium, which had previously served as the summer theater stage.[93]

The Jockey Club's longest relationship was with San Antonio bicycle clubs, which were racing at the track by 1895. Bicycle races had become the nation's top spectator sport, and many Texas towns had at least one professional rider. Houston and Dallas built velodromes that could seat more than two thousand spectators to watch cyclists compete around quarter-mile ovals of high-banked wooden boards. San Antonio joined the Texas circuit with a track of boards banked on the outer rim of the Jockey Club's half-mile horse track. Introduced at one race was "the first" tentuplet bicycle, with seats for ten. Bicycle races drew national stars like Marshall "Major" Taylor—the first Black person to win the title of world cycling champion—and Otto Zeigler, "the California Demon." Extra streetcars went out River Avenue on race days.[94]

Yet the Jockey Club struggled. By June 1897 some fifty subscribers had pledged fifty cents a month—today's equivalent of fifteen dollars monthly—to help "reestablish the former prestige" of the club by repairing the track and resodding the paddock. A year later there had been no notable races since "a small attendance" watched Hermann Kampmann's horse Nedwood nose out Theodore Banks's Princess in the quarter-mile heats in January 1898. No fall season had been announced. Stables waited to be cleaned, the clubhouse needed repair, and weeds were growing everywhere.[95]

An unexpected bonanza landed in the club's lap in September 1898. The First US Volunteer Cavalry—Theodore Roosevelt's Rough Riders—had left its training ground in Riverside Park four months earlier to become the first American force in Cuba at the outset of the Spanish-American War. Soon five wartime militia regiments were organized in Texas, including the Fourth Texas Volunteer Infantry, formed in Houston in July and ordered to San Antonio in September. It was assigned to Fort Sam Houston but planned to bivouac in Riverside Park. Five days before the Fourth Texas was to arrive, however, Riverside Park's water supply was deemed inadequate.[96]

The army scrambled and signed a lease for the entire Jockey Club complex, one of the few alternative sites with enough open ground, an accessible water main, and adequate bathing facilities—the waterworks canal—in close proximity. Like Riverside Park's fairgrounds, it had permanent structures that could be adapted to military use. Government rent checks were better than the uncertain revenues of fall racing and Wild West shows, at least while they lasted.[97]

On September 29, 1898, the 1,282 members of the Fourth Texas Volunteers arrived on trains from Houston. Space was found for two companies at nearby Fort Sam Houston, and the remaining ten companies went to the Jockey Club. Soldiers pitched their tents and began cleaning up the place. Soon all companies were at the club, named Camp Mosby, presumably after the Confederate cavalry hero Col. John S. Mosby.[98]

"The bright blaze of the camp fire was kindled for the first time in the Fourth's history last week, and during the latter part of the nights and early mornings kept burning in the various company streets," reported one dispatch from Camp Mosby. Tents faced south, their floors of wood and the walls "stoutly staked down and quite a number planked up with lumber." There were tents for the hospital and a large lounge tent, set up by the YMCA. Soldiers, after several hours of calisthenics and drills, bathed in the waterworks canal until tubs and showers were installed. Enlisted men went to the canteen under the grandstand for beer, officers to their club in the former jockey clubhouse. The Fourth had its own newspaper, the *Soldier*, edited by Chaplain W. D. Robinson and published on Fridays.[99]

Kitchens were enclosed on all four sides, and mess sheds were built. Some stables were converted as a commissary, and the rest were occupied by soldiers. The adjutant, 1st Lt. Spencer Hutchins, turned two stalls into a single room for his quarters, chinking walls to keep out the cold. He cut a door from his quarters into an adjacent office created by combining the next three stalls into one room. Clerks were kept comfortable with "a good stove." Arriving from New York were thirteen hundred overcoats, useful during a winter so cold that the temperature hovered around zero for several days and the San Antonio River froze. Other than the cold, soldiers' main complaint was the dust kicked up from parades on the former racetrack.[100]

In December, soldiers with little to do began carrying off the furnishings of Limburger's Beer Garden, a mile up River Avenue across from today's Witte Museum and closed for the winter. A quartermaster general investigation used testimony from a streetcar motorman and other passersby to verify Henry Limburger's allegation that soldiers threw 95 eight-foot wooden tables and 152 benches over his fence and took them back to Camp Mosby along with lumber, electric wires, two iron pots, a butcher block, and more. Limburger inspected the camp with the commander and identified some items, which were

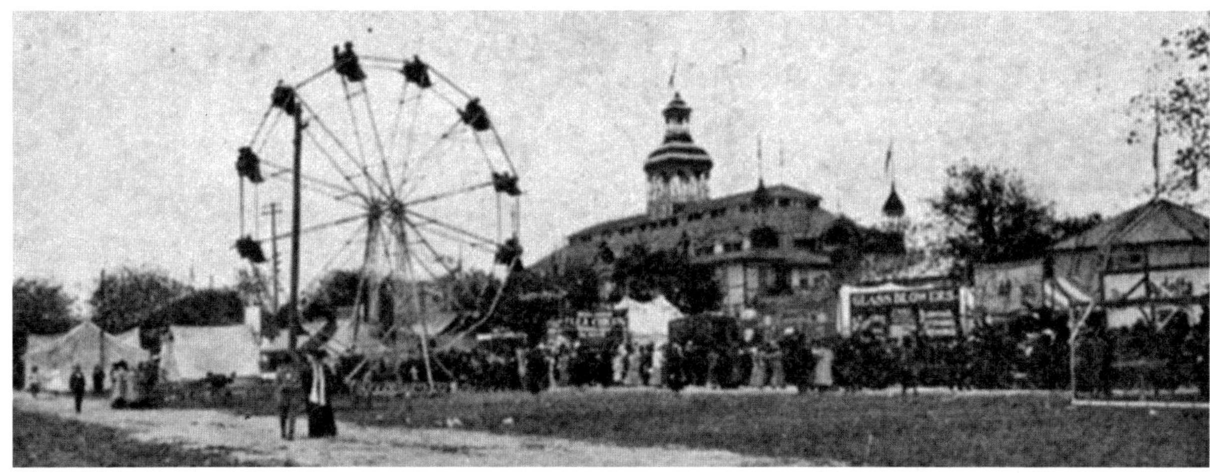

The Jockey Club sought to lure the thriving International Fair away from Riverside Park in 1893.

promptly returned. He submitted a claim for loss and damage of $1,091.25, today's equivalent of $35,000. The secretary of war recommended that Congress pay him.[101]

Soon the neighborhood would quiet down. The Spanish-American War ended in mid-December 1898, three months after soldiers arrived at Camp Mosby. In January its soldiers spread rumors that the real reason for a round of vaccinations was to keep them healthy so they could be held on duty longer, perhaps to go to the Philippines or replace the Third Texas Volunteers on the Mexican border. But in March the Fourth Texas Volunteers were discharged from service and Camp Mosby was dismantled. Those who would be going home to McKinney, its newspaper reported, "are looking forward with glad anticipation to the day that will see them again in civil life."[102]

With a paying tenant gone and chances of reviving a racing season dim, Jockey Club members found their goal of luring the International Fair at risk of going unmet. The fair's Riverside Park leaseholder had offered to sell the Fair Association its eighty-acre park outright for $20,000.

Jockey Club owners decided to match the Riverside price. The Jockey Club package for hosting the fair included the twenty-six acres from River Avenue west to the waterworks canal plus twenty-four adjacent acres west from the canal to the San Antonio River owned by George Brackenridge, for a total of fifty acres. Brackenridge, whose terms for cooperation with Jockey Club owners were not revealed, did specify that his waterworks reserved the right to use the canal if needed.[103]

Fair directors, who included Brackenridge, split evenly on which proposal to accept. The board president, Vories P. Brown, announced he would cast his tie-breaking vote according to what the majority of fair shareholders thought. He set up a special voting place at fair director T. C. Frost's bank for shareholders to cast their ballots four days later, with each share counting as one vote.[104]

A burst of sparring indicated the Jockey Club had the edge on ease of access from downtown, a drive one newspaper reporter measured as seventeen minutes compared with thirty minutes to Riverside Park. Its facilities were judged to be in far better condition and more compactly arranged, the water supply superior, and access up the broad River Avenue from downtown more impressive. A "magnificent grove" of several hundred pecan trees would provide welcome shade in the area between the canal and the river where new buildings would need to be constructed.[105]

The Riverside Park site, on the other hand, was larger and had direct rail access for both passengers and freight for exhibits. The thousands of out-of-town visitors could arrive directly by train only at Riverside. Its main building, however, required major repair, as did other buildings and the grandstand. The racetrack, a quarter-mile longer than the Jockey Club's half-mile track, had to be rebuilt. Park owners lined up commitments for street access to at last be paved and for streetcar

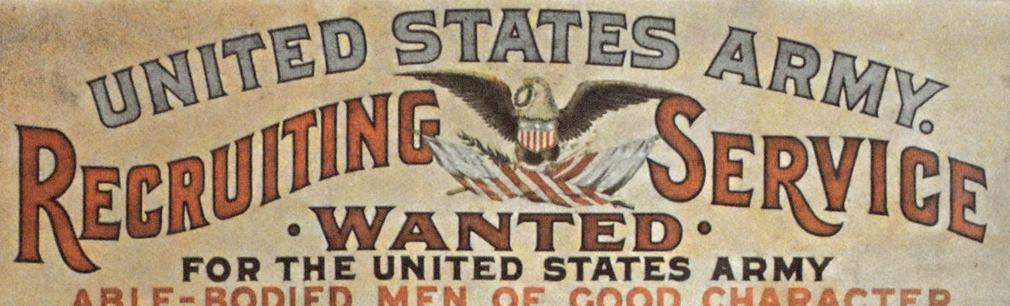

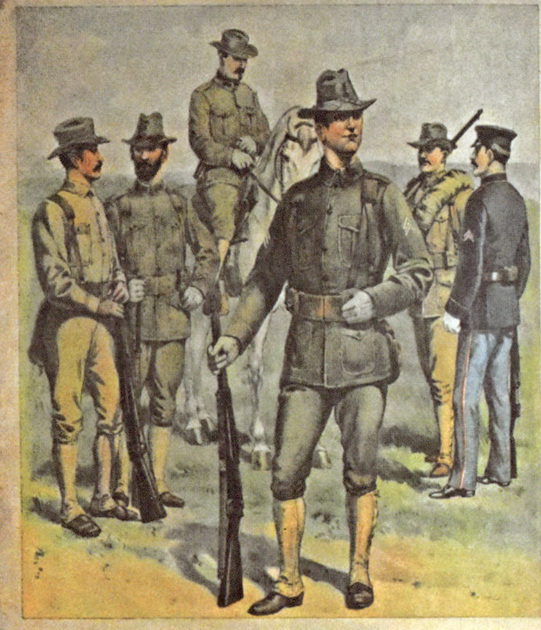

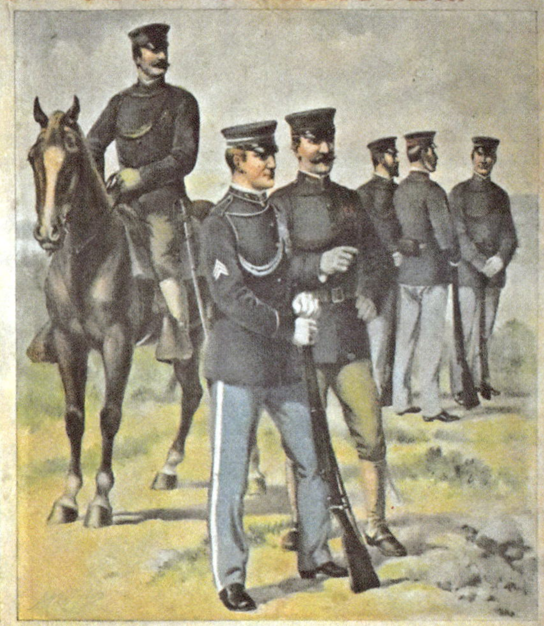

Recruiters sent Camp Capron some twelve hundred men.

rail improvements that would minimize transfers. They also promised to make all other necessary improvements and offered convenient lease terms until the purchase price was due.[106]

When votes were counted, 165 shareholders favored moving to the Jockey Club and 147 preferred staying at Riverside Park. But in the deciding number of shares, 2,558 were voted in favor of Riverside Park and 1,483 in favor of the Jockey Club.[107]

Camp Capron came to the rescue of the forlorn Jockey Club complex two months later, if only for two more months.

In mid-July 1899 the tents previously used by the Fourth Texas Volunteers and stored at Fort Sam Houston were taken out, aired in the sun, and hauled in wagons with other supplies down Grayson Street and up River Avenue to the Jockey Club, this time leased to house and train recruits for the new Thirty-Third Infantry of the US Army. The installation was named Camp Capron by the Thirty-Third's commander, Col. Luther Hare, to honor Capt. Allyn K. Capron, a Rough Rider who died in combat while serving with Hare in Cuba. Regimental headquarters was set up in the clubhouse, which also housed the camp post office. Hospital tents were staked southwest of the grandstand. Recruiters opened an office and fanned out across Texas.[108]

Recruits began arriving at the rate of seventy-five to a hundred a day, knowing they would be sent to face postwar insurgency raging in the Philippines. Some were seasoned veterans reenlisting, among them a Rough Rider who had been standing next to Capt. Capron when he was struck by the fatal bullet. Recruits took the train a hundred miles west to Fort Clark for ten days of target practice.[109]

There were three hundred recruits in camp by August 5, when the canteen reported the night's beer consumption at nineteen half-barrels. Ten days later the regiment was nearing its full complement of some twelve hundred men. At the end of the month the new regimental band drew both soldiers and San Antonians to a nighttime concert, followed by dancing on a platform between the clubhouse and the grandstand.[110]

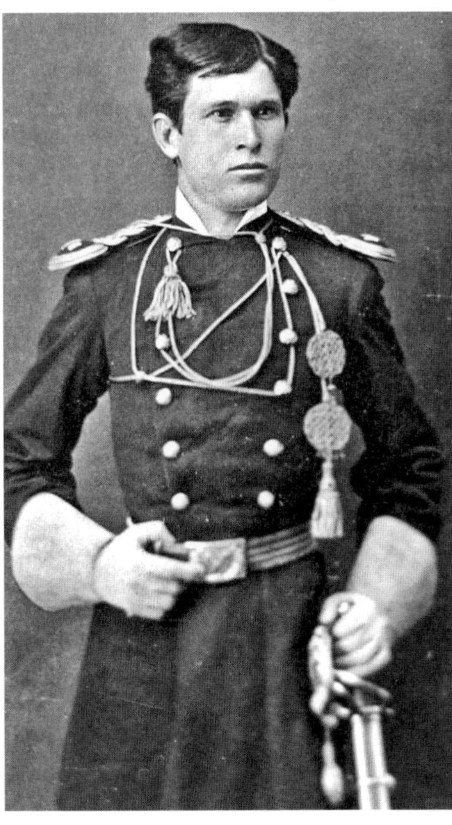

Luther Hare, shown as a second lieutenant, was a colonel when he commanded Camp Capron in the future park.

By mid-September the regiment was at full strength and judged combat ready. Reveille sounded at 5 a.m. on September 15. Two hours later the soldiers were taking down their tents, packing their gear, and lining up in the shade of the grandstand, entertained by the regimental band as they waited to be marched in formation down River Avenue to the Southern Pacific depot. There they boarded four waiting trains that would take them to San Francisco for a troop ship bound for Manila and fame as a top American combat unit during the Philippine Insurrection of 1898–1902. By the end of the month remaining government property had been moved to Fort Sam Houston, and Camp Capron was turned back to the Jockey Club.[111]

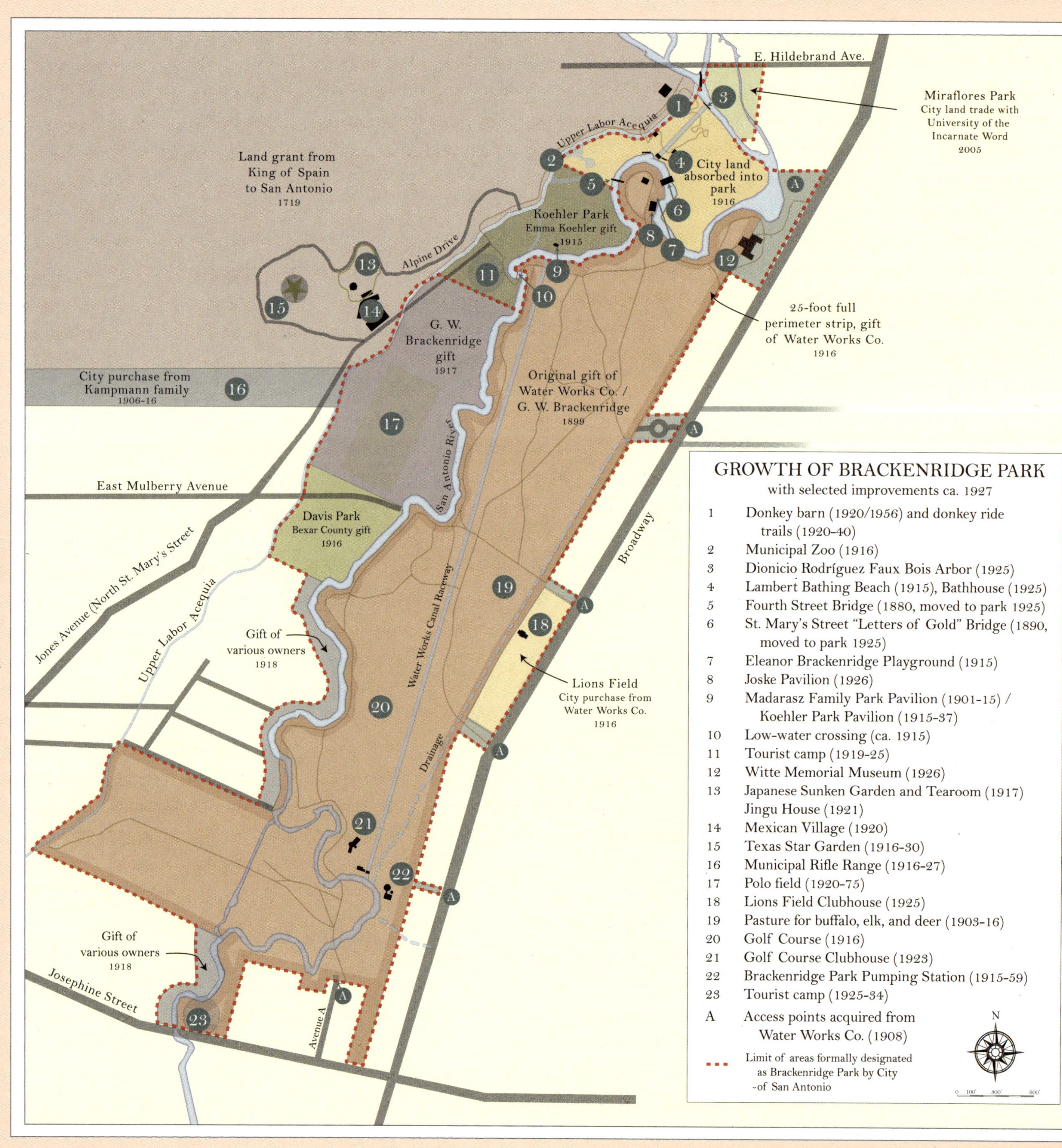

E. Hildebrand Ave.
Miraflores Park
City land trade with University of the Incarnate Word
2005
Upper Labor Acequia
Land grant from King of Spain to San Antonio
1719
City land absorbed into park
1916
Koehler Park
Emma Koehler gift
1915
Alpine Drive
G. W. Brackenridge gift
1917
25-foot full perimeter strip, gift of Water Works Co.
1916
City purchase from Kampmann family
1906-16
Original gift of Water Works Co. / G. W. Brackenridge
1899
San Antonio River
East Mulberry Avenue
Davis Park
Bexar County gift
1916
Broadway
Jones Avenue (North St. Mary's Street
Upper Labor Acequia
Gift of various owners
1918
Water Works Canal Raceway
Lions Field
City purchase from Water Works Co.
1916
Drainage
Gift of various owners
1918
Josephine Street
Avenue A
GROWTH OF BRACKENRIDGE PARK
with selected improvements ca. 1927
1 Donkey barn (1920/1956) and donkey ride trails (1920–40)
2 Municipal Zoo (1916)
3 Dionicio Rodríguez Faux Bois Arbor (1925)
4 Lambert Bathing Beach (1915), Bathhouse (1925)
5 Fourth Street Bridge (1880, moved to park 1925)
6 St. Mary's Street "Letters of Gold" Bridge (1890, moved to park 1925)
7 Eleanor Brackenridge Playground (1915)
8 Joske Pavilion (1926)
9 Madarasz Family Park Pavilion (1901-15) / Koehler Park Pavilion (1915-37)
10 Low-water crossing (ca. 1915)
11 Tourist camp (1919-25)
12 Witte Memorial Museum (1926)
13 Japanese Sunken Garden and Tearoom (1917) Jingu House (1921)
14 Mexican Village (1920)
15 Texas Star Garden (1916-30)
16 Municipal Rifle Range (1916-27)
17 Polo field (1920-75)
18 Lions Field Clubhouse (1925)
19 Pasture for buffalo, elk, and deer (1903-16)
20 Golf Course (1916)
21 Golf Course Clubhouse (1923)
22 Brackenridge Park Pumping Station (1915-59)
23 Tourist camp (1925-34)
A Access points acquired from Water Works Co. (1908)
Limit of areas formally designated as Brackenridge Park by City of San Antonio
N

PART 2

Brackenridge Park Takes Shape

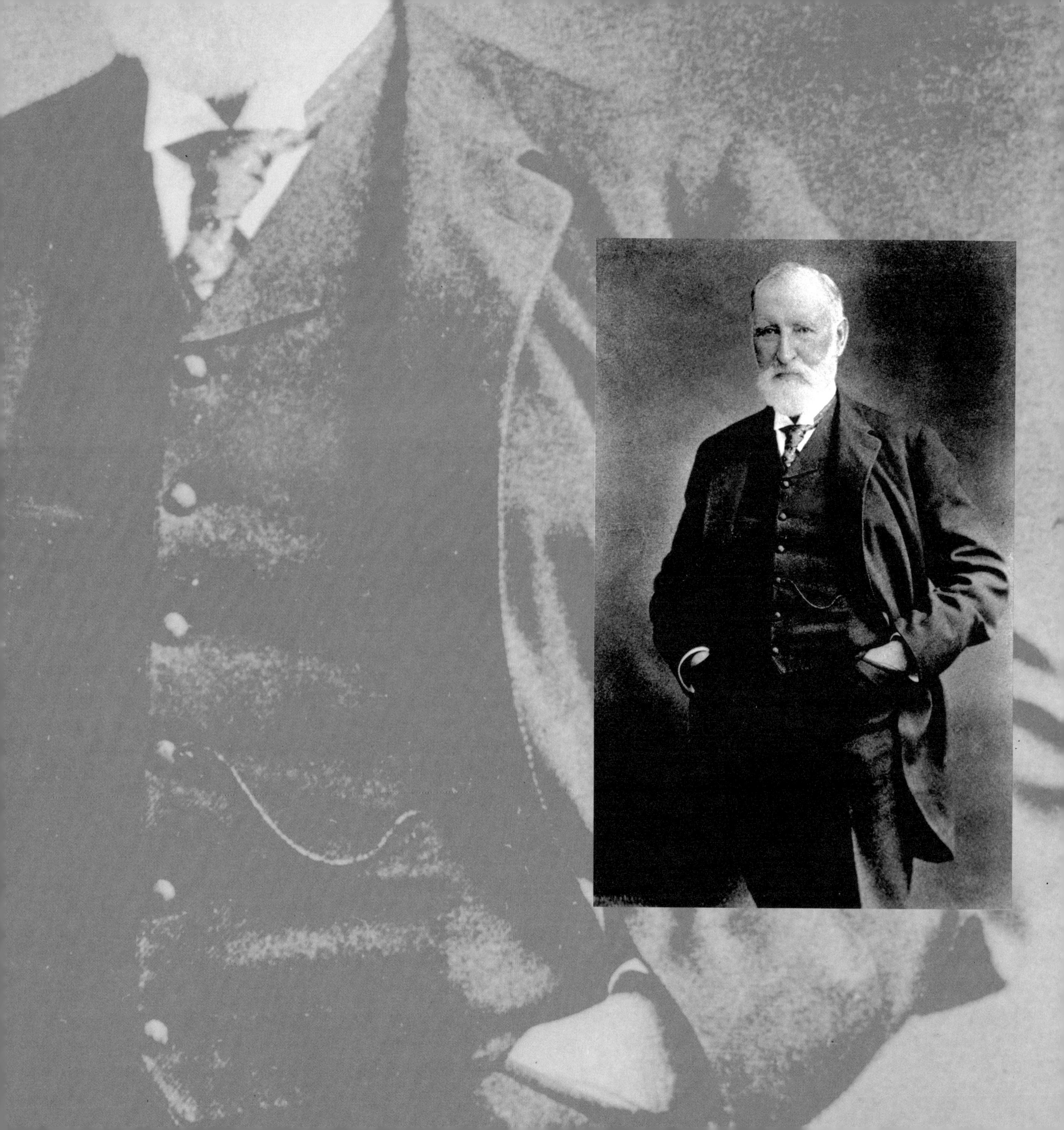

San Antonio Gets a Driving Park

When New York City officials decided in 1853 that they needed an eight-hundred-acre park uptown, a location was decreed, talented planners went to their drawing boards, experienced construction crews set to work, and five years later Central Park was open to the public.

In San Antonio, things worked a little differently.

A half century after Central Park opened, San Antonio may have been, like New York, the largest city in its state. But San Antonio's fifty-three thousand residents were a fraction of Manhattan's nearly two million and came up seriously short in comparisons of industry, philanthropy, outlook, and general prosperity.

That did not keep San Antonio from getting an uptown park fully one-fourth the size of Central Park, however. Residents just had to wait for circumstances to coalesce on their own. Stars finally aligned in 1899, when land for a major park was donated by the city's top financier.

Other cities had their Carnegies, Rockefellers, and Mellons. San Antonio had George Washington Brackenridge. Brackenridge, San Antonio's lone nineteenth-century mogul, stood out when he arrived after the Civil War in a rough-hewn frontier town that hardly resembled the industrial Pittsburghs or New Yorks of the time.

"Six feet tall, erect of carriage, with piercing dark eyes and bristling beard," as Brackenridge was described by his biographer, Marilyn McAdams Sibley, he did not quite fit in. A steely eyed financier, Republican, and prohibitionist in a town of cattlemen, Democrats, and fun-lovers, he was "domineering, caustic, tactless, and given to outbursts of anger," and one who tended to "take unpopular positions perversely just for the sake of controversy." A strong advocate of the rights of Blacks and of numerous civic causes, Brackenridge once grumbled that he was ahead of his time—"too large for Texas"—but he made it a practice not to respond to criticism, believing it "a result of living in a country which you have outgrown."[112]

Financier George Brackenridge donated land for the park in 1899.

Brackenridge ended his first year of college in his native Indiana to come to East Texas with his family. He later entered Harvard Law School but left in his first

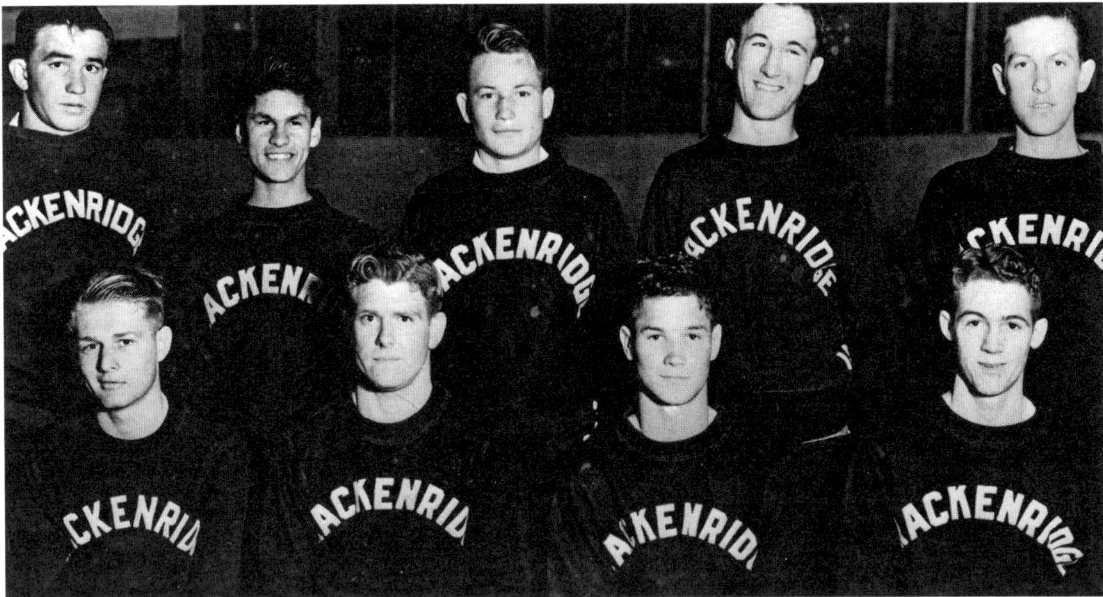

Though George Brackenridge was unmarried and had no children, beneficiaries carry his name on school shirts like these worn by 1979 basketball players at Brackenridge High School, which he helped establish in 1917.

year with the outbreak of the Civil War. During the war he made a fortune profiteering in the cotton trade with Mexico and became a US treasury agent in New Orleans after it fell to the Union in 1863. As his new home Brackenridge chose San Antonio, which had voted in 1861, if barely, to oppose secession. It was the closest he could come to the former Confederate stronghold of East Texas and get by with his wartime record as a Union Loyalist, though he was still made to feel uneasy by San Antonio's hardline former Confederates, who never forgave him for his sympathies.[113]

Using his connections and wartime profits, in mid-1866 Brackenridge opened San Antonio National Bank. It was soon chosen as the US Army's main depository in the city, making Brackenridge the one local banker with a reliable major source of funds. He launched his career as a financier by backing ranchers and trail drivers moving cattle to Kansas. In 1869 he bought an estate surrounding the head of the river; the property had first been owned by an alderman and future mayor, James R. Sweet, who had purchased the land in 1852 when San Antonio sold its water source to raise money. Since "bracken" is the word for a common type of fern in his family's native Scotland, Brackenridge named his new home Fernridge.[114]

Brackenridge, unmarried, regretted that his education was incomplete and encouraged others to finish theirs. He had a special focus on the University of Texas. In 1886, three years after the university opened, he became a major financial contributor and influential member of the UT board of regents, sometimes serving as chairman, for a record-setting twenty-seven years. He also made substantial contributions to Black colleges in Texas and backed San Antonio's first public school for Blacks, built in 1869 with stones from the old Confederate army tannery.[115]

A longtime San Antonio school board member and president, Brackenridge in 1916 gave $40,000—today's equivalent of $2 million—to the San Antonio school district for the new Brackenridge High School, the fourth local public school to bear a Brackenridge family member's name. When he died, in 1920, he left the bulk of his estate to a trust for educational purposes, one of the first of its type in the nation; it became the George W. Brackenridge Foundation.[116]

By the 1890s Brackenridge was losing interest in his property at the upper reaches of the San Antonio River. In 1886 he had built a showplace house for his mother, whom he lived with, beside his smaller stone home, built three decades earlier by onetime mayor Sweet. The new stylish Victorian three-story featured imported tiles, mirrors, carpets, chandeliers, and a dining room with immense mahogany beams, large sideboards laden with crystal and silver, a ten-foot-long dining table with carved chairs, and one wall covered with hand-tooled elephant hide. But his mother died the year it was

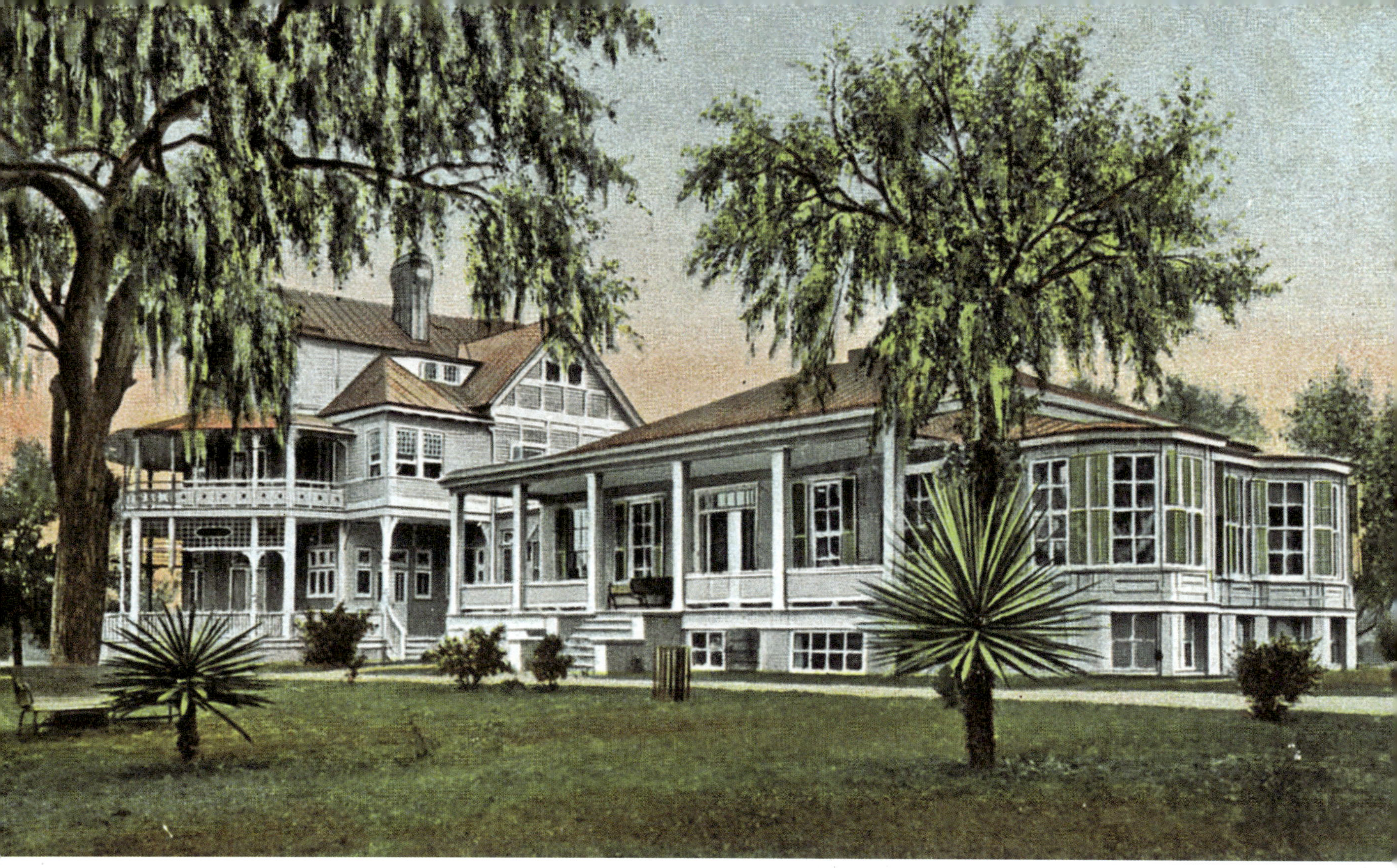

In 1886 Brackenridge built an elaborate three-story Victorian house next to his 1852 home.

finished, and Brackenridge moved to the roof townhouse of his new Moorish-style San Antonio National Bank building on Commerce Street.[117]

Brackenridge's melancholy over the death of his mother was worsened by the declining surroundings of his headwaters home, as new artesian wells throughout the city lowered the water table and the lush springs began to dry up. The city wanted the water system he owned, though an effort in 1872 to buy it had foundered on price and hard feelings over challenges to his ownership of the water rights. In 1890 he set the price at $2 million—some $58 million today—for the waterworks, his home, and six hundred acres of adjoining property, which the city could use for a park. The funding proposal went to voters that September.[118]

Mayor Bryan Callaghan, with whom Brackenridge often clashed, nonetheless recognized a bargain and backed the purchase. He faced strong opposition from the Taxpayers Association, which opposed paying for most improvements needed to forge a modern city. Despite his own fiscal conservatism, Callaghan had managed construction of a grand Second Empire city hall in the center of Military Plaza and added handsome iron bridges across the river downtown. Atop trusses spanning either side of the wide Saint Mary's Street bridge were two medallions in black with the letters of Callaghan's name and

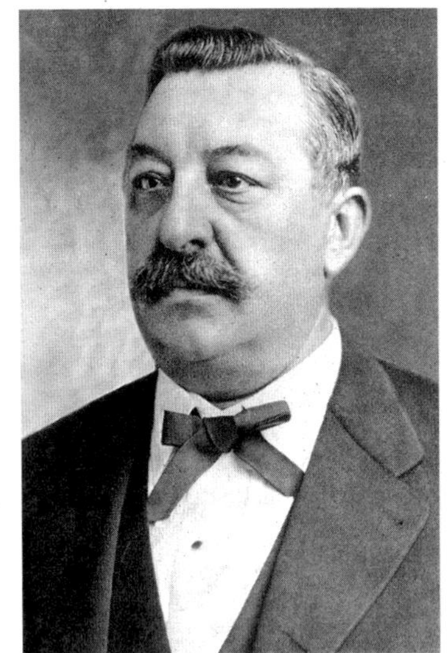

Park commissioner Ludwig Mahncke was a major designer for the new Brackenridge Park.

others painted in gilt. The Letters of Gold bridge was attacked as an example of municipal extravagance and nearly cost Callaghan reelection. The bridge would be reborn nearly four decades later in a most unexpected place.[119]

Brackenridge's offer was soundly rejected by voters who wondered why their taxes should be raised to buy a waterworks that was already giving them water. The defeat left the Water Works Company stuck with land of little use, and Brackenridge could see no need to keep it. Maintaining water rights and easements would be quite sufficient.

So Brackenridge started to sell off his property piecemeal. In 1897 French-born Louise (Mother Madeleine) Chollet, cofounder of the Sisters of Charity of the Incarnate Word, asked to buy 40 acres of his headwaters estate. But Brackenridge would sell only the entire 180-acre estate, including the houses and furnishings. He gave her nine days to come up with $120,000, today's equivalent of $3.1 million. To his apparent surprise, she did, and the estate eventually became the campus of the University of the Incarnate Word. Brackenridge's two houses remain intact. He was less successful in disposing of land farther downstream and ended up with title to the entire Jockey Club tract when sale to the International Fair fell through.[120]

Brackenridge's frequent adversary, longtime mayor Bryan Callaghan, was "San Antonio's most skilled defender of the traditional consensus favoring low taxes, an inactive government, and minimal public improvements," according to historian David Johnson. But in February 1899 Callaghan was soundly defeated by reform candidate Marshall Hicks. Brackenridge's sentiments were now aligned with those at city hall.[121]

Reform sympathizer Ludwig Mahncke was elected to a second term as alderman. The German-born Mahncke once ran a beer garden on South Alamo Street and owned the Mahncke Hotel on East Houston Street, formerly the Vance Hotel and future site of the Gunter. He shared his friend George Brackenridge's love of nature to the point that, as park commissioner with no money left in the city's park fund, he wrote his personal check for today's equivalent of $9,000 to pay for planting cypress saplings that grew into the towering trees along today's downtown River Walk.[122]

After Mayor Hicks confronted the city's dire financial situation—illuminated when some of the former tax collector's records were found hidden behind a steam radiator—the new mayor went forward with elements of the City Beautiful Movement in vogue in major cities elsewhere.[123]

City Beautiful adherents emphasized aesthetics but also addressed broad urban issues of the time. Activists worked on political reform to improve urban living conditions and the environment. Proponents urged that more streets be paved, billboards be removed, schools and playgrounds be built, and public hygiene be improved. Coincidentally, capitalists decided that upgraded surroundings and major parks would subtly improve workers' states of mind and increase their productivity in the workplace.[124]

Worker efficiency was not as important in a nonmanufacturing city like San Antonio, nor had there been a sense of urgency for new parks within city limits. Not only did San Antonio not have the means to pay for significant park development, demand was less due to low urban density and easy access to a vast countryside for outings. But there was growing awareness that the fast-developing city would eventually need a major park and that urban parks with "beautiful natural scenery" enhanced cities' appeal to affluent tourists more than parks with "cheap thrills of the Coney Island type." San Antonio's

San Pedro Springs Park was the city's historic center for amusements and recreation.

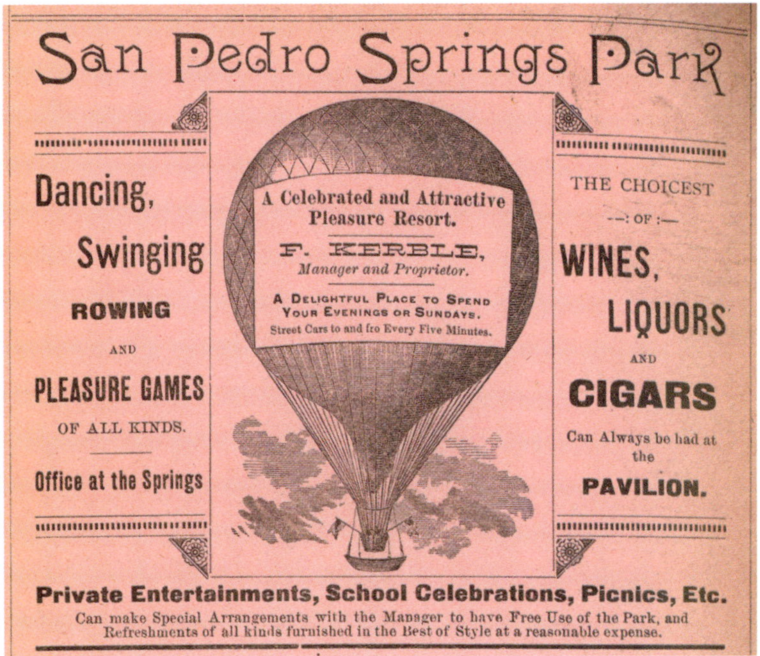

historical monuments were already drawing substantial numbers of visitors. The lure of more tourism revenue added pressure for a large municipal park.[125]

Nine months after Hicks ushered in a more enlightened regime at city hall, Mahncke helped convince Brackenridge that he should donate the land around his waterworks since the city would not buy it. The donation would double the total area of San Antonio's parklands. The tract stretched nearly two miles along the river from the future Hildebrand Avenue south to Josephine Street, and most of it was still in a natural state as development leapfrogged beyond. In November 1899 Brackenridge invited city council members and civic leaders to inspect the proposed park. One alderman was "surprised and astounded at its grandeur and beauty."[126]

The size of Brackenridge's donation was given as 199 acres. One ingrate at the time thought the donation should be listed as 174 acres—the number the complainer said the waterworks used for property tax reporting purposes—though if the 48 acres with retained water rights were deducted, the gift would be 127 acres. Unofficial references have ranged to 265 acres and higher. A more accurate computer-generated count, however, replacing hand-drawn calculations complicated by difficult river and acequia borders, puts the total original donation at close to 213 acres.[127]

Two years earlier Callaghan had abolished the short-lived post of park commissioner. Hicks named Ludwig Mahncke chairman of a parks and plazas committee to oversee development of what the city council accepted in December 1899 and named Brackenridge Park.

Brackenridge Park was more than four times the size of the city's next-largest park, San Pedro Springs Park, set aside for public use by the King of Spain in 1729. The forty-six acres around the spring had been designated an official city park in 1852 and leased to Swiss-born John Jacob Duerler, who built his home there.[128]

Duerler landscaped the park and added bathhouses, paddleboats, a small zoo, racetrack, food concessions, and a concert and dance pavilion. After Frederick Kerble bought the lease in 1882, sports events flourished and a small natural history museum, zoo, and balloon rides were added. In 1891 the city took over when Kerble's lease expired. Mayor Callaghan authorized a two-year cleanup and renovation costing today's equivalent of $630,000. The park reopened, along with many of its old attractions, in August 1899.[129]

Brackenridge Park was not intended to be another San Pedro Springs Park with races and balloon rides. Mahncke planned it as the sort of driving park pioneered by New York's Central Park a half century later. When it opened in 1858 Central Park featured landscaping, scenic enhancements, and a system of carriage roads, pedestrian walkways, and bridle paths—and no major buildings. Visitors were to experience "rural scenery with an appropriate sense of isolation."[130]

Such park settings were becoming passé by the time Brackenridge Park was formed, as municipal park design trended toward terraced promenades, sunken gardens, and shaded boulevards with broad vistas rather than greenswards and rambles. But Brackenridge Park encompassed enchanting woodlands and

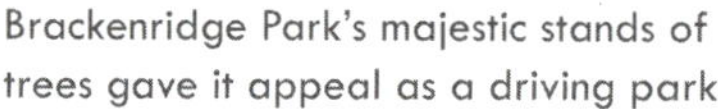
Brackenridge Park's majestic stands of trees gave it appeal as a driving park.

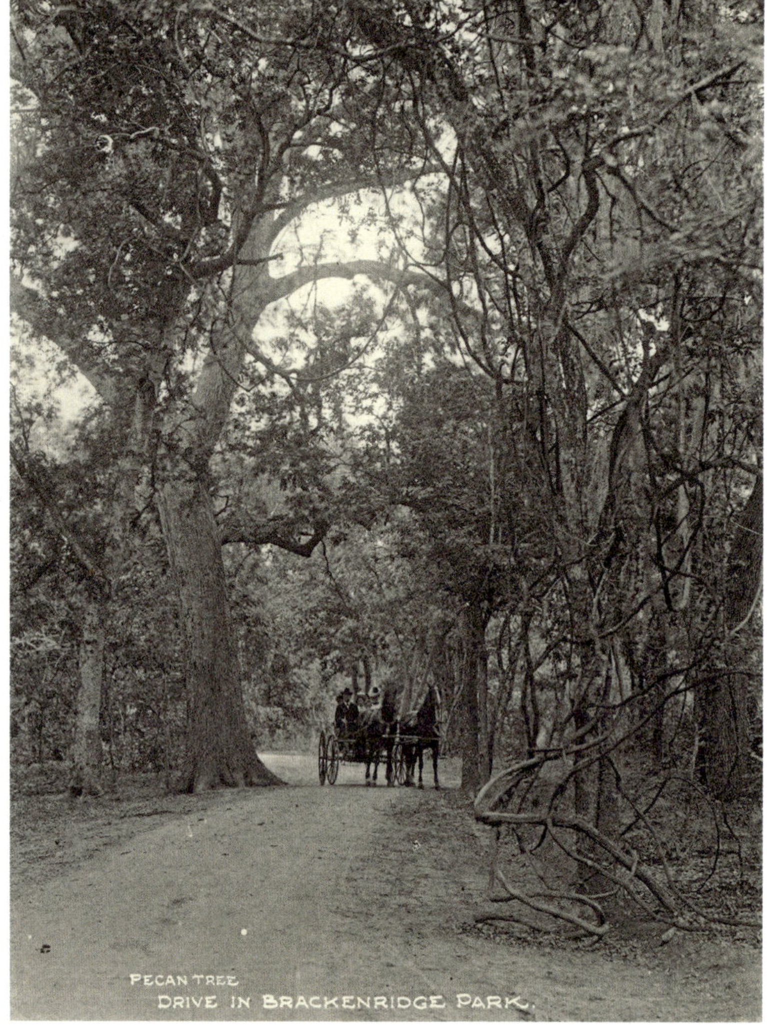

paths beside a winding river, and San Antonians did not want to pay for extras anyway. A rural driving park it would be.[131]

Ludwig Mahncke's second term as alderman soon expired, ending his assignment as park committee chair. But he found a new job in the revived post of park commissioner. Mahncke kept Brackenridge Park workers busy "clearing out the underbrush and blending the wild, natural beauty of the grove with park effect," he wrote in his section of the mayor's report to the city for 1901. Care was taken to preserve all major trees. Labor costs were kept down by using prisoners transported to and from the park on city buses. Brackenridge paid for materials.[132]

Both Brackenridge and Mayor Hicks assisted Mahncke in planning a seven-mile network of meandering sylvan drives, the last of which was completed in September 1902. As visitors arrived in late summer 1900, four miles were already paved with macadam and converged in the park's center. The project added $2,500—today's equivalent of $78,000—finally appropriated by the city to add to funds already eked out from existing budgets. A reporter taking a spin on his bike in August 1900 tried out a new road through the former Jockey Club entrance down to the river, then cycled beneath moss-covered oaks and elms, past workers clearing mesquite and underbrush, and around to exit at River Avenue by the future site of the Witte Museum. "Scarcely a ray of sunlight penetrates the entire distance," the reporter marveled.[133]

As the park neared completion in 1901, more visitors drifted in. Wires were strung that September for electric lights along walks and drives. The total cost for getting the park in shape was a scant $5,000, some $160,000 today, a fourth of what was spent rehabilitating the smaller but still heavily used San Pedro Springs Park.[134]

Brackenridge had specified that the Jockey Club entrance be kept open so individual cyclists and bicycle clubs could access the track. A month after the park was created, the track hosted the city's first motorcycle races and, later, a few automobile races. In 1901 a blue-ribbon group of more than thirty San Antonians successfully petitioned the city for permission to use the track for horses. Local horse owners began organizing occasional races, keeping the Jockey Club's spirit alive for a few more years. The grandstand and stables were taken down early in 1900, but the track remained and the clubhouse became the home of park gardener Louis Schunke and his wife, Amelia.[135]

For visitor appeal, Mahncke wanted to add exotic animals to the deer that gathered in the park's more open area to the south. He ran afoul of quirky legislation prohibiting wild game from being shipped on railroads into the county for zoological purposes, which remained in effect as his trip to Austin in August 1901 did not succeed in getting an amendment. But things changed, for a year later Mahncke brought in several bison and elk by rail. Brackenridge had purchased them for the

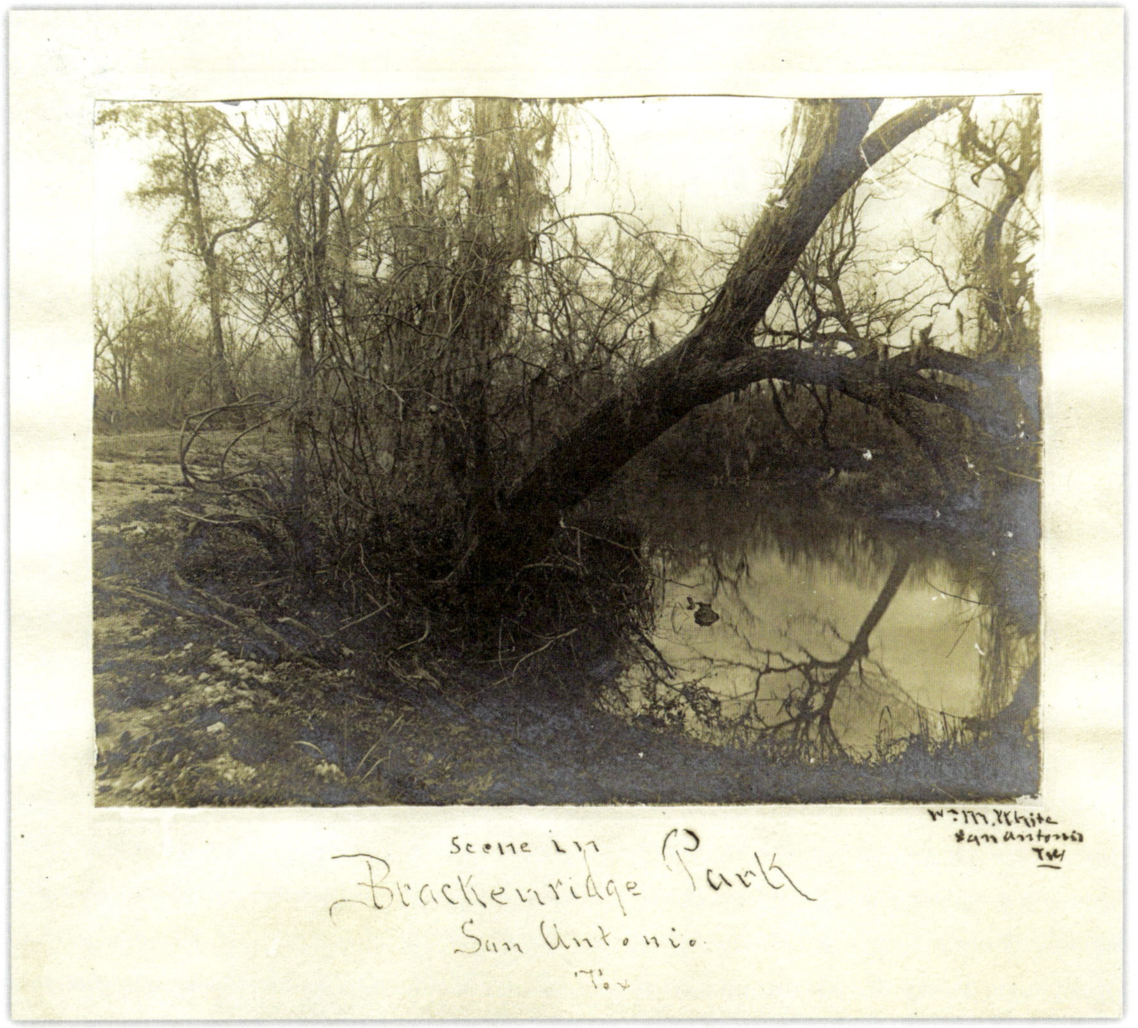

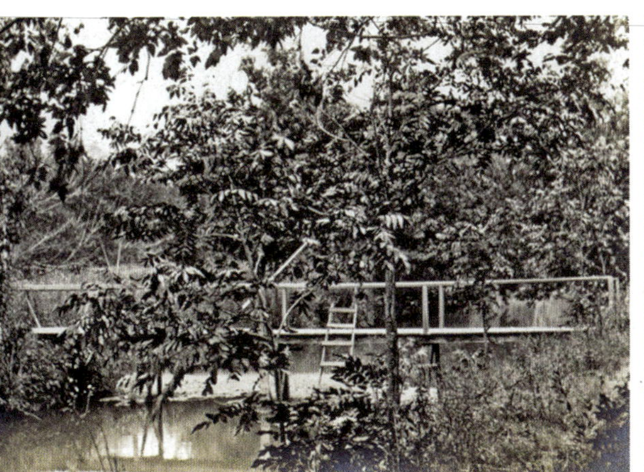

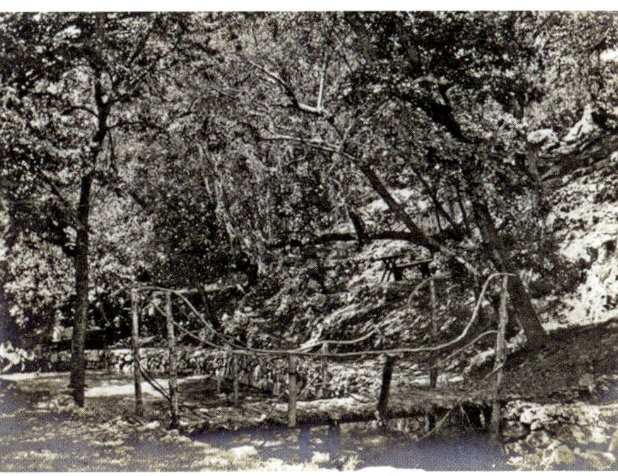

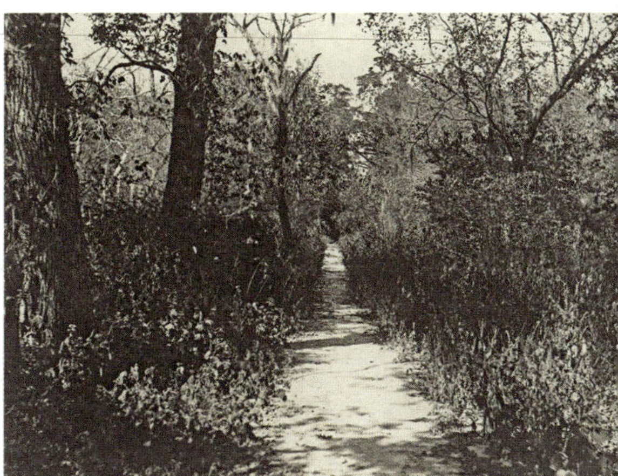

Brackenridge Park opened in 1901 as a driving park, featuring shaded drives for carriages, walking paths, river ponds, and rustic bridges—one with a ladder to a swimming hole and another with a picnic table nearby.

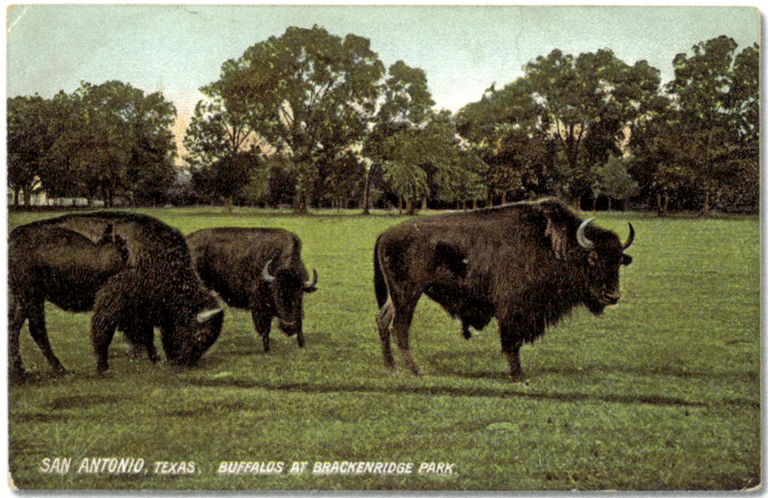

George Brackenridge stocked one section of the park with bison (then referred to as "buffalo") purchased from North Texas rancher Charles Goodnight.

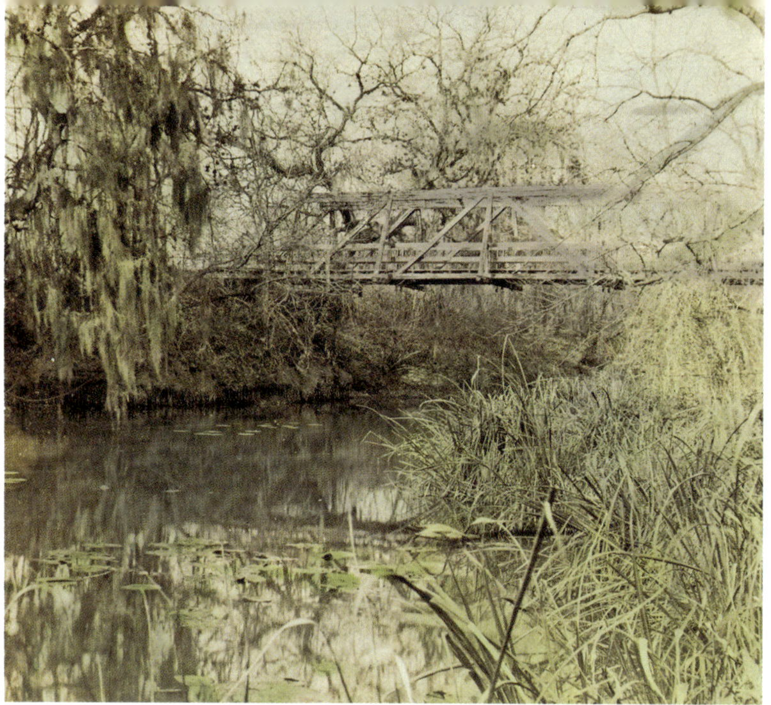

A hand-colored photograph shows a footbridge crossing a pond overhung by a tree dripping with Spanish moss.

park from legendary Texas Panhandle rancher Charles Goodnight, who had developed his latest ranch into a major tourist attraction featuring zoo-like enclosures of bison, elk, antelope, and other animals. He was also supplying zoos in eastern cities and in Europe.[136]

In December 1903 Goodnight sold Brackenridge a bison bull and a heifer, bringing park herds up to five head of bison and twelve elk. Maintenance was an issue, as some of the animals became ill or died and the deer herds multiplied. Although large amounts of hay were harvested in the park to feed the animals, additional feed was costing the city $700—now $20,000—a year, too much for the tight-fisted Callaghan, back in office as mayor in 1905. Venison lovers benefited in 1908 when he had the herd of forty-three deer culled by ten, which were sold to local butchers. The next year ten of the twenty-five elk were sold for $250 to furniture dealer G. A. Stowers, who moved them to his ranch near Kerrville. Mahncke stocked the river in the park in May 1903 with eleven thousand black bass from the state fish hatchery in San Marcos.[137]

By this time the park was "full of people." One carriage rider described the drive along the river as winding "with the sinuosity of the river channel, curving and dipping with the natural lay of the land" as it passed "splendid old trees, with their crowns high in the sunshine and their trunks in the shade. At every turn there is a delightful surprise; now you are descending seemingly into a darker, more secluded portion of the forest, to rise again into an open spot." Visitors could leave their carriages in clearings and take a walk through the woods.[138]

For carriage riders one pastoral scene seemed to blend into another. Hicks's 1901 report to the city included three images of the new park, all along the river—a small waterfall, a lily pond, and a "pool of the fairies." Hicks added a quote beneath the pool photo from Shakespeare's *Merry Wives of Windsor*: "They are fairies; he that speaks to them shall die. I'll wink and couch; no man their works must eye." Although Shakespeare is seldom quoted in San Antonio municipal reports, the lines evoke the ethereal sentiments of the late Victorian era captured in the folds of a forested driving park.[139]

If outside observers could not rise to the eloquence of Shakespeare, they did their best. A reporter from semiarid El Paso called the park "a recreation spot fit for the Gods. Its beauty is beyond description, and the greatest effort of the writer would but feebly portray its wonders." A Boston magazine editor wrote that it was the "most magnificent piece of parking

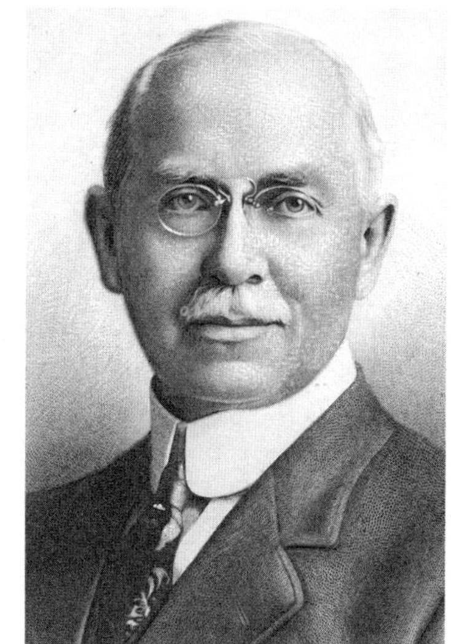

Brewer Otto Koehler took exception to the prohibition of alcoholic beverages in Brackenridge Park and opened Madarasz Family Park across the river, complete with bandstand and beer garden, in 1901.

in the United States that has come under my observation" with "a woodland that is unsurpassed," one "into which it is a boon to plunge for an hour or two to relieve the fatiguing monotony of city life."[140]

The park was barely open when the Business Men's Club breathlessly titled a new promotional foldout "Beautiful San Antonio Texas: The Commercial & Industrial Center of the Southwest, The Great Health Resort of America." It trumpeted that Brackenridge Park "in point of natural beauty is not excelled on the continent." More restrained guidebooks initially listed the more familiar San Pedro Springs Park first, but by 1909 a chamber of commerce guide had joined others in shifting Brackenridge Park to top billing, touting it as "a primeval forest which has not been despoiled by the hand of man."[141]

There were two main caveats to Brackenridge's gift of the park. One was a ban on the use of alcoholic beverages. He feared that strong drink would make the park disreputable and unattractive to women and children. He decreed that violation of the ban would trigger the transfer of park ownership from the city to one of his favorite charities, the University of Texas. His belief was endorsed by his sister, Mary Eleanor Brackenridge, a noted advocate of temperance and women's suffrage in Texas and a member of Texas Woman's University's first board of regents.[142]

Although George Brackenridge maintained a fine wine cellar and occasionally enjoyed good whiskey, his stern Calvinist background reinforced his fear that ordinary citizens could not handle the temptations and needed protection from their weaknesses. For justification he needed look no further than the city itself. At the time of the park's opening San Antonio had six breweries and more than two hundred saloons, one for every 250 inhabitants.[143]

Wags began referring to "Prohibition Park." The *San Antonio Light* suggested that for "refreshments" visitors might have to cross River Avenue / Broadway to Limburger's Beer Garden, reopened after being stripped two years before by boisterous soldiers from Camp Mosby. But Henry Limburger's park clientele was soon targeted by German-born brewer Otto Koehler, age forty-six. Koehler spotted fourteen acres for sale across the river from the new park—the shuttered Ilka Nurseries, on the site of the Confederate army tannery. He saw a chance to one-up the straitlaced George Brackenridge.[144]

Ilka Nurseries had closed after being beset by tragedy. Its founder, Helen Madarasz, had prospered and become close friends with upriver neighbors Brackenridge and his sister, as had Helen's son Ladislaùs, who was employed for a decade as a bookkeeper at Brackenridge's bank. In April 1895 the bank announced plans to begin rotating duties among employees. The day before that was to take effect, Ladislaùs confessed to his mother that his accounts were short by today's equivalent of $92,000. He took the night train to Galveston, fled the country on shipboard, and was last reported living in Argentina.[145]

The day after Ladislaùs left, Helen grimly reported her son's circumstances to the bank and became reclusive, remaining in her isolated frame house in a picturesque grove on the nursery grounds and tending to its operation. During a robbery in April 1899 she was murdered and her home set afire to destroy the evidence. Two suspects were apprehended but were later cleared, and the criminals were never found.[146]

Koehler thought the nursery site would make a fine park for San Antonians to relax in with a good beer. They had only to cross a short bridge to escape the alcoholic beverage ban in Brackenridge Park. He bought the land through his San

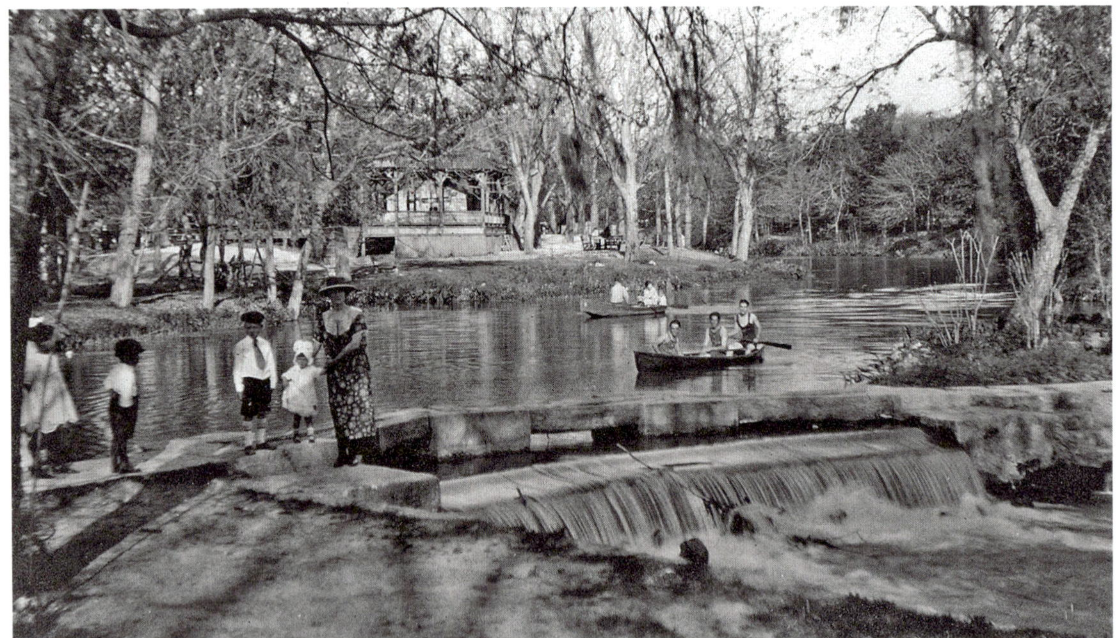

Boaters head down the San Antonio River below a bandstand built by Otto Koehler in 1901.

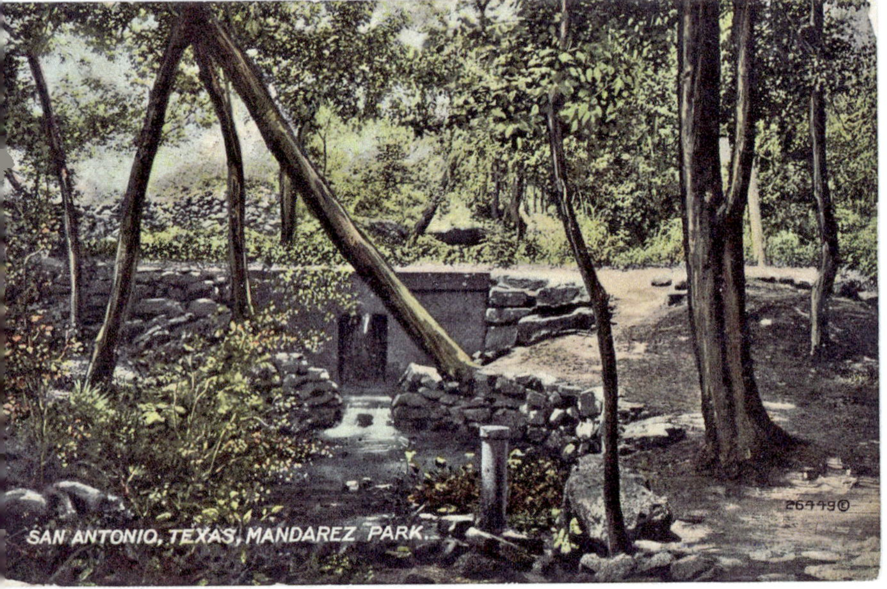

A stone bridge crossed the Upper Labor Acequia's overflow channel in what is correctly spelled Madarasz Park, which in 1915 became Koehler Park.

Antonio Brewing Association, the holding company of City Brewery, which produced Pearl beer in a large complex a mile downriver. Rather than set up a naming confrontation with Brackenridge, Koehler chose to name his park Madarasz Family Park, for the site's recent owner.[147]

In May 1901 brewery workers were building a bandstand and placing benches in a shady riverside setting that made one reporter think "this promises to be a more attractive park than Brackenridge Park itself." The next month the public was welcomed to a sort of beer garden in Madarasz Family Park for "picnics and jollifications" and to order "sandwiches, ice cream, cream cheese, milk of all descriptions," with "the famous Triple XXX Pearl Beer and soda water and cigars always on hand." Custodians Leo Dethleffsen and his wife, Pauleen, promised to "make all who come feel at home."[148]

The new park's appeal to San Antonio's numerous German-born beer lovers and to those from elsewhere was obvious only three months after it opened. On a Saturday afternoon in September 1901 some two hundred delegates in town for the joint national conventions of the Hermann Sons fraternal group and the Krieger Bund of North America—veterans of the German Army—trekked to Madarasz Family Park for an evening of music, fireworks, and convivial dining and dancing, plus a display of military drills, though the mood was dampened by the death of President William McKinley.[149]

The second major requirement of Brackenridge's gift limited access across a twenty-five-foot perimeter around the entire park. He originally fenced the perimeter strip and allowed the public access only at two ends. Newspapers referred to it as a "Chinese wall." Nor did his donation include a 250-foot setback along River Avenue, which vexed those dealing with the park through the years perhaps as much as his ban on alcoholic beverages. The setback requirement ultimately deprived the park of the identity offered by unobstructed boundaries at parklands like New York's Central Park.[150]

The issue seems to have stemmed from years of mistrust and frustration in dealing with a recalcitrant city hall. Brackenridge's stated intention was long-term protection of the park. If it was surrounded by a buffer and was thus inaccessible from the street, how could a moody city council sell it? His fears were well founded. As late as 1962 a city councilman proposed sale of a 250-foot former setback section the city had purchased nearly fifty years earlier to extend the park out to Broadway, an area now known as Lions Field. The city stood to gain today's equivalent of $17 million and finances were, as usual, tight. Only an uproar from conservationists halted further council consideration.[151]

Even when he presented the city with its largest park, critics carped that Brackenridge gave the land only as a way to rid himself of taxable land while keeping his company's water rights. Unfazed, in 1905 Brackenridge donated seventy-two acres for another park, including the old reservoir and the sloping strip east of Broadway that had accommodated pipes up the hillside to the reservoir. He named it in honor of his old friend Ludwig Mahncke, the park commissioner who had helped design Brackenridge Park.[152]

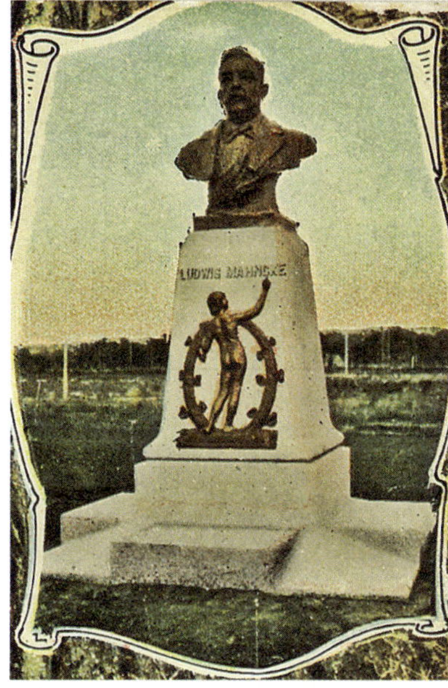

A bust by Pompeo Coppini in memory of park commissioner Ludwig Mahncke was placed by the former Jockey Club clubhouse and later moved to Mahncke Park.

Mahncke resigned his post the following January after running athwart of Callaghan, who had gotten back in office as mayor and roundly criticized Mahncke for going over his park budget. "I have done my duty and treated him with courtesy," Mahncke fumed, "and in return have been treated like a dog." Two months later Mahncke died of pneumonia. Friends commissioned a four-foot bust of him by well-known sculptor Pompeo Coppini. It was placed in Brackenridge Park near the former jockey clubhouse in 1908 and moved sixty years later to the foot of Mahncke Park.[153]

Brackenridge also disposed of a small tract beside Brackenridge Park on the west side of River Avenue south of what later became Hildebrand Avenue. He donated it to the Salvation Army for building a rescue home for "fallen women and their infants," a euphemism for unwed mothers. "Puritan elements" were so outraged at the idea of having such a place next to the park that they lobbied city hall to block the plan in court. But

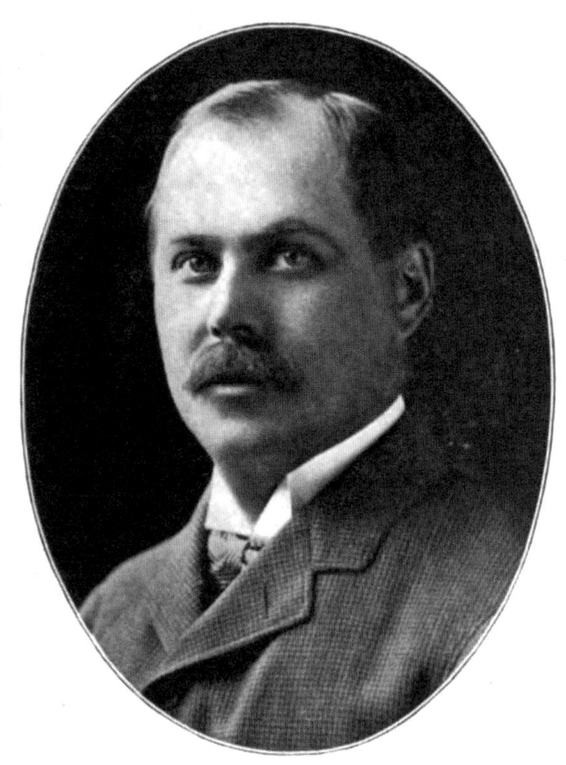

Saint Louis investors led by George J. Kobusch purchased the San Antonio Water Works from George Brackenridge.

the court ruled in favor of the Salvation Army. Brackenridge contributed to the home's construction in 1910 and to an endowment fund. The rescue home was in use for sixty years, and its final structure survives as part of the Boardwalk shopping complex on Broadway.[154]

By 1905, when Brackenridge was seventy-three, he was ready to be rid of the Water Works. Though still in charge, he did not resolve the new park's controversial perimeter strip, perhaps relishing the idea of Callaghan, back in as mayor that year, having to wrangle over the issue with another owner for a change. This time the city showed no intention of buying the company. Brackenridge asked a friend heading to Chicago to see if he could find a purchaser there. The friend found none, but on his way home stopped in Saint Louis to visit relatives. He ended up meeting with streetcar manufacturing magnate George J. Kobusch, who by nightfall sent Brackenridge's friend home with $100,000 in cash for an option to purchase the company. Kobusch gathered investors, bought the Water Works, and became the majority shareholder.[155]

The new owners reincorporated in 1906 as the San Antonio Water Supply Company. They had little interest in allowing public access across their land to the park, so the city filed a condemnation suit in 1908. The parties settled when the water company agreed to sell the city six entrances to the park, five along River Avenue and one on the southern perimeter at Josephine Street. Five entries were narrow, but the sixth and northernmost covered eight acres that became the site of the Witte Museum, Pioneer Hall, and the Reptile Garden.[156]

In 1911 Mayor Callaghan openly accused Brackenridge of malice by including the park's perimeter strip in the sale to the Saint Louis investors without providing legal access to the park. Moreover, Callaghan complained, Brackenridge was unfairly credited in the naming of a park that had actually been owned by the Water Works Company, however much of it Brackenridge may have owned. Callaghan got the council to change the name and signage to Water Works Park. Brackenridge dismissed the slight, saying: "Whether the park bears my name or not, it will meet the purposes and wishes of the donors fully as well under any other name." San Antonians still used the original name. After Callaghan died in 1912 while in office, the succeeding mayor and council changed the name back to Brackenridge Park.[157]

The matter of the remaining strip enclosing the park, however, pierced though it may have been by new entrances, was yet to be resolved.

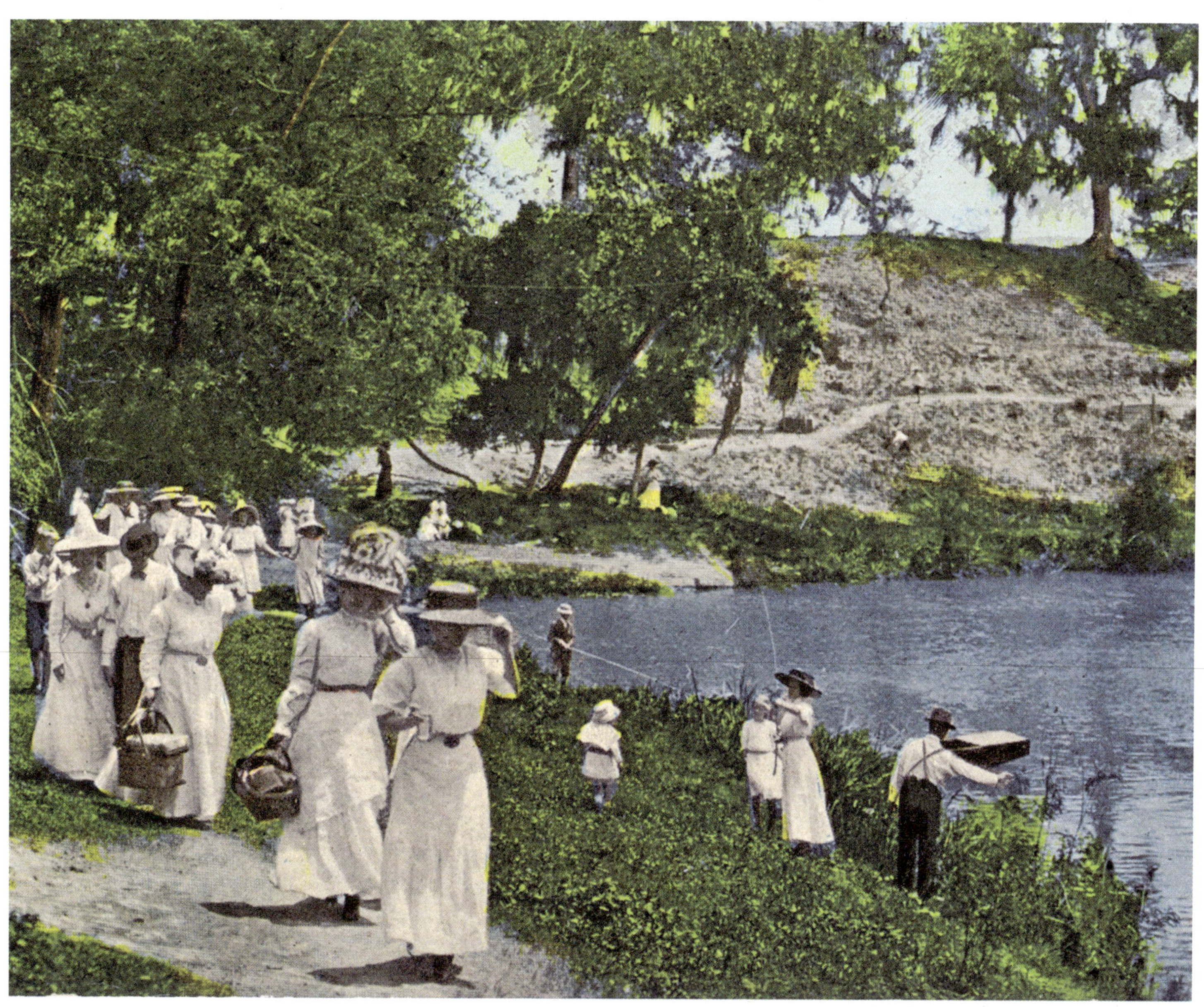

By 1910 the upper reaches of Brackenridge and Madarasz Parks were favorite spots for fishing and Sunday picnics.

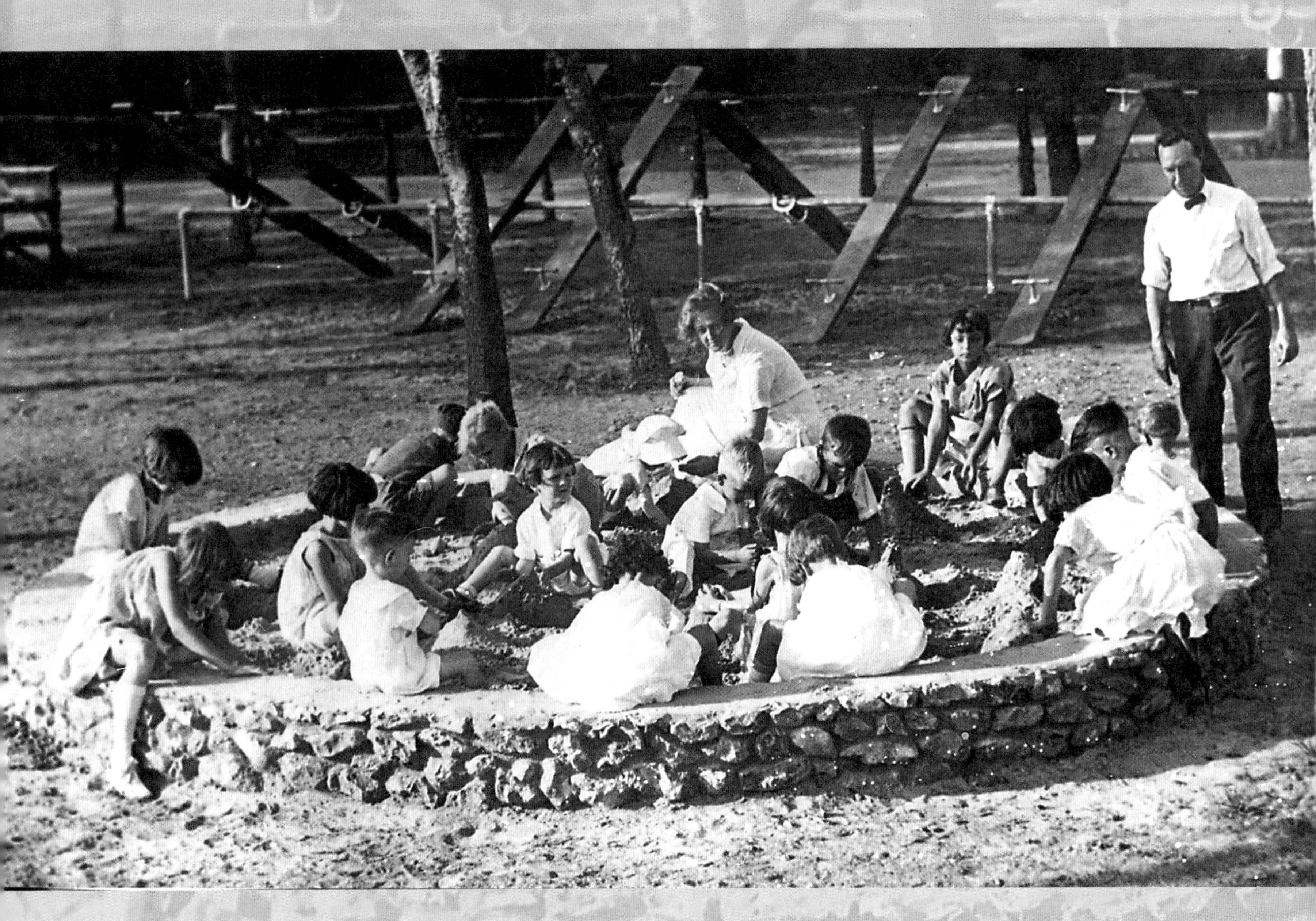

A Pivotal Year

John Raymond Lambert, forty-seven, leapt into his new role of parks commissioner on June 1, 1915, with a lengthy agenda for Brackenridge Park. On his first day he started building San Antonio's first public playground. He tried to keep it secret long enough to finish and make a dramatic unveiling, but word leaked out and he had to tell the press what he was up to.

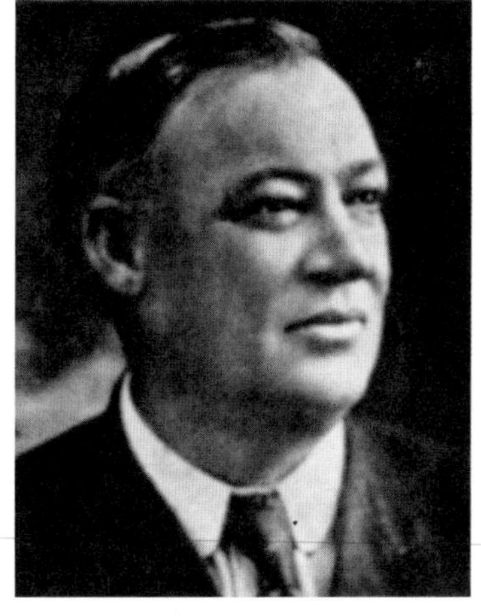

Parks commissioner Ray Lambert.

Lambert wanted to make Brackenridge Park "the finest playground in the South." As weeks went on he seemed to be heading in every direction at once. In hardly a year he changed the location planned for the zoo and moved in a herd of bison and elk to make way for the state's first public golf course. Along a river bend he began a bathing beach complete with water slide, picnic tables, and a concession booth that doubled as a bandstand. He planned to make a quarry pit-turned-garbage dump into a lush fern garden, then changed it to a Japanese lily pond. A chimney top was to look like a pagoda roof but ended up bizarre in a different way.

Quirkiness seemed inevitable as rapid-fire projects were adapted to fit minimal budgets. Some ideas were abandoned altogether, like Lambert's thought to illuminate the park by building a river-powered electric plant within park boundaries. One tract swung from becoming a botanical garden to a polo field.[158]

Nearly a decade after Lambert began transforming the contemplative driving park into a full-blown major municipal park and playground, a crowd celebrated him at the Koehler Pavilion on Ray Lambert Day. He told those present: "This work is just begun."

Lambert's first day as parks commissioner marked the start of commission government in San Antonio. Under the new charter, aldermen were called commissioners and elected at large rather than representing specific districts. Each was put in charge of a department. Lambert became commissioner of sanitation, parks, and public property, though he was usually referred to simply as parks commissioner. Having more political clout than appointees who previously headed departments, commissioners like Lambert could bring greater effectiveness to their assignments.

San Antonio's first municipal playground, named for George Brackenridge's sister, Eleanor, opened near Lambert Beach in 1915.

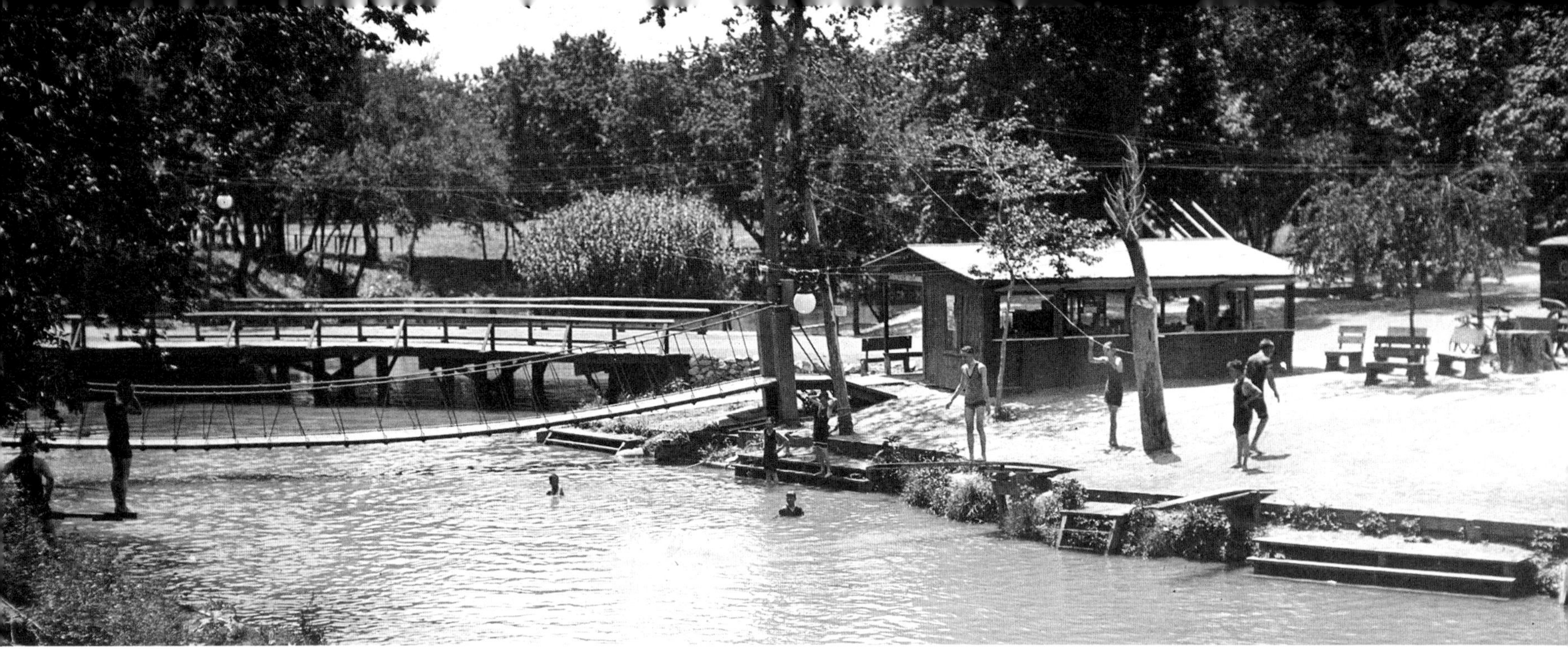

Lambert Beach still had few permanent facilities in 1920.

Lambert was first voted into office in 1903 as one of several candidates picked by Mayor Bryan Callaghan, a traditional political boss, to represent the old guard. But as reformers on the council gained strength, Lambert broke ranks with conservative aldermen and began voting with them. Like his new compatriots, he embraced change and became an energetic advocate for making San Antonio more functional and attractive.[159]

"I am a stonecutter and carver by trade," Lambert once noted, of his knack for some projects, "and I guess that helped me some." He stood "tall, broad, fleshy, with sandy hair and blue eyes to match, big hands callused by his one-time trade." Born in West Virginia in 1870, trained as a stonecutter in Iowa and apprenticed as one in Chicago in 1887, he left for Mexico in search of gold. "I was ripe for adventure," Lambert explained. "I went." By the mid-1890s he was in San Antonio cutting stone for construction of the Bexar County Courthouse. A few years later he began running the San Jacinto, a corner saloon a mile down South Flores Street from city hall and across from the San Antonio and Aransas Pass Railroad depot.[160]

When he became parks commissioner in 1915, social reformers were championing municipal playgrounds, and San Antonio as yet had none. His M. Eleanor Brackenridge Playground, named to recognize George Brackenridge's sister's interest in child welfare, was finished above a bend in the river soon known as Lambert's Bathing Beach. Seesaws and swings were made by city carpenters. The sand pile was given by a contractor. Also donated were poles and tin to make chutes for children to slide into the river, deep enough for swimming.[161]

Work began nearby on a seven-unit tin bathhouse for use until the adjoining unused pump house could be converted into a bathhouse. Ropes supported a swinging bridge across the river. Concrete walks beneath the spreading shade trees led to a new baseball diamond, croquet grounds, and four tennis courts. The thrifty parks commissioner was happy to announce that the project, including the playground, cost taxpayers less than $150.[162]

The San Antonio Municipal Band played for "thousands" at the formal opening of Lambert Bathing Beach in April 1916. Lambert himself presented "two fine bathing suits" to winners of the men's and women's swimming races. The band performed a series of concerts there each summer. Movies were shown on a screen hung on the south wall of the pump house.[163]

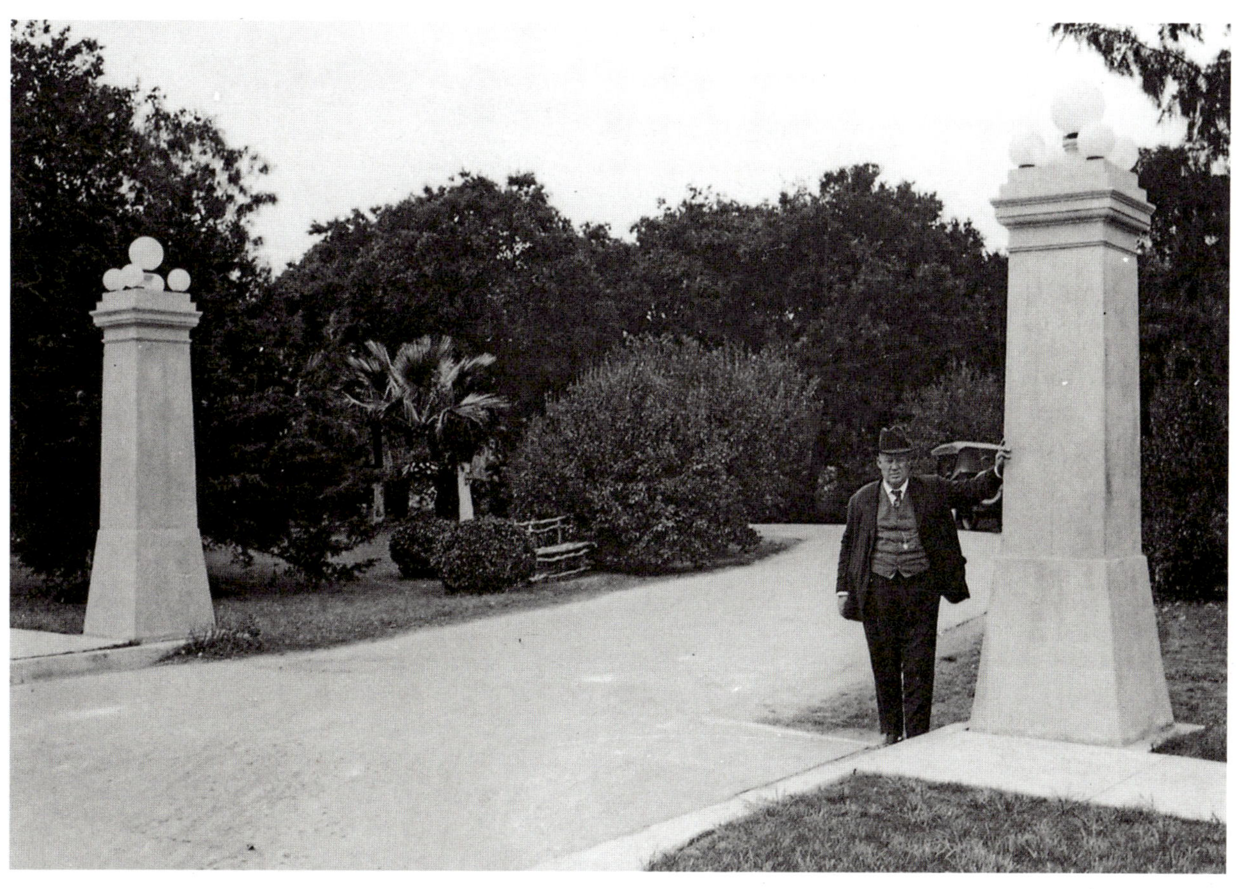

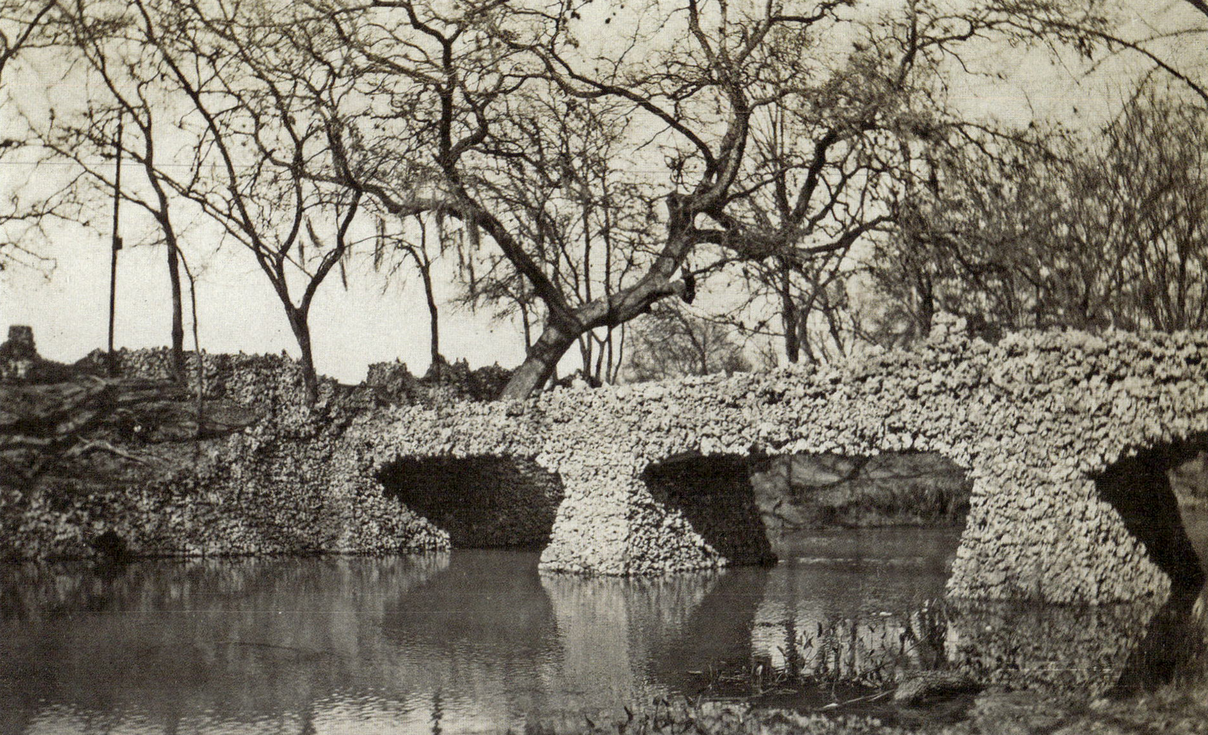

Ray Lambert stands at a gate where streetcars dropped passengers at the park's northern end. From there they could cross this arched shell stone bridge and make their way to Lambert Beach and the zoo.

By summer 1915 extra streetcars were being added every ten minutes to the run from downtown up River Avenue / Broadway to the park. On Sundays they dropped off as many as six thousand San Antonians at the park's northernmost entrance, where Lambert placed two gateway pillars. Passengers disembarked to a winding path and a shortcut to the beach over a new bridge across the river behind today's Witte Museum—a striking four-arched narrow pedestrian span of Texas shell stone, soft honeycombed rocks mortared together.[164]

Quite different to deal with was the southern half of the park, its area more open due in part to one recent development, years in the making. In June 1912 park commissioner Henry Steingruber had taken state horticulturist Harvey Stiles, the acting mayor, and three aldermen to view the "nearly complete destruction" of an immense swath of five hundred pecan trees near the river in the southern part of the park. The trees, part of the larger stand that for a decade shaded the new park's roads and pathways, were among those the Jockey Club had promoted as offering shade for the proposed site of International Fair buildings.[165]

Stiles had been monitoring the pecans' decline for three years. Public attention was at last drawn to the problem of the "immense amount of fungus" on the trees. Stiles placed the cause not on disease or a shortage of water during two recent droughts but on chronic lack of water due to increasing numbers of artesian wells that had lowered the water table and decreased the river's nourishing flow from the headwaters springs upstream.[166]

Two months later, aldermen went back to the park to discuss Stiles's recommendations for saving the trees. The next month they appropriated $300 to divert water from a main along River Avenue to water the trees. But it was too late. Three months later, in December 1912, Stiles pronounced the five hundred water-starved trees dead.[167]

Three years after purchasing San Antonio's water system from Brackenridge's company, in 1909, the Saint Louis investors cashed out and sold 90 percent of their stock to a Belgian syndicate based in Antwerp. Tensions in Europe were starting to simmer, and the United States was a safe place to invest. The new owners renamed the Water Works Company the Compagnie des Eaux de San Antonio—Water Company of San Antonio—and designated the Mississippi Valley Trust Company in Saint Louis as its agent.[168]

Germany's invasion of Belgium in 1914 disrupted the company's communications with its American agent. Interest and dividends that previously went to Antwerp began accumulating as surplus funds, which could be used for water system development. With San Antonio's population nearly doubling every ten years, the remaining American investors saw plenty of development needing to be done.[169]

The $250,000 Brackenridge Park pumping station—costing $14.7 million in today's dollars—was completed in 1915 to augment the Market Street pumping station downtown. Its wells varied from eight hundred to a thousand feet in depth and gave the Brackenridge plant a pumping capacity of twenty million gallons a day, equaling Market Street's. The hilltop reservoir was no longer needed, nor the old stone pump house nearby, nor the older one upstream. Water would be pumped directly to users through cast iron pipes branching out from Brackenridge Park.[170]

Excavating three thousand cubic feet of soil created a pump pit fifty feet wide and forty-five feet—three stories—deep to enhance hydrostatic pressure for the two steam-powered centrifugal pumps. Three curving vertical sections of concrete were maneuvered into the pit to form a cylindrical caisson walling the interior. The flat-roofed circular fourth story rose sixteen feet above ground and for ventilation was rimmed with arched windows, resembling, from a distance, a turret on a Civil War

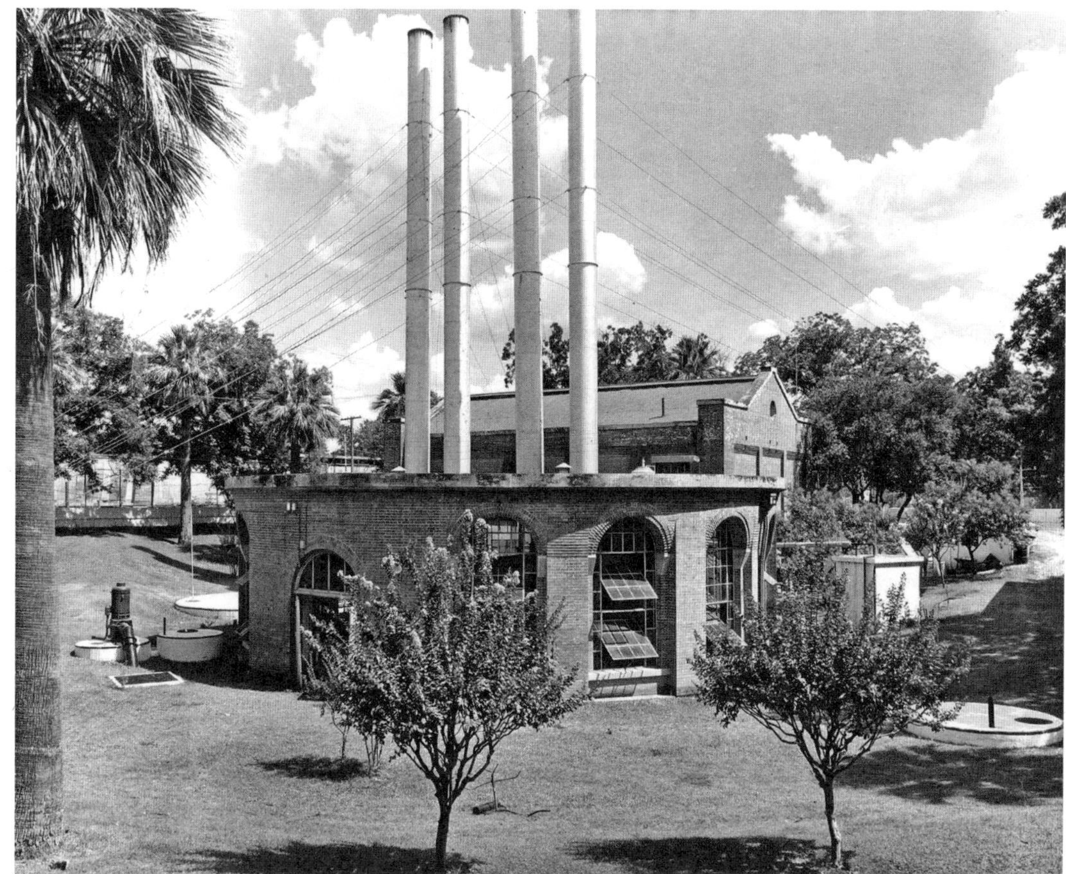

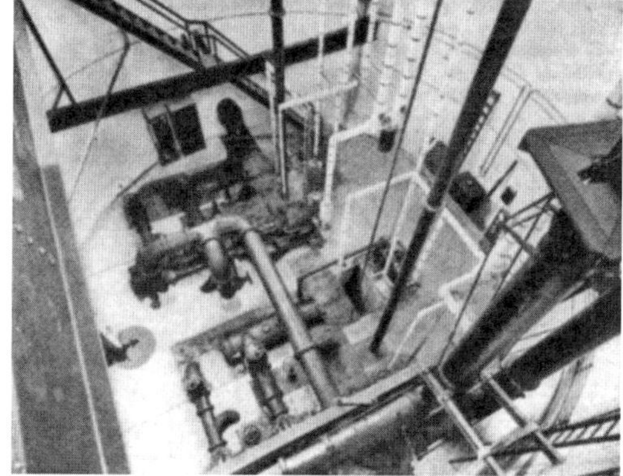

In 1915 the Brackenridge Park pumping station replaced the older pump houses. Park visitors could peer from a viewing balcony into the circular pit three stories below ground level. A brick power plant was nearby.

ironclad. An underground passage linked the pump pit with the gabled brick power plant beside it that housed three oil-fueled boilers, their narrow chimneys rising outside.[171]

The Compagnie des Eaux de San Antonio was well aware that the plant was in a municipal park, and its general manager sought to make it "one of the show places of the park." Surroundings were landscaped with flowerbeds and trees. Its biggest attraction was the pump pit, left open at all hours so visitors could walk around the gallery circling the top level and peer through the network of pipes to the pumps at work three levels below.[172]

As the pumping station was being built, Ray Lambert was settling into his new post. He found himself among leaders trying to position San Antonio, which its promoters dubbed "the largest city in the largest state," as a major destination for tourists, "the place where the sun spends the winter."

But golfers frozen out of courses in the North had few options for playing in San Antonio, as the city's few private courses were not open to them. The southern half of Brackenridge Park, even more open with loss of the water-starved pecans, was seen as an excellent site for a course. And the land was already owned by the city. Longtime amateur golfer and Texas Golf Association cofounder Frank M. Lewis took Mayor Clinton Brown to dinner at the San Antonio Country Club to make the case for a public golf course in the park.

Brown was drawn in by Lewis's enthusiasm. Lambert signed on as well, though he knew little about golf. "So much interest has been displayed in the matter that I guess I'll have to learn to play," he said. In June 1915, his first month as parks commissioner, Lambert took along an avid golfer, former alderman A. B. Weakly, to scout the potential site of the course.[173]

But first a home had to be found for the southern park's roaming menagerie of bison, elk, and other wild animals, favorites with visitors. Lambert wanted to keep them by creating a zoo. One potential location had already been picked.

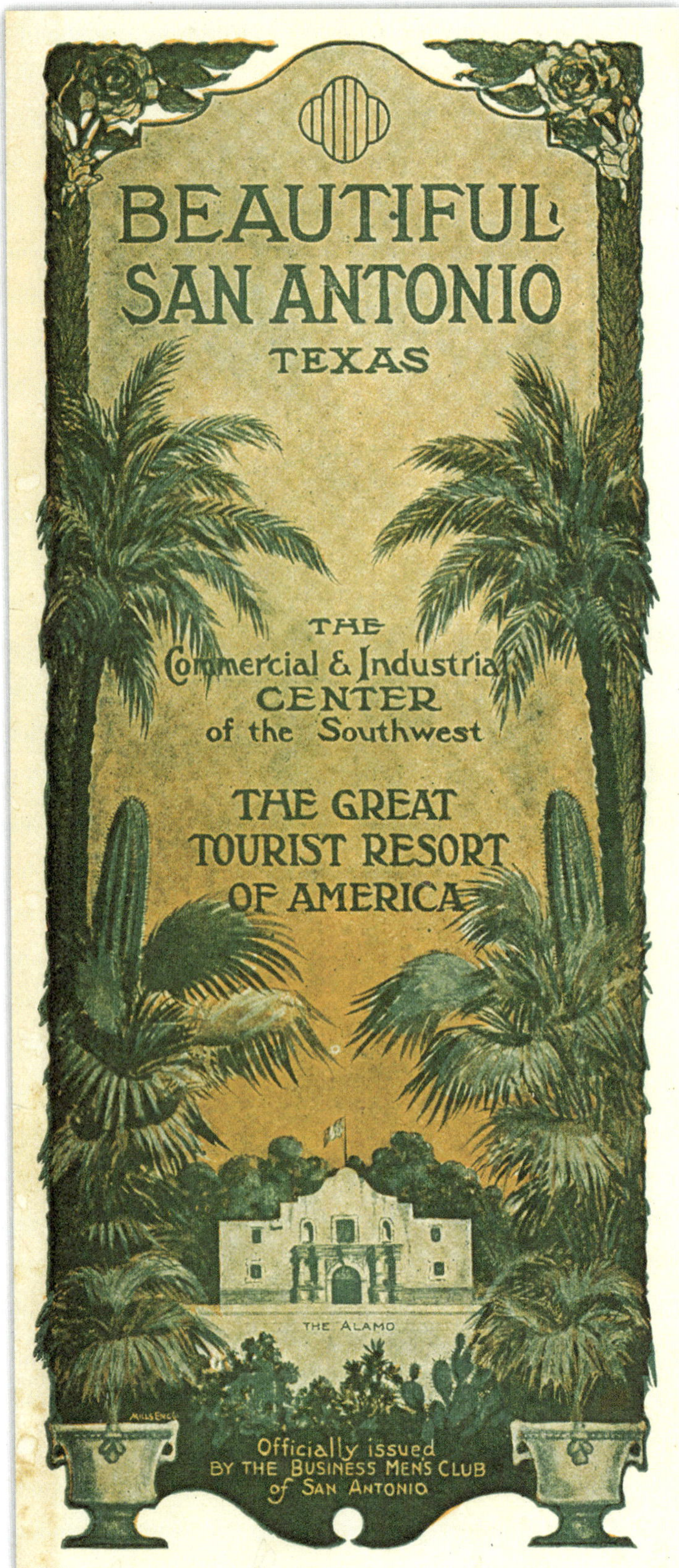

Boosters made exaggerated claims in this 1904 brochure to attract tourists as they waited for sure-fire amenities like an eighteen-hole golf course.

Four years before, the city had lost what passed for its natural history museum and its zoo, "the only zoo in Texas." Their establishment, demise, and the stalled plans to replace them were typical San Antonio hard-times tales of earnest but shoestring efforts and of half-thought-out solutions.

The city's first zoological garden had opened in San Pedro Springs Park. In 1888 a newspaper reported that when an order for "a box of monkeys" arrived, the zoo "will then have quite a nice little collection of animals." Before long it featured leopards, badgers, and coyotes pacing inside raised wooden cages and in pens, though in 1897 its bear pit was shut down and covered by a bandstand. The zoo's last owner, Jacob Amreihn, died in 1908. The longtime operator of the park's small frame natural history museum, Hungarian-born Gustav Jermy, died soon after. Jermy, about to retire as Texas state geologist and botanist, had been elected director when the museum formed in 1884. He donated most of his collection of regional plants, fossils, and minerals as core exhibits for the museum, which opened the next year.[174]

In 1911 city officials, alleging to have just discovered that the museum and zoo were located on city property but paid no rent, decreed that the operators take no further advantage of taxpayers and stop charging admission. Both the museum and zoo closed. The zoo owner's heirs sold their animals to a circus supplier in Kansas City for $530, today's equivalent of $15,000.[175]

Vocal over the loss of both was the Scientific Society of San Antonio, established in 1904, which saw itself as successor to earlier learned societies in the city. The society met on the second floor of the stylish Stevens Building on West Commerce Street, where it maintained a four-thousand volume library and elegantly cased exhibits of natural history artifacts and curiosities. The collection, eventually opened to the public two afternoons a week, was to aid one of the society's founding goals: establishing a distinguished natural history museum in San Antonio.[176]

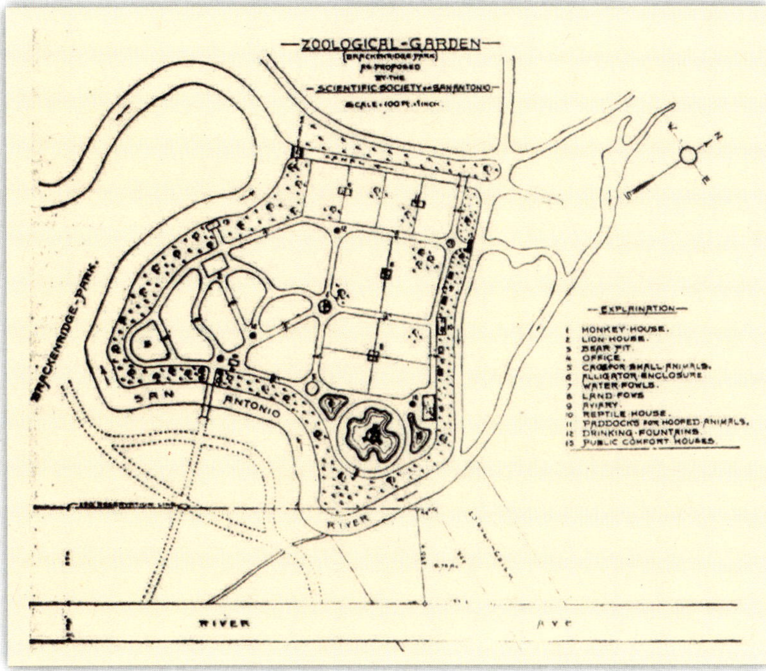

Today's zoo was originally to be at this site beside the San Antonio River. Ray Lambert saw the wisdom of moving the zoo to higher ground. The Witte Museum was eventually built near the street at lower center.

The society began advocating for both a new natural history museum and a zoological garden. In spring 1914 a society committee gained city council approval of a twelve-acre site in northeast Brackenridge Park. The zoological garden would take the western portion of the site, east of the pump house raceway. A museum would take the adjoining section farther east, facing Broadway—just as New York's Metropolitan Museum of Art in Central Park faced Fifth Avenue. Once the city authorized the society to establish the zoo, the group began fundraising and had donations of numerous animals lined up but lost interest when Mayor Brown reneged on his promise of a $500 monthly budget item for zoo maintenance, claiming it would require a tax increase.[177]

There the matter stood until Lambert took office a year later and had to hustle the bison, elk, and other animals out of the way for the new golf course.

The parks commissioner had only to take a quick look at the proposed zoo site to see problems. The riverside land was subject to flooding. Building stand-alone cages would be expensive. Why couldn't the zoo be on the other side of the river, higher up around the abandoned quarry's towering rim of cliffs, which could be adapted for cages? It would be at the eastern edge of the old rock quarries, on city property. That, Lambert said, "will be a world better and won't cost too much. Nature has done the work."[178]

As a veteran alderman, Lambert enjoyed a level of credibility no private organization's committee could achieve with city hall. Three months into his role as parks commissioner, he had official approval for his department to organize a zoo in his chosen spot below the cliffs. Squatters there were ordered to move to an old quarry nearby where Lambert hoped they would build "picturesque" adobe homes "like those in old Mexico" and offer typical Mexican curios for sale to tourists. Thirty-seven shacks of wood and tin were moved away to house tuberculosis patients at the Southton Road Convalescent Center.[179]

Despite his refusal to seek new taxes for the Scientific Society to operate the zoo, with Lambert in charge Brown proposed a tax increase for 1916 that would yield nearly $200 a month—about $48,000 a year today—for the new zoo, though its expenses soon increased by half. Lambert would keep feed costs down by using scraps from the city market house and packing houses, and by harvesting oats and Johnson grass planted on city-owned property.[180]

In early September 1915 Lambert announced that the city was ready to accept donated animals. This was a good season to find bargains, he said, as circuses were slimming down as they went into winter quarters.[181]

Within ten days Lambert had the zoo's first two bears, donated by real estate man Travis Jones from his ranch in Arizona. The back wall of the bears' cage was a limestone cliff, the other three walls made of reinforced steel rods salvaged from the recently demolished city hospital. A rock ledge inside allowed the bears to sun themselves. They were joined by a third bear, donated by candy manufacturer G. A. Duerler, and by a fourth from Yellowstone National Park, which, through the US Department of the Interior, also supplied several beavers.[182]

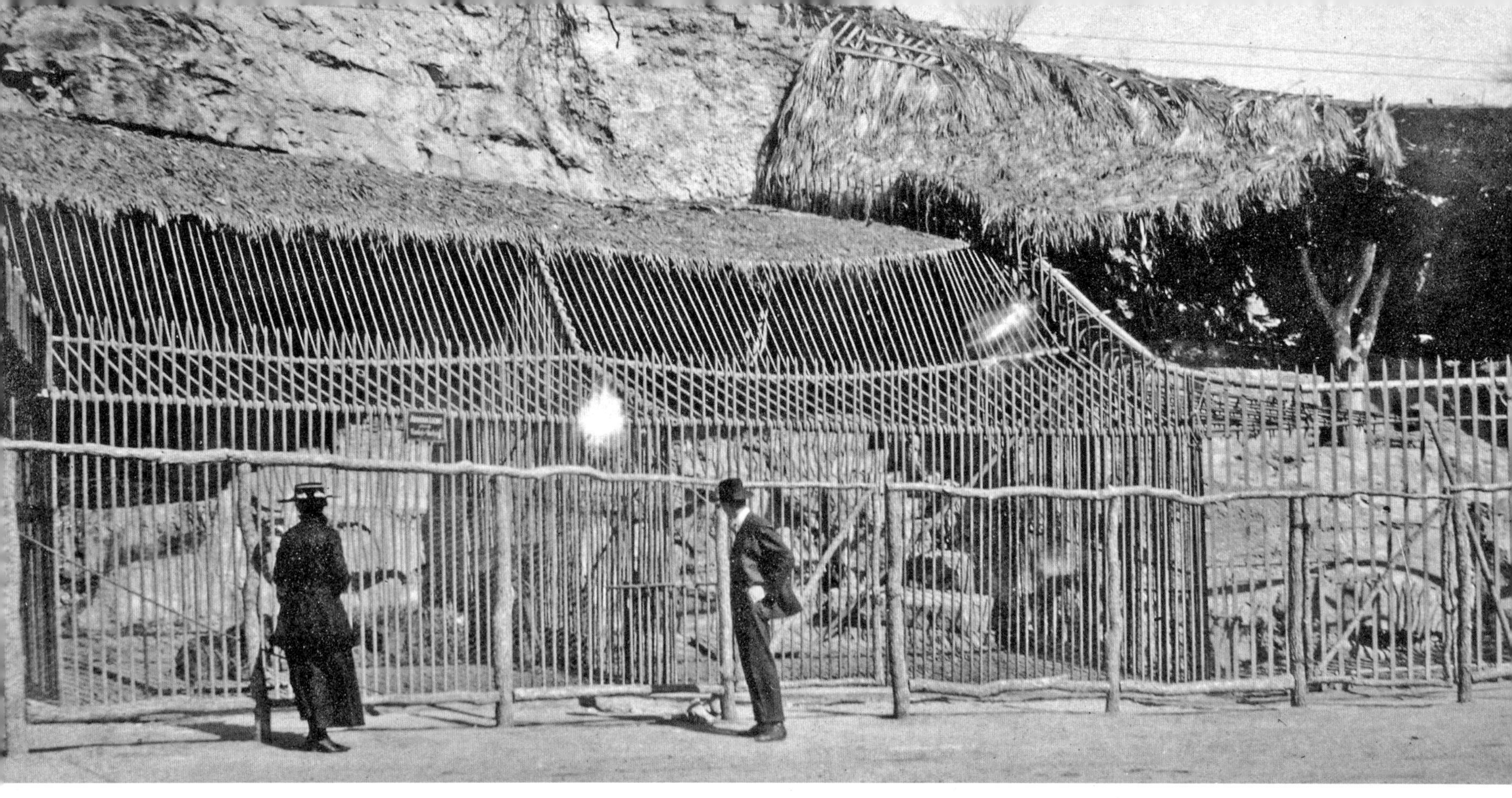

A similar neighboring cage was built for a pair of young male and female lions purchased by two local residents from a dealer in Los Angeles. An aviary was supported by poles donated by lumberman Albert Steves and enclosed with wire mesh salvaged from fencing that George Brackenridge had once stretched around the park. Gifts of Texas animals included an armadillo from Sutherland Springs, a wildcat from Seguin, a black wolf from Gruene, and a Mexican eagle from Adkins. Lambert gave a pair of Egyptian geese. Two kangaroos did not survive their new surroundings.[183]

For nearly six months San Antonians were treated to progress reports of sea lions promised by Albert Steves, who hired two San Francisco–based fishing crews to find them off the Pacific coast. Sea lions proved elusive. One set was caught but broke out of the nets, and storms interfered. Finally, in November 1917, a trio of year-old seals arrived in San Antonio. Their new home was a cold spring-fed pool, opposite the wolf den and lined with rock salvaged from the newly razed city hospital. The Upper Labor Acequia nearby was already closed, but water mains were near in case the spring went dry.[184]

Another drama was relocation of the five bison, in September 1915, from the golf course site a mile north to a twenty-acre pasture in a former quarry pit above the zoo. How to move the bison perplexed Lambert, as "they cannot be led and they will not be driven." Worse, they could attack unpredictably; three bison were killed while being loaded in North Texas for the trip to Brackenridge Park. "And that," Lambert said, "was when the work was done by experts at the Goodnight Ranch."[185]

A scheme to cut a path to the new zoo pasture and lure the bison by placing feed along the route was scrapped in favor of a plan devised by park superintendent Alfred Hansen. He kept the bison in a pen south of the new waterworks pumping station and deprived them of feed for several days. Then he put feed inside crates made of heavy timbers and set at the edge of the pen. Four buffalo were enticed into the crates with little difficulty. But the fifth, the

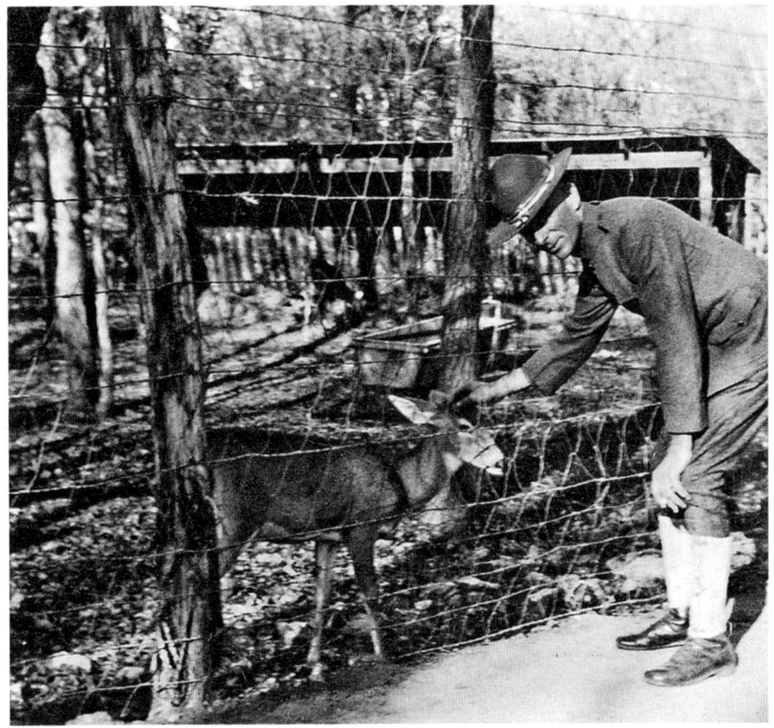

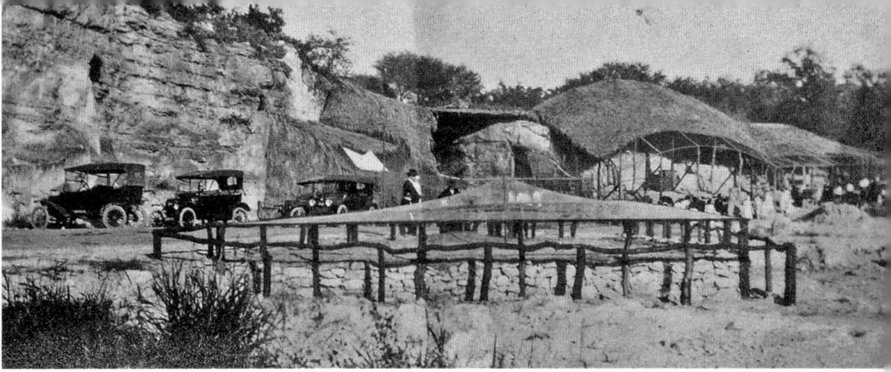

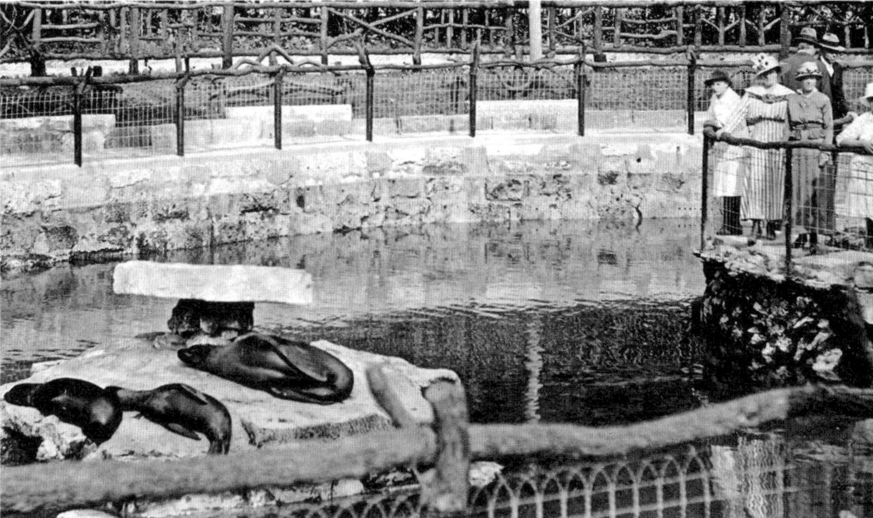

Animals began moving into the Municipal Zoo's cliffside cages in 1915. Deer were penned nearby, and sea lions went into a spring-fed pool.

"old bull buffalo," one newspaper reported, "broke every rope cast over him" and made "wild dashes against the heavy stockade." He finally gave in to the bait and, like the others, was hauled by wagon to the zoo.[186]

Hansen had to look no further for a zookeeper than Glenn Shockley, age forty-two. Born in Missouri, Shockley was fifteen when his parents told him he had to get rid of the assortment of animals he kept in their backyard. He ran away and joined a circus as an animal attendant and trainer. He had settled in San Antonio in 1901 as keeper at the zoo in San Pedro Springs Park during its last years. His philosophy: "You can't tame a animal by a-beatin' him just the same as you can't make a man your friend by a-kickin' him around. You gotta be his pal."[187]

A crew from the French-based Gaumont Film Company arrived at Brackenridge Park in February 1916 to record the crowds and animal feedings at the newly opened zoo for a *Mutual Weekly* news event summary, silent clips shown in motion picture theaters throughout the country.[188]

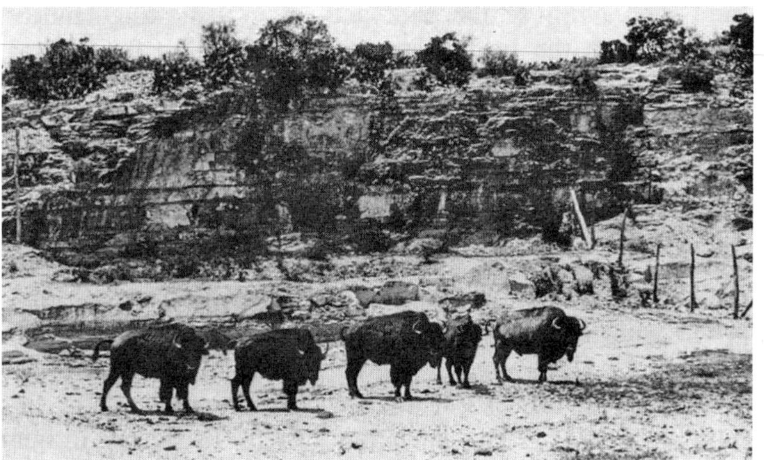

Bison arrived at the zoo after their tricky move off the golf course site.

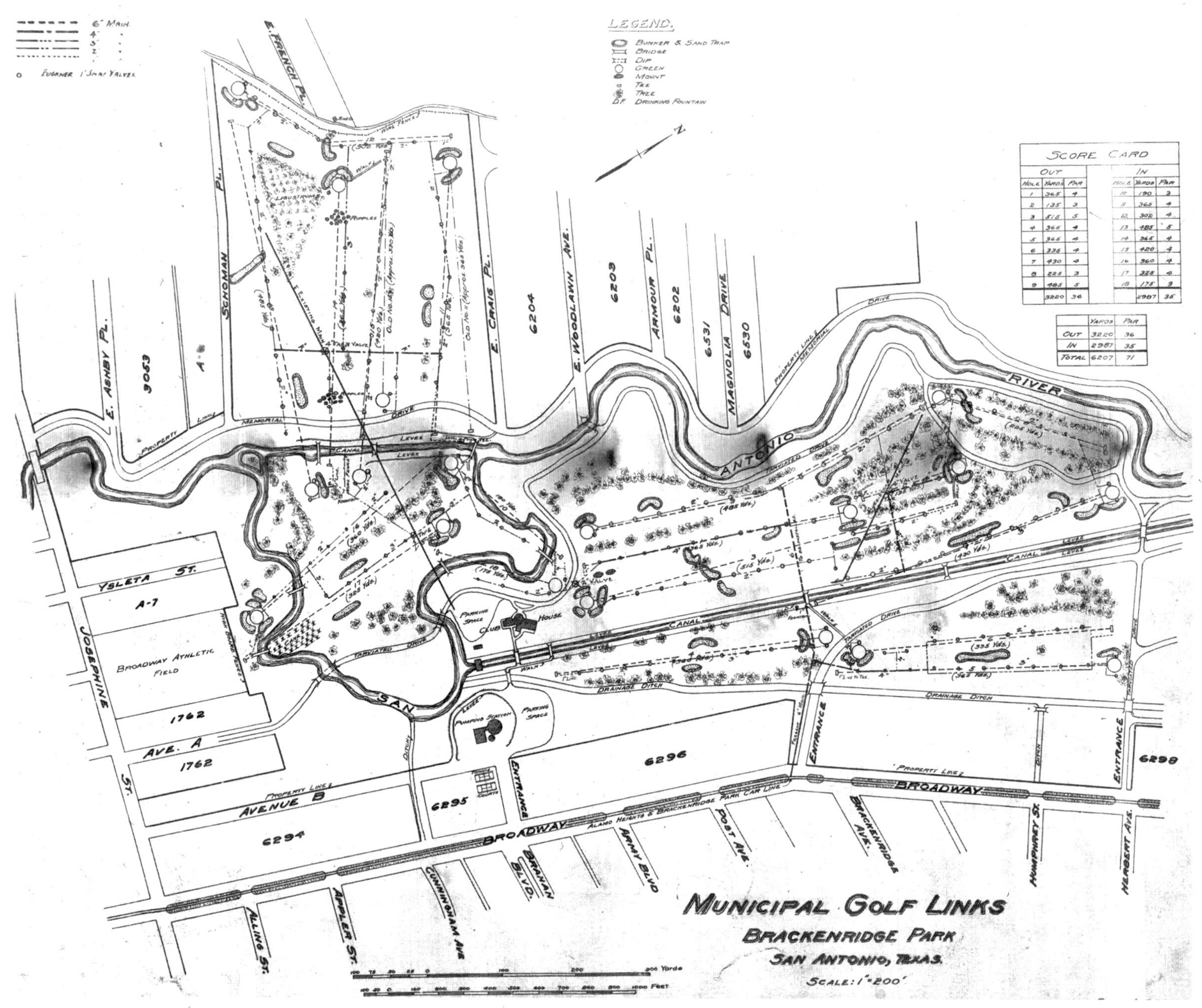

In the early 1920s the Water Works raceway canal and scenic drives still cut through Brackenridge Park's golf course. Mulberry Avenue was later extended over the drive at far right to meet Broadway. The open area left of the intersection became Lions Field, bordered farther left by the entrance road first used for the 1893 race track.

With work on the zoo underway, in October 1915 the city hired golf course designer Albert Warren Tillinghast, who remembered arriving to start even before the bison had been lured off the future course. Tillinghast's prolific career included original design of some seventy courses, redesign of another seventy, and consultation on more than a hundred others, many still on the national circuit for championship events. San Antonio's would be the first public golf course in Texas.[189]

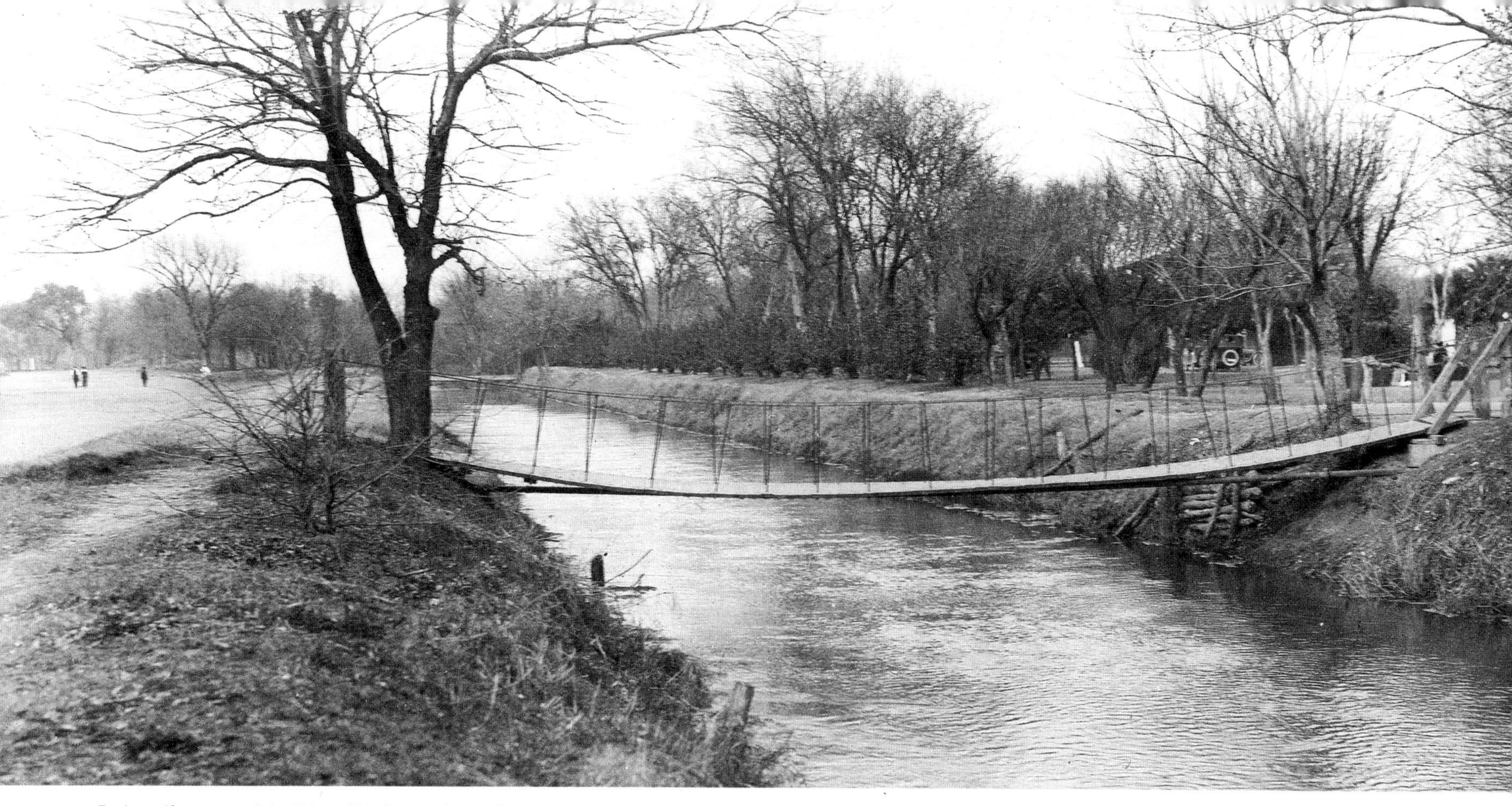

Early golfers crossed the Water Works canal on a footbridge at the third tee to reach the fairway.

Tillinghast began work under his fourteen-day contract on October 5, 1915. Construction would be continued by assistant city engineer W. S. Delery, for whom Tillinghast had high regard. Tillinghast stressed that he would be available for consultation for the following ten days while he was designing the eighteen-hole Funston Moor Golf Course at Fort Sam Houston. He left detailed sketches and specifications for each hole. Delery promised that in clearing undergrowth "it will not be necessary to damage trees of any size."[190]

For the clubhouse, Tillinghast picked a location near the raceway canal just up from the lower pump house, which offered close access to River Avenue. The first three holes—which covered the Jockey Club's racetrack site—swung north from there, and the next six arced back to the clubhouse, the second nine then spreading westward and returning. The twenty-one-year-old racetrack clubhouse, most recently residence of a park gardener, stood nearby and could be used until the new golf clubhouse was built. It was rewired and got new plumbing for hot and cold showers, and eighty lockers were installed. To help avoid admission fees, the Gunter Hotel provided towels at no charge. The first floor was reserved for male golfers, the second for female golfers.[191]

A particular design challenge was the raceway canal, still filled with water and bisecting the course's upper nine holes. Memorial Drive along the west side of the river and two scenic drives across to the east also continued to pass through the course. Tillinghast finessed the obstacles in part with his signature "reef bunkers," a series of sand bunkers that crossed the fairway diagonally at holes three and eight. The toughest hole was the seventh, where the raceway split the fairway from the left of the tee box nearly halfway to the green. Harder still were three holes on the back course, where seven of the nine holes had to contend with the meandering San Antonio River.[192]

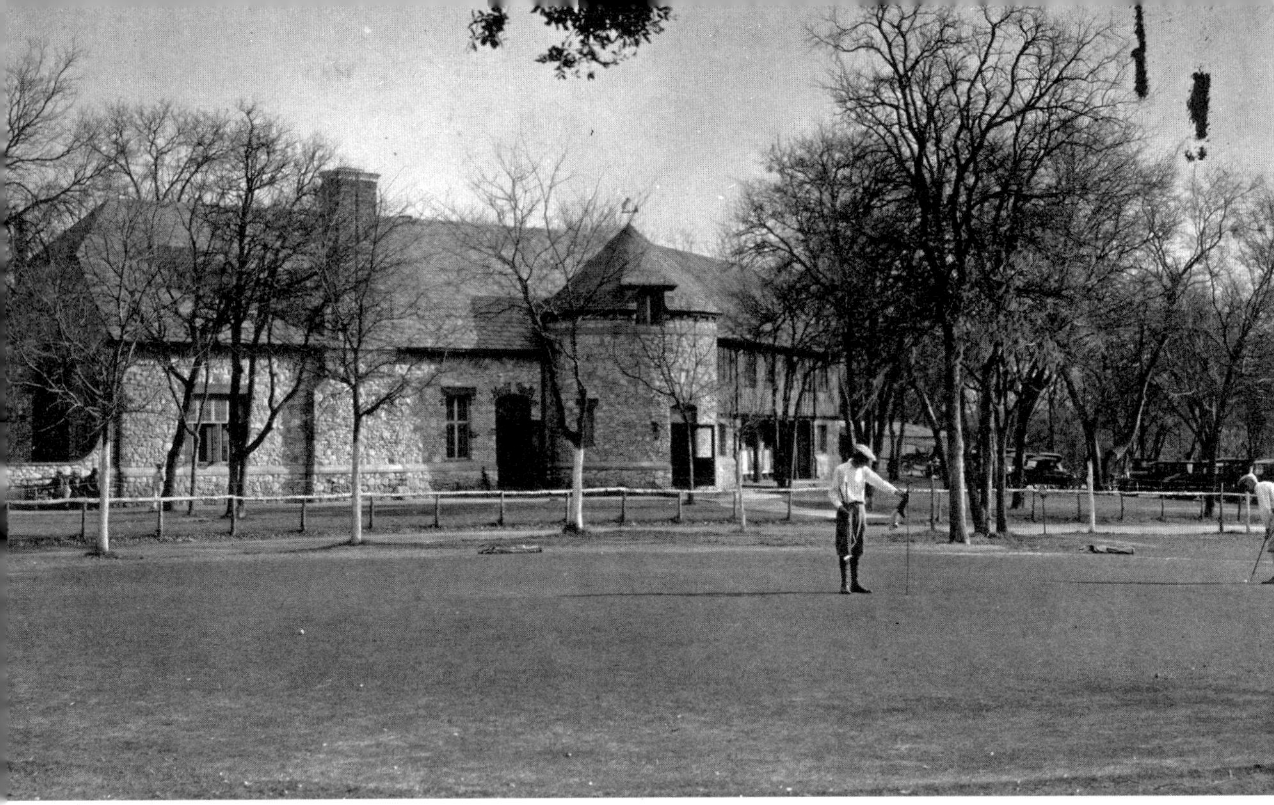

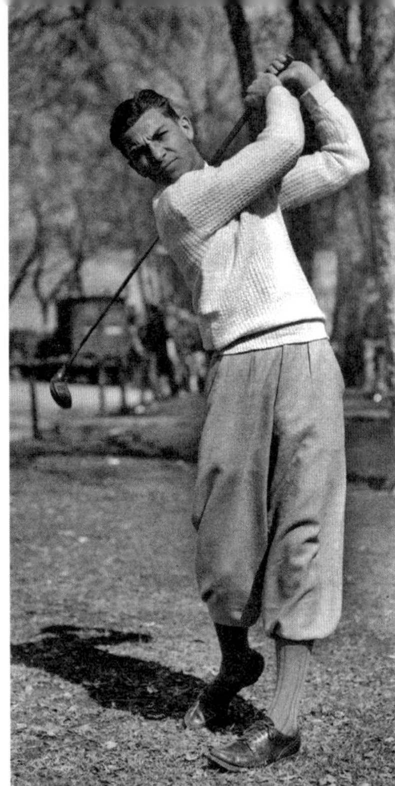

A Tudor-style clubhouse opened in 1923 in time for the second Texas Open, a longtime annual event that drew such legendary golfers as Ben Hogan, shown at the Brackenridge course.

At one point Tillinghast thought clearing the "jungle" was going too slowly. He complained to Mayor Brown and to Lambert, who agreed to put fifty prisoners on the job for ten days. "The next day," Tillinghast recalled, "the work force was comprised of fifty men, not forty-nine or fifty-one, mind you, exactly fifty prisoners, all huskies, caught the night before at illegal cockfights and crap games."[193]

The first nine holes of what city council named Brackenridge Park Golf Links opened on February 20, 1916, the second nine to a one-day tournament on September 30. The *San Antonio Light* contributed a silver loving cup for the winner. The course was so successful that Jack O'Brien, sports editor of the *San Antonio Evening News*, teamed up with John Bredemus, the course's golf pro, to organize the state's first professional golf event, the Texas Open, held in February 1922. With a purse of $5,000—today's equivalent of $75,000—more than three times that of the U.S. Open, it drew golfers from across the country and more than six thousand fans daily to watch. It was an annual event at the park for another thirty-seven years, as the Brackenridge course attracted golfers from Ben Hogan to Arnold Palmer to Lee Trevino.[194]

Hosting the Texas Open merited a new clubhouse. Civic leaders raised $8,000 and hired architect Ralph H. Cameron, who also designed two Alamo Plaza landmarks, the Medical Arts Building / Emily Morgan Hotel and the US Post Office and Courthouse. Cameron's two-story Tudor-style stone clubhouse near the lower pump house featured a great room with open beams and a large fireplace on the north wall. He designed a weathervane silhouette of a golfer putting a ball for the conical-roofed rotunda. After the clubhouse opened in 1923, in time for the second Texas Open, the old clubhouse, built in 1894 for the Jockey Club, was razed.[195]

Local golfing enthusiasm ran so high that the Brackenridge Women's Golf Association, among the first women's golf groups in Texas, was organized the same year as the first Texas Open. An early member was Elizabeth Fucals, among the first Black women welcomed to play on a Texas course in those years of segregation.[196]

Mexican American golfers had little trouble playing on San Antonio municipal courses, though at the outset the city required Hispanics to prepay for their tournaments. Brackenridge was the home course for the National Pan American Golf Association, organized by Mexican American players in San Antonio in 1938. The nation's largest Hispanic golf organization, with more than forty chapters in nine states, it purchased in 1985 a former golf shop just outside the Brackenridge course, on Millrace Street, as its headquarters.[197]

Racial segregation rules of the times limited Blacks to using parks designated for them in their own neighborhoods, mostly in eastern San Antonio. Since Brackenridge Park's new golf course did not extend as far as the park's southern border along Josephine Street, Lambert saw that area as a place to include Blacks in at least part of the park. In May 1916 he asked the city council to create "a park for Negroes" in the section east of the river and north of Josephine Street for several hundred feet to the southern edge of the golf course.[198]

Lambert said the new park could be ready in a few weeks for the Blacks' Emancipation Day celebration on June 19, now the national holiday known as Juneteenth. Lambert thought a city permit for the event would be granted "provided the celebration is confined to this new park," but the council took no action on his park proposal. Nor is there a record of a response four years later to a petition from the local chapter of the National Association for the Advancement of Colored People asking that Blacks be allowed to "enjoy the pleasures of Brackenridge Park," though other official permissions were being granted for Juneteenth celebrations in Brackenridge Park as well as in San Pedro Springs Park as restrictions on Blacks' use began fading.[199]

Six months after Lambert became parks commissioner, one of his biggest fears was allayed. Otto Koehler, who owned the beer-selling Madarasz Family Park across the river, had died in late 1914. Madarasz Park's fourteen acres formed a wedge into the angle between the new zoo's site and Brackenridge Park, and Lambert feared heirs would lose interest and sell it for residential development. Koehler's Saint Louis–born widow, Emma Bentzen Koehler, fifty-seven, took over the brewery's operation and apparently found the park / beer garden business distracting. Instead of selling, on the day before Christmas 1915 she announced the gift of Madarasz Family Park to the city in memory of her husband. It was to bear his name.[200]

The city agreed to allow beer to still be sold in the park and to forbid any future municipal ban on its sale there. It also agreed to apply Koehler Park concession proceeds toward maintaining the new golf course and enlarging the zoo.[201]

Another of Emma Koehler's conditions precipitated the final solution of George Brackenridge's bothersome twenty-five-foot-wide "Chinese wall" perimeter, which surrounded the entire park. Its title had transferred to recent purchasers of the water company. Different ownership may not in practice have kept beer-drinkers from crossing between Koehler and Brackenridge Parks, but the perimeter between the two parks gave its owners the legal right to prevent any crossing. That left the only legal public entry to Koehler Park at Rock Quarry Road / North Saint Mary's Street on the park's distant western edge. What would be the point of donating a park that offered little legal access?[202]

Thus Emma Koehler made her gift dependent on the water company deeding to the city the entire "Chinese wall" perimeter chokehold around the park. Given public enthusiasm over Koehler's new donation, longtime water company shareholders in Missouri felt obliged to agree. But majority ownership was based in Belgium, where there was a war going on and Belgian directors were hard to reach. Eventually they were found and approved transferring title of the strip to the city.[203]

A father leads his children through the Municipal Zoo.

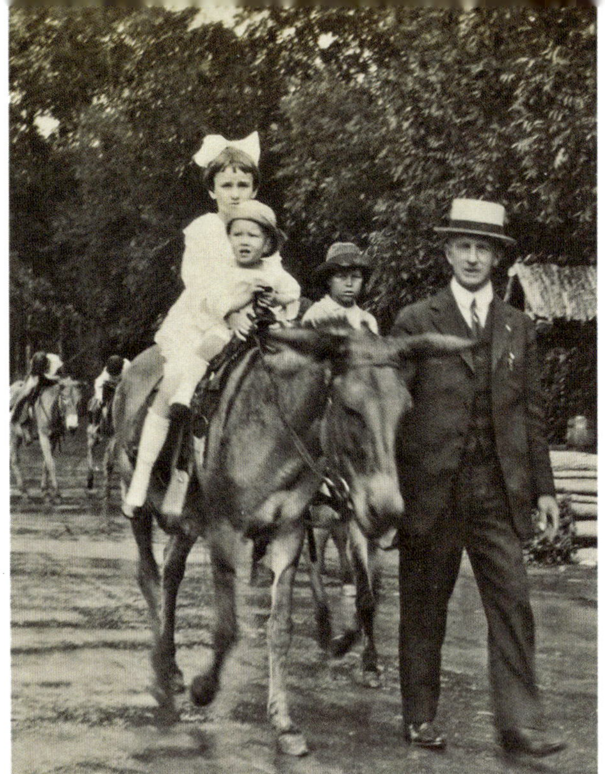

Koehler Park provided a launch point for a new scenic drive around the rim of former Alamo Cement quarries to the west. In June 1916 Lambert put a crew of city prisoners to work breaking rocks and clearing the path for Alpine Drive. It was built west from the zoo and across a reconstructed cement plant bridge. Half a mile of ridges offered spectacular views of the city's growing skyline. Some passages were so narrow that the route was limited to one-way traffic and edged with large rocks embedded in cement to keep cars from going over the precipice. Once smoothed by a twenty-ton roller, the road was covered by a thick chemical residue donated by San Antonio Gas and Electric to hold a top layer of gravel in place. Alpine Drive descended to pecan tree–lined Rock Quarry Road for the return to Koehler Park.[204]

Lambert planned Alpine Drive as both an automobile drive and a burro trail. On hand for its opening in 1916 were a dozen burros, purchased at a pop-up burro market at Lambert Beach organized by a Rotary Club committee headed by Studebaker dealer Frank A. Winerich. Rotarians added saddles and bridles to the burros, decked them out in ribbons, and two days later ceremoniously presented them for children's rides along the Alpine Drive trail. Receiving the burros on behalf of the city were the twin sons of Mayor Brown. Four years later the burros moved to a new network of trails north of Lambert Beach.[205]

Making the transition from Alpine Drive to the new trails was the good-natured burro guide Ernest Smith. Children nicknamed him Peg for the wooden shaft that served as his lower left leg, lost when Smith was twenty-seven and working as a San Antonio and Aransas Pass Railroad switchman in Yoakum. He became a street crossing guard near the railroad's depot in San Antonio, across from the saloon run by future parks commissioner Lambert, and later took a job with Lambert's parks department.[206]

"I was working out here doing something else," Smith once explained, "and they said, 'You'd better take care of the burros.' And I said, 'All right.' I came over here, and first thing you know the children were calling me 'Peg' and jest lovin' me." By 1921 Smith had hundreds of postcards and letters from children across the country he had helped on and off one of the park's more than thirty donkeys. Some children wrote Smith the name of the donkey they wanted to ride the next time they came.[207]

Children sent nickels and dimes to a fund to aid Smith after he suffered a paralyzing stroke on the job in 1924. He returned to visit the donkey trails once, on a stretcher, before he died three years later, at age fifty-seven. His death was front-page news.[208]

With the golf course, zoo, Lambert Beach, and Koehler Park in operation before Lambert had been parks commissioner for even a year, Brackenridge Park's traffic infrastructure of former carriage drives and paths was bound to prove inadequate. One balmy Sunday in February 1916 park policemen had to be stationed in front of the zoo to keep ten thousand park visitors moving. Some pressure was relieved by a rustic bridge built across the river as an exit at the park's upper end, at what would become Hildebrand Avenue, but a $5,000 network of connecting roads and bridges was deemed essential. Moreover, some

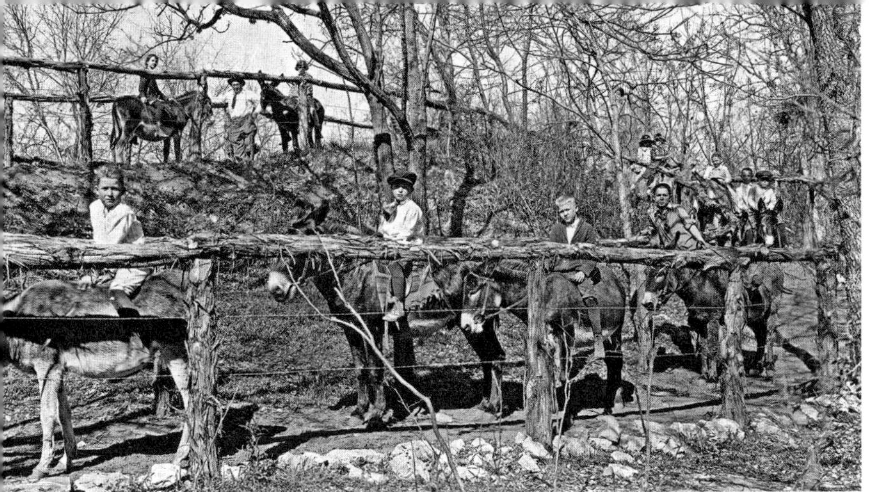

Beloved burro guide Ernest Smith stands near top left in a 1920s view of children descending a trail above Lambert Beach.

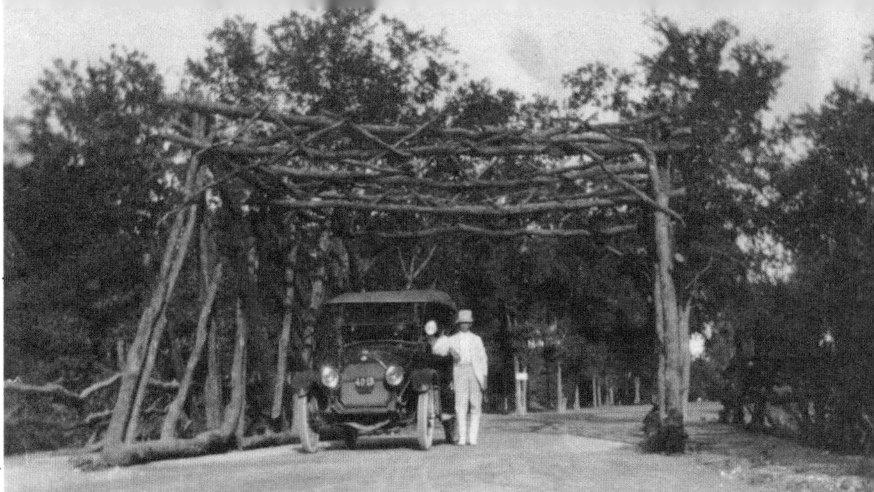

Improvements to the park by 1916 included a rustic bridge near Lambert Beach.

sort of bridge across the river was needed to link Brackenridge and Koehler Parks.[209]

This time a protest erupted not from unhappy taxpayers but from the City Federation of Women's Clubs, whose component clubs had 2,200 members. In a session at the Gunter Hotel two months after the city's announcement of Emma Koehler's gift, members unanimously demanded that the city build no bridges across the river between the two parks and, moreover, that they be separated by fences without gates. George Brackenridge, the federation's resolution declared, had required that his park "should be free from any of the injurious environment inseparable from the sale of intoxicating beverages; therefore be it." Beer-drinking patrons of Koehler Park should not be allowed to wander over and despoil Brackenridge Park, keeping it a place "where the young people of our city may find healthful and wholesome recreation."[210]

Lambert, attending the session to discuss city beautification but aware of the growing strength of the Prohibition movement, assured the ladies that he had "asked for the best and most reliable men on the police force to be placed in the park" and believed they had already been "particularly strict" in enforcing Brackenridge Park's drinking ban. Little more was heard about the matter.[211]

A visible reminder of Prohibition is a rustic marker dedicated in the park in 1925 on the first anniversary of the death of George Brackenridge's sister, Eleanor, a leader in the temperance movement. It was placed along a wooded path at

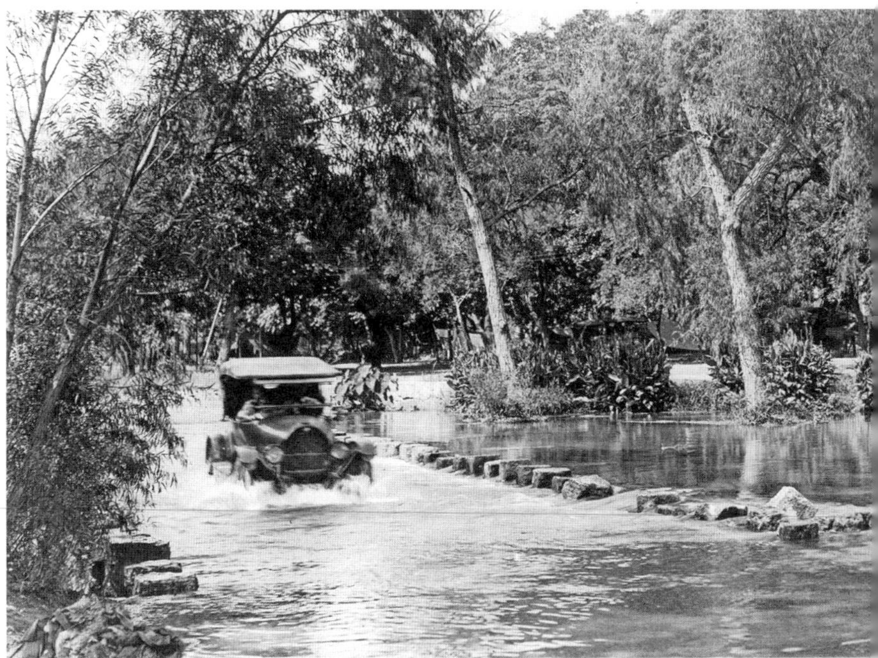

By the 1920s a stone low-water crossing over the San Antonio River linked Brackenridge and Koehler Parks.

the base of a large oak tree by the Woman's Christian Temperance Union, identified as WCTU.

A stone low-water crossing was built through the river so automobiles could pass between Brackenridge and Koehler Parks and pedestrians could gingerly step across on stone uprights on both sides. At the lowest point cars often slowed so children sitting on the running boards could dangle their feet in the water.

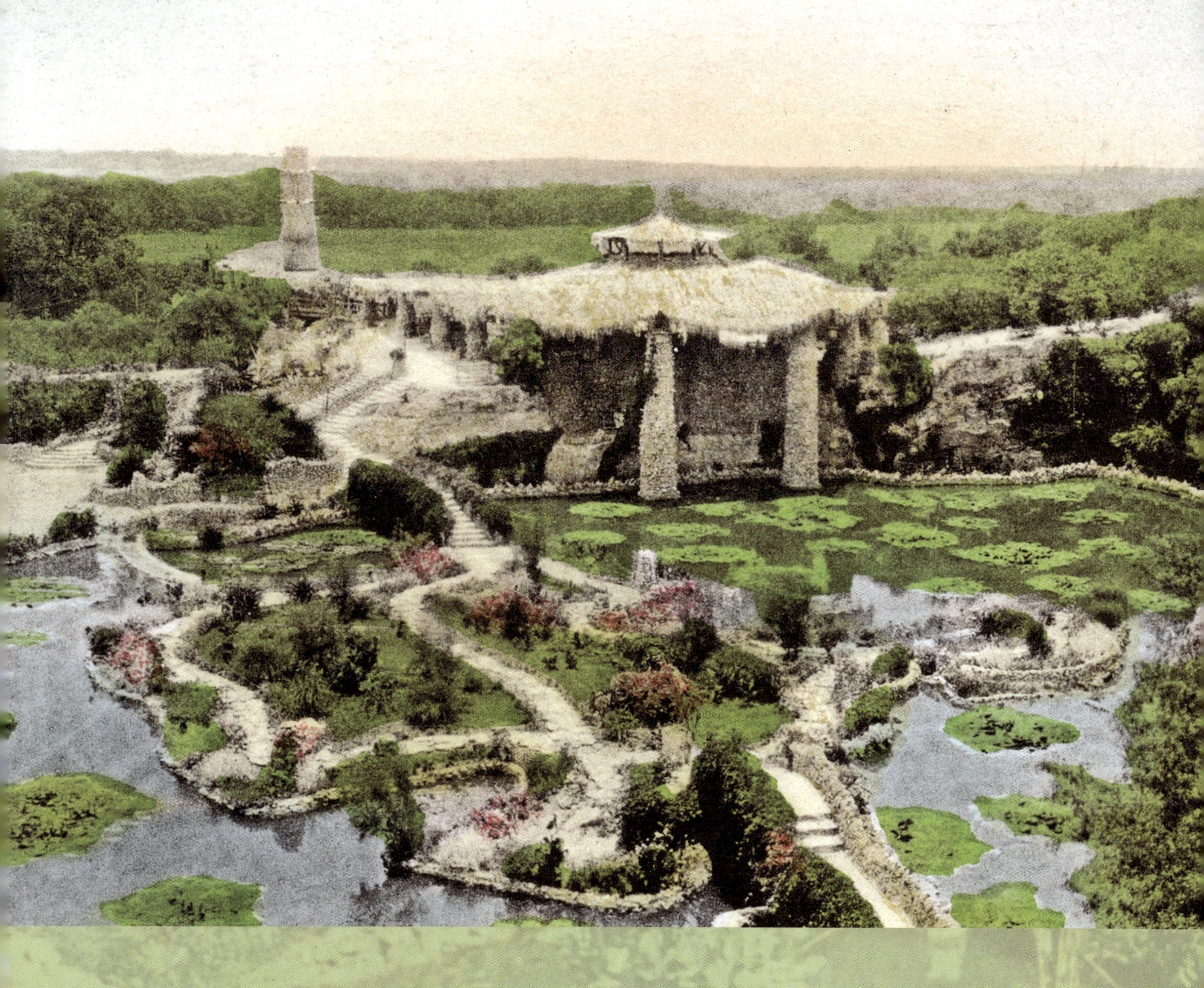

The Japanese Tea Garden

Hardly a year into his post as parks commissioner, Ray Lambert was looking down from Alpine Drive in 1916 when he had an epiphany.

On one side below him, rock cliffs plunged forty feet to a pit three to four hundred feet in diameter. Quarried by a cement company that had departed seven years earlier, the pit had been turned into a garbage dump. "The stench has become unbearable," neighbors complained. They were adamant that "the most exclusive residential district of San Antonio should not be made the dumping ground for the entire city." Some suggested the quarry become part of the adjoining Brackenridge Park.[212]

"As I looked down over the precipice, a vision I had seen as a boy and almost forgotten was suddenly recalled to my mind," Lambert remembered. "It was while on a fishing trip in the Old Baldy Mountains in California that one day in wandering about I suddenly came upon just such a scene in a huge natural depression in the mountains where a lake had been formed. Cattails and other water plants were swaying on the surface, and the clear water contained all sorts of fish darting in and out among the rushes. I never will forget what a thrill of pleasure I experienced as I looked down at it from above. I guess that is what gave me the idea."[213]

The ultimate idea was to transform the pungent pit into a Japanese sunken garden, which would become, after the Alamo, the most photographed sight in San Antonio. Its cornucopia of cliffside overviews, scenic close-ups, and picturesque exotic plantings made perfect backgrounds for snapshots to send folks back home—and prime fodder for municipal promotions.

"What do you think about building a lily pond in there?" Lambert asked a predecessor in charge of parks, Henry Steingruber. "It can't be done, Ray," came the reply. He asked Rudolph Gras, park foreman from 1913 to 1953, who replied, "With money, yes."[214]

Lambert loved overcoming obstacles and completing large projects heavy on inspiration and light on municipal cash outlay. He started this one at the beginning of 1917.

By the 1920s a sunken garden created from a former cement quarry pit had become one of the city's most photographed scenes.

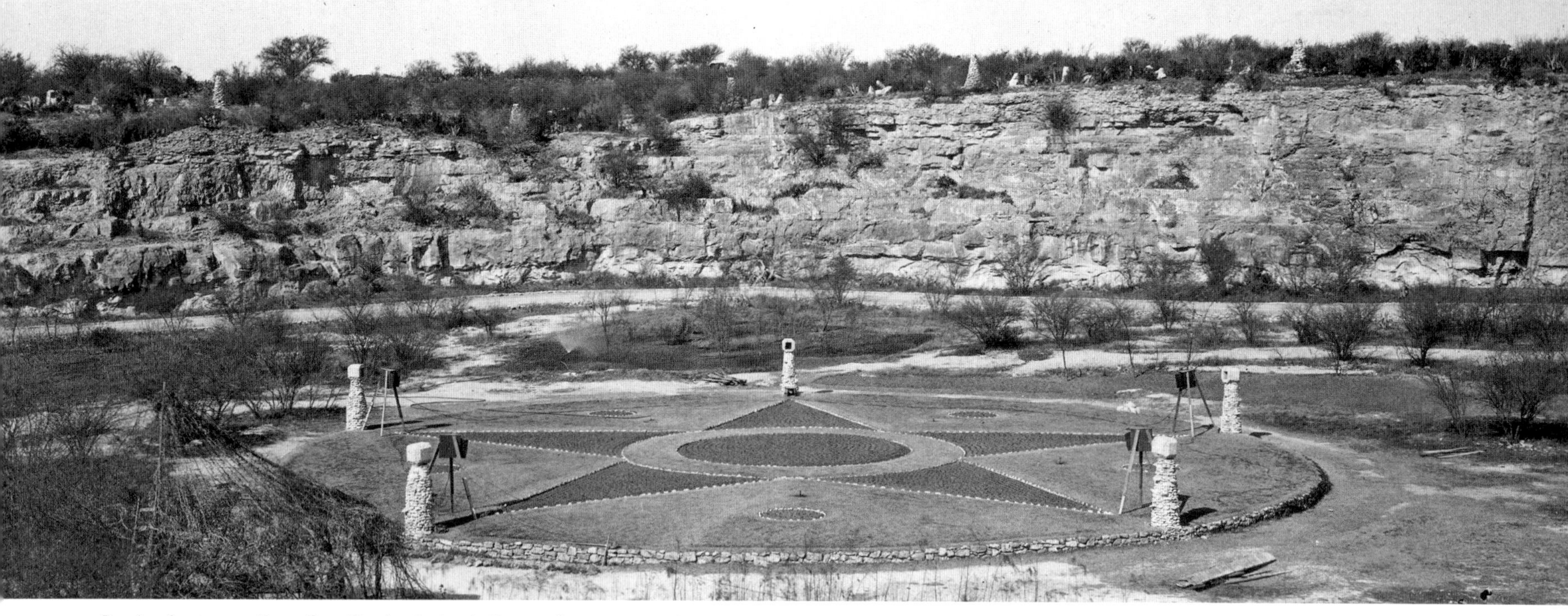

Ray Lambert put a Texas Star Garden in the shallower of two quarry pits. Fieldstone pylons stretch along Alpine Drive in the background.

A lily pond was Lambert's second idea for the old quarry pit. He first thought it would make a fine fern garden. While hunting the previous year on Clear Fork Creek, a tributary of Cibolo Creek thirty miles northeast of San Antonio, he followed the stream around the foot of a high bluff. The trickle of spring water over the bluff's edge sustained a moist area below, matted with ferns. "It is a spot of great sylvan beauty," Lambert said in mid-1915, "and I think if we supply the conditions as to moisture and soil we can reproduce it at the old rock quarry." He planned a perforated pipe around the quarry pit's rim that would drip water over the edge to beds of ferns below.[215]

There was also a shallower pit to the east, over the ridge that became the route of Alpine Drive. Lambert planned a different garden there, this one in the outline of a star encircled by a low rock border. It was illuminated by lights on low fieldstone pylons, later removed, near each of the star's five points. He named it the Texas Star Garden.

Lambert decided to make the larger pit not a fern garden but a lily pond, a quintessential feature of Japanese gardens. The change was no coincidence. A fascination for all things Japanese, termed Japanism, had been spreading throughout the West when, in 1893, the allure of the Japanese temple pavilion at Chicago's Columbian Exposition sparked the craze in the United States.

Women in San Antonio, like those elsewhere, began dressing in vibrantly colored Japanese garb for garden parties lit by Japanese lanterns hanging from trees. Flowers adorned the wheels of a rickshaw pulled by costumed participants in a Battle of Flowers parade. Exposition Park sponsored a Japanese carnival. Carl Hahn, director of the first San Antonio Symphony, gathered musicians in 1908 to produce *Princess Chrysanthemum*, a three-act Japanese operetta performed in Beethoven Hall. One reviewer termed it a "musical triumph." Its chorus of sixty kimono-clad young ladies represented Japanese girls in the garden of the emperor.[216]

One San Antonio department store sold four- and six-cup Japanese teapots for 25 cents and hundred-piece sets of Japanese china for $35.75. Kimi Iwama ran the Japan Art Company on Alamo Plaza, and T. K. Matsuoka advertised "first class service" for chop suey and yaka mein at Main Plaza's Japanese Restaurant, its diners perhaps unaware that those dishes were of Chinese origin. The Hot Wells Hotel was promoting open-air

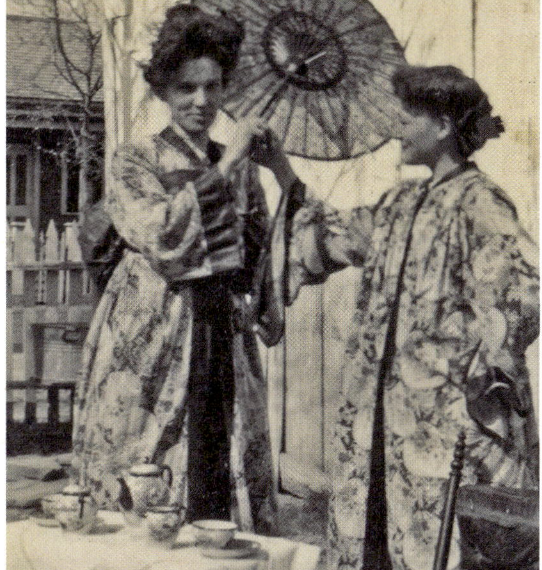

As national enthusiasm for things Japanese reached San Antonio, friends had Japanese tea parties in their backyards, a rickshaw entered a Battle of Flowers parade, and hotels opened their own Japanese gardens, one promoting artist Kimi Eizo Jingu, future proprietor of the Japanese Tea Garden.

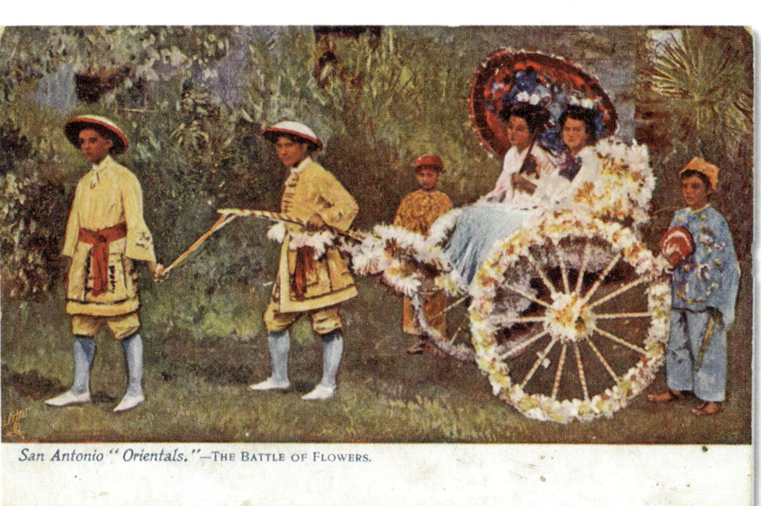

San Antonio "Orientals."—The Battle of Flowers.

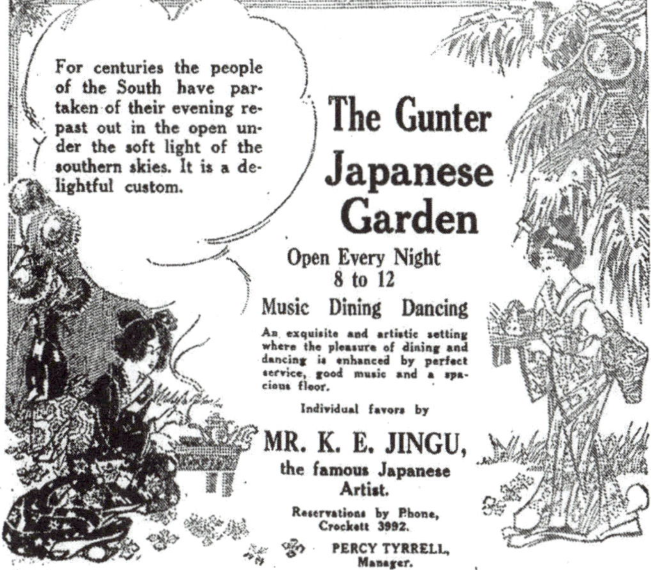

For centuries the people of the South have partaken of their evening repast out in the open under the soft light of the southern skies. It is a delightful custom.

The Gunter Japanese Garden

Open Every Night
8 to 12

Music Dining Dancing

An exquisite and artistic setting where the pleasure of dining and dancing is enhanced by perfect service, good music and a spacious floor.

Individual favors by

MR. K. E. JINGU,
the famous Japanese Artist.

Reservations by Phone, Crockett 3992.

PERCY TYRRELL, Manager.

dining in its Japanese Tea Garden in 1918. Not to be outdone, the Gunter Hotel built a dance floor over tennis courts next to its new Japanese Garden. Diners entered through what the *San Antonio Light* described as "a Japanese temple gate done in white, orange and black, with Japanese characters painted on the heavy posts by Mr. Jingu," or Kimi Eizo Jingu, who would become a key figure in Lambert's grand undertaking.[217]

When Lambert announced in December 1916 that the cement plant would be turned into a Japanese tea garden, he said it would be "modeled somewhat" after the one in San Francisco's Golden Gate Park, created for an exposition in 1894 and maintained after that by a Japanese landscape architect and his family. A Japanese tea garden opened for a 1915 exposition in San Diego's Balboa Park also continued with its own resident Japanese family.[218]

In British Columbia, Victoria had a sunken garden in the limestone quarry pit of a former cement plant, though without Japanese trappings. Begun in 1902, the plant's industrial remnants were preserved in what became the city's Butchart Gardens, now a National Historic Site of Canada.[219]

Worthy a model though Golden Gate Park's tea garden may have been, San Antonio was not San Francisco. Its Asian community was comparatively small, and short on architects who could address the finer points of Japanese design. Golfers may have persuaded the city to hire a top national professional to design Brackenridge Park's golf course—A. W. Tillinghast, nabbed at the beginning of his career—but it was Lambert's job to create a Japanese garden out of a quarry pit.

Lambert immersed himself in books he could find on the subject. In evaluating his creation in 1918, the *San Antonio Light* summarized local understanding of Japanese gardens and what Lambert was aiming for: "A true Japanese garden must suggest solitude and repose. It must be an ideal spot for meditation,

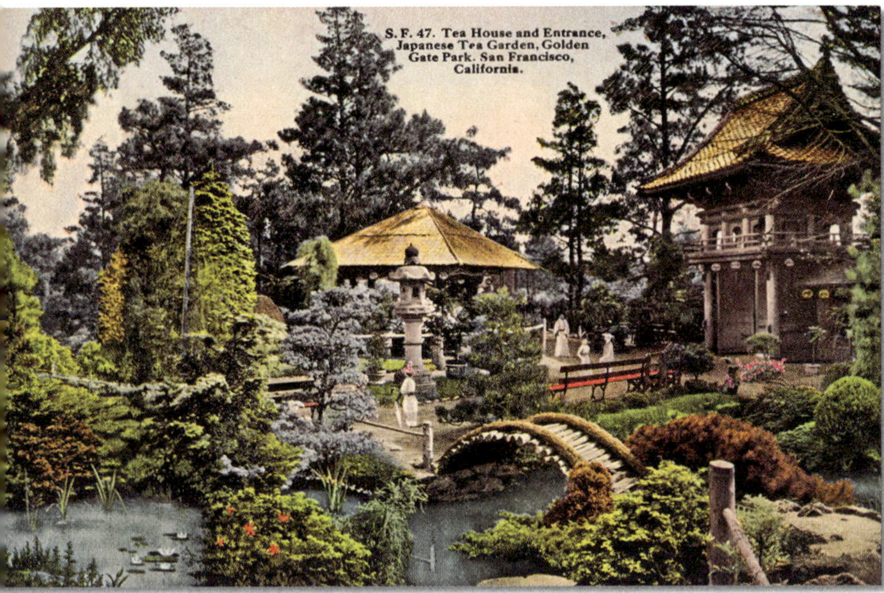

Brackenridge Park's Japanese Tea Garden was "modeled somewhat" after the one in San Francisco's Golden Gate Park.

leisure, and seclusion, although to be truly Japanese it should be somewhat wild in character. There must be many winding paths and nooks and corners with rustic seats, partially obscured by trailing vines and shrubbery, where a person can dream the hours away, inhaling the flower-scented air and listening to the sweet song of the birds."[220]

Creating such a mood was within Lambert's grasp, and his knowledge of how to cut and shape the quarry's rock helped in designing walls and bridges. But achieving the exquisite precision of a garden like Golden Gate Park's was too much to expect from a thinly stretched city parks department in remote San Antonio.

Hewing to the art of the possible, Lambert set out to at least try. Using his characteristic salesmanship, he drove Alamo Cement president Charles Baumberger around Alpine Drive. As they looked into the pit Baumberger and his company had created, Lambert said he wished he had cement to fill in the cracks so the pit would hold water. Baumberger sent two thousand bags. Businessman Albert Steves got the Alpine Drive treatment and donated fifteen carloads of sand. Kuntz-Albaugh Lumber gave wire to reinforce the concrete. The San Antonio Sewer Pipe Company gave two carloads of eight-inch drainage tile. The utility company provided electric lights. San Antonio Water Supply promised water at no charge, "one of the best gifts of all," Lambert thought, given the pond's unending need for water. City commissioners authorized use of prisoners at the city jail to do the labor. It became one of at least four of Lambert's projects throughout Brackenridge Park to utilize prisoners, a practice begun by Ludwig Mahncke in the earliest days of the park.[221]

By March 1917 all garbage had been hauled out and remaining machinery disposed of. A rock-strewn but "rich and fertile" island was built in the center of the irregularly shaped pond, measuring between three hundred and four hundred feet across. It was connected to the northern shore by a triple-arched stone bridge—called the "dragon bridge"—and by a single-arched bridge to the southern shore, its reflection in the water intended to establish a circle and suggest a full moon. A walkway of stepping stones beside the cliffs reached a ledge on the south side. A concrete reservoir at the top of the hill to the west could supply a waterfall over another cliff.[222]

Throughout the pond's base, workers built more than five dozen wooden boxes that would not rise above the water line, filled them with soil, and planted them with lilies, including the Queen Victoria variety that grew pads up to six feet in diameter. Donors gave nearly $800 to gather most of the lilies, and some unusual varieties were unexpectedly found south of town at Mitchell Lake, where, it was supposed, "the seeds were carried from afar by ducks."[223]

Beneath the pond, assistant city engineer W. S. Delery designed a system of pipes. They could fill the pond with water or drain it for maintenance and removal of moss and algae from the bottom. When cleaning time came, the several thousand goldfish added to the pond would be transferred to holding tanks built nearby.[224]

On the island and elsewhere workers set in bulbs and seasonal bedding plants taken from the park's nursery and greenhouses or donated by San Antonians. Blooms rotated throughout the year. Ranunculus and anemones were to

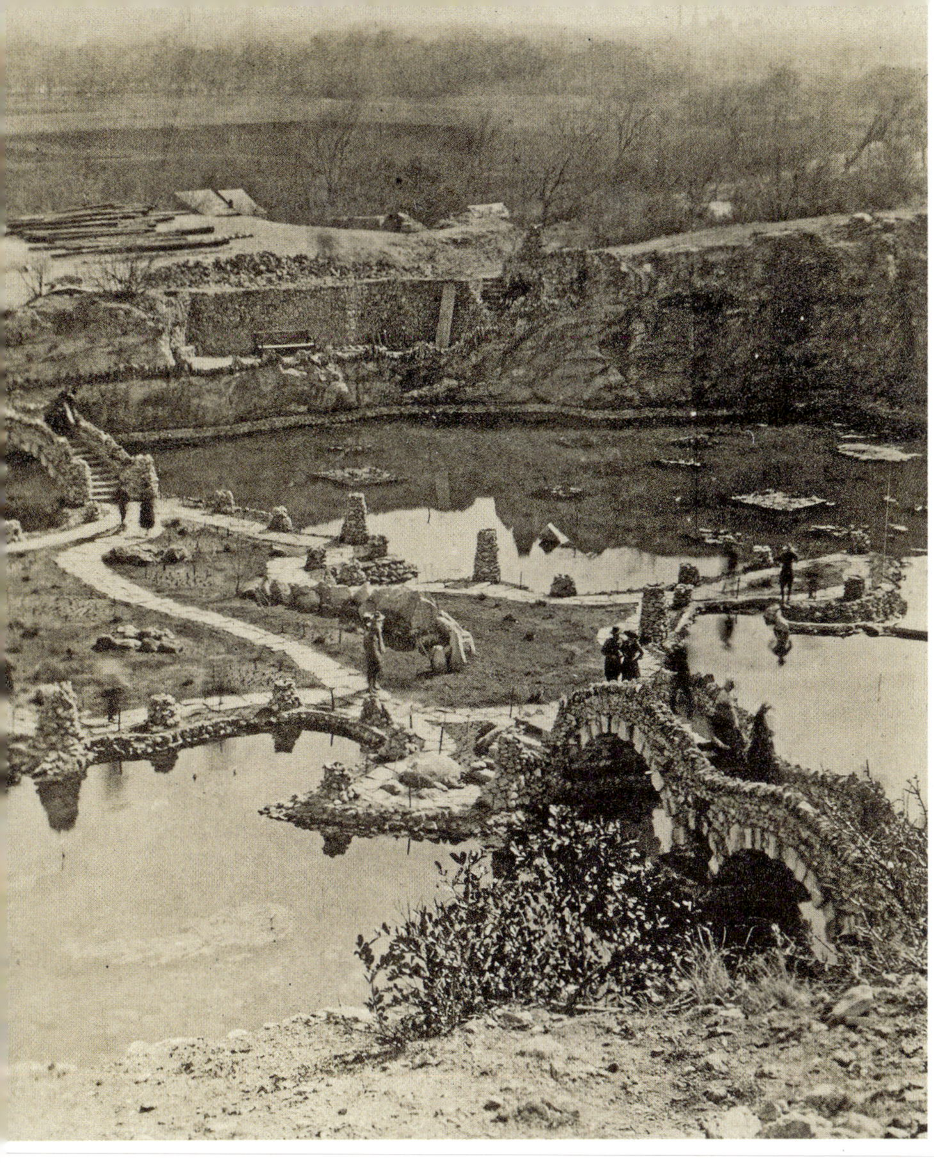

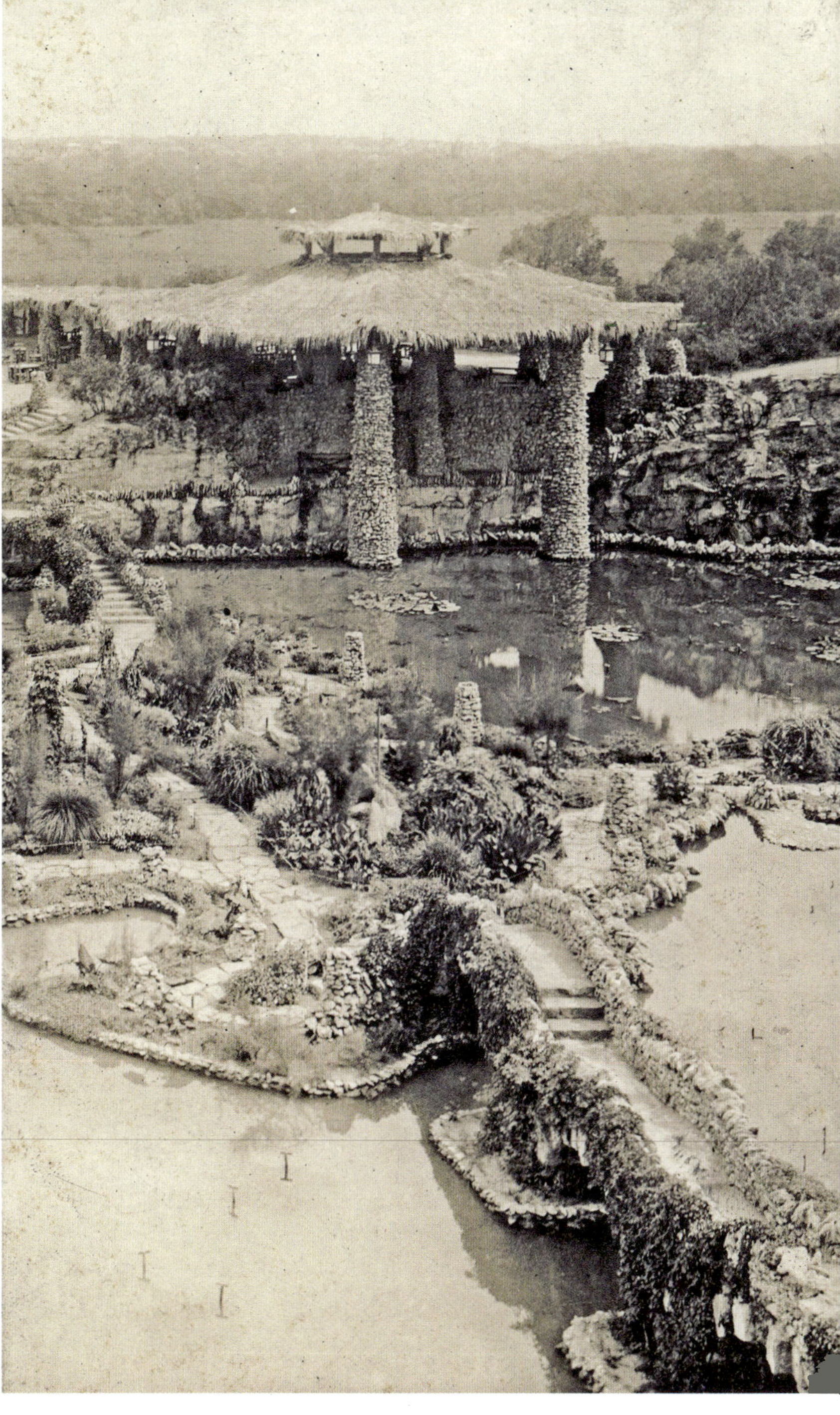

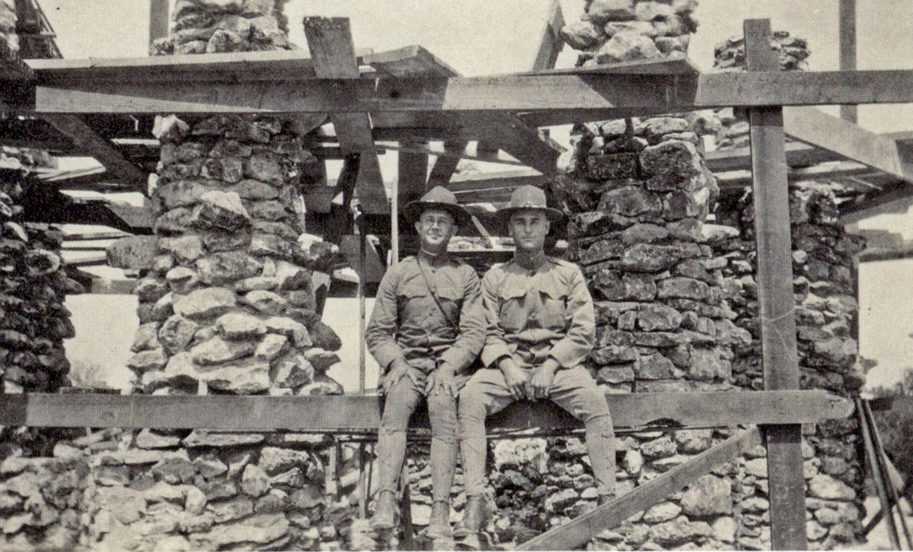

As work on the tearoom pavilion progressed in 1917, donated pine logs waited on site, two soldiers from Camp Travis posed on scaffolding during construction, and a thatched roof covered the finished structure and terrace.

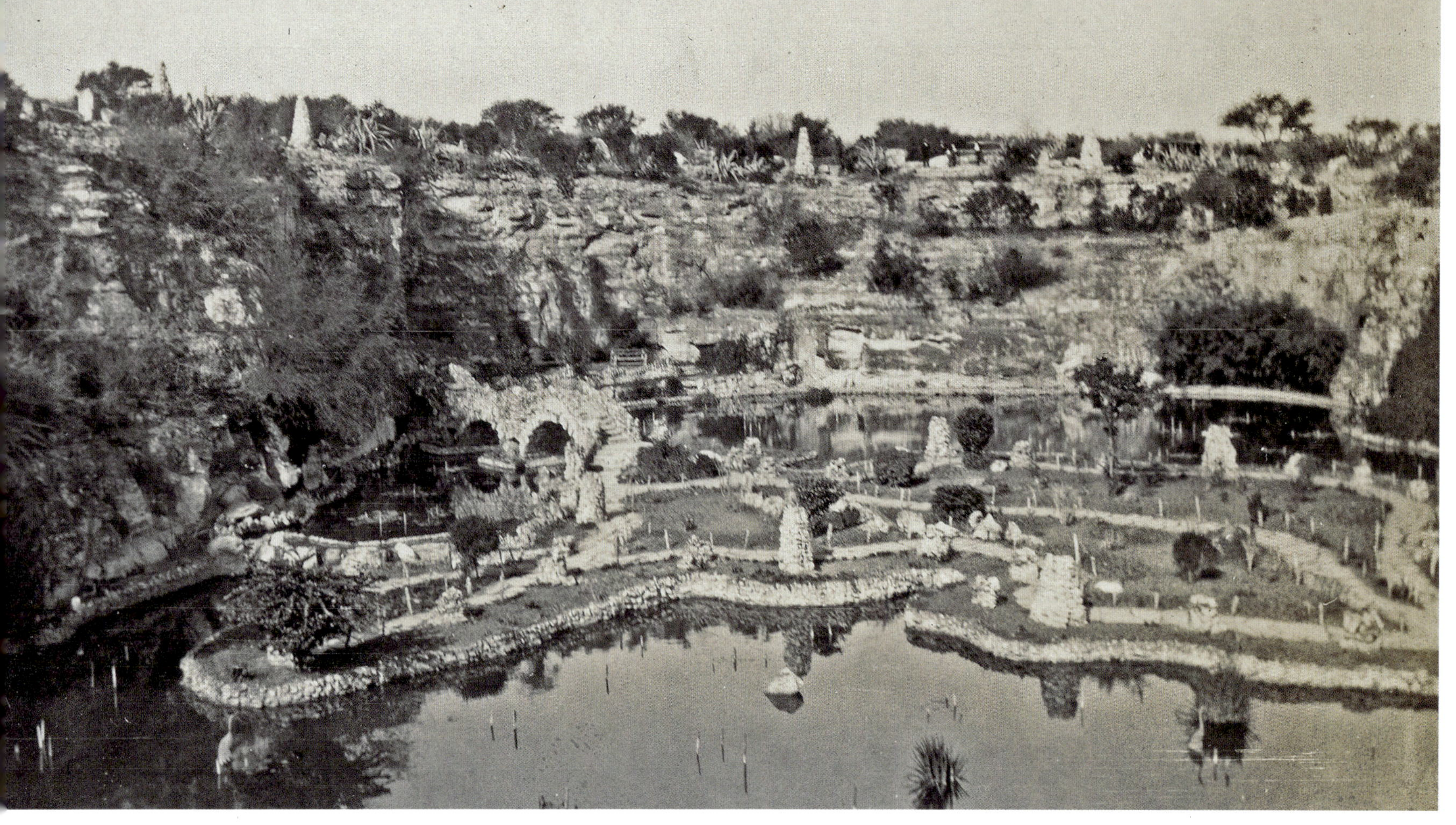

The tearoom pavilion overlooked an island separating two lily ponds. Along the rim of the former quarry pit, stone pylons with lights marked Alpine Drive.

blossom in January, and cannas, iris, and tulips a few weeks later. Blooming summertime plants ranged from giant zinnias to cosmos and larkspur, followed by salvia, petunias, and phlox. Flowering shrubs included rose bushes, bananas, and crape myrtle. A sprinkling of distinctly non-Japanese cactus and other southwestern plants sheltered by cliff walls from harsh weather along with palm trees would keep the setting "tropical always."[225]

Electric lights concealed among flowers and shrubs lit walkways and strings of lights mixed with vines overhanging the cliffs. More lights were visible on Alpine Drive's low fieldstone pylons above, all creating a Japanese garden's "uncanny sense of unreality" in the moonlight.[226]

As the yearlong tea garden project neared completion, two major areas remained to be dealt with: the broad southern ledge overlooking the garden and the open former cement production area below it, around the base of the kilns and chimney.

Simple though the outcome may seem today, the decision process was complicated. Steves Lumber Company early on sent the city a freight car load of pine logs the buyer had not paid for and charged the city only its original freight cost. Lambert thought the logs could be used to build "a Chinese temple" as a tearoom at the base of the old kiln. Next came the notion of stripping the logs to resemble bamboo for use instead in a three-tier tearoom structure rising from the pond up the side of a quarry wall. The top level would be above the quarry rim and offer a view of the city skyline.[227]

By April 1918 plans had moved to placing a "Japanese" tearoom pavilion on the firm rock base of the lily pond's south rim. Lambert kept the physical connection with the pond by replacing the tiers of "bamboo" intended to support

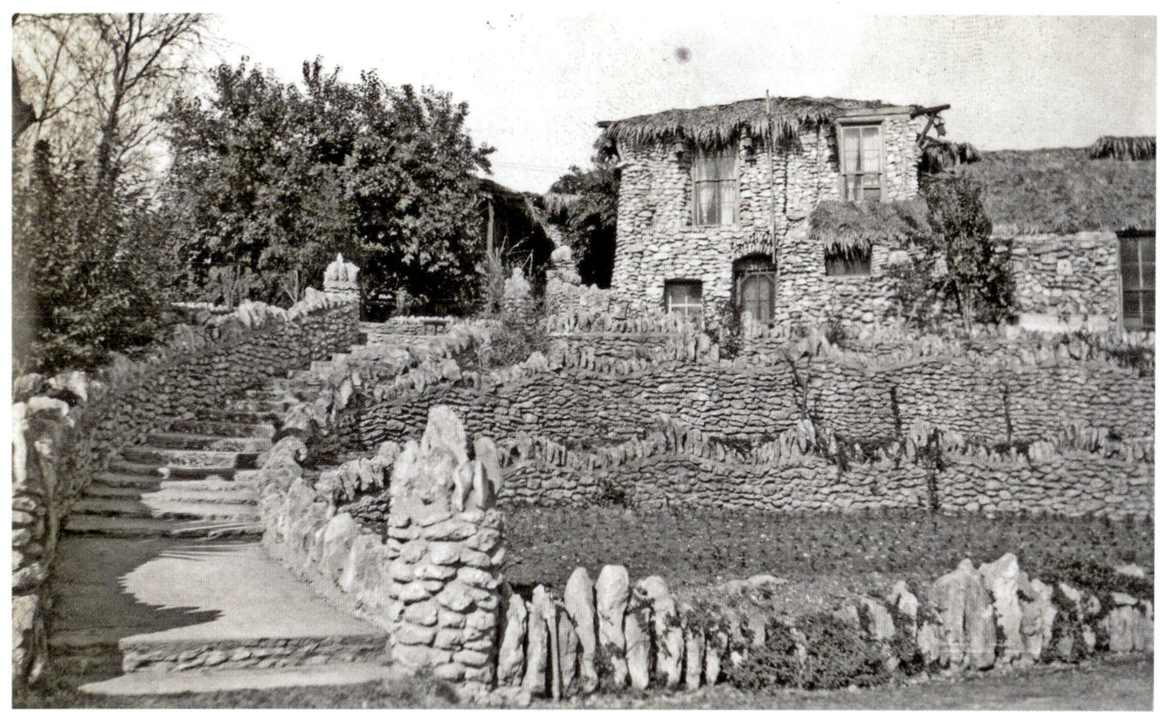

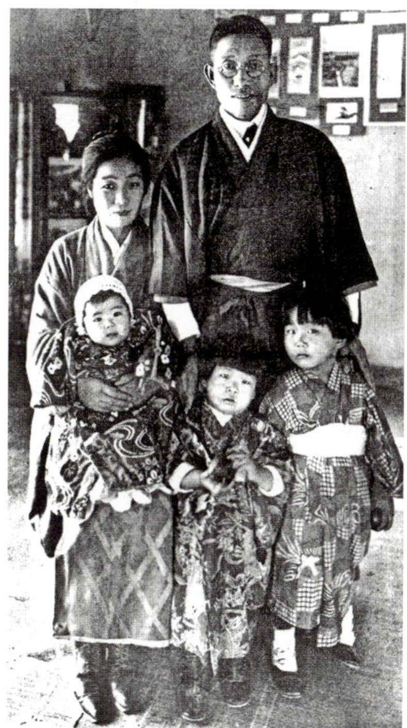

Kimi Eizo Jingu and his wife, Miyoshi, raised eight children beside the tearoom pavilion in a rock home, shown in 1929. A family portrait shows daughter Rae, named for Ray Lambert, at front center.

a tearoom at one side with two round fieldstone columns that would rise from the pond's edge to support an extension of the pavilion's roof.[228]

The load of pine logs finally became roof supports for what Lambert called, with a straight face, a Japanese pagoda. Round stone pillars supported a one-story octagonal roof thatched with palm leaves salvaged from cuttings previously piled in the quarry dump. The only nod to the multiple levels that define traditional pagodas was a small thatched open-sided cupola rising a few feet to shield an opening at the center of the main roof that ventilated warm air from below.

Soon to arrive on the scene were Kimi Eizo Jingu and his wife, Miyoshi Otsuki Jingu—she went by Alice—who had met through their Methodist church in Japan. They settled in Seattle, where Jingu met a Texan who offered him a job on a peanut farm in Texarkana. From there they moved to San Antonio, where in 1918 Kimi, an artist, worked at the Gunter Hotel's Japanese Garden and did drawings for guests. There he met Lambert, who learned that Jingu also knew plants. That was enough for Lambert to offer him

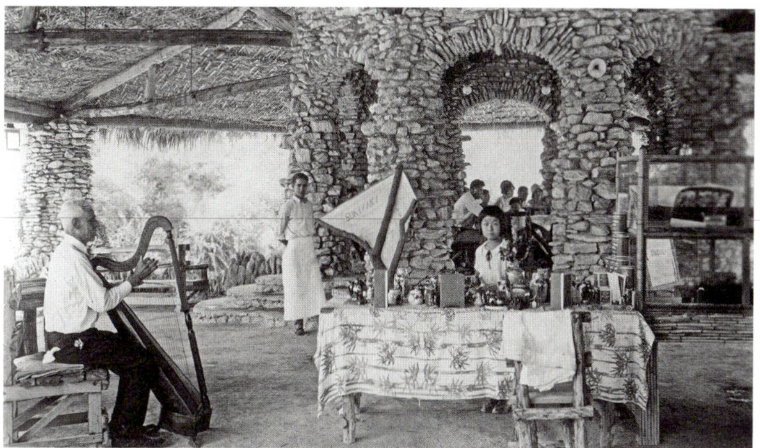

Santana Perez plays his harp for diners.

management of the park's tearoom and to advise on Sunken Garden plantings.[229]

The Jingus moved into a two-story thatch-roofed stone house built for them a few steps from the "Japanese pagoda," on a site once used for a small kiln and rock crushing equipment. Their third child was their first born in the house, a

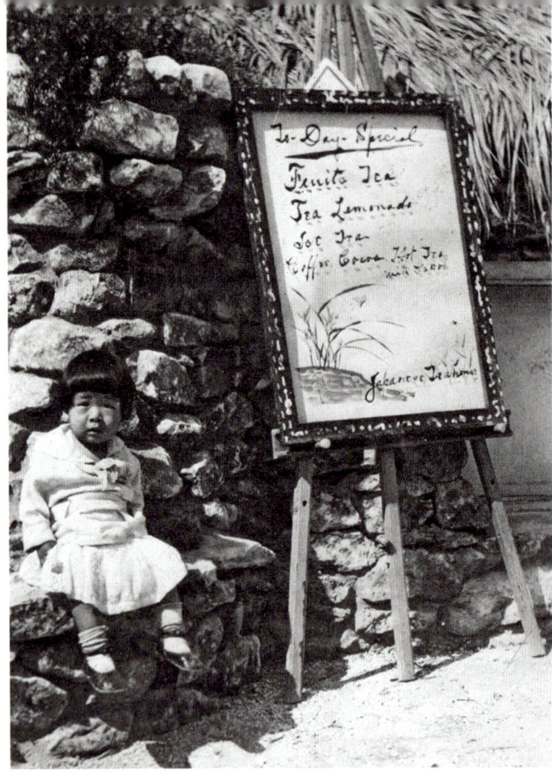

Mary Jingu sits beside the tearoom menu in 1918.

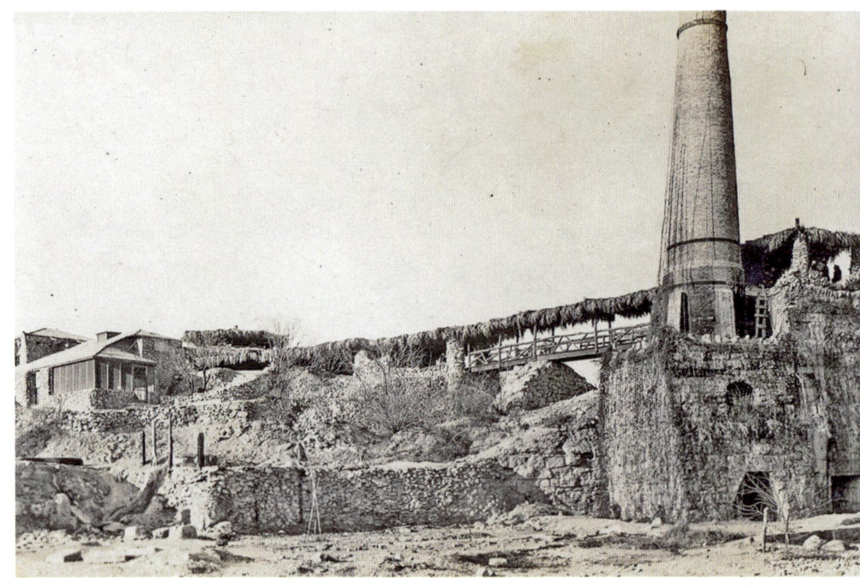

A thatched-roof walkway led from the tearoom and the Jingus' home to a lookout atop the old cement company's kiln.

daughter they named Rae for Ray Lambert. Eventually the Jingus had eight children. They grew up playing in the garden and park and working in the tearoom, which long featured Santana Perez at the entrance playing Mexican tunes on his thirty-five-string harp.

In addition to serving tea in the pavilion, in 1926 the Jingus opened a room of their home, the Bamboo Room, for light lunches. Its walls were covered with bamboo Jingu harvested, split, and burnished. On the ceiling he painted watercolors of the four seasons. San Antonians and tourists were served green tea, also sold powdered in lacquered canisters, but many considered it too bitter. So the Jingus created iced green tea by mixing the tea leaves with a tablespoon of sugar and filling the glass with ice and a slice of lemon. The local Borden Dairy created green tea ice cream for them to serve.[230]

The third component of Lambert's sunken garden complex was the former cement manufacturing area below, its focal point the brick chimney rising above the remains of two kilns.

The chimney seems to have been a particular challenge for Lambert, for he came up with two unconventional solutions to deal with it. The first was in December 1916, when a Chinese tearoom had originally been planned near the base of the old kiln. At the chimney base Lambert planted English ivy that would cover a concave wire frame affixed to the top, giving the appearance of "a pointed concave roof" and making the chimney, from a distance, resemble "a vine-clad pagoda or Chinese temple." Conceded Lambert: "We may not be able to get these vines grown sufficiently to give the pagoda effect this year, but given a little time this will be one of the prettiest features of the park system."[231]

When the tearoom went elsewhere, Lambert settled on making the brick chimney appear as a castellated yet inaccessible observation tower, as it is identified on one map. Cuts were made in its decorative rim to resemble battlements. Two steel bands spaced below ringed the chimney/tower and held a dozen simulated gun barrels pointed outward to suggest a formidable defense. At ground level, the kiln remains could be seen as resembling a whimsical castle. The dragon's-tooth style of jagged rocks lining the tops of the kilns' stone walls implied ramparts and matched the decor of the rest of the tea garden area.[232]

A flight of stone steps from the former kiln rose up the rim of the old quarry pit to the tearoom. From there visitors could take a thatched-roofed walkway to a thatched observation shelter overlooking the kilns and enjoy the vista out to the polo field. A short distance away, an arrow-straight trellised walkway known

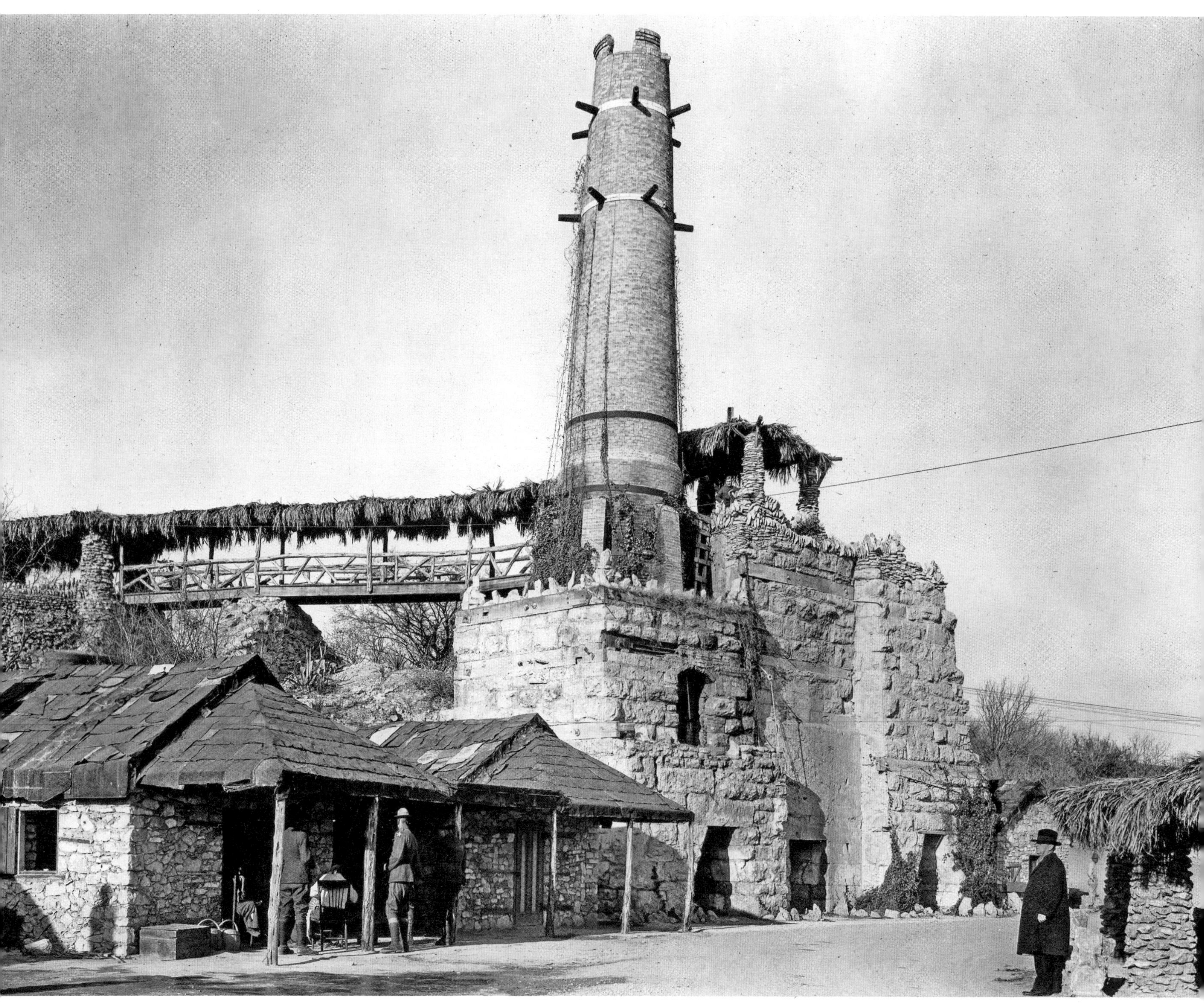

Charles Baumberger gazes toward two new "Mexican Village" homes in 1921. The kiln's chimney top was notched to resemble a battlement, with two bands below holding simulated gun barrels. Behind him is part of a large thatched shelter where Mexican food was served.

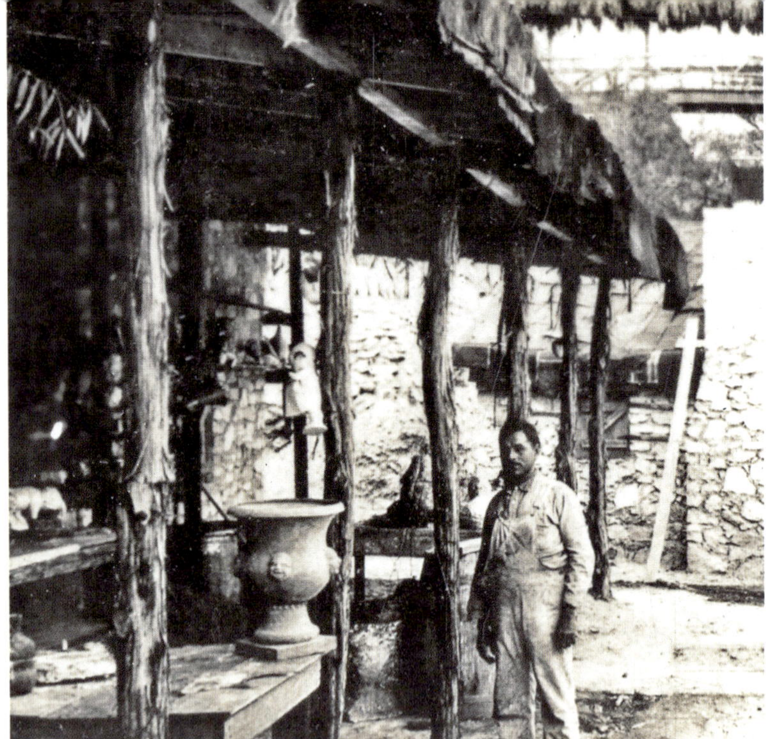
Resident artisans included Bacilio Aguilar, a potter and sculptor.

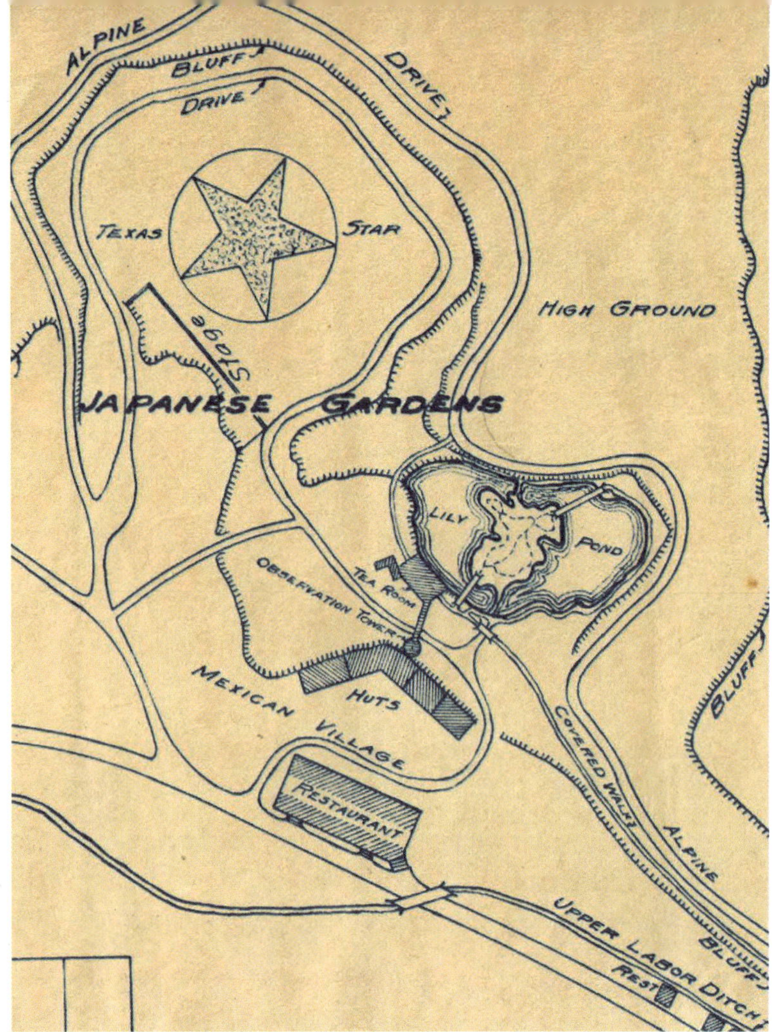

In 1926 the Texas Star Garden got its first stage, precursor to its replacement by the Sunken Garden Theater.

as Lover's Lane followed the path of an old quarry tramway toward the zoo, a short walk beyond.

The kiln area diverged from the Japanese theme and catered to tourists by becoming a "Mexican Village." It was "the result of another dream," the *San Antonio Express* reported, "of the artist of the Lily Pool, Ray Lambert, Commissioner of Parks." On one side of the kilns three "little rock houses with rusted, scrappy tin roofs," including many flattened cans, were built in 1920 for artisans and their families. One housed "a very able potter," another a blanket and basket weaver, the third a needle worker from Mexico who sold lace and crochet work. A fourth house on the other side of the kilns was for cooking Mexican food to be served in an open thatched-roofed restaurant nearby. Seven tabletops were millstones once used for grinding cement.[233]

Looking more authentically Mexican were the picturesque small homes scattered beyond and known as "Little Mexico." The dwellings were first built for cement plant workers and then occupied by squatters, most of Hispanic origin. Thus, thought the *Express*, "the newly made Mexican Village is appropriately placed even though it does touch elbows and back yards with Japan."[234]

Thanks to donations, Lambert completed his tea garden complex, including the Mexican Village, for just $7,000, today's equivalent of $140,000.[235]

The Japanese theme struck an immediate chord with San Antonians and tourists. Over the years uncounted thousands of visitors have come through. In their enthusiasm local boosters saw the sunken garden and tearoom as nothing less than purely Japanese. A chamber of commerce booklet in 1920 enthused that the sight "has become far famed throughout the country for its beauty and artistic design" and that "it is probable that no park feature in any city of the country has attracted more attention and favorable comment than this beauty spot."[236]

Tour buses headed for the tea garden as soon as it was completed in 1918. Menus on dining cars along the Southern Pacific Railroad's Sunset Route helped to spread its fame from New Orleans to Los Angeles.

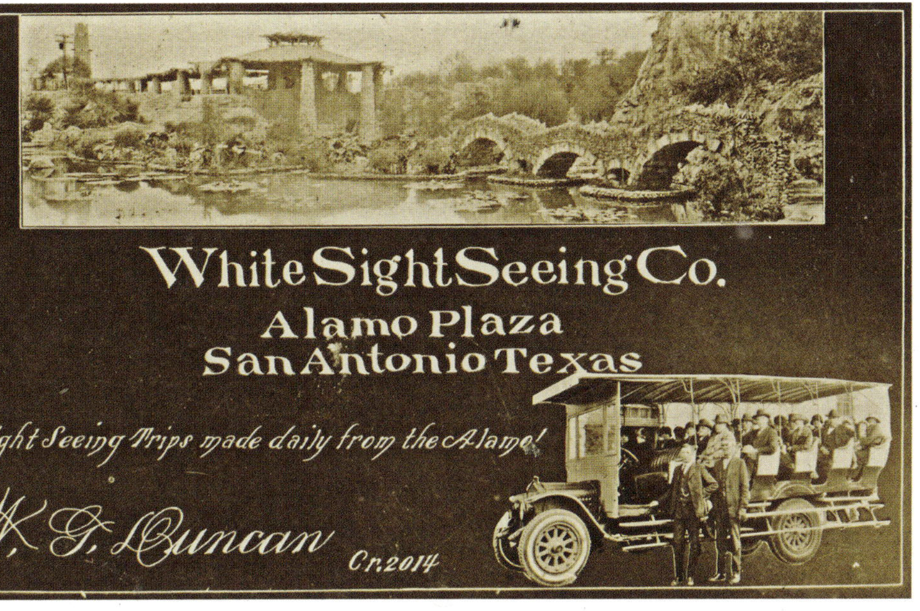

SUNKEN GARDENS IN BRACKENRIDGE PARK, SAN ANTONIO, SUNSET ROUTE

Southern Pacific Menu

Some observers, though, took a more dispassionate look and found quite different aspects to praise. One was an architectural writer from New York. "We rather expect stereotyped ideas in public works because of the omnipresent politician" and to see "some pre-conceived scheme" forced on park planners, wrote I. T. Frary in *Architectural Record* in 1919. He found, instead, "a rare exception to this rule, and a remarkable example of intelligent adaptation of design to existing conditions."

Frary saw the "Japanese pagoda" as only "a curious pavilion." But he was charmed by "the precipitous walls around the edges of the lily-strewn pools" and by the arched bridges that led one through "a bit of fairyland nestled into a hollow scooped from the mesquite plain." He added that at night, "as one follows the 'Alpine Drive' and looks down into this weird pocketful of loveliness, lighted apparently by large fireflies, the contrast with the city park on one side and the mesquite waste on the other produces an eerie feeling that lingers long about one."[237]

"The Tea Garden is many things," noted Jay Louden, a present-day architect who worked on the site's restoration. "But it is definitively not Japanese. Many features of the garden are more Chinese than Japanese—the dragon's tooth masonry and the so-called Dragon Bridge—and the rest is really just a pastiche of readily available materials that could be worked by the ever-present prison labor. The precision, clarity, and maintenance-intensive aspects of true Japanese landscape work were entirely out of reach.

"But Lambert's achievement is all the more astonishing for that. It is an extraordinary translation of possibility into a unique reality."[238]

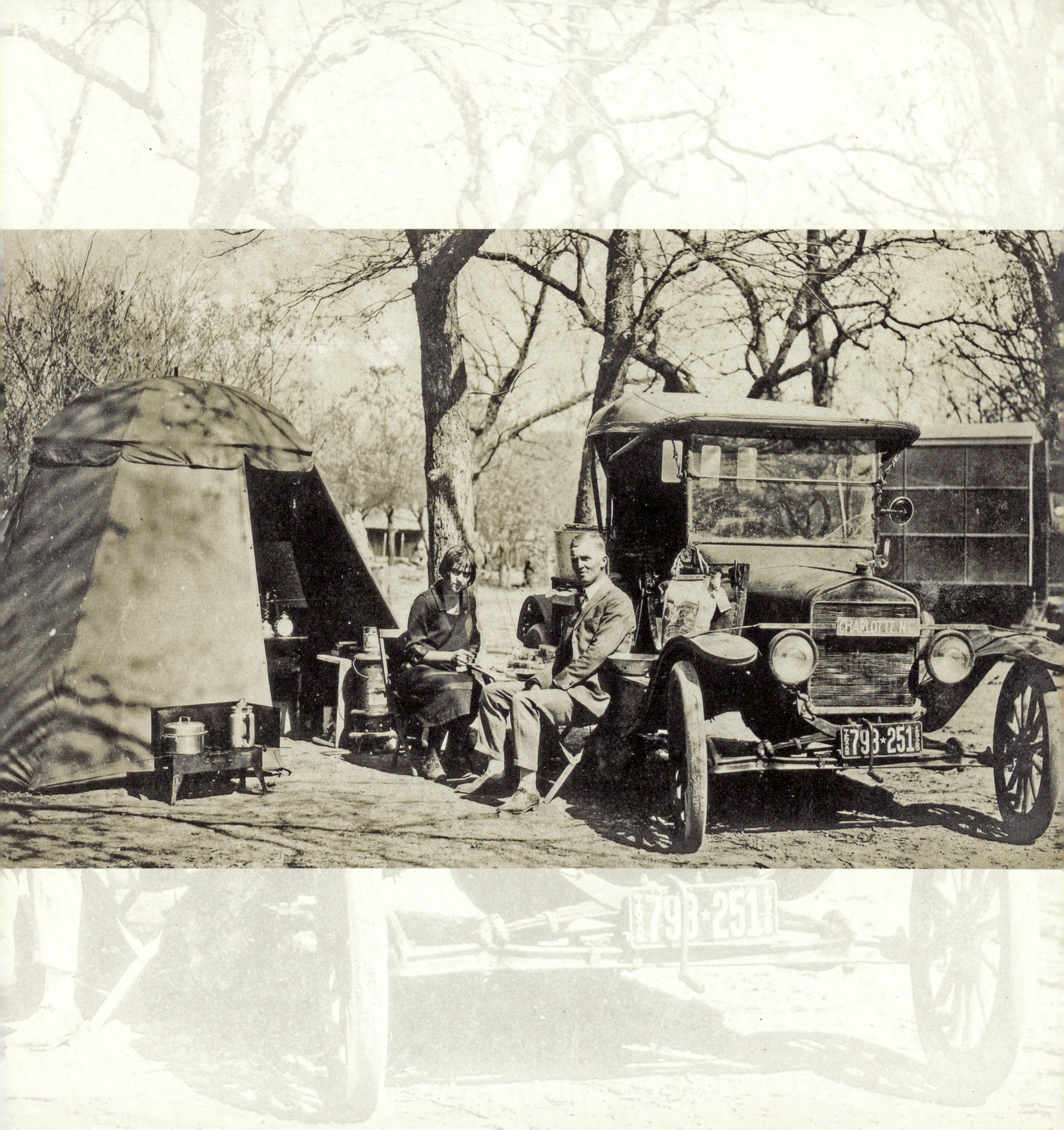
CHARLOTTE N.C.
TEXAS

Ray Lambert's Park

With a golf course anchoring one end, a zoo the other, and a sunken garden and recreation areas in between, Brackenridge Park by the mid-1920s was beginning to resemble its present appearance. Like the city, it was evolving as much by happenstance as by plan. The addition of some sixty acres in various transactions did little to smooth the ragged boundaries. But, happily, helping hands at home were creating a municipal park as beloved by its residents—and as significant a place—as those crafted by professional designers elsewhere.

As the largest city in the state, San Antonio aspired to the heights advocated by the City Beautiful Movement sweeping the nation. But the city was still only a regional commercial hub, and its entrepreneurs lacked the resources of those in hard-charging places like Dallas and Houston. Its development was handicapped, observes urban historian David Johnson, because local businessmen of the time "persistently refused to learn the lessons of city-building." The few who did "could not consistently overcome the basic cultural bias against organized development."[239]

In Dallas, the influential George B. Dealey gained wide support in 1911 for hiring his friend George E. Kessler, a nationally recognized planning professional, to design the sort of sophisticated system of parks and shaded boulevards being implemented in cities throughout the nation. In San Antonio, Dealey's counterpart, George W. Brackenridge, had to come up with a boulevard plan himself.[240]

In 1905 Brackenridge proposed a fifteen-mile boulevard around the city's northern and eastern edges. From a start at San Pedro Avenue it would go east, south through the rock quarries and the northern tip of Brackenridge Park, east past Mahncke Park, and south to end near the Southern Pacific depot on East Commerce Street. Along the last leg Brackenridge would donate twenty acres for a new park. "The entire proposition can be arranged easily with perhaps a small bond issue," he thought. Six years later, Adams & Adams Architects proposed widening existing streets into boulevards in a circuitous path linking Brackenridge and San Pedro Springs Parks, Alamo Plaza, and three smaller parks. Both proposals, and others, went nowhere.[241]

In February 1925 a couple from Charlotte, North Carolina, stayed in the tourist camp opened by Ray Lambert in Koehler Park.

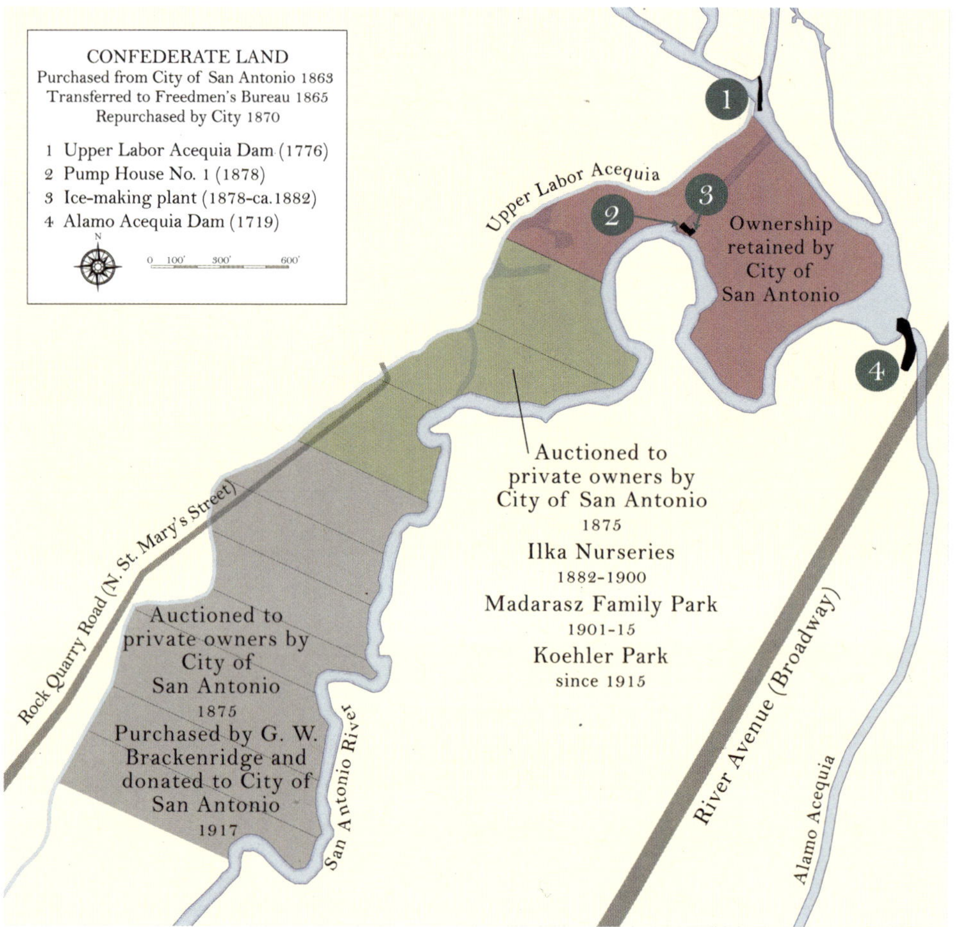

Months after he took office, parks commissioner Ray Lambert began quietly conjuring up his own boulevard plan, featuring narrow roadways on both sides of the San Antonio River from Brackenridge Park through downtown to the southern city limits. Northbound traffic would presumably go up the eastern side of the river, southbound traffic down the western side. Though mostly unrealized, Lambert's proposal happened to result in the largest addition of land to Brackenridge Park since George Brackenridge's original gift.

Lambert seems to have first worked out the section of his unannounced boulevard plan along the river through Brackenridge Park. There the probable northbound lane along the river's east bank was already in place as the narrow Avenue A.

For the probable southbound lane on the west side of the river, however, only a portion of the route lay within Koehler and Brackenridge Parks. More than a mile of the western bank south of Koehler Park remained in private hands. In addition to wanting a roadway there, Lambert sensed the danger of that bank becoming "dotted with houses and outbuildings of all kinds," spoiling parkgoers' riverside view. Lambert had the foresight to mount a preemptive strike.[242]

The largest block of privately owned property along the west bank was thirty-five vacant acres from Koehler Park south to East Mulberry Avenue, held by three owners. It was the last of the Confederate army tannery property auctioned by the city in 1875 still in private hands.

All three owners gave Lambert options to purchase their lots for a total of $27,500, today's equivalent of nearly $10 million. But that amount of money could not be found in the city budget. Lambert asked Mayor Clinton Brown to approach banker George Brackenridge, who sometimes made loans to help the city through financial difficulties. Brackenridge at once agreed to advance the full amount and to hold the land for a year, at no interest, when the city was to repay him. The thirty-five acres were purchased in Brackenridge's name.[243]

South of Mulberry down to Josephine Street were fields of the county's former poor farm and another dozen properties. Many owners were believed unwilling to sell outright, but perhaps, thought Lambert, all could be persuaded to donate 250-foot strips at the ends of their properties as setbacks from the river. That would allow room for a narrow roadway and, also down to the river, a green buffer for the park. An incentive for owners to donate would be the lure of property values enhanced by access to a new road.[244]

All twelve landholders, plus Bexar County, donated their 250-foot riverside strips. County commissioners went further and gave the remaining ten acres of the former county poor farm as far west as the Upper Labor Acequia. In January 1917 the city accepted the county's donation and agreed that the tract be named Davis Park in honor of the incumbent county judge, attorney James R. Davis.[245]

George Brackenridge was sufficiently impressed with the execution of Lambert's plan to cancel the city's obligation to repay his loan for the upper thirty-five acres, and he donated them to the city in January 1917. This donation remains the largest addition to the park since Brackenridge's initial gift in 1899.[246]

From the future Tuleta Drive in Koehler Park south through the golf course to Josephine Street, Lambert got the city to build more than a mile of what Lambert named Memorial Drive in honor of Bexar County residents who died in World War I. While that was under construction in January 1918, Lambert at last publicly revealed his entire proposal of a riverside boulevard from Brackenridge Park to the southern city limits. One newspaper writer indicated the widespread skepticism that greeted the idea by beginning a story, "While a few citizens are shaking their heads over the announcement of Commissioner Lambert . . . " Lambert's boulevard plan shared the fate of its predecessors and went no further. But nearly half of Memorial Drive survives as River Road.[247]

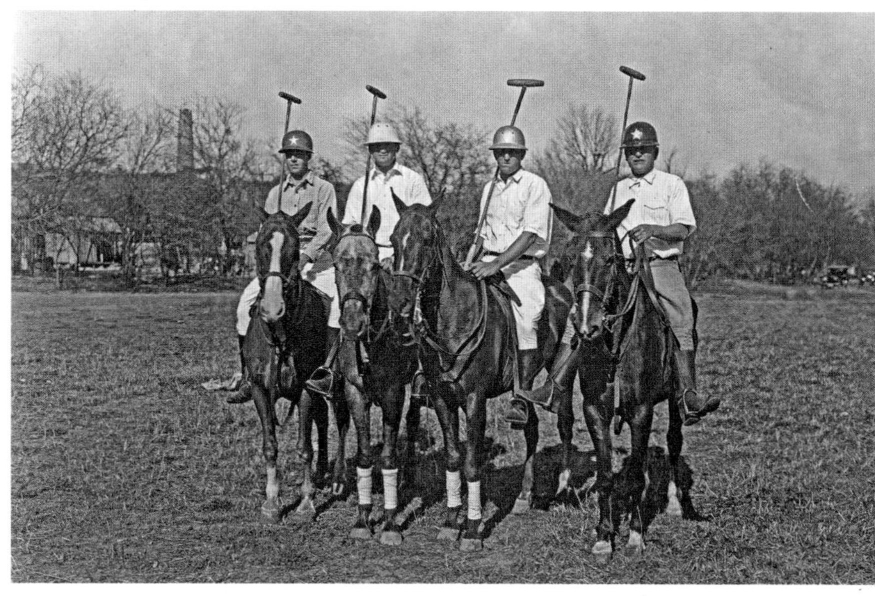

The kiln chimney rises behind the park's polo field, with homes of former workers in the brush at center left. San Antonio Polo Club players, *from left*, are George Drought, Carl Crawford, Arthur Meckel, and William Meadows.

Brackenridge's newest donation became the largest open space in the park. In 1919 Lambert had park engineer W. S. Delery draw plans to make it a Texas botanical garden, as the San Antonio Federation of Women's Clubs was urging. But polo players were also eyeing the site. Polo spread from England to the Northeast in the 1870s and had reached San Antonio by July 1883, when the Texas Polo Club began matches in San Pedro Springs Park. The San Antonio Polo Club joined the national Polo Association in 1920 with an elite roster of players that included former mayor Clinton Brown.[248]

Botanical garden plans were set aside, and the new San Antonio Polo Club was allowed, at no cost to the city, to prepare a grass polo field three hundred feet long by one hundred sixty yards wide. There, in 1920, two teams of four players, each on horseback, began seeking to drive a wooden ball between goalposts eight yards apart at each end. Army cavalry officers at Fort Sam Houston had been honing their riding skills by playing polo since before World War I. Competition between civilian and military teams helped fill Brackenridge Park bleachers with spectators.[249]

Some local players rose to international polo fame. Brothers Charles and Tom Armstrong, both on the 1920 club roster, began one of the longest polo lineages in North America, including children and grandchildren Charles M., John, and Stewart Armstrong. Other famed local players at the park were Bert Beveridge and his son, Robert D. A continuing national polo tradition began in San Antonio in the 1930s when famed local bootmaker Cosimo Lucchese, who sold a line of polo boots, presented the silver Lucchese Cup to the winner of an annual tournament held in the park and, later, elsewhere.[250]

A spinoff of polo connections between the park and Fort Sam Houston came in 1917, when Maj. Gen. James Parker, a cavalry officer who commanded Fort Sam Houston, suggested that his officers and other riders would welcome a bridle path through the park. Lambert picked up on the idea and invited Parker along as they went through the woods to mark out the park's first bridle path. It entered the woods near the original golf clubhouse and wove to Lambert Beach, a path made narrow and winding so that few trees had to be cut.[251]

A plot of 1.33 acres, outside formal park boundaries, was sold back to the city in 1916 by heirs of John H. Kampmann to be used "for park purposes." It was the last portion of Kampmann's rock quarry tract west of the park. The next year it became the Municipal Rifle Range, supervised by the parks department and managed by W. J. Reed, a sergeant stationed at Fort Sam Houston, who lived with his family in the old Kampmann quarry workers' house on the land. Eleven years later, as residential development drew near, the rifle range was closed. The site, near the present-day Tuesday Musical Club, is overgrown and fenced.[252]

Meanwhile, the legacy of the park's 250-foot setback from River Avenue, renamed Broadway in the mid-1920s, was becoming a major source of public discontent. Ownership of that strip of land had transferred to new owners of the Water Works in 1908. In 1915 the city assessed property owners along River Avenue to help pave the street. The unexpected cost caused the by-then-Belgium-based Water Supply Company to put its River Avenue property on the market as individual building lots, giving the city right of first refusal to purchase them. The strip was undeveloped, making passersby accustomed to the visual extension of the park to the street. Fear of construction that would block views of the park caused the City Federation of Women's Clubs to arise in "alarm and indignation."[253]

A federation resolution in May 1916 declared: "That 265 [*sic*] acres of such matchless beauty should be marred by a row of close-together houses and a view of this wonderful natural beauty obstructed is a blow to urban beauty that the clubwomen of San Antonio most vigorously protest against." Secretaries of each of the federation's twenty-six clubs were asked to write Ray Lambert and request that he propose a council resolution to purchase the entire strip.[254]

Lambert promised his cooperation, agreeing that the land's loss would be "a material detriment to the park." The federation organized its own central committee, chaired by Jeanette (Mrs. A. H.) Cadwallader, to lead a drive to expand the park fully out to River Avenue. The Water Supply Company temporarily suspended sale of additional lots along the park's perimeter but denied the federation's request to donate them. Recent purchasers of five lots along Broadway agreed to sell them back for the same price. A fund-raising plan adopted the slogan "Buy a foot of the park for the city!"[255]

In July 1916 the city purchased from the Water Supply Company a section of the Broadway strip south of what became Mulberry Avenue. The eight acres cost $30,000, today's equivalent of $720,000, and were later known as Lions Field. Private efforts to buy more faltered, and Lions Field ultimately provided the only extended view into the park from Broadway. Park vistas north and south of Lions Field became mostly blocked for future generations by a mile dominated by motels, fast-food restaurants, and secondhand shops.[256]

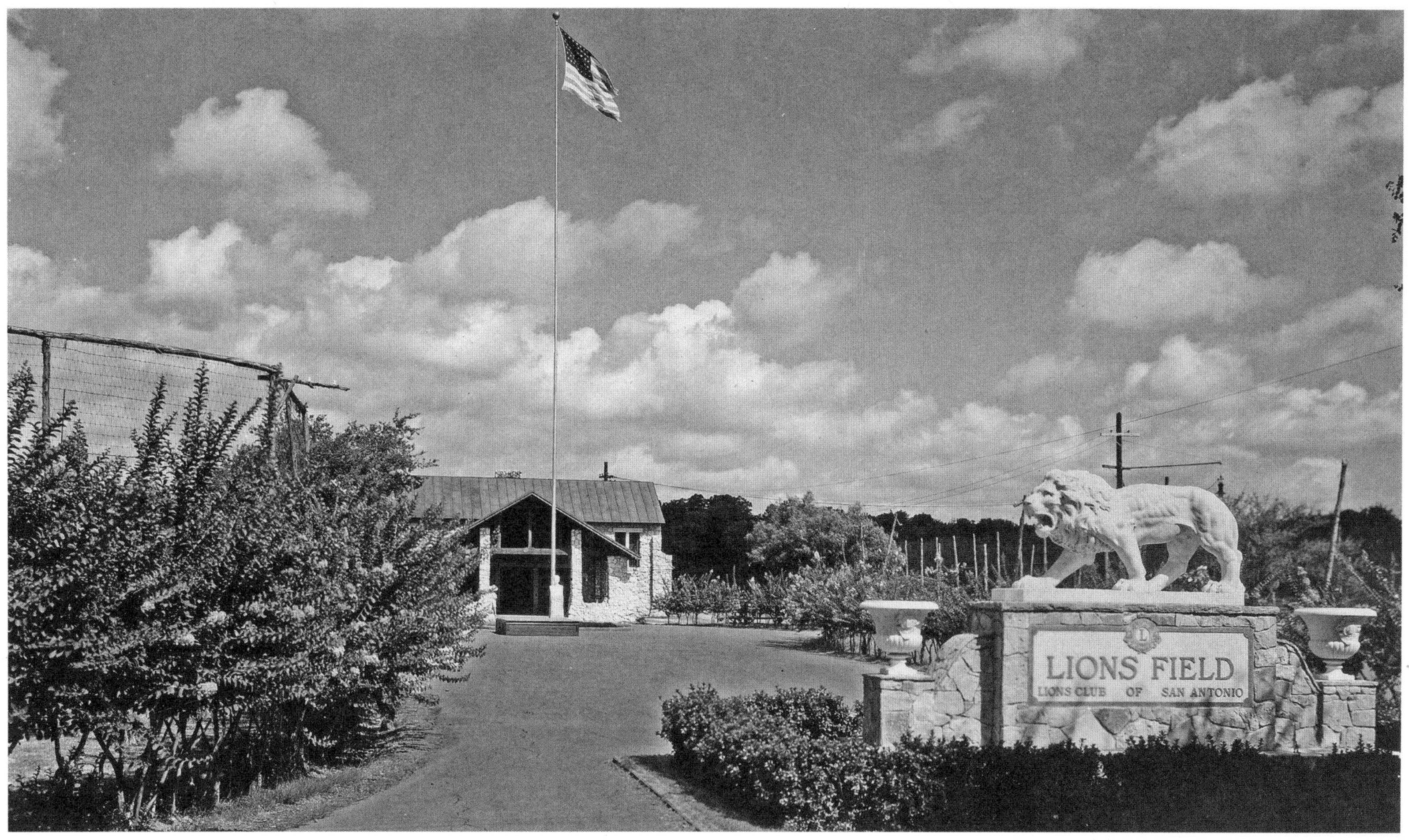

Lions Field had the first professionally managed and supervised playground west of the Mississippi.

For seven years the park's Broadway frontage lay vacant. In 1923 Lambert suggested to the San Antonio Lions Club that it pick that site for a supervised children's playground the club planned to build. The club agreed. Members sought assistance from the Playground Association of America, formed in 1908 to foster a sense of community by developing socialization at an early age. No professionally managed and supervised children's playground had yet been built west of the Mississippi.[257]

The New York–based Playground Association sent its field secretary to check the site and then dispatched Eswald Petter to plan its development. Robert C. Oliver moved from suburban Chicago to direct the playground and its clubhouse, built with $10,000 from the Lions Club and $15,000 from city bond funds. The Lions Club would run the operation with an annual stipend from the city covering three-fourths of the cost and the club contributing the remainder, a financial agreement that does not seem to have survived the Depression.[258]

An indication of Lions Field's popularity came on Easter Sunday afternoon in 1925, two months before the park opened, when more than six thousand children searched the area for twelve thousand eggs, including dozens of gold and silver prizewinners.[259]

On June 17, 1925, Texas governor Miriam Ferguson joined San Antonio mayor John W. Tobin, parks commissioner Lambert, Lions Club president William G. Higgins, and an estimated ten thousand spectators at the dedication of Lions Field, complete with ball field and playground. For thirty minutes six hundred children demonstrated how they used the playground equipment. More played tag. Five months later the Lions Club formally presented the city with

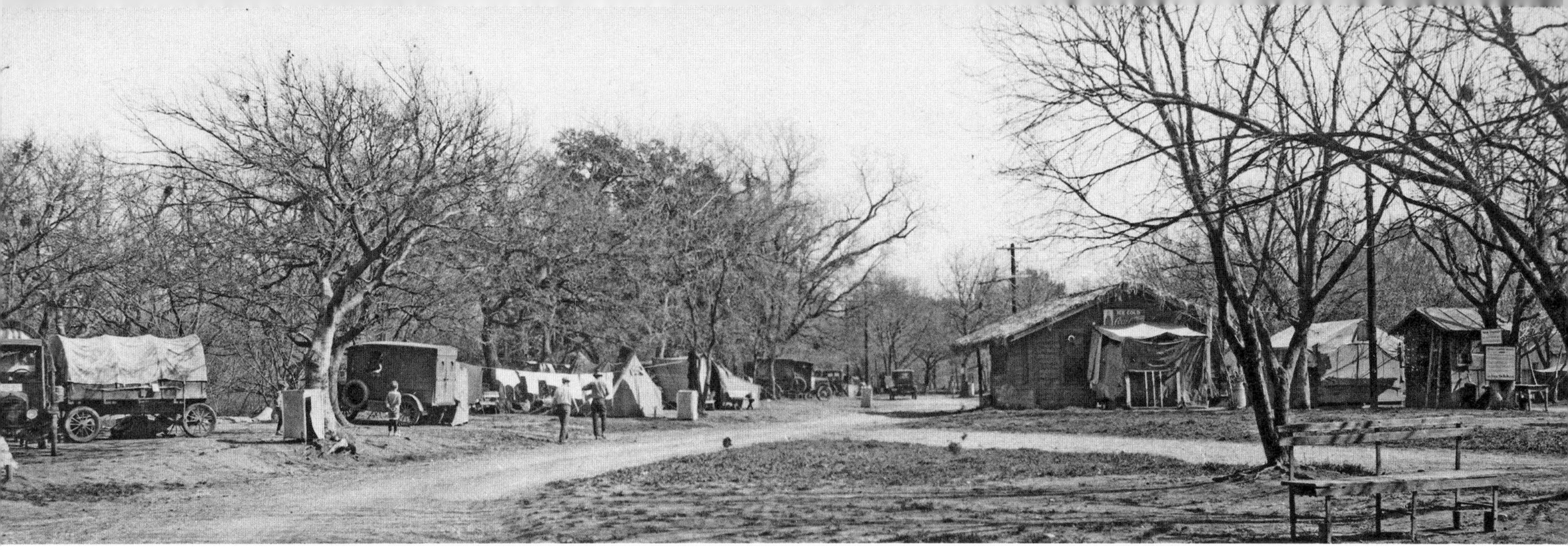

In the early 1920s several thousand tourists a year put up tents in Koehler Park's tourist camp.

the completed clubhouse, set back from Broadway near its intersection with East Mulberry Avenue and including an auditorium, restrooms, and lockers. Nearer Broadway, the club's symbol was placed on a pedestal, a lion eight feet tall and fourteen feet long sculpted in Carrara marble by club member and monument company owner Louis Rodríguez.[260]

At the same time, Ray Lambert was upgrading the park's first playground as part of improvements to its surrounding Lambert Beach, now that danger of flooding there had lifted.

Lambert Beach had historically caught the first rush of the river's periodic floodwaters, which jumped the winding banks, spread through the park to city streets, and then surged toward downtown. In the absence of weather reporting, the upper pump house became an early warning center of sorts. As one unexpected tempest in the early morning darkness of February 26, 1903, brought a sudden rise of the river into Brackenridge Park, the engineer on duty at the pump house phoned an alert to Fire Chief William G. Tobin. It was Tobin's first warning of the approaching torrent and gave his men time to prepare for rescues.[261]

Ten years later, San Antonio's flood warning system consisted of a fireman sent out to Brackenridge Park during heavy rains to check overflow from the park onto River Avenue. The fireman found water at waist level at 2 a.m. on December 4, 1913, and phoned Fire Chief Phil Wright. An hour later Wright still had to call Fort Sam Houston for troops to help save stranded San Antonians.[262]

By 9 p.m. on September 9, 1921, three hours after torrential thunderstorms broke out, water in Brackenridge Park was rising one foot every five minutes. That sent a hundred campers scurrying for higher ground at the tourist camp Ray Lambert had opened two years earlier southwest of the low-water crossing in Koehler Park. Campers' effects were swept from tents pitched along the lighted camp streets, near restrooms with showers and an auto supply store. No injuries were reported. Downstream, the park's six-year-old Water Works complex's pump pit three levels below ground was equipped with a pump that could remove storm water at the rate of two thousand gallons a minute.[263]

The 1921 flood, worst in San Antonio's modern history, submerged nearly a square mile of downtown under two to twelve feet of water, and several dozen residents along three creeks farther downstream drowned. The disaster sped construction of a dam a half-mile north of Brackenridge Park near the mouth of river tributary Olmos Creek's watershed, blocking the most serious source of floodwaters. The sharp reduction of flood risk protected not only the city below but also Brackenridge Park. Ray Lambert could now begin major upgrades around the oak-shaded narrow riverbanks known as Lambert

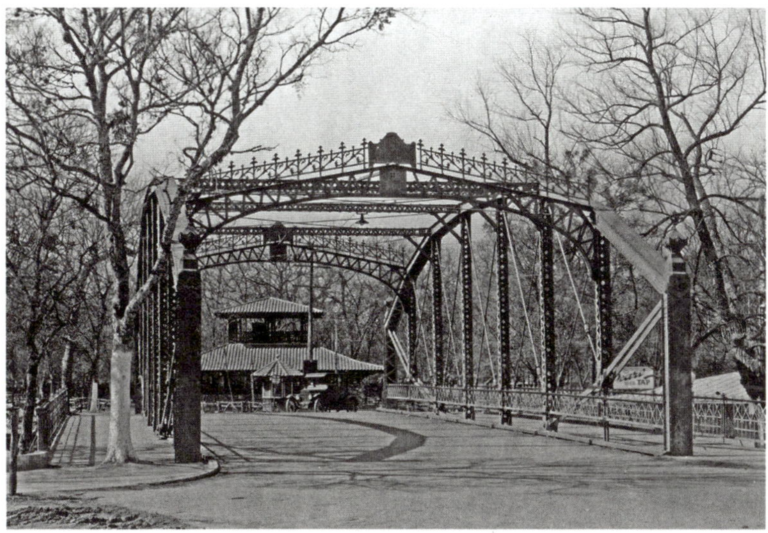

The Letters of Gold iron bridge framed a tile-roofed refreshment stand topped by a cupola for a band. The sign visible through the near right trusses enticed beachgoers to cross the river to Koehler Park, where beer could be legally served.

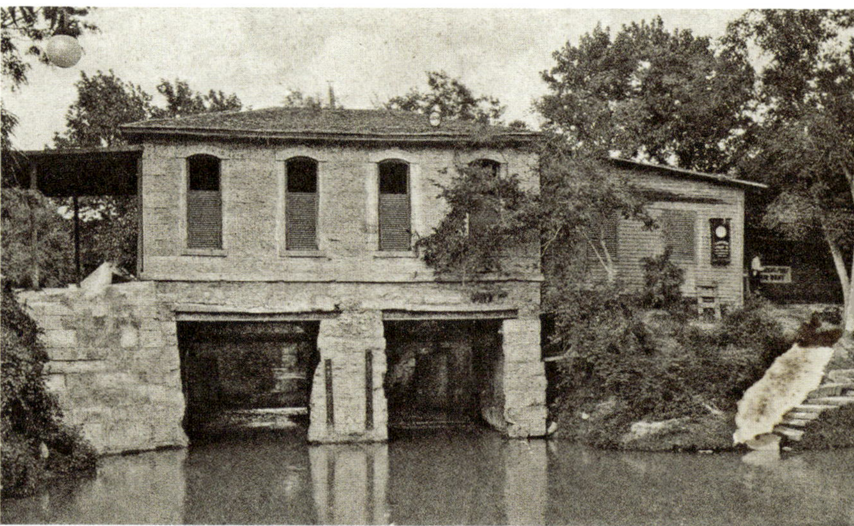

New shutters reflect the Lambert Beach pump house's conversion to a bathhouse in the early 1920s. Remaining at right is the 1878 frame structure where surplus water power was once used to manufacture ice.

Beach with reasonable assurance of safety from rising water. Existing playgrounds, tin bathhouses, and swinging bridges could be safely joined with more permanent structures.

San Antonio's landmark iron bridges were damaged in the 1921 flood. Most could be repaired, but it was thought better to just replace some with larger, concrete bridges. One to be removed was the grand ninety-foot iron bridge across the river on St. Mary's Street near St. Mary's Catholic Church. When dedicated in 1890, its builder, the Berlin Bridge Company of East Berlin, Connecticut, drove a steamroller to the middle of the bridge to prove its structural strength to skeptics. A narrower bridge, with curving side trusses, was also being replaced. It had been installed across Fourth Street / Lexington Avenue by the King Bridge Company of Cleveland, Ohio, in 1880, two years after the company supervised construction of the Water Works pump house.[264]

Ray Lambert saw the opportunity to salvage both bridges and add useful and dramatic features to Brackenridge Park at minimal cost. In 1925 the Fourth Street Bridge became a pedestrian bridge across the river to the zoo at the western end of Lambert Beach. Bridge aficionados believe it to be one of the few surviving bowstring pony-truss iron bridges in Texas. In the same year the St. Mary's Street Bridge was placed to the east, crossing the river near the pump house where a rustic wooden bridge, perhaps damaged by the flood, had been built nine years earlier. It is thought to be the last lenticular through-truss iron bridge in the state.[265]

With the St. Mary's Street Bridge Lambert imported to Brackenridge Park not only a significant piece of San Antonio's architectural legacy but also a bit of political history. Overhead trusses at both ends bore medallions originally painted black and highlighting in gold the names of Mayor Bryan Callaghan and others, sparking the "Letters of Gold Campaign" controversy over whether Callaghan, who managed to win, had overspent on the bridge and, therefore, could be expected to make unnecessary splurges elsewhere, as well.[266]

In addition to rescuing the two bridges, Lambert was likely responsible for saving the park's oldest surviving building—the derelict 1878 pump house—from destruction. Despite the prevailing municipal proclivity to simply remove troublesome antiquated structures, when Lambert Beach opened in 1915 the new parks commissioner could see the former pump house's potential as a bathhouse, much as he saw the wisdom of adapting the picturesque deserted cement kiln and chimney as features of the Japanese Tea Garden.[267]

But a small tin bathhouse had to suffice until the mid-1920s, when the pump house's equipment could be cleared out and the two water outlet stone arches at the river level could be removed so steel beams could be inserted to support the upper floor. The inlet arches on the opposite raceway side remained, though eventually buried by landfill for a roadway. Beside the east wall, bathers also used the surviving frame addition built in 1878 for the short-lived ice factory.

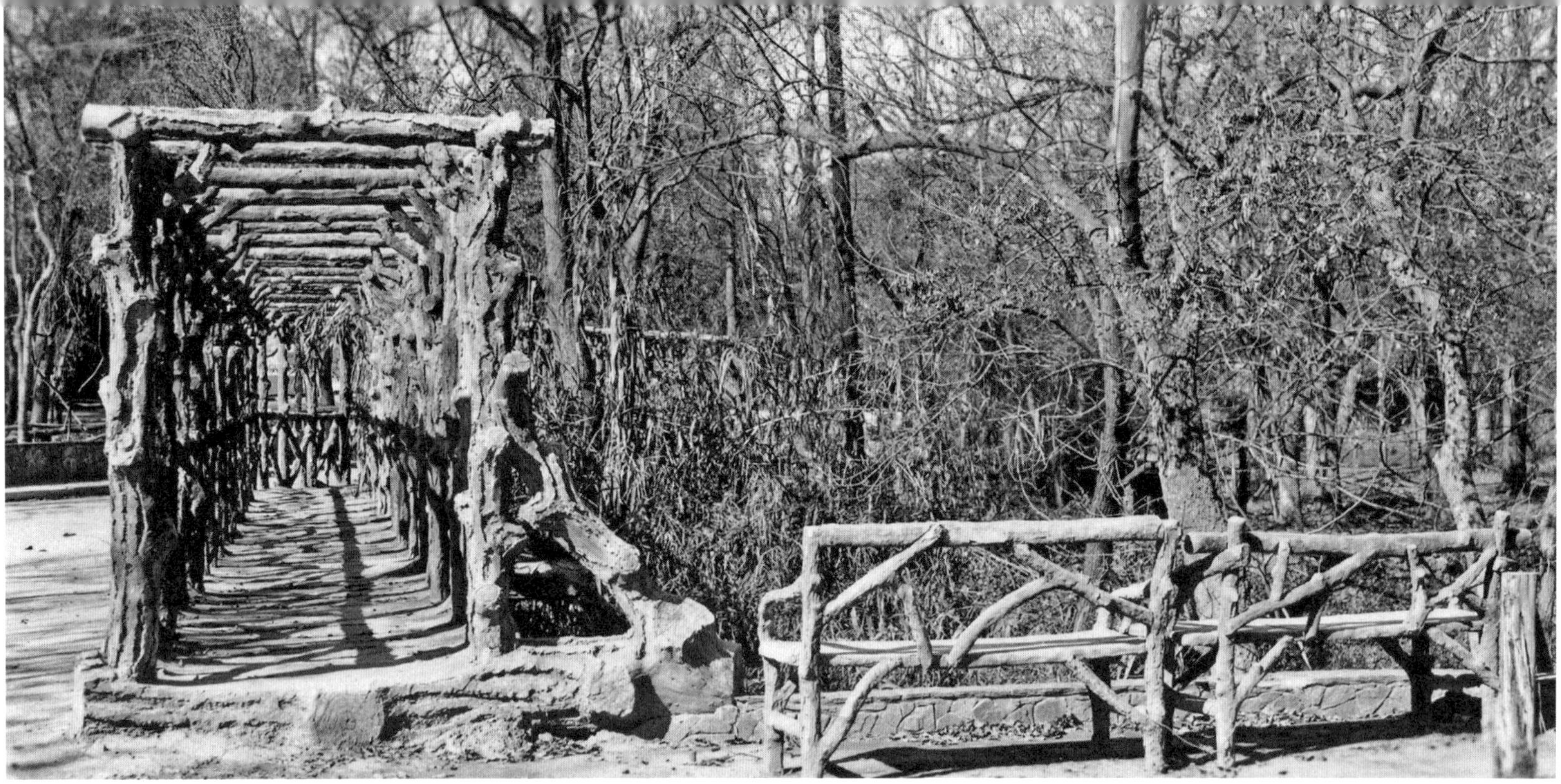

Just west of the pump house, Emmett Jackson designed in 1925 an elongated bathhouse of concrete and rubble stone veneer with twenty-two changing rooms on each side. Nearby, Will Noonan designed the surviving men's and women's restroom buildings of stone rubble with narrow ventilation boxes atop hipped roofs of green tile. In March 1925 the swimming area gained a gravel base and new concrete steps leading down to the water. New streetlights along both sides of the river appear to be like those designed by the economy-focused Ray Lambert, who developed an inexpensive process for making light posts by filling molds with used cans and metal scraps and covering them with concrete. That type of ornamental light post normally cost the city thirty-four dollars each, but Lambert could make each for seven.[268]

North of Lambert Beach, winding donkey ride trails crossed the pump house raceway on one narrow stone-arched bridge and returned over a similar bridge. Close to the northernmost span was the higher 1878 Water Works vehicular bridge over the raceway. Beside it donkey riders in 1925 saw an unusual sight: a pedestrian bridge being built in the form of an elongated arbor of cement *faux bois*—"false wood," also known as *trabajo rústico*, or "rustic work." It has become an iconic feature of Brackenridge Park.

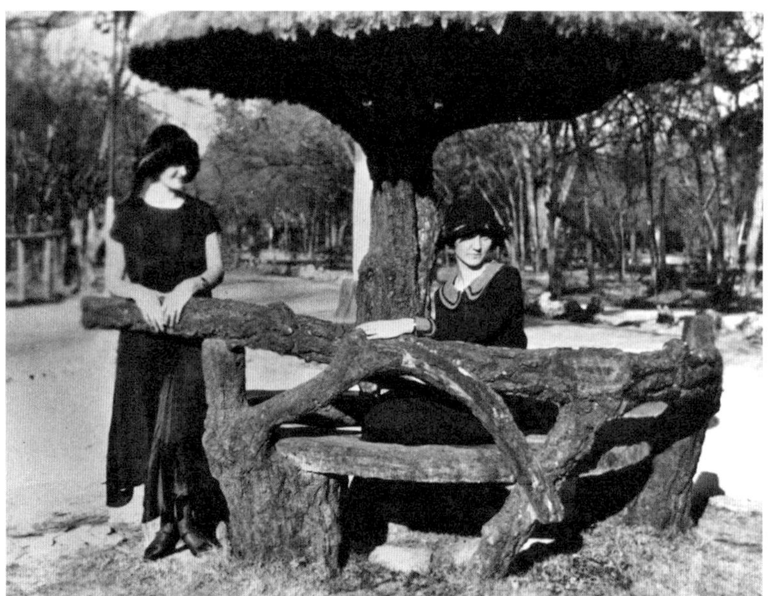

This palapa is among Rodríguez's other painted cement pieces in the park.

Faux bois tree trunks fashioned by Dionicio Rodríguez form an elongated arbor along a bridge in northern Brackenridge Park.

The bridge is among the masterpieces sculpted by Dionicio Rodríguez, thirty-four, recently arrived from Mexico and destined for national acclaim. He used reinforced concrete to create natural forms and textures of trees and rocks. Thirty-three pairs of "tree trunks" along both sides of the bridge supported a ceiling of false branches, which also intertwined handrails. *Faux bois* crosscut planks formed the arbor floor. Rodríguez applied his own formula for lifelike colors before the cement dried, and added such details as knotholes and insect borings, making the sculpted trees difficult to distinguish from nature. According to park passersby, even woodpeckers were fooled.[269]

Elsewhere in the main park are three more Rodríguez works—a hollow tree trunk with a hipped roof and two small structures with palapa-style faux thatched roofs, one with a small round table and two curved benches.

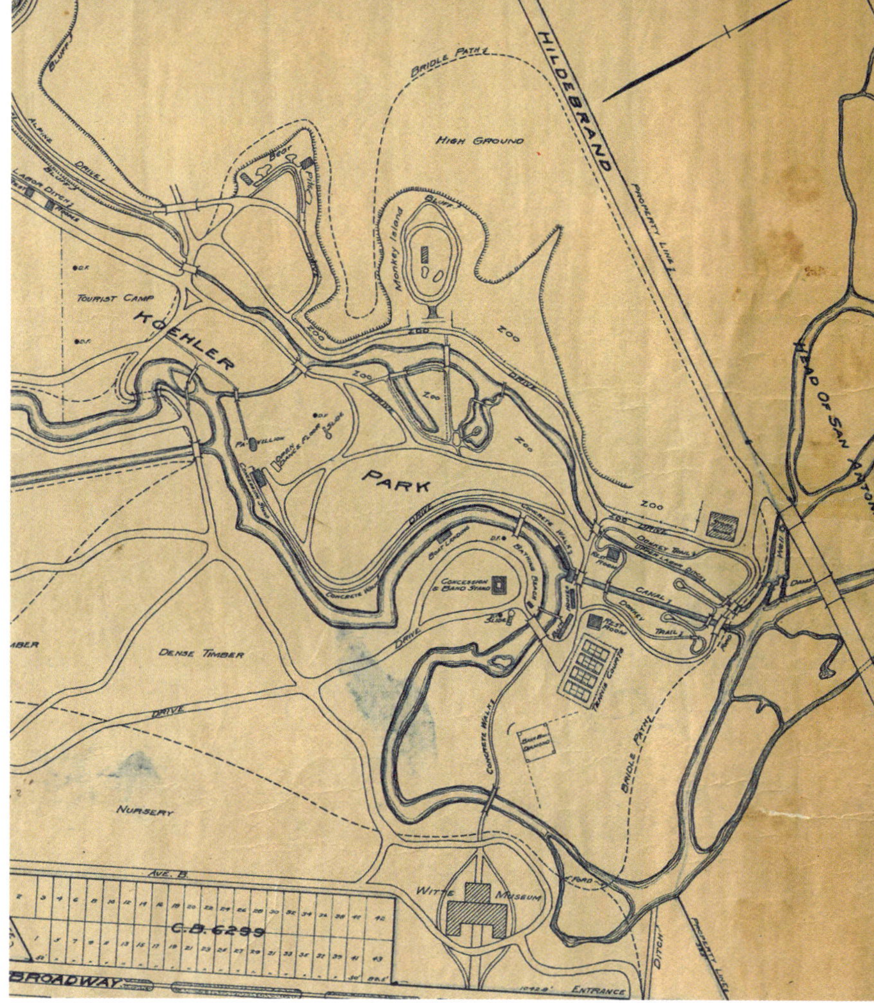

The southern portion of Lambert Beach benefitted from a bequest of local department store magnate Alexander Joske, who left Brackenridge Park $10,000—nearly $150,000 today—if the city would provide a matching amount for an unspecified improvement. Ray Lambert needed a large greenhouse but decided a pavilion would benefit more people. The result shows how he could produce a landmark of the highest quality on the rare occasions when his hands were not tied by funding difficulties.[270]

Completed in 1926 and designed by Emmett Jackson, who was also working on Municipal Auditorium plans, the Joske Pavilion's thick walls were a mosaic of battered, multicolored sandstone broken by five arched openings on either side. The spacious and whimsical interior had a concrete-beamed ceiling, with buttressed chimneys at each end. At the south end rose a massive stone fireplace. On the north end an operatic stone stairway with a wrought iron railing climbed to a balcony overlooking the playground and the river.[271]

Between the Joske Pavilion and the southern banks of Lambert Beach, Will Noonan designed a refreshments stand forty feet square with a green tile roof and a large cupola as a bandstand. The building, later replaced with a new one, was strategically located near the point of a peninsula formed by the looping river so, in those years before the reach of electronic audio systems, band music from the cupola could project throughout the beach area.[272]

The refreshments stand was built by Brackenridge Park's first major concessionaire, Greek-born Alexandre Demetrius Politis. He was running a café on Houston Street in 1921 when the city awarded him the concession contract for Brackenridge and Koehler Parks, and, soon, for San Pedro Springs and Roosevelt Parks as well. The contract included selling gasoline and auto supplies at Koehler Park's tourist camp and running the thatch-roofed Mexican Village restaurant below the Japanese Tea Garden.[273]

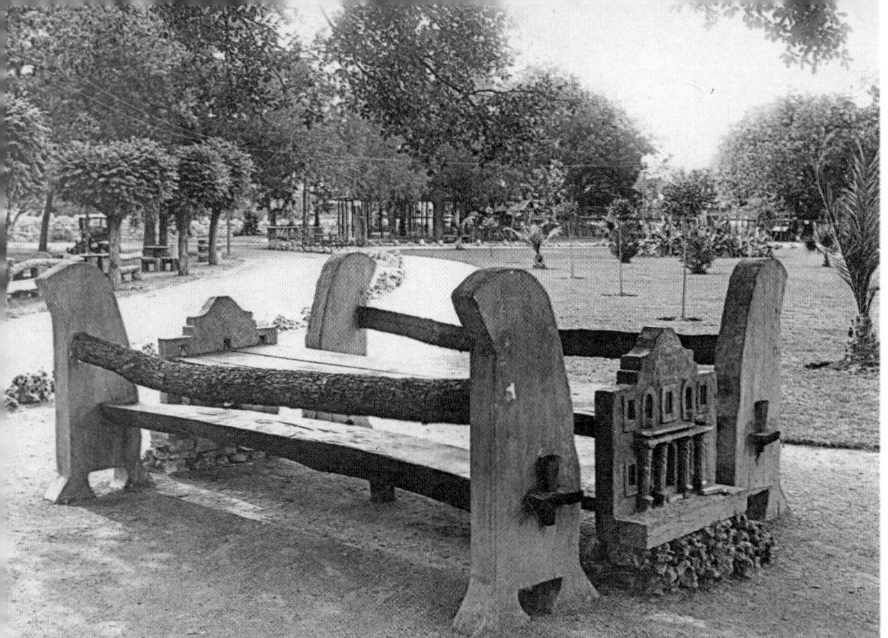

One vanished feature of the 1920s is this rustic picnic table with images of the Alamo at either end.

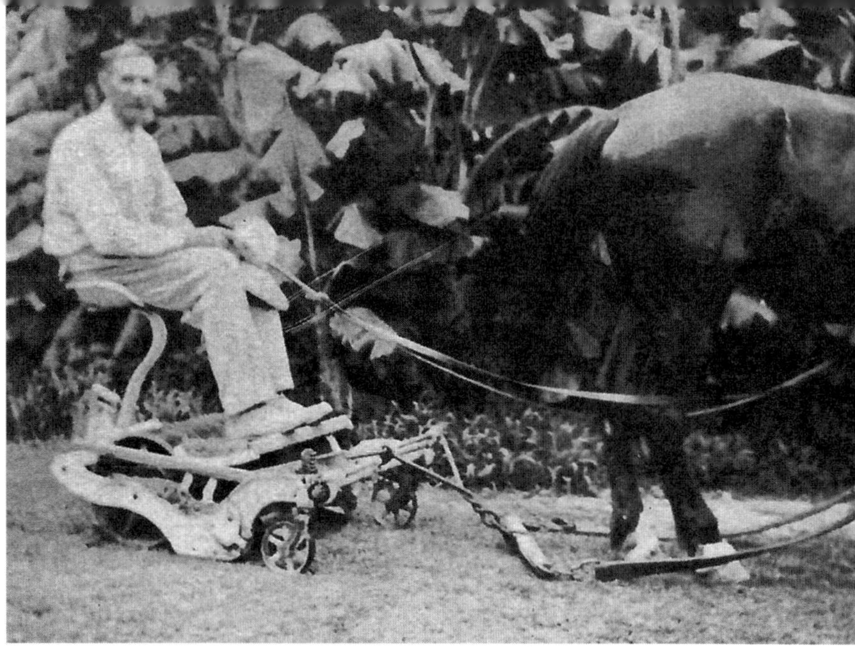

Unproclaimed pillars of the park include groundskeepers like Hermann Leesch, who guided this roller in 1927.

A secondary recreation area was developing to the west, across the river around the pavilion in Koehler Park. Just east of the pavilion, concessionaire Politis ran his "Swiss Inn," also known as the Koehler Park Inn. From there a surviving stairway of Ray Lambert's signature dragon's tooth limestone construction led down to a boat landing. To the north was an open dance floor and near it a playground with a slide and drinking fountains. Zoo cages were scattered across the open landscape beyond in the years before zoo grounds were fenced and admission was charged.

In 1925 the city purchased the municipal water system from the privately owned San Antonio Water Supply Company. That allowed the city to accommodate a new arrival—Gutzon Borglum, fifty-eight, in San Antonio to do a monumental sculpture of Texas trail drivers, commissioned by the Old Trail Drivers Association, to be placed in the plaza in front of Municipal Auditorium. Borglum spotted the vacant lower pump house near the golf course and saw its possibilities as a studio. The city's new San Antonio Water Board let him remodel and rent it.[274]

Initial donations for the monument included $1,000—today's equivalent of $14,000—from cowboy humorist Will Rogers, given at a fundraising barbecue in Brackenridge Park in 1926. But the goal of today's $1.2 million was not reached, and only a quarter-scale bronze casting was finally made. Borglum used the studio for another eleven years, opening it to the public on many afternoons.[275]

The wide range of Borglum's creations in his park studio included early models for his sculpture of the four presidents on Mount Rushmore. Two of his works had different fates during World War II. A monumental bronze of Woodrow Wilson commissioned by Polish president Jan Paderewski in 1929 to recognize Wilson's support of the country was erected in Poznań but taken down by invading Nazi troops and melted into ammunition. Borglum's statue of Thomas Paine was saved by being buried at the foundry in Paris just before Hitler's invasion.[276]

Julian Onderdonk, José Arpa, and other, less prominent painters, were also drawn to the park. Favorite subjects were the picturesque homes of squatters near the former cement plant. Many of the squatters were workers who refused to leave when the company moved in 1908, when fifty-two were counted as still living there.

The city began evicting these residents in 1920 and was finishing the job six years later when artist Hugo Pohl happened through and began sketching those who remained. Pohl got Lambert's permission to build a house and studio from scrap

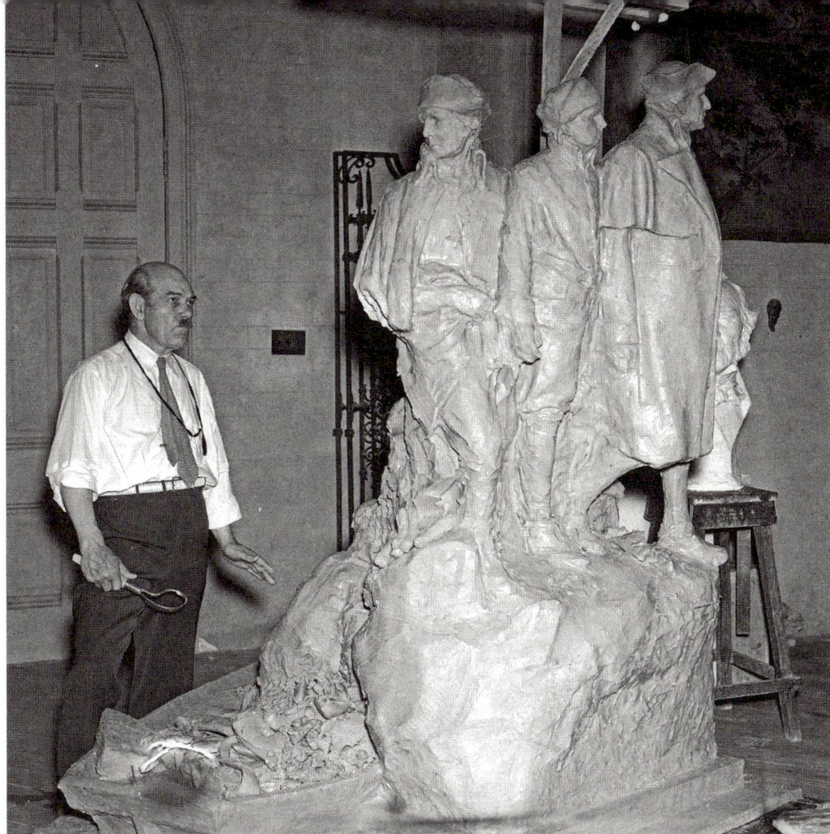

Among the sculptures Gutzon Borglum created in his Brackenridge Park studio was *Spirit of the Westward Movement*.

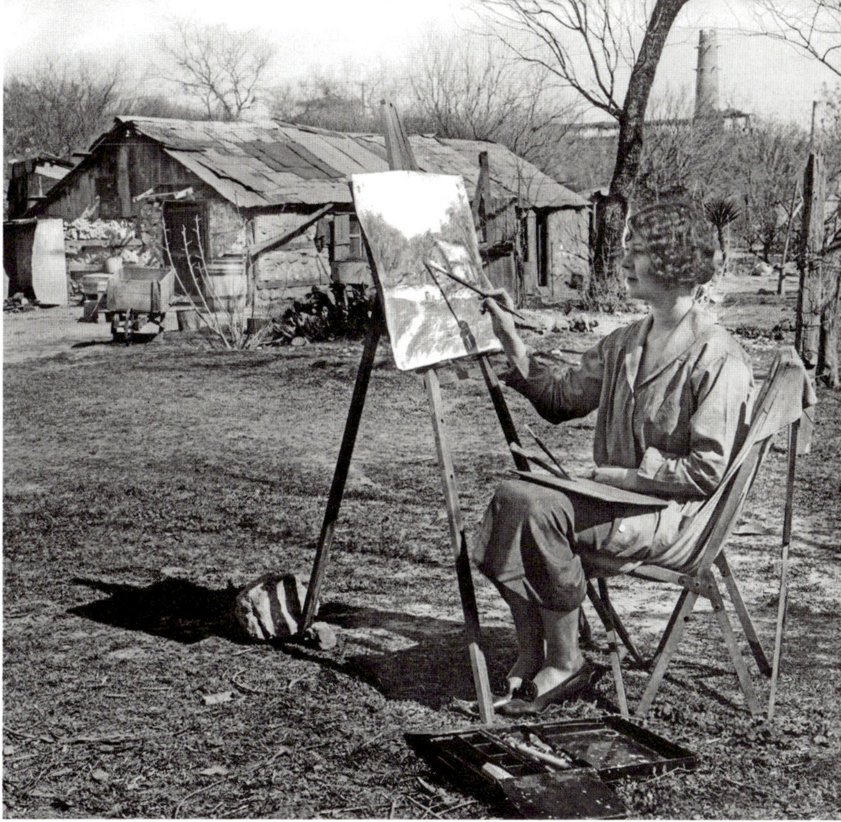

Margaret Jamison was among the artists attracted by rustic homes built for cement plant workers.

lumber across from the zoo entrance and began offering art classes. A painstaking "academician of the old school," he was the first teacher of the noted Paul Rodda Cook. After three years the city evicted Pohl himself so the new zoo superintendent could live in the house.[277]

Brackenridge Park almost missed getting the Witte Museum. A last-minute bequest changed the start of construction at San Pedro Springs Park to begin anew at Brackenridge Park, where backers had given up on a decade-old plan by the Scientific Society to build a natural history museum next to the zoo.

The insular, all-male membership of the Scientific Society, though it owned museum-quality collections and had secured a site in the park from the city, engaged only occasionally with the larger community, and its hopes for a natural history museum went unrealized. Instead Ellen D. Schultz, who taught botany at Main Avenue High School, and Emma Guttzeit, the school's vice principal, launched a public effort to establish what would

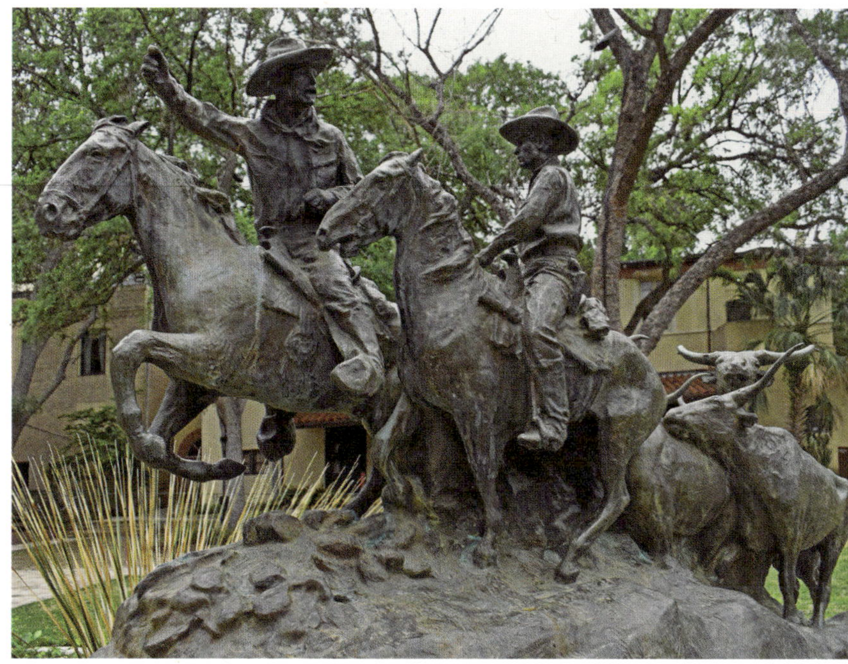

The quarter-size bronze casting of Borglum's portrayal of Texas trail drivers is at the Witte Museum.

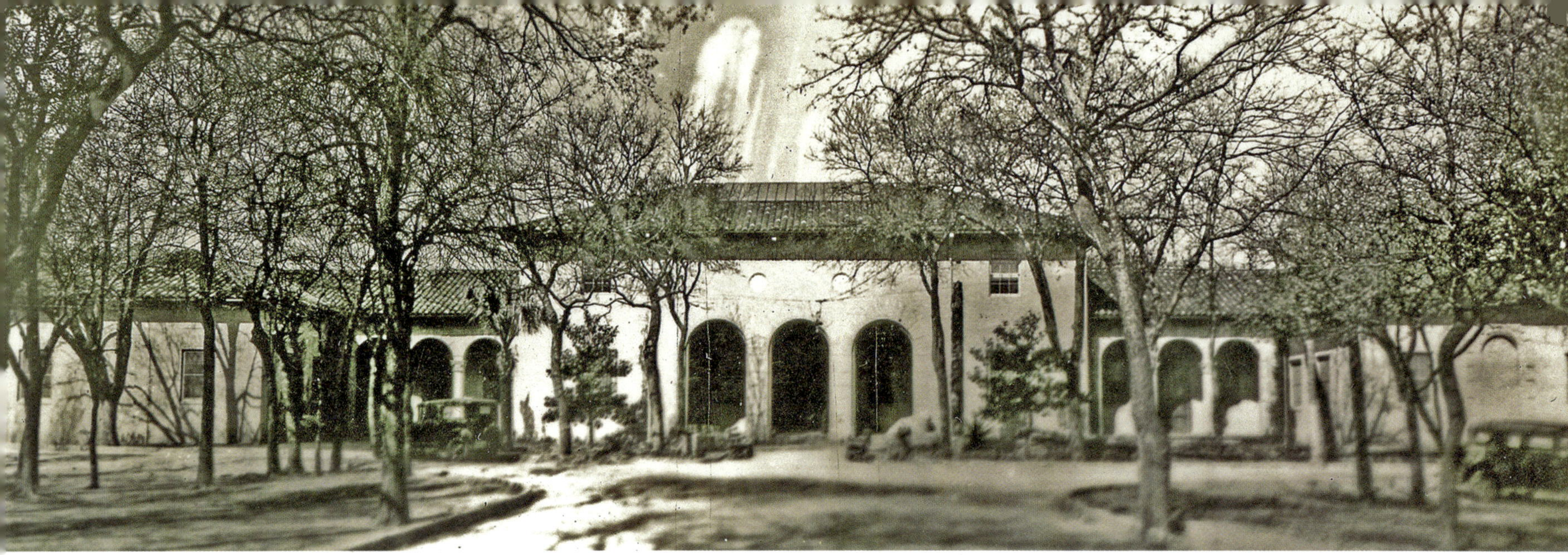

The Witte Memorial Museum opened facing Broadway in 1926.

become, at last, a major museum for San Antonio. The women succeeded where men had failed.

In 1923 the two formed the Museum of San Antonio Association and raised $6,000 to buy the natural science collection gathered by H. P. Attwater of Houston. A newspaper reporter watching the three-ton acquisition being unpacked in San Antonio was particularly impressed by its encyclopedic array of edible nuts of Texas, including as many as fifty varieties of pecans. There were also samples of prize-winning wools and stuffed birds and mounted wild animals, similar to those in Gustav Jermy's small natural history museum in San Pedro Springs Park, which had closed twelve years before. Exhibits from the Attwater Collection were set up in two empty Main Avenue High School classrooms, and public support for a museum building grew. Mayor John W. Tobin promised a site in San Pedro Springs Park and $7,500 in city funds toward a building. Robert M. Ayres volunteered his firm to design it.[278]

The day after test drilling began for the museum's foundation in San Pedro Springs Park came news that recently deceased real estate man Alfred G. Witte had left $65,000—today's equivalent of nearly $1 million—for a museum specifically in Brackenridge Park and named in his parents' honor. Witte had apparently been unaware that the city museum once planned in Brackenridge Park was being built instead in San Pedro Springs Park. If the site were moved back to Brackenridge Park, however, Witte's bequest would cover not only a fundraising shortfall but would allow for a second floor.[279]

Mayor Tobin, Lambert, museum leaders, and others inspected the museum's originally planned site in Brackenridge Park. They agreed the new museum should go there.[280]

Just as the zoo initially counted on donations of armadillos, javelinas, and coyotes from area ranchers, so did the museum issue an appeal to local residents for gifts of family heirlooms and other treasures. A donation of items brought home from their travels by the late congressman James L. Slayden and his wife, Ellen, were among exhibits featured at the grand opening of the Witte Memorial Museum in Brackenridge Park on October 6, 1926.[281]

The Scientific Society declined an invitation to display its collections, leaving more space for three other groups. The north wing highlighted the museum association's natural history collection, the fifty varieties of pecans displayed in rows of glass jars along the west wall. The south wing featured Texas history and was overseen by the San Antonio Conservation Society, active in the museum's formation. The second floor held works from the San Antonio Art League's collection. An active program of events and exhibits included the first show in Texas by Mexican muralist Diego Rivera. Acquisitions ranged from early

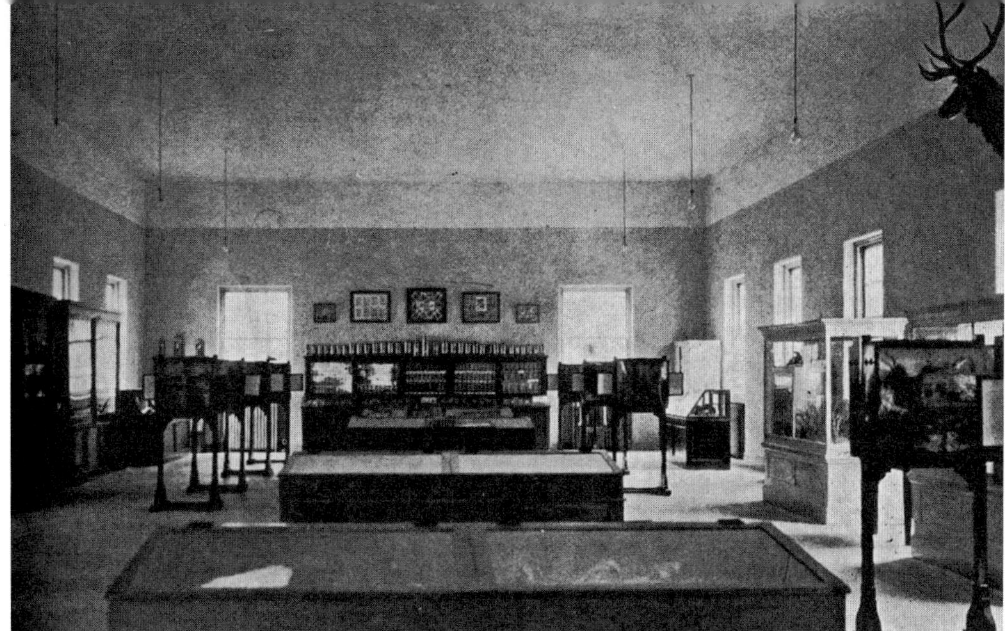

The Witte's natural history hall included, along the far wall, glass jars displaying varieties of pecans.

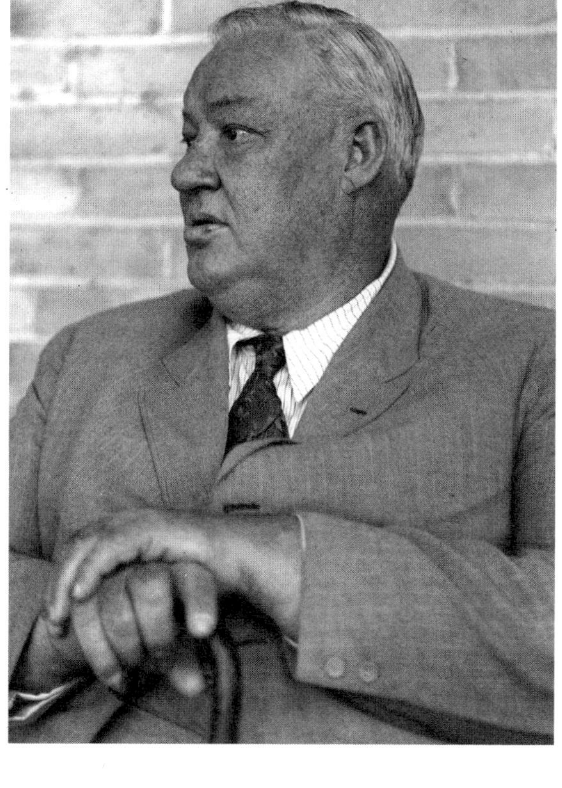

As he looked back at Brackenridge Park's transformation, Lambert said, "This work is just begun."

southwestern Native American baskets and pottery to early Texas paintings and even Davy Crockett's fiddle.[282]

Ellen Schultz was hired as museum director at a salary of one dollar a year. She soon married Magnolia Petroleum Company staff worker Roy Quillin, a noted Texas ornithologist who carefully cataloged his collection of more than ten thousand eggs from fifty-three species of birds and built wooden cabinets to house them. Quillin's ability to blow out contents of the eggs through one small hole rather than the usual two enhanced the quality of the collection, now housed in study drawers at the Witte Museum.[283]

Though still able to carry on as parks commissioner, Lambert by the mid-1920s was in declining health. San Antonians grateful for his park reforms set Ray Lambert Day for a Sunday in October 1924, though an afternoon shower sent several hundred people crowding into the pavilion in Koehler Park. An opening concert by the San Antonio Municipal Band included the "Ray Lambert March," described by one newspaper as "a pleasingly original composition."[284]

Chaired by future mayor and congressman Maury Maverick, the event included addresses by Mayor Tobin, chamber of commerce president Albert Steves, and clergy from Saint Cecelia's Catholic Church and Central Christian Church. A member of the Woodlawn Lake Civic Club read a poem extolling Lambert's accomplishments in all of the city's parks. Mary Jingu, daughter of the proprietors of the park's Japanese tearoom, "was swung up on a table in her picturesque Japanese costume" and presented Lambert with a bouquet of flowers. Lambert spoke of his early training as a stonecutter and expressed gratitude to park donors George Brackenridge and Emma Koehler. But, he stressed, "This work is just begun."[285]

In December 1927 Lambert, fifty-nine, succumbed to acute bronchial pneumonia. He was survived by his wife, two sons, and four stepchildren. Municipal buildings were draped in mourning, city hall's flag was lowered to half-staff, and Lambert's body lay in state in Municipal Auditorium for two hours before his funeral at Saint Mary's Catholic Church.[286]

Ray Lambert, alderman and saloonkeeper trained only as a stonemason, had been the right man in charge during the dozen critical years he served as San Antonio's parks commissioner. Starting with little but energy and imagination, he parlayed meager resources in order to transform Brackenridge Park, crown jewel of the municipal parks system, for future generations.

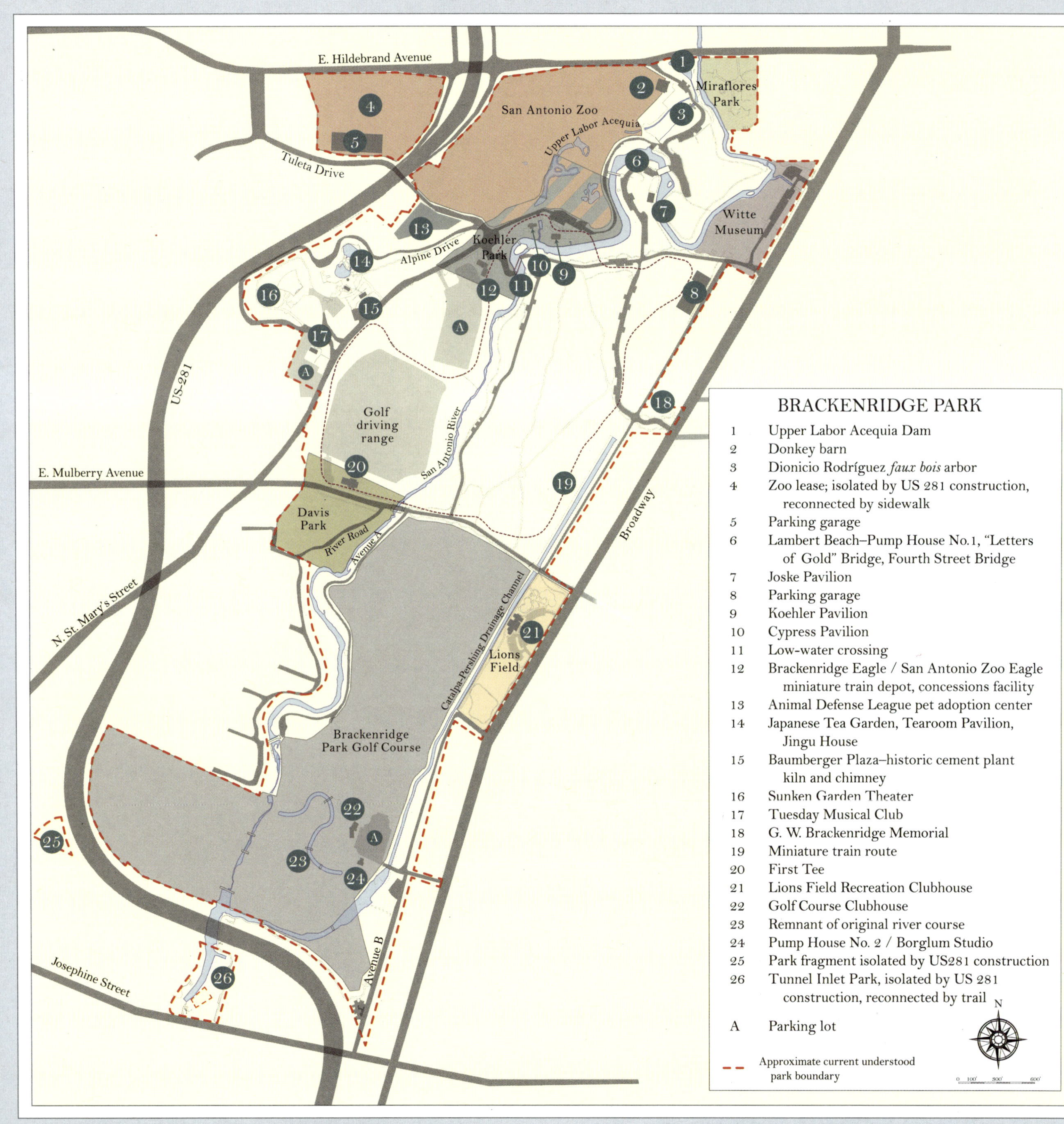
E. Hildebrand Avenue
San Antonio Zoo
Miraflores Park
Upper Labor Acequia
Tuleta Drive
Witte Museum
Koehler Park
Alpine Drive
US-281
Golf driving range
San Antonio River
E. Mulberry Avenue
Davis Park
River Road
Avenue A
Broadway
N. St. Mary's Street
Catalpa-Pershing Drainage Channel
Lions Field
Brackenridge Park Golf Course
Josephine Street
Avenue B
BRACKENRIDGE PARK
1 Upper Labor Acequia Dam
2 Donkey barn
3 Dionicio Rodríguez *faux bois* arbor
4 Zoo lease; isolated by US 281 construction, reconnected by sidewalk
5 Parking garage
6 Lambert Beach–Pump House No. 1, "Letters of Gold" Bridge, Fourth Street Bridge
7 Joske Pavilion
8 Parking garage
9 Koehler Pavilion
10 Cypress Pavilion
11 Low-water crossing
12 Brackenridge Eagle / San Antonio Zoo Eagle miniature train depot, concessions facility
13 Animal Defense League pet adoption center
14 Japanese Tea Garden, Tearoom Pavilion, Jingu House
15 Baumberger Plaza–historic cement plant kiln and chimney
16 Sunken Garden Theater
17 Tuesday Musical Club
18 G. W. Brackenridge Memorial
19 Miniature train route
20 First Tee
21 Lions Field Recreation Clubhouse
22 Golf Course Clubhouse
23 Remnant of original river course
24 Pump House No. 2 / Borglum Studio
25 Park fragment isolated by US281 construction
26 Tunnel Inlet Park, isolated by US 281 construction, reconnected by trail
A Parking lot
Approximate current understood park boundary
N

PART 3

The Modern Park

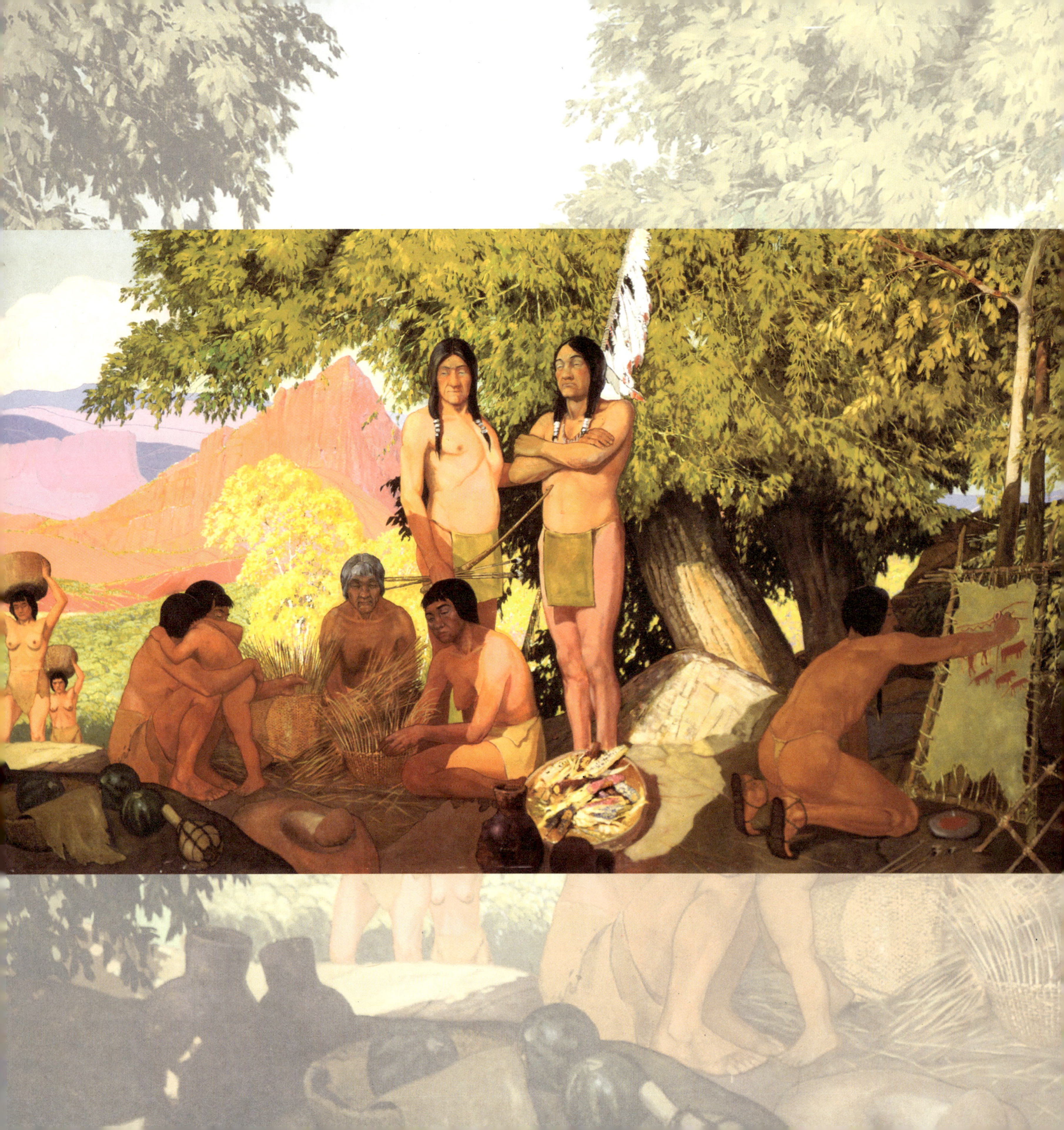

The New Deal

New Deal relief programs had a profound effect on Brackenridge Park and its tenant institutions. By the time the Great Depression ended with the onset of World War II, federal funding had enhanced the park's landscape, facilities, and traffic patterns, ushering in a new era.

The full force of the Depression struck San Antonio in 1931, but the appetite for city-sponsored public improvements and tourism development had already diminished. Fiscal conservatives had taken over city hall in 1930, three years after parks commissioner Lambert's death, limiting the options of his successor, Jacob Rubiola.[287]

A sharp decline in construction in 1931 signaled rising unemployment in San Antonio. Banks began closing. In September the city, faced with declining tax collections, lost deposits of $509,000, nearly 20 percent of its annual budget, with the failure of its largest bank, City Central Bank and Trust Company. That caused further layoffs of policemen, street crews, and public health personnel as the city slashed its budget for the coming year by 40 percent. The parks department took a particularly hard hit with the dismissal of sixty workers.[288]

With no new city projects, no plans for more, and no funds in sight in any event, the New Deal came to the rescue. Federal aid programs were supporting improvements nationally in parks, important places of entertainment and recreation for the millions of unemployed with nowhere else to go. A city had only to fund 10 to 25 percent of a project's cost. The federal government would pay the rest and hire unemployed workers to do the work. By mid-1939 the New Deal had changed the face of Brackenridge Park and its tenant institutions with spending exceeding today's equivalent of more than $10 million.[289]

The Texas basketmaker Indians mural by Harry Anthony De Young.

In 1933 the Franklin D. Roosevelt administration was scrambling to sync its evolving cornucopia of federal relief programs with state and local efforts. In November 1933 the Civil Works Administration (CWA) formed as a short-term agency to get jobless Americans off direct financial relief and onto employment rolls at prevailing wages. Several thousand San Antonians were put to work at tasks ranging from road building to teaching adult education.[290]

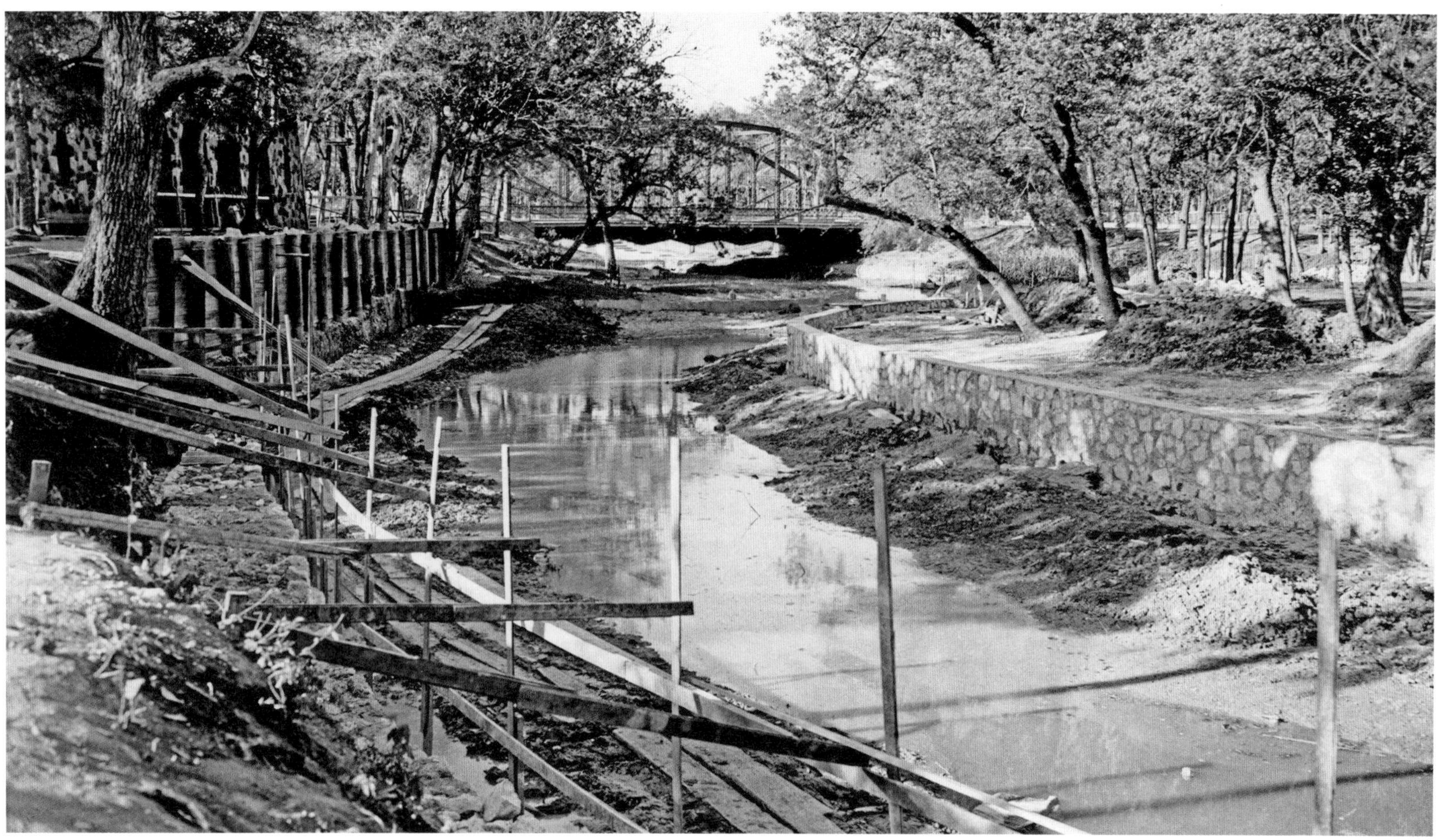

NYA workers replaced retaining walls along the river in Brackenridge Park.

In the first New Deal effort in Brackenridge Park, Harry Anthony De Young was commissioned to paint a Texas basketmaker Indians mural for the Witte Museum. The oil on canvas, sixteen feet long by eight feet tall and inspired by the Witte's archeological excavations in the Lower Pecos Canyonlands, hung in the Witte's entrance hall from 1934 until it went into storage several decades later, when some aspects were determined to be more imaginary than historically accurate. De Young was one of eight artists to paint murals for public buildings in the city in the CWA's Public Works of Art Project.[291]

CWA programs helped get four million previously unemployed Americans through a dire winter, but ended in mid-1934. Many of administration's projects and staff members transferred to the Works Progress Administration (WPA), the New Deal's largest and most diverse public works program, formed in May 1935 and renamed Work Projects Administration in 1939. Rather than having other entities do the hiring, the WPA employed workers directly for projects requested at the local level and approved by state and federal officials.[292]

There was also the National Youth Administration (NYA), formed a month after the WPA. Unlike the Civilian Conservation Corps, which employed young men primarily in forestry projects, the NYA took both women and men and provided a wider variety of work and training. The NYA targeted youth ages sixteen to twenty-four needing financial assistance to continue their education and unemployed youth ages sixteen to twenty-five who were in financial need and were not in school. By January 1936 more than 1,600 San Antonians were signed up with the NYA, and 4,130 older workers had WPA jobs.[293]

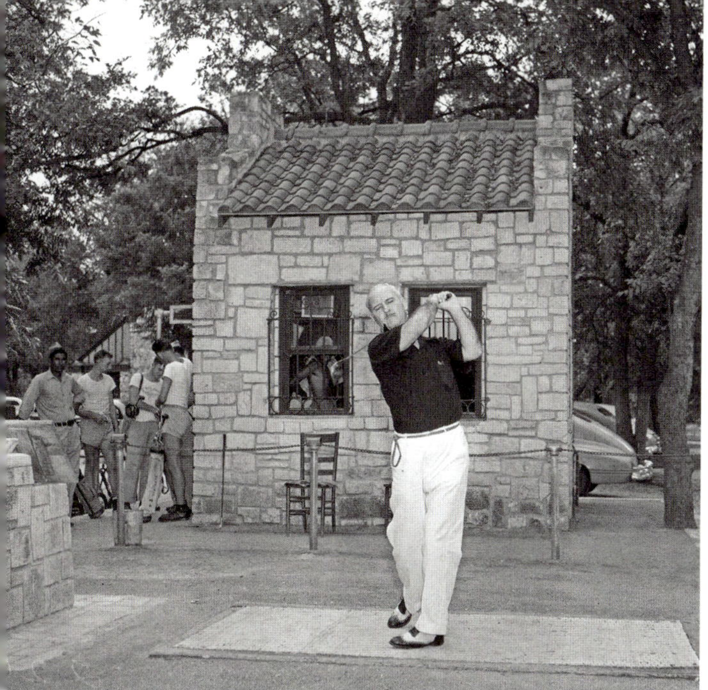

Murray Brooks tees off at the stone starter house, built by NYA workers along with the drinking fountain at its left. San Antonio architect Otto Ransleben was working for the NYA when he designed a three-span bridge for Brackenridge Park's golf course in 1939.

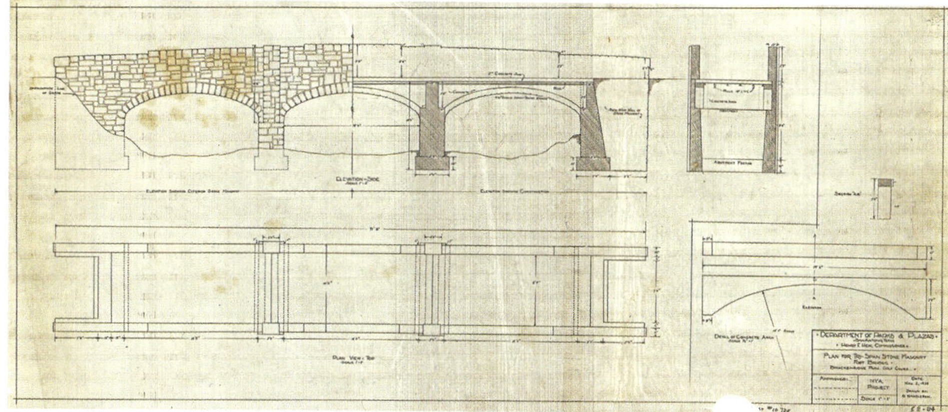

NYA workers replaced long stretches of crumbling rock retaining walls beside the river in the park's northern section, paved a low-water crossing south of East Mulberry Avenue, across from the River Road neighborhood, and built stone-curbed parking lots. At the Municipal Golf Course, they built a quaint stone starter house, a caddy house, tee boxes, drinking fountains, and five bridges for golfers crossing the old waterworks canal and the river. The projects were planned by Murray Brooks, course manager since 1923 and a pro at the city's courses for more than forty years. In 1934 the city extended Mulberry Avenue through Brackenridge Park along the golf course's northern border east to Broadway, making the new park road a major east-west thoroughfare.[294]

WPA workers replaced picnic tables south of the Joske Pavilion with nineteen tables made of concrete, each with a glazed number tile on its end and concrete benches on either side. They stood on concrete pads beside barbecue pits. Across the river, the WPA replaced Otto Koehler's 1901 bandstand and pavilion with the Koehler Pavilion, whose central frame structure supported a hipped metal roof. But the largest number of the park's WPA workers were at the zoo.[295]

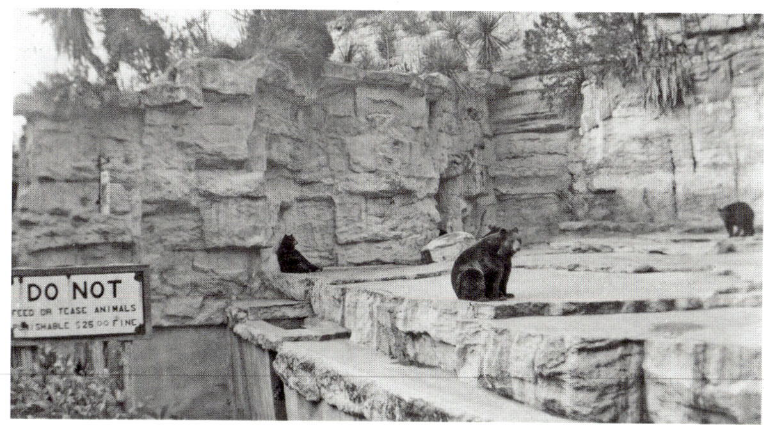

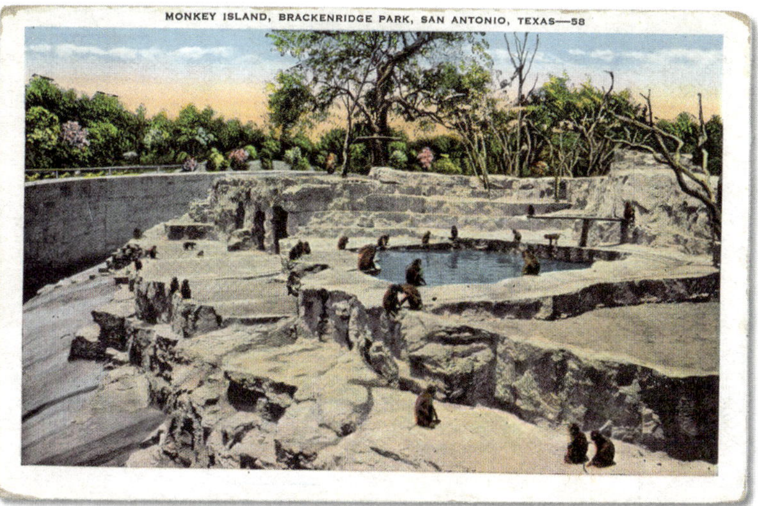

In 1929 the zoo pioneered barless cages for bears. Primate Paradise, better known as Monkey Island, soon followed.

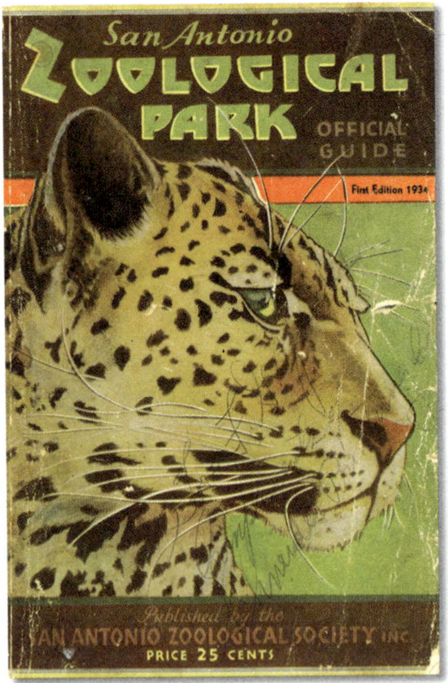

The zoo's first guidebook came out in 1934.

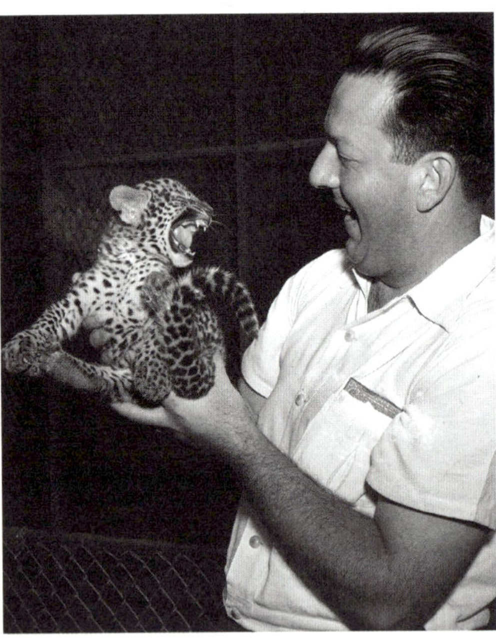

Fred Stark, shown getting acquainted with a baby leopard.

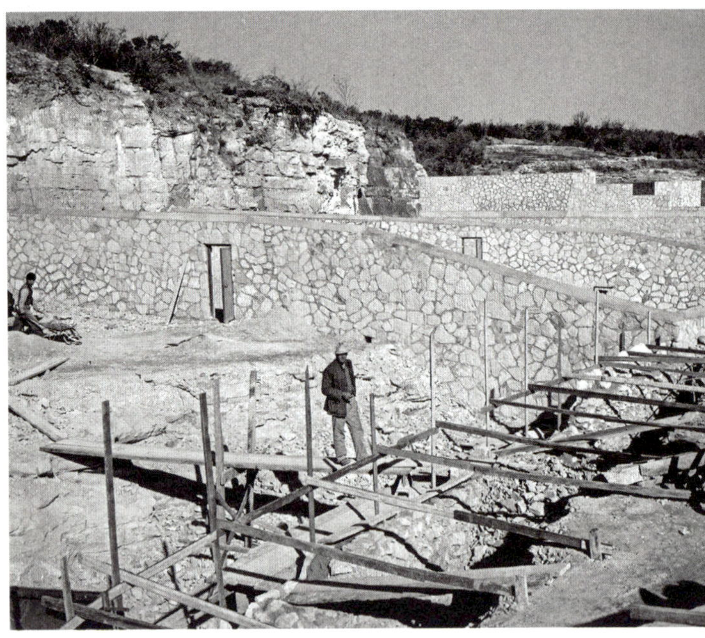

The zoo's African Panorama, built by the WPA, was a series of open habitats set against limestone cliffs.

While Americans with little else to do were visiting zoos as never before, zoos' municipal subsidies were dropping and longtime benefactors were cutting their contributions. To delight families that could afford few other diversions, the WPA launched zoo projects by employing workers who soon outnumbered permanent employees at most zoos, including San Antonio's.[296]

Operated by the parks department, the municipal zoo was ready for change. In 1929 its supporters had chartered the San Antonio Zoological Society, which helped open two cageless habitats still uncommon in more established zoos—barless bear terraces along the old quarry cliffs and Primate Paradise, better known as Monkey Island, designed by architects Adams & Adams. More than forty monkeys, freed from their old cages, frolicked around the moated expanse of large rocks and scattered trees. Quarters for three chimpanzees and cages for a fast-growing collection of birds followed the next year.[297]

As 1931 turned economically catastrophic, the struggling parks department turned over zoo operations to the zoological society, though the zoo still relied on some municipal funding. Society member Fred A. Sullivan, advertising director of a local shoe company, was made the zoo's first private director. He was succeeded three years later by Fred W. Stark, age twenty-six, curator of birds, who remained director for the next thirty-three years.[298]

The San Antonio Zoo got its first rush of WPA workers—a hundred—in 1935. Believing that "every well-equipped zoo" should have a monkey island, the WPA was adding them at a dozen zoos, from San Francisco to Detroit to Pittsburgh. But San Antonio's zoo was ahead of that curve, so the WPA simply improved Primate Paradise and built administration, hospital, and commissary buildings. New exhibit areas designed by Adams & Adams were begun in 1935 for animals from elephants to gazelles to hippos. A new aviary at the entrance accommodated birds as large as eagles and condors.[299]

The zoo's biggest project was the African Panorama. As many as 160 workers at a time survived nearly three years of fund shortages and attempted budget cuts to complete, in 1939, a series of barless cages backed by high limestone cliffs. Old cages were cleared away and small dens were built for the animals' shelter. Workers dug moats and built barriers to keep viewers at a safe distance and put up walls of limestone blocks

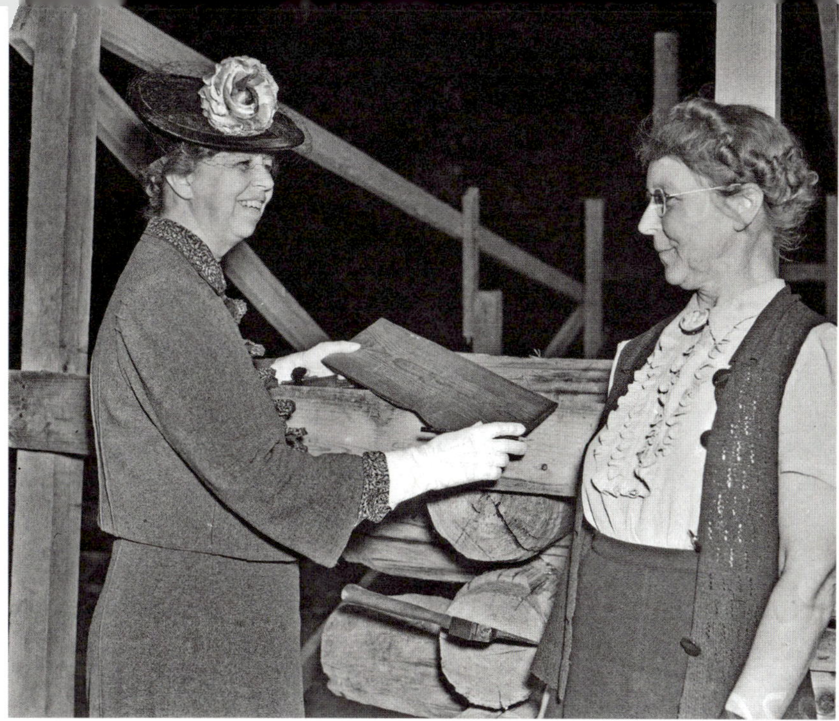

Eleanor Roosevelt signs the first handmade roof shingle for a log cabin being built by the NYA at the Witte Museum, as Witte director Ellen Shulz Quillin, *right*, looks on.

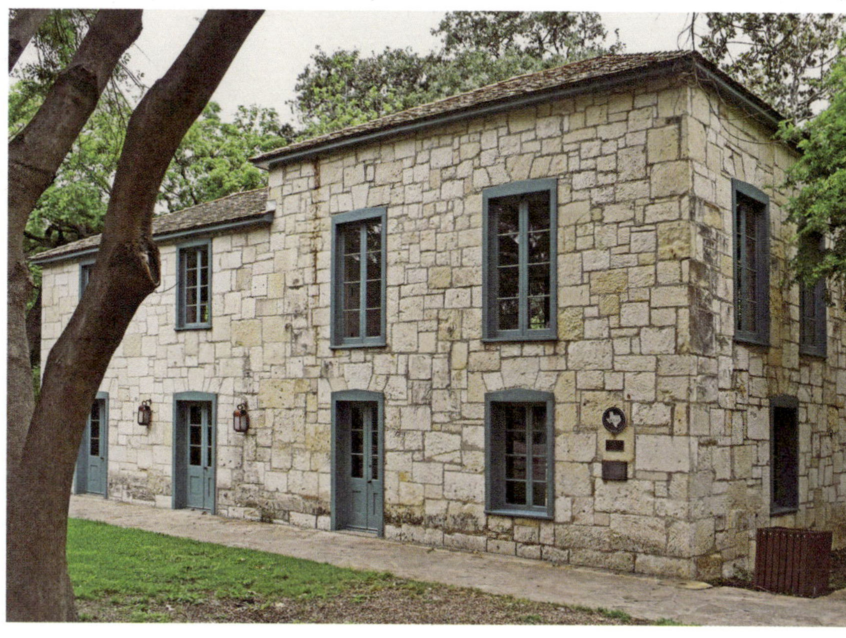

Moving the Twohig House to the Witte Museum was the last WPA project completed in Texas.

quarried nearby to separate habitats of lions, tigers, elks, wolves, and others.[300]

The zoo's last WPA project, in 1942, was a reptile house with eighteen glass-fronted displays for more than a hundred varieties of snakes.[301]

In 1939, the days of living in remote log cabins were still within some Texans' memory. Witte leaders believed that new generations needed to be reminded of those pioneer times. Cabins within a hundred miles of San Antonio were studied and measured, and plans for a new cabin were drawn up. The San Antonio Public Service Company contributed telephone poles as the logs. The cabin, an East Texas type surrounded by a split-rail fence, had two front rooms separated by an open dog-run, or breezeway, and a roof of sixteen thousand cypress shingles hand-cut on site by NYA workers.[302]

As the cabin was under construction in March 1939, First Lady Eleanor Roosevelt was on a train trip through the Southwest. She stopped in San Antonio to tour a garment maker's shop, drive through needy neighborhoods, visit with local leaders, and inspect several WPA and NYA projects. These included the cabin at the Witte, where she was hosted by director Ellen Shulz Quillin and signed the cabin's first handmade shingle. Roosevelt mentioned the visit in her daily national newspaper column.[303]

The WPA was winding down its work at the end of 1941 when the local Historic Buildings Foundation swung in to save one of the San Antonio River Walk's choice landmarks, the century-old two-story rock home of banker John Twohig, which was about to be torn down by neighboring San Antonio Public Service. The utility company's president, Chester Chubb, agreed to donate the house to the Witte Museum, have it dismantled under the direction of architects, and deliver it. It was rebuilt by a WPA crew at the edge of the Witte property beside the river.[304]

Washington approval for the last-minute project was obtained by San Antonio–based state WPA director Harry Drought, whose wife, Ethel, had helped establish the Witte and was one of Roosevelt's escorts on her San Antonio visit. Parks commissioner Henry F. Hein, Jacob Rubiola's successor, used city trucks to deliver Alamo Cement president Charles Baum-berger Jr.'s donation of 430 bags of the cement for the project

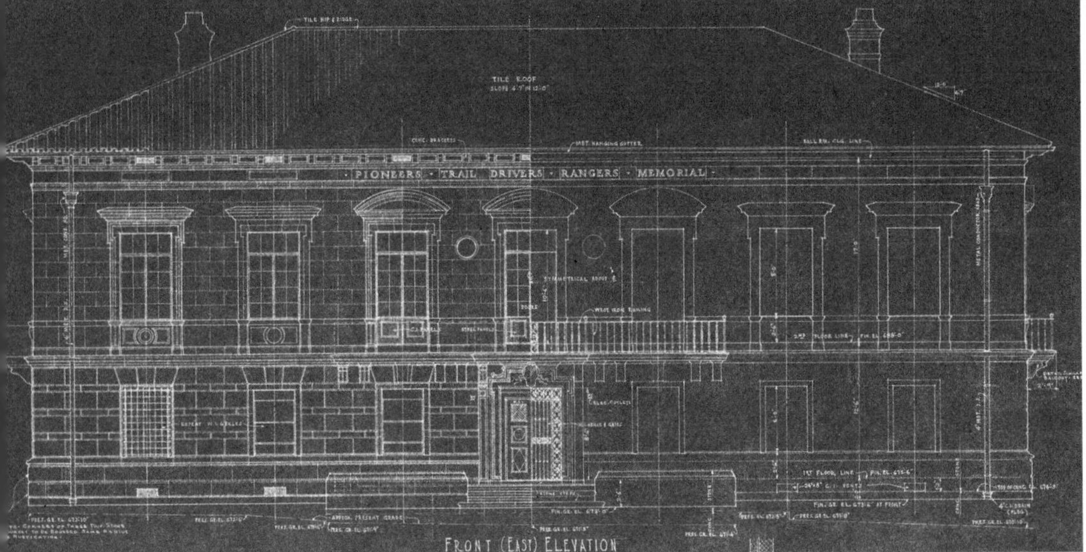

Building plans for the Texas Pioneers, Trail Drivers, and Rangers Memorial.

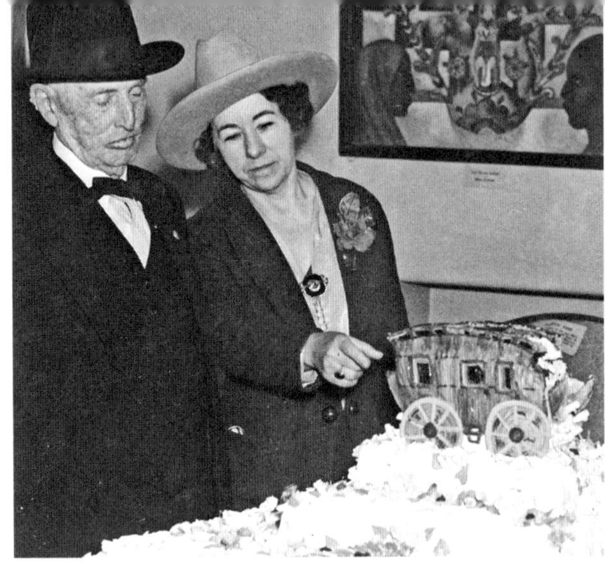

A stagecoach topped a cake at the Old Trail Drivers Association 1936 Christmas party, attended by W. T. Jackman, *left*, and Bessie Terry Lesser, *right*.

precisely at 5 p.m. on August 1, 1942. That was the last moment cement for nonmilitary use could be delivered anywhere. The Twohig House, finished the next year, was the last WPA project completed in Texas.[305]

The Twohig House was the first of three noteworthy stone homes built in the second quarter of the nineteenth century and relocated to the Witte grounds, adding a new dimension to Brackenridge Park's historic resources. In 1943 the hurricane-damaged one-story home of Texas Declaration of Independence signer José Francisco Ruiz was moved from Military Plaza and rebuilt near the Twohig House. Four years later the home of Celso Navarro, Ruiz's uncle and father of Declaration signer José Antonio Navarro, was rescued from harm's way on Camaron Street and reconstructed near the other two homes.[306]

In the midst of the New Deal the centennial of Texas independence came up. The state wrangled $3 million in federal funds to help mark the anniversary by citing the precedent of a $5 million federal appropriation for the Louisiana Purchase Exposition in Saint Louis in 1903 and the need for Depression relief.[307]

The big prize was hosting a centennial exposition, to be the equivalent of a world's fair. San Antonio leaders wanted it badly enough to propose sacrificing northern Brackenridge Park for the exposition grounds. Those would extend westward into an abandoned rock quarry dubbed San Jacinto Park, though its sole amenity was a ball diamond. But the extravaganza went to Dallas, which now uses the site for the Texas State Fair. Brackenridge Park stayed intact, and the so-called San Jacinto Park ended up as the new campus of Trinity University.[308]

Brackenridge Park, however, gained major benefits from the centennial. Nearly two-thirds of the $3 million in federal Texas centennial appropriations, to be matched by the state, were going to memorial projects throughout Texas. Veterans of the iconic cattle trail drives and frontier law enforcement were in their eighties and nineties, and it was a fine opportunity to preserve the memory of their achievements with a building in Brackenridge Park in San Antonio. Such a memorial was indeed already in the planning stages, to face Broadway just north of the Witte Museum. The project was granted $98,278 in centennial funds, today's equivalent of $1.8 million.[309]

Building plans had begun in 1933 with Ellen Shulz Quillin, director of the Witte Museum, which had a founding goal of honoring early Texas settlers. In 1934 the Witte board approved building plans by Ayres & Ayres, joined later by Phelps & Dewees. The museum allied itself with the Old Trail Drivers Association, headed by W. T. Jackman, who had driven cattle up the Chisholm Trail to Kansas in the 1870s and served for twenty years as sheriff of Hays County. Additional support came from the Trail Drivers Memorial Association, led by Bessie Terry Lesser. By October 1936 discussions with federal, state, and local

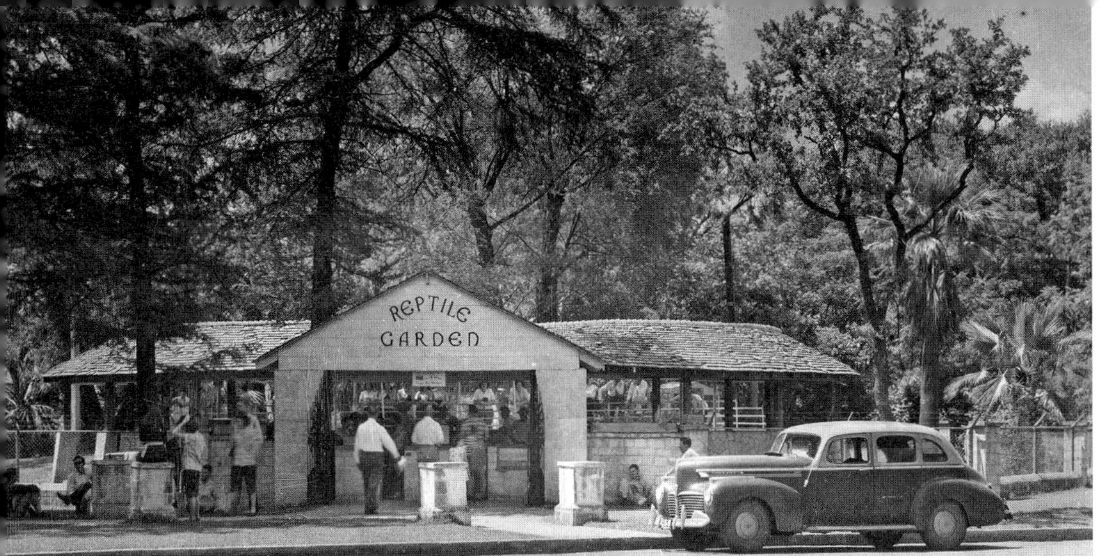

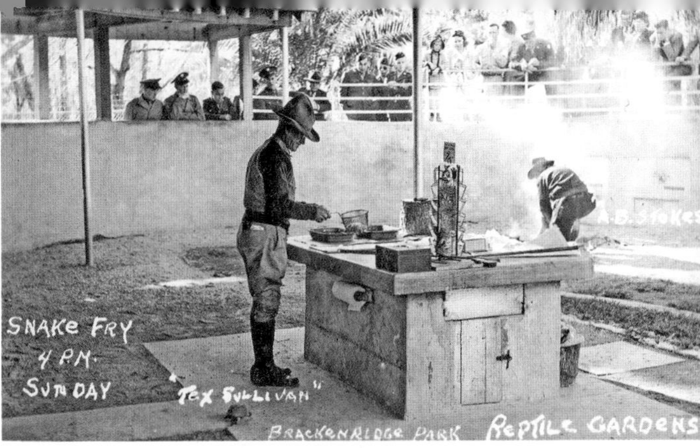

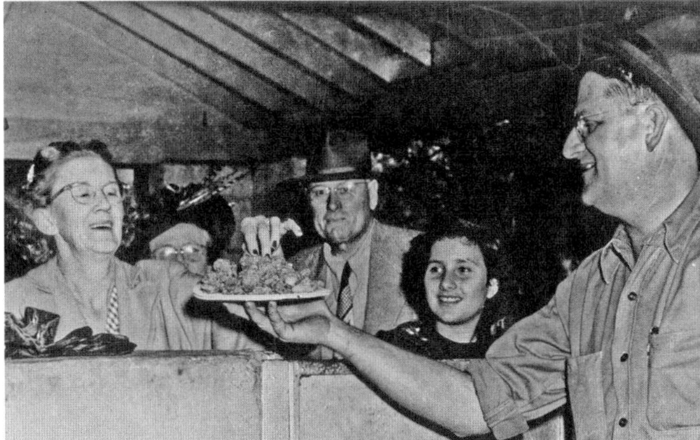

The Witte Museum's new Reptile Garden, built by the WPA in 1939, featured Sunday afternoon snake fries.

officials over who would manage and use the building tilted away from the Witte, and the museum withdrew from the project.[310]

The Texas Pioneers, Trail Drivers, and Rangers Memorial, as lettered in gold leaf above the entrance, opened on New Year's Day 1938 with an afternoon dedication and an evening ball. Along Broadway north of the Witte, the two-story cream-colored limestone structure, better known as Pioneer Hall, featured Renaissance classical detailing. An architectural guide terms it a "boldly scaled yet simple building" in the prewar style of many public structures. On the first floor were exhibit halls and on the second a large room for lectures and "old-time parties."[311]

Construction of Pioneer Hall directly over an access road disrupted the park's traditional main pedestrian entrance from Broadway, though the number of streetcar and bus passengers dropped off there had already declined as more people had automobiles and drove directly in. The NYA was on hand to create a direct northern automobile entrance by opening Tuleta Drive east from North St. Mary's Street at Koehler Park through to Broadway, passing just south of the Witte Museum. NYA workers built the surviving low stone perimeter wall with wrought iron letters to mark the new entry and created a landscaped parking area in front of the museum building. The four-arched honeycomb limestone rock bridge across the river behind the Witte, no longer needed by pedestrians, was taken down.

Another problem remained. Along the entrance path north of its building the Witte had put in a reptile garden, a popular snake pen shaded by a flat metal roof and now quite close to the new Pioneer Hall. The Trail Drivers Association didn't like it. In a letter to the editor of the *Light*, Bessie Terry Lesser compared the situation to one before encroachments were removed around the Alamo. She declared: "Today we are faced with another, even worse desecration, a rattlesnake pen in front of another shrine to Texas heroes." Texas pioneers hated rattlesnakes, she explained, "yet in front of their memorial the rattlesnake reigns supreme. . . . Why this desecration to our Texas heroes?"[312]

The Witte was not about to shut down the popular revenue producer, begun after a jobless snake lover, W. C. Bevan, appeared at the Witte in mid-1933 when the museum had $2.47 left in its maintenance fund for the next three months. Bevan suggested that the museum raise funds with a snake garden and agreed to set one up in exchange for quarters on the grounds, as others had done in compensation for their services. The Witte took him up on it. Bevan found himself

New Deal Projects in Brackenridge Park

1934
Texas Basketmaker Indians Mural in Witte Museum *CWA*

1935
Administration, hospital, and commissary buildings in zoo *WPA*

1935–36
Elephant, hippo, impala exhibit areas in zoo *WPA*

1935–37
Koehler Pavilion *WPA*
Peccary House in zoo *WPA*

1936–37
Perimeter wall at Witte Museum *WPA*
Additional bathhouses at Lambert Beach *WPA*

1936–39
African Panorama in zoo *WPA*

1937
Reptile Garden for Witte Museum* *WPA*
Sunken Garden Theater completion *WPA*

1937–38
San Antonio River retaining walls *NYA*
Letters of Gold Bridge retaining walls *NYA*
Sunken Garden Theater concession area *NYA*

1938–40
Picnic area south of Joske Pavilion *WPA*
Aviary in zoo *WPA*

1939
Low-water crossing bridge off River Road *NYA*
Tuleta Drive extension to Broadway *NYA*
Walls, fences, sea lion exhibit, drainage in zoo *WPA*
Dog-trot cabin replica at Witte Museum** *NYA*

1940
Starter House, Caddy House,* bridge, tee boxes,* drinking fountains* on golf course *NYA*
Drainage and culvert improvements at Witte Museum *NYA*

1941–43
Twohig House reconstruction at Witte Museum *WPA*

1942
Reptile House in zoo *WPA*

CWA–Civil Works Administration
NYA–National Youth Administration
WPA–Works Progress Administration (1935–39)
Work Projects Administration (1939–43)
* Not surviving ** Disassembled, moved to storage

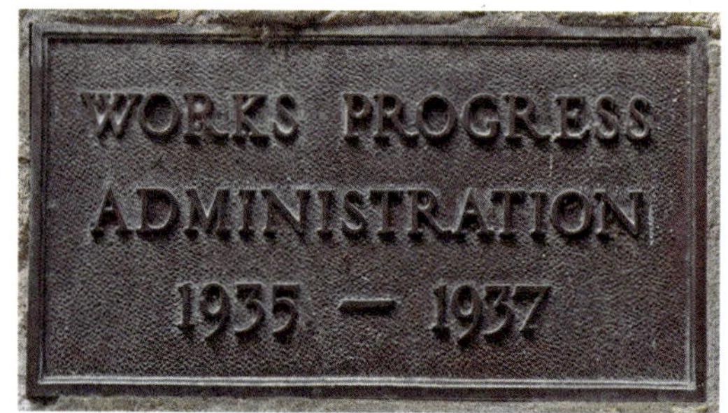

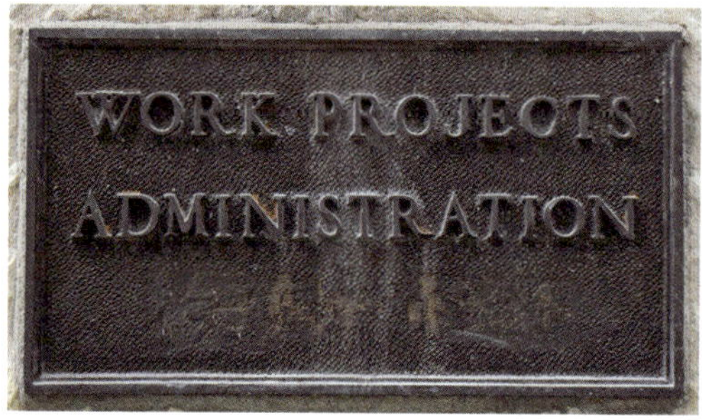

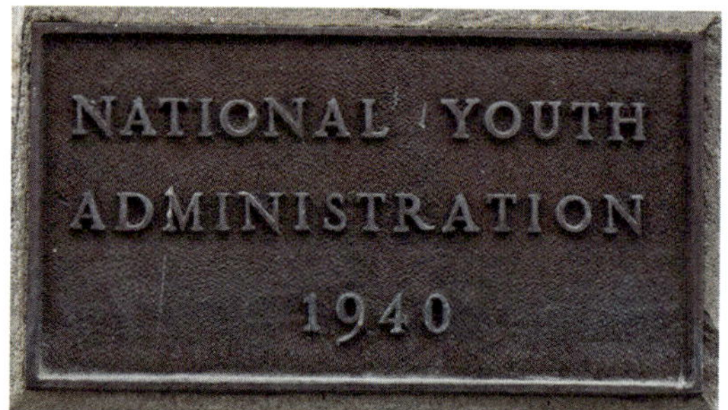

Plaques on Brackenridge Park projects.

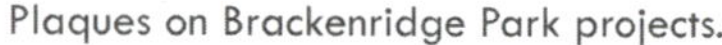

Sculptor Pompeo Coppini with his bust of Albert Steves, now displayed at the Witte Museum.

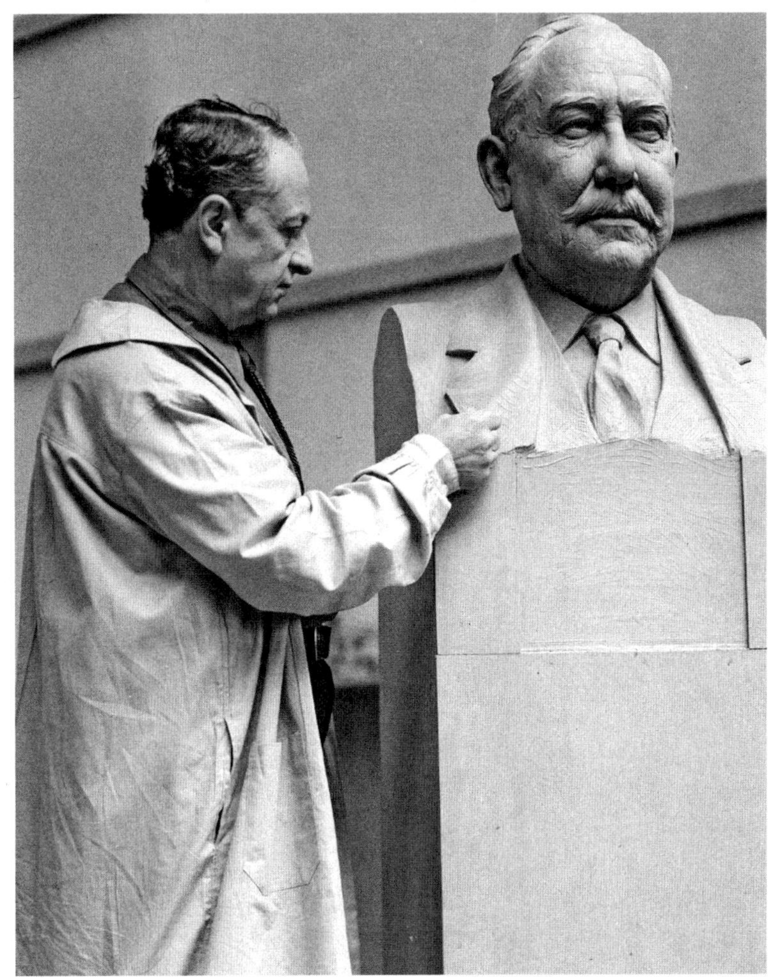

sleeping in a donated antique streetcar. When word got out that the Witte was paying as much as fifteen cents a pound for rattlesnakes, seven hundred pounds of snakes were brought from surrounding ranchlands. Crowds of viewers came to watch handlers show the snakes.[313]

New Deal crews were on hand to solve the rattlesnake desecration issue. In November 1939 the WPA finished a reptile garden some distance from the farther side of Pioneer Hall where the park's northern entrance pillars once stood. The new facility, a fifty-foot concrete and rock enclosure with a peaked roof, included cages and a small amphitheater for daily shows and Sunday afternoon snake fries. Most snakes were moved three years later to the zoo's WPA Reptile House, though snake fries continued until the Witte closed the Reptile Garden in 1950.[314]

A second Brackenridge Park beneficiary of Texas centennial funds was the Sunken Garden Theater, begun in 1930 on the site of the Texas Star Garden in a shallow quarry pit near the deeper pit that held the Japanese Tea Garden. After seven years the theater was still not completed, though performances were being held. Proponents landed a centennial grant of $59,457, with the requirement that the theater be a memorial to Texas heroes. At its entrance a concrete bas-relief sculpture of pioneers with a covered wagon bears the inscription "Memorial to the Heroes of the Texas Revolution."[315]

The spot was long known for its acoustical quality, confirmed when San Antonio's noted Italian-born sculptor Pompeo Coppini met Ray Lambert there in 1919. "We even went so far as testing the acoustics," Coppini recalled. "I sang, and Lambert stood at the far north end at the bottom of the cliff, telling me that it was splendid."[316]

Seven years later, in May 1926, came a more formal acoustical audition. A temporary stage was built at the site for a half-hour presentation by the Chaminade Choral Society, whose leader suggested the site for an amphitheater. The society was part of the Tuesday Musical Club, founded in 1901 by six women in the Euclid Street home of Anna Goodman (Mrs. Eli) Hertzberg, club president for its first thirty-six years.[317]

At the time, noted Coppini, "there was a mad race between two musical leaders in San Antonio," Hertzberg and English-born Mabel Clarke (Mrs. Lewis) Krams-Beck, life president of the San Antonio Musical Club. Krams-Beck, Coppini wrote, "was tremendously ambitious also to become a leader of society and to lay the foundation of something more enduring than just being leader of a club."[318]

The resolute Krams-Beck and her San Antonio Civic Opera Company took over advocacy of the site and got the Sunken Garden Theater done. Only three companies in the nation were staging outdoor operas at the time, reported the

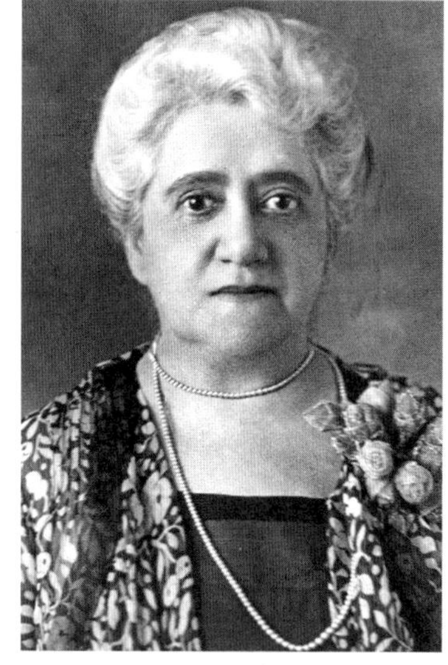

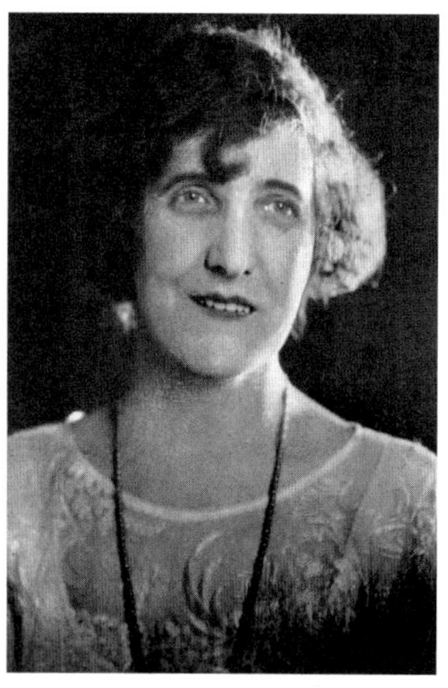

Anna Hertzberg, *left*, whose Tuesday Musical Club built its auditorium in the park, and Mabel Krams-Beck, *right*, whose San Antonio Civic Opera Company was instrumental in construction of the Sunken Garden Theater.

San Antonio Express. A stage thirty by forty feet was built of planks, with light bulbs strung across the front. Old billboards formed stage wings, funeral tents were loaned as dressing rooms, and on the evening of July 12, 1928, wooden folding chairs were set up for Gilbert and Sullivan's *Pirates of Penzance*, the first of six light operas performed through the next year.[319]

It was a good time to be doing light operas, as the 1920s ushered in a national wave of their popularity, which lasted through the 1950s. Grand opera, as performed in San Antonio by visiting companies at the Opera House or the new Municipal Auditorium, relied on "extraordinary human voices not likely to be found locally," noted Trinity University music historian Carl Leafstedt, while light operas "feature large casts of walk-on or minor roles that can be given to the local community." This allowed large numbers of residents a chance to play a role or two on stage before their peers.[320]

"All you need is a few good dramatic leads who can sort of sing well, but they have to be good actors," Leafstedt observed. "Good actors are in better supply in most cities—then and now—than good singers."[321]

Grounds of the makeshift theater worked so well for the Civic Opera Company that in 1930 the city agreed to replace the Texas Star Garden with the outdoor Sunken Garden Theater. Sculptor Gutzon Borglum submitted plans for a front stage width of more than a hundred feet, but they were rejected as impractical. Krams-Beck and parks commissioner Rubiola agreed instead on architect Harvey P. Smith's plans for a front stage width of sixty feet; widening either side of the stage would screen storerooms on one side and dressing rooms on the other. But the first phase would include only the stage.

The unfinished Sunken Garden Theater opened on June 24, 1930, to an audience of fifteen hundred with Gilbert and Sullivan's *Yeomen of the Guard*. Dedication ceremonies on July 15 featured the theater's official presentation to the city's citizens by Mayor C. M. Chambers and an address by Henry Kiel, who as mayor of Saint Louis in 1917 had established the nation's first municipally owned outdoor theater.[322]

As the Depression worsened, performances continued without a completed theater until 1937, when the Texas centennial funds arrived. Then $2,000 from the city triggered $6,000 more from the WPA. Harvey Smith was joined by architects George Willis and Charles Boelhauwe. With mechanical engineer Lloyd Royer they devised a stage curtain that rose as it unrolled from a cylinder fifteen feet beneath the floor.

Colonnades on either side of the stage were completed and WPA workers laid a sloping concrete floor for two thousand permanent seats and thirty boxes. Behind the last row of seats, a restroom building was topped by a projection room. Rededication ceremonies on July 8, 1937, featured Victor Herbert's comic operetta *Mlle. Modiste*.[323]

From 1936 to 1943 the Sunken Garden Theater was home to San Antonio's WPA-sponsored Tipica Orchestra for rehearsals, offices, music library, and instrument storage. Under direction of versatile Mexican-born musician Dan Silva, its thirty to forty members played familiar Latin American and Mexican music at the theater and at parks, churches, meeting halls, and civic events throughout the city. Also based there was the twenty-eight-member Federal Symphony Orchestra, which changed its name to the WPA Orchestra when the independent

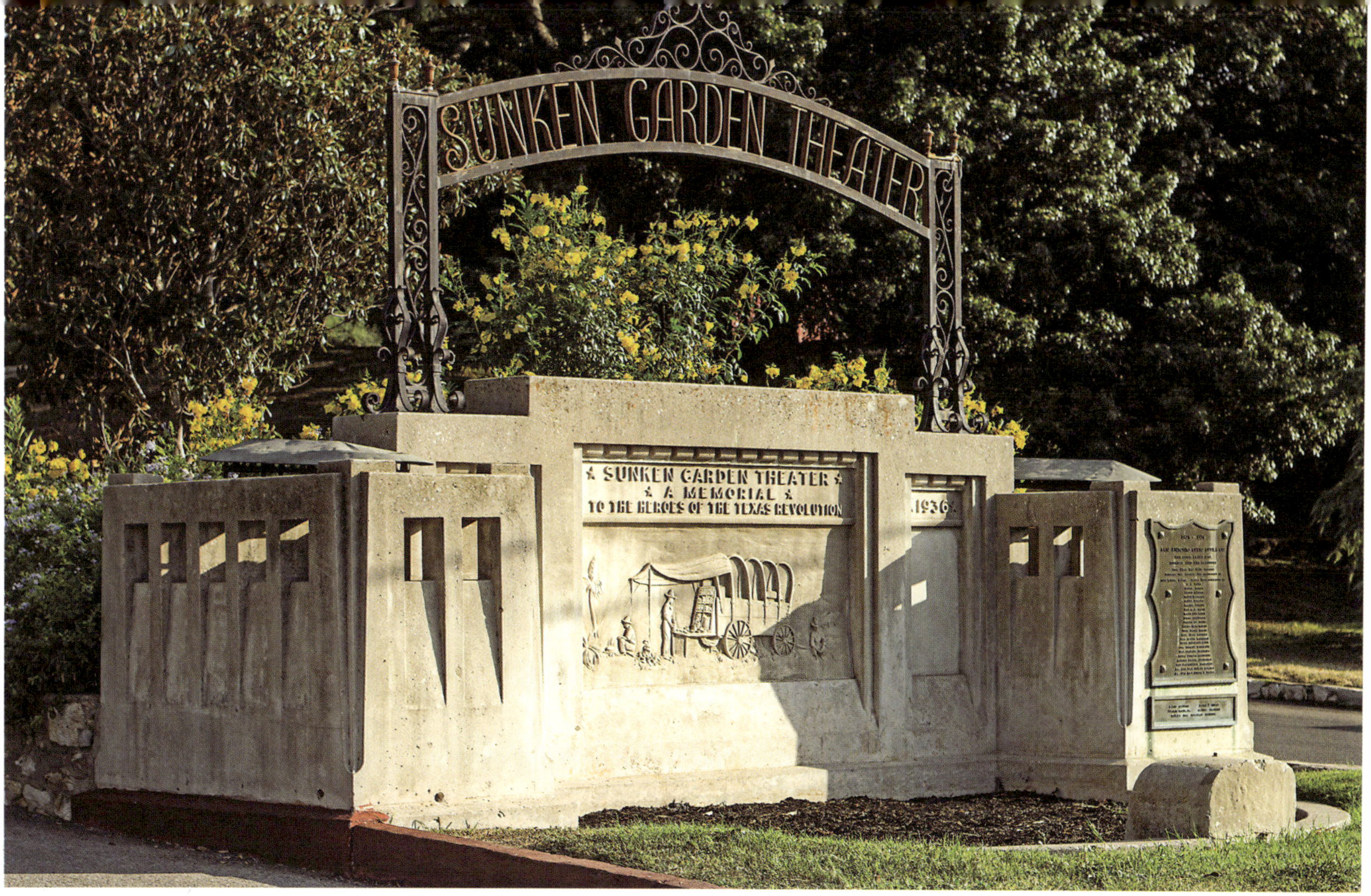

Sunken Garden Theater construction was aided by federal and state Texas Centennial funding as a memorial to heroes of the Texas Revolution.

San Antonio Symphony was formed in 1939. The symphony performed its first concert at the Sunken Garden Theater on June 2, 1939, before an audience of 2,500.[324]

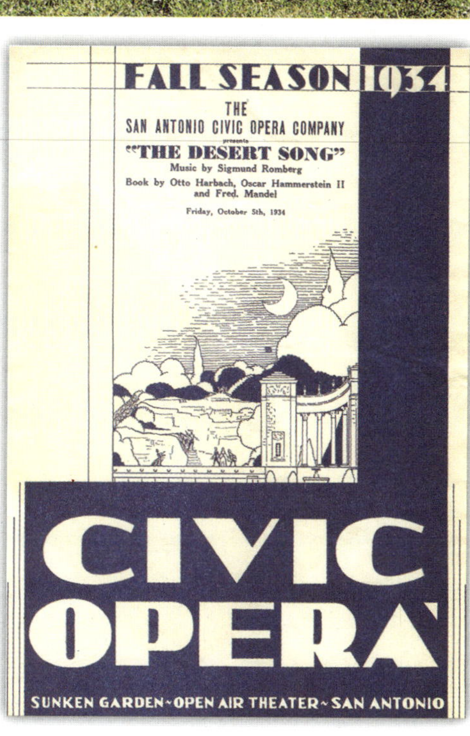

National popularity of civic opera drew crowds to the Sunken Garden Theater.

If there was indeed a "mad race" between music mavens Mabel Krams-Beck and Anna Hertzberg, it ended in a draw. Twenty years after a bronze plaque marked dedication of the Sunken Garden Theater to Krams-Beck, "Anna Hertzberg Music Memorial" was inscribed across the front of a new building less than two hundred yards away.

By the 1940s the Tuesday Musical Club needed a replacement for its Anna Hertzberg Hall of Music, a converted house next door to its late founder's home on Euclid Street. Mayor

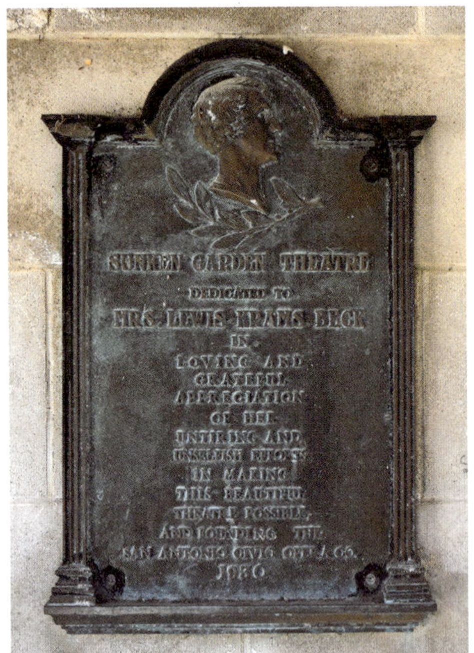

The theater is dedicated to Mabel (Mrs. Lewis) Krams-Beck, whose profile appears on a bronze plaque.

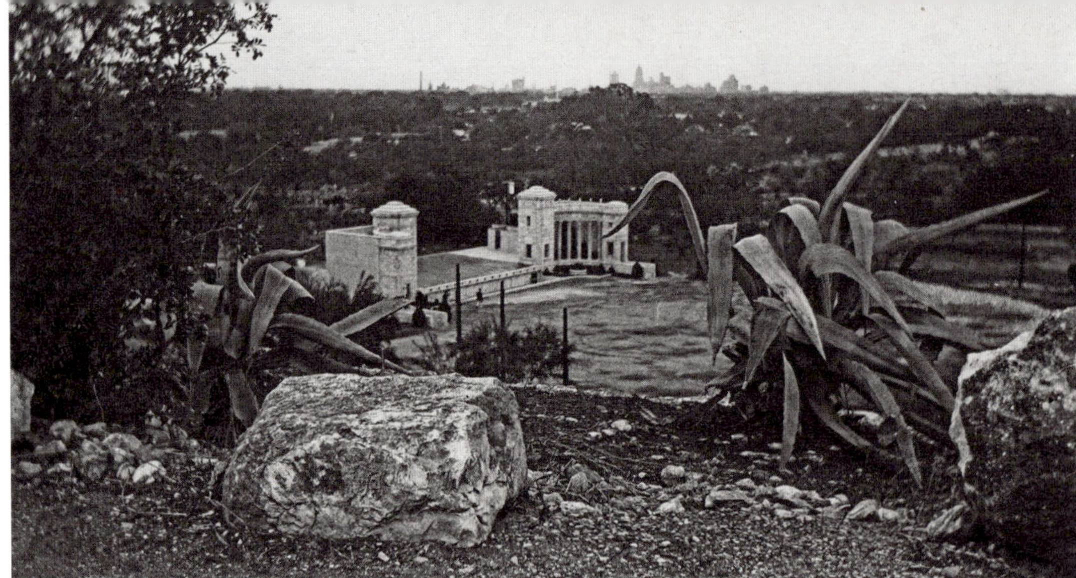

The San Antonio skyline rises above the cliffs surrounding the Sunken Garden Theater.

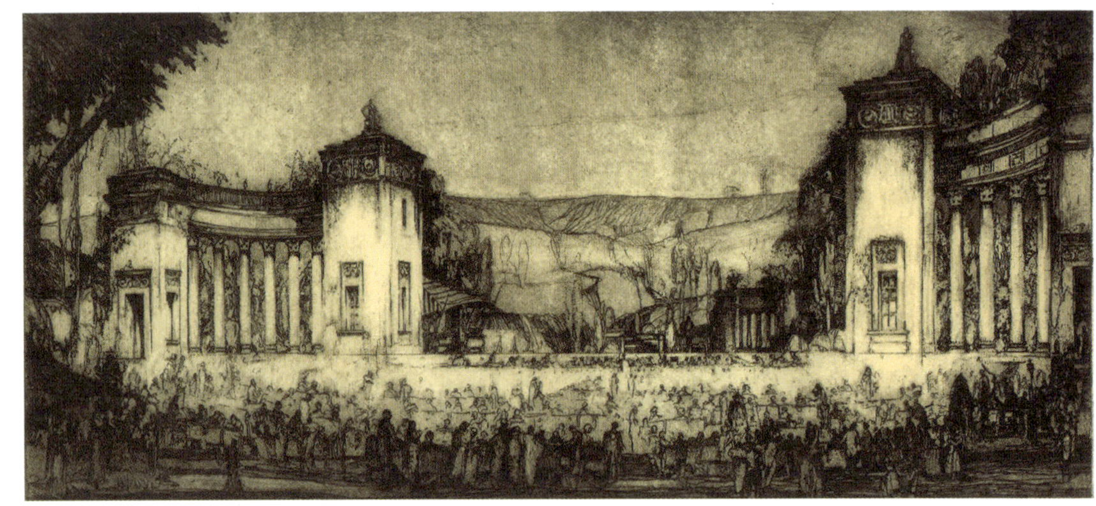

The majesty of the classical theater stage is captured in this etching by John A. Griffith.

Gus Mauermann suggested some unused city property near the entrance to the Sunken Garden Theater. While that was within what was commonly considered Brackenridge Park, Mauermann felt he could offer the site since it was free of the use restrictions on nearby tracts donated by George Brackenridge and Emma Koehler.[325]

The Tuesday Musical Club hired architects Atlee B. and Robert M. Ayres to design a one-story modified classical-style white building with a curved entry portico. Its auditorium could seat three hundred for the club's half dozen annual performances. Parks commissioner Henry Hein donated landscaping. The dedication on March 19, 1950, featured "three beautiful selections" sung by the club's choir.[326]

Coppini and his protégé Waldine Tauch were commissioned in 1951 to do a sculpture in memory of Hertzberg to go on a pink granite base in front of the new building, the name across its front changed from Anna Hertzberg Music Hall to Tuesday Musical Club. The bronze, Genius of Music, was of a young boy representing Pan playing a fife, an instrument on which children traditionally developed their musical ability. Coppini changed his design from the usual portrayal of the mythological Pan playing pipes in the wilds partly because, he wrote, "the sounds of Pan's pipes were so horrible that the word 'panic' came from it."[327]

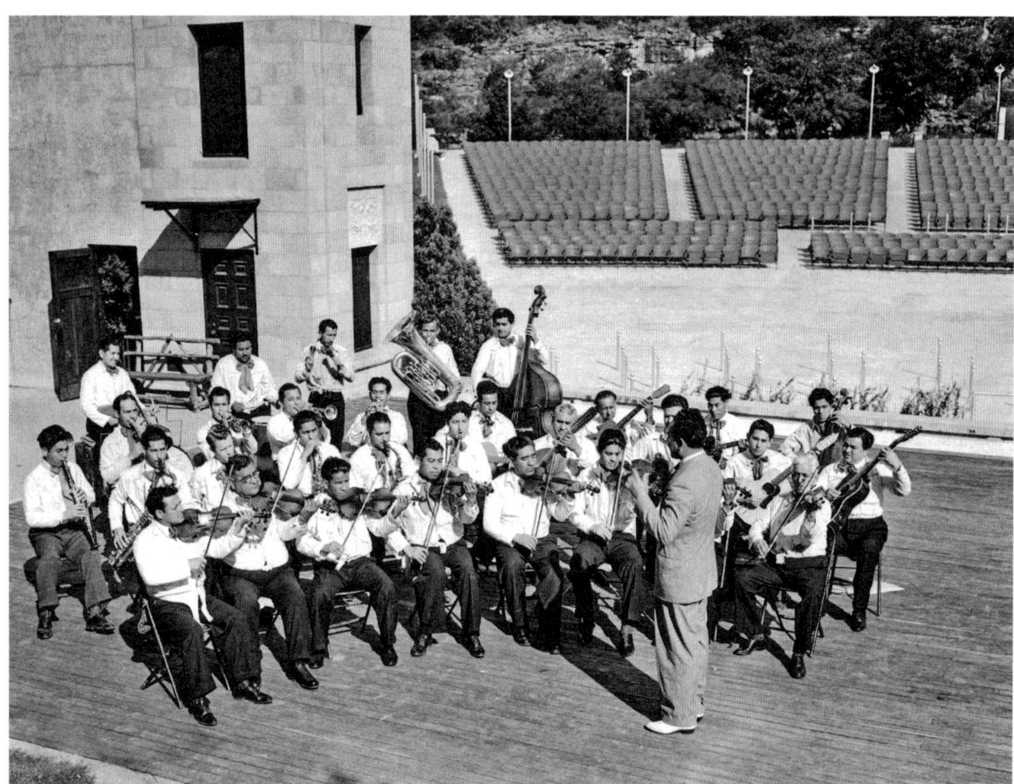

Dan Silva directs a Tipica Orchestra rehearsal on the Sunken Garden Theater stage.

The Tuesday Musical Club opened its new building in 1951 as the Anna Hertzberg Music Memorial.

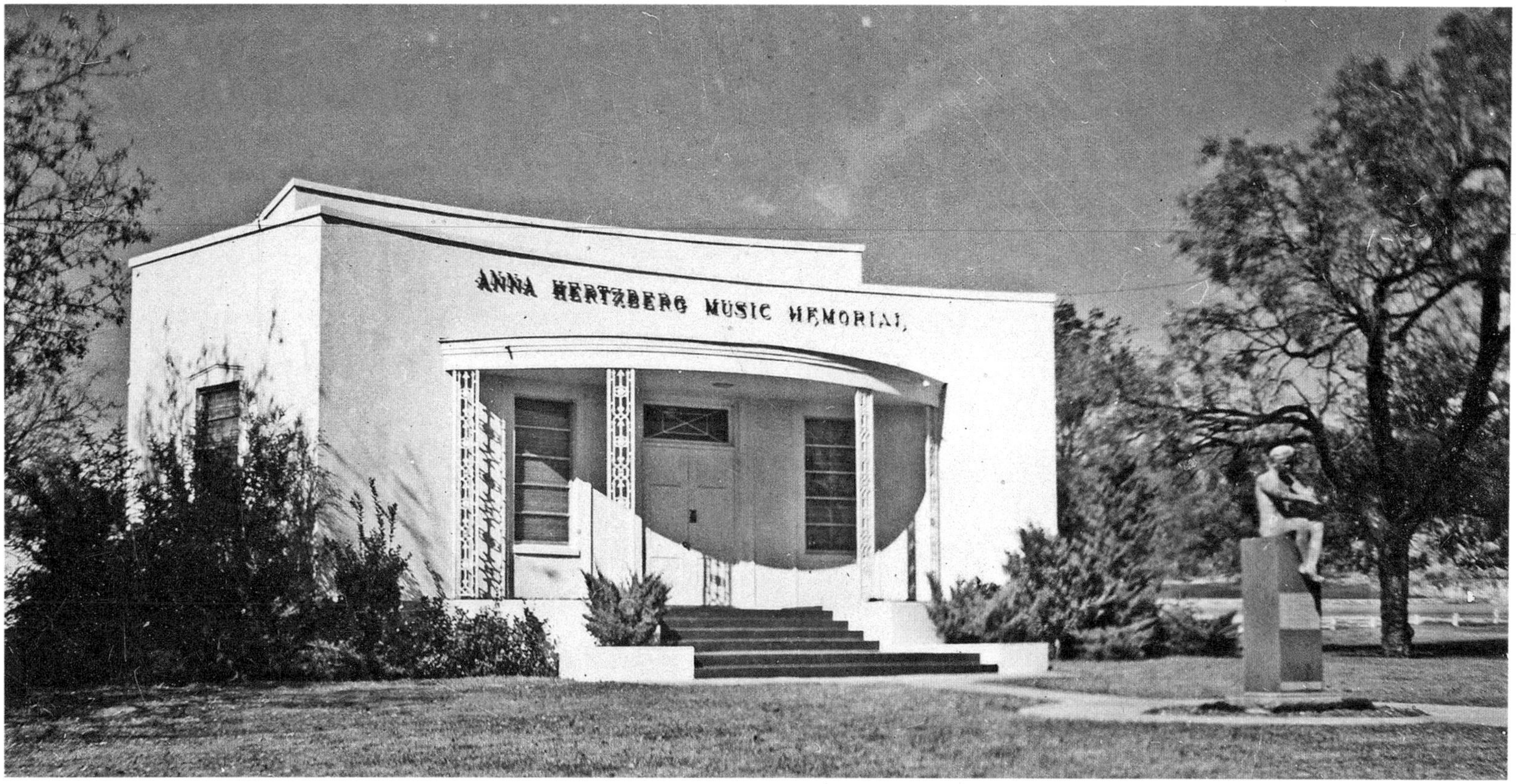

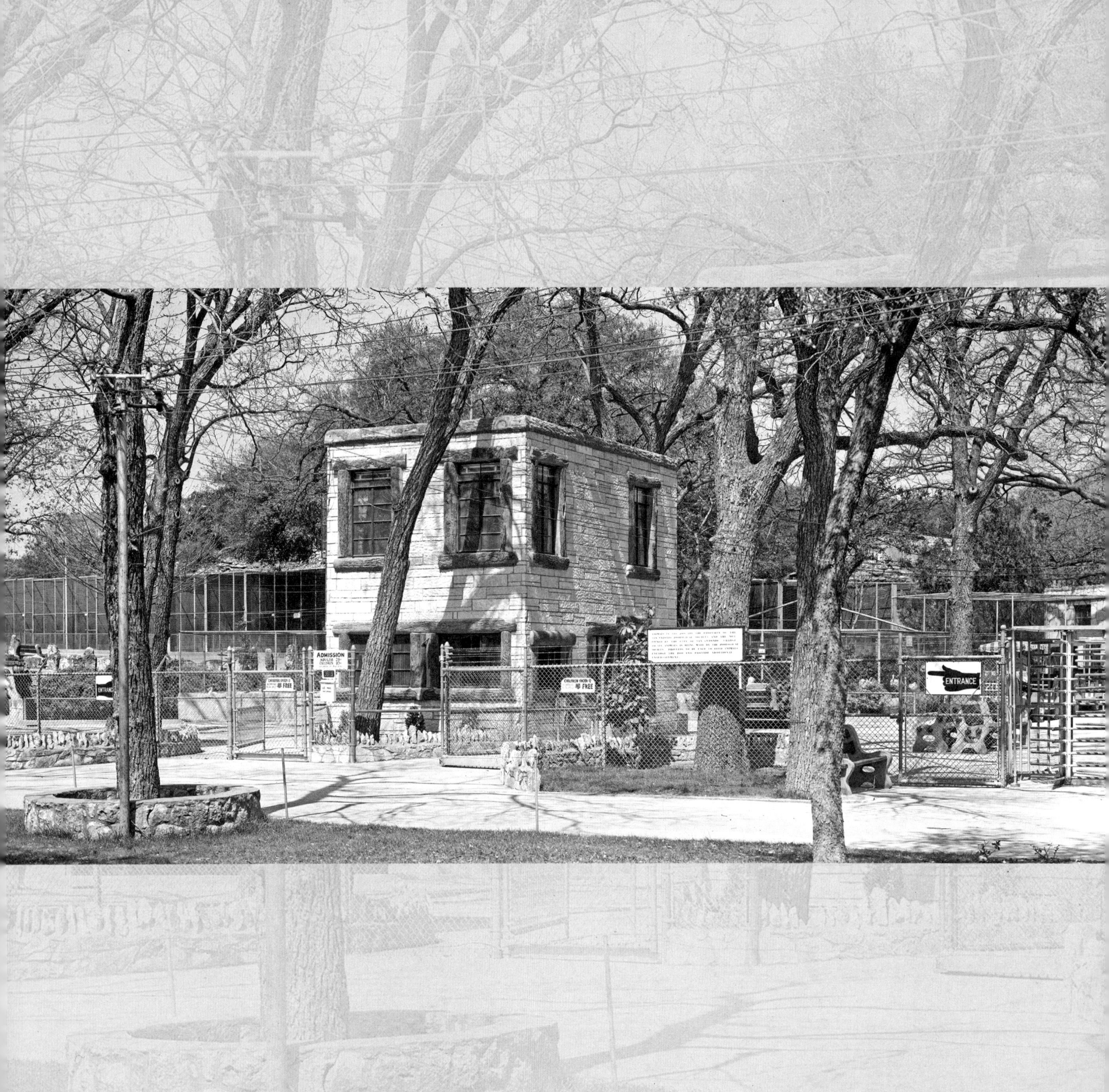

Admission
FREE
ENTRANCE

Adrift

It seemed in the 1940s that Brackenridge Park was drifting down some sort of rabbit hole to a place where things were upside down, backward, and sideways.

Impressive though federally funded New Deal improvements were, years of municipal budget cutbacks had taken their toll on the park. Prisoners were sent in twice a week to help cut weeds and remove trash, but that didn't help much.[328]

The *San Antonio Express* in 1946 thought the zoo was shipshape but called the river through the park a "sluggish stream clogged with scum, algae, and lily pads," as well as being "a secondary garbage dump" for picnickers' papers, bottles, and boxes. A park bench was half submerged, playground equipment had disappeared, and restrooms were "so dark, dismal, and unsanitary" that they should be closed. It was all due, the paper said, to "lack of sufficient care spread over a long period of time."[329]

Six years earlier the situation had already blown a fuse at the *San Antonio Light*. When "a haze of smoke and smell" began wafting over the park from a reactivated city incinerator to the west, the *Light* headlined a full-page exposé "Brackenridge Park Neglected." Nine photos revealed "clouds of smoke laden with [the] stench of garbage." Others pictured untended goats grazing at the polo grounds, rock piles blocking bridle paths, golfers having to search through a maze of sunflowers for lost balls, and a "neglected" Alpine Drive studded with weeds and grass. Text declared that the disheveled park had reverted to "its raw, primitive state," and ended: "We give you Brackenridge Park. You can have it."[330]

Nearly three months later the city stopped using the offending incinerator, but new problems kept surfacing.[331]

A territorial issue erupted between Koehler Park and the zoo. Ethnic prejudice convulsed the Japanese Tea Garden. Five parks directors spun through the job in five years as political upheaval rocked city hall. An expressway carved chunks from Brackenridge Park's perimeter. San Antonio's park spending per capita ranked sixty-sixth in the nation. Then there was the occasional oddity like the performance on horseback by the Royal Oak Mounted Square Dance Team. When the park's miniature train was stopped at gunpoint things really did seem to have gone over the edge. It was the first train robbery in the United States since 1923.

The zoo, fenced at last in 1940, got this new entrance building a decade later.

Emma Koehler, shown with a bottle of beer at her Pearl Brewery the day Prohibition ended.

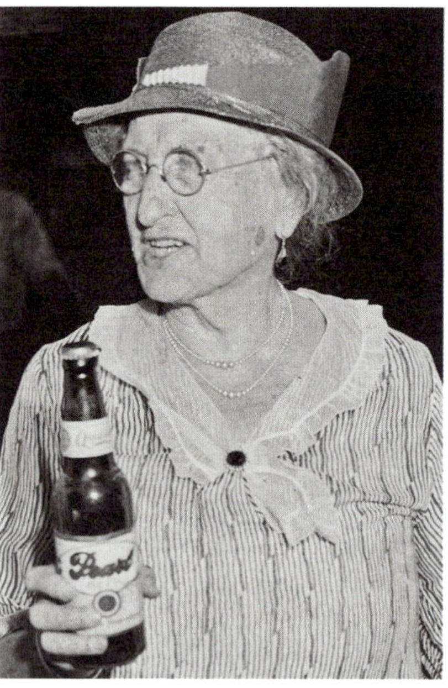

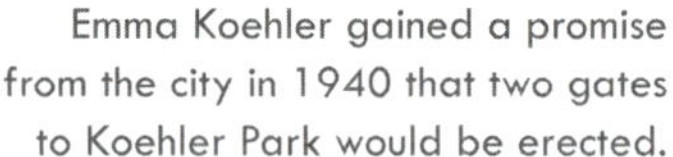

Emma Koehler gained a promise from the city in 1940 that two gates to Koehler Park would be erected.

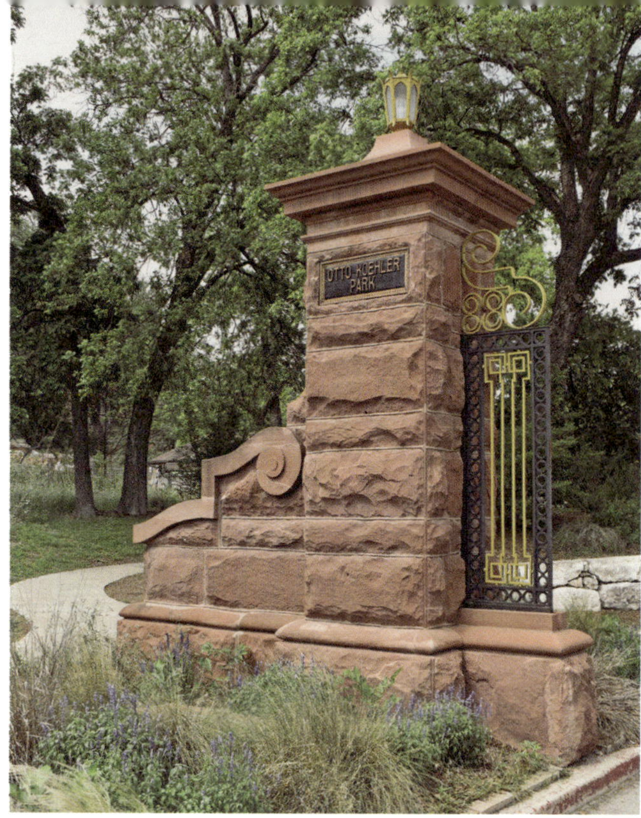

The unfenced zoo faced security issues. "Vandals and the unthinking have cost the city and the zoo society heavily," the *Express* reported in mid-1940. As miscreants roamed through, "many animals have been killed or freed in the keeper's absence." Parks commissioner Henry Hein discovered that feeding zoo animals was costing the city $45,000 a year, today's equivalent of $820,000. He believed that was too much of a burden for taxpayers and should be shared by zoo visitors, whom he thought should start paying admission.[332]

The zoo had opened in 1916 on part of the city's land grant from the King of Spain. The zoo built an aviary on adjacent property donated by Emma Koehler and overseen by the city as an extension of Brackenridge Park. By 1940 the zoo, operated by the private San Antonio Zoological Society, had spread onto half of Koehler Park's fourteen acres. That didn't bother the park's donor until the zoo wanted to charge admission to what she had given twenty-five years before as a free-entry park.[333]

Stirring up the formidable Emma Koehler, eighty-two, was not a good idea. City council ended up having to pass an eight-page ordinance to placate her. The ordinance authorized a contract in which Koehler agreed to let the zoo use most of the part it had appropriated with the stipulation that it be known as "the Zoological Area" of Koehler Park. The Zoological Area could be separated from the rest of the park with a wire fence, but otherwise it would "to all appearances be as though it were a portion or extension of Otto Koehler Park." The zoo was also required to move cages and facilities that were spilling into the park beyond the new Zoological Area.[334]

But Emma Koehler was not done. Koehler Park was on the western bank of the winding San Antonio River, Brackenridge Park on the eastern side. No other visible boundary identified Koehler Park. Koehler gave the city six months after the Zoological Area was fenced off to complete, at no expense to her, two pairs of entry columns at the northern and southern entrances to Koehler Park. Each set of columns would be at least ten feet tall and bear bronze plates with, in part, "Otto Koehler Park" in "letters large enough to be visible and readable by persons entering said park." Koehler also required the city to build and maintain a street sixteen feet wide between the two gates.[335]

The street was completed, but only the southern entry columns were built. Those red sandstone pillars with ironwork and lamps remain a distinctive landmark, but they have little context, leaving visitors wondering even today what they are

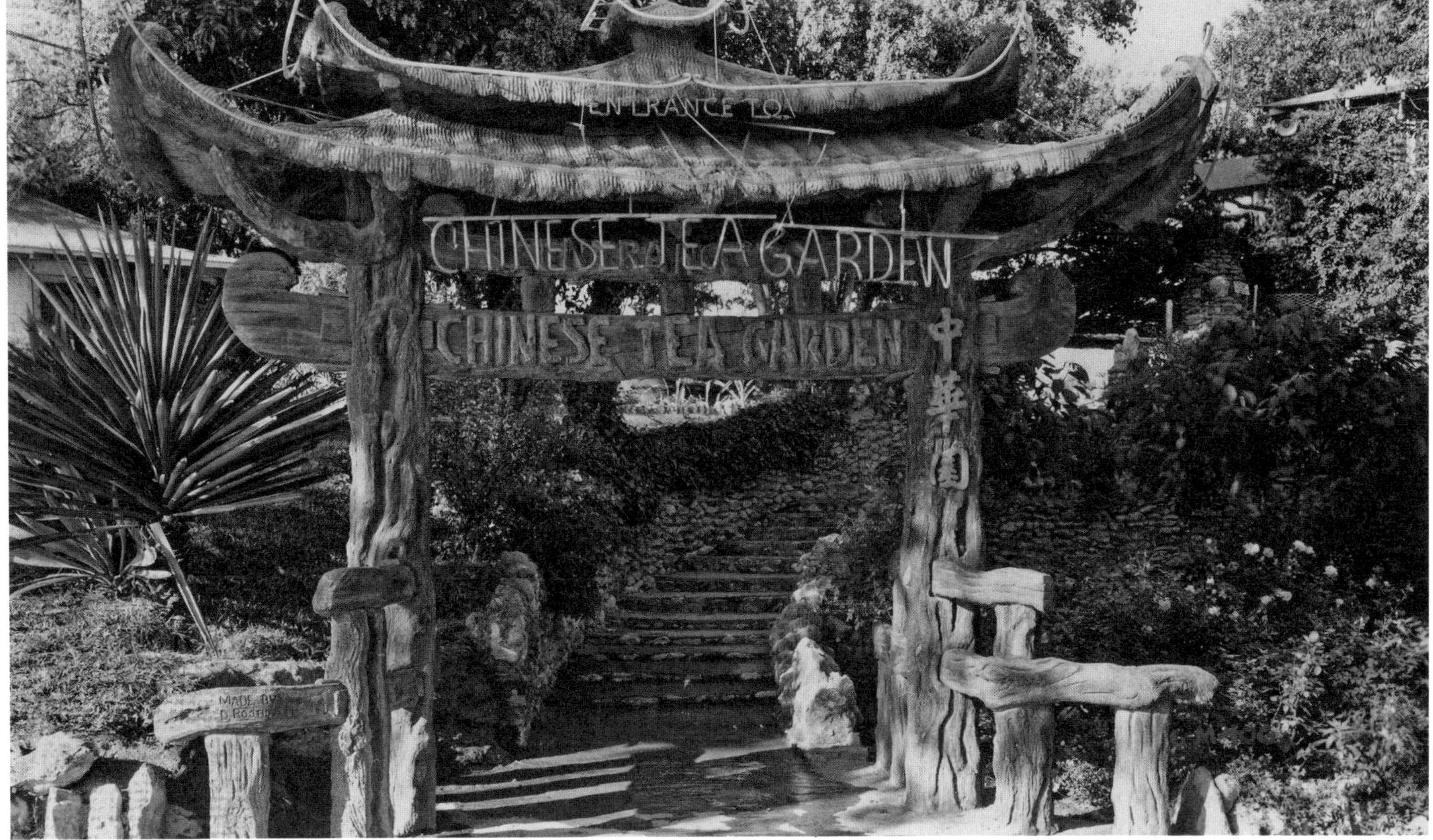

Neon lettering was added to this *faux bois* gateway built for the Japanese Tea Garden in 1942, when wartime sentiment caused it to be renamed the Chinese Tea Garden.

entering or exiting and confused about whatever happened to the Brackenridge Park they thought they were in.[336]

As terms of the agreement with Koehler were being dealt with, in early July 1940 the zoo put up a perimeter chain link fence topped by barbed wire with an entrance at the southeast corner. Tickets were priced at twenty-five cents for adults and ten cents for children. Complaints caused adult tickets to be cut by ten cents, and the next Sunday's attendance of 1,971 set a day's record. Ticket sales were boosted by adding displays of animals and birds, and the number of animal performances was increased. For the previous year donkey rides along the traditional trails near Lambert Beach had cost five cents. Now the rides were moved inside the zoo and their fees covered by zoo tickets.[337]

More unsettling than effects of the zoo's creep into Koehler Park was that the longtime fascination with all things Japanese would be abruptly replaced with virulent prejudice against anything Japanese. Families identified even with tranquil Japanese tea gardens in park settings were suddenly targets.

In 1939 the city renewed Miyoshi Jingu's contract to operate the Japanese Tea Garden. Parks commissioner Hein announced plans to improve that facility, including adding bamboo furniture from the Japanese tea garden at San Francisco's Golden Gate International Exposition on Treasure Island once the event closed the next year. But attitudes changed with the bombing of Pearl Harbor in December 1941.[338]

After the United States declared war against Japan, Japanese tea gardens throughout the country were closed and some homes of resident Japanese-born operators were vandalized, torn down, or burned. At parks in San Francisco, San Diego, and Chicago tea garden proprietors and their families were shipped off to internment camps for the duration of the war.[339]

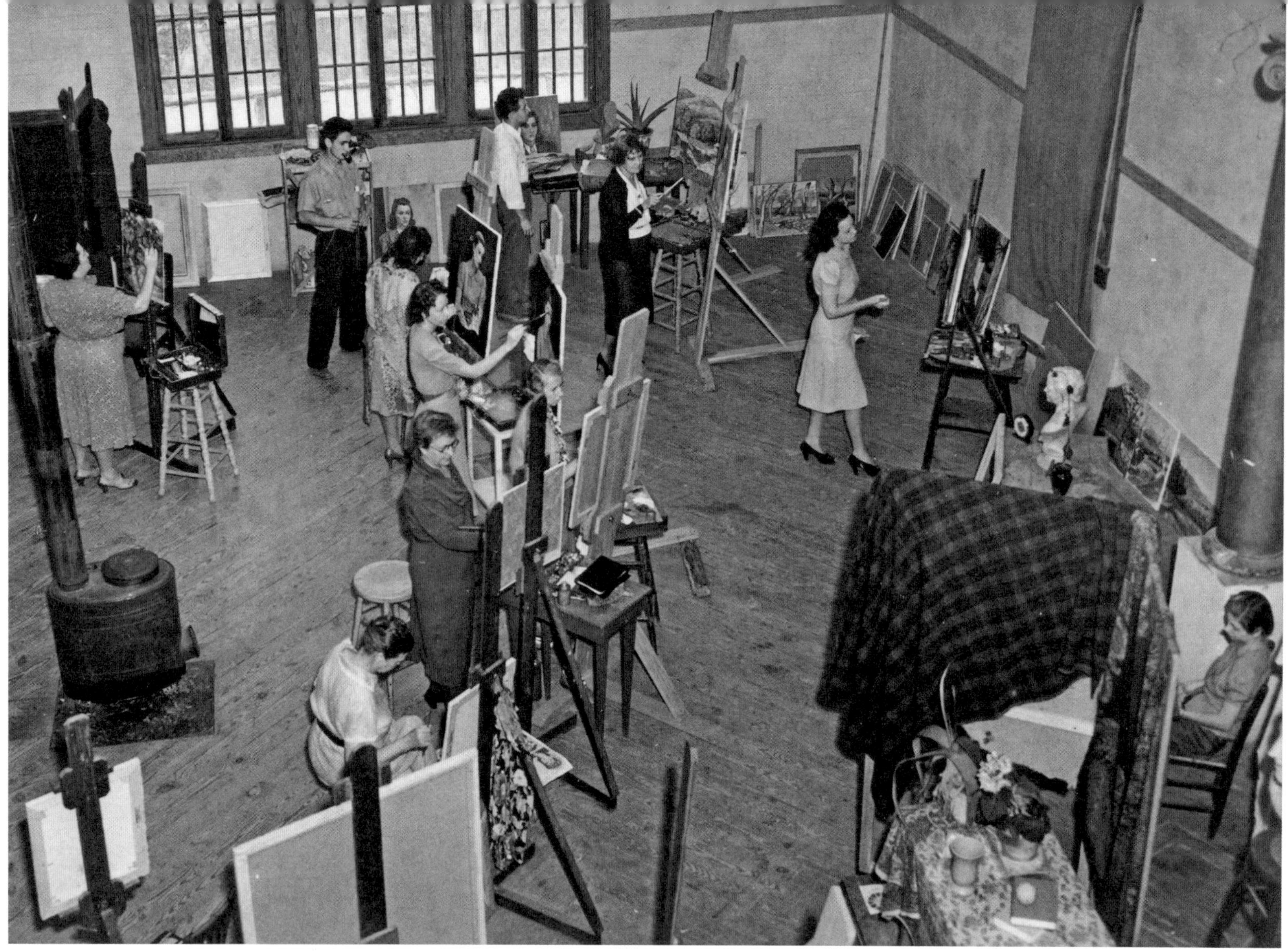

The Borglum Studio was rented by painter Henry Lee McFee, shown standing with his pipe as he taught a San Antonio Art League class there in 1940.

In San Antonio, soon after Pearl Harbor Mayor C. K. Quin ordered police to pick up and interrogate all San Antonians of Japanese descent. In July 1942 the city council voted to evict the widowed Miyoshi Jingu and her children from the city-owned home next to the tea garden she and her late husband had opened in Brackenridge Park twenty-five years before. Jingu protested that she and the five children still living with her had no other means of support and nowhere else to live. When the city cut off their water and electricity, she got the message.[340]

Located far from the large concentrations of Japanese Americans elsewhere, perceived as highly dangerous, the Jingus at least avoided confinement in an internment camp. With assistance from members of Travis Park Methodist Church, which had helped bring them to America and which the family attended, Jingu found a home, though family heirlooms and furnishings were confiscated and never returned. Two daughters got jobs as clerks in a flower shop, a third as a gift wrapper at Joske's department store. Both sons enlisted in the army. James received a Purple Heart in Europe with the 442nd

Richard Howard Hunt, one of the most important Black sculptors of the twentieth century, stands with his sculpture *Fragmented Head*, completed when he rented the Borglum Studio in 1959.

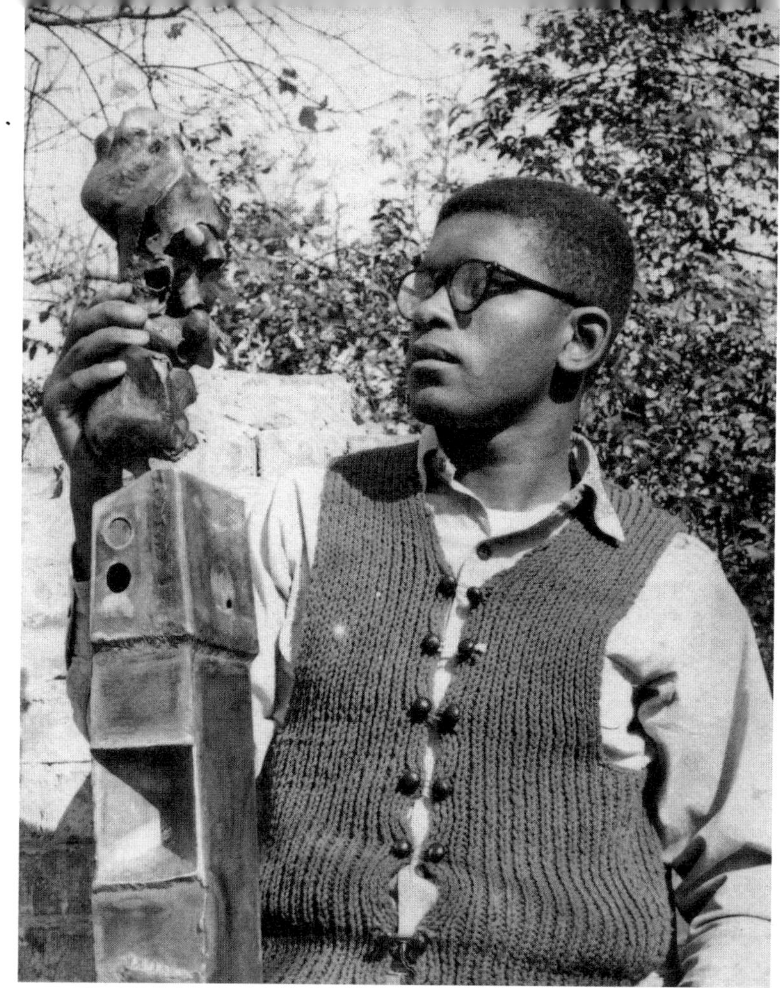

Regiment's combat team, composed primarily of Japanese American soldiers. In the 1950s the Jingus moved to California. There Miyoshi Jingu, at age sixty-five, became an actress. Her first film role was a bit part in *The Teahouse of the August Moon*.[341]

Since China was an American ally against Japan, city council decreed that the Japanese Sunken Garden be renamed the Chinese Sunken Garden and that its tea garden, also renamed Chinese, be run by those with family origins in China. Chinese Americans Ted and Rose Wu, who lived a few blocks away and operated a Chinese grocery on South Alamo Street, were selected to run it. San Antonio's Asian community was small, and there was no animosity between the Jingus and the Wus. "They were friends," daughter Mabel Jingu Enkoji, the Joske's gift wrapper, recalled when she was eighty-six. "The Wus more or less apologized to my mother because it wasn't their idea."[342]

A monumental Chinese-style *faux bois* entry gate replaced the simple Japanese wooden torii Kimi Jingu had erected. Done by sculptor Dionicio Rodríguez in collaboration with associate Maximo Cortés, it was completed within months of the Jingus' eviction and is considered a *faux bois* masterpiece. Four tree trunks supported lintels and a thatched roof with four upturned corners and two successively smaller palapa roofs above. Chinese calligraphy on a righthand post and on the largest lintel translate as "China Garden." The city made certain this was no longer taken for a Japanese tea garden even at night, installing neon lighting reading "Chinese Tea Garden" atop the gate's own lettering. In 2004 the gate was listed on the National Register of Historic Places.[343]

Wartime developments elsewhere in Brackenridge Park were more benign. An influx of soldiers enjoyed the park, a few coming to study art in Brackenridge Park's lower pump house, which Gutzon Borglum had rented as a studio for eleven years. After him American cubist painter Henry Lee McFee rented the studio with seascape painter Boyer Gonzales. In 1939 McFee was hired by the San Antonio Art League to begin the Museum School of Art there. Though McFee left for Los Angeles the next year, painting classes continued. When they were about to end in 1942 the school was rescued by Marion Koogler McNay and moved to the aviary of her home three miles north. As the San Antonio Art Institute it grew as a companion to what became the McNay Art Museum.[344]

The former pump house was reopened by Alice Naylor as the Mill Race Art Studio in 1943 to teach art to servicemen and women stationed at local military installations. By war's end 150 military personnel, calling themselves the Mill Race Artists, had studied there.[345]

Most notable of the postwar artist lessees was Richard Howard Hunt, who rented the pump house from early 1959 through mid-1960 while serving as an army illustrator at Fort Sam Houston. Hunt, age twenty-four, had studied at the School of the Art Institute of Chicago and was an accomplished sculptor.

While in the park studio he created the metal sculpture *Fragmented Head*, now at the Smithsonian Institution's Hirshhorn Museum and Sculpture Garden.[346]

Hunt happened to be among the first Blacks served, peacefully, at the Woolworth's lunch counter on Alamo Plaza on March 16, 1960, the day seven San Antonio lunch counters began serving people of color. Eight years later he was the first Black visual artist named to the National Council on the Arts. He went on to become one of the nation's most prolific public sculptors, with more than 160 commissions plus works in collections of more than a hundred museums.[347]

Farther north in the park, on the grounds of the Witte Museum, Harding Black turned the restored Ruiz House into a studio he named the Pottery Shop, built a kiln behind it in 1945, and became part of the American studio ceramics movement while teaching classes to adults and children. "Each Saturday we did a different animal," remembers Mary McMillan Fisher, then eight. "Once we made a poodle, pushing clay through screen wire for the pom-poms." Noted particularly for his stoneware and porcelain glazes, Black moved to his own studio farther north on Broadway some two decades later.[348]

Mill Race Art Studio director Alice Naylor, who later chaired the art department of Incarnate Word College, became a leader of artists who called themselves the Lime Kiln Colony or the Sunken Garden Art Colony. For a decade after World War II the city rented them the cluster of four stone houses beside the old cement kiln earlier known as the Mexican Village. Alice Naylor's two-room casita had "rough rock walls and peep-size windows," a fireplace, and a much-patched tin roof that looked leaky but wasn't. By 1949 nine artists were working there and dozens more came by to talk shop. Some formed the River Art Group and began the annual River Art Show, a pioneering event along the then mostly deserted River Walk. Others organized the Texas Watercolor Society.[349]

By the end of World War I, Brackenridge Park's dominance of San Antonio city parks was diminishing. From 1930 to 1950, the city's population rose by more than 75 percent, from 231,000 to 408,000. Brackenridge may still have been San Antonio's flagship park, but there were now more than two thousand acres of city parks, and Brackenridge's area had dropped from half of city parkland to barely 15 percent. With administrative oversight spread thin, no overall plan to guide development, and no specific advocate of its own, Brackenridge Park was heading into uncertain times.

Being in a city with a low tax base and prevailing aversion to higher taxes made it increasingly difficult to manage growing needs for municipal services. Parks commissioner Jacob Rubiola and his successor, Henry Hein, could not keep their budgets on par with those of other departments. That did not sit well with Stewart King, designated by Hein as superintendent of parks. In 1950 King, who began as city forester, calculated that in the previous twenty years the city budgets for garbage pickup, street cleaning, cemeteries, and sewage disposal had more than doubled. The parks budget, however, had fallen by a sum that amounted to a drop of 31 percent. Moreover, labor costs had doubled, leading to thirty-eight fewer parks jobs.[350]

Also distressing, King noted, was that fact that an average $1.70 per capita was being spent on parks and recreation by sixty-eight major American cities in 1950. San Antonio ranked sixty-sixth, spending a paltry 61 cents. Houston spent $1.08 per capita, Fort Worth $1.58, Austin $1.97, and Dallas $2.30. King left city employment to become a landscape architect with architect O'Neil Ford and planner Sam Zisman.[351]

King's successor in 1951, Hugo Traupmann, thought King "did the best he could with what he had to work with" but added that city parks in general "have been on the downgrade" since his arrival in 1930. In his first year Traupmann's citywide projects included, in Brackenridge Park, new plantings and clearing

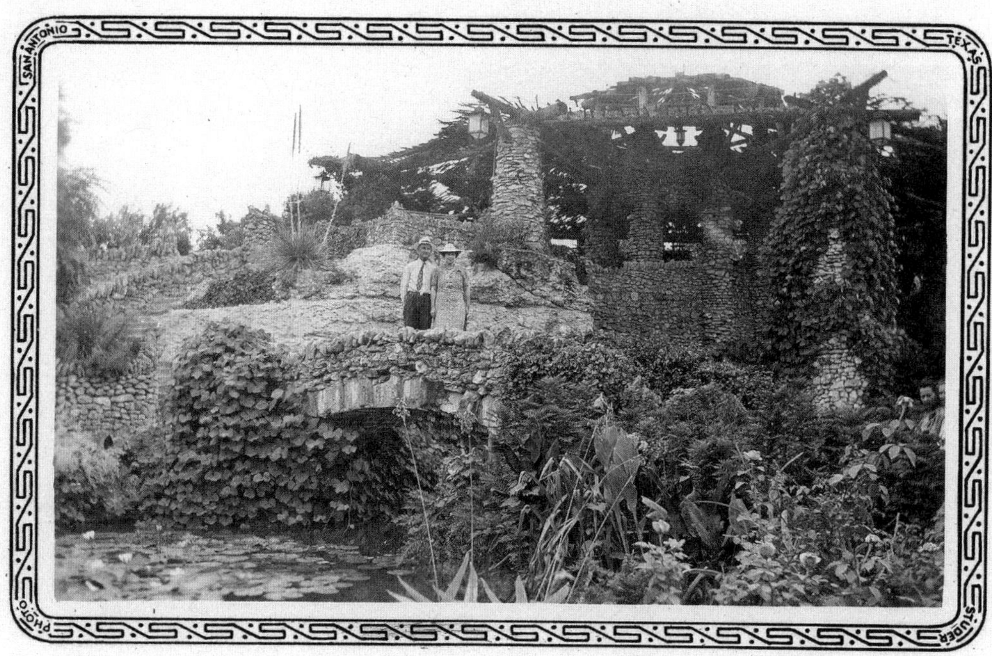

Tourists continued to visit the Japanese Tea Garden in the 1940s even though the lily pond was overgrown and the pavilion was in desperate need of a new thatched roof.

underbrush along the river for fifty new concrete picnic tables, benches, and brick barbecue units. Most paved park streets were widened, with paved parking spaces added; the number at the Joske Pavilion more than doubled.[352]

But the outlook for Brackenridge and other parks was about to worsen. Pressure to abolish the commission form of government and have all operations under a city manager led to a new city charter in 1952. The mayor and councilmen had less authority and were no longer in charge of anything in particular, like parks. The new city manager hired six hundred employees during the next year, trying to build "a respectable city operation."[353]

Still remaining was the challenge, noted historian David Johnson, of "how to create a political system that could replace professional politicians with well-organized amateurs who could consistently win elections—and successfully run a government." Near chaos at city hall led to changing city managers and, in the parks department, five different directors from 1951 to 1955.[354]

Until the city government could get itself under control, irate conservationists and news writers had to be the front line of defense against those who would encroach on city parks, their open spaces an easy target for parking lots and office buildings. Developers' schemes—most ultimately unsuccessful—spread from downtown plazas and parks up Broadway to Mahncke Park, where in 1958 the City Water Board had to be dissuaded from building a headquarters facing Broadway in Mahncke Park or, at the park's upper end, facing North New Braunfels Avenue. Four years later came the short-lived proposal to raise nearly $2 million for the city treasury by selling Brackenridge Park's Lions Field for retail development.[355]

Crowds still flocked to Brackenridge Park, oblivious of its underlying issues and ready to enjoy diversions added by a range of entrepreneurs, some of whom avoided the inconvenience of city franchises by operating outside the park. Starting in the mid-1930s, riders could take bridle paths through the park by renting horses from the Blue and White Stables or the Brackenridge Stables and Riding Academy, both off Mulberry Avenue just outside the park's western boundary.

Jim Hasslocher bought fifty army surplus bicycles in 1947 and began renting them from a lot by his mother's home on Broadway near the Tuleta Street entrance. He also offered cold watermelon slices. The next year he opened his first Frontier Drive-In nearby to sell charcoal-grilled hamburgers. Within fifteen years Hasslocher had a growing restaurant chain and

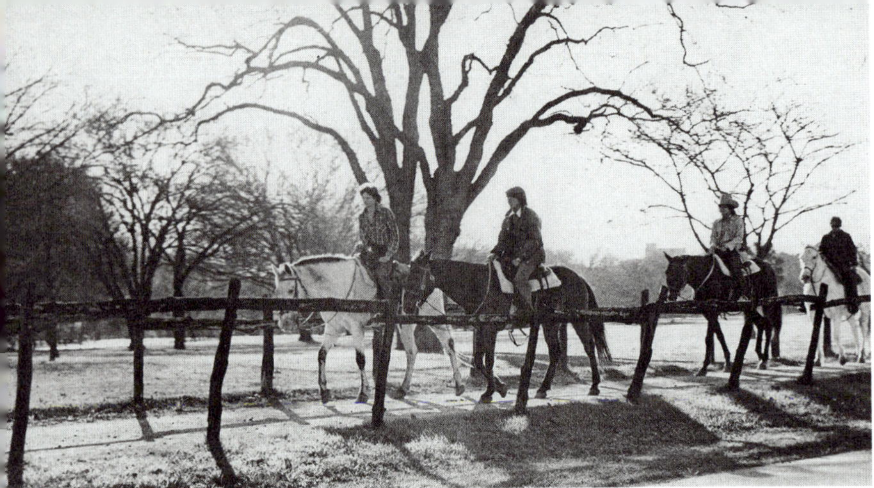

Bridle paths drew riders who rented horses from two stables outside the park.

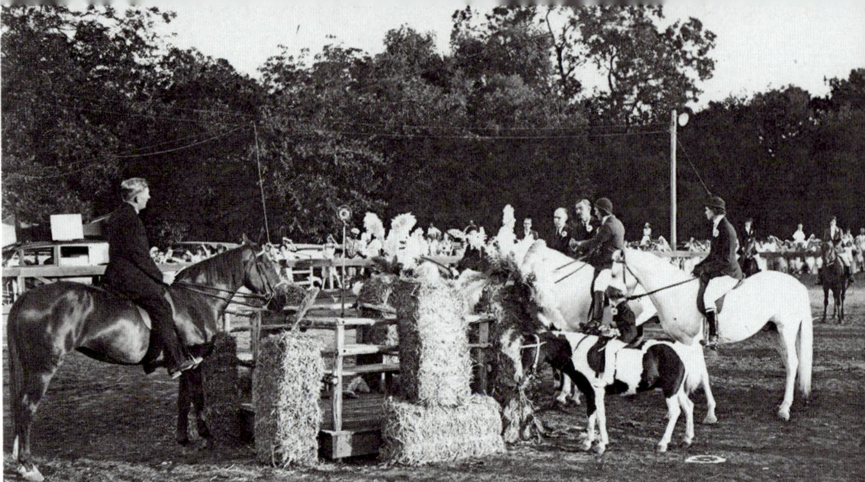

Virginia Hope and Jay B. Moore met on a bridle path in the park. They were married there in a ceremony on horseback on September 10, 1933, presided over by Justice of the Peace John F. Onion. The altar was made of baled hay and pampas grass.

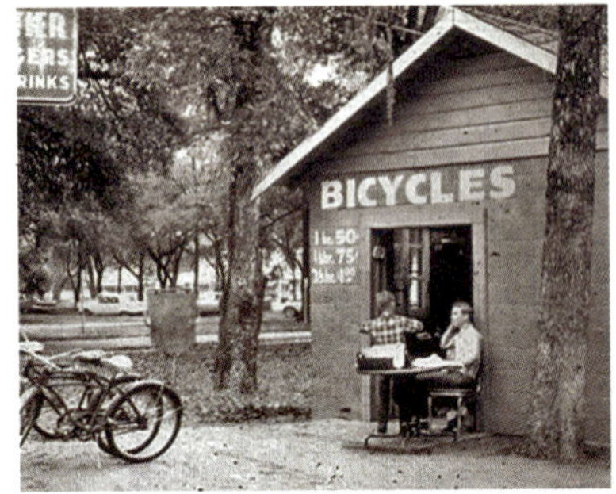

Outside the eastern boundary future restaurateur Jim Hasslocher opened a bicycle stand for park bikers in 1947.

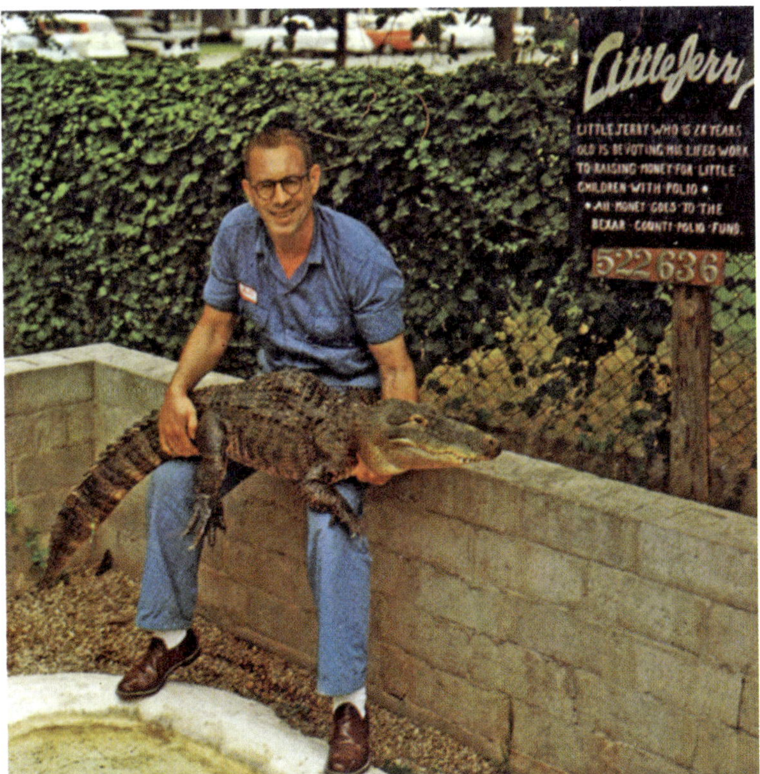

Alligator Garden operator Bill Kimbrell holds Little Jerry, one of the alligators who drew tossed coins donated to the county's polio fund.

several park food franchises, including a restaurant and tap room near the Brackenridge Eagle depot in Koehler Park.[356]

After the Witte Museum closed its Reptile Garden, the city leased the site as a franchise operation to Bill Kimbrell, who, with his wife, Vera, had been running the Texas Alligator Farm on Roosevelt Avenue. In 1952 the Kimbrells reopened the defunct Reptile Garden as the Alligator Garden, fitted out with ten sunken open-air tanks that at one point held seventy-five alligators. Children could "ride" some. "Old Joe would be the one they usually sat on because he hardly ever moved," the Kimbrells' son Richard once recalled. "You could only get close to the other ones in the winter, because they go dormant in cold weather."[357]

During their twenty-three years of operation, the Kimbrells donated $10,000 in coins thrown into alligator tanks to the county's polio fund. They closed the Alligator Garden when Bill Kimbrell retired in 1975 and shipped the animals to an alligator farm in Hot Springs, Arkansas. The Witte Museum eventually razed the building for a planned Center for Rivers and Aquifers.[358]

Another longtime park franchisee was George Evers, who in the 1930s got the concession for renting river canoes and paddleboats from a landing near the Joske Pavilion. He later added half-mile rides in a speedboat. Evers counted up to 1,200 customers a day, but in 1946 he got a six-month franchise fee waiver for revenue lost during the polio epidemic that emptied

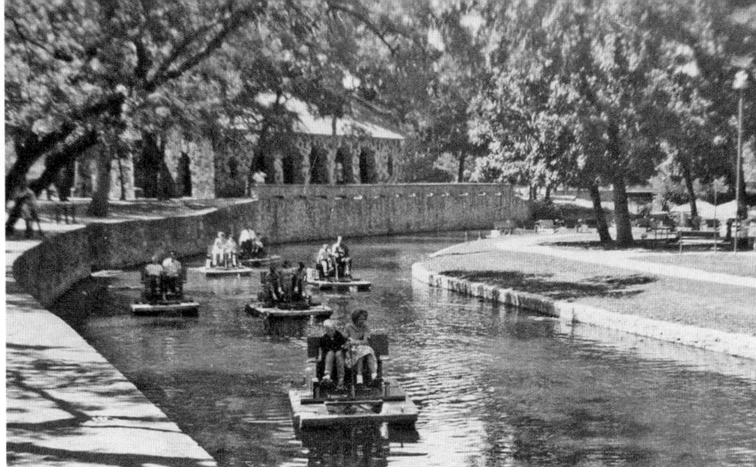

The Joske Pavilion provided the backdrop for paddleboats, a concession dating from the 1930s.

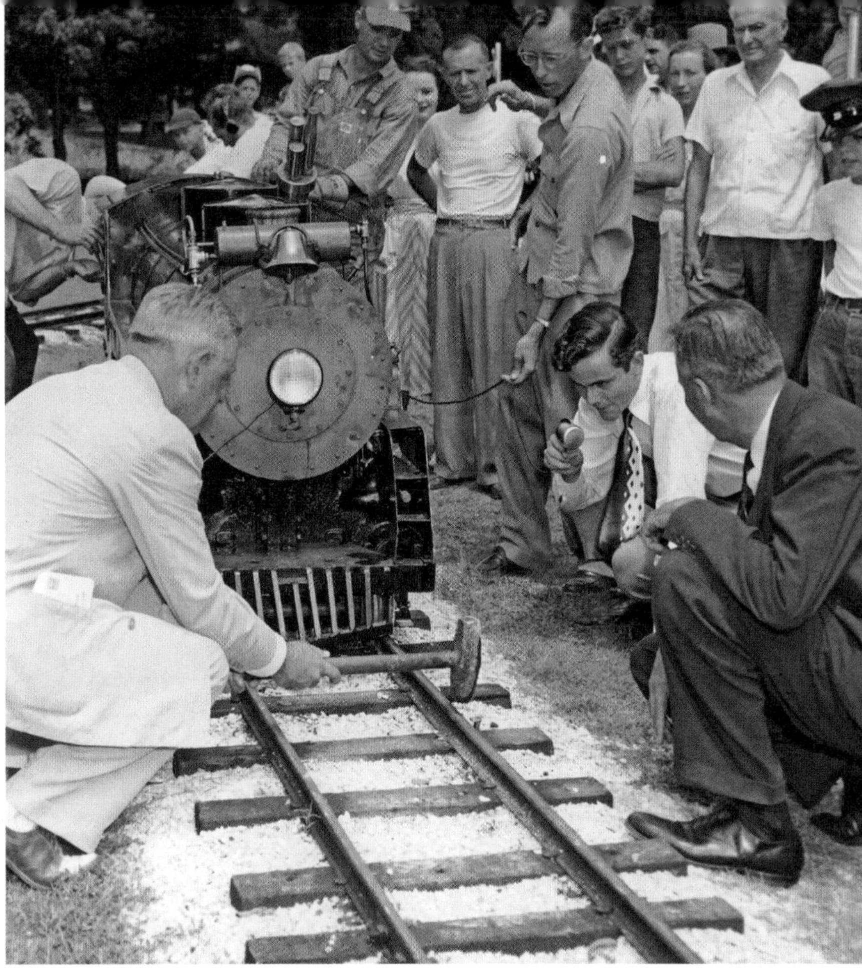

Parks commissioner Henry Hein drove a miniature golden spike in 1948 to launch Brackenridge Park's first miniature train, a steam locomotive with four coaches near the Joske Pavilion. Concessionaire David Martin was also the engineer.

the park. In 1959 he won a 40 percent fee reduction to offset a competitive problem, as large numbers of potential customers were opting instead for the most lucrative concession in the park, the new miniature train.[359]

Brackenridge Park's first train began running on June 28, 1948, when parks commissioner Henry Hein drove a golden spike two and a half inches long to mark the opening of a miniature rail line near the Joske Pavilion. Known as the Junior MK&T Line, the concession was operated by David B. Martin, age twenty-five, who served as engineer, fireman, conductor, brakeman, track walker, and general maintenance supervisor. His quarter-size steam locomotive, named No. 412, left a miniature station to travel a 1,250-foot oval track fourteen inches wide. The engine pulled four twelve-passenger coaches and at full throttle could go twenty miles an hour. By 1954 No. 412 was the last steam train engine operating in San Antonio.[360]

The steam age of railroads in San Antonio ended altogether in 1956 when investors headed by Austin-based G. L. Smith Enterprises picked up the Brackenridge Park train franchise and chose diesel engines rather than ones powered by steam. Named the Brackenridge Eagle, the new line turned into one of the most popular and enduring attractions in the park, now carrying some 350,000 passengers annually.[361]

In the postwar years, when waning private railroad companies still advertised for passengers, the first Brackenridge Park train's display of the Missouri-Kansas-Texas "Katy" Railroad's

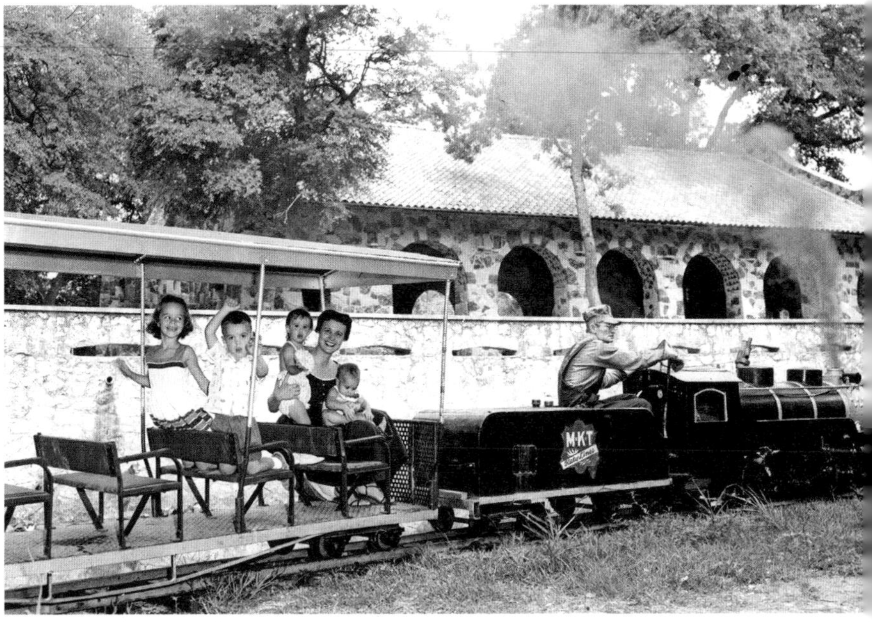

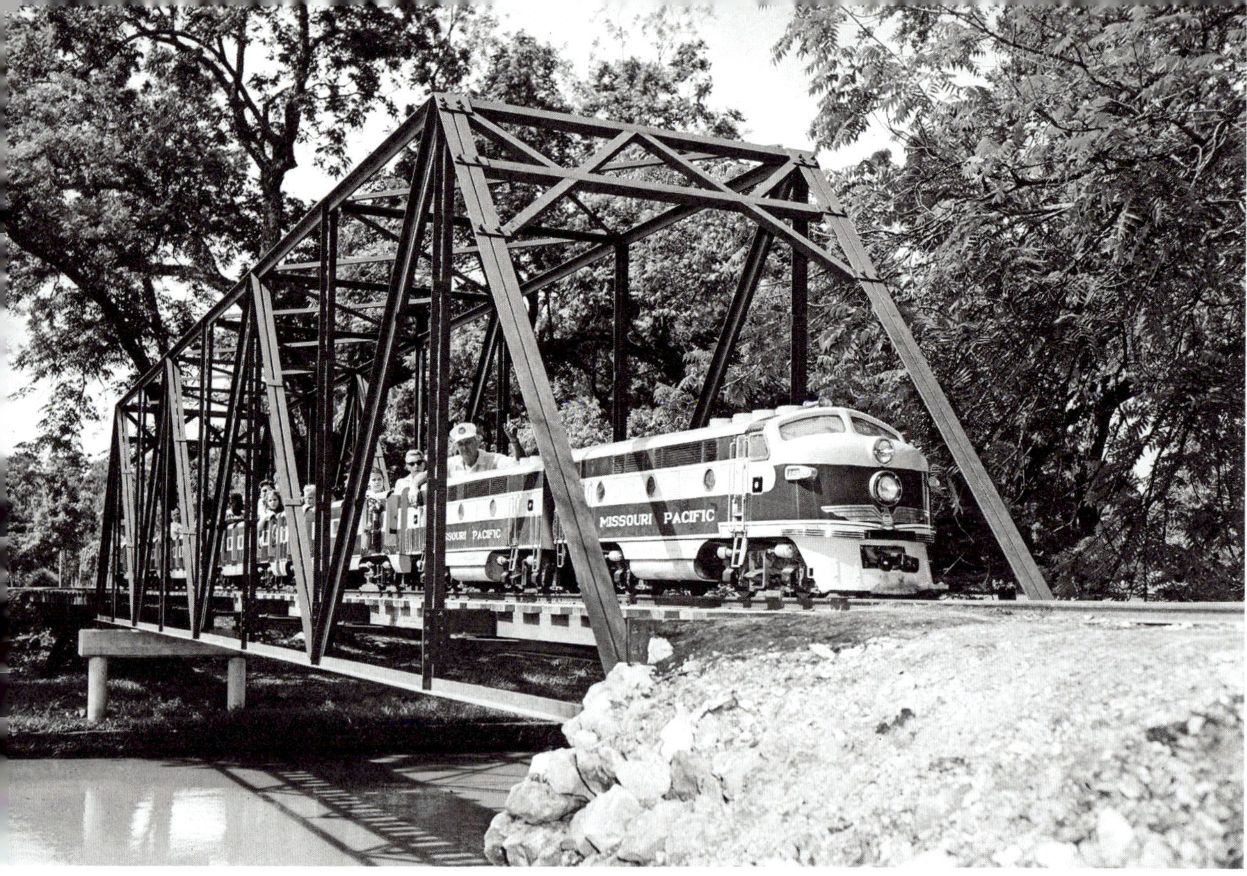

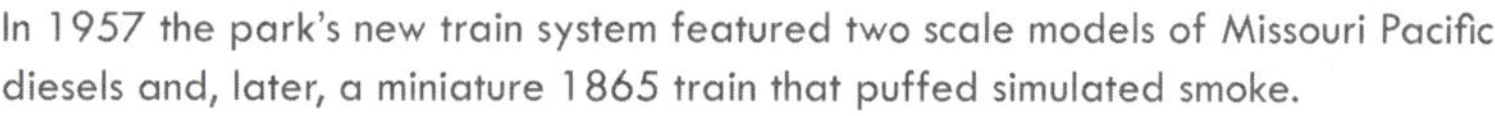

In 1957 the park's new train system featured two scale models of Missouri Pacific diesels and, later, a miniature 1865 train that puffed simulated smoke.

logo suggests an MKT promotional subsidy aimed at boosting awareness of passenger travel by rail. Display of the Missouri Pacific Railroad's symbol by its successor, the Brackenridge Eagle, indicates a similar effort. The Eagle's two trains were one-fifth scale model replicas of a sleek new Missouri Pacific diesel train. Each drew cars carrying up to forty-eight passengers. The Missouri Pacific furnished a construction crew to build the Eagle's two-mile track bed. Trains crossed the San Antonio River twice, once on a wooden trestle and again on a new seventy-foot steel span technically termed a Warren through-truss bridge.[362]

The Eagle was proclaimed "the World's Longest Miniature Railroad." It had been running for three months and carried 35,000 passengers by the time of official opening ceremonies on June 14, 1957. At peak times trains left every eight minutes from the main depot, a concrete block structure an eighth of a mile east of the zoo entrance. A round trip took fifteen minutes. To give the feel of a mainline railroad and help the railway even serve as a people mover among multiple destinations in the park, three small wooden shelters bore the names of stops where passengers could board or disembark—the Witte Museum, the golf driving range at the former polo field, and the then-named Chinese Sunken Gardens.[363]

Two years later the Eagle route expanded from two miles to more than three with additional tracks reaching even closer to the Witte Museum. The tracks then passed not through dense woodlands, as had previous trains, but some two hundred yards farther east, roughly paralleling Avenue B to reach Mulberry beside a drainage canal across from Kiddieland, facing Broadway and adjacent to Kiddie Park. That spot presented an opportunity for a new depot to draw passengers from the crowded children's amusement park as well as from nearby street traffic, Lions Field, and the golf course across the street.[364]

The Kiddieland Depot was built to be an attention-getter, "an authentic reproduction" of the historic Missouri Pacific station at Buda, sixty-five miles northeast of San Antonio.

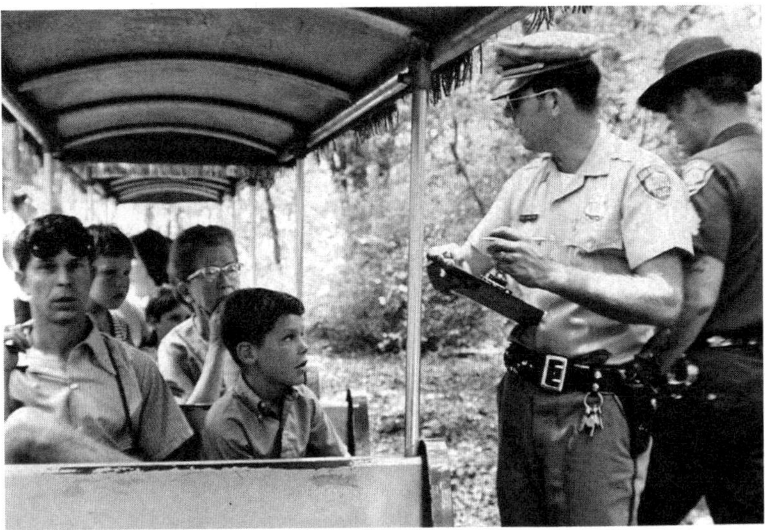

Policemen interviewed stunned riders of the Brackenridge Eagle after a heist in 1970, the nation's first train robbery since 1923.

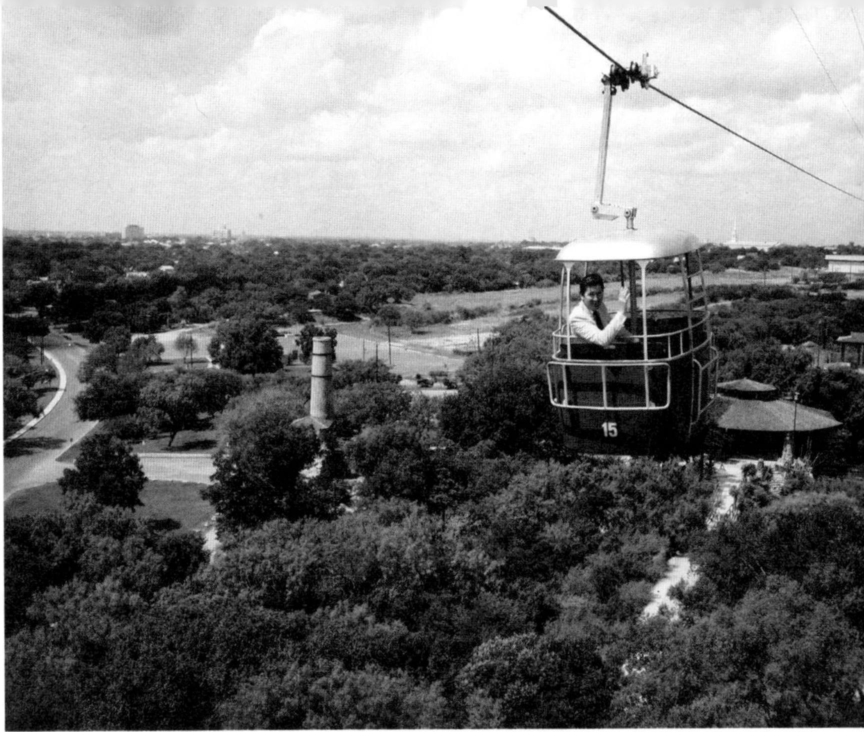

Fess Parker, star of the movie *Davy Crockett: King of the Wild Frontier*, took the Sky Ride over the Sunken Garden while on a visit to the Alamo in 1965.

Buda mayor Bruce Ferguson cut the ribbon at the July 1959 dedication ceremony, emceed by Henry Guerra and attended by dignitaries including San Antonio mayor pro-tem Mike Passur, Bexar County judge Charles W. Anderson, postmaster Dan Quill, the local Missouri Pacific Railroad general manager, and the station telegrapher from Buda.[365]

But at a time when rail passenger stations were closing throughout the United States as more travelers preferred to drive or fly, the Brackenridge Eagle's satellite stations failed to catch on. All were eventually removed. Unnamed replacement shelters at a few of the sites now serve the occasional rider getting off or on.

Eagle staffers were finding that riders wanted more than just miniature superliners promoting modern passenger rail travel. Some nostalgia would do. In 1963 the Missouri Pacific diesels were joined by a one-fifth scale model of an 1865 steam locomotive, gray and blue with brass trimmings and pulling passenger cars with white-fringed blue canopy tops. The train was manufactured in Buffalo, New York, at a cost of $42,000—$363,000 today—and powered by two fifty-horsepower engines. Simulated smoke puffed from a diamond-shaped stack.[366]

The Brackenridge Eagle made news in 1961 when a train jumped the track and tipped over, causing minor injuries to six people. But those headlines paled in comparison to national reports of an incident in mid-July 1970. Shortly after the Eagle exited the tunnel near the Kiddieland station one afternoon, two masked men, one armed with a pistol, leapt from the brush. The pair stopped the train and took $500, car keys, checkbooks, and credit cards from the seventy-five dumbfounded passengers. One passenger who thought the robbery a joke was roughed up, the *New York Times* reported. The crime gained renown as the first train robbery in the United States since 1923 and the first of a miniature train. The perpetrators, found to be soldiers at Fort Sam Houston, went to prison.[367]

The most spectacular concession in Brackenridge Park was opened by the Aerial Transportation Company, headed by Randall Clay. Investors included auto dealers B. J. "Red" McCombs and Austin Hemphill. On its first weekend in 1964, more than four thousand riders boarded bright-colored, four-foot-wide gondolas across from the zoo entrance and took the 1,200-foot Sky Ride, which quickly became one of the city's top attractions. Viewers ascended a hundred feet for seven minutes of dramatic sights of the San Antonio skyline and the Sunken Garden, directly below.[368]

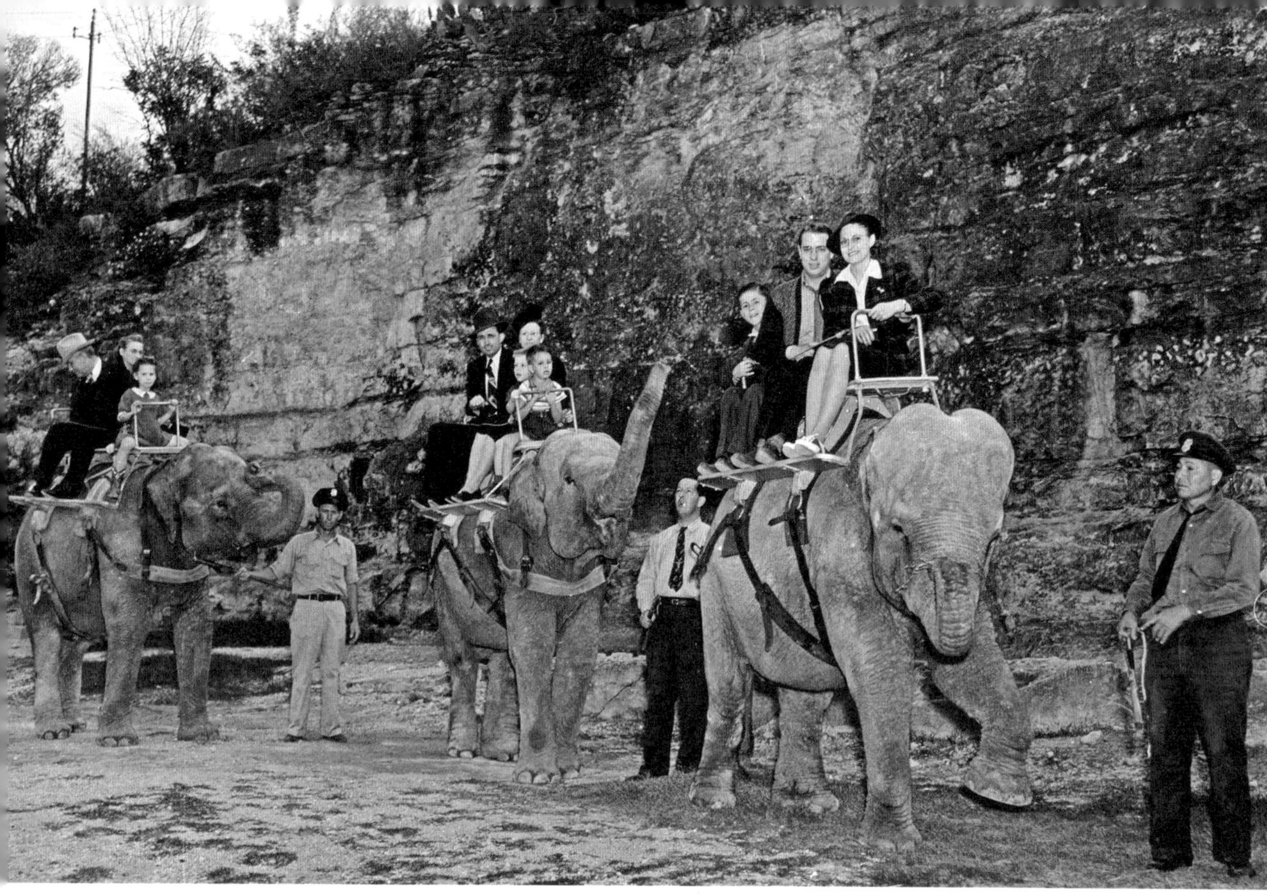

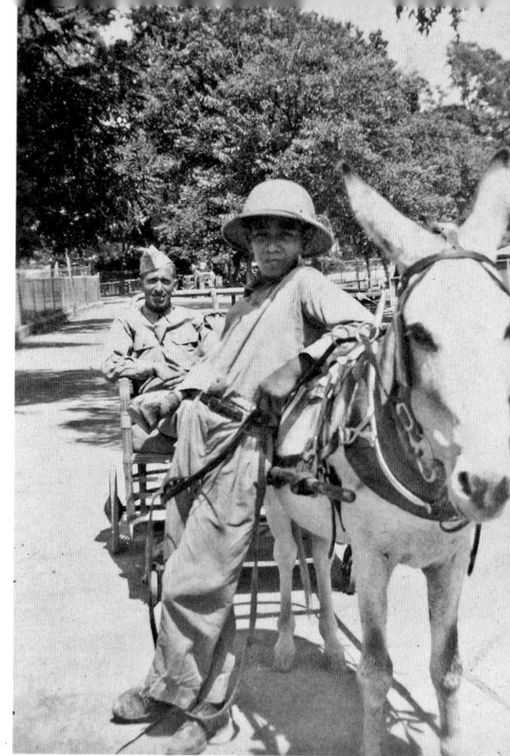

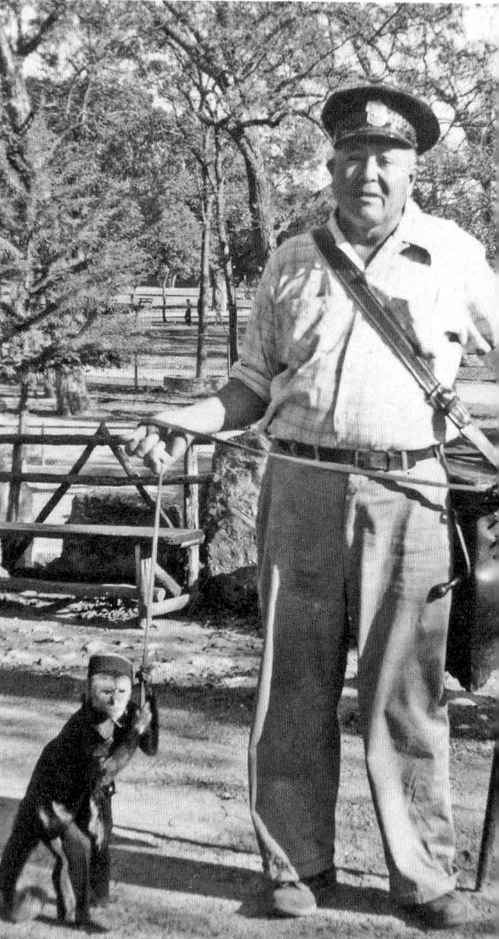

In 1940 the zoo purchased three elephants to star in three-ring circuses, and spectators could ride them afterward. Visitors could also travel in burro-drawn carts and enjoy an organ grinder with a monkey.

Brackenridge Park's three largest tenant institutions—the San Antonio Zoo, Municipal Golf Course, and Witte Museum—were, in comparison with city hall, paradigms of stability. All three were guided through the Depression, wartime, and into the 1960s by managers whose tenures ranged from thirty-three to forty-five years.

The zoo drew the most visitors. Under Fred Stark, director from 1934 to 1967, five thousand animal specimens went on display, more than half of them birds. In 1940 the newly fenced zoo bought three trained elephants and launched a three-ring circus that performed twice on weekdays and three times on Saturdays and Sundays. Spectators flocked to see elephants skip on two feet, seals balance balls on their noses, a mule named Rabbit mount a pedestal unaided, and performances by lions and tigers. A uniformed monkey leashed to an organ grinder took coins from passersby and clinked them into a tin cup. Peacocks roamed the grounds.[369]

Stark also presided over expansion of African wildlife displays and construction of the Hixon Bird House. In 1956, he was charged with breeding Rosie, one of sixteen whooping

In 1956 the donkey barn was cloaked in rubble stone and gained a second story with an Alamo-style parapet.

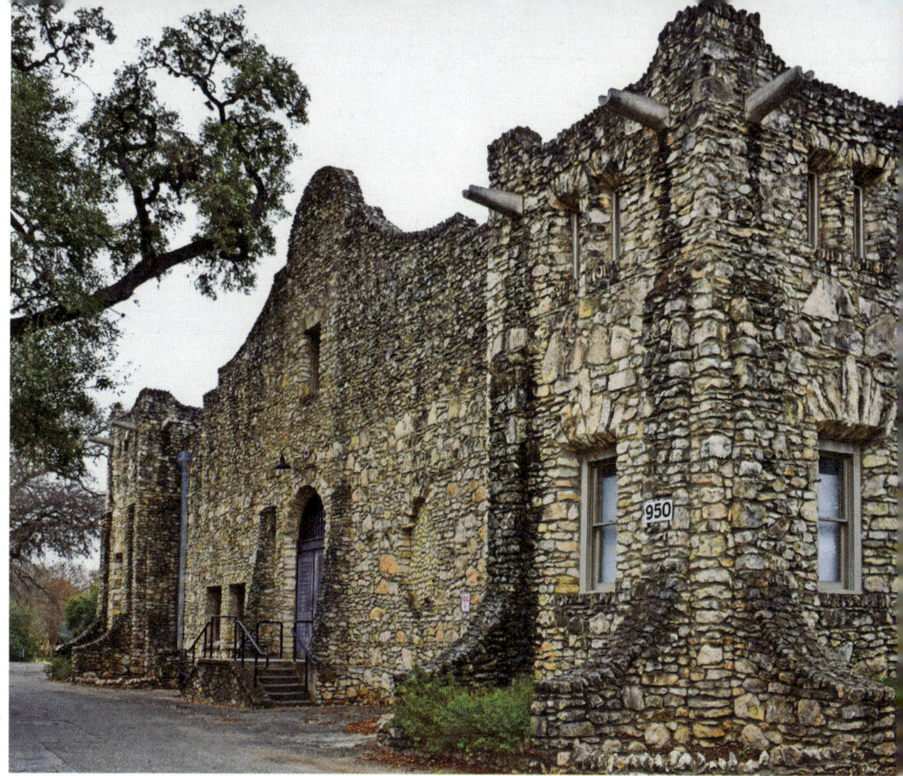

cranes then in existence and the only whooping crane in the world consistently displayed in a zoo.[370]

A. W. Tillinghast, who designed the park's golf course in 1916, visited twenty years later. He had high praise for the city's golf operations manager, Murray Brooks, in charge of the Brackenridge course from 1923 to 1968, but warned of the dangers of complacency. "So popular is the Brackenridge course and so heavy is the play that the city appears to adhere to the policy of 'standing pat,'" he said. "There seems to have been little effort to keep pace with the advance of golf." The annual Texas Open, held at more than a half dozen courses in San Antonio, was hosted in Brackenridge Park twenty-one times, but as private clubs invested more in amenities the Brackenridge course held its last Texas Open in 1959.[371]

The Witte likewise was out of step with museum developments elsewhere. It risked being dismissed as the city's attic, taking pride as it did in support from "citizens willing to entrust to its care their family treasures." The editor of *Arts* magazine gave an unvarnished appraisal. Visiting from New York in 1957, he expressed dismay at what he considered the museum's poor lighting, inadequate explanatory material, and "seeming stagnancy." His column elicited a retort from the director of the San Francisco Museum of Art. She got to the heart of difficulties by writing that the Witte should be cut some slack, as it "represents the sort of thing that happened in museums all over the country, and indeed all over the world, in their formative stages," when funds and broad support were hard to come by.[372]

Ellen Schulz Quillin, the Witte's founding director, soldiered on, whatever outsiders may have thought about the Native American skeleton on display near the entrance, the shrunken head nearby, or the caged tarantula in the front hallway. San Antonio children loved them. She kept developing strong collections and retired in 1960 after dedication of renovations and expansions that increased museum space by more than half and included a new entrance to the main building. Eight years later the museum gained international attention with the theft of its 49-plus carat McFarlin diamond, described in the *New York Times* as "a pale yellow stone as big as a hen's egg" and valued at today's equivalent of nearly $2 million. The crime was never solved.[373]

As city hall got a grip on things, stability also returned to the parks department. Robert Lee Fraser, a landscape architect with a master's degree in horticulture from Texas A&M University, was named parks and recreation director in 1955 and stayed in the job for eighteen years. "I remember visiting Brackenridge Park as a child," Fraser said when he was appointed. "I thought it was the next thing to heaven." In 1956 he moved his department to Brackenridge Park, into the 1920s barn built for donkeys and hay at the park's northern entrance. A second story was added and the entire structure cloaked in a rubble stone facade topped by an Alamo-style gabled parapet.[374]

Addition of "recreation" to Fraser's title reflected the role recreation was gaining in the nation's parks over passive activities like picnics or enjoying the beauty of gardens. In 1940 Brackenridge Park offerings included a network of bridle paths plus five tennis courts and free swimming at Lambert Beach.

Picnic spots are held days in advance for families' Easter picnics and campouts, a Brackenridge Park tradition going back at least seventy-five years.

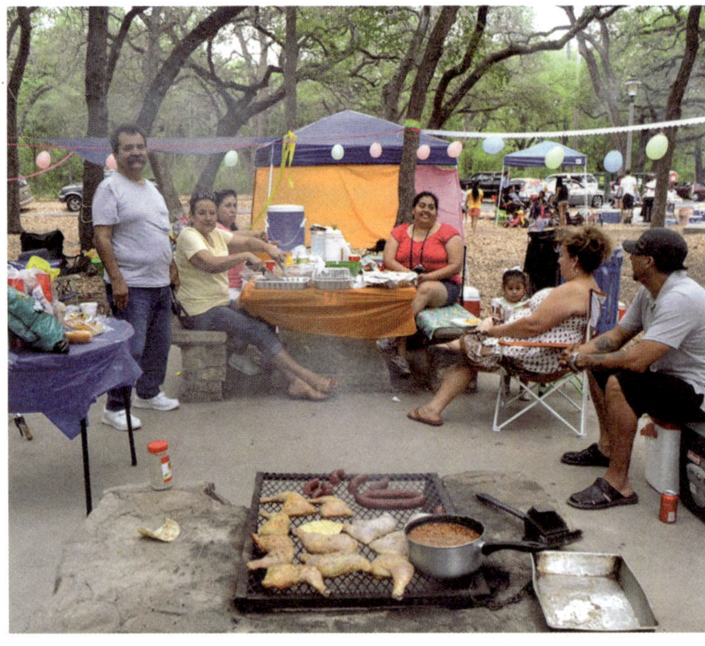

There were softball fields near Lambert Beach, in Koehler Park, and at Lions Field. In 1952 the Polo Club began sharing the southern part of its field on nonmatch days with a golf driving range opened by Frank Machock, who set up a putting green and miniature golf course and built a snack shop.[375]

The San Antonio Horse Association maintained stables and a show ring at the edge of Davis Park, which were used by the San Antonio Charro Association for rodeos prior to Freeman Coliseum's opening in east San Antonio in 1949, when the Sheriff's Mounted Posse of Bexar County took over the facilities. Two hundred entries and three thousand spectators were drawn to a weekend horse show in 1950. The Royal Oak Mounted Square Dance Team performed between events.[376]

The 1930s had seen a sharp increase in picnickers at Easter. As evening curfews were lifted for Easter weekends, many San Antonians began reserving campsites there. This was particularly true of Mexican American families, who developed a strong loyalty to the park. Former state senator Leticia Van de Putte, whose family came to San Antonio from Mexico in 1922, recalled: "Mexican Americans were not welcomed at all parks then, but [they] were at Brackenridge Park, and our family's been going there ever since. We picnicked a lot near Lambert Beach. I jumped into the river when I was five years old, and my grandfather dived in to save me."

When Covid pandemic restrictions began lifting in 2021, Van de Putte asked her aged mother, Belle San Miguel Ortiz, where she wanted to go. "My mother said, 'The park, of course,' meaning Brackenridge. We picked up hamburgers and sat at a picnic table beside the river."[377]

In 1950 Easter sunrise services drew two thousand worshippers to the Sunken Garden Theater. By 7 a.m. all picnic areas were occupied or being held for later use. As many as one hundred thousand people came to the park that day. Attendance reached sixty-five hundred at two baseball games and a polo match, five thousand on the Brackenridge Eagle train and river paddleboats, forty-three hundred at the Witte Museum and Reptile Garden, and seventeen thousand at the zoo, which park superintendent Stewart King thought made it the zoo's biggest day on record. The next morning King's crews were "snowed under" cleaning up the litter, notably remains of *cascarones*, confetti-filled eggshells cracked on heads.[378]

On Easter Sundays "the sound of conjunto music and the smell of smoking barbecue pits filled the air" throughout the park, as "children raced along the trails near the river on bikes and scooters" and others played kickball. Protocols evolved and families developed their own Easter weekend traditions.[379]

"Some people chain up their lawn chairs to trees or put tape around their area," and others usually respect the claim, said John Ortega Jr., who arrived at 6 a.m. on Holy Thursday in 2016 with his girlfriend. They set up near the ball diamond where his family had camped every Easter for seven years. To be safe, Ortega defined their camping area with caution tape and relatives took shifts throughout Thursday and Friday until all forty family members were there on Saturday.[380]

In 2019 the Cernas, Easter regulars since 1953, assigned fifteen members to rotate through several days of preholiday "hanging out and cooking" to hold the traditional family spot. A weekend succession of bamboo-pole fishing, piñata

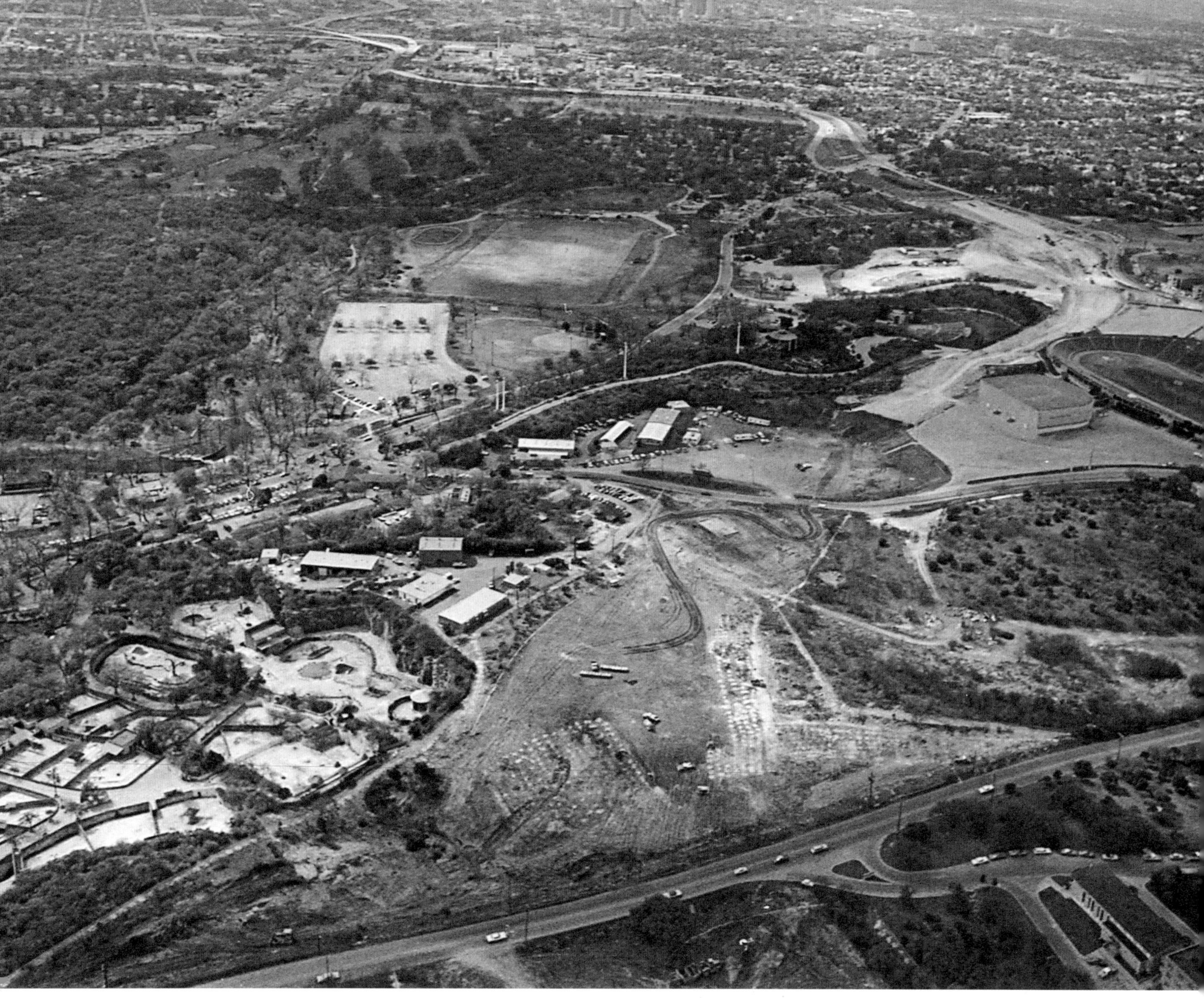

When completed in 1978, US 281 would continue, skirting the zoo as it reached a new interchange at Hildebrand Avenue, *left foreground*. At left center, a parking lot turns toward the polo field. The far side of the wooded area at left center is bordered by Broadway. Completing this section required US 281 to squeeze between Alamo Stadium, *far right center*, and the Sunken Garden Theater, across highway construction to its left. A section of Alpine Drive that once rose around and behind the theater had already been removed in this view.

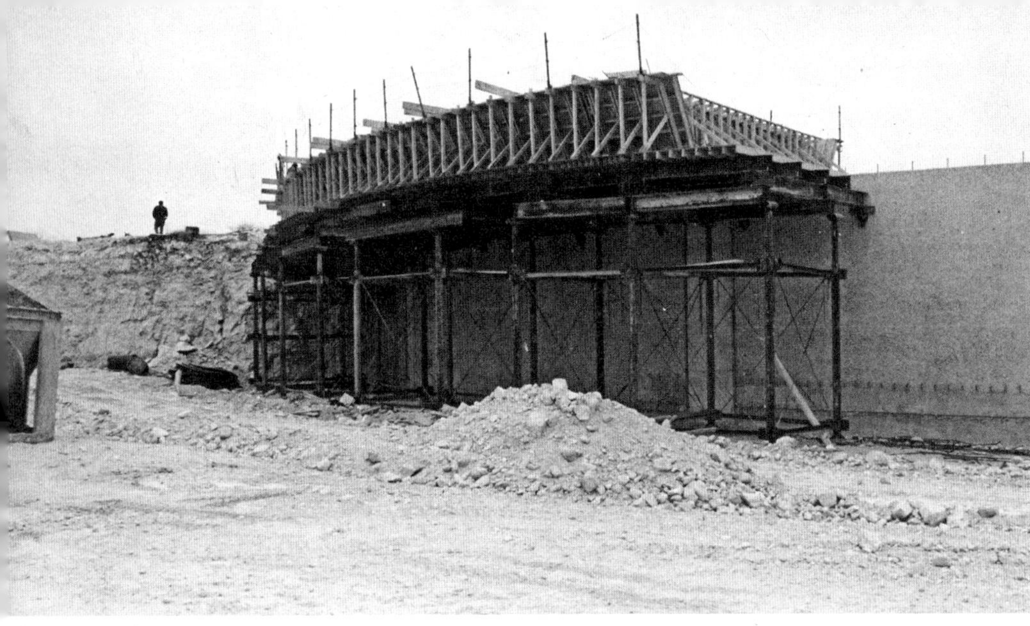

The solution to fitting US 281 between Alamo Stadium and Alpine Drive above and behind the Sunken Garden Theater's lawn seating was to widen the route by shortening an arc of Alpine Drive and cantilevering the new shorter section to curve above one lane of the new expressway.

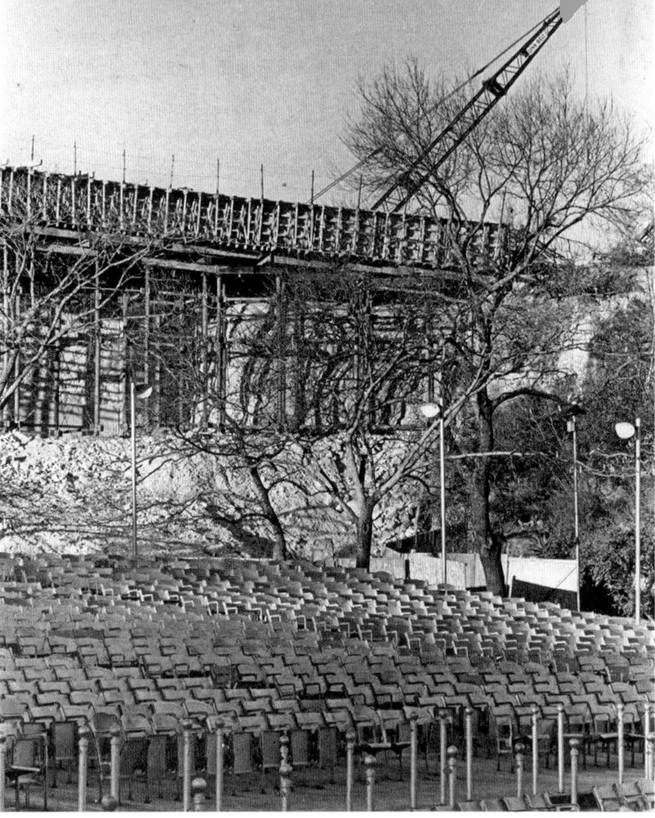

competitions, and sack races ended by dividing the family into four age categories for a raw egg toss. Rose Cerna Castillo estimated the record throw at "about 50 yards."[381]

Trash and recycling bags were periodically passed out, and on Easter Monday volunteers from the Parks and Recreation Department and the Brackenridge Park Conservancy cleaned up what was left behind. The weekend total for 2015 was five tons of trash and half a ton of recyclables.[382]

No upheaval brought as many headaches to Brackenridge Park as the interstate highway program, authorized by Congress in 1956. There was no quick route between San Antonio's International Airport and downtown nine miles south. Broadway, McCullough Avenue, and San Pedro Avenue were lined with development, and converting any of them to an interstate highway would be prohibitively expensive and disruptive. If the proposed link could go straight through Olmos Basin and Brackenridge Park, transportation time from the airport to downtown would be cut in half, to less than fifteen minutes.

The Texas Highway Department's solution, proposed in 1960, was a route that would cut south through Olmos Basin, cross Hildebrand Avenue, and take the zoo's old buffalo paddock. After that came the route's biggest challenge, how to funnel traffic through the narrow gap between Alamo Stadium and the Sunken Garden Theater, where the limestone ridge behind the theater made that section too narrow for a six-lane interstate.

Engineers proposed removing the ridge and replacing it with a much narrower concrete buffer. But the ridge also carried Alpine Drive up around the rear of the theater area. So that section of the drive was replaced by a slightly shorter roadway over the top of the narrower new concrete wall. Where the new Alpine Drive would still conflict with the expressway, a new cantilevered section curved outward above the highway's easternmost lane and returned, able to carry Alpine Drive traffic while providing ample room for highway traffic to pass below.

The golf course lost its twelfth hole, cut in two so US 281 could swerve east around the edge of the course as best it could. As it crossed Broadway the highway blocked Brackenridge Park's southern access to Josephine Street. One point where it met the street disappeared altogether under an access road. The park still reappeared past a gap of commercial buildings to the west, where its southernmost four acres extended on either side of the San Antonio River as far as Josephine Street.[383]

San Antonians were divided over the plan to use parkland for an interstate highway, whether it was Brackenridge Park or

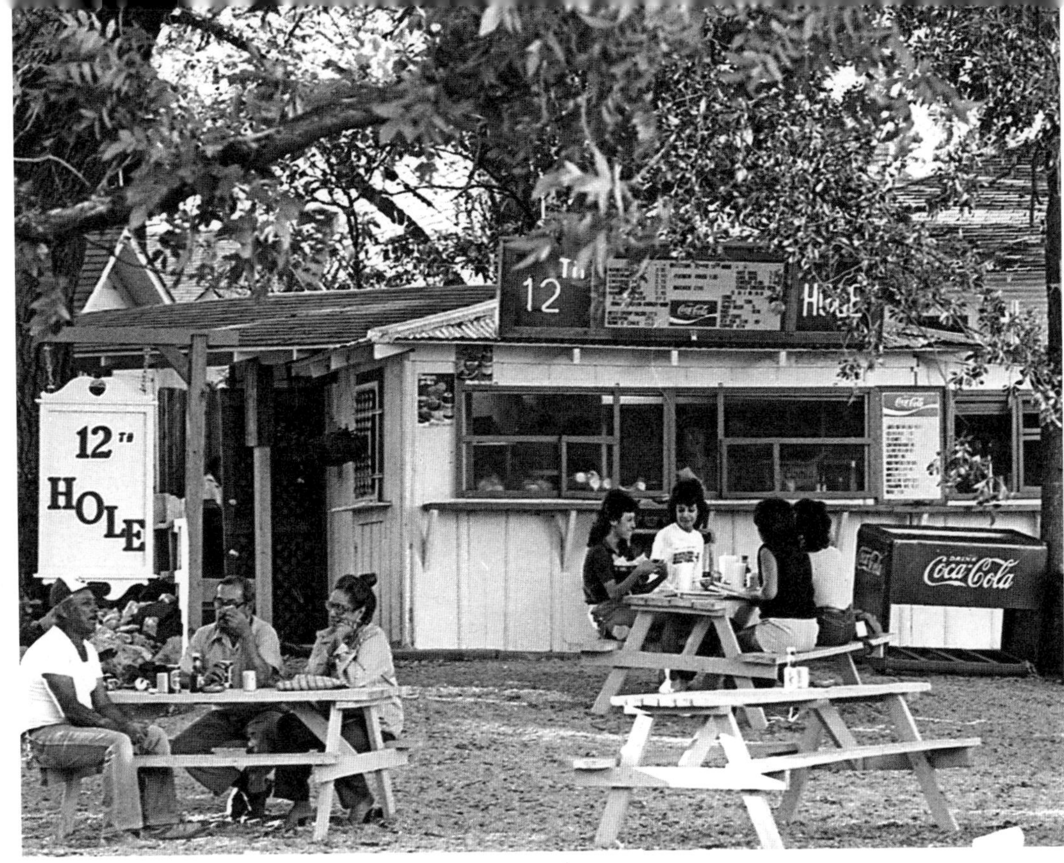

Severed from its clientele when US 281 cut through the golf course's twelfth hole, a popular sandwich and drink stand once across the street was renamed the 12th Hole but finally closed.

Olmos Basin, a flood plain with less legal standing as a park. The resulting uproar took more than a decade to resolve. The leading opponent on behalf of the parks was the San Antonio Conservation Society, while the city, led by Mayor Walter McAllister, strongly supported the highway. Public meetings, marches, court battles, and legislative standoffs made the issue a national cause célèbre.

When a US Senate resolution engineered by Texas senator Ralph Yarborough passed in 1966, the secretary of transportation was prohibited from approving federal funds for a highway through a public park if there was a reasonable alternative. Conservationists asserted that there was such an alternative. To circumvent the impasse, McAllister got the state, which had no such funding prohibition, to agree to build the crucial section, designated US 281, without federal funding. On February 7, 1978, a broadly grinning McAllister, age eighty-eight, was at the opening of what was named the Walter W. McAllister Sr. Freeway, termed "freeway" rather than "expressway" because the *San Antonio Light* objected to any usage calling to mind the name of its bitter rival, the *San Antonio Express*.[384]

Many golfers considered the biggest consequence of US 281 construction to be their loss of the traditional twelfth holeand their access from the course to one of their favorite destinations.

In 1926 Austrian-born Elizabeth Schriever, whose Terry Court home faced the twelfth green across the street, built a ten-by-ten-foot building in her backyard and named it the Oaks. She set picnic tables outside and began selling what many considered to be the best egg salad sandwich and lemonade in town. She also offered a wide selection of beer, banned on the golf course since its land was donated by prohibitionist George Brackenridge in 1899.[385]

Before construction of US 281, "play stopped at The Oaks as a part of every round of golf," wrote golf course historian Reid Meyers. "Golfers developed a protocol to finish playing #12, sit at the table for ten minutes and enjoy a lemonade or beer and sandwich, then move on to #13 tee. The next foursome would do the same."[386]

Schriever's refuge tried soldiering on using the name the 12th Hole, but with its main customer base blocked on the far side of a six-lane expressway, the bistro eventually closed.

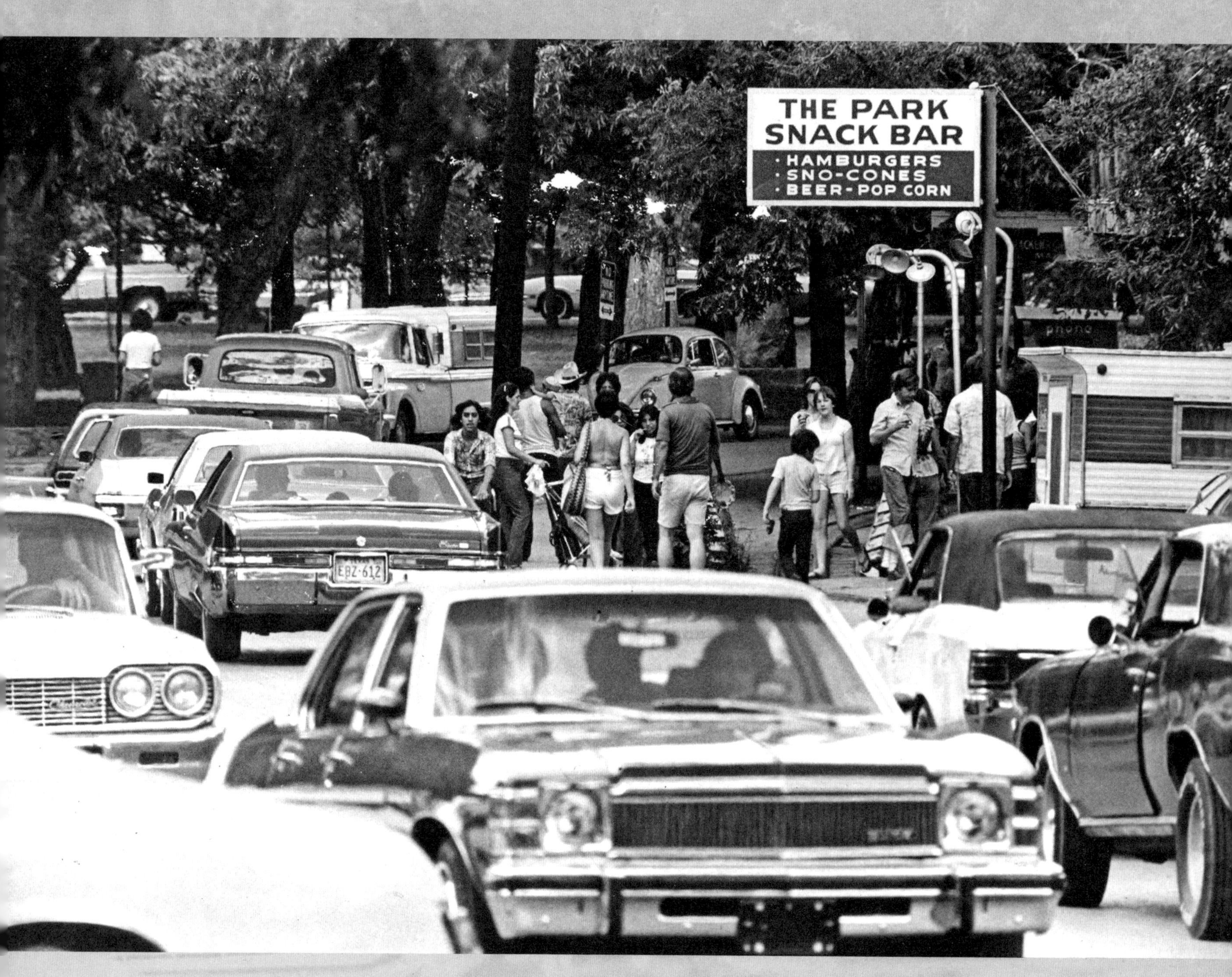
THE PARK
SNACK BAR
· HAMBURGERS
· SNO-CONES
· BEER-POP CORN

Renewal

After three decades marked by drift and discord, in the 1970s Brackenridge Park still seemed to be lurching forward with no clear sense of direction. As the onetime sylvan refuge was veering toward becoming an amusement park, realization came that it was time to step back and take a look.

For starters, there was no formal record of exactly what was in the park nor of how and when it got there, much less an assessment of what needed fixing and how. So in 1976 when the city commissioned the local architectural and engineering firm C-G-R Inc. to prepare the park's first master plan, the initial step was to get a professional archeological and historical assessment of the entire park. Susanna Katz and Anne Fox of the University of Texas at San Antonio's Center for Archaeological Research were hired for the job. Three years later, their twenty-six-page published report listed fifteen prehistoric and twenty-seven historic sites within the park.[387]

By mid-1977 a citizens advisory committee headed by neighboring River Road resident Arthur P. "Hap" Veltman Jr. was meeting frequently to review master planners' progress reports on issues ranging from public recreation use to signage, lighting, flood control, excess traffic, and parking lots. "It cannot be stressed too strongly that this master plan reflects an enormous amount of thinking and planning by professionals and lay people," C-G-R wrote when the plan was finished and adopted in 1979. Working closely with the master planners was Ron Darner, a landscape architect who succeeded Robert Fraser as parks and recreation director in 1973 and held the post for twenty-four years.[388]

The only significant effort stemming from the master plan's adoption seems to have been a short-lived $1 million palm garden planted northeast of the Koehler Pavilion. The six-acre site with winding walkways through the palms opened with a celebration in November 1982. A picnic shelter known as the Cypress Pavilion was constructed nearby. On the Koehler Pavilion went the project's commemorative plaque, entitled "Brackenridge Park Rehabilitation."[389]

Weekend traffic snarls in the 1970s were only one indication that Brackenridge Park needed help.

Into the unsettled 1970s strode Philip J. Sheridan, hands down the most colorful and influential concessionaire in the park's history. A onetime school principal, he

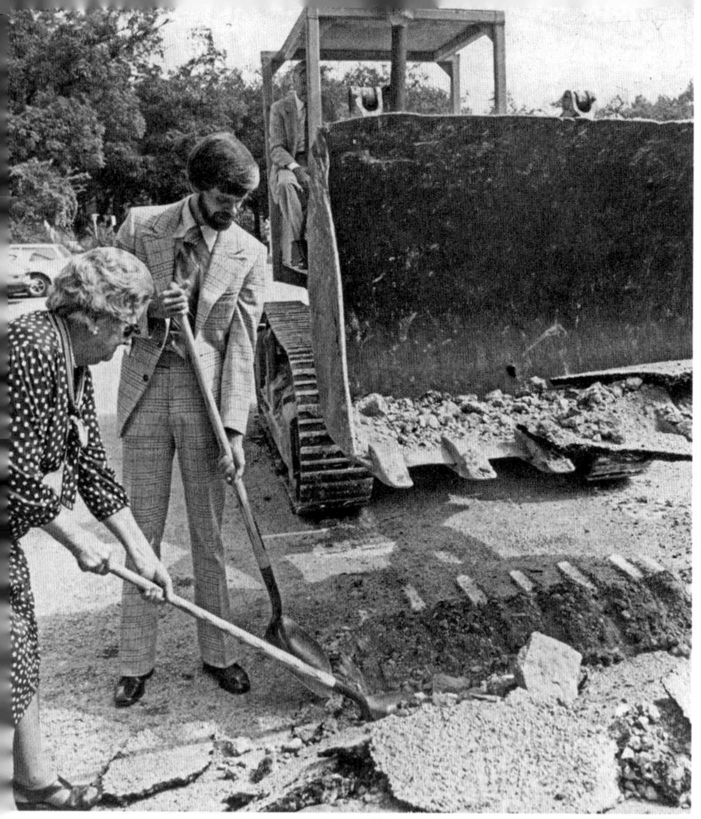

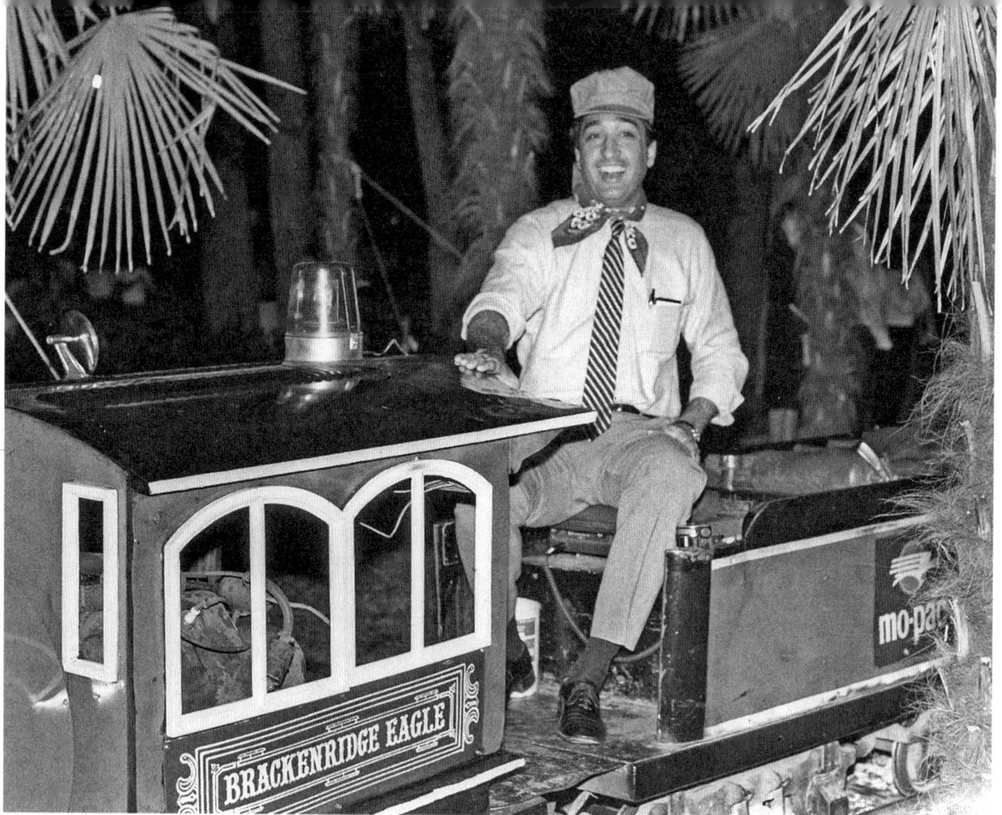

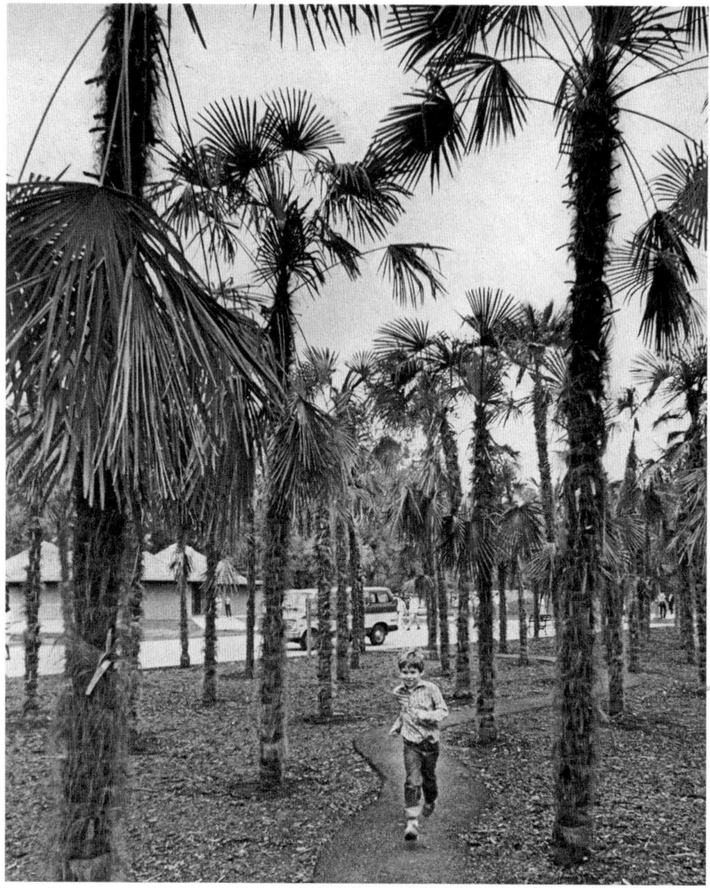

In 1981 city councilman Van Archer was in the operator's seat at the groundbreaking for a $1 million palm garden. Wielding shovels were park master plan committee member Tom Brereton and Marie Clark, whose brother, George Carson, helped fund the effort. The next year Maverick Fisher, age seven, dashed through the newly planted palms, and Mayor Henry Cisneros engineered the Brackenridge Eagle as it broke through the grand opening banner stretched across the track.

had parlayed a summer food services agreement with the Alamo Heights city swimming pool into a HemisFair '68 food concession contract and then into carnival and food concessions for rodeo and Fiesta events. He got his first contract for Brackenridge Park in 1973. Two decades later he had all six of the park's concession contracts and, with his other contracts, was the city's largest concessionaire.[390]

Sheridan's reputation, however, was mixed. His obituary in 2017 noted that he was an Eagle Scout and a Marine Corps officer, held master's degrees in theology and in school administration, and was a published scholar of Latin American history. But in 1993 Sheridan was free on bond after pleading guilty to charges of tax evasion. The next year he was indicted on a charge of sexual assault of a child, and in 1996 he was

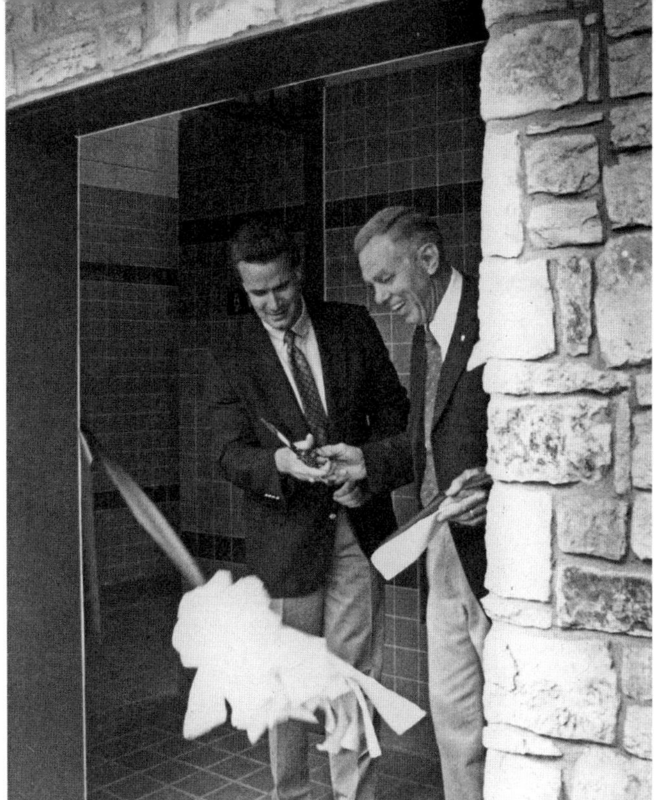

City councilman Lyle Larson cut the ribbon in 1992 on a new train depot restroom building with its donor, concessionaire Philip Sheridan, *right*.

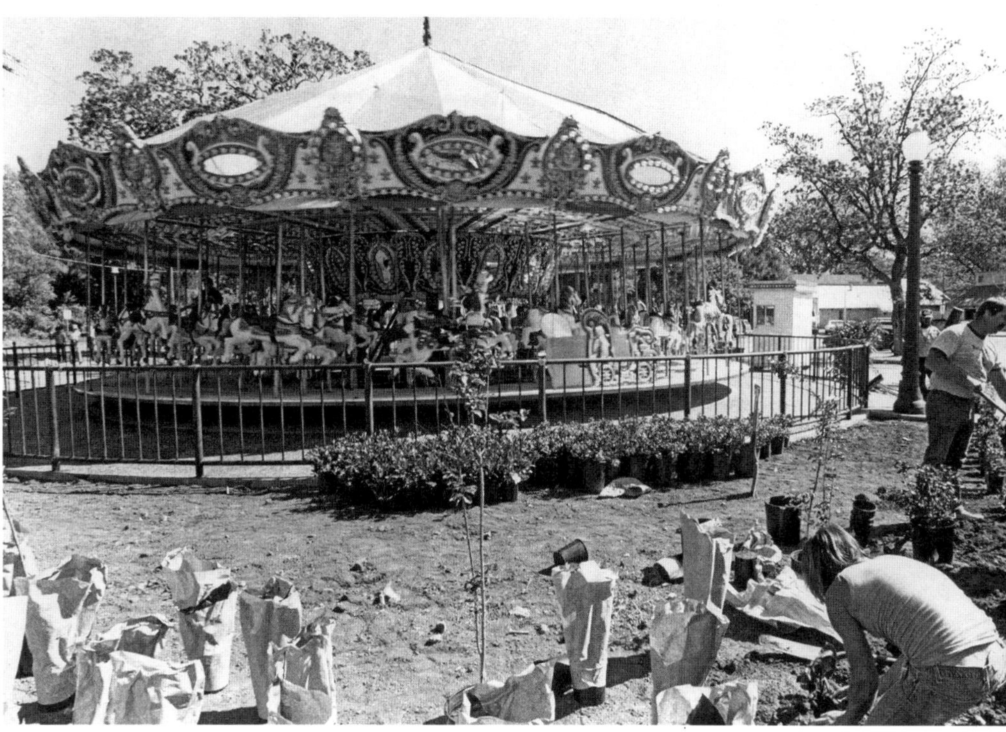

A carousel begun in Koehler Park in 1986 had to be moved across the river into Brackenridge Park to escape deed restrictions.

indicted on two felony counts of lying on an application to sell alcoholic beverages.[391]

Sheridan was as adept at negotiating plea agreements as he was at gaining political favor, in part by financing new concession buildings in Brackenridge Park. He was praised in 1997 for a $100,000 donation credited with rescuing the Fiesta Commission from insolvency. Despite opposition from city staff, city council continued renewing his contracts, pleading ignorance of charges against Sheridan and promising to research them.[392]

Sheridan's first Brackenridge Park contract was a nine-year agreement for the Koehler Park concession stand next to the Brackenridge Eagle depot. Eight months later, in April 1974, he survived charges of poor food service under his Convention Center contract but was in hot water for chopping down a tree in Brackenridge Park without permission and building a concession stand while ignoring guidelines. "No, no, that's not our plan," declared architect Ed Mok of Marmon & Mok, the firm that drafted the approved design, when he saw the nearly completed facility. "That's outlandish, outrageous. We certainly don't want to be credited with that." The assistant city attorney did not know "exactly what our cause of action would be." A month later parks department director Ron Darner said the matter was "still under consideration." Sheridan's agreement continued.[393]

As he gained contracts to operate the Brackenridge Eagle, the Sky Ride over the Sunken Garden, and paddleboats near the Joske Pavilion, Sheridan thought the park should have a carousel. In 1986 he started building one in Koehler Park, not bothering to get a permit.[394]

The watchdog San Antonio Conservation Society feared the carousel would help turn Brackenridge into little more than an amusement park. A Koehler heir, Margaret Pace Willson, agreed and charged that the carousel violated terms of Emma Koehler's gift. She deeded the society a reversionary legal interest in Koehler Park, giving the society grounds on which to sue the city. In November 1986 a judge ordered work on the carousel site to stop until a formal hearing could be held. Two

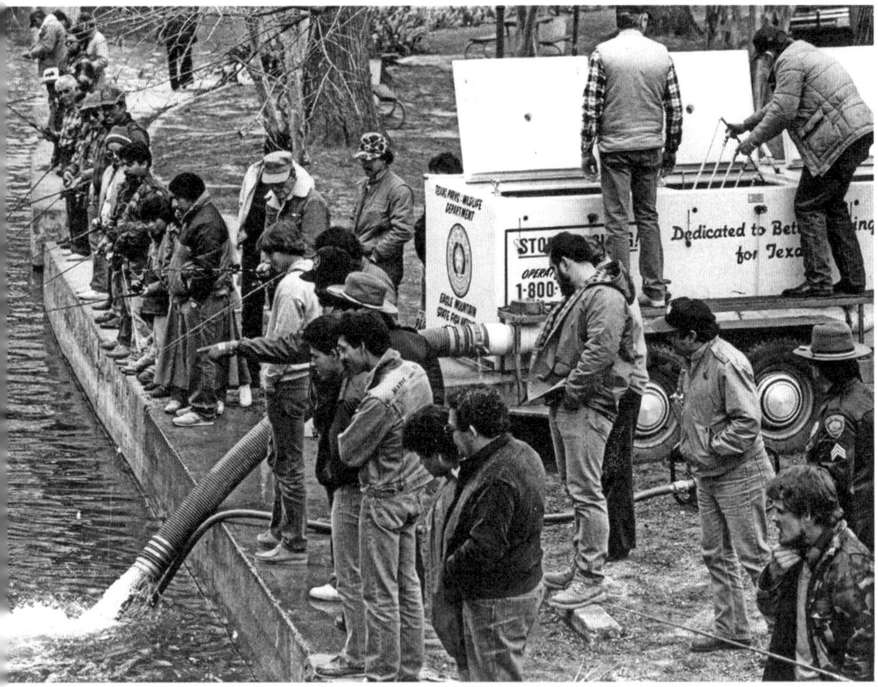

Fishermen held their poles at the ready in January 1987 as the river at Lambert Beach was restocked with two thousand rainbow trout.

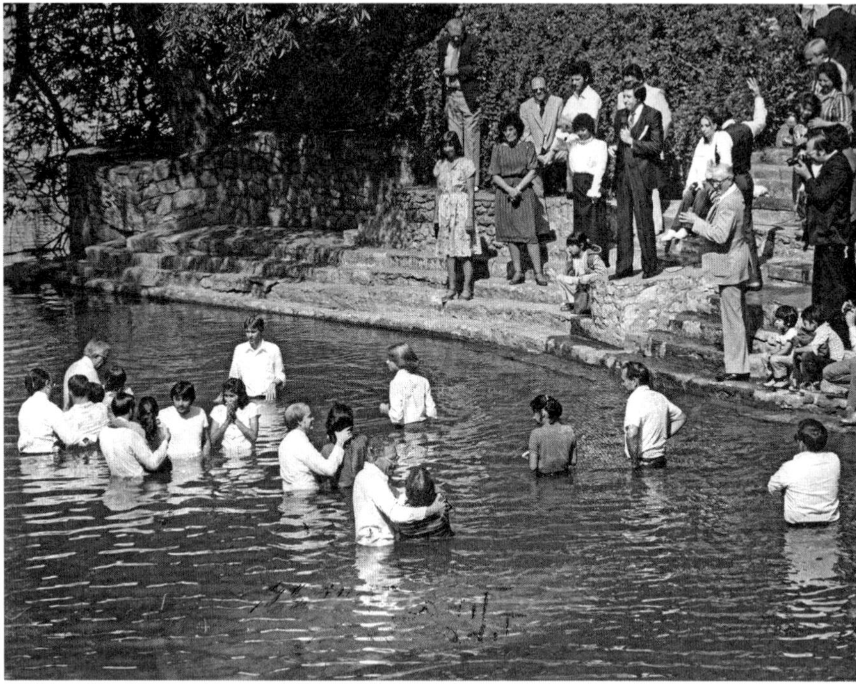

Members of the Seventh Day Adventist Church of Highland Hills were baptized at Lambert Beach one Sunday in October 1982.

weeks before the scheduled hearing, the city granted Sheridan a permit to build the carousel in a new location across the Koehler Park line inside Brackenridge Park, complicating the conservation society's standing to sue.[395]

The carousel and a popcorn wagon were finished in time for Easter 1987, but litigation continued. Both parties settled two years later. The conservation society withdrew when city council agreed to permit no more amusement rides in Brackenridge or Koehler Parks, a prohibition that did not extend to the San Antonio Zoo.[396]

A decade later, as legal problems tarnished his luster, Sheridan's paddleboat contract had expired and he was down to two contracts in Brackenridge Park. He transferred to the San Antonio Zoo his contracts for the Sky Ride, idled in 1999 by problems with safety regulations, and the Brackenridge Eagle, no longer running after derailing seven times in less than two years. The Sky Ride required maintenance and repairs estimated to cost several million dollars. When the city ruled that a sky ride did not benefit the zoo's educational purposes and declined to help, the Sky Ride was disassembled in 2002. A sale disposed of fourteen gondolas at $1,000 each within an hour.[397]

As concessionaire, the zoo fixed the train's track bed on its own and by 2001 had the trains running again, one named the San Antonio Zoo Eagle and the other for zoo supporter Mary Rogers Barrett. A new main depot closer to the zoo entrance opened with a gift shop. Next door went the Eagle Nest Café, its space remodeled in 2019 to become a Starbucks. A third train was added, and in 2021 the first of the old trains' colorful replacements left the station as the San Antonio Zoo Train.

There had been changes in nearby attractions as well. Horseback riders following rustic wooden-railed bridle paths along Mulberry Avenue had been a familiar sight since 1937. Rentals from Brackenridge Stables just outside the park reached an annual high of thirty-two thousand in 1981. But seven years later, with rentals down by more than a third, the stables closed and horseback rides ended.[398]

The number of polo matches had also been dwindling, and stopped altogether when the Retama Polo Center opened

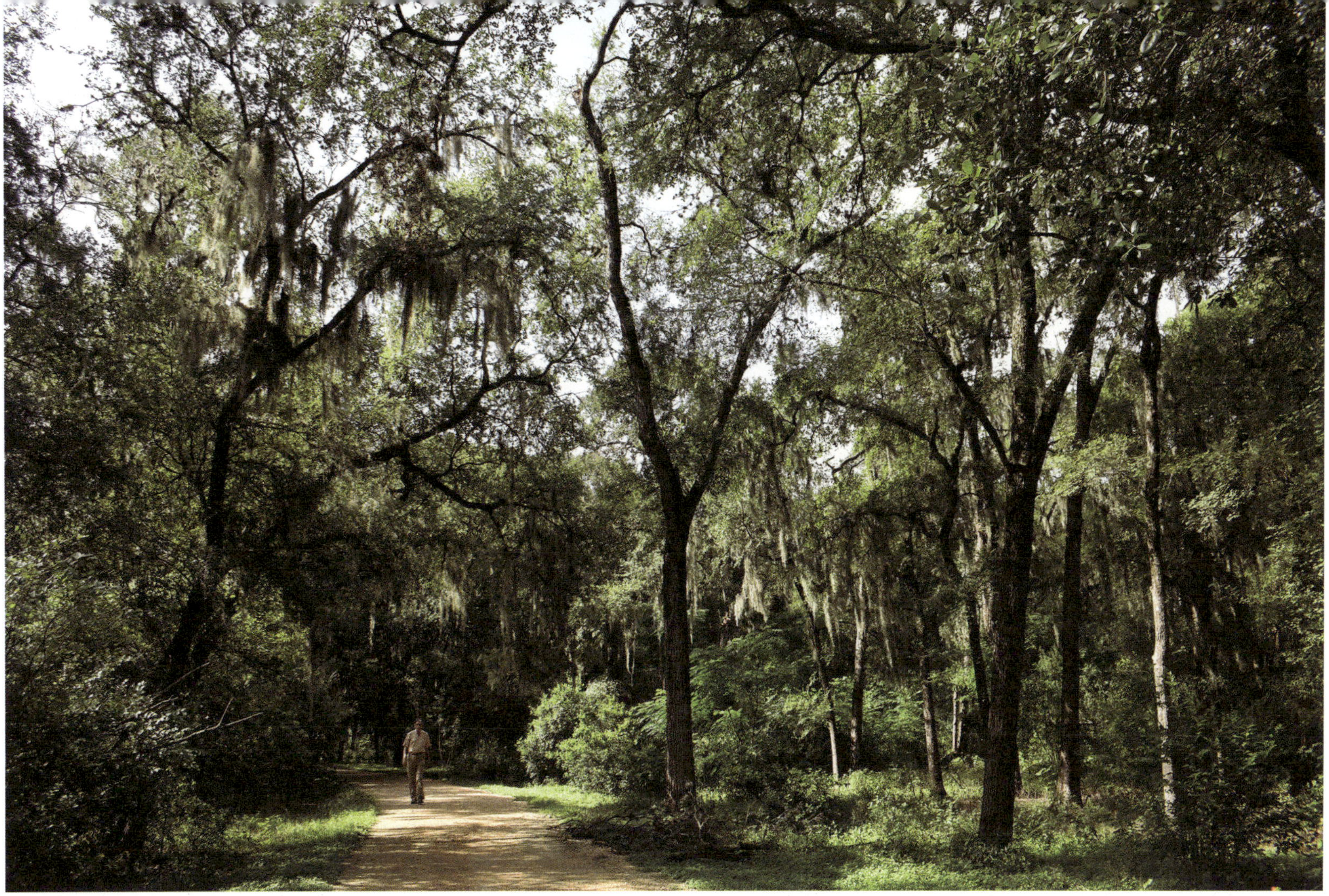

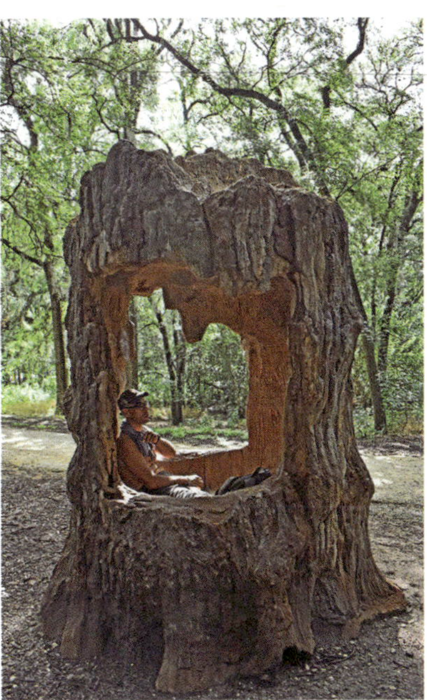

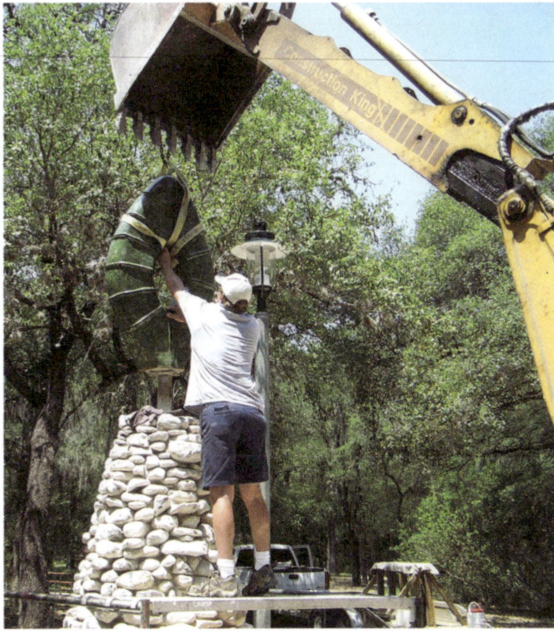

Spanish moss still clung to the trees when park improvements begun in 2003 converted some roadways to pedestrian trails. Jogger Jason Martinez rested by one trail inside a *faux bois* stump in 2021. A parks department worker in 2006 lowers a trailside sculpture by Susan Budge into place.

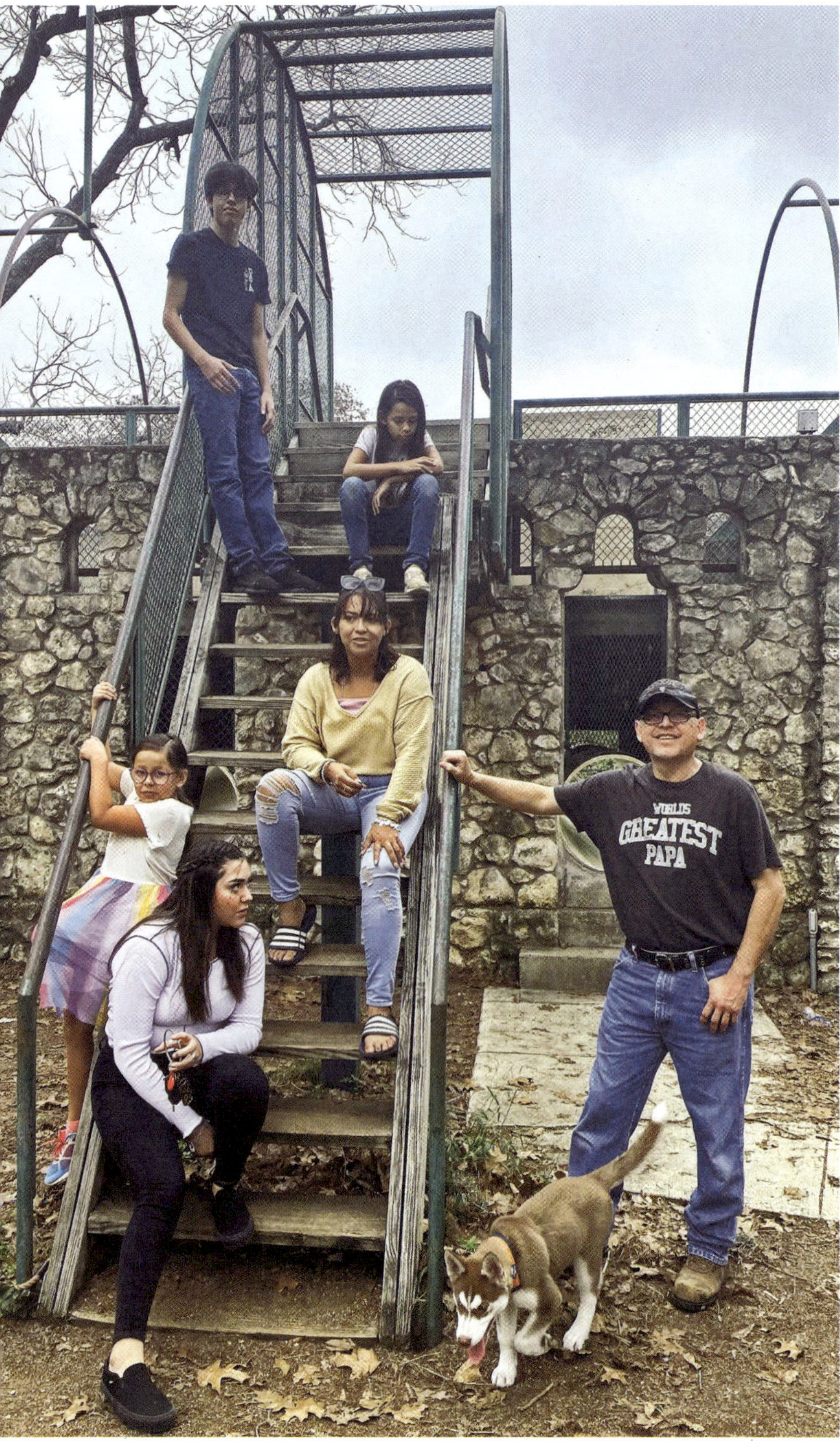

The Martinez family gathered at a stairway installed when the roofless Lambert Beach bathhouse was renovated as a playscape in 1992.

fifteen miles north in 1975. The driving range concession using the southern edge of the field was taken over in 2001 by Golf San Antonio, granted the entire field for its First Tee Learning Center to teach golf to inner-city children. A First Tee clubhouse was built nearby.[399]

Ongoing park improvements included, in 1992, renovation of Lambert Beach's deteriorating 1925 stone bathhouse. End units were restored to their original appearance. The roof was removed from the rest of the building and recreational equipment mixed in to create a playscape. Upgrades elsewhere, including landscaping north of Lambert Beach, were funded by $7.5 million in city bonds approved in 1994 and 1997.[400]

Malcolm Matthews began a decade as parks and recreation director in 2002. The next year he began guiding a three-year renovation of facilities using $6.5 million in newly approved city bond funds. The Lions Field playground, Dionicio Rodríguez arbor, pedestrian bridges near the Koehler Pavilion, and Joske Pavilion and adjacent playground were repaired and improved. Since "too much of the park has been overrun by cars," as one project manager said, some interior roadways were converted to pedestrian trails, more walking trails were built, and public art was installed.[401]

Another attempt was made at dramatizing Brackenridge Park's near-midpoint entrance across from Mahncke Park, a cut through the Broadway commercial strip purchased from the Water Works Company in 1908 and widened to 170 feet with a small traffic circle in 1916. "It's always been the official entrance, but most people don't know it's there," said the parks department's Rodney Dziuk. In 2005 the city added stone entrance pillars with decorative metalwork by George Schroeder and removed the traffic circle, which for thirty years had featured a statue of George Brackenridge.[402]

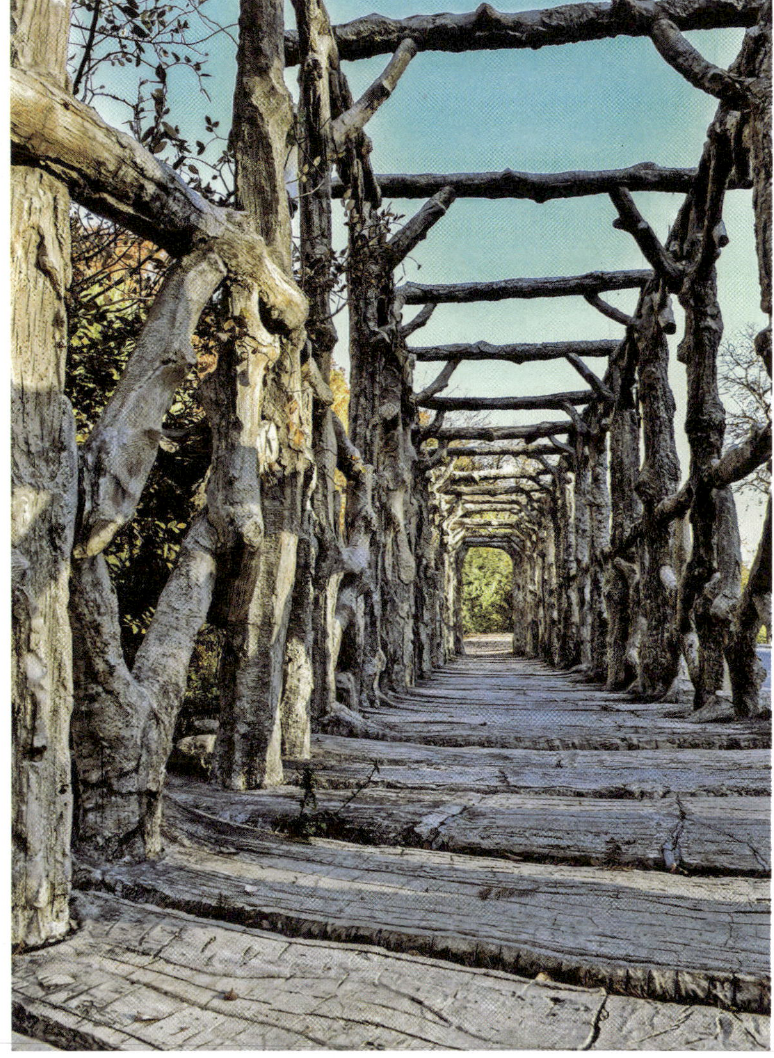

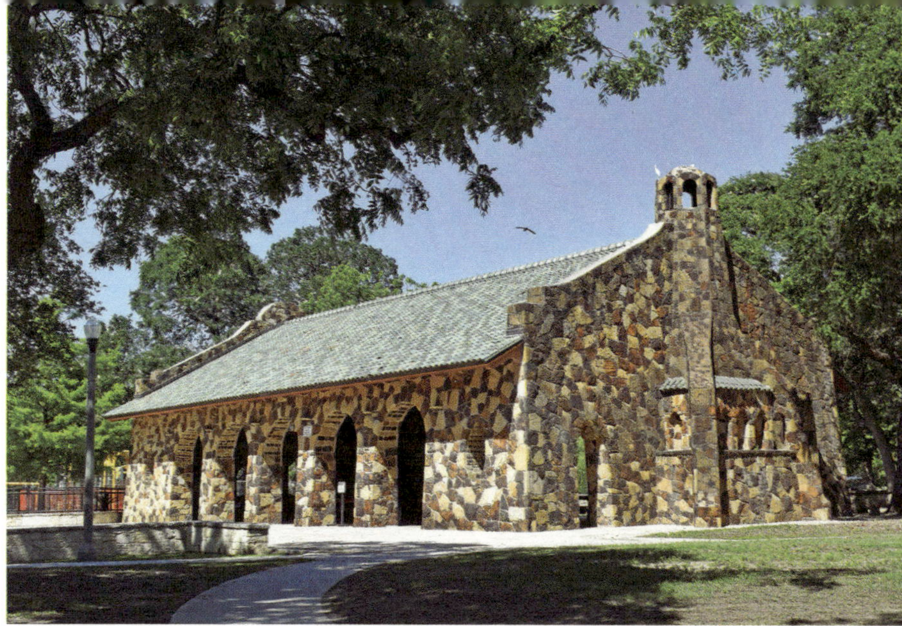

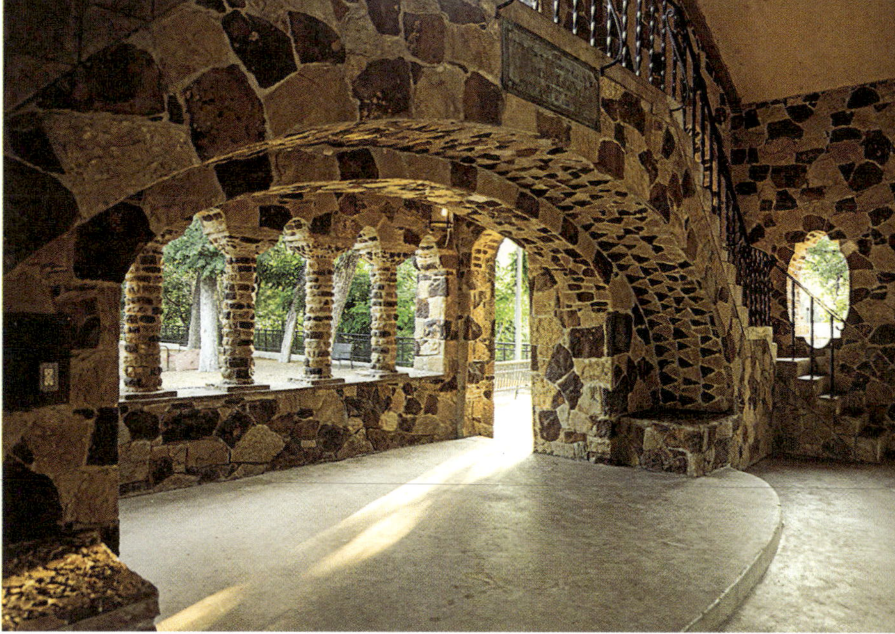

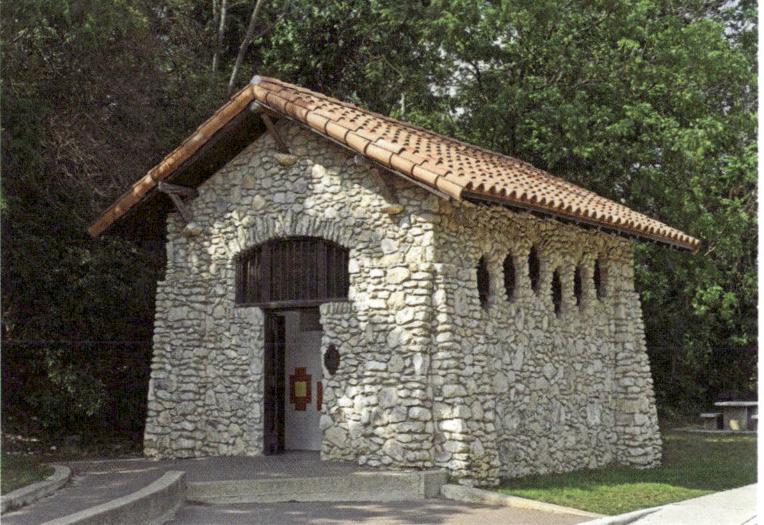

Park improvements from 2003 to 2006 restored 1920s landmarks, including the *faux bois* bridge, a restroom building near Koehler Park, and the Joske Pavilion's interior and exterior.

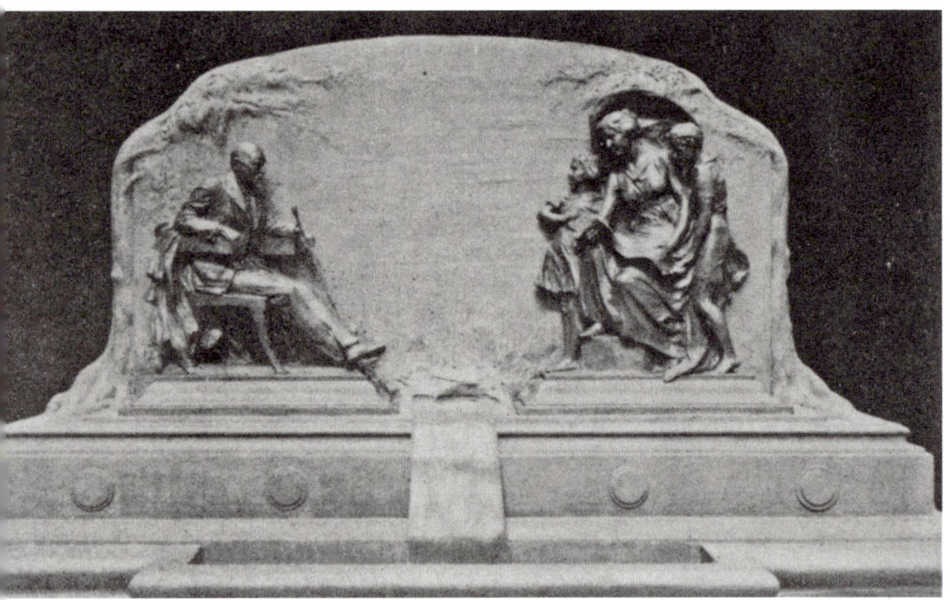

A monument to George Brackenridge was designed by Pompeo Coppini in 1951 with bronze reliefs separated by a chiseled map of Brackenridge Park. As this plaster model indicates, a stream of water representing the river was to flow down the middle into a pool at the base.

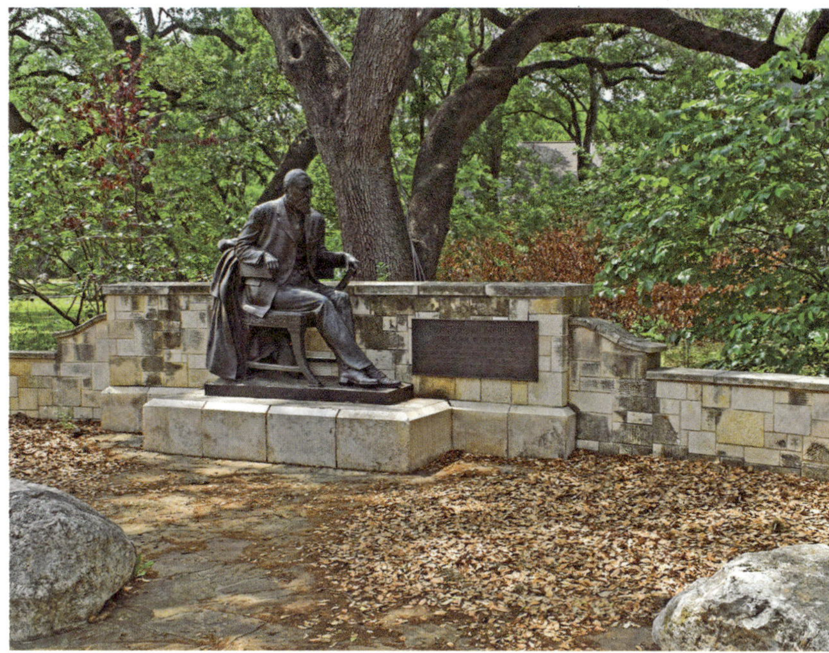

Only one figure of Coppini's proposed monument to Brackenridge was cast, in 1969, and placed at the park entrance in the 3400 block of Broadway.

In a short distance the entry road crossed Avenue B and narrowed as it entered the park through a wooded area. With no other park feature obvious or even close, passersby still felt little sense of arrival, and the intended grand entrance remained infrequently used.[403]

The changes had included a small adjacent plaza designed by J. Harris Hein to feature the relocated bronze relief of a seated George Brackenridge, part of a larger design by Pompeo Coppini. Its story dated from 1951, when *Express* publisher Frank G. Huntress sought to rectify the lack of a Brackenridge memorial by commissioning Coppini, then eighty-two, for a major sculpture to go in the park.[404]

Coppini designed a rough-cut stone vertical slab set on a raised stone base, the monument about thirty-four feet long and rising some eighteen feet. At the left would be a bronze relief of a seated Brackenridge leaning across to a bronze relief of a small girl and boy with their teacher, representing Brackenridge's philanthropy in education. A relief map of the park, sculpted on the stone between the two bronze reliefs, would be angled back. Water, representing Brackenridge's development of San Antonio's modern water system, would flow down the outline of the San Antonio River in the park relief to a stone chute and fall into a small pool at the statue's base.[405]

Huntress sought contributions ranging from "the pennies of school children to large donations of business leaders." He was able to raise little more of the $25,000 cost than what covered a plaster model of the Brackenridge relief portion ready for bronze casting. Coppini died in 1957. There things stood for another twelve years, until Coppini's longtime student Waldine Tauch took matters in hand.[406]

Tauch, a member of the city's Fine Arts Commission, convinced the other members to approve shipping the plaster model to Italy for bronze casting with the promise that the city would pay. She apparently mentioned it to Mayor Walter McAllister, but no contract was authorized by city council or even brought up before the order was placed. When the finished bronze casting arrived in 1969 with a bill for $30,000, council members, caught unaware, vowed never to pay. Private fundraising resolved the matter. The casting of Brackenridge was mounted on a pedestal in the center of the traffic circle and unveiled in November 1970.[407]

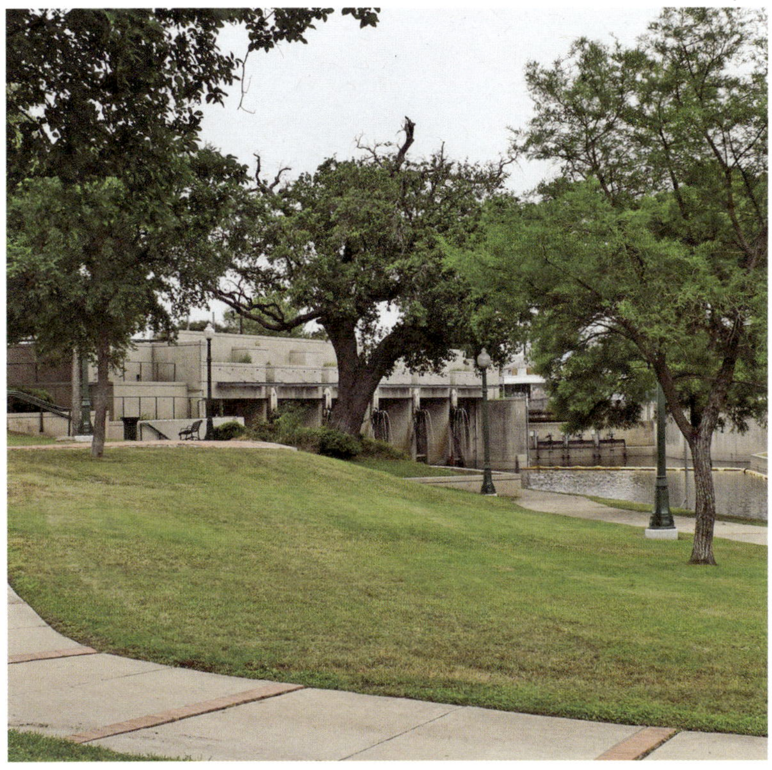

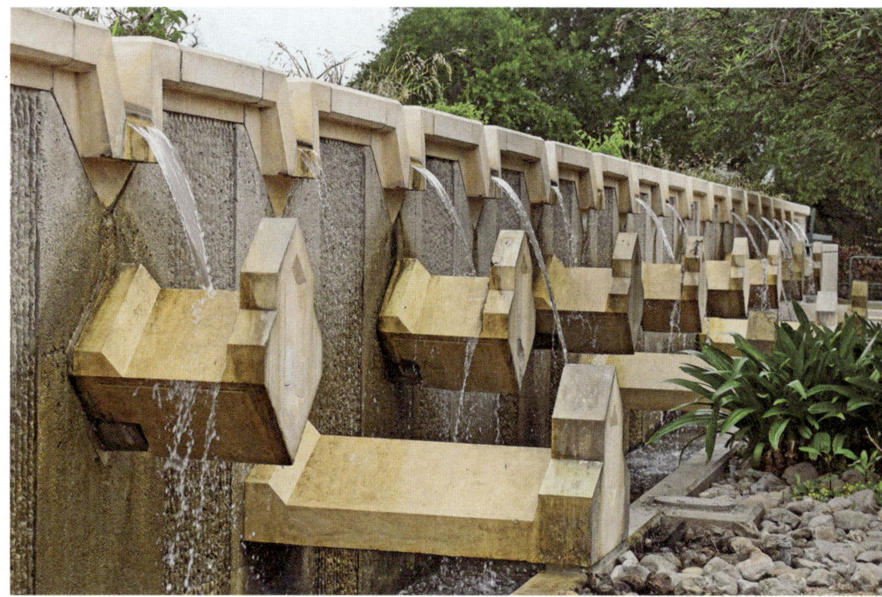

At Brackenridge Park's southern tip on Josephine Street, a flood tunnel intake structure dominates the four-acre Tunnel Inlet Park. A decorative structure on the opposite side aerates water sent up the tunnel at non-flood times for recirculation downstream through the River Walk.

The narrow greensward beside the newly improved park entrance covered an underground drainage pipe that since the park's earliest days had carried storm water from Mahncke Park under Broadway and a short distance into Brackenridge Park, where it flowed into an open dirt ditch along the edge of the golf course. In 1977 the drainage system was enlarged with the Catalpa-Pershing Project, a two-mile storm drainage system named after streets upstream in the Mahncke Park neighborhood, which it crossed from northeast to southwest. Neighborhood residents succeeded in having their section of the channel covered. But soon after it crossed Broadway into Brackenridge Park, the new concrete channel was left uncovered as it continued southwest along Avenue B and swung west around the golf course to empty into the San Antonio River north of US 281.[408]

South of US 281, the river's stormwaters have been diverted since 1998 at Tunnel Inlet Park, the four acres forming the southernmost tip of Brackenridge Park at Josephine Street. There the diverted stormwater drops some 150 feet through an inlet shaft into a concrete tunnel twenty-four feet in diameter beneath downtown San Antonio. Three miles later it exits from the outlet shaft back into the river. The $111 million tunnel project took the US Army Corps of Engineers four years to complete, and is among the world's longest.[409]

Reducing the risk of flooding through the downtown area allows riverside hotels and restaurants to open patios closer to the river level with little fear of high water. In normal weather the tunnel helps maintain the water level along the River Walk by diverting some river flow at the tunnel outlet downstream and pumping it up the tunnel to the inlet, where the water is aerated and recirculated down the river channel. Three artesian wells in Brackenridge Park that once pumped five million gallons daily through the River Walk are no longer needed.[410]

Of the citywide park bond funds approved in 2003, nearly half were earmarked for badly needed structural repairs to Brackenridge Park's crown jewel since 1917, what was again called the Japanese Tea Garden after being renamed the Chinese Tea Garden during anti-Japanese sentiments at the start of World War II. When the United States broke with China during the Cold War, the Chinese designation was dropped, and the feature became just the Sunken Garden.[411]

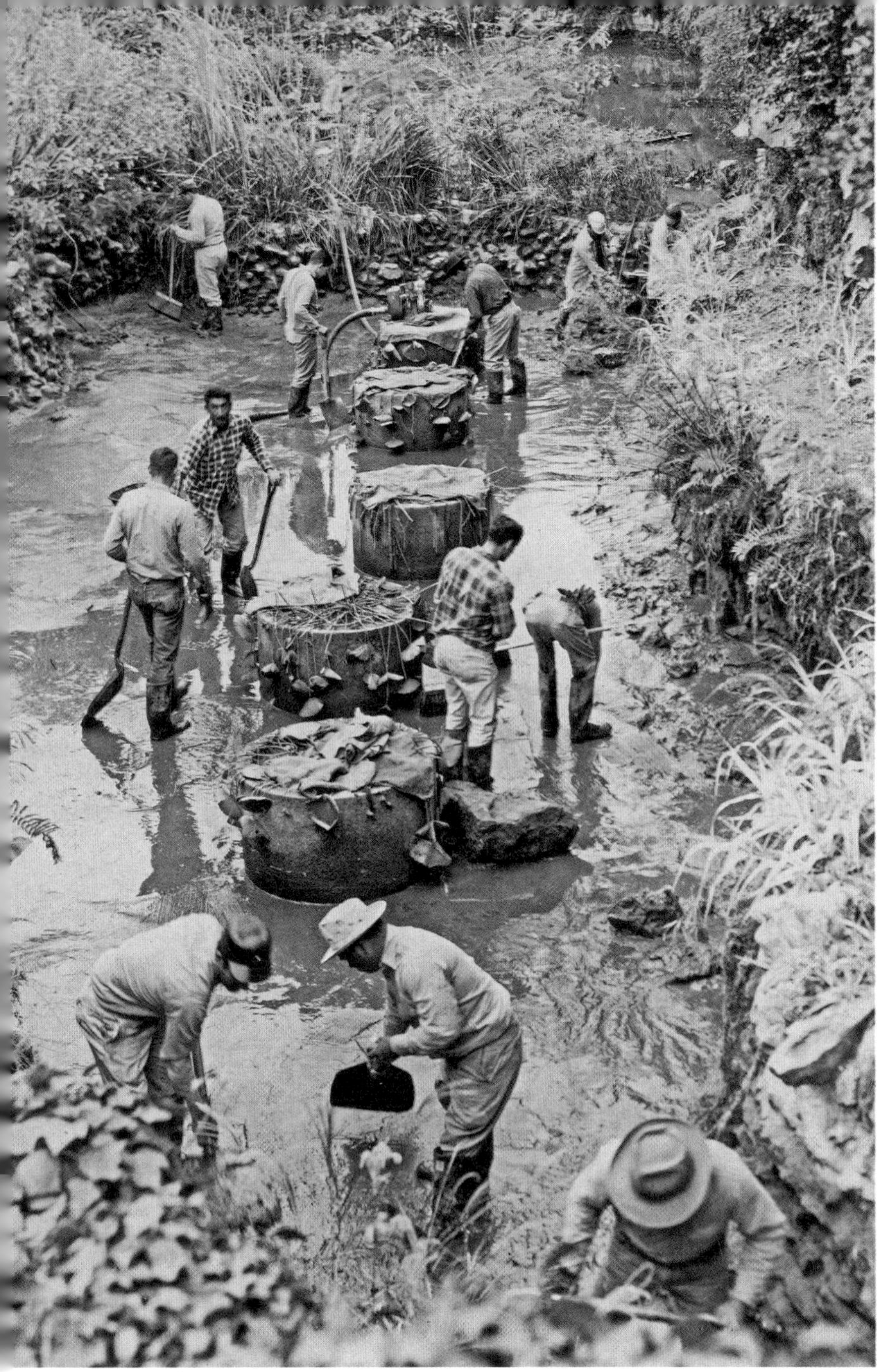

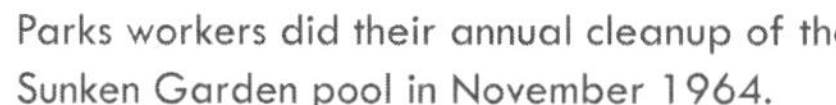

Parks workers did their annual cleanup of the Sunken Garden pool in November 1964.

The matter resurfaced in the public eye when city councilman Van Archer suggested "Japanese" be restored as "at least a small and symbolic reparation for the wrongs suffered by an American minority group caught in the madness and hysteria of war." Under Mayor Henry Cisneros, the council unanimously approved the change in July 1983, in line with a nationwide trend of restoring names of landmarks once designated Japanese.[412]

Japan's US ambassador and twenty-five members of the Jingu family that had once lived in San Antonio's garden, including seven children of the late Kimi and Miyoshi Jingu, several grandchildren, and a great-granddaughter, attended a rededication ceremony in October 1984. Although the landmark archway still bore the name Chinese Tea Garden, Mary Jingu Onodera unveiled a plaque beside it explaining that name.[413]

A new look at fully repairing and restoring the complex put estimates at $6 million, twice what was available in public funds. There would have to be private funding to fix the severe disrepair. The pavilion's thatched roof had been replaced with wood shingles that were failing, and support beams had weakened. The base of the pond below leaked so badly it had to be left drained, exposing cracks amid the empty lily pots once concealed below the water line. Garden maintenance had been punted to volunteers from three gardening groups, but they could not keep up. The city tried turning over the tea garden to a private company to restore and operate, but with a franchise fee of $2.5 million there were no bidders.[414]

Bond funds were used to make structural repairs to the garden pavilion and to put on a roof with synthetic thatch that, unlike the original natural thatch, resisted fire and bugs. To help with funding, the San Antonio Parks Foundation, established in 1981 and headed by former mayor Lila Cockrell, came forward to help with its auxiliary Friends of the Parks, organized under leadership of former city council member Bonnie Conner. Houston's landscape and design firm SWA Group did master planning, with architectural design by San Antonio's Alamo Architects.[415]

The San Antonio Parks Foundation launched a campaign to raise matching funds. The first phase, begun in 2005, was completed in 2007. The pavilion was restored and the two-story stone Jingu House, built at the edge of a cliff without sufficient support, was stabilized through emergency fundraising and given

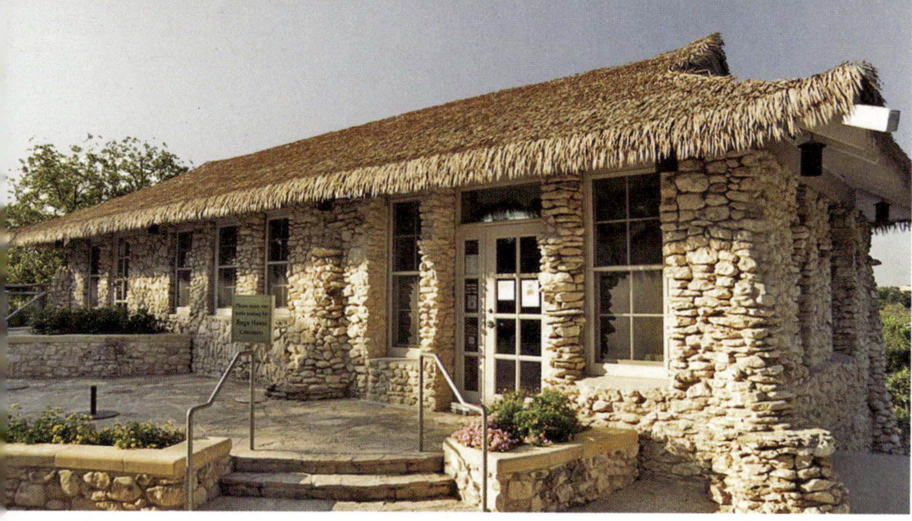

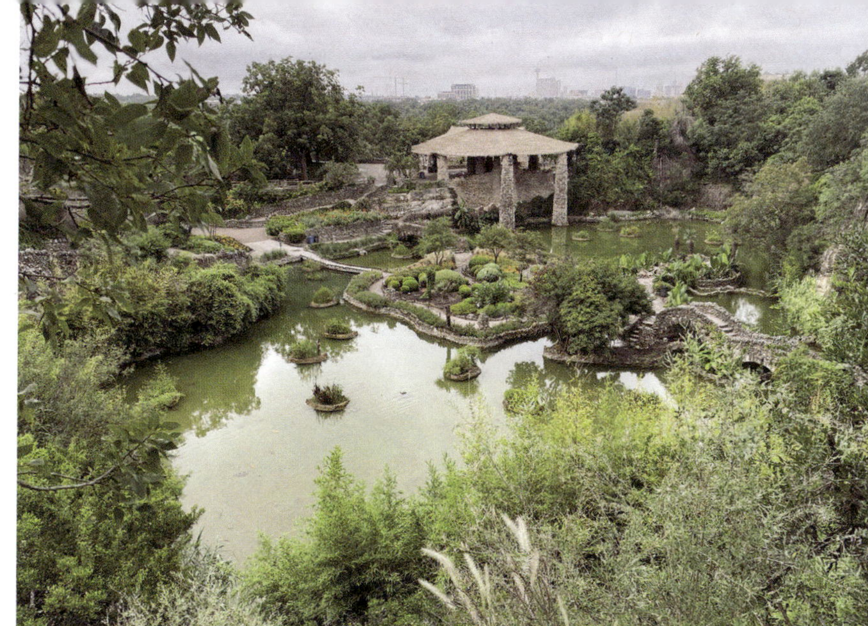

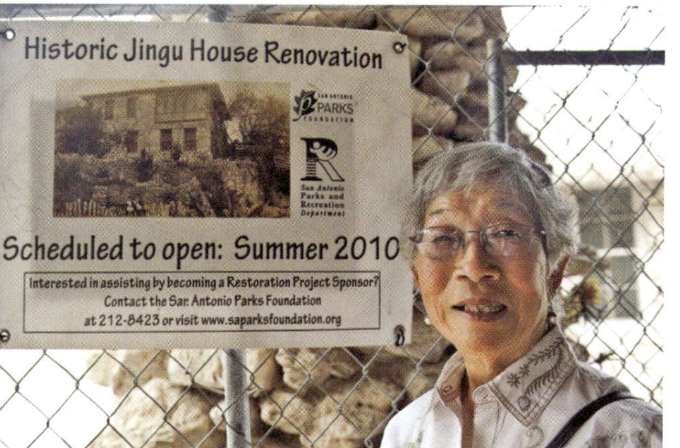

Mabel Jingu Enkoji's childhood home was restored by the San Antonio Parks Foundation.

Restoration by the San Antonio Parks Foundation in 2005–2010 revitalized the Japanese Tea Garden complex, restoring water to the pond and reviving the cliffside waterfall.

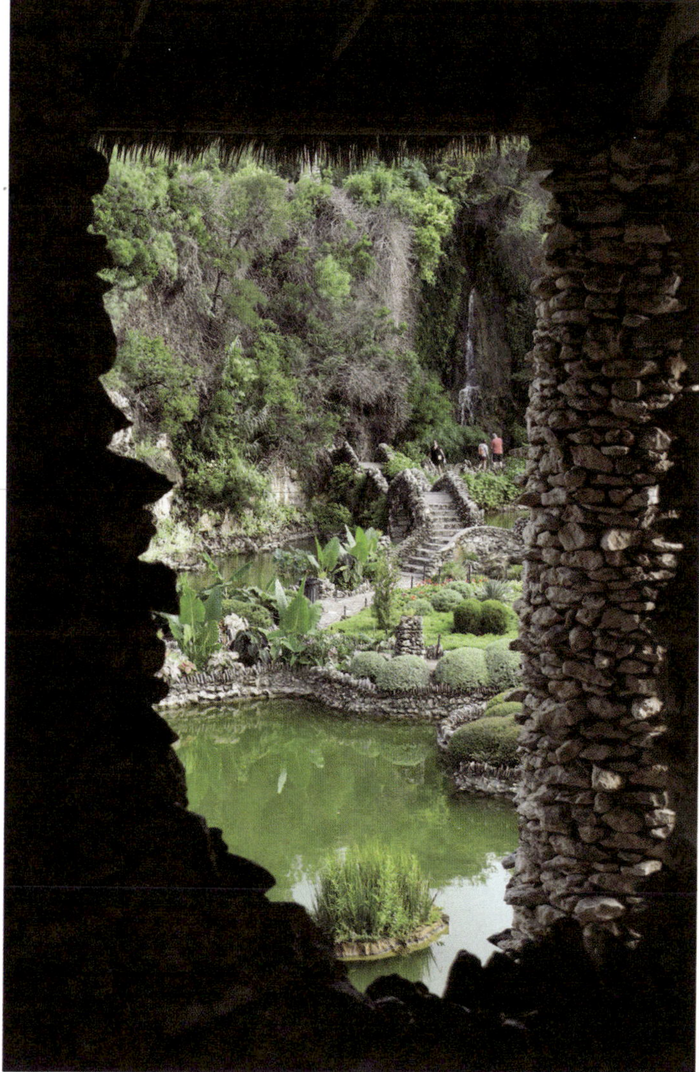

a retrofitted foundation. Then the San Antonio Parks Foundation raised $850,000 toward the $1.2 million second phase. This restored the sixty-foot waterfall and repaired walkways and ponds, which gained a synthetic lining and a recycling water system that supported Koi and aquatic plants. The tea garden reopened in March 2008 to great fanfare. Celebrants included Mabel Jingu Enkoji, one of the three surviving Jingu children.[416]

Next the foundation raised more than $1 million for a two-year renovation of the Jingu House, which opened in 2010 as a fund-raising facility for the foundation. Under a franchise with caterer Caryn Hasslocher, who was followed in 2022 by restaurateur Cappy Lawton, the Jingu House served lunch and was available for special events, along with the upper garden, patio, and pavilion, for up to three hundred people. A romantic nook for weddings could fit up to fifteen on a ledge of the lower garden beneath the waterfall.[417]

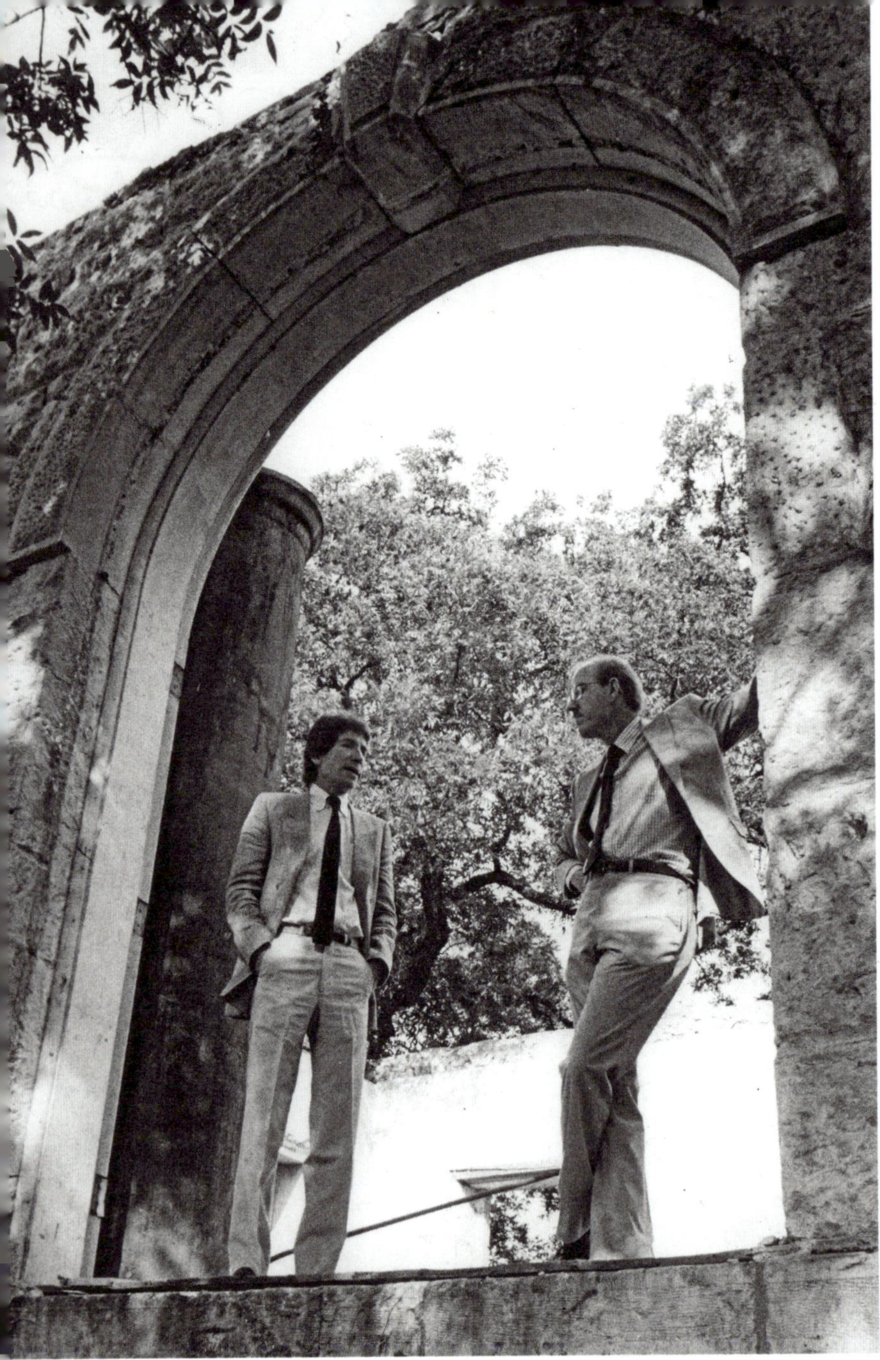

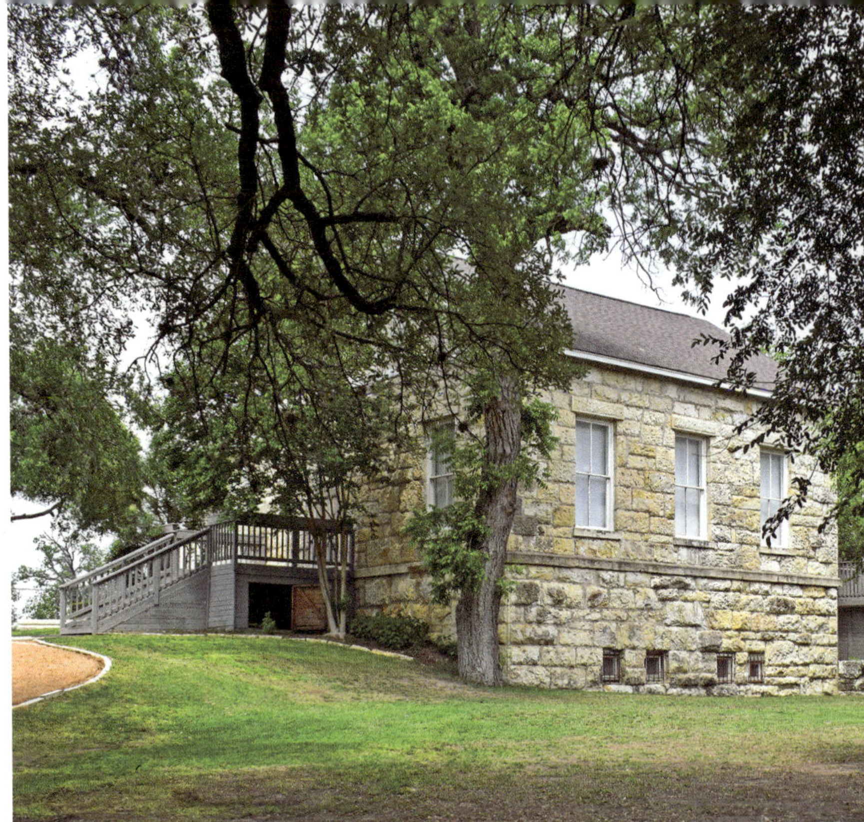

Architects Richard Mogas, *left*, and Joe Stubblefield leased the roofless lower pump house in 1978 and restored it as their office. It is now rented out by Alamo City Golf Trail members as the Borglum Studio.

Of the independent institutions within Brackenridge Park, the golf course was changed most by the intrusion of US 281. Reconfiguring the nine holes at the course's western end in 1968 erased the original Tillinghast design. Two ponds were added to that section and a third to the eighth hole. The first nine holes changed as the long-dry waterworks canal to the 1885 pump house and most of the river's remaining meander nearby were filled in. Three of the five New Deal–era bridges were removed.[418]

Nearly forty years later, in 2005, incoming mayor Phil Hardberger picked as city manager Sheryl Sculley, who held that post in Kalamazoo, Michigan. She hired Pat DiGiovanni, also from Kalamazoo, as her deputy. DiGiovanni, an avid golfer, was unimpressed with the condition of San Antonio's seven public courses, particularly that of Brackenridge. He drafted Jim Roschek, Kalamazoo's director of golf operations, to move to San Antonio as head of the new Municipal Golf Association-SA, which took over Brackenridge course management. MGA-SA closed the course for a yearlong $4 million–plus redesign funded by the city and overseen by an Arlington, Texas, firm headed by John Colligan that specialized in restoring historic golf courses.[419]

As San Antonio River Improvements Project earthmoving equipment sought to avoid newly discovered archeological sites, the riverbed meander through the back nine holes was reopened. Massive oaks and pecans were trimmed, and a hike-and-bike path was created around the course to Avenue B,

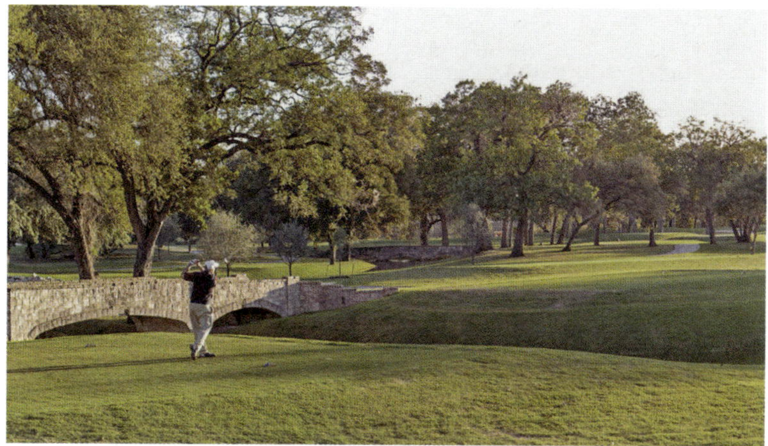

Golf Digest reported that Brackenridge Park golfers played "one of the most fun" municipal courses in the country.

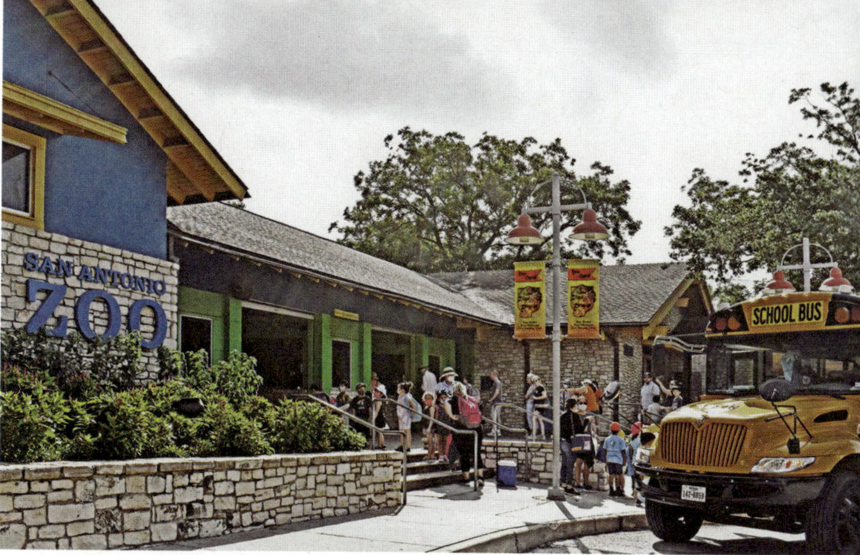

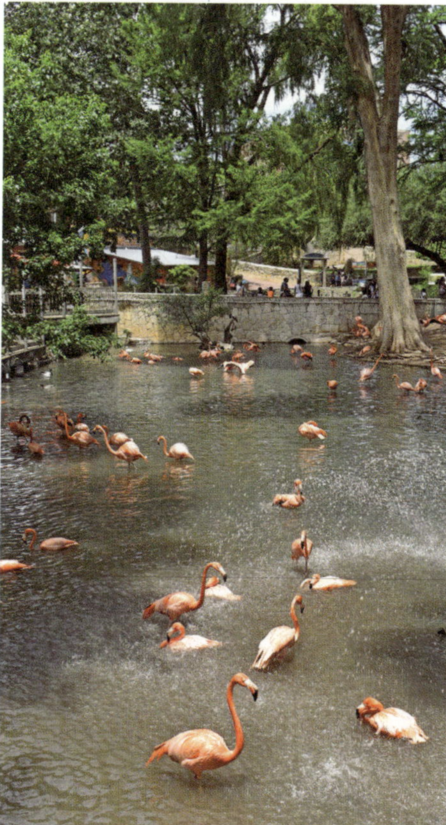

Annual attendance exceeds two million at the San Antonio Zoo. Here, flamingos gather in a pool that was once part of the Upper Labor Acequia.

which paralleled Broadway. Fifteen of the eighteen holes were restored to A. W. Tillinghast's original design, including rectangular-shaped greens and flat-bottom bunkers with steep grass faces. The restored clubhouse included a Texas Golf Hall of Fame and Museum and an outdoor Walk of Fame with plaques telling of local golf highlights.[420]

A stone's throw from the clubhouse, the roof of the unused 1885 pump house had collapsed before the city leased it in 1978 to architects Joe Stubblefield and Richard Mogas. The two restored the building and opened it six years later as their studio. The Municipal Golf Association, also known as Alamo City Golf Trail, has since rented out the renovated pump house as the Borglum Studio for special events.[421]

Nearby and closer to Broadway the view was more open after the 1915 Brackenridge Park pumping station was closed in 1959 and razed, though unobtrusive wells continued in use.[422]

"Brackenridge Park Golf Course has never looked this good," GolfTexas.com declared when the course reopened in December 2008. *Links Magazine* called Brackenridge, one of Tillinghast's few public courses, "a sleeper," offering "affordable golf with great 'bones.'" *Golf Digest* termed it "one of the most fun" municipal courses in the country.[423]

In 1968, a year after longtime director Fred Stark's death, Louis DiSabato, thirty-six, director of the Seneca Park Zoo in Rochester, New York, was named director of the San Antonio Zoo. Five years later DiSabato developed a plan, with architect Tom Pressly Jr., that began with a new animal nutrition center, followed by a veterinary center. A new natural habitat area with overlooks in onetime quarry areas showcased animals from Africa, Australia, and the Americas. The city added three new acres of Koehler Park to the zoo for a $3 million children's zoo, opened in August 1987.[424]

Steve McCusker, whose career included positions at zoos in Fort Worth, Portland, and Tucson, succeeded DiSabato in 1994. The zoo celebrated its centennial in 2014 with the opening of an $8 million Zootennial Plaza, complete with a restaurant that seats three hundred and a carousel with sixty hand-painted animals. McCusker moved zoo offices into the park's former donkey barn, vacated as parks department headquarters five years earlier.

Annual zoo attendance doubled from 1.1 million after completion of Africa Alive!, a sprawling grotto with a wide window providing eye-level underwater views of the hippopotamus pool. In 2004 the zoo opened the nature-based school for preschoolers that in 2018 moved to a $17 million two-acre campus on Tuleta Drive to the west. The Will Smith Zoo School was based in the former ten-classroom building of the Sunshine Cottage School for Deaf Children. It could serve up to two hundred children.[425]

San Antonio native Tim Morrow was named zoo director in 2014. His eighteen years with SeaWorld Park and Entertainment included vice presidency of its San Antonio water park. Morrow supervised expansion of a $1 million rhinoceros habitat with a viewing deck and construction of a new habitat for endangered whooping cranes, which joined the zoo's breeding program of rare snow leopards, golden lion tamarins, Andean and California condors, and more. Added to these were the first American flamingos and white rhinoceroses born in any zoo. Morrow also took on planning for a $200 million, twenty-year master plan that would include developing twelve acres beneath a US 281 overpass as part of the zoo.[426]

In 2019 the zoo repurposed a parking lot near its entrance to house Kiddie Park, originally opened on Broadway adjacent to Brackenridge Park in 1925. Billing itself as "the nation's oldest children's amusement park," the zoo's latest addition featured a classic carousel with hand-carved animals, built in 1918 and brought to Kiddie Park in 1935.[427]

Across from the zoo entrance, a $5 million pet adoptions center operated for the city by the Animal Defense League was built in 2012. It was on the site of the city pound, in the park since the 1920s. Demolition of the pound building four years earlier had followed growing anger over the pound's policy of sending all strays not claimed or adopted within five days to its gas chambers. The no-kill center could house up to fifty dogs and thirty cats and had a fenced lawn for trial walks for dogs and their potential adopters.[428]

Another transformation was occurring across the park at the Witte Museum. In 2004 Marise McDermott became the seventh director of the Witte since Ellen Shulz Quillin's retirement in 1960. McDermott had previously served for six years as head of Iowa's Cedar Rapids History Center, as well as in earlier positions on the Witte staff and as a reporter for the *San Antonio Light*. She reversed the Witte's fortunes with a successful series of fundraising efforts for projects totaling $100 million. The number of visitors rose to 600,000 a year.

The Witte succeeded the Trail Drivers Association as custodian of Pioneer Hall, incorporated in a museum master plan by Lake Flato Architects as a South Texas heritage center. After its restoration and addition of a rear wing under architects Ford, Powell & Carson, Pioneer Hall reopened in 2012. On the south it was linked to the Witte's main building by a soaring great hall and dinosaur gallery completed in 2017. On the north it was connected to a new exhibit hall and events center.

Between the Witte buildings and the San Antonio River, a courtyard featuring three historic homes rescued in the 1940s joined Texas impressionist artist Julian Onderdonk's frame studio, moved in 2008 from behind his old home in the Monte

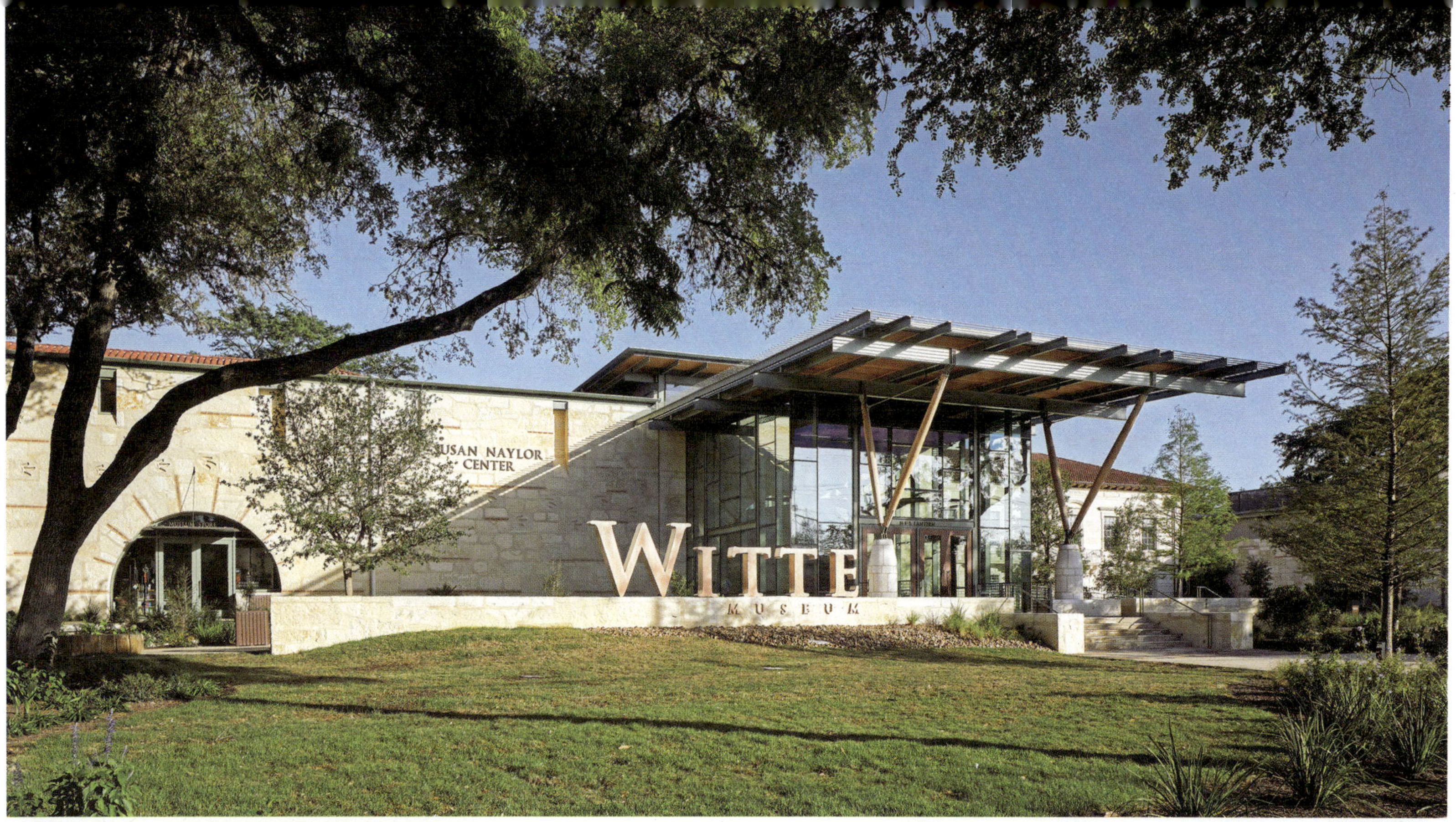

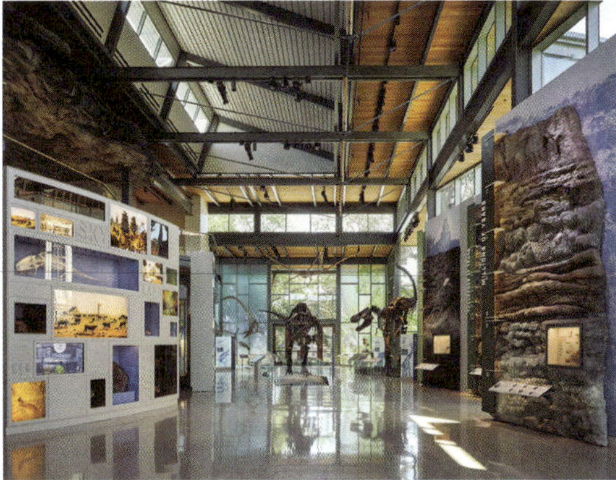

Part of the former Pioneer Hall is visible at right of the renovated Witte Museum's main building, which gained a great hall.

A darker section of paving beside the Witte Museum marks the path of the Alamo Acequia's main channel.

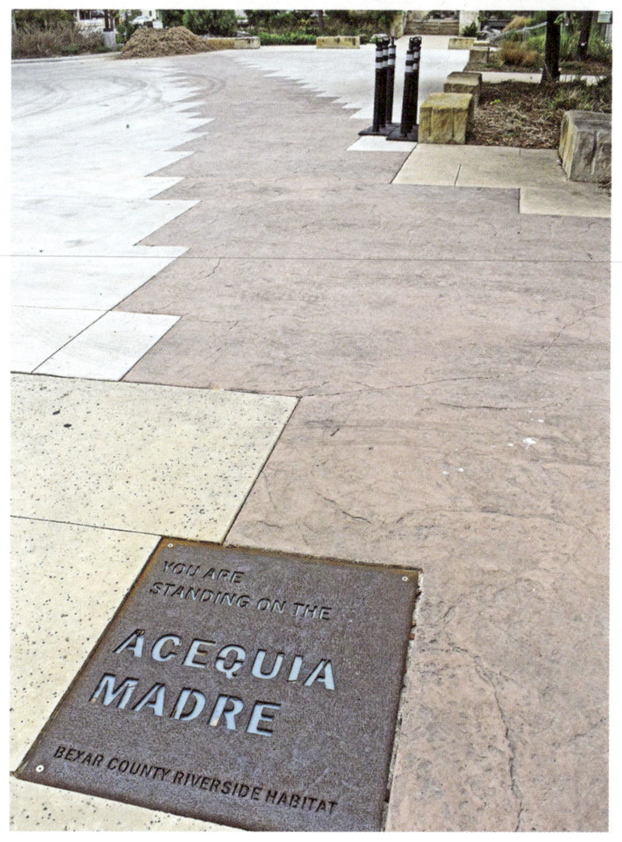

Vista neighborhood. The bronze quarter-scale casting of Gutzon Borglum's monument to Texas trail drivers went nearby. Beside the river near the south end of the courtyard, a science treehouse at Tuleta Drive and the river, designed by Lake Flato Architects in 1997, became an interactive health learning center. At the northern end stone seats and a stage for a small open-air riverside theater were added near the marked course of the Alamo Acequia that once crossed the grounds.

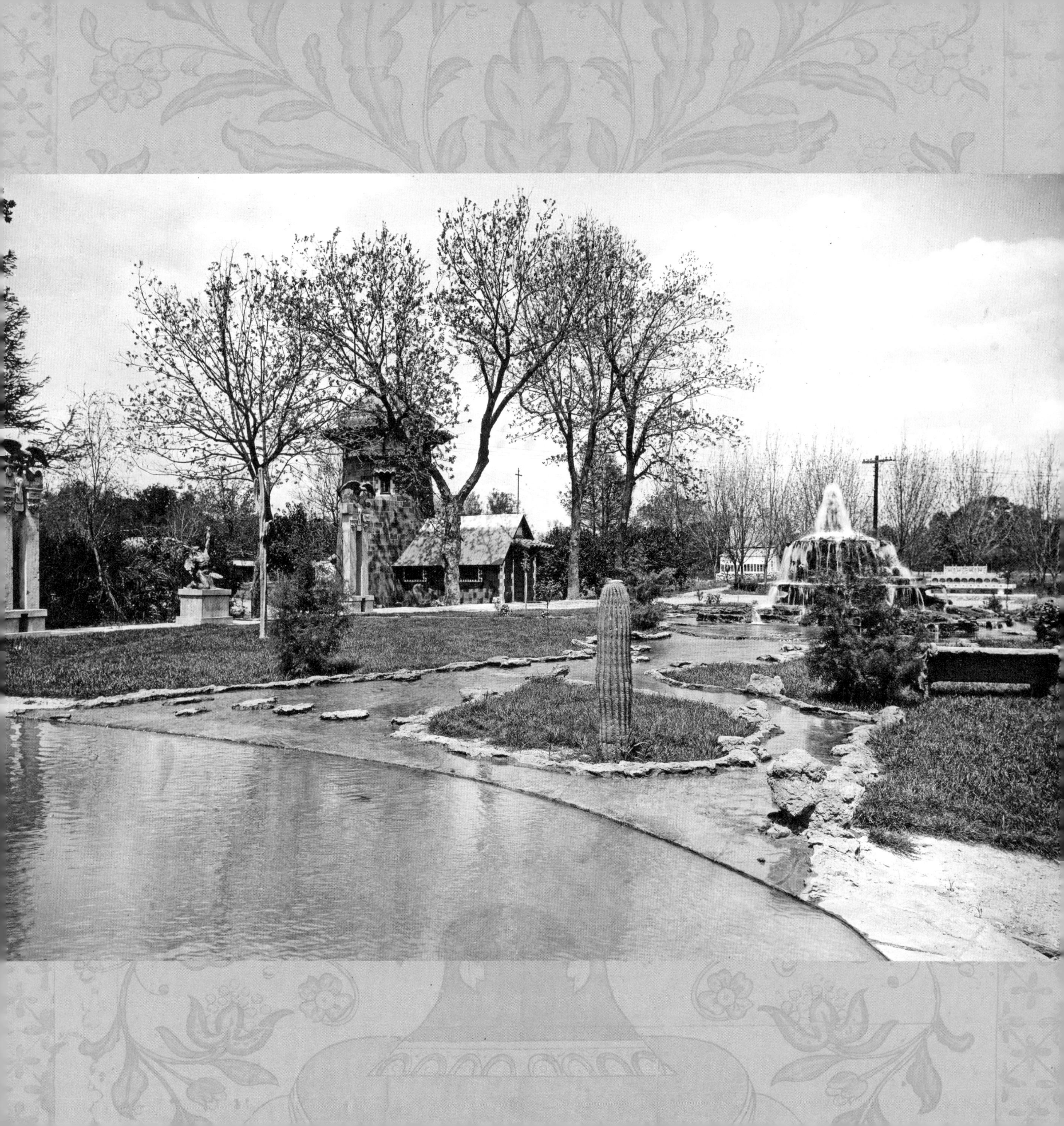

Miraflores

In 2005 the remains of a contemplative garden were added to Brackenridge Park. The garden had been intended for patients of an adjacent sanitarium that was never built. The 4.5-acre site at the park's northeastern edge was once part of a dairy farm pasture, its fencing apparently so poor at keeping in cows that Carey / Hildebrand Avenue along the pasture's northern border was first known as Cow Street.[429]

Like so many features contributing to the distinctive charm of San Antonio and Brackenridge Park, the garden's design sprang from the mind of an untrained planner. Dr. Aureliano Adolpho Urrutia was a prominent refugee of the Mexican Revolution who named his garden Miraflores and put in plantings, monuments, and symbols that evoked his homeland. Inconsistencies that would have been resolved differently by a professional designer were masked so cleverly, one landscape architect observed, that they gave "an ingenuous appeal" to its overall "grandiose concept, which could have been wearisome and overbearing if executed in a more polished manner."[430]

Miraflores evolved from 1921 to 1946. By 2005 what remained brought fewer comparisons to Mexico City's Chapultepec Park and Urrutia's Xochimilco birthplace than to an overgrown cemetery. The garden narrowly escaped being cleared for a parking lot. Yet three dozen elements surviving in one form or another were sufficient to win Miraflores a listing in 2006 on the National Register of Historic Places. Restoration slowly began.[431]

Miraflores included a tower and library and a twelve-foot fountain of rock and concrete by Dionicio Rodríguez that tapped an artesian well.

Before the Mexican Revolution forced him into exile, Urrutia had been one of Mexico's most prominent surgeons and minister of the interior for three months under President Victoriana Huerta. He was personal physician to longtime president Porfirio Díaz and director of the national school of medicine and of the Hospital General. With his wife, Luz Fernandez, daughter of an international shipping magnate, he built a hospital and sanitarium complex, Sanatorio Urrutia, with surrounding gardens, in the Mexico City borough of Coyoacán.[432]

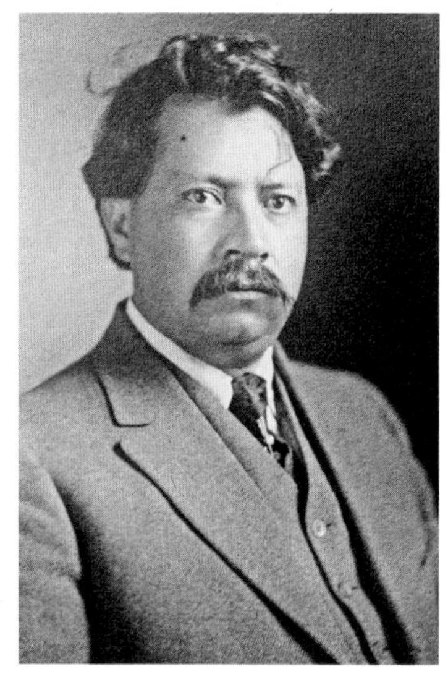

Aureliano Urrutia was a prominent surgeon in Mexico, where he served as minister of the interior for three months.

After a hasty escort out of Mexico in 1914 under protection of sympathetic members of the American military, Urrutia and his family, like thousands of other refugees from the Mexican Revolution, came to San Antonio. He built Clínica Urrutia near Santa Rosa Hospital and reestablished a medical practice, gaining fame for successfully separating a set of conjoined twins and becoming a dramatic figure as he strode about in a cape, carrying a straight cane. Several sons and sons-in-law joined his clinic as physicians, and some daughters ran the nearby Farmacia Urrutia. He died in 1975 at age 103, leaving his fifth wife and seven sons, eight daughters, fifty-one grandchildren, and fifty-five great-grandchildren.[433]

In 1916 Urrutia purchased a wooded site from the Water Supply Company in the 3200 block of Broadway, where he built a dramatic one-story residence he named Quinta Urrutia, incorporating Aztec, Toltec, Moorish, and Spanish motifs. On the roof above the front doorway was an eight-foot cement reproduction of the Winged Victory of Samothrace. The five-acre tract included formal gardens and pools.

While working in his clinic downtown, Urrutia dreamed of having his own hospital and adjoining gardens that would resemble Sanatorio Urrutia in Coyoacán. By 1921, notes great-granddaughter Elise Urrutia, he was recovering from the death of his first wife, Luz, and realizing that he might not be able to return to his native Mexico. That year he purchased nearly fifteen acres at the southwest corner of Broadway and Hildebrand Avenue, less than a mile north of his home. He saw it as becoming "not the usual type of hospital, but a hospital composed of pleasant, homelike bungalows surrounded by flowered lawns, clustered around a central House of Administration."[434]

The hospital complex was never built, although an elaborate entrance gate was constructed facing Broadway with the medical identification "Doctor Urrutia" on a bronze plaque at the top. The arch of pinkish brown volcanic stone was resplendent in its colorful covering of Talavera tiles of tigers, peacocks, flowers, and the Virgin of Guadalupe.

Low walls flanking the arch ended in columns bearing the name of what was completed at the far end of the property: "Mira Flores," which can be translated as "vista of flowers," the would-be sanitarium's showplace gardens. Urrutia began working on them as soon as he purchased the tract. A straight single-lane gravel road led from the planned sanitarium's entrance through groves of giant live oaks across the flat upper two-thirds of the property to the gardens. There the site sloped gently south and west toward the banks of the San Antonio River, which Urrutia slightly reengineered, across from the old Upper Labor Dam.

GET DR. URRUTIA OUT OF VERA CRUZ

Fugitive Ex-Minister Now on His Way to Galveston on American Transport.

HOPES TO BE AN AMERICAN

Will Settle in New Orleans and Seek Naturalization—Funston Glad to Get Him Away Safely.

Special Cable to THE NEW YORK TIMES. From a Staff Correspondent.

VERA CRUZ, May 23.—Dr. Aureliano Urrutia, the former Minister of the Interior in Huerta's Cabinet, whose arrival here from Mexico City caused a riot among Mexicans, sailed with his family for Galveston this afternoon on the navy transport Hancock.

Dr. Urrutia, who was saved from serious harm in the rioting by the vigilance of the United States authorities here, was quietly smuggled out of the city by the army and navy officers. He thanked the Americans for their protection and for the kind treatment and consideration which he and his family had received.

Dr. Urrutia would say nothing about political conditions in Mexico. It is understood that he will take a train from Galveston for New York City.

Persistent rumors reach here that a military uprising is imminent in Mexico City.

All is quiet in Vera Cruz, and everything is going on here as if there was not an American soldier in the city.

Admiral Fletcher shifted his flag from the Florida to the Arkansas as commander of the first division of the Atlantic Fleet this afternoon. The battleship South Carolina sailed for Hayti tonight.

Urrutia came to San Antonio after a dramatic escape in 1914 during the Mexican Revolution.

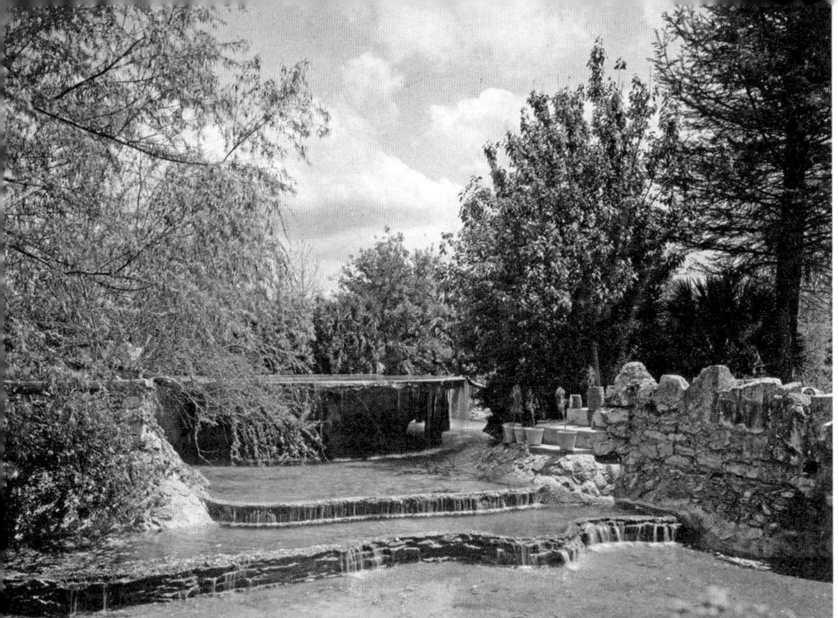

Water features in Miraflores recalled the features of Urrutia's native Xochimilco.

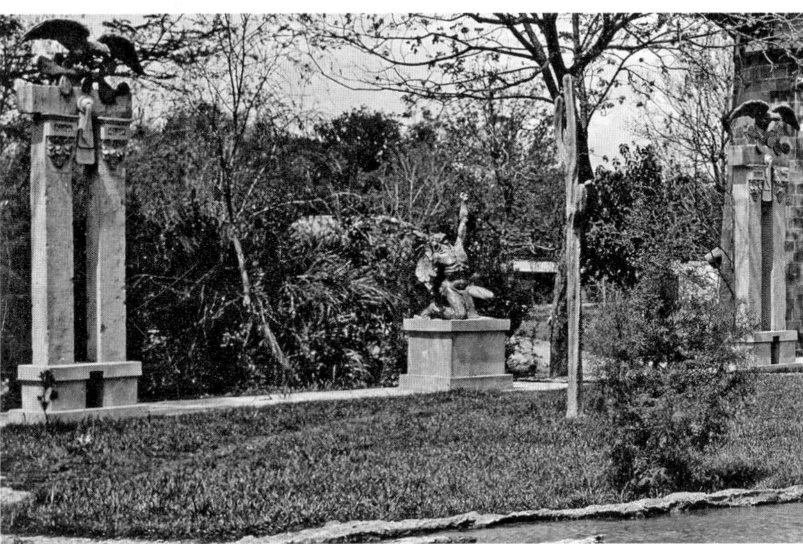

Columns topped by Mexican eagles flanked a sculpture of Cuauhtémoc raising a clenched fist in defiance of Hernán Cortés.

This western third of the property was ideally suited for a lush garden atypical of those in the semiarid Southwest, observed landscape architect Sarah Westkaemper Lake. Its soft alluvial soil, of higher quality than most soils in the city, was free of rocks and watered by an abundance of springs, supplemented by a new artesian well that assured an ample supply of water for fountains and ponds. Large cypress trees near the riverbanks offered shade from the hot afternoon sun. Lake said she thought the prevailing southeast breeze was cooler there, which she attributed to the wooded river bends at the windward side. Here tropical plants San Antonians long sought to nourish elsewhere "are actually suitable to the site," she wrote, if some suffered from fluctuations in the water table.[435]

Though fond of classical design, Urrutia, untrained in landscape architecture, apparently began with no overall plan. He laid out Miraflores with features similar to European parks and Mexico City's Chapultepec Park. Plantings and water features were like those of his Coyoacán sanitarium gardens, recalling the landscape and water features of his native Xochimilco.[436]

There were flowering crape myrtles and magnolias along with pecans, some planted as allées along esplanades. Roses climbed fences. Masses of shrubs included palms, nandina, and broad-leafed evergreens. Lawns were planted in Saint Augustine grass. There were sunny zones around large pools and gardens in shaded areas. Urrutia's clay pots filled with herbs and tropical plantings personalized the garden. At Miraflores, Urrutia would say, "you can visit the only parts of Mexico I have left—her flowers and her plants."[437]

Rather than adhering to a symmetrical system of roadways following consistent axes, Urrutia improvised as he added features at different times, then "joined the dangling axial roadways as best he could," Lake wrote. He did not terrace the site, causing some features, unlike those in more formally designed gardens, to lie on an uneven slope. Adjoining elements were not always in scale, and craftsmanship of decorative ceramics and metalwork was inconsistent. Miraflores, restorative in its tranquility, became in many ways "an idiosyncratic personal playground, full of vitality in its juxtapositions and eccentricities."[438]

The garden's main entrance was at the midpoint of its northern border on Hildebrand Avenue, originally a side street from Broadway dead-ending at the river. Guests passed through a classical gate larger than the one on Broadway and designed by Mexico City architect Marcelo Izaguirre. Its iron pickets were modeled on lances of conquistadores, and its tile panels on flanking pilasters commemorated conquistador Hernán Cortés and the founding of today's Mexico City.[439]

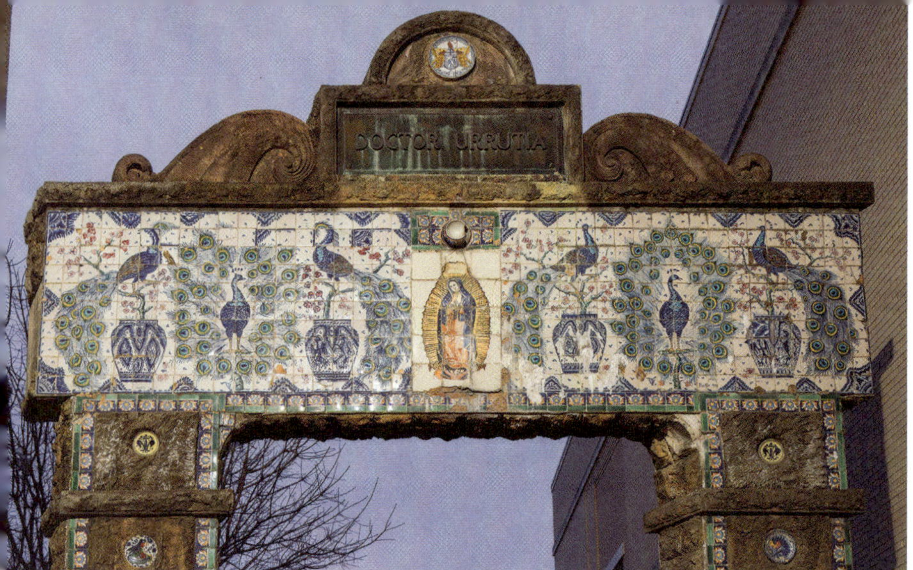

A tiled arch now at the San Antonio Museum of Art formed an entrance gate over a path leading to a side entrance to Miraflores.

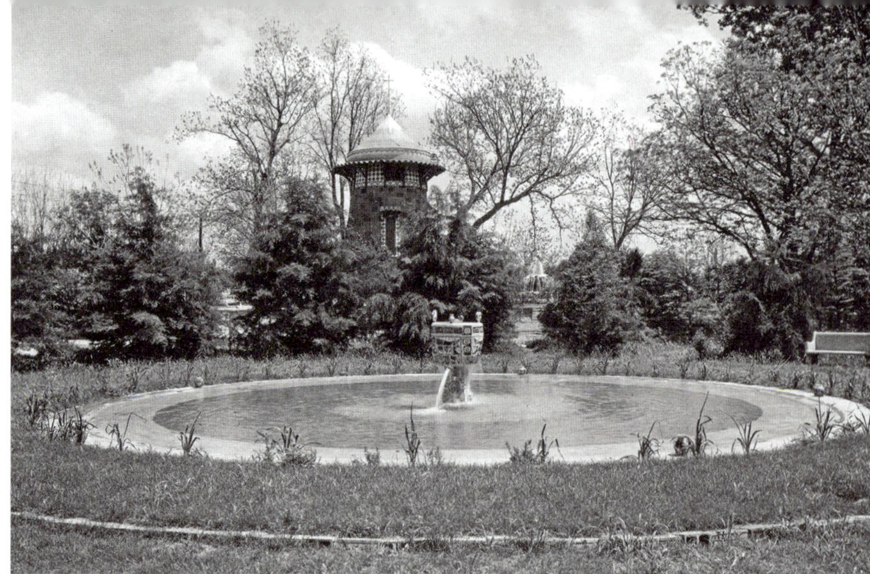

Brightly colored tiles accented a thirty-foot stone tower with a conical roof. The fountain's centerpiece was replaced in 1946 with a bronze statue of Urrutia.

An esplanade extended from the gate. A straight tree-lined gravel road with flat concrete curbs for automobiles and pedestrians turned at a focal point, a mounted bust of Porfirio Díaz. Nearby was a six-foot concrete sculpture of Cuauhtémoc, the last Aztec ruler, kneeling as he raised a clenched fist in defiance of Cortés. Luis L. Sanchez completed the work in 1921, precisely four hundred years after Cuauhtémoc's defeat by Cortés. It is among five Miraflores sculptures listed in the Smithsonian American Art Museum's *Inventories of American Painting and Sculpture*.[440]

A unique pedestrian entrance from Hildebrand at the northwest corner of Miraflores led down steps through a sculpted hollow tree, typical of *faux bois* cement work by Dionicio Rodríguez, brought from Mexico City in 1924 by Urrutia to design works for the garden. Urrutia launched Rodríguez's career in the United States by introducing him to parks commissioner Ray Lambert, who began commissioning his work for Brackenridge Park.[441]

Among the more than half a dozen works in Miraflores identified as Rodríguez's was the garden's defining feature, a twelve-foot irregular fountain of honeycomb limestone and concrete. Water piped to its top from an artesian well cascaded into a shallow pool and flowed through two five-foot-wide channels to a concrete swimming pool twenty feet away, where Urrutia took a daily 5 a.m. swim. At the pool's west end, water overflowed into two stone-rimmed ponds with water plants. The water cascading, spraying, and dripping into pools, and bubbling along natural-appearing channels produced "a demonstration garden of water effects," according to Lake, making the sound of water audible throughout the garden.[442]

Two buildings stood in the garden, both decorated with bands of brightly colored ceramic tiles. Quinta Maria, near the river, constructed in 1923 as a tile-roofed guesthouse prototype of those planned for sanitarium patients, survives. The other, a thirty-foot stone tower with a flattened conical roof and a small ell used as a library, does not. Their strong accent colors matched the bright designs and profuse ornamentation popular in Mexico and some parts of San Antonio, as did the garden's statues, benches, pedestals, and urns. One of three surviving concrete benches designed by Atlee B. Ayres for Miraflores is fifteen feet long and inlaid with tiles that Urrutia insisted came from the castle where Hernán Cortés was born in Spain.[443]

Miraflores, mostly completed by 1930, served for civic and social events, including, in good weather, weekend Urrutia family gatherings, otherwise held at Quinta Urrutia. In 1931 several hundred members of the American Institute of Architects visited during their national convention in San Antonio. A significant change came in 1946, when an urn in the center of the circular pool was replaced by an oversized full-length bronze statue of Urrutia wearing his signature cape. Commissioned by one of his admirers in Mexico and completed

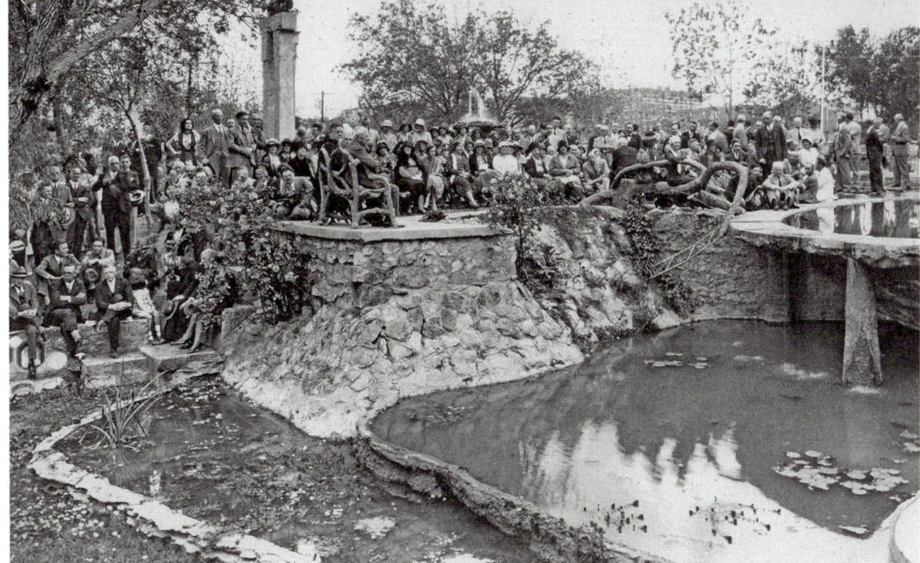

Miraflores hosted those attending the 1931 American Institute of Architects national convention.

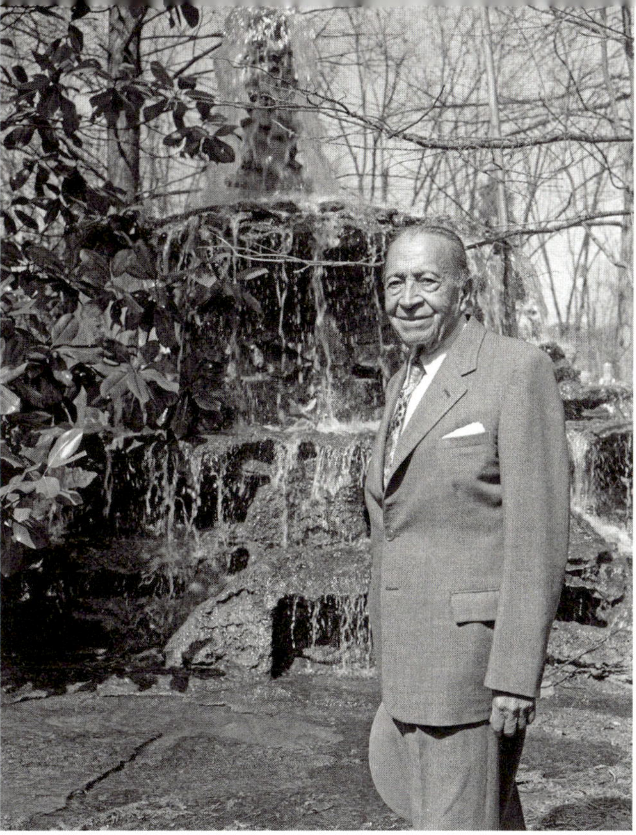

Urrutia, shown in the 1950s, retained ownership of Miraflores until he was ninety.

by Ignacio Asúnsolo in 1940, it was intended for Coyoacán, but resentment over Urrutia's alleged activities during the Huerta government lingered. Placement in Coyoacán was considered "problematic," and the statue was shipped to Miraflores.[444]

In 1953 Urrutia sold the vacant ten acres once planned for his sanitarium to the fast-growing insurance company USAA for a nine-story headquarters. The monumental tile arch facing Broadway was moved to the northeast corner of Miraflores.[445]

Two years after he retired from medical practice in 1960, at age eighty-eight, Urrutia finally put Miraflores and his home, Quinta Urrutia, on the market. Quinta Urrutia was razed for a Volkswagen dealership. Several elements were salvaged and moved to Miraflores, including a palapa bench by Dionicio Rodríguez, crouching lions that flanked the house's entrance, a stone rendering of the head of the Aztec moon goddess Coyolxauhqui, and the reproduction of the Winged Victory above the front entry.[446]

USAA purchased Miraflores to complete its property ownership from Broadway west to the river and the next spring built a pavilion and restroom, opening Miraflores as a summer day-care camp run by the YWCA for children of its employees. The camp was termed "one of the first in the country to recognize the special needs of single and working parents and their children."[447]

When Urrutia's home on Broadway was razed, the rooftop copy of the Winged Victory of Samothrace was brought to Miraflores.

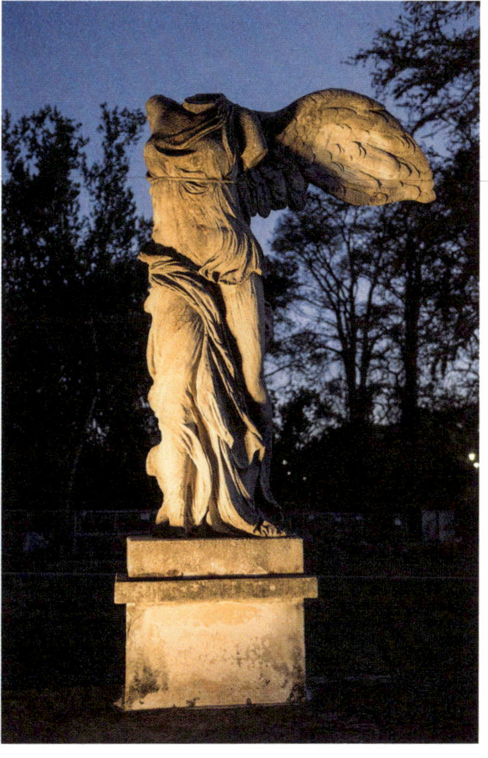

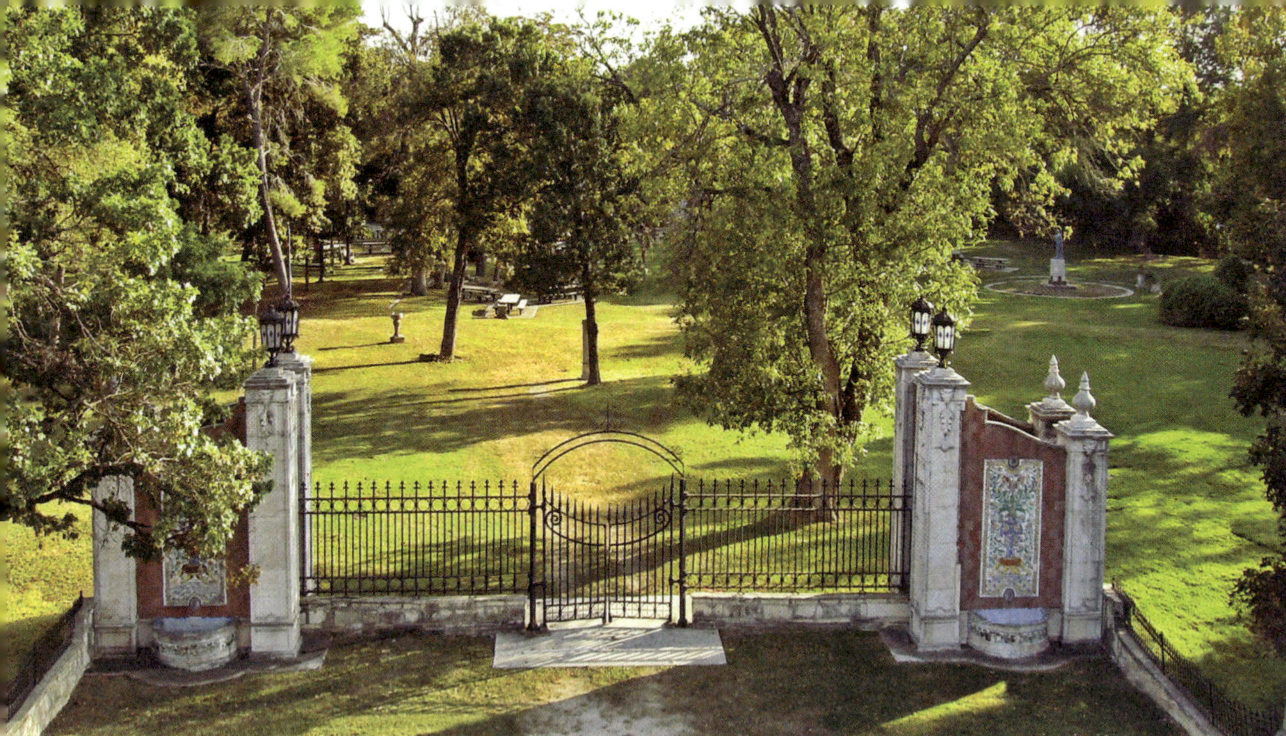

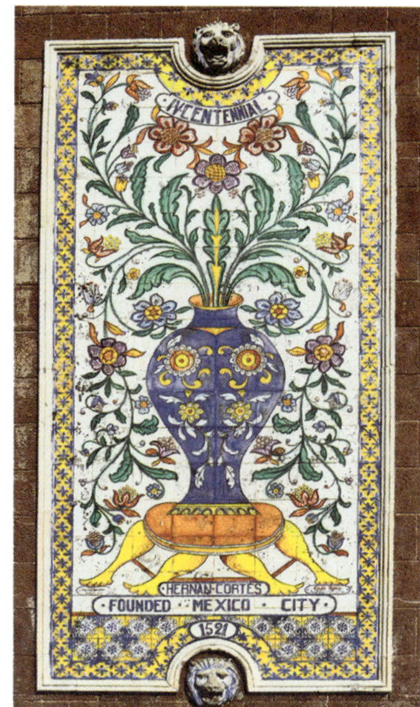

By 1978 Miraflores's main gate on Hildebrand Avenue, which once opened onto an esplanade, led instead to picnic tables on concrete pads in what became Pioneer Park.

USAA moved to northwestern San Antonio in 1974 and sold its property to Southwestern Bell. At this point, few traces remained of the library tower and its adjoining structure. Many of the garden's sculptural and decorative elements had disappeared or were in varying stages of deterioration. Southwestern Bell planned eventual expansion on the site but in the meantime turned Miraflores over to retirees in the local chapter of Telephone Pioneers of America. Members cleaned the grounds, poured concrete pads for two dozen picnic tables, built an open-air pavilion, filled pools, and leveled the area. The grounds opened as Pioneer Park in mid-1978 and got a swimming pool, later filled in.[448]

In 1981 Southwestern Bell cited vandalism in its request to the city to demolish the guest cottage, Quinta Maria, but relented and restored it after objections from the San Antonio Conservation Society and the city's first historic preservation officer, Pat Osborne. After more leveling and filling, by the end of the decade most of the original gardens lay buried up to a depth of four feet. A drainage system was installed and paved parking extended another twenty feet over the garden, slicing off the northeast corner to straighten the border for more parking. Sculpture in the way was to be relocated farther in, but the monumental arch, moved from Broadway, was left marooned in the parking lot.[449]

By 2001 Southwestern Bell had apparently decided the drainage problems in the rest of Miraflores were not worth risking construction there and addressed further parking issues with a multilevel garage next to its building. The company donated what remained of Miraflores to the University of the Incarnate Word across Hildebrand Avenue.

Incarnate Word, headed by Dr. Lou Agnese, began plans to clear Miraflores for a university parking lot. The monumental arch went to a courtyard at the San Antonio Museum of Art. Missing were the crouching stone lions from Quinta Urrutia, the bust of Porfirio Díaz, assorted urns and statuary, and the last fragments of balusters of the stone railing once behind the statue of the defiant Cuauhtémoc, missing his lower right arm. In 2002 the deteriorated Dionicio Rodríguez cascade fountain was quietly demolished during work on a reported leak of the artesian well that supplied the fountain.[450]

Incarnate Word thought it had clear title to Miraflores. But preservationists alarmed by the garden's impending destruction

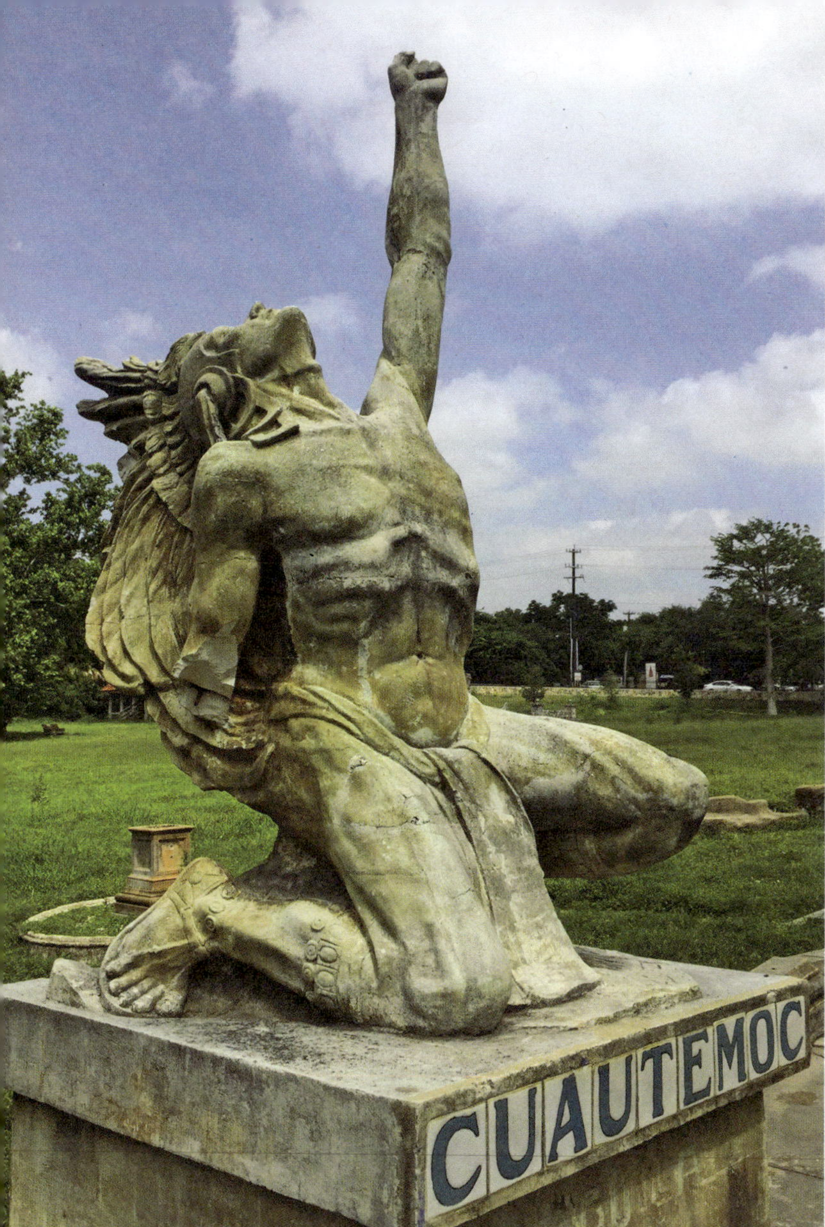

The dramatic sculpture of the last Aztec ruler remains at Miraflores.

A master plan prepared in 2008 by RVK Architects shows Miraflores's features.

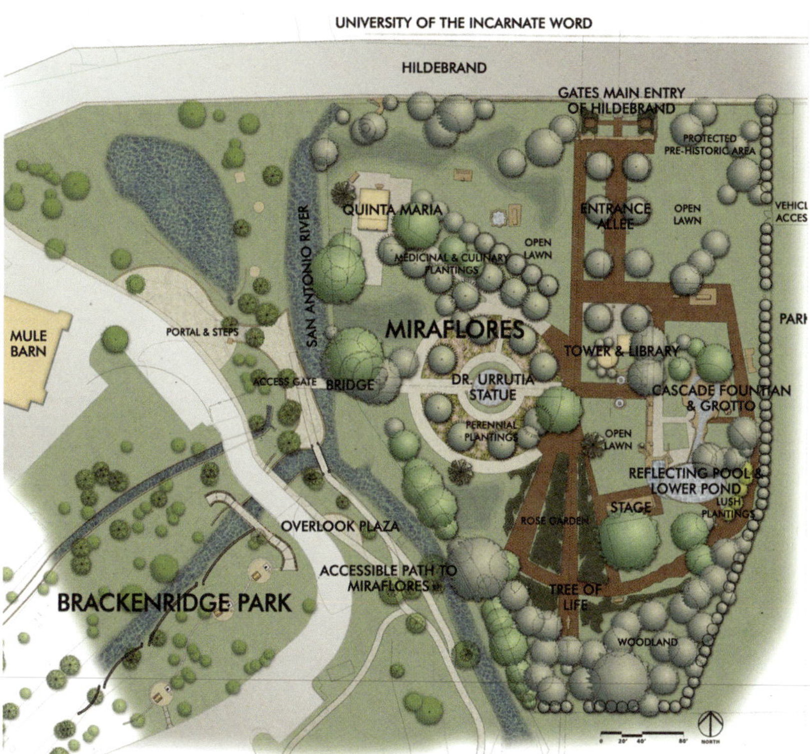

learned that a western portion deeded to the university had never been properly conveyed to Southwestern Bell, nor had any change in title been recorded for that parcel since it was included in a grant to San Antonio by the King of Spain in 1719. The San Antonio Conservation Society cried foul, and the city sued.[451]

Incarnate Word settled in 2005 by turning over the Miraflores tract to the city, accepting in return flood-free city property up the hill at the corner of Hildebrand Avenue and Devine Road, and making a cash settlement for the difference in value. The university built a pharmacy school on its new property, and the city added Miraflores to Brackenridge Park.

The parks department, under its director of the previous four years, Xavier Urrutia—not known to be related to Aureliano Urrutia, and succeeded in 2019 by Homer Garcia III—wasted no time trying to figure out what it had. Miraflores gained a listing in the National Register of Historic Places in 2006 and as a state antiquities landmark three years later. In 2008 a University of Texas at San Antonio archeological study revealed Native American artifacts and identified numerous buried garden elements. That same year a team led by Kimberley Wolf of RVK Architects finished a master plan commissioned by the city to bring Miraflores back to life. Recommendations included

A fifteen-foot bench designed by Atlee B. Ayres included, according to Urrutia, tiles from Hernán Cortés's birthplace in Spain.

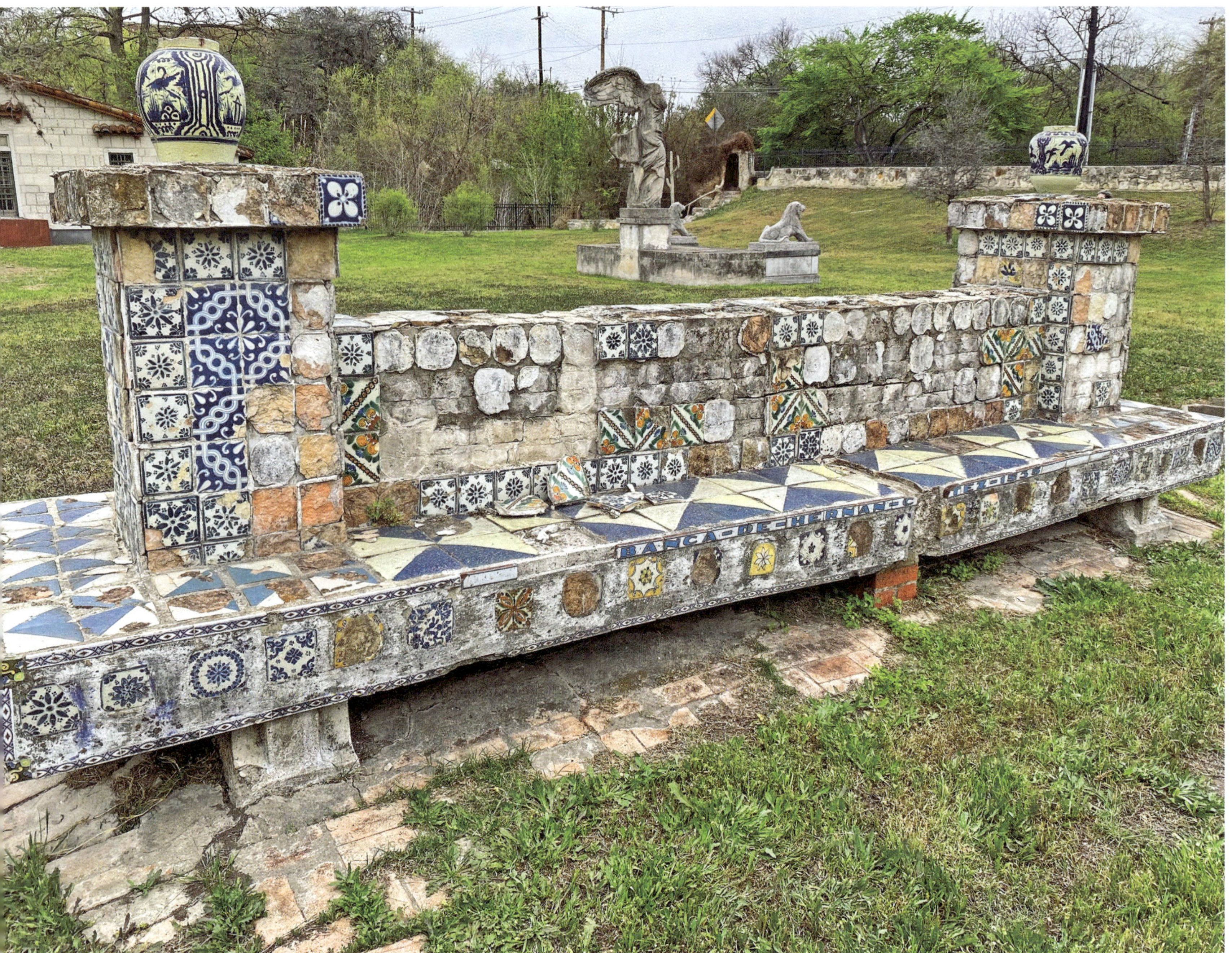

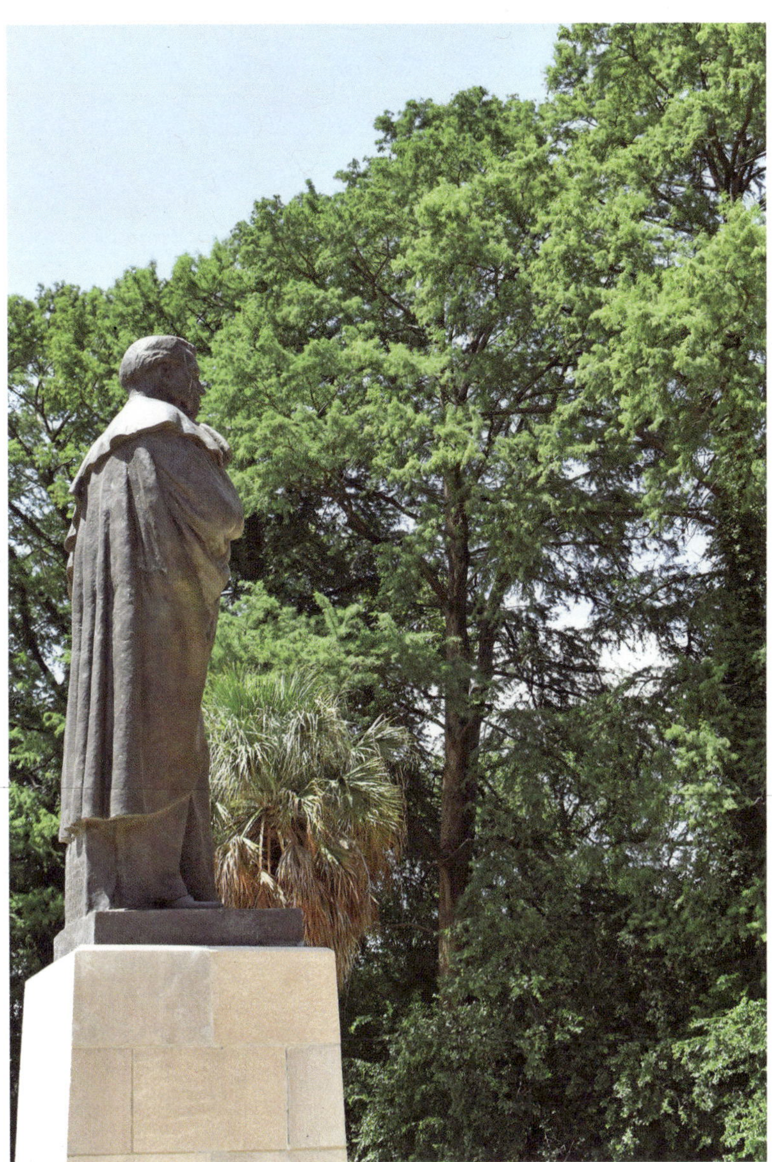
Visitors crossing the river bridge into Miraflores are greeted by a bronze statue of a caped Urrutia by Ignacio Asúnsolo.

reconstructing the razed Rodríguez cascade fountain and adding something resembling the lost library tower.[452]

The city placed Miraflores under the auspices of the recently formed Brackenridge Park Conservancy, and in 2009 a pedestrian bridge linking Miraflores with the park was built across the river. The full-length bronze statue of Urrutia in the center of what would again be a pond was restored in 2021 and rotated to face those who would cross the bridge from Brackenridge Park when Miraflores could be opened to the public. Excavations begun by the city in 2018 uncovered brick pathways to be restored and original benches pushed over and buried when the land was filled.

The San Antonio Conservation Society planned to return original Miraflores pieces it had held in storage and provided a grant in 2011 to repair a Dionicio Rodríguez sculpture and palapa bench. Four years later the Hildebrand entrance gate and its Talavera tiles were painstakingly restored. Hope that objects lost to the park would start coming back rose with Pat and John Jimenez's return of a main section of one of two pillars carved to commemorate Urrutia's directorship of a medical faculty in Mexico. Originally standing beside the Miraflores entrance esplanade, the section had been in their garden since John Jimenez found it abandoned in a vacant lot. The other pillar survives in place.[453]

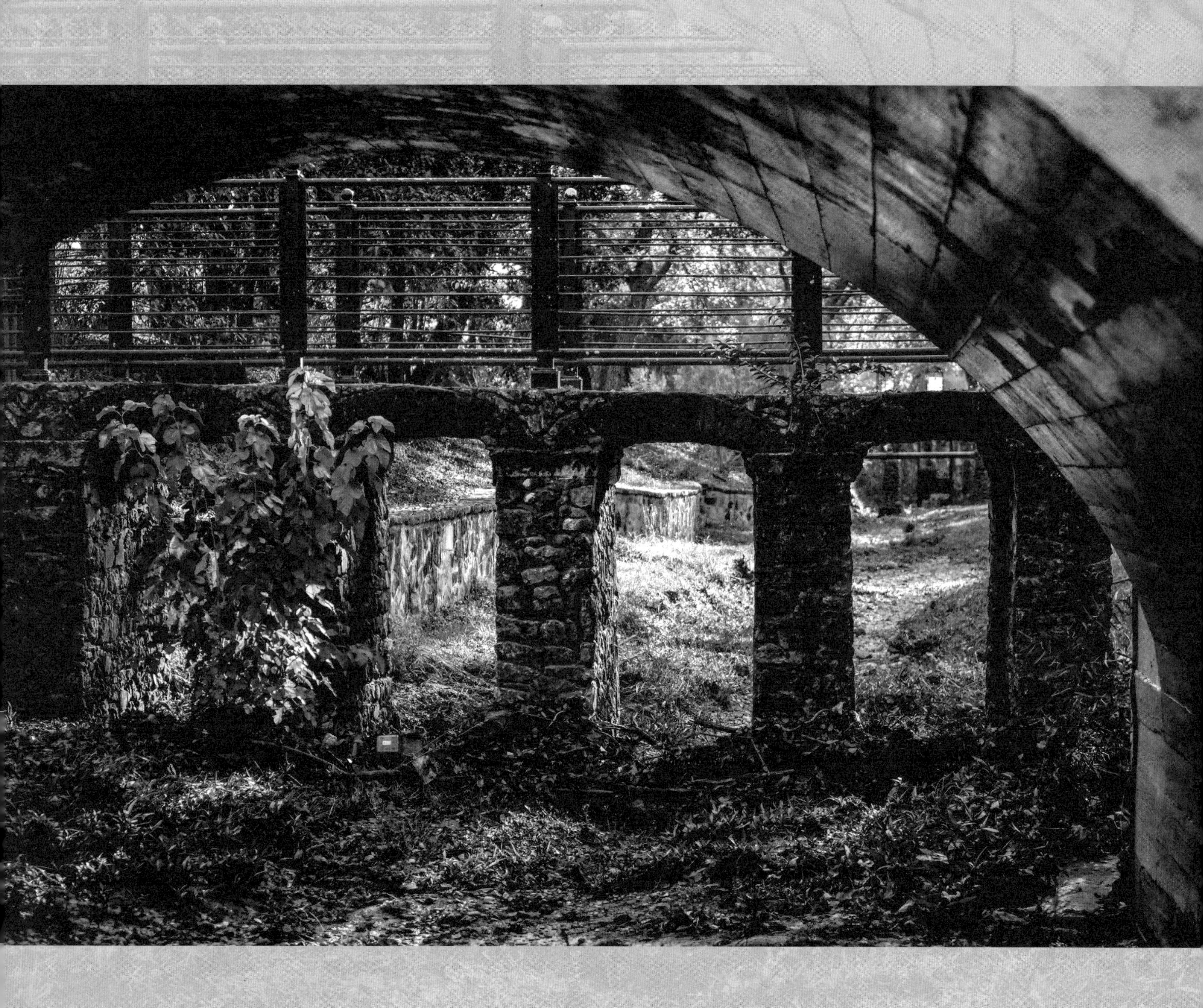

A Sustainable Park

Some of Brackenridge Park's components may have been in stages of renewal during the early twenty-first century, but overall the park was suffering. A blue-ribbon study in 2020, confirming the fears of close observers, concluded: "Brackenridge Park is in decline."[454]

Brackenridge Park may have appeared to be flourishing. Annual visitor numbers were approaching two million, as major traffic arteries provided convenient access from all sectors of the city, and many visitors came from vibrant neighborhoods nearby.

But the San Antonio River through the park was "no longer healthy or safely accessible," according to the new Cultural Landscape Report. Natural vegetation and soils were threatened, and historic tree canopies and native plants were dwindling. Moreover, its authors added, entry and arrival areas were "not entirely evident or inviting," and circulation through the park was "confusing." As "the park currently has no public face or physically defined presence in the community," its "historic and public value have become less and less comprehensible."[455]

San Antonio parks in general had not shown much improvement in spending compared with major American cities since 1950, when parks superintendent Stewart King reported the survey ranking San Antonio sixty-sixth among sixty-eight parks in municipal outlay per capita. Since then San Antonio had become the nation's seventh most populous city and the twenty-fourth largest metropolitan statistical area. Yet despite being run by a modernized parks department, the Trust for Public Land in 2020 ranked its parks no better than seventy-fifth among the nation's one hundred largest cities, ahead of Houston (seventy-eighth) and Fort Worth (ninety-fourth) but behind Dallas (fifty-fourth) and Austin (thirty-seventh).[456]

Brackenridge Park's underworld emerges in Charlotte Mitchell's eerie 2018 view peering through the arches of a former donkey trail bridge and down the empty raceway of the 1878 pump house.

A blueprint for upping San Antonio's game at its traditional flagship park was the 2020 *Brackenridge Park Cultural Landscape Report*, nearly two years in the making. At 676 pages and weighing 5.5 pounds, it was the first careful examination of the 120-year-old park by nationally recognized professionals.

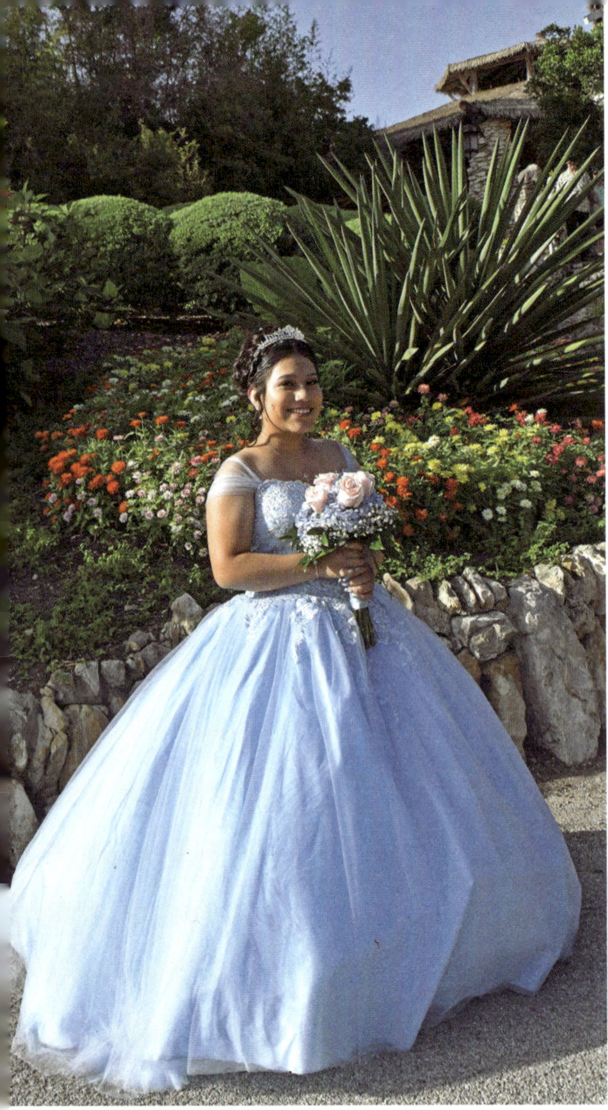

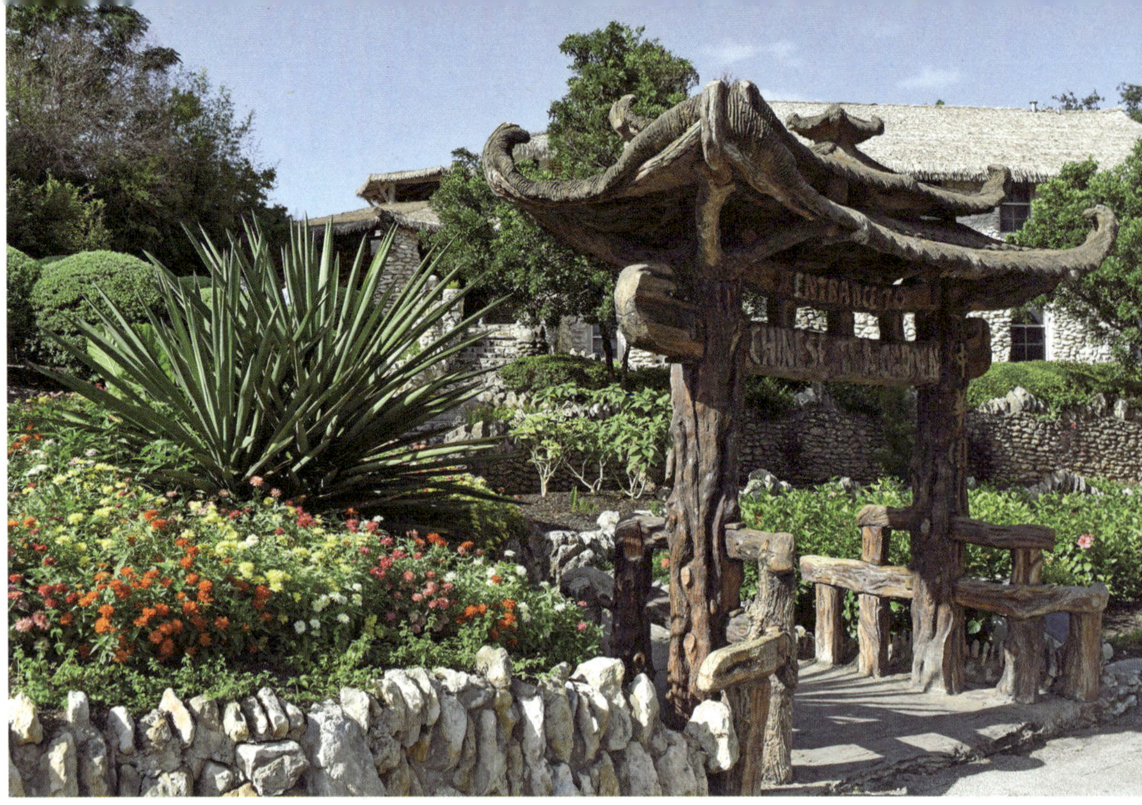

Miranda Mendosa picked a setting beside the *faux bois* gate to the Japanese Tea Garden—for a time named the Chinese Tea Garden—for her quinceañera portrait in 2021.

Funded by the San Antonio Parks and Recreation Department, the San Antonio River Authority, and the Brackenridge Park Conservancy, the cultural landscape report was undertaken by two landscape architecture research, planning, and design firms: Reed Hilderbrand of Cambridge, Massachusetts, and Suzanne Turner Associates of Baton Rouge, Louisiana. They collaborated with the University of Texas at Austin's Lady Bird Johnson Wildflower Center, which produced a separate seventy-two-page *Ecological Site Assessment* of the park, with detailed recommendations for improvements.

The studies supplemented the park's new ninety-four-page master plan and would aid in prioritizing development and rehabilitation proposals. The master plan, which took two years to complete, was commissioned by the city and completed in 2017. The previous plan, finished in 1979 but not updated for nearly thirty years, was mostly forgotten, its primary outcome a $1 million palm garden that did not survive and was turned into a parking area.[457]

The cultural landscape report urged an end to such "plop and drop" additions, a "piecemeal approach to funding and isolated development" practiced so often in Brackenridge Park that it "has only added to the site's fragmentation over time." It recommended that a thorough knowledge of the park's basic ecological and cultural issues first be achieved to understand the impact of future additions and changes.[458]

Experts had not expected to discover that Brackenridge Park, dismissed nationally as a crazy-quilt development lacking overall design, in fact had good bones. Its elements were distinctive and obviously popular, and the park's fabric needed only to be made more coherent and rescued from the consequences of maintenance shortfalls and long environmental decline.

Also noted was that the park's development happened to coincide with the five evolutionary stages of American park design. Its opening as a driving park matched the Pleasure Ground / Picturesque Park Movement of 1850–1900, pioneered by New York's Central Park. Lambert's improvements

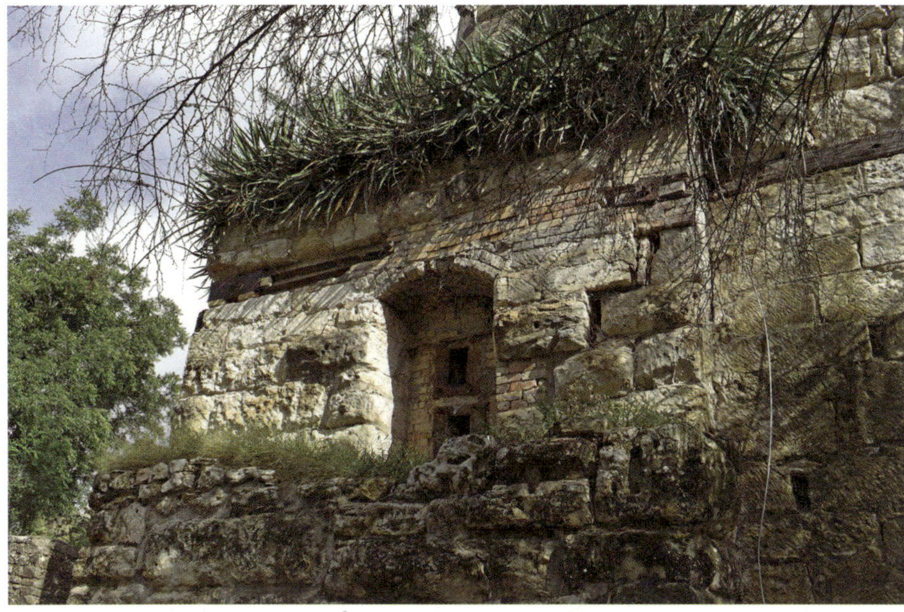

Remains of the 1880s cement plant in Brackenridge Park produce scenes worthy of the ruins of classical Rome.

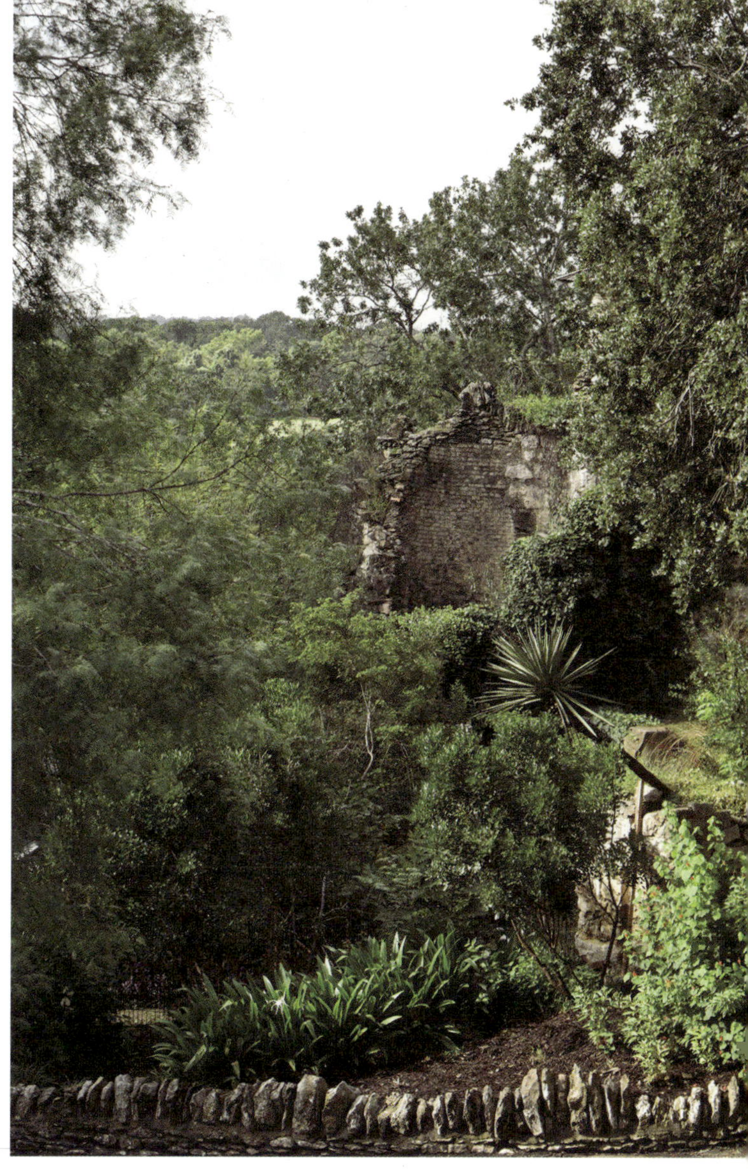

fit the Reform Park / City Beautiful Movement of 1900–1930. Works Progress Administration additions coincided with parks' emphasis on recreation facilities in 1930–65. Restoration of the Sunken Garden and renovations followed parks' national shift toward an open-space system valuing historic preservation in 1965–95.

Cultural landscape report authors observed that supporters, consciously or not, were moving the park in the newest direction—becoming a sustainable park, one self-sufficient in material resources, while creating new standards for aesthetics and landscape management and broadening citizen participation.[459]

They were convinced that Brackenridge Park deserved to be "elevated in the eyes and minds of the local community and widely known outside of San Antonio."[460]

Entry into the new era was being led by the Brackenridge Park Conservancy, formed by the San Antonio Conservation Society, a self-appointed guardian of parks, among other things, since its founding in 1924. Given the park's complex issues, the society believed Brackenridge Park needed its own advocate.

Native San Antonian Elizabeth Barlow Rogers, a landscape designer in New York City, had addressed Central Park's deepening deterioration in the 1970s. She was made Central Park's first administrator in 1979 and helped organize and became first president of the private Central Park Conservancy that dramatically reversed the decline. The San Antonio Conservation Society enlisted her help back home. In 2005 the Central Park Conservancy, led by its planning director, Lane Addonizio, produced a sixteen-page strategic assessment with recommendations for Brackenridge Park. It identified now familiar issues—fragmentation, ill-defined borders and entries, maintenance problems—and suggested formation of a conservancy similar to Central Park's.[461]

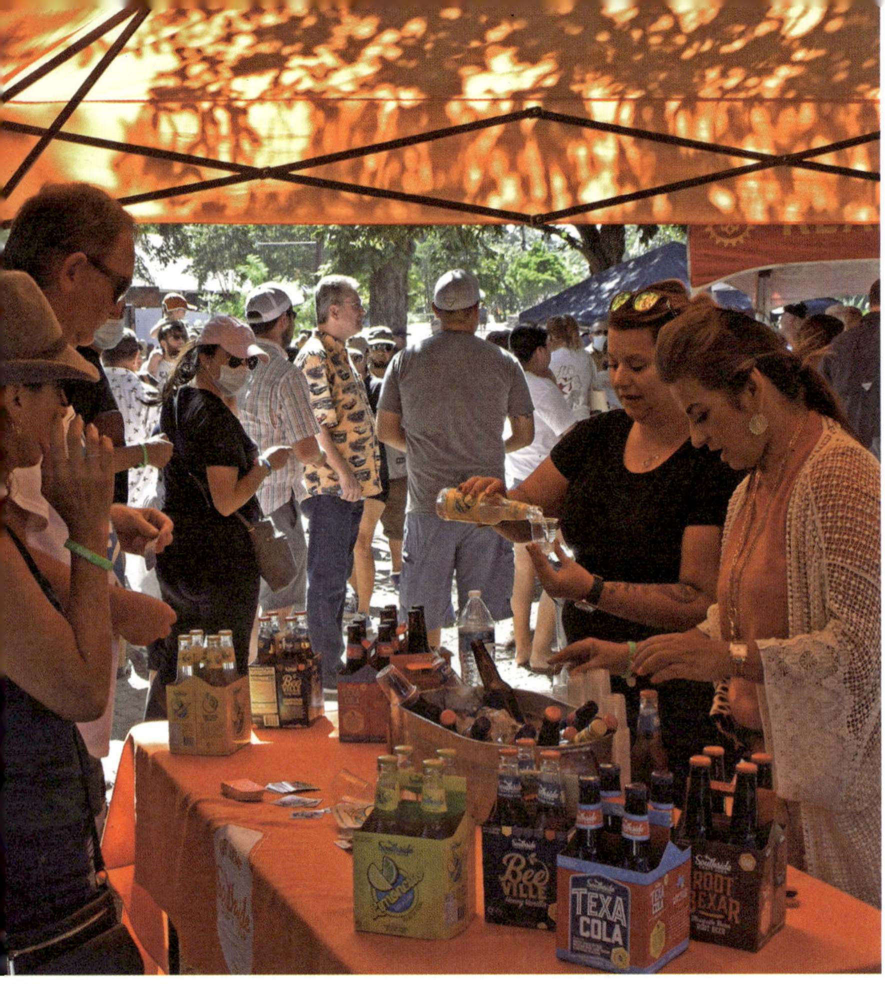

A server pours in the Southside Craft Soda tent at the Brackenridge Park Conservancy's tenth annual Parktoberfest in 2021 near the Koehler Pavilion.

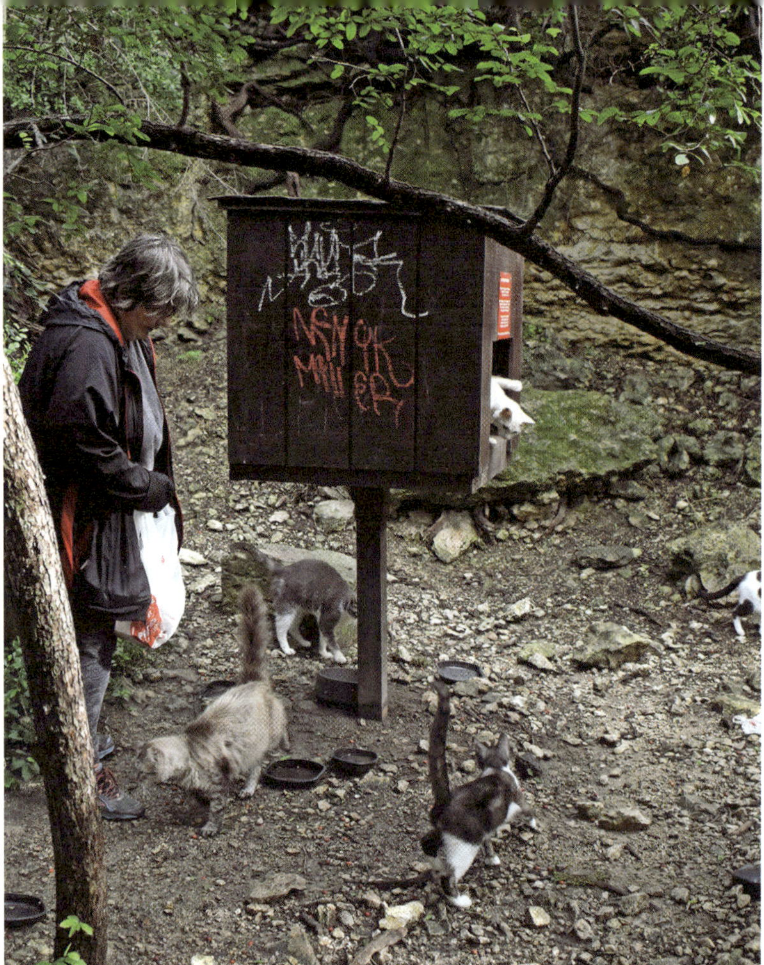

Volunteer Margaret Sendrow stands by a feeding station for cats, neutered and released in an effort to manage the park's feral cat population.

The Brackenridge Park Conservancy was organized in 2007, incorporated in 2008, and elected its first board the next year. With seed money from the conservation society, community planner Leilah Powell was hired as part-time director. A prime goal was determining precisely what was in the park and how it got there. An archeological and historical report made a start three decades before, but gave no detailed description of the park's creation nor of its structures. Mysteries were solved through the sleuthing of historian Maria Watson Pfeiffer, aided by archeologist Steve Tomka. Their 114-page compendium, funded by the San Antonio Conservation Society, landed Brackenridge Park in the National Register of Historic Places in 2011.

One chronic problem addressed early on involved the park's several hundred feral cats, most dumped illegally. They were decimating the park's population of small mammals. During a biodiversity study conducted in 2011–12 for the conservancy, 240 traps to measure the park's mammals were set out in four zones for three nights. They collected only one small mammal, a nonnative house mouse. The most abundant larger mammal found, and the only one trapped in all four zones, was the feral cat.[462]

Using a grant from the San Antonio Area Foundation, conservancy board member Tom Christal launched an effort to reduce the feral cat population by rounding up as many as could be gathered. After receiving veterinary care, some were given for adoption. Others were neutered and released back to the park, where they could keep cat numbers down by defending their territories from fertile feline invaders. Volunteers fed the five cat colonies in the park.[463]

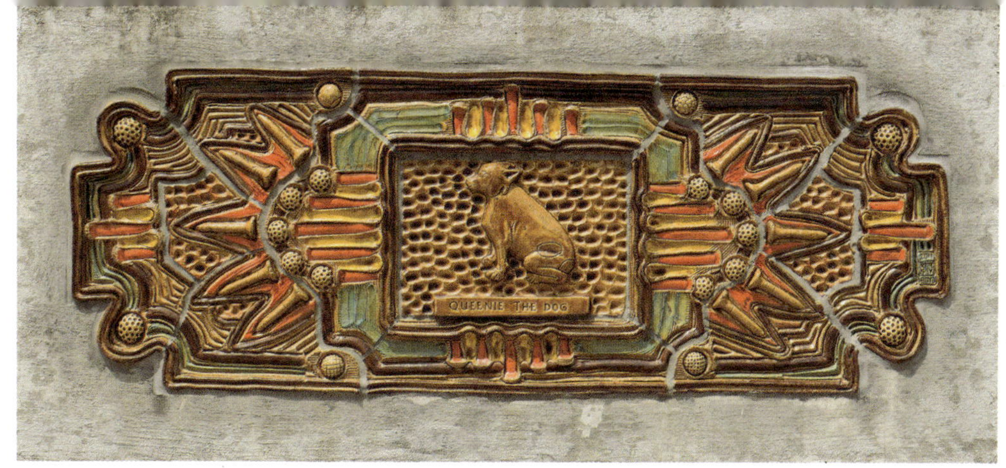

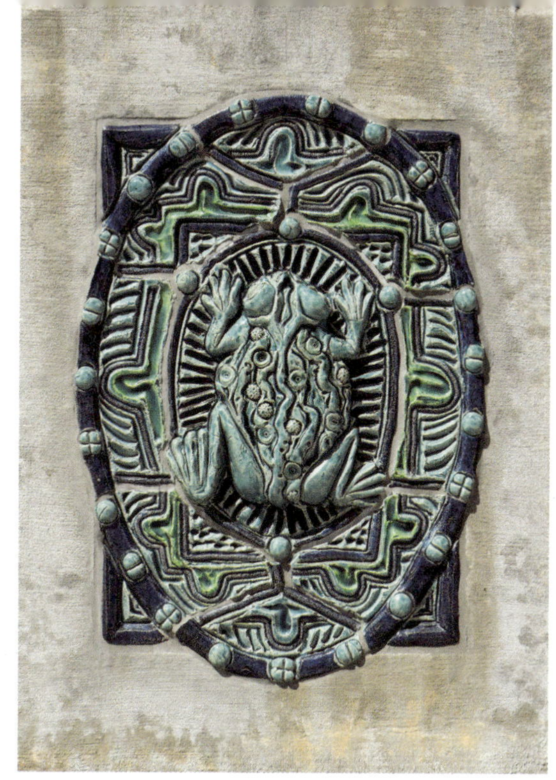

Diana Kersey's ceramic panels adorn two bridges over the Catalpa-Pershing drainage channel. One, on the Millrace Street Bridge to the golf course, shows Queenie the Dog, pet of newspaper editor Jack O'Brien, who helped organize the first Texas Open at the nearby course in 1922. The other, from the Mulberry Avenue Bridge series, portrays the life cycle of the toad.

More intractable were problems like compacted soil along riverbanks, erosion, and invasive species that choked out native plants and diminished the park's health. One area facing these challenges was at the eastern edge of the park around Mulberry Avenue, disrupted by the deep concrete drainage channel built during the Catalpa-Pershing Project in 1977. Methods were being studied to improve soils and plantings and reduce the channel's sharp slopes to permit more natural meanders, much as a concrete channel through the River Walk's Mission Reach south of the city had been broken up to restore the river's natural contours.[464]

Visual improvements above the channel included, in 2011, a rebuilt East Mulberry Avenue bridge with a series of twenty-four ceramic panels by Diana Kersey embedded in both sides of the bridge's sidewalk guardrails. To link the bridge with water, the panels depicted the life cycle of the ubiquitous Gulf Coast toad, though the bridge became known by the misnomer "Frog Bridge."

Kersey's golf-related ceramic tiles on the new Millrace Street bridge over the Catalpa-Pershing channel at the golf course included, among others, an image of course designer A. W. Tillinghast. Another, *Queenie the Dog*, portrayed the longtime companion of *San Antonio Evening News* sports editor Jack O'Brien, who helped organize the first Texas Open on the course in 1922.[465]

When Leilah Powell resigned in 2015 to become chief of policy for then-mayor Ivy Taylor, she was succeeded by a full-time director, Lynn Osborne Bobbitt, a former conservation society president later instrumental in opening a National Public Radio station in San Antonio. Joe Calvert, a great-great-grandson of Ludwig Mahncke, the park commissioner who first laid out Brackenridge Park, served as conservancy board chair in 2018–22.

The Brackenridge Park Conservancy signed an agreement with the Parks and Recreation Department and moved into the stone building concessionaire Phil Sheridan erected in 1979 on the site of the original Lambert Beach concession building. As the conservancy became a part of planning and decisions regarding the park, it also developed such programs as Parktoberfest, held each October at the Koehler Pavilion with music by local bands and beer from local brewers. An annual outdoor fundraising gala at varying locations in the park often included train rides for all. The four hundred attending the 2019 gala, held near the main low water crossing, honored Betsy Rogers for her aid in organizing the Brackenridge Park Conservancy.

The conservancy's ten-year management agreement renewed in 2018 with the city's Parks and Recreation Department assigned the conservancy control of six facilities "as is,"

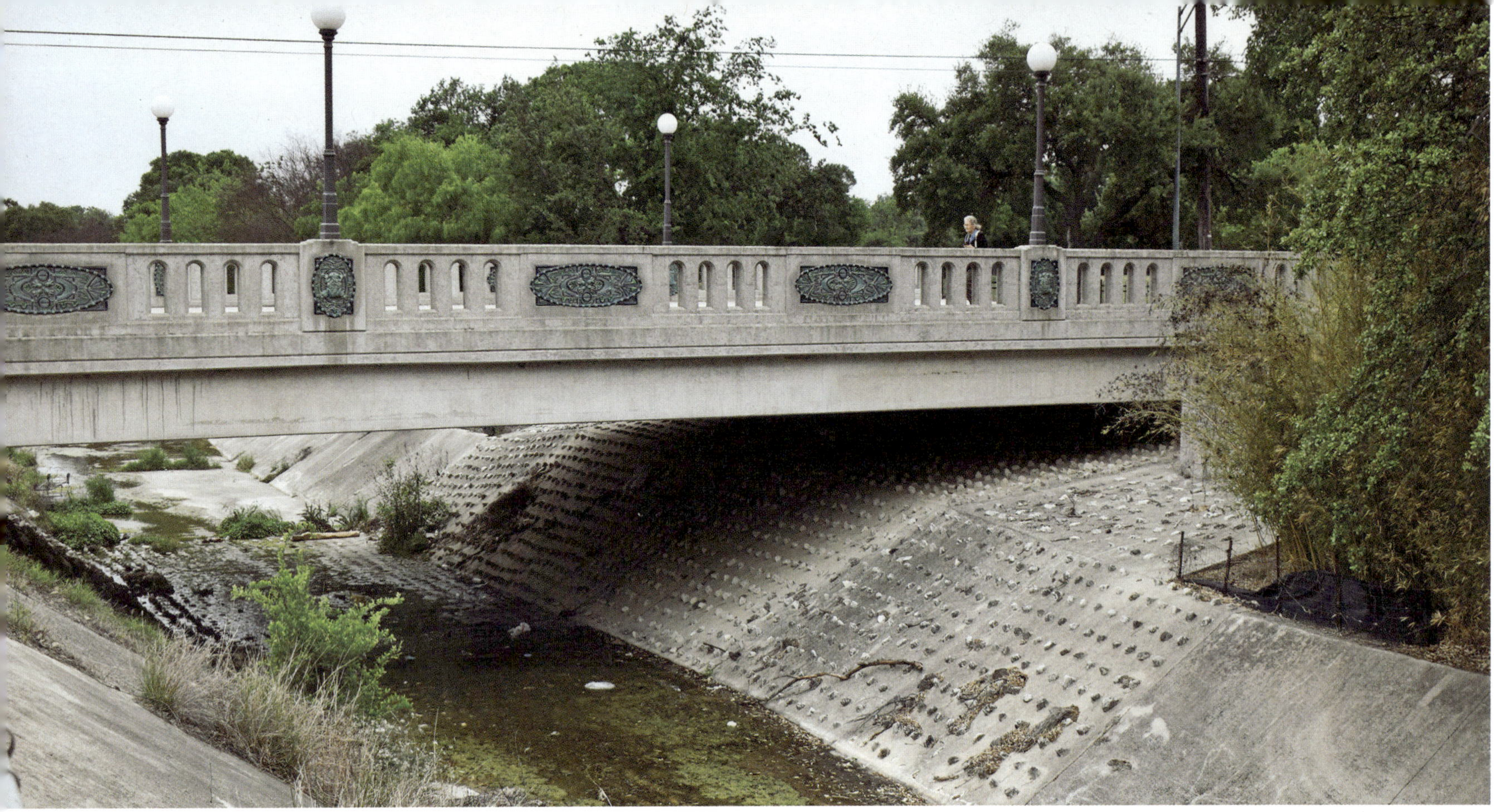

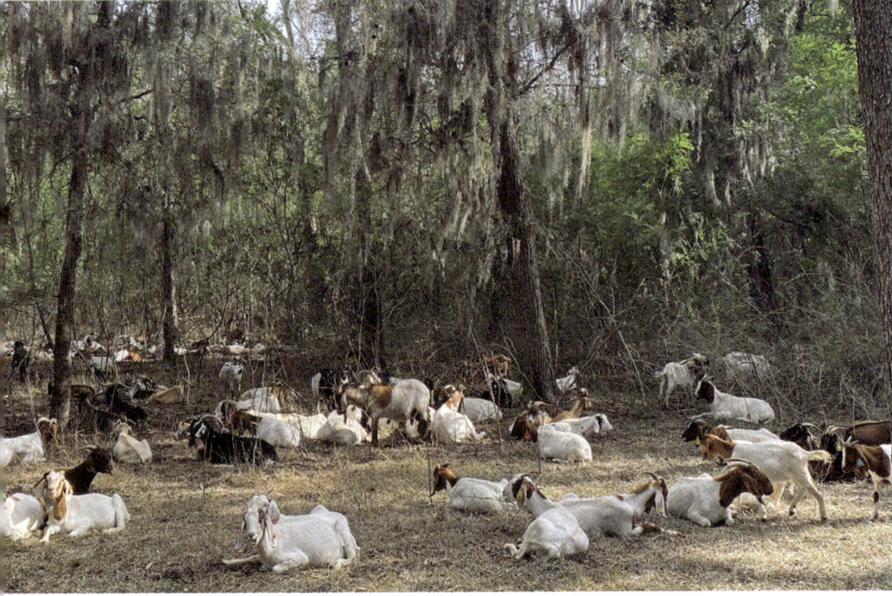

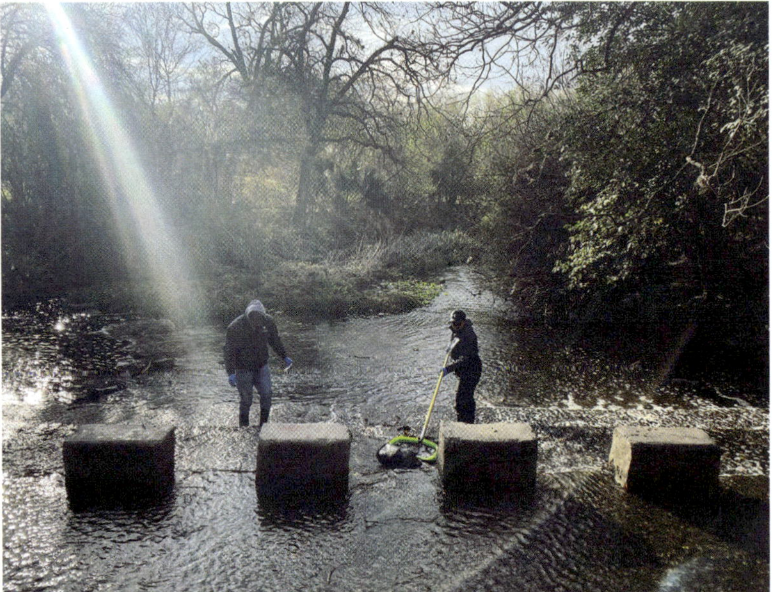

Park environmental challenges include returning the Catalpa-Pershing drainage channel to a natural state; removing invasive undergrowth, aided for one week in May 2022 by a herd of 160 goats, shown taking a break after clearing the area in the foreground; and removing silt and invasive species near a low-water river crossing, where maintenance workers skimmed out debris on a cold January morning in 2022.

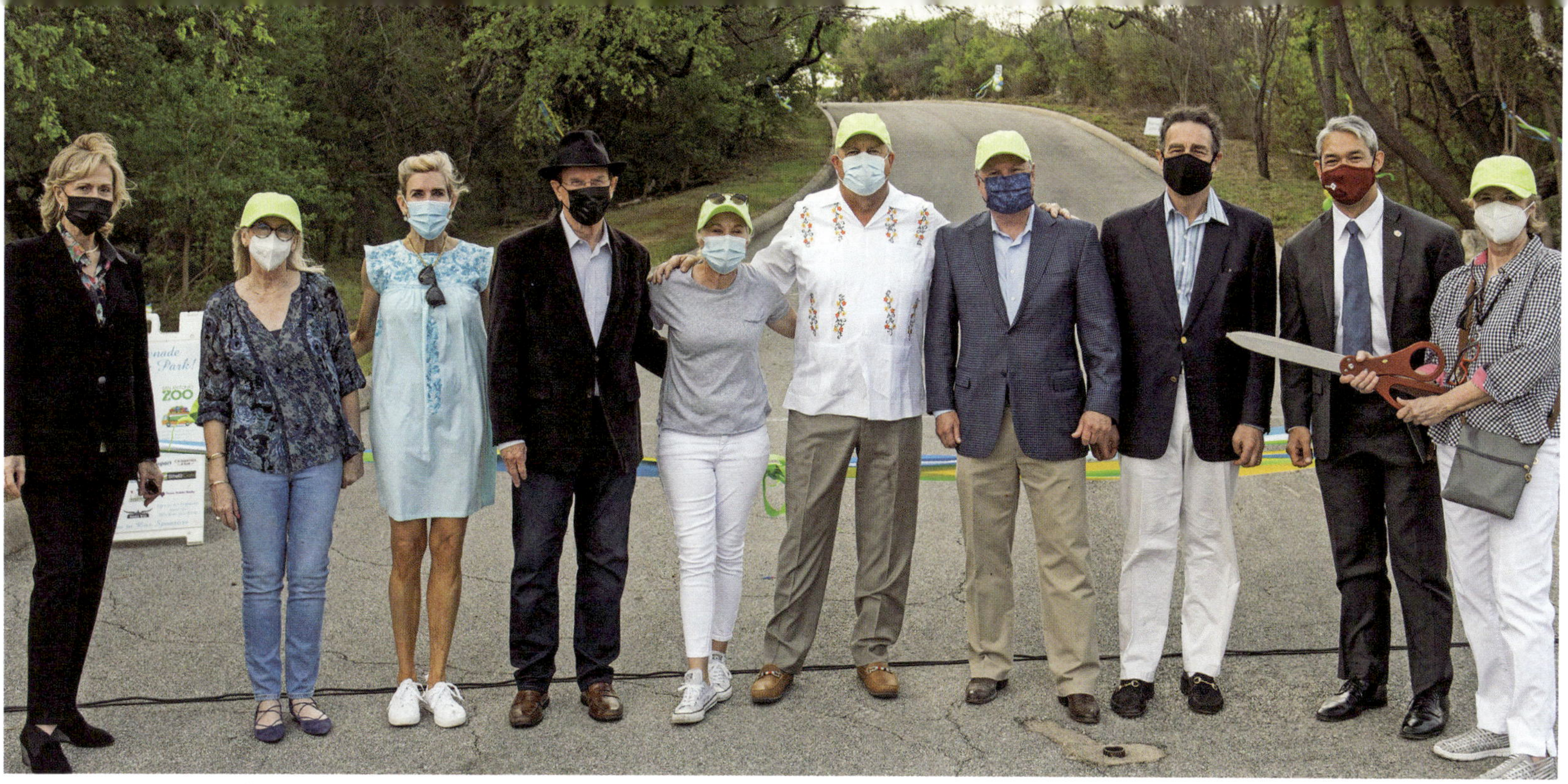

A moment in time was captured at the Brackenridge Park Conservancy's gala in March 2021, when effects of the COVID-19 pandemic required protective masks. Conservancy director Lynn Bobbitt, *far right*, stands ready to hand scissors to Mayor Ron Nirenberg beside her to cut the ribbon for the main feature, when gala-goers with boxed dinners would drive in their cars up and around Alpine Drive for picnics at a safe distance from others. Also in the masked lineup are, *from left*, Tracy Wolff; tri-chairs Vivienne Bathie and Liecie Hollis; Bexar County judge Nelson Wolff; event tri-chair Robin Howard; conservancy board chair Joe Calvert; treasurer Lukin Gilliland Jr.; and vice president Nick Hollis.

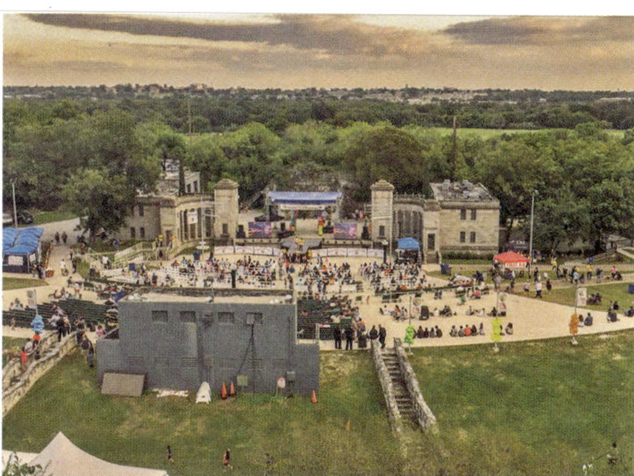

An audience gathers in 2017 for an evening performance at the Sunken Garden Theater, scheduled for renovation and management by the Brackenridge Park Conservancy.

including Miraflores Park and the 1878 pump house. The conservancy was also granted exclusive rights to redevelop and operate the Sunken Garden Theater, long struggling with maintenance issues but promising major revenue-generating potential for the conservancy once renovated and brought up to date, an effort that could cost as much as $62 million.[466]

One new conservancy board member was Joe Turner, who had recently retired to nearby New Braunfels after thirteen years as director of Houston's Parks and Recreation Department. A highlight of his tenure was revitalization of Houston's 445-acre Hermann Park, designed by nationally known landscape architects in 1914. In 2015 the American Planning Association named the renewed park one of the Fifteen Great Places in America. Turner, soon made director of special projects for the conservancy, in 2021 was named executive director to succeed Lynn Bobbitt, who became director of development and special events. He noted similarities between Brackenridge and Hermann Parks.[467]

"Both were donated in the same era by successful businessmen," Turner said. "Each park has a zoo, a natural science museum, an eighteen-hole golf course, an outdoor theater, and a train. One has a bayou, the other a river. Each has an effective conservancy organization, though Hermann Park's started

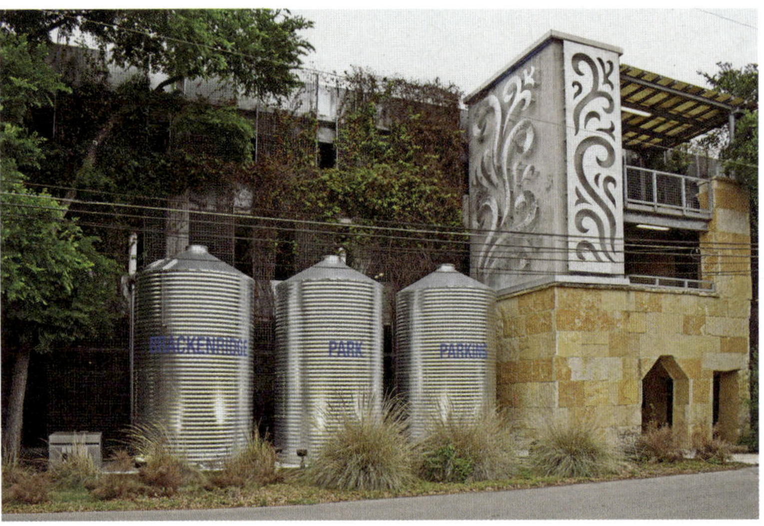

Three cisterns are part of a rain catchment system irrigating landscaping around the parking garage opened in 2009 near the Witte Museum.

sixteen years earlier than Brackenridge Park's." The issues facing Brackenridge Park resemble those facing Hermann Park when he began there. "Hermann Park had declined. Landscape elements were in serious need of recovery. Facilities had deteriorated. There was no front door, and the park was difficult to enter. Getting around inside was confusing. Sound familiar?"[468]

With the start of Broadway's planned reconstruction and reimagination as a prime commercial and cultural corridor from downtown north to Hildebrand Avenue, efforts to upgrade Brackenridge Park gained new significance. Expansion at the Witte Museum and Mahncke Park's San Antonio Botanical Garden was joined by construction of the $47 million DoSeum for children, opened in 2015 on nearly six acres across Broadway from Lions Field.

A turning point for Brackenridge Park and its conservancy came in March 2017, when the Cultural Landscape Foundation held its third Leading with Landscape Conference in San Antonio. The foundation was established in Washington, DC, in 1998 by its president and CEO, Charles A. Birnbaum, a landscape architect who coordinated the National Park Service Historic Landscape Initiative for fifteen years. Birnbaum had already spent time in San Antonio, at the invitation of the conservancy, and was intrigued with the potential of what he saw.

Leading with Landscape conferences usually focused on the host city's general landscapes but in 2017 concentrated only on Brackenridge Park. Four hundred attendees filled the Pearl Stable for the daylong program. Nineteen nationally prominent landscape designers and local officials spoke. Suddenly, San Antonians who had hardly given the state of Brackenridge Park a second thought were hearing perceptive people making unexpected appraisals. Former conservancy director Leilah Powell said the event amounted to "an intervention" for the park.[469]

Kinder Baumgardner, managing principal of the Houston-based landscape design firm SWA, reported to those present that he had trouble finding Brackenridge Park. "I did find the park eventually," he said, but thought nearly every business on Broadway had better street presence than the park did. Gina Ford, principal at the Boston-based firm Sasaki, believed the park's features comprised a surprising amount of "story in this landscape that's partly visible but mostly hidden." Doug Reed, principal of the firm Reed Hilderbrand, which later helped produce the park's cultural landscape report, saw promise in "revealing and interpreting of its cultural heritage," adding that with its range of resources Brackenridge "may in fact be more like a national park than any city park."[470]

Enthusiasm generated by that event, along with city council ratification of the park's new master plan two days before, helped clear the way for voter approval in May 2017 of a bond issue that included $21.5 million to improve Brackenridge Park.[471]

Nearly two-thirds of those bond funds addressed a shortage of shared parking for two of the park's major institutions. The first targeted enlarging the parking garage opened near the Witte Museum in 2009.

Since 2004, Witte Museum leadership had stressed that additional parking was critical to turning the museum's operation around. The most likely place to find sizable new parking space was on costly land on the other side of Broadway, a busy thoroughfare museumgoers would not like to cross. More attractive was a park nursery site close by on Avenue B on the

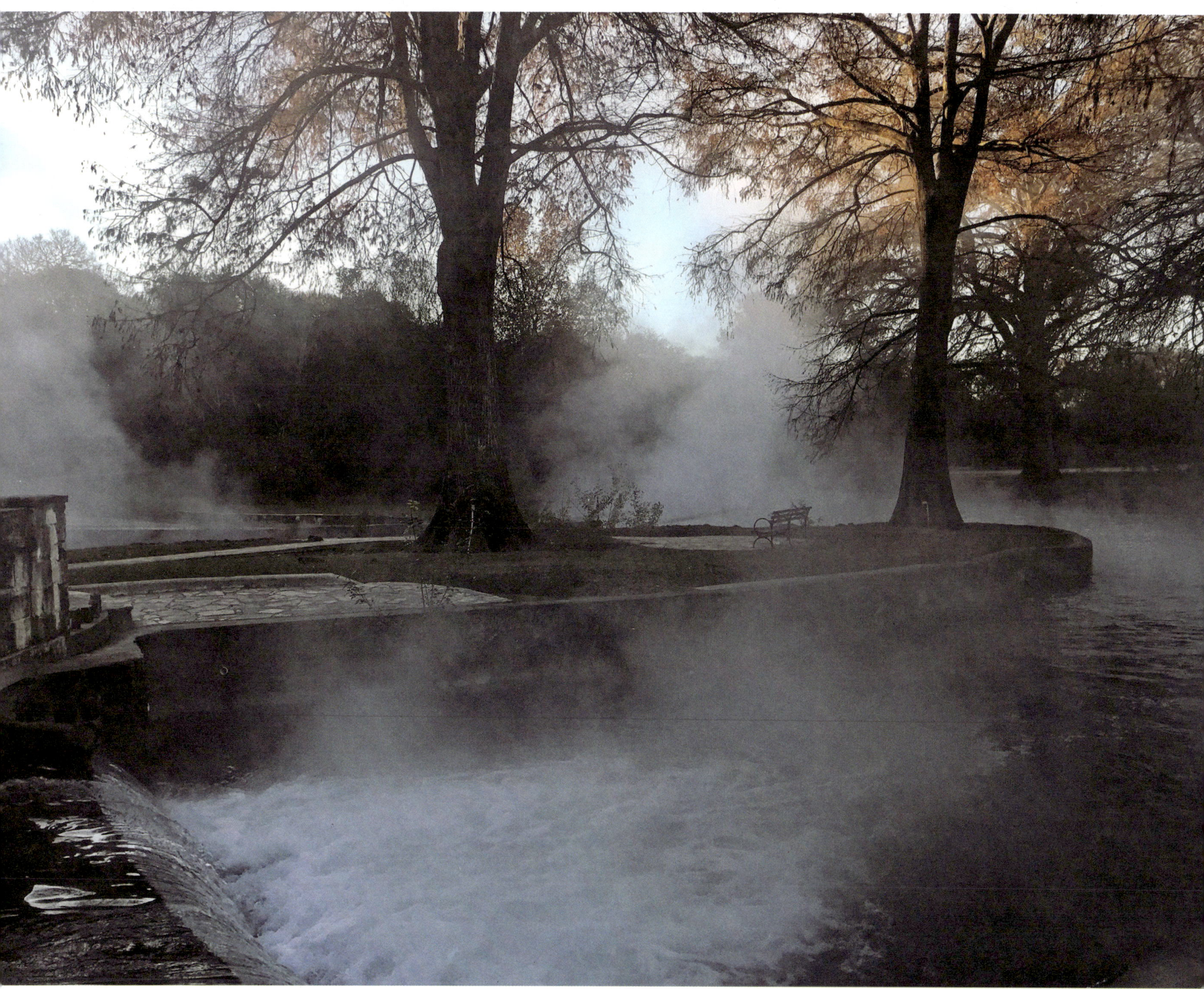

Early morning mist shrouds the river near the main low-water crossing in December 2018.

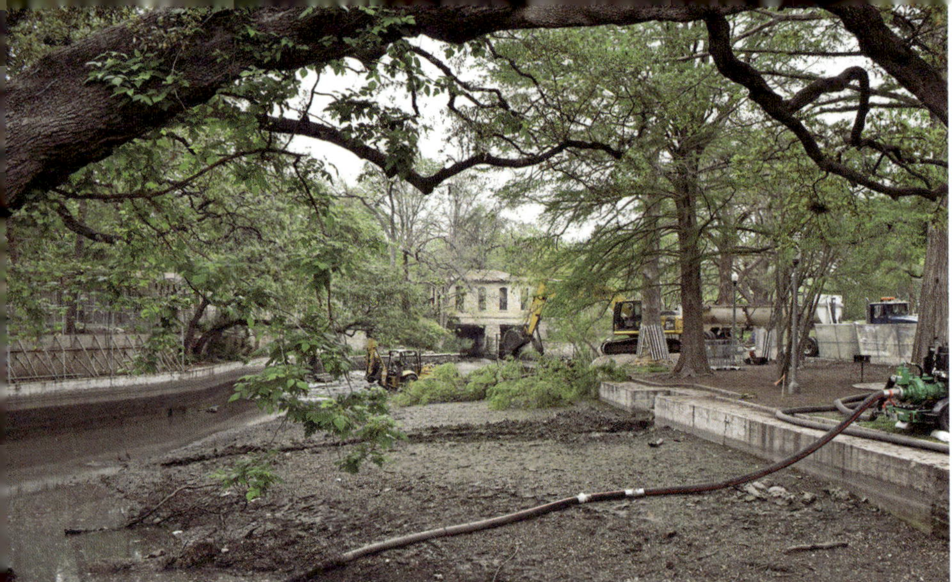

After the river was drained at Lambert Beach in March 2020, silt was dredged and repairs made to the banks and foundations of the 1878 pump house, center, prior to its restoration.

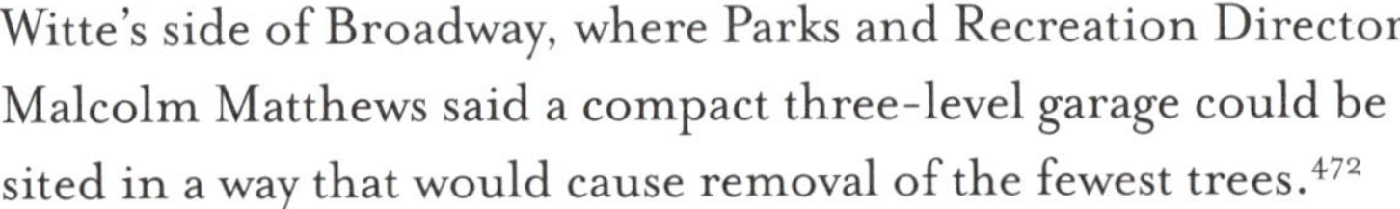

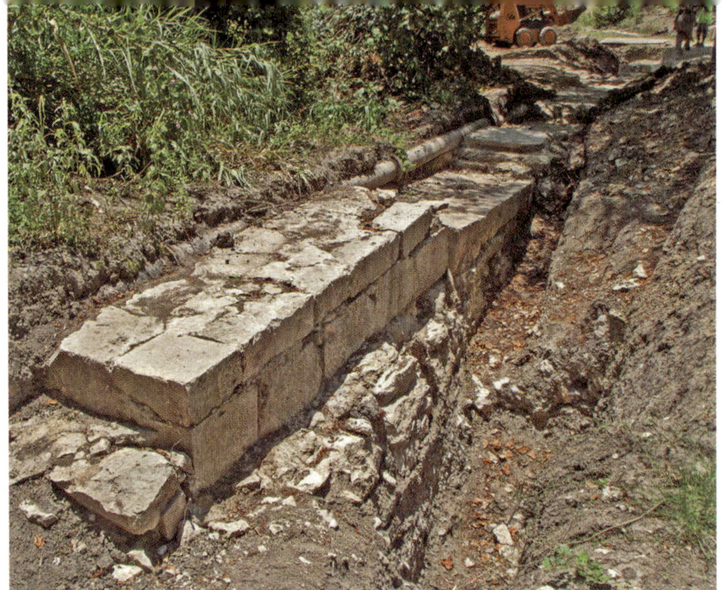

Archeologists went to work after a 1995 flood exposed remains of the 1776 Upper Labor Acequia dam. Top rows of evenly cut stones were added by Confederate army engineers in 1863.

Witte's side of Broadway, where Parks and Recreation Director Malcolm Matthews said a compact three-level garage could be sited in a way that would cause removal of the fewest trees.[472]

Members of the River Road Association, representing an isolated neighborhood adjoining the far side of the park, charged that "up to four hundred trees" would have to be cut and that using the land for such a non-park purpose would trigger deed restrictions and park ownership would revert to the University of Texas. The museum, however, concluded that only sixty-eight trees would have to be removed—some might be replanted—and the city attorney determined that no deed restrictions would be violated. The dustup delayed completion by more than a year.[473]

The garage was worth the wait. Some considered it "the first truly modern parking garage in the city," a milestone toward creating a sustainable park. Its design by Lake Flato Architects included panels of mesh allowing vines to trail down the facade, helping mask the garage's presence among the trees. A rainwater catchment system drained into three cisterns to irrigate landscaping. Motion-activated lights brightened as cars approached and dimmed when the garage was not in use. Artist Cakky Brawley added brushed aluminum images evoking water and vegetation to the front of the garage. The $2 million fourth level added to the garage in 2019 brought its capacity to more than four hundred vehicles.[474]

A second parking garage opened the same year on a scrub-covered hillside of Tuleta Drive across US 281 from the zoo. Designed by Alamo Architects, the $11.75 million five-level garage held more than six hundred spaces and was linked to the zoo and the park by a sidewalk beneath the expressway. Decorated with colorful large images of animals, it, too, bore mesh panels to be covered by vines.[475]

Circling back to address the water that gave birth to both city and park, the remaining 2017 bond funds for the park were earmarked for repairing and restoring the area around the river's northernmost segment. The 2020 *Ecological Site Assessment* confirmed the earlier biodiversity study indicating that the river's northern portion had very poor aquatic health, with many of its banks heavily compacted and eroding from too little maintenance. The solution was to sustain the riparian buffer by slowing and filtering runoff, building soil, and planting trees to provide additional shade. The area would be woven with trails, raingardens, bioswales, and soil-protection areas. The fixes would be consistent with recommendations in the cultural landscape report and in the city's master plan.[476]

Architect Steven Tillotson had an epiphany in 1995 when he happened by the river in the park below Hildebrand Avenue and noticed that a flash flood had exposed a row of aged

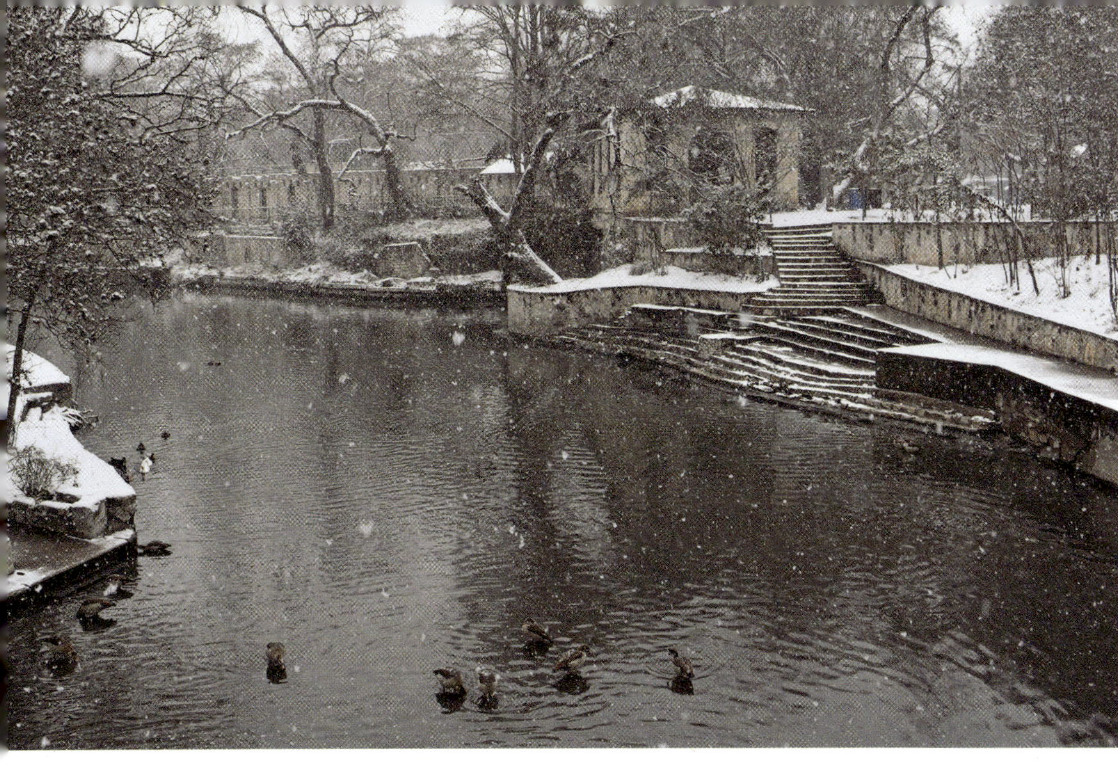

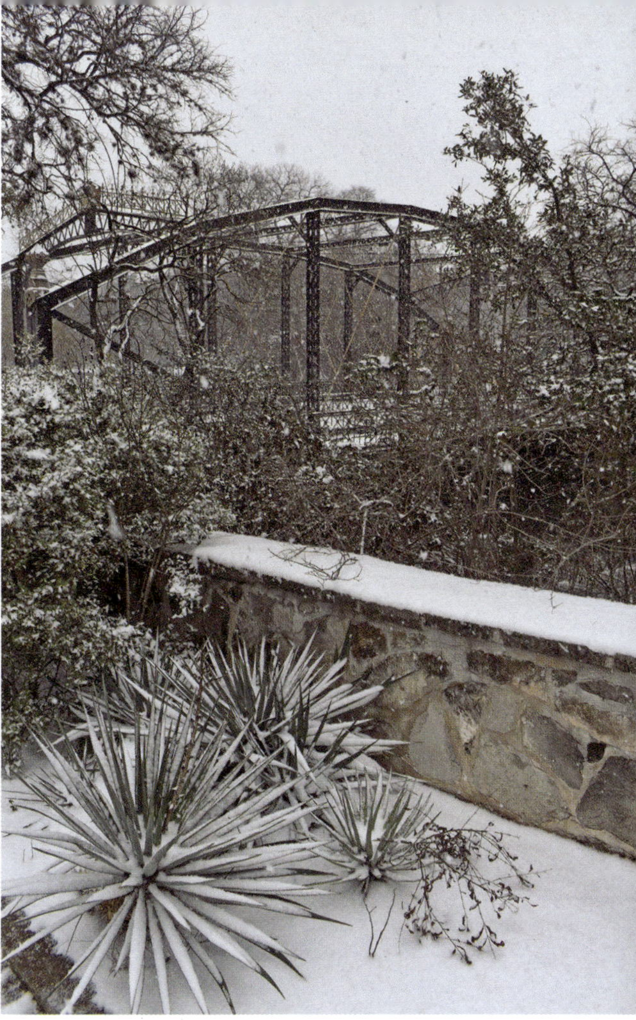

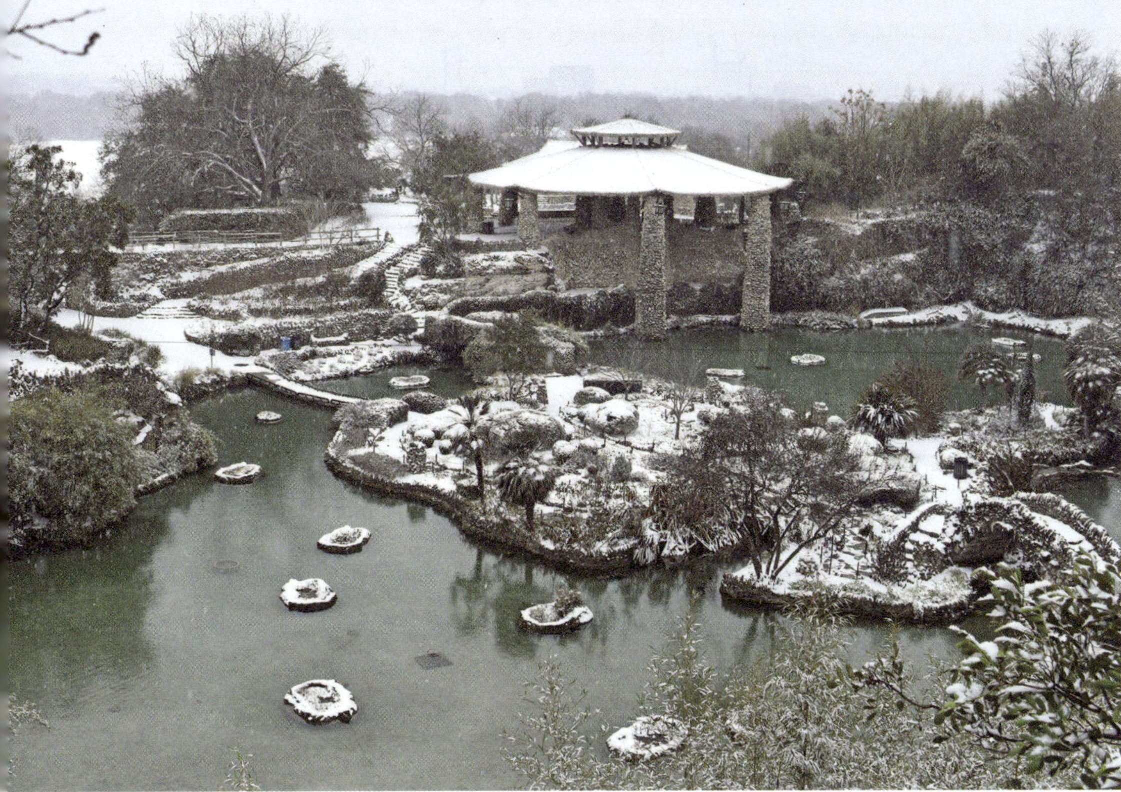

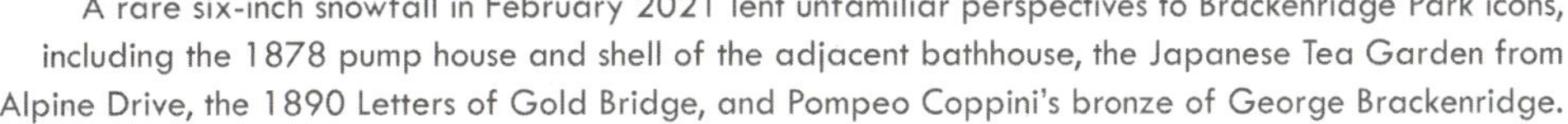

A rare six-inch snowfall in February 2021 lent unfamiliar perspectives to Brackenridge Park icons, including the 1878 pump house and shell of the adjacent bathhouse, the Japanese Tea Garden from Alpine Drive, the 1890 Letters of Gold Bridge, and Pompeo Coppini's bronze of George Brackenridge.

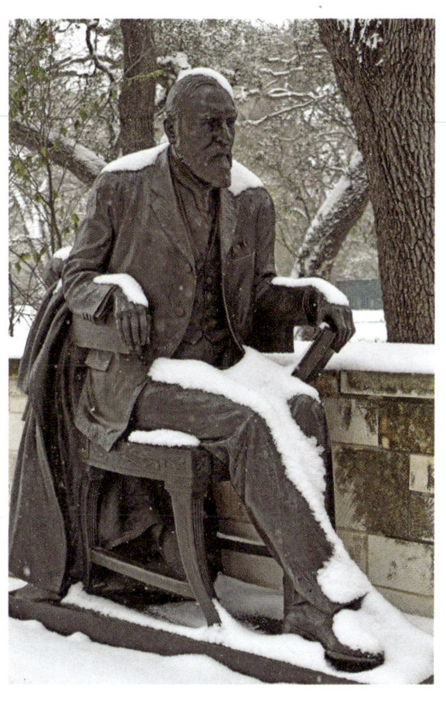

limestone blocks beneath a newer concrete pad. He knew that was the location of the 1776 Upper Labor Dam, previously thought destroyed, and sounded the alarm. The shallow concrete pad that happened to protect what was below was removed. City archeologist Kay Hindes confirmed that the dam had been found. There were further excavations in 2013–14.[477]

Interest in San Antonio's Spanish heritage had been rising with the successful effort to make the city's five former Spanish missions a UNESCO World Heritage Site. Now came realization that the Upper Labor Dam was also a Spanish colonial landmark. The dam for the still-functioning Mission Espada acequia remained in use, and the buried Mission San Juan acequia dam had been located, but the Upper Labor Dam was a rare survivor of the city's civilian acequias, closed and filled for more than a century.[478]

Restoration of the Upper Labor Dam area became the focal point of the Brackenridge Park Conservancy's first involvement in a major park project. The group would support rehabilitation of an area at the northern end of Brackenridge Park, a deteriorated ten-acre section extending south from the dam to the 1878 pump house and Lambert Beach.[479]

Though public concerns arose over the number of trees to be cut to repair river walls and restore other areas, the $13.5 million project was to get underway in 2022. Funding came from 2017 city bond funds ($7.75 million), the City of San Antonio ($1 million), Bexar County ($1 million), the Conservation Society of San Antonio ($300,000), and the Brackenridge Park Conservancy ($3.5 million). The conservancy's privately raised funding would provide amenities not covered by public funds, much as completion of the publicly funded San Antonio River Walk's Museum Reach and Mission Reach were enhanced with private funds raised by the San Antonio River Foundation, once chaired by Nick Hollis, who became the conservancy's board chair in 2022.

Following design plans of the SWA Group, which had worked on the Japanese Tea Garden restoration, the dam's confusing and overgrown surroundings of dry channels and irregular elevations would be transformed into a premier park setting. Nowhere are so many layers of Brackenridge Park's cultural landscape more visible.

The proposed closing of nearby Hildebrand Avenue access to all but supply vehicles would allow greenswards to replace expanses of asphalt no longer needed for roads and parking. A stagnant basin originally walled as a holding pond for the Confederate army tannery and later repaired as a lily pond by the NYA was again to be fresh and ready for water lilies. Added to the mix would be a relaid stone channel section salvaged a decade earlier from a tannery sluiceway farther down the acequia.

The area's water flow was planned to resemble its late nineteenth century pattern. The partially revealed 1776 dam would again divert water into an original segment of the Upper Labor Acequia. Water would flow once more into the pump house raceway, cleared and relandscaped to create a vista south to a restored pump house. Close by, fill that supported a latter-day road over a section of raceway would be removed and replaced by a steel pedestrian bridge leading westward to a new plaza, much of it replacing a stretch of pavement.

At the end of the raceway, removing fill would reveal the pump house's two lower-level stone arches that water once flowed through to power turbines. The pump house's opposite wall, beside the river, would regain similar arches, replacing the pair removed during repairs a century before. Riverbank walls downstream were to be rebuilt and the banks creatively landscaped.

A new trail from the pump house to the acequia dam would meet the ten-mile hike and bike trail along the San Antonio River from Mission Espada north through

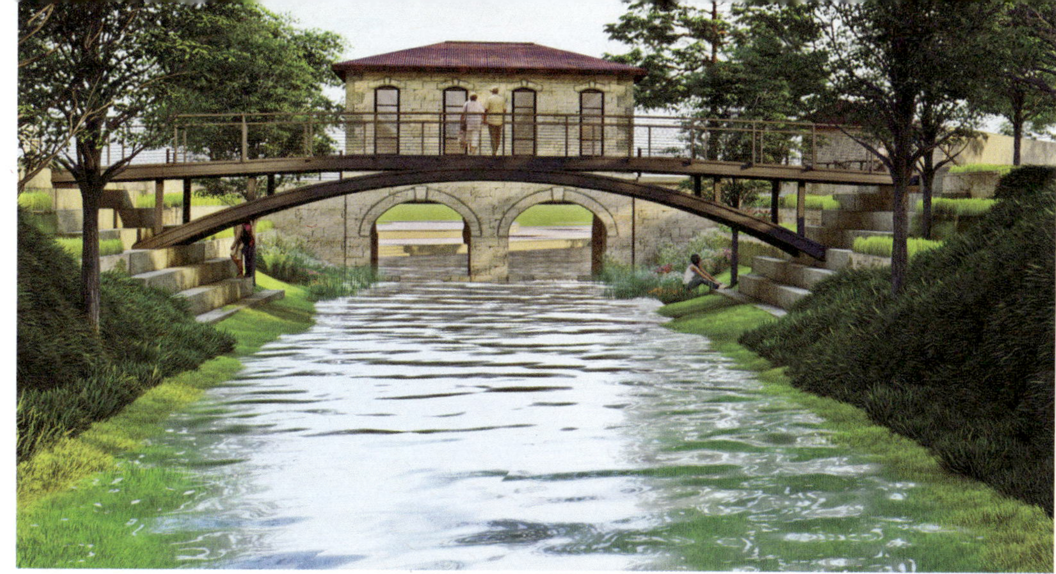

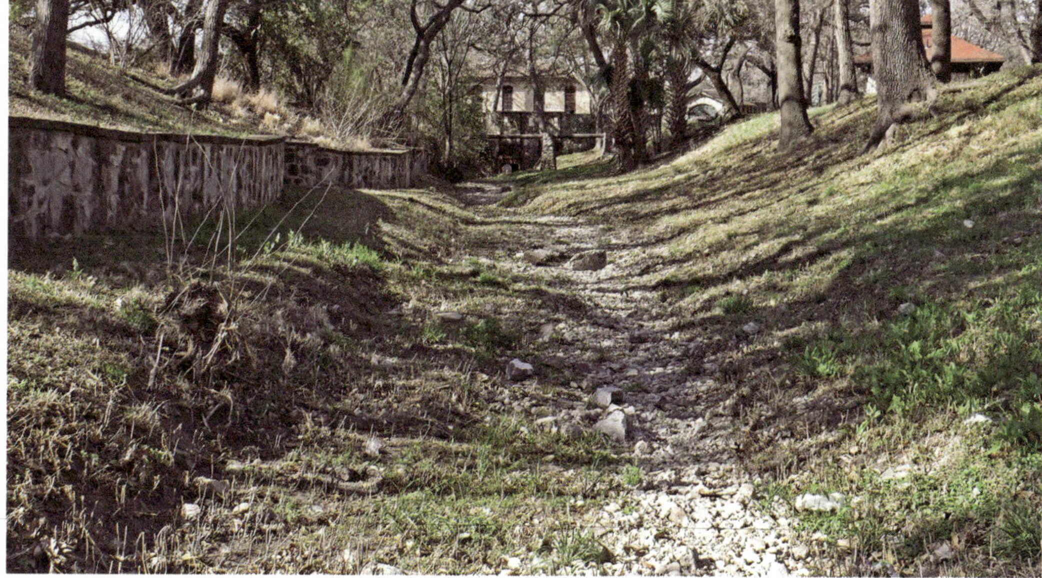

The raceway restoration, shown in a conceptual drawing, will replace a bridge supported by landfill with a steel span and reveal original arches supporting the 1878 pump house.

downtown and up the Museum Reach into Brackenridge Park. Just north of the dam area a passage engineered beneath a Hildebrand Avenue bridge would take the trail through the University of the Incarnate Word campus and to the Blue Hole, the traditional headwaters spring of the San Antonio River. Volunteers maintain it as part of the fifty-five-acre Headwaters Sanctuary, a ministry of the Sisters of Charity of the Incarnate Word.

From there the trail is to connect with the Great Springs Project, a network of trails to the Edwards Aquifer's three other historic main springs—at New Braunfels, San Marcos, and Austin—slated for completion by 2036.

As trails link the six parks in Boston's seven-mile Emerald Necklace park system, linking the Headwaters Sanctuary with the fifteen-mile River Walk would complete a necklace of historic areas downstream to the Spanish missions. That could become a linear National Heritage Area, a type of national park that joins lived-in landscapes with significant historic, cultural, and natural resources. There are already more than fifty National Heritage Areas elsewhere in the country. This would be the first in Texas.

As Brackenridge Park innovator Ray Lambert observed in 1924 of what he had achieved, so could park advocates a century later say of their accomplishments, "This work is just begun."

Notes

Abbreviations Used in the Notes

BCDR Bexar County Deed Records
CCM San Antonio City Council Minutes
NAC National Archives Catalog
NR National Register of Historic Places Registration Form
Express *San Antonio Express, San Antonio Daily Express, San Antonio Express-News*
Light *San Antonio Light, San Antonio Daily Light, San Antonio Light and Gazette*

Foreword

Frederick Law Olmsted quotations are from his *A Journey through Texas: or, A Saddle-Trip on the Southwestern Frontier; with a Statistical Appendix* (New York: Edwards and Co., 1857), 150, 156; accessible online at https://quod.lib.umich.edu/m/moa/AAW3927.0001.001?rgn=main;view=fulltext.

Introduction

1 *Texas Sun*, Feb. 1878.
2 "Where Is The Park?" *Express*, May 15, 1974.
3 Reed, Grove, Turner, et al., *Brackenridge Park Cultural Landscape Report*, xxvi.

Riverside Haven

4 Hester, *Digging into South Texas Prehistory*, 39–45.
5 Katz and Fox, *Archaeological and Historical Assessment*, 5–11.
6 Hester, *South Texas Prehistory*, 44–46.
7 Stothert, *Archaeology and Early History*, 31.

Water and Stone for a Spanish Outpost

8 The Spanish ford was marked on 1870s maps by reliable city engineer Gustave Frieslaben and corresponds with the 1764 Menchaca map. The path later moved north, above the headwaters and along today's Nacogdoches Road.
9 Cox, *Spanish Acequias*, 17–18, 35.
10 McKenzie, *Archaeological Investigations*, 18–21.
11 Pfeiffer and Tomka, NR, 37; Betje Black Klier, "Guilbeau, Francois, Jr.," *Handbook of Texas Online*. A de la Garza mill once thought to have been within Brackenridge Park has been located farther south.
12 De la Teja, *San Antonio de Béxar*, 75, 81–83; McKenzie, *Archaeological Investigations*, 26–27; Cox, *Spanish Acequias*, 19. Farmlands were organized into *labores*, or blocks, made up of several *suertes*, sections assigned by the drawing of lots.
13 De la Teja, *San Antonio de Béxar*, 82–83; Pfeiffer and Tomka, NR, 35.
14 Maverick, Green, and Fisher, *Memoirs of Mary A. Maverick*, 18.
15 Pfeiffer and Tomka, NR, 40.
16 Katz and Fox, *Archaeological and Historical Assessment*, 16; Pfeiffer and Tomka, NR, 36–37.

A Confederate Industrial Zone

17 Maj. T. A. Washington to Maj. A. G. Dickinson, Dec. 23, 1862, NAC, 156–57, accessed Oct. 9, 2020, catalog.archives.gov/id/51399394; Washington to Lt. Gen. E. Kirby Smith, Mar. 30, 1863, *War of the Rebellion, Official Records* (hereafter OR), Serial 21, 1029, accessed Oct. 9, 2020, https://ehistory.osu.edu/books/official-records/021; Maj. E. C. Wharton to Capt. Edmund P. Turner, Oct. 13, 1863, OR, Serial 42, 308–9; Maj. Joseph E. Dwyer to Col. A. C. Jones, Sept. 1, 1864, NAC, 21. While stating the quartermaster department's intent to concentrate all shoe production in San Antonio, Major Wharton noted that production would continue at existing shops at Tyler, Austin, and Houston. Numerous publications state erroneously that additional facilities were completed near the San Antonio tannery—as does a Texas Historical Commission marker on the tannery site—citing as their authority only the published intention that they would be built. The *Galveston Weekly News* quoted a *San Antonio Herald* report that the cotton and woolen factories would be water-powered and built of stone (May 20, 1863, 2).
18 William T. Windham, "Problem of Supply in the Trans-Mississippi Confederacy," *Journal of Southern History* 27:2 (1961): 149–55; Washington to Brig. Gen. H. P. Bee, Dec. 4, 1862, NAC, 143.
19 *Twenty-Sixth Annual Reunion of the Association of the Graduates of the United States Military Academy*, June 10, 1895, accessed Oct. 6, 2020, https://penelope.uchicago.edu/Thayer/E/Gazetteer/Places/America/United_States/Army/USMA/Cullums_Register/1439*.html; Col. Earl Van Dorn to L. P. Walker, Secretary of War, Mar. 30, 1861, OR, Serial 114, 37.
20 Col. A. C. Myers to Washington, June 19, 1862, NAC, 156, and Oct. 30, 1862, NAC, 160; Washington to Smith, Mar. 30, 1863; Washington to Bee, Dec. 4, 1862.
21 Dwyer to Jones, Sept. 1, 1864.
22 BCDR, K2:428–30, Nov. 22, 1862, and S-2:497–99, Jan. 13, 1863, in Pfeiffer and Tomka, NR, 38.
23 CCM, C:339–40, 392, Apr. 20, 1863; McKenzie, *Archaeological Investigations*, 29–30; Dwyer to Jones, Sept. 1, 1864.
24 Washington to Dickinson, Dec. 23, 1862.
25 Dwyer to Jones, Sept. 1, 1864; Washington to Dickinson, Dec. 23, 1862.
26 Dwyer to Jones, Sept. 1, 1864.
27 Myers to Washington, June 19, 1862; Dwyer to Jones, Sept. 1, 1864. Sumac was the tanning agent for the tannery's small production of high-grade leather.
28 Dwyer to Jones, Sept. 1, 1864.
29 Ibid.
30 Ibid. San Antonio's regional supply depot utilized the arsenal buildings built by the US Army; the depot used some of the buildings for arms production.
31 Ibid. There were also storage sheds, a carpenter's shop, a storeroom for hides, a harness room with grain storage, a small lime storage house, and a tool house.
32 Ibid.; Fred Mosebach, "San Antonio's Early Possibilities," *Express*, Oct. 18, 1936, 3-C. François Guilbeau left the country in 1863 and the Washingtons lived there until early 1865, when the home was requisitioned as the replacement for a military hospital. Washington to Maj. Gen. Jonathan G. Walker, Jan. 14, 1865, NAC, 151.
33 Washington to Smith, Mar. 30 and Nov. 23, 1863, NAC, 86.

34 Dwyer to Jones, Sept. 1, 1864. In September 1864 the tannery had four tons of baled japonica on hand in San Antonio and another four hundred tons stashed in Matamoros, along with twenty-five tons of sumac and fifty tons of huisache beans. Nine tons of hides were on hand in San Antonio as well as twelve tons of tallow, nearly fourteen hundred gallons of oil, and an unspecified number of barrels of lime.

35 Dwyer to Jones, Sept. 1, 1864; Turner to Dickinson, Nov. 23, 1863, OR, Serial 42, 459.

36 Washington to Smith, Nov. 23, 1863.

37 Turner to Dickinson, Nov. 23, 1863; Dickinson to Maj. S. T. Fontaine, Nov. 30, 1863, OR, Serial 42, 460.

38 Dwyer to Jones, Sept. 1, 1864.

39 Ibid.; Washington to Maj. Gen. P. O. Hébert, Sept. 5, 1864, NAC, 136.

40 Mosebach, "Early Possibilities," 3-C; Washington to Hébert, Sept. 5, 1864.

41 Dwyer to Jones, Sept. 1, 1864.

42 Washington to Capt. E. S. Gaines, Jan. 11, 1865, NAC, 140.

43 Washington to Lt. H. Burns, Feb. 2, 1865, NAC 90; Lt. A. W. Wallace to Maj. R. W. Keyworth, Feb. 3, 1865, NAC, 87–88.

44 "Thornton Augustine Washington," accessed Oct. 10, 2020, https://civil-wartalk.com/threads/washington-thornton-augustine.164848; Mosebach, "Early Possibilities," 3-C.

45 "Government Sale," *San Antonio Herald*, Jan. 24, 1867.

46 Richter, *Overreached on All Sides*, 210, 229–30; "Terrible Hail-Storm in Texas," *New York Times*, June 5, 1868, 1; CCM, C:588, Feb. 20, 1867, in Pfeiffer and Tomka, NR, 38, and McKenzie, *Archaeological Excavations*, 31; CCM, C:655.

47 Richter, *Overreached*, 230; Sibley, *Brackenridge*, 166; "A Distinguished Citizen," *Light*, Jan. 14, 1903, 6.

48 CCM, D:134 and BCDR, 2:236–37 in McKenzie, *Archaeological Excavations*, 31. Brackenridge, as one of three local board members of the Freedmen's Bureau, had advocated the bureau's donation of tannery stone for construction of the Rincon School. Sibley, *Brackenridge*, 166; Mason, *African Americans and Race Relations*, 131–32.

49 *American Florist Company's Directory* (Chicago: American Florist, 1902), 195–98; James Patrick McGuire, "Újházi, László," *Handbook of Texas Online*; Pfeiffer and Tomka, NR, 44. We are left to wonder the origin of Ilka, a Hungarian girl's name.

50 *American Florist Directory*, 198; Uecker, *Cultural Resources Survey*, 11; 5, L. W. Madarasz, *Price List of Ilka Nurseries 1888–89*, 9–13, https://www.biodiversitylibrary.org/item/162098#page/3/mode/1up; Mosebach, "Early Possibilities," 3-C.

Turbines and Kilns

51 Morris A. Pierce, *Documentary History of American Water-Works*, accessed Oct. 26, 2020, waterworkshistory.us.

52 Ibid.; Johnson, *In the Loop*, 88–90.

53 Porter, *Spanish Water*, 102, 104–5; Johnson, *In the Loop*, 65.

54 Goff, *San Antonio*, 100–1; Baker, *Manual of American Water-Works*, 2:582; McLean, *San Antonio's Water Supply*, 21–22.

55 Gould, *Alamo City Guide*, 84; Baker, *Manual*, 2:582; W. P. Trowbridge, *Statistics of Power and Machinery Employed in Manufacturers, Reports on the Water-Power of the United States, Part II* (Washington, DC: Government Printing Office, 1887), 254; *Tenth Census of the United States, 1880: Water Power* (Washington: US Census Office, 1880), 254. Diggers threw up the semi-impervious caliche as a perimeter berm banked against the walls. A hundred stone piers were spaced within to support a stone roof, but plans to add a covering were apparently not carried out. Several piers were preserved by the Botanical Garden to support an arbor. A small lake was beyond the northern embankment and a small reservoir in what is now the Botanical Garden parking lot.

56 *Tenth Census*, 254; *Worthington Pumping Engines, Steam Pipes, and Hydraulic Machinery, August 1st, 1883*, 22, accessed Oct. 26, 2020, waterworkshistory.us/tech/Worthington/1883Worthington.pdf. Pump house construction began on Jan. 28, 1878, with laying of the foundation. San Antonio's only industrial building known to be older is Simon Menger's San Antonio Soap Works, a limestone building dating from the 1860s or early 1870s on San Pedro Creek.

57 *Tenth Census*, 254; *Worthington Pumping Engines*, 22; *Victor Turbine*, Stillwell & Bruce Mfg., Dayton, Ohio, 1882, 62, accessed Oct. 26, 2020, https://archive.org/details/stillwellbiercem00unse/mode/2up.

58 *Express*: "Water Works," Aug. 25, 1877, 4; "Mammoth Puddle," Feb. 18, 1879, 4; "Our Waterworks," Apr. 9, 1879, 4.

59 "Our Waterworks," 4; Morris A. Pierce, "Documentary History of American Water-Works: San Antonio, Texas," accessed June 8, 2021, waterworkshistory.us/TX/San_Antonio/.

60 "Visit to the Waterworks," *Galveston Daily News*, July 28, 1878, 8; "David Boyle," accessed June 8, 2021, www.hevac-heritage.org/built_environment/biographies/surnames_B-G/boyle/B1-BOYLE.pdf.

61 "Visit to the Waterworks." *Express*: "Important Project," Feb. 18, 1879, 4; "Meat Exportation Movement," Mar. 2, 1879, 3.

62 "Waterworks," *Express*, June 15, 1879, 4; Pfeiffer and Tomka, NR, 41.

63 Sibley, *Brackenridge*, 131; Porter, *Spanish Water*, 109–10, 114; *Tenth Census*, 254; Pfeiffer and Tomka, NR, 42.

64 Sibley, *Brackenridge*, 131–32; Porter, *Spanish Water*, 112.

65 Ibid.; *Tenth Census*, 254; McLean, *San Antonio's Water Supply*, 21–22; "Only a Few," *Light*, Sept. 26, 1886, 1.

66 Porter, *Spanish Water*, 113.

67 Pfeiffer and Tomka, NR, 42, 64; Maria Pfeiffer to Lewis F. Fisher, email, Aug. 3, 2021. Brackenridge made the Maverick purchase with his brother John, who conveyed his interest to George nine years later.

68 Stubblefield, Tillotson, and Hardy, NR, 2; Metcalf & Eddy Consulting Engineers, *Report to City of San Antonio, Texas* (Boston, 1920), 23; Baker, *Building the Lone Star*, 220; *Worthington Pumping Engines*, 31.

69 Fisher, *American Venice*, 19.

70 Ibid., 20.

71 Black, *Historical and Archaeological Assessment*, 2; "City's Water Consumption," *Express*, Oct. 26, 1922, 16–17A. In October 1911 a fifty-horsepower pump powered by compressed air and housed in the 1878 pump house began drawing more than a million gallons a day from a well next to the pump house, for the first time sending water down the river to increase its flow, flush out refuse, and make the river more attractive through downtown. *Express*: "Start Pump," Oct. 6, 1911; "Million Gallons," Oct. 13, 1911, 7.

72 Sibley, *Brackenridge*, 155; Porter, *Spanish Water*, 115; "Power Streams," *Express*, Jan. 30, 1920, 1-D.

73 Lesley, *Portland Cement*; Charles F. Kalteyer, "Portland Cement Plant," typescript in Texana Collection of San Antonio Public Library, 7.

74 Lesley, *Portland Cement*, 7.

75 Gould, *Alamo City Guide*, 90; Charles Baumberger, "Making a Success," *Compressed Air Magazine* 28:10, Oct. 1923, 657–60.

76 Gould, *Alamo City Guide*, 90; Baumberger, "Making a Success," 657–60.

77 Baumberger, "Making a Success," 657.

78 Ibid., 658; Gould, *Alamo City Guide*, 91.

79 Kalteyer, "Portland Cement Plant," 3; Andrew Morrison, *Prosperity and Prospects of San Antonio* (San Antonio: Metropolitan Publishing, 1887), 133.

80 Baumberger, "Making a Success," 658.

81 Baumberger, "Making a Success," 658; Charles F. Kalteyer, "George Henry Kalteyer," *Handbook of Texas Online*, accessed Nov. 7, 2020.

82 Baumberger, "Making a Success," 659. The rotary kiln at the San Antonio plant switched to fuel oil after oil was struck in East Texas in 1901.

83 Kalteyer, "Alamo Cement Company," 2; Baumberger, "Making a Success," 660. The plant beside Alamo Heights closed in 1984, and Alamo Quarry Market was built on part of the site. The vast quarry pit floor was turned into a golf course. The company has since operated at additional quarries successively farther north and under new ownerships while keeping the name Alamo Cement Company.

84 Baumberger, "Making a Success," 657.
85 Pfeiffer and Tomka, NR, 59; "Poor Farm," *Light*, Dec. 14, 1886, 1.

The Jockey Club and the International Fair

86 *Light*: "Jockey Club," Nov. 6, 1893, 8; "Jockey Club," Apr. 27, 1894, 5.
87 *Light*: "Only a Few," Sept. 26, 1886, 1; "Membership," July 31, 1893, 8; "Jockey Club," Nov. 6, 1893, 8. Express: Paula Allen, "Horse Races," Feb. 3, 2019, 4-A.
88 *Light*: "Only a Few," Sep. 26, 1886, 1; "In the Hands of a Trustee," Dec. 11, 1893, 8; "Jockey Club," Nov. 6, 1893, 8; "Jockey Club," Apr. 27, 1894, 5.
89 *Light*: "Jockey Club," Oct. 28, 1893, 8; "Jockey Club," Nov. 6, 1893, 8; "Jockey Club," Apr. 27, 1894, 8.
90 *Light*: "Jockey Club," Oct. 28, 1893, 8; "Success," May 7, 1894, 8; "Fall Race," Nov. 13, 1894, 8. Express: "Holiday Races," Dec. 13, 1893, 5.
91 *Light*: "Jockey Club," Oct. 28, 1893, 8; "Jockey Club," Apr. 24, 1894, 8.
92 *Light*: May 7, 1894, 8; "Opened Successfully," June 13, 1894, 8; July 28, 1894, 12; "Buck Will Entertain," Feb. 26, 1897, 8; "Light Flashes," May 17, 1897, 8.
93 *Light*: "Corbett's Quarters," Sept. 15, 1895, 8; "Corbett in Training," Oct. 5, 1895, 8.
94 *Light*: "Cycle Brevities," Oct. 27, 1895, 8; "S.A. Racing," June 5, 1938, 10-A. Hugh Hemphill, *San Antonio on Wheels* (San Antonio: Maverick Publishing, 2009), 9, 13–14.
95 Light: "City News," June 11, 1897, 8; "The Fourth's Camp," Sept. 25, 1898, 1; "Races Yesterday," Jan. 22, 1898, 1; "At Camp Mosby," Oct. 15, 1898, 8.
96 "Texas Militia Regiments–Spanish-American War," accessed Nov. 1, 2020, globalsecurity.org/military/agency/army/militia-tx.htm. *Light*: "Our New Soldiers," Sept. 11, 1898, 1; "Only Two More," Sept. 24, 1898, 8; "Fourth's Camp," 1.
97 *Light*: "City News," June 11, 1897, 8; "Fourth's Camp," 1; "Races Yesterday," 1; "At Camp Mosby," 8.
98 *Light*: "Fourth's Camp," 1; "At Camp Mosby," 8.
99 *Light*: "It's Camp Mosby," Oct. 1, 1898, 8; "Volunteers Will Move," Nov. 26, 1898, 8. "Fourth Texas Regiment," *Cuero Daily Record*, Oct. 25, 1898, 6.
100 "Fourth Texas Regiment"; "Volunteers Will Move"; "Camp Mosby Notes," *McKinney Democrat*, Mar. 2, 1899, 1.
101 *Spanish-American War Claims* (Washington: 56th Congress, 1st Session, House of Representatives, doc. 460, 1900), 407–13.
102 "To Vaccinate," *Denton County News*, Jan. 5, 1899, 4; "Camp Mosby Notes," 1; Patrick McSherry, "A Brief History of the 4th Texas Volunteer Infantry," accessed Nov. 2, 2020, spanamwar.com/4thtexas.htm.
103 "Seeking Site," *Express*, May 28, 1899, 13.
104 "Notice to Subscribers," *Light*, May 28, 1899, 12.
105 "Seeking Site."
106 Ibid.
107 "Fair Site Chosen," *Light*, May 30, 1899, 8.
108 *Light*: "Recruiting for the Thirty-Third," July 18, 1899, 12; "Matters Military," Aug. 1, 1899, 8; "Camp Is Named," Aug. 2, 1899, 2; "Rough Riders" and "Matters Military," Aug. 8, 1899, 5, 8. *Express*: "Col. Hare Gets More Recruits," Aug. 16, 1899, 7.
109 "Matters Military," *Light*, Aug. 31, 1899, 8.
110 *Light*: "Matters Military," Aug. 6, 1899, 12; "Matters Military," Aug. 31, 1899, 8. *Express*: "Col. Hare," 7.
111 "Off for Manila," *Light*, Sept. 16, 1899, 8; "Galveston," *Express*, Sept. 23, 1899, 10; Brian M. Linn, "Thirty-Third Infantry," *Handbook of Texas Online*, accessed Oct. 2, 2021.

San Antonio Gets a Driving Park

112 Sibley, *Brackenridge*, 10.
113 Ibid., 22, 34.
114 Ibid., 80–83, 91, 129, 141; Johnson, *In the Loop*, 77.
115 Sibley, *Brackenridge*, 166–69, 172.
116 Ibid. In San Antonio he also subsidized construction of Brackenridge School on Centre Street for Black children and Eleanor Brackenridge School, in honor of his sister, on Brooklyn Avenue; with his brother Tom, he built J. T. Brackenridge Memorial School for Black students. Named in Tom's memory, the latter school, like Brackenridge High School, survives.
117 Ibid., 139–40, 150–54.
118 Ibid., 170.
119 Johnson, *In the Loop*, 130, 133; Fisher, *American Venice*, 14.
120 Sibley, *Brackenridge*, 140, 142.
121 Johnson, *In the Loop*, 154–55. Callaghan's forty-two years in city politics included sixteen as mayor.
122 Fisher, *American Venice*, 25.
123 Johnson, *In the Loop*, 156–59.
124 Wilson, *City Beautiful*, 36–37.
125 Ibid.; Johnson, *In the Loop*, 159.
126 Pfeiffer and Tomka, NR, 47–48; "City Solons' Session," *Light*, Nov. 28, 1898, 8; "Col. Brackenridge Also Donates," *Light*, Dec. 23, 1899, 16.
127 "Col. Brackenridge Also Donates," 16; "Clubwomen Will Protest," *Express*, May 14, 1916. In suggesting reasons for the wide discrepancies in the reported size of Brackenridge's gift, architect Jay Louden noted that determining the area was "extremely difficult by hand" and that "thirty minutes of computer work for me is a full day of work of a junior drafter with less precision" and, perhaps, limited capability and interest. Of the 213.2 acres, Louden tallied 164.4 acres east of the river and 48.8 west of it. Jay Louden to Lewis F. Fisher, email, June 18, 2021.
128 Dorothy Steinbomer Kendall, "San Pedro Springs Park," *Handbook of Texas Online*, accessed Nov. 12, 2020.
129 Ibid.; Crook, *San Pedro Springs Park*, 72–73; Hicks, *Annual Message*, 14.
130 Carr, *Wilderness by Design*, 19–22, 37–38.
131 Pfieffer and Tomka, NR, 48.
132 Ludwig Mahncke, "Parks and Cemeteries," in Hicks, *Annual Message*, 36–37; "You Don't Have to Test It," *Light*, Aug. 7, 1901, 2.
133 Hicks, *Annual Message*, 14; James P. Newcomb, "Beautiful Brackenridge Park," *Express*, Sept. 29, 1902; Pfeiffer and Tomka, NR, 48. *Light*: "Notes of the Parks," Mar. 27, 1900, 8; "Brackenridge Park," Aug. 24, 1900, 4.
134 Mahncke, "Parks and Cemeteries," 36–37; "Black Bass Received," *Austin American-Statesman*," May 21, 1903. *Light*: Aug. 27, 1900, 3; "Light Flashes," Sept. 16, 1901, 8.
135 *Light*: "Col. Brackenridge," Dec. 23, 1899, 16; "Match Race," Jan. 3, 1900, 8; "Jockey Club," Aug. 24, 1900, 5; "For a Speedway," May 14, 1901, 6; "Speedway Opened," July 15, 1901, 4; "Good Trotting," Sept. 3, 1901, 7; "Winter Racing," Dec. 16, 1904, 3; "S.A. Racing," June 5, 1938, 10-A.
136 *Light*: "Mission Failed," Aug. 30, 1901, 1; "City News," Oct. 17, 1902, 6. H. Allen Anderson, "Charles Goodnight," *Handbook of Texas Online*, accessed Mar. 12, 2021; Reed et al., *Cultural Landscape Report*, 218–19.
137 *Light*: "Fish from the Hatcheries," May 20, 1903, 4; "More Buffalo," Dec. 3, 1903, 12; "Found Deer Were Becoming Expensive," May 8, 1908, 7; "Offers Elk," Mar. 11, 1910, 4; "G. A. Stowers Buys Elk," Mar. 14, 1910, 7. On Jan. 31, 1906, the *Express* reported the menagerie had grown to six bison, nineteen elk, forty-three deer, four goats, one sheep, four swans, three geese, forty-nine peafowl, thirteen white turkeys, twelve bronze turkeys, two silver pheasants, two Mexican pheasants, and three guineas. Ten tons of hay harvested in the park were stored for feed.
138 Pfeiffer and Tomka, NR, 49; Newcomb, "Beautiful Brackenridge Park," *Express*, Sept. 29, 1902.
139 Hicks, *Annual Message*, facing 41.
140 Reed et al., *Cultural Landscape Report*, 215; Pfeiffer and Tomka, NR, 49.
141 *Visitors Guide* (San Antonio: Nic Tengg [1903]), 25–26; *San Antonio* (San Antonio Printing, 1909), 7–8.
142 Sibley, *Brackenridge*, 161.

143 Ibid.; *General Directory and Blue Book of the City of San Antonio, 1903–1904* (New York: Jules A. Appler, 1902).
144 *Light*: "Real Estate," June 2, 1901, 5; "Riverside Park," Feb. 15, 1901. Sibley, *Brackenridge*, 161.
145 McGuire, *Hungarian Texans*, 107–8.
146 Ibid; "Negro Suspect's Story," *Express*, June 28, 1899.
147 "Real Estate," 5; "Madarasz Family Park," *Express*, June 16, 1901, 32.
148 "Light Flashes," *Light*, May 8, 1901, 4, 5; "Madarasz Family Park," 32.
149 "German Conventions," *Light*, Sept. 16, 1901.
150 "City Makes an Offer," *San Antonio Gazette*, Apr. 4, 1908; Sibley, *Brackenridge*, 162. Through cooperation with the University of Texas, alcoholic beverage consumption restrictions on Brackenridge-donated lands have loosened in recent years, notably at the golf course clubhouse in Brackenridge Park and the Botanical Garden in Mahncke Park.
151 Sibley, *Brackenridge*, 162; Fisher, *Saving San Antonio*, 274.
152 Pfeiffer and Tomka, NR, 49; notes by city engineer F. M. Giraud show the strip between Broadway and North New Braunfels Avenue as 15.78 acres and the hilltop donation across North New Braunfels Avenue at 27.46 acres, not including 6.17 acres of the immediate reservoir area that was reserved for the Water Works Company (Map Showing Brackenridge & Mahncke Park, San Antonio Parks & Recreation Dept.). "Additional Land for Mahncke," *Light*, May 12, 1905, 5.
153 Pfeiffer and Tomka, NR, 49.
154 Sibley, *Brackenridge*, 148; Morgan, "George W. Brackenridge," 96–97; US Bureau of the Census, *Benevolent Institutions, 1910* (Washington, DC: Government Printing Office, 1913), 250.
155 Sibley, *Brackenridge*, 158; McLean, *San Antonio's Water Supply*, 12.
156 Sibley, *Brackenridge*, 163; "Ordinance Condemning Land," *Express*, Feb. 4, 1904, 5; Newcomb, "Some Notes," 10.
157 Sibley, *Brackenridge*, 163–64.

A Pivotal Year

158 *Light*: "Lambert Has New Plan," June 29, 1915, 2; "Work Started," Jan. 14, 1917, 8; "Federation in Final Session," May 13, 1917, 7.
159 Johnson, *In the Loop*, 189, 191.
160 *Express*: "How Famed Beauty Spot Grew," Oct. 13, 1918, 1-B; "Body of Commissioner Lambert to Lie in State," Dec. 20, 1927, 18. The characterization is in Woolford and Quillin, *Witte*, 37; Pfeiffer and Tomka, NR, 52.
161 "City Playground," *Express*, June 16, 1915.
162 Ibid.; "Municipal Park," *San Antonio Evening News*, Apr. 26, 1919, 12. *Light*: "Plans Formal Opening," Apr. 11, 1916, 3; "Thousands Enjoy Opening," Apr. 24, 1916, 7.
163 "City Playground"; Municipal Park," 12. *Light*: "Plans Formal Opening," 3; "Thousands Enjoy Opening," 7.
164 "Thousands at Park," *Light*, Aug. 18, 1915, 5. Lambert erected a second set of pillars at what was known as "the old racetrack entrance." Originally marked "George W. Brackenridge Park," they survive without the word "Park," which was removed once park entry through the golf course was blocked by removal of a bridge across a drainage ditch. As the United States entered World War I, Lambert announced plans to accommodate soldiers stationed in San Antonio by extending the beach half a mile and providing facilities for twenty-five thousand, an effort that did not materialize. "Park Beach," *Light*, June 12, 1917, 2.
165 "Trees in Park," *Light*, July 17, 1912, 14.
166 Ibid.
167 *Light*: "Will Inspect," Aug. 20, 1912, 2; "Provides for Raise," Sept. 17, 1912, 7; "Park Grove," Dec. 1, 1912, 40.
168 McLean, *San Antonio's Water Supply*, 12–14.
169 Ibid. The Belgian syndicate, seeking funds to rebuild Belgium in 1920, sold two-thirds of its stock to a dozen San Antonio investors. The remaining third went to Mississippi Valley Trust and was later purchased by the San Antonians.
170 Ibid., 13–15; William Wren Hay, "Concrete Rings, Superimposed," *Engineering Record*, 71:24, June 12, 1915, 742; "Turbine Pumping Station," *Engineering News*, 75:24, 1125. The company's vice president and general manager, Robert J. Harding, handled project design and direction.
171 Hay, "Concrete Rings," 741–42; "Turbine Pumping Station," 1125–28.
172 Hay, "Concrete Rings," 741; "Turbine Pumping Station," 1127–28.
173 *Light*: "Block Out Golf Course," June 13, 1915, 3; "Texas' 30 Golf Years," May 25, 1936, 6-A.
174 Scott E. Stover, "San Pedro Springs, Texas," *Design* (Winter 1996), 9. *Light*: "Progress of Culture," May 1, 1884, 1; "At San Pedro Springs," July 7, 1888, 4; "Jacob Amreihn," Jan. 7, 1908; "Gustav Jermy," July 13, 1908, 5. Jermy operated the museum for the sponsoring Texas Museum, Scientific and Literary Association. His personal encyclopedic collection of the flora of Gillespie County was purchased in 1897 by the Missouri Botanical Garden in Saint Louis, which opened the Jermy Herbarium.
175 "San Pedro Zoo," *Light*, Nov. 2, 1911, 1.
176 *Express*: "City Should Have Zoo," Aug. 12, 1911, 16; "Plans Museum," Sept. 7, 1912, 4; "Natural History Museum for City," Oct. 1, 1916, 6; "Opening the Vault of Science," Sept. 16, 1917, 25; "Rare Lizard Specimen," Dec. 4, 1925, 7. The Scientific Society's founding president was George Brackenridge, who seems to have taken no further leadership role in the group.
177 *Light*: "IGN Would," Apr. 28, 1914, 5; "Preparing," Apr. 29, 1914, 7; "Zoo Offered," June 14, 1914, 5; "Mayor Will Oppose," June 29, 1914, 1. "Ideal Site," *Express*, May 19, 1914, 7.
178 Pfeiffer and Tomka, NR, 51; "It's Just Like Home," *Light*, Jan. 21, 1917, 9.
179 *Light*: "Lambert Seeking," Sept. 2, 1915, 7; "Specimens," Sept. 15, 1915, 14. "Southton Road Convalescent Center," Bexar County Historical Commission files.
180 *Light*: "Find Tax Rate," Mar. 5, 1916, 2; "Plans Formal Opening," Apr. 11, 1916, 3; "It's Just Like Home," 9.
181 "Lambert Seeking," 7.
182 *Light*: "Travis Jones Gives Two Bears," Sept. 12, 1915, 4; "It's Just Like Home," 9; "Plans Formal Opening," Apr. 11, 1916, 3.
183 *Light*: "Gift of Two Lions," Nov. 8, 1915, 1; "Bird House," Mar. 17, 1916, 5; "Three Sea Lions," Mar. 22, 1917, 8; "It's Just Like Home," 9; "Beach Open," Apr. 11, 1916, 2.
184 *Light*: "Preparing an Outdoor Tank," Oct. 11, 1916, 4; "Hunting Sea-Lions," Jan. 30, 1917, 12; "Three Sea Lions," 8.
185 "Seeks Way," *Light*, Sept. 14, 1915, 5.
186 Ibid. *Light*: "Buffalo Removed," Jan. 26, 1916, 9; "It's Just Like Home," 9; "Donkey Trail," Sept. 26, 1940, 11-A.
187 "To Tame a Wild Animal," *Light*, Mar. 19, 1916, 2.
188 "Zoo in Motion Pictures," *Light*, Feb. 28, 1916, 14.
189 Meyers, *Ghosts*, 22, 97.
190 *Light*: "Golf Course to Be 6000 Yards Long," Oct. 4, 1915, 3; "Finishes Work on City's Free Golf Course," Oct. 17, 1915, 7. In 1922 Tillinghast designed a course for Alamo Country Club, now Oak Hills Country Club.
191 *Light*: "City Golf Course," Oct. 4, 1915, 3; "City to Make," Jan. 4, 1916, 10; "City Course," Feb. 20, 1916, 1.
192 Meyers, *Ghosts*, 25.
193 Ibid., 23.
194 *Light*: "City Course," 1; "Attractive Trophies," Sept. 19, 1916, 13; "Expect Big Crowds," Sept. 29, 1916, 3. Meyers, *Ghosts*, 32–33.
195 Meyers, *Ghosts*, 22, 27–28, 97; "Texas' 30 Golf Years," 6-A; "A. W. Tillinghast, Architect," friendsofbelmontgolfcourse.com/a-w-tillinghast-architect, accessed Nov. 6, 2020.
196 Meyers, *Ghosts*, 69, 71.
197 Ibid., 64–67.
198 "Park Strip," *Express*, May 23, 1916, 9.

199 Ibid.; CCM, July 1, 1920; Everett L. Fly to Lewis F. Fisher, email, Aug. 31, 2021. In 1934 the Witte Museum included an admission-free "Negro Day" to showcase an exhibit of Italian paintings, a type of open house planned "for other population groups or for the community as a whole." "Think," *Express*, June 11, 1934, 1. Other use of Brackenridge Park by Blacks before segregation's official end is mentioned later in this book.

200 "Madarasz Park Is Christmas Gift," *Light*, Dec. 24, 1915, 1. The gift was put at 10.93 acres on the deed and at 12 acres on a plaque placed on a red granite boulder by the Zoological Society, but present-day calculations give the size, including the nearly half of Koehler Park occupied by the zoo, as 13.83 acres.

201 "Plan to Move," *Light*, Sept. 8, 1916, 3; BCDR, 582–85, Sept. 25, 1916.

202 "Madarasz Park Is Christmas Gift," *Light*, 1.

203 Ibid.

204 *Light*: "Alpine Trail," June 13, 1916, 14; "Working on Burro Trail," June 29, 1916, 5; "Park Alpine Drive," Sept. 10, 1916, 3. Alpine Drive was to be the key link in Olympian Way, "a beautiful scenic driveway" between Laurel Heights and Alamo Heights. It was expected to spur suburban development by providing easy access to recreational facilities in Brackenridge Park but never caught on. "Heights Are Connected," *Light*, Apr. 1, 1917, 22.

205 *Light*: "Alpine Trail," 14; "Rotarians to Give," June 7, 1916, 8; "Buys Twelve Burros," June 8, 1916, 3; "Movies to Chronicle," June 10, 1916, 10. Rides remained free until 1939 and were moved inside the zoo the next year. "Free Donkey Rides Abolished," *Express*, June 23, 1939, 8.

206 *Light*: "Wooden-Legged Man Is Hero," Apr. 8, 1917, 20; Bess Carroll, "Donkey Man, Beloved 'Peg' to S.A. Children," Aug. 26, 1927, 1.

207 *Light*: "Wooden-Legged Man," 20; "Peg and Park Burros," Aug. 14, 1921, 1-B.

208 "Kiddies Swell Fund," *Light*, Sept. 2, 1924, 1; "Donkey Man," 1.

209 *Light*: "Driveways," Feb. 11, 1916, 3; "Thousands Enjoy," Feb. 21, 1916, 5; "Plans Formal Opening," Apr. 11, 1916, 3.

210 "Women Want," *Light*, Feb. 13, 1916, 12.

211 Ibid. No one seemed to object to assigning "the best and most reliable men on the police force" to enforce prohibition in Brackenridge Park, thus leaving the worst and least reliable men to combat crime elsewhere in the city.

The Japanese Tea Garden

212 "Location of Incinerators," *Light*, Oct. 31, 1915, 11.

213 "How Famed Beauty Spot Grew," *Express*, Oct. 13, 1918, 1-B.

214 "Sunken Garden," copy of an undated historical description in San Antonio Parks Department Maintenance Division files, 1; Pfeiffer and Tomka, NR, 52. Lambert particularly valued the work of Henry Steingruber, head of city parks for six years and abruptly replaced with S. R. Walker in 1913. After Lambert became parks commissioner he hired Steingruber as chief gardener for city parks. "Mayor Cited for Failure to Pay," *San Antonio Evening News*, Aug. 5, 1920.

215 "Lambert Has New Plan," *Light*, June 29, 1915, 2.

216 "Operetta Proves Musical Triumph," *Light*, Nov. 26, 1908, 2.

217 "Japanese Garden," *Light*, May 5, 1918, 7.

218 "Japanese Tea Garden San Francisco," accessed Dec. 12, 2020, japaneseteagardensf.com/about; "Japanese Friendship Garden San Diego," accessed Dec. 12, 2020, niwa.org/aboutniwa.org/about.

219 "Butchart Gardens," accessed Dec. 12, 2020, butchartgardens.com/our-story.

220 "Famed Beauty Spot," 1-B. When lit at night, the *Light* added, the Japanese garden "takes on an air of weird, ethereal beauty. The lights are soft and dim, and many of them are partially overshadowed by a hanging vine or the branch of a tree, and softly reflected in the clear waters of the pond. It is then that it really answers the definition of Kobori, a famous landscape gardener of old Japan, when he described an ideal garden as 'the sweet solitude of a landscape clouded by moonlight, with a half gloom between the trees.'"

221 Ibid. The *Express* put Baumberger's donation at 25,000 bags, but another story reported the total at "something like 1,700 sacks." In an interview three years later Baumberger said his donation was two thousand bags. "Lily Pond for Park," *Light*, Dec. 18, 1916, 3; J. B. Grinstead, "Sidelights of History," *Grinstead's Graphic* 2:10, Mar. 15, 1921, 27.

222 *Express*: "Work on Lily Pond," Mar. 18, 1917; "Famed Beauty Spot," 1-B. "Magic at Work in San Antonio's Playground," *Light*, June 10, 1917, 11.

223 "Work on Lily Pond." *Light*: "Rare Lily Bulbs," Apr. 17, 1917, 13; "Magic at Work," 11.

224 *Light*: "Magic at Work," 11; "Sunken Garden," 2; "Sunken," Mar, 7, 1926. "Work on Lily Pond."

225 *Light*: "Magic at Work," 11; "Sunken Garden," 3–4.

226 I. T. Frary, "Sunken Gardens," *Architectural Record* 45:2, Feb. 1919, 185.

227 *Light*: "Tea Garden," 9; "Magic at Work," 11. The first tier, at pond level, would be a raft or floating platform "where tea could be served as on a tiny boat."

228 "Pagoda Plans," *Light*, Apr. 4, 1918, 5.

229 "Japanese Garden," 7; "Japanese Tea Gardens," accessed May 2, 2021, at https://japaneseteagardensa.org. The website is maintained by members of the Jingu family.

230 "Japanese Tea Gardens."

231 "Tea Garden," 9.

232 "Sunken Garden in Brackenridge Park," 4. The bands of faux gun barrels were removed during maintenance work in 1963. Remains of the chimney's original decorative rim not already cut out for "turret" openings were also removed, and the top of the chimney was capped with concrete.

233 "Down Little Mexico-Way," *Express*, Aug. 29, 1920, 15.

234 Ibid. In 1944 the open area around the "Mexican Village" was named Baumberger Plaza in honor of Charles Baumberger, who had started at the cement company in 1880, risen to its presidency, and was a major original donor to the Sunken Garden.

235 Historical description in Parks Department Maintenance Division files, 2.

236 *San Antonio* (Chamber of San Antonio, Texas, [1920]), 24.

237 Frary, "Sunken Gardens," 186.

238 Jay Louden to Lewis F. Fisher, email, May 29, 2021.

Ray Lambert's Park

239 Johnson, *In the Loop*, 226.

240 Wilson, *City Beautiful Movement*, 259, 263–64.

241 *Light*: "May Be Given," June 30, 1905; "Scenic Driveway," Mar. 26, 1911.

242 *Light*: "Has Plan to Enlarge," May 14, 1916, 12; "Buys Land to be Added to Park Holdings," Nov. 16, 1916, 1.

243 "Buys Land," 1.

244 *Light*: "Has Plan to Enlarge," 12; "Buys Land," 1.

245 *Light*: "Has Plan to Enlarge," 12; "County Gives," July 4, 1916, 5; "O'Hara's Job," Jan. 9, 1917, 9. West of the acequia path, the county held on to the former poor farm's remaining 8.5 acres, which included the buildings, until selling them in 1920 for development. In the 1950s Davis Park became known locally as Allison Park after N. Dwight Allison, managing editor of the *San Antonio Light* and a brigadier general in the US Army Reserves, whose home on Allison Drive faced the southern boundary of the park.

246 "Gives Tract to City for Use as Park," *Light*, Jan. 16, 1917, 10; Pfeiffer and Tomka, NR, 58. The latter gift carried the same prohibition on the sale or consumption of alcoholic beverages.

247 "Lambert's Plan," *Express*, Jan. 16, 1918, 2-A; Pfeiffer and Tomka, NR, 57.

248 Pfeiffer and Tomka, NR, 62; Laffaye, *Polo in the United States*, 16, 89; Marin Fenwick, "Just Among Ourselves," *San Antonio Evening News*, Feb. 12, 1919, 6.

249 "Work on Lily Pond." In polo jargon the Brackenridge Park grounds were known as a "Sunday field," which distinguished a major playing field from more informal playing grounds. Stewart Armstrong, "Sunday Field," *World Polo News*, June 8, 2020.

250 "Polo," *Air Corps News Letter* 21:1, Jan. 1, 1938, 22; Laffaye, *Polo*, 90, 149; "Museum of Polo," accessed July 8, 2021, uspolo.org/news-social/news/museum-of-polo-and-hall-of-fame-announces-2021-hall-of-fame-inductees.

Robert Beveridge's son Bert "Bertito" Beveridge played polo in San Antonio as a youth but ended up in Austin making Tito's Handmade Vodka.

251 "Mark Out Bridle Path," *Light*, Aug. 6, 1917, 10.

252 Pfeiffer and Tomka, NR, 37, 54.

253 Ibid., 56.

254 "Clubwomen Will Protest."

255 *Light*: "Not to Comply," May 30, 1916, 1; "Ready to Sell," June 8, 1916, 3; "Lot Sale Suspended," June 10, 1916, 2; "Committee Seeks," June 24, 1916, 8; "Clubwomen Inspect," Jan. 28, 1917, 3.

256 "City to Buy," *Light*, May 26, 1916, 3. Notable exceptions to the blight were Quinta Urrutia, the exuberantly styled home of the noted Dr. Aureliano Urrutia, built in 1918 and replaced in 1963 by a Volkswagen dealership designed by O'Neil Ford and Associates. Its immediate wooded neighbor to the north featured a 1918 home designed by Atlee Ayres; the house afterward served as architectural offices for Bartlett Cocke, and later was the Acorn, a school for young children.

257 Pfeiffer and Tomka, NR, 56–57; Wilson, *City Beautiful*, 81–82; Fisher, *Saving San Antonio*, 274.

258 Pfeiffer and Tomka, NR, 56–57. *Express*: "Playground Director Here," Nov. 2, 1924, 12; "Lions to Retain," July 24, 1929, 11. A disagreement with the city five years later over control ended with the Lions Club still in charge, an outcome helped by Mayor C. M. Chambers being president emeritus of the club. The coming year's $10,000 budget, $7,500 of that contributed by the city, included costs for a director, a coach, and a director of dancing, plus addition of a director of dramatics and music and miscellaneous operating expenses.

259 "Br'er Rabbit Delights," *Light*, Apr. 13, 1925, 1.

260 Pfeiffer and Tomka, NR, 57; "Miniature Machine Is Favorite," *Light*, Sept. 21, 1925. When the lion was struck by a falling tree in a 2002 storm, it was repaired by the late sculptor's nephew, Lupe Rodríguez. Lions Club involvement in the park has long been limited to maintaining the lion statue and the flower garden around it.

261 "Highest Water," *Express*, Feb. 27, 1903, 7.

262 "Rescue Work Prompt," *Light*, Dec. 4, 1913, 2.

263 Fisher, *American Venice*, 51; Pfeiffer and Tomka, NR, 60; "Park Campers Find," *Light*, Jan. 28, 1923, 10-C; "Turbine Pumping Station," *Engineering News*, June 15, 1916, 1128. Tourists in as many as three thousand cars used the campgrounds in 1921–22. The congestion caused Lambert to move the camp in 1925 to the far southern border of the park, east of the river at Josephine Street. When commercial tourist courts nearby during the Depression complained of competition from the camp's low rates, city council closed the tourist camp in 1934.

264 Fisher, *American Venice*, 14.

265 Baker, *Building the Lone Star*, 273; "Brackenridge Park Bowstring," accessed Dec. 8, 2020, https://bridgehunter.com/tx/bexar/bh47388/, and "Brackenridge Park Bridge," accessed Dec. 8, 2020, https://bridgehunter.com/tx/bexar/brackenridge/.

266 "'Letters-of-Gold Bridge' Moved," *Express*, June 16, 1915.

267 "City Playground," *Express*, Dec. 16, 1925, 8.

268 *Express*: "City Playground," June 6, 1915; Paula Allen, "Free River Beach," Oct. 15, 1980. "Texan's Magic," *Dearborn [MI] Independent*, Apr. 16, 1921, 6; Pfeiffer and Tomka, NR, 62.

269 Light, *Capturing Nature*, ix, 12, 41–42, 48.

270 "New Park Building," *Express*, Nov. 1, 1925, 1; Pfeiffer and Tomka, NR, 12–13. Joske also left $100,000 to build an elaborate rustic two-story Boy Scouts clubhouse in the 2500 block of Broadway, backing onto Brackenridge Park. The building was razed after the scouts moved to the new McGimsey Scout Camp in Castle Hills in 1969. *Express*: "Boy Scouts Will Dedicate," Feb. 3, 1926, 9; "Boy Scouts Sell," May 24, 1969, 56.

271 Pfeiffer and Tomka, NR, 62.

272 Pfeiffer and Tomka, NR, 62. As the United States entered World War I, Lambert announced plans to accommodate soldiers stationed in San Antonio by extending the beach a half mile and providing facilities for twenty-five thousand persons, an effort that did not materialize. "Park Beach," *Light*, June 12, 1917, 2.

273 Pfeiffer and Tomka, NR, 62.

274 Woolford and Quillin, *Witte*, 130; "Old Pump House," *Express*, Feb. 28, 1927, 7. Private San Antonio investors had purchased control of the water company from Belgian investors, who needed cash to rebuild after World War I.

275 "Old Pump House," 7.

276 Andrew Gaul, Pump Station No. 2, retrieved July 13, 2021, uiw.edu/sanantonio/pumphouse.html. A video of Borglum at work on the Wilson statue in his Brackenridge Park studio was retrieved July 13, 2021, at criticalpast.com/video/65675052206_sculpture-of-Woodrow-Wilson_Gutzon-Borglum_men-work-on-sculpture_ordered-by-Poland.

277 "Park 'Squatters,'" *San Antonio Evening News*, Feb. 21, 1920, 7. *Light*: "Artist Paints," Nov. 30, 1926; "Artist to Lose," July 14, 1929. Steinfeldt, *Art for History's Sake*, 225. Pfeiffer and Tomka, NR, 59.

278 *Express*: "San Antonians Enthused," Feb. 11, 1923, 6; "Attwater Collection Being Unpacked," Aug. 4, 1923, 8. Woolford and Quillin, *Witte*, 39; Pfeiffer and Tomka, NR, 59.

279 Woolford and Quillin, *Witte*, 40–47.

280 Ibid., 47. Four years later San Pedro Playhouse was built on the abandoned museum site in San Pedro Park.

281 Fisher, *Saving San Antonio*, 102.

282 Ibid.; Woolford and Quillin, *Witte*, 47.

283 Woolford and Quillin, *Witte*, 47; "Mexican Artist to Exhibit," *Express*, Sept. 23, 1927, 9; Terry C. Maxwell, "Three Men," *Bulletin of the Texas Ornithological Society* 12:1, June–July 1979, 6.

284 "Thousands Pay Tribute," *Light*, Oct. 6, 1924, 1.

285 "Tribute Given," *Express*, Oct. 6, 1924, 15; "Thousands Pay Tribute," *Light*, Oct. 6, 1924, 1.

286 "Body of Commissioner Lambert to Lie in State," *Express*, Dec. 20, 1927, 18.

The New Deal

287 Johnson, *In the Loop*, 236–38.

288 Mary Maverick McMillan Fisher, "San Antonio I: The Hoover Years," in Robert C. Cotner, ed., *Texas Cities and the Great Depression* (Austin: Texas Memorial Museum, 1973), 56–58.

289 "S.A. Zoo," *Light*, June 25, 1939, 6-B. Federal payments at the time totaled $183,483, those of the city $54,119.

290 "Civil Works Administration," accessed Dec. 23, 2020, https://livingnewdeal.org/glossary/civil-works-administration-cwa-1933/; Lyndon Gayle Knippa, "San Antonio II: The Early New Deal," in *Texas Cities and the Great Depression*, 78–79.

291 "Texas Basketmaker Indians Mural," Texas Public Archaeology Network, accessed Dec. 23, 2020, https://txpan.txstate.edu/Projects/History-of-the-Witte-Memorial-Museum/The-New-Deal-and-the-Witte/ND-Projects-at-the-Witte-Museum/TX-Basketmakers-Mural.html. The mural was taken down for renovations in 1960 and put in storage, as museum officials believed it did "not reflect current scholarship regarding the lifeways of the people of the Lower Pecos Canyonlands."

292 "Works Progress Administration," accessed Dec. 23, 2020, https://livingnewdeal.org/glossary/works-progress-administration-wpa-1935/.

293 "National Youth Administration," accessed Dec. 23, 2020, https://livingnewdeal.org/glossary/national-youth-administration-nya-1935/; Knippa, "San Antonio II," 85. One major National Youth Administration project in San Antonio was the La Villita restoration in 1939–41.

294 Pfeiffer and Tomka, NR, 13, 20; Meyers, *Ghosts*, 30. As Mulberry Avenue was extended east across the old Upper Labor Acequia and on to Broadway, it crossed Memorial Drive. A section of Memorial Drive to the south, later known as River Road, was left intact, but the half-mile that continued from the new intersection north between the river and the polo field to the future Tuleta Drive was closed.

295 Pfeiffer and Tomka, NR, 20, 65; "Koehler Pavilion," accessed Dec. 24, 2020, https://livingnewdeal.org/projects/koehler-pavilion-san-antonio-tx/.
296 Bender, *Animal Game*, 115–16, 126.
297 Matthews, *San Antonio Zoo*, 9–18.
298 Ibid., 19, 36.
299 Ibid., 26; Bender, *Animal Game*, 126, 129; "New Zoo Plans," *Light*, Mar. 24, 1929, 10; "Building at Zoo," *Light*, Nov. 23, 1935, 16.
300 *Light*: "Building at Zoo," 16; "Bring Africa," Feb. 28, 1936, 3-B; "Funds for Zoo," Nov. 5, 1937, 2-A; "Zoo Project," Jan. 16, 1938, 5; "S.A. Zoo," 6-B.
301 Matthews, *San Antonio Zoo*, 29.
302 Woolford and Quillin, *Witte*, 79–81.
303 Eleanor Roosevelt, "My Day, March 20, 1939," *Eleanor Roosevelt Papers Digital Edition* (2017), accessed Dec. 24, 2020, www2.gwu.edu/~erpapers/myday/displaydoc.cfm?_y=1939&_f=md055218. The cabin was moved west of the museum building in 1946, where it gained a neighbor the next year with construction of a replica Hill Country cabin. It was disassembled and moved into storage during museum renovations in 2016.
304 Woolford and Quillin, *Witte*, 99–101; Fisher, *Saving San Antonio*, 228–29.
305 Woolford and Quillin, *Witte*, 101.
306 Ibid., 88, 92.
307 Ragsdale, *Year America Discovered Texas*, 77.
308 Ragsdale, *Year America Discovered Texas*, 62, 168; Maria W. Pfeiffer and Kristi Miller Ulrich, "Historical Background," in Ulrich, *Intensive Survey and Testing*, 21.
309 Ragsdale, *Year America Discovered Texas*, 113, 175; "2 Centennial Jobs Receive Approval," *Express*, Oct. 21, 1936, 18; Maria W. Pfeiffer and Kristi Miller Ulrich, "Historical Background," in Ulrich, *Intensive Survey and Testing*, 21.
310 "Old Trail Driver," *Express*, Feb. 11, 1939, 8; Pfeiffer and Ulrich, "Historical Background," 19–25.
311 "Pioneers Plan," *Light*, Sept. 19, 1937, 4; "Maverick Creates," *Express*, May 30, 1939, 10-A; Lewis F. Fisher and Maria Watson Pfeiffer, *San Antonio Architecture* (AIA San Antonio, 2007), 224.
312 "Letters to the Editor," *Light*, June 30, 1939, 20.
313 Woolford and Quillin, *Witte*, 60–64.
314 Ibid., 77–78. "Snake Garden Nearly Ready," *Light*, Nov. 11, 1939, 2-A.
315 Ragsdale, *Year America Discovered Texas*, 77, 113, 175; "2 Centennial Jobs Receive Approval," 18; Pfeiffer and Ulrich, "Historical Background," 21.
316 Pfeiffer and Tomka, NR, 60; Coppini, *Dawn to Sunset*, 252–53.
317 Braubach, *Always on Tuesday*, 3, 46; Pfeiffer and Tomka, NR, 60; Maria Watson Pfeiffer, "Sunken Garden Theater," manuscript in Public Library Texana collection; "Sunken Gardens," *Light*, May 3, 1926.
318 Coppini, *Dawn to Sunset*, 253.
319 "Outdoor Opera Plans Revived," *Express*, May 16, 1928; "Open Theater," *Light*, June 11, 1938, 1-B; Marie Braun Berry, "San Antonio Civic Opera," 1942, typescript in San Antonio Public Library Texana Room files.
320 Carl Leafstedt to Lewis F. Fisher, email, Jan. 19, 2021.
321 Ibid.
322 *Light*: "Work on Open Air Theater," Apr. 2, 1930, 37; "Light Opera," June 25, 1930, 12-A.
323 *Light*: "Sunken Garden Theater," Apr. 22, 1937, 1; "Curtain Rises," July 2, 1937, 1; "Operatic Voices," June 11, 1938, 1-B. Pfeiffer and Tomka, NR, 17. National Youth Administration workers completed the theater's concession area in 1938.
324 "Concert Set," *Light*, May 15, 1941, 12-B; Carl Leafstedt to Lewis Fisher, email, Apr. 22, 2021.
325 Braubach, *Always on Tuesday*, 3, 46, 56–57.
326 Pfeiffer and Tomka, NR, 18; Braubach, *Always on Tuesday*, 61–62.
327 Braubach, *Always on Tuesday*, 67–69.

Adrift

328 "Brackenridge Park Neglected," *Light*, June 30, 1940, 12-A.
329 "Park's Care Hits Slump," *Express*, Apr. 21, 1946, 1-B.
330 "Brackenridge Park Neglected," 12-A. The incinerator had been built near the future site of Alamo Stadium in 1924 but abandoned three years later, "when Mayor C. M. Chambers bowed to the protests against smoke, stench, and flies." It was put back in service in 1940 after its replacement, near Stinson Field, was destroyed by its collapsing chimney.
331 "Exposition Park Used as Dump," *Express*, Sept. 17, 1940, 2-A.
332 "Zoo to Start," *Express*, July 7, 1940, 5-A.
333 "Council Gives Zoo," *Light*, July 11, 1940, 11-A.
334 Ibid.; Ordinance 2118, CCM, Book R, 185–87, July 10, 1940.
335 Ibid.
336 The bronze plates do not bear the promised inscription "Dedicated to the use of the public December 24, 1915, by Mrs. Emma Koehler."
337 *Express*: "Free Donkey Rides Abolished," June 23, 1939, 8; "New Fence," July 5, 1940, 10-A; "Zoo to Start," 5-A; "Zoo Charges," July 21, 1940, 11; "Zoo Reduces," Aug. 17, 1940, 1; "Cut in Admission Charge," Aug. 19, 1940, 1; "Zoo Office," Sept. 22, 1940, 1-A; "Donkey Trail Moved," Sept. 26, 1940, 11-A. The burro rides, however, were discontinued within a few years.
338 *Light*: "Council Acts," Aug. 3, 1939, 8-A; "Tea Garden," Sept. 15, 1939, 14-A.
339 "100 Years of Japanese Legacy in Balboa Park," *San Diego Uptown News*, Apr. 24, 2015; Meyer Gorelick, "Japanese American Family at Heart," accessed Dec. 31, 2020, sfexaminer.com/news/japanese-american-family-at-heart-of-beloved-golden-gate-park-garden/; Nara Schoenberg, "Garden of the Phoenix," *Chicago Tribune*, Aug. 14, 2016. In California, San Diego's Japanese Tea Garden in Balboa Park was closed and the Asakawa family, resident operators since the tea garden opened in 1917, were shipped to an internment camp in Arizona for Americans of Japanese origin. At the nation's oldest public Japanese tea garden, in San Francisco's Golden Gate Park, members of the Hagiwara family, which had operated the garden since it opened in the 1890s, ended up in an internment camp in Utah; their home was torn down. In Chicago, Japanese-born Shoji Ōsato and his wife had run a teahouse since 1935 in Jackson Park, site of the Japanese Tea Garden on the grounds of the 1893 Columbian Exposition, credited with sparking America's early interest in Japan. When the war began Osato was sent to an internment camp and the teahouse closed. In 1946 it was vandalized and burned.
340 Robyn Ross, "Sign of the Times," *Texas Observer*, Jan. 5, 2012.
341 Thomas K. Walls, *Japanese Texans* (San Antonio: University of Texan Cultures at San Antonio, 1987), 156–58; *San Antonio City Directory* (Dallas: John F. Worley, 1946), 505; David McLemore, "Garden Trip Revisits," *Dallas Morning News*, Apr. 7, 2002, 43-A. Miyoshi Jingu was also with Fred McMurray on the television show *My Three Sons*. Her last role before her death in 1969 was with Cary Grant in *Walk Don't Run*, a comedy set in Tokyo.
342 Ross, "Sign of the Times." The Wus later gained note for their longtime Tai Shan Restaurant backing up to the park at 2611 Broadway.
343 Light, *Capturing Nature*, 44–46.
344 Woolford and Quillin, *Witte*, 121–23. Borglum abruptly left San Antonio over a studio maintenance disagreement with the city and gave his key to Witte Museum director Ellen Shulz Quillin, who negotiated its use by the Witte. The San Antonio Art Institute closed in 1992.
345 "Mill Race Art Studio," *Express*, Nov. 11, 1945, 11-A.
346 Scott Huddleston, "Sculptor Recalls," *Express*, Apr. 14, 2021, 1; "Fragmented Head," Hirshhorn, accessed Apr. 20, 2021, https://hirshhorn.si.edu//collection/artwork/?edanUrl=edanmdm%3Ahmsg_66.2523.
347 Huddleston, "Sculptor," 1; Jonathan Rinck, "Richard Hunt," *Sculpture: A Publication of the International Sculpture Center*, retrieved Apr. 20, 2021, https://sculpturemagazine.art/richard-hunt-2/.
348 Pfeiffer and Tomka, NR, 43; Woolford and Quillin, *Witte*, 323–25.
349 "Lime Kiln Art Colony," *Express Magazine*, Jan. 2, 1949; Roger Allen Cook, "Sunken Garden Art Colony," *Southern Artist* 2:1 [1954]; Pfeiffer and Tomka, NR, 43; Woolford and Quillin, *Witte*, 323–25.

350 Stewart King, "Little Known Department Facts," paper delivered at President's Council, February 6, 1950, typescript copy in San Antonio Conservation Society Library parks files, 5, 6.

351 King, "Little Known Department Facts," 6; David Dillon, *Architecture of O'Neil Ford* (Austin: University of Texas Press, 1999), 84. King was quoting statistics in the March 1949 *Park Maintenance* magazine.

352 "Park Picnic Units," *Light*, July 29, 1951, 18-A.

353 Johnson, *In the Loop*, 275–77.

354 A listing compiled by Maria Pfeiffer shows Hugo Traupmann as parks director in 1951, Gus Haycock in 1952–53, Alvin Schmidt in 1953–55, and, also in 1955, Clyde McCullough and Robert Fraser.

355 Fisher, *Saving San Antonio*, 262, 265, 273–74; "Water Board Retreats," *Light*, Jan. 10, 1958, 8; "What Is the Value?" *Express*, Feb. 14, 1962, 4-A.

356 "Things to Know," accessed Sept. 2, 2021, mysanantonio.com/business/local/slideshow/12-things-to-know-about-Jim-s-Restaurant-in-San-127718.php; "City of S.A. Concessions," *Express*, July 5, 1963, 8-D. Jim Hasslocher's daughter, caterer Caryn Hasslocher, later had the food concession at the Japanese Tea Garden's Jingu House.

357 Richard A. Marini, "When Kids Rode Reptiles," *Express*, Aug. 29, 2021, 1-E.

358 Marini, "When Kids Rode," 1-E.

359 "City of S.A. Concessions," 8-D. *Light*: "Concession Man Asks Rental Waiver," Aug 8, 1946, 2-A; "Around the Plaza," Apr. 30, 1946, 1-B.

360 Bill Freeman, "City's Lone Steam Engine," *Express*, Mar. 29, 1954, 3-H. *Light*: "Shoe Tract for Rail Tracks," Mar. 18, 1948, 12-A; "Hein Drives," June 24, 1948, 4-B. Ten years earlier Charles Miller, owner of Miller's Park / Kiddieland adjacent to Kiddie Park, replaced the miniature steam train circling his small park with a miniature diesel streamliner he named Miller's Zephyr. *Light*: "Streamlined Toy," Apr. 6, 1938,1-B; "Don't Forget," May 27, 1938, 4-G.

361 "Council Indicates," *Express*, May 18, 1956, 2-A; "Tiny Train Pact Approved," *Light*, June 7, 1956, 19. Teams at Brackenridge High School were named the Brackenridge Eagles.

362 *Light*: "Railroad in Park," Mar. 17, 1957, 1-E; "Park Miniature Railroad," June 11, 1957, 37; "Eagle Ride," Feb. 3, 1958, 16; "San Antonio Zoo Railroad Bridge," accessed Dec. 1, 2020, https://bridgehunter.com/tx/bexar/bh48862/. The Eagle's original route wound east to approach the Witte Museum, then turned southwest through the park's densest woodlands to East Mulberry Avenue and west to circle around the former polo field to return to the main depot.

363 *Light*: "Railroad in Park," Mar. 17, 1957, 1-E; "Park Miniature Railroad," June 11, 1957, 37; "Eagle Ride," Feb. 3, 1958, 16. Although a sign at the main Brackenridge Park depot touted "The World's Largest Miniature Railroad" as late as 2021, the claim was invalid by the late 1980s. By then the miniature Train Mountain Railroad in Chiloquin, Oregon, stretched twenty-five miles. It is now thirty-six miles long. http://trainmtn.org/tmrr/pages/about_us.shtml.

364 The old tracks through the woods were later removed, returning the line's length to two-plus miles.

365 "New Depot Inaugurated," *Light*, July 17, 1957, 9-A. A fifth satellite passenger shelter was built past the Witte Museum stop after the landmark Intercontinental Motors opened in 1963 on the site of Quinta Urrutia, between Avenue B and Broadway. The new stop was named Wolfsburg for the German city where the dealership's Volkswagens were manufactured.

366 "Steam Engine on S. A. Run," *Light*, Aug. 3, 1963, 17.

367 Pfeiffer and Tomka, NR, 11, 19, 26, 69; "San Antonio Zoo Railroad Bridge"; "Two Masked Men," *New York Times*, July 19, 1970, 64; Madalyn Mendoza, "Almost 50 Years Ago," *Express*, July 18, 2019.

368 Tony Irizarry, "Sky Ride," accessed Jan. 9, 2021, uiw.edu/sanantonio/SkyRide.html. The city received 25 percent of gross annual profits after the company recovered the initial construction cost of $300,000.

369 Matthews, *San Antonio Zoo*, 29–33; *Guide to the San Antonio Zoo* (San Antonio Zoological Society, [1941]), 4-8; "Donkey Trail Moved," *Light*, 11-A.

370 Matthews, *San Antonio Zoo*, 29.

371 A. W. Tillinghast to President of the PGA, Jan 6, 1936, in Meyers, *Ghosts*, 31, 44, 83. The Texas Open has been held at more than six other courses in San Antonio and is the PGA's oldest professional tournament held in the same city for its entire existence. It was held in Brackenridge Park in 1922–26, 1929–40, 1950–55, and 1957–59. "History Overview," accessed Jan. 10, 2021, https://valerotexasopen.com/history-overview/.

372 Woolford and Quillin, *Witte*, 335; John MacArthur, "Spectrum," *Arts*, January 1957, 11; Grace L. McCann Morley to John MacArthur, *Arts*, March 1957.

373 "$256,000 Diamond Is Stolen," *New York Times*, June 15, 1968, 26.

374 "New Director Sets," *Light*, Aug. 28, 1955, 11; Pfeiffer and Tomka, NR, 10.

375 *Texas: A Guide*, 325; Pfeiffer and Tomka, NR, 68, 69. A few years later Lambert Beach's pool closed for a decade as runoff from new streets contaminated the water. A proposal for an Olympic-size pool in Koehler Park did not materialize. Public swimming at Lambert Beach eventually ended altogether as swimmers shifted to well-equipped public pools elsewhere.

376 Ibid., 325; "3000 Fans Watch Posse Horse Show," *Light*, June 20, 1950, 10-A. *Express*: "Horse Show," June 15, 1950, 5-B; Paula Allen, "Brackenridge Log House," Dec. 9, 2001. Pfeiffer and Tomka, NR, 68. The stables burned in 1951 but were rebuilt and used by the Posse throughout the decade. A small clay tile structure north of Mulberry Avenue remains from the Posse days.

377 Leticia Van de Putte to Lewis F. Fisher, email, May 18, 2021.

378 "Park and Zoo Draw," *Light*, Apr. 10, 1950. Maria Watson Pfeiffer remembers one Easter Sunday in the park when her mother, Elsa Watson, wearing a bright pink dress, got out of their car, which was stranded in the traffic jam, and started directing traffic. Olmos Basin and Concepción Parks were also "flooded" with Easter picnics. The Easter camping and picnic tradition in Brackenridge Park began so gradually the origins were not recorded.

379 Camille Garcia, "Easter Campers Leave Piles of Trash," *San Antonio Report*, Mar. 28, 2015.

380 Camille Garcia, "Easter Weekend Campers," *San Antonio Report*, Mar. 25, 2015.

381 Emilie Eaton, "San Antonio Family Has Celebrated Easter at Brackenridge for 66 Years," *Express*, Apr. 21, 2019.

382 Garcia, "Easter Campers Leave Piles of Trash."

383 After World War I, the section between the points had been the Broadway Athletic Field. In 1925 it became the home of League Park, San Antonio's first modern ballpark. In 1930 Babe Ruth scored a first-inning home run for the New York Yankees there in an exhibition game with the San Antonio Indians. League Park closed when its stadium burned in 1932. David King, *San Antonio at Bat: Professional Baseball in the Alamo City* (College Station: Texas A&M University Press, 2004), 59, 67.

384 This account of the US 281 saga is from Fisher, *Saving San Antonio*, 283–333.

385 Meyers, *Ghosts*, 53–57. Adolph and Elizabeth Schriever's son Bernard worked as a youth at the Brackenridge Golf Course pro shop and won the city golf championship; he went on to become a four-star general in the US Air Force.

386 Ibid., 56.

Renewal

387 Katz and Fox, *Archaeological and Historical Assessment*, 6, 22.

388 CGR Inc., *Synopsis of a Master Plan* (1980), 6.

389 Reed Harp, "Banner (Tearing) Day for Park," *Light*, Nov. 19, 1982. When the palms did not survive, the area was used for parking.

390 Carlos Guerra, "New Sheridan Deal Déjà Vu All Over Again," *Express*, Nov. 28, 2000; "Philip John Sheridan" obituary, accessed Jan 15, 2021, legacy.com/obituaries/sanantonio/obituary.aspx?n=philip-john-sheridan&pid=184627667&fhid=8911.

391 Ken Dilanian, "Sex Charge Clouds Park Contract," *Express*, Oct. 27, 1996, 1; Hernández-Ehrisman, *Fiesta City*, 191; "Philip John Sheridan" obituary.

392 Hernández-Ehrisman, *Fiesta City*, 192.

393 *Express*: Joy Cook, "City Staff Opposes Phil Sheridan," Dec. 5, 1971, 4-H; Deborah Weser, "Was Park Work Illegal?" Apr. 19, 1974, 3; "Park Stand Decision Still Pends," May 15, 1974.
394 "Philip John Sheridan" obituary; Hernández-Ehrisman, *Fiesta City*, 191.
395 "Judge: No More Work on Carousel," *Express*, Nov. 14, 1986, 2-B; Fisher, *Saving San Antonio*, 461.
396 "Great Carousel Caper," *San Antonio Conservation Society Newsletter*, May–June 1987, 4; "City Council Vetoes," *Express*, Sept. 8, 1989, 2-B.
397 "New Sheridan Deal"; Scott Huddleston, "Pieces of the Sky," *Express*, Feb. 22, 2002, 1-B; Irizarry, "Sky Ride."
398 Paula Allen, "Happy Trails Have Ended," *Express*, 2001
399 Pfeiffer and Tomka, NR, 19; "First Tee," accessed Jan. 14, 2021, firsttee sanantonio.org/partners/first-tee-learning-center/.
400 Pfeiffer and Tomka, NR, 12.
401 Nicole Lessin, "Park's Entryway," *Express*, Aug. 3, 2005; Tricia Lynn Silva, *San Antonio Business Journal*, May 20, 2001.
402 Ibid.
403 Ibid.
404 "Torres, McAllister," *Express*, Aug. 29, 1969, 7-C.
405 "Brackenridge Statue," *Express*, Dec. 2, 1951, 20.
406 *Express*: "Brackenridge Was Great Contributor," Sept. 9, 1951, 1-B; "Torres, McAllister," 7-C.
407 *Express*: "Torres, McAllister," 7-C; "Brackenridge Statue," Nov. 11, 1970, 71.
408 *North San Antonio Times*, Apr. 27, 1978; Anderson, Pfeiffer, and Harris, *Archeological Monitoring*, 17, 21–23.
409 "San Antonio River Tunnel," accessed Feb. 21, 2021, sariverauthority.org/services/flood-management/engineering-projects/san-antonoio-river-tunnel.
410 Fisher, *American Venice*, 172–73.
411 Dropping "Chinese" from the garden's name change did not involve evicting its tearoom operators of Chinese origin. Ted and Rose Wu continued to run it for a decade until they turned it over to a niece and nephew, Fred and Kan Jean Wu, who did not renew their lease in the mid-1960s. New operators made the tearoom a snack bar serving hamburgers and ice cream, but it soon closed. Paula Allen, "Japanese Family," *Express*, Oct. 10, 2004.
412 Similar reconciliations were occurring in California. In 1974 a new plaque in San Francisco's Golden Gate Park commemorated the evicted Japanese family that established its Japanese Tea Garden. San Diego's onetime Japanese Tea Garden in Balboa Park had been demolished in 1960 to make room for a zoo expansion, but in 1990 a new one opened as the Japanese Friendship Garden. In Chicago, the site of Jackson Park's ill-fated Japanese garden and teahouse was restored and in 1993 named the Osaka Japanese Garden.
413 Ross, "Sign of the Times"; Patricia Manson, "Restoring Tea Garden Name," *Houston Post*, Oct. 14, 1984, 25A.
414 *Express*: Jan Jarboe Russell, "Return to Glory?," Oct. 24, 2004; "Gardens a Treasure," Oct. 30, 2004, 10-B; Christopher Anderson, "Tea Gardens Pavilion," June 8, 2005.
415 Cockrell, *Love Deeper*, 262–63; Anderson, "Tea Gardens Pavilion."
416 Cockrell, *Love Deeper*, 263–65; "Historic Japanese Tea Garden," accessed Jan. 20, 2021, https://jinguhousesa.com/history/. For food services the San Antonio Parks Foundation hired Fresh Horizons, which agreed to return a portion of its profits to maintain the Jingu House.
417 "Historic Japanese Tea Garden."
418 Meyers, *Ghosts*, 83, 101–8; "Brackenridge Park Golf Course," accessed Feb. 1, 2020, golftexas.com/golf-courses/south/san-antonio/brackenridge.htm. This appears to be the time when the remaining public drives through the golf course were eliminated, including the pillared entrance road from Broadway marked "George W. Brackenridge Park."
419 Meyers, *Ghosts*, 101–3, 106.
420 Ibid., 109–16; Mike Bailey, "Old Brackenridge Park Golf Course Is Better Than Ever in San Antonio," accessed Feb. 1, 2020, golftexas.com/departments/coursereviews/brackenridge-park-golf-course-review-11884.htm.
421 Sally Booth-Meredith, "Architects Restore," *Express*, Aug. 26, 1984, 1-J.
422 "$6,900 Razing Tag," *Express*, July 29, 1961. Two wells at the site remain in use.
423 "A. W. Tillinghast, architect," friendsofbelmontgolfcourse.com/a-w-tillinghast-architect, accessed Nov. 6, 2020; Thomas Dunne, "Illustrious Career of A. W. Tillinghast," *Links Magazine*, accessed Nov. 29, 2020, linksmagazine.com/the_essential_a_w_tillinghast/; Stephen Hennessey, "Best A. W. Tillinghast Golf Courses," *Golf Digest*, Aug. 22, 2018.
424 Matthews, *San Antonio Zoo*, 37–44, 51.
425 *Express*: Vincent Davis, "Zoo Celebrates," Mar. 8, 2014, 1; Scott Huddleston, "Donkey Barn," Jan. 3, 2013, B-1.
426 Matthews, *San Antonio Zoo*, 72–78; Shari Biediger, "$200M Zoo Plan," *San Antonio Report*, Aug. 16, 2018.
427 "San Antonio Zoo Taking over Historic Kiddie Park," *Express*, April 19, 2019.
428 *Light*: "City Has Eight Lives," Aug. 9, 1926, 1; "Five Days to Live," May 21, 1937, 1-B. *Express*: Lisa Sandberg, "Death by the Pound," Nov. 14, 2004; "Animal Adoption Center," Oct. 1, 2012, 9-A; "Animal Shelter Reopens," Jan. 5, 2017, 3-A.

Miraflores

429 Sarah C. Westkaemper [Lake], "Three Twentieth Century Gardens: A Heritage of Excellence in San Antonio" (master's thesis, School of Landscape Architecture, Louisiana State University, 1985), 55.
430 Ibid.
431 Ibid., 56.
432 Nancy Aguirre and Elise Urrutia, "Place in Exile," in *Three Hundred Years of San Antonio and Bexar County*, edited by Claudia R. Guerra (Trinity University Press, 2019), 55.
433 Ibid., 55. The intrigues that led some Mexican factions to make Urrutia "one of the favorite villains in our history" are highlighted in a Spanish-language biography by granddaughter Cristina Urrutia Martínez, *Aureliano Urrutia: Del crimen político al exilio* (Barcelona: Tusquets Editores, 2008).
434 Elise Urrutia, "Miraflores at 100," accessed Jan. 26, 2021, quintaurrutia.com/home/2021/01/04/miraflores-at-100; "Relief of Suffering," *Express*, Oct. 29, 1929, 15.
435 Westkaemper, "Twentieth Century Gardens," 45–46, 57; *Miraflores: Our Culture, Our Heritage / Nuestra Cultura, Nuestro Patrmonio, Master Plan and Improvements* (San Antonio: RVK Architects, 2007), 44.
436 Westkaemper, "Twentieth Century Gardens," 49.
437 Ibid., 54; Martínez, *Aureliano Urrutia*, 250.
438 Westkaemper, "Twentieth Century Gardens," 48, 50, 55.
439 Ibid., 49–50, 53.
440 Ibid., 49–50; *Miraflores*, 16, 49. Also listed are the full-length bronze statue of Urrutia by Ignacio Asúnsolo, the Aztec moon goddess Coyolxuahqui by Luis L. Sanchez, and the Grotto and the Palapa Bench by Dionicio Rodríguez.
441 Light, *Capturing Nature*, 27.
442 Maria Pfeiffer, "History of Miraflores," in *Miraflores*, 18; Westkaemper, "Twentieth Century Gardens," 51–52.
443 Westkaemper, "Twentieth Century Gardens," 50–53, 57.
444 Pfeiffer, "History of Miraflores," 16, 21.
445 Paul T. Ringenbach, *USAA: A Tradition of Service* (Brookfield, MO: Donning, 1997), 143–44.
446 Pfeiffer, "History of Miraflores," 21.
447 Ringenbach, *USAA*, 202–3.
448 Pfeiffer, "History of Miraflores," 22–23.
449 Ulrich, *Archaeological Services*, 9; Pfeiffer, "History of Miraflores," 23–24, 46.
450 Ulrich, *Archeological Services*, 9; Pfeiffer, "History of Miraflores," 24; Light and Pfeiffer, "Miraflores Park," 20.
451 Fisher, *Saving San Antonio*, 501–2.
452 Ulrich, *Archaeological Services*, 17–40.
453 Elise Urrutia, "Local Couple Returns Miraflores Monument," *San Antonio Report*, Oct. 31, 2016; Elise Urrutia, "Miraflores to Resprout," *San Antonio Report*, June 11, 2017.

A Sustainable Park

454 Reed et al., *Cultural Landscape Report*, xxv.

455 Ibid., xxvi, 38–39.

456 "2020 ParkScore Rankings," Trust for Public Land, accessed Feb. 8, 2021, tpl.org/parkscore.

457 *Brackenridge Park Master Plan* (City of San Antonio, 2017), 2, accessed Feb. 5, 2021, brackenridgepark.org/files/large/b163e99c63315d1.

458 Reed et al., *Cultural Landscape Report*, 37.

459 Ibid., 85–86, 488. Treatment of the park's evolution cited updates of analysis by Galen Cranz.

460 Ibid., xxvi.

461 Two other former San Antonians had leadership roles with major New York City parks. In 1994 Warrie Lynn Smith Price was founder and first president of the Battery Conservancy, which revitalized the historic twenty-five-acre Battery Park at the southern tip of Manhattan. Robert Hammond cofounded and was the first executive director of Friends of the High Line, a linear park that opened in 2009 along what had been an abandoned elevated railway structure through 1.45 miles of Manhattan's west side.

462 *Brackenridge Park Biodiversity Study*, 20–22, 57.

463 Berit Mason, "Lost Cats of Brackenridge Park," *78209 Magazine*, Oct. 5, 2017.

464 *Express*: Steve Bennett, "Mulberry Bridge," June 23, 2011; Paula Allen, "Queenie Likely Rests," Jan. 13, 2013.

465 Lady Bird Johnson Wildlife Center, *Ecological Site Assessment*, 60–61.

466 "Brackenridge Park Conservancy Management Agreement," accessed Feb. 7, 2021, https://webapp9.sanantonio.gov/FileNetArchive/%7B3BCEDEAB-9033-4EE6-9B25-2A9D2E0C6FF1%7D/%7B3BCEDEAB-9033-4EE6-9B25-2A9D2E0C6FF1%7D.pdf. Scheduling and operations management were granted "as is" to the conservancy for the Lambert Beach Bathhouse, Kampmann House, 1878 Pump House, Mexican Village, Miraflores, and the Restroom / Storage Building used for conservancy offices.

467 "Hermann Park Recognized," *Houston Chronicle*, Oct. 22, 2015.

468 Joe Turner to Lewis F. Fisher, email, Feb. 10, 2021.

469 Iris Dimmick, "Brackenridge Park's 'Intervention,'" *San Antonio Report*, Mar. 4, 2017.

470 Dimmick, "Park's 'Intervention'"; Raj Mankad, "Beyond the Riverwalk," *Dirt*, Mar. 21, 2017.

471 Vianna Davila, "Council Approves," *Express*, Mar. 2, 2017.

472 Guillermo Garcia, "Plan for Witte Garage," *Express*, June 28, 2007, 1. The nursery site was identified on a 1958 map as "Botanical Gardens."

473 Guillermo Garcia, "UT Now Part of Battle," *Express*, July 21, 2007, 1.

474 Richard Marini, "New Generation of Garages," *Express*, Dec. 1, 2019.

475 Marini, "New Generation."

476 Lady Bird Johnson Wildlife Center, *Ecological Site Assessment*, 36, 38.

477 I. Waynne Cox, Edgar D. Johnson, and C. Britt Bousman, "Excavations for the Upper Labor Dam Site," Index of Texas Archaeology, accessed Feb. 9, 2021, https://scholarworks.sfasu.edu/ita/vol1999/iss1/4/; Maria Watson Pfeiffer to Lewis F. Fisher, email, July 29, 2021. Then a staff member at the parks department, Pfeiffer oversaw the excavation for the city.

478 McKenzie, *Archaeological Investigations*, 32. The Alamo Acequia Dam nearby at the park's northeast corner had been leveled before the 1930s, though substantial portions remained buried.

479 Other structures in the tract included, near the dam, the 1925 Dionicio Rodríguez arbor pedestrian bridge, an 1878 Water Works vehicular bridge, the nearby 1920s donkey trail bridge, and, farther south, the arches of a second donkey trail bridge since adapted to support a pipe. Nearer the pump house, a long-closed decorative stone 1920s restroom building would be renovated and reopened. A 1940 one-room limestone electric pump station that once sent water up to a municipal tank at Hildebrand Avenue and Devine Road would remain unchanged, as would the stone shell of the 1925 bathhouse.

Selected Bibliography

Archeological Reports

CAR Center for Archaeological Research, University of Texas at San Antonio

Anderson, Nesta J., Maria Pfeiffer, and Brandy Harris. *Archeological Monitoring of the Catalpa-Pershing Channel Improvements*. Austin, TX: Atkins, 2012.

Black, Stephen L. *An Historical and Archaeological Assessment of the Proposed San Antonio Botanical Center*. CAR Report No. 24, 1976.

Cox, I. Waynne. "Historical and Archival Documentation for Pioneer Park, San Antonio, Bexar County, Texas." CAR Research Survey Report No. 196, 1990.

Figueroa, Antonia L., and Jon J. Dowling. *Additional Phase II Testing at 41BX323 in Brackenridge Park, San Antonio, Bexar County, Texas.* Principal Investigator Steve A. Tomka. CAR Archaeological Report No. 377, 2007.

Katz, Susanna R., and Anne A. Fox. *Archaeological and Historical Assessment of Brackenridge Park, City of San Antonio, Texas.* CAR Survey Report No. 33, 1979.

McKenzie, Clinton M. M. *Archaeological Investigations of the Alamo Dam and Upper Labor Dam, Brackenridge Park, San Antonio, Bexar County, Texas.* With contributions by C. Stephen Smith. Principal Investigator Raymond Mauldin. CAR Report No. 444. Vol. 1 (redacted), 2017.

Stothert, Karen E. *The Archaeology and Early History of the Head of the San Antonio River.* Southern Texas Archaeological Association, Special Publication No. 5. Incarnate Word College Archaeology Series No. 3. San Antonio: Southern Texas Archaeological Association in cooperation with Incarnate Word College, 1989.

Uecker, Herbert C. *A Cultural Resources Survey for the San Antonio Animal Care Spay and Neuter Adoption Facility Project, Bexar County, Texas.* San Antonio: South Texas Archaeological Research Services Report of Investigations No. 182, 2011.

———. *Cultural Resources Survey for the San Antonio Parks and Recreation Department's Zoo Water Treatment Plant Project.* San Antonio: South Texas Archeological Research Services Report of Investigations No. 149, 2008.

Ulrich, Kristi Miller. *Archaeological Investigations at the Lily Pond in Brackenridge Park, San Antonio, Bexar County, Texas.* Principal Investigator Steve A. Tomka. CAR Technical Report No. 35, 2011.

———. *Archaeological Services Associated with Improvements to Miraflores at Brackenridge Park, San Antonio, Bexar County, Texas.* With contributions by Antonia L. Figueroa. CAR Report No. 387, 2008, prepared for Rehler Vaughn & Koone, San Antonio, Texas.

———. *Intensive Survey and Testing Associated with the Rediscovery of the Acequia Madre (41BXS) and Alamo Dam, San Antonio, Bexar County, Texas.* With contributions by Maria W. Pfeiffer. CAR Report No. 417, 2011.

Books, Articles, National Register Nominations, and Miscellaneous Manuscripts

Baker, Moses, ed. *Manual of American Water-Works.* New York: Engineering News, 1889.

Baker, T. Lindsay. *Building the Lone Star: An Illustrated Guide to Historic Sites.* College Station: Texas A&M University Press, 2000.

Bender, Daniel E. *The Animal Game.* Cambridge, MA: Harvard University Press, 2016.

Brackenridge Park Biodiversity Study. Round Rock, Tex.: Bio-West Inc., 2012.

Braubach, Marian N. *Always on Tuesday: One Hundred Years of Music, a History of the Tuesday Musical Club Inc., 1901–2001.* San Antonio: Tuesday Musical Club, 2000.

Carr, Ethan. *Wilderness by Design: Landscape Architecture and the National Park Service.* Lincoln: University of Nebraska Press, 1982.

Cockrell, Lila Banks. *Love Deeper Than a River: My Life in San Antonio.* San Antonio: Trinity University Press, 2019.

Coppini, Pompeo. *From Dawn to Sunset.* San Antonio: Naylor, 1949.

Cox, I. Waynne. *The Spanish Acequias of San Antonio.* San Antonio: Maverick Publishing, 2005.

Crook, Cornelia E. *San Pedro Springs Park: Texas' Oldest Recreation Area.* San Antonio: Self-published, 1967.

De la Teja, Jesús F. *San Antonio de Béxar: A Community on New Spain's Northern Frontier.* Albuquerque: University of New Mexico Press, 1995.

Fisher, Lewis F. *American Venice: The Epic Story of San Antonio's River.* San Antonio: Maverick Publishing, 2015.

———. *Saving San Antonio: The Preservation of a Heritage*. 2nd ed. San Antonio: Trinity University Press, 2016.

Goff, George P. *San Antonio and Environs*. Lancaster, PA: Inquirer Printing, 1881.

Gould, Stephen. *The Alamo City Guide*. New York: Macgowan & Slipper, 1882.

Hernández-Ehrisman, Laura. *Inventing the Fiesta City: Heritage and Carnival in San Antonio*. Albuquerque: University of New Mexico Press, 2008.

Hester, Thomas R. *Digging into South Texas Prehistory: A Guide for Amateur Archaeologists*. San Antonio: Corona Publishing, 1980.

Hicks, Marshall. *Annual Message of Marshall Hicks, Mayor of the City of San Antonio*. San Antonio: Guessaz & Ferlet, 1901.

Johnson, David R. *In the Loop: A Political and Economic History of San Antonio*. San Antonio: Trinity University Press, 2020.

Kerby, Robert L. *Kirby Smith's Confederacy: The Trans-Mississippi South, 1863–1865*. New York: Columbia University Press, 1972.

Lady Bird Johnson Wildflower Center. *Ecological Site Assessment, Brackenridge Park*. University of Texas at Austin, 2019.

Laffaye, Horace A. *Polo in the United States: A History*. Jefferson, NC: McFarland, 2011.

Lesley, Robert W. *History of the Portland Cement Industry*. Chicago: International Trade Press, 1924.

Light, Patsy Pittman. *Artisans of Trabajo Rústico: The Legacy of Dionicio Rodríguez*. Photographs by Kent Rush. College Station: Texas A&M University Press, 2021.

———. *Capturing Nature: The Cement Sculpture of Dionicio Rodríguez*. College Station: Texas A&M University Press, 2008.

———, and Maria Pfeiffer. "Miraflores Park National Register Nomination." San Antonio, Nov. 2003, rev. Mar. 2006.

Mason, Kenneth. *African Americans and Race Relations in San Antonio, Texas*. Milton Park, UK: Taylor & Francis, 1998.

Matthews, Wilbur L. *History of the San Antonio Zoo*. San Antonio: San Antonio Zoo, 1991.

Maverick, Mary A., Rena Maverick Green, and Maverick Fairchild Fisher, eds. *Memoirs of Mary A. Maverick: A Journal of Early Texas*. San Antonio: Maverick Publishing, 2005.

McGuire, James Patrick. *The Hungarian Texans*. San Antonio: University of Texas Institute of Texan Cultures, 1993.

McLean, Bert J. *The Romance of San Antonio's Water Supply and Distribution*. San Antonio: Water Supply Co., 1927.

Meyers, Reid E. *The Ghosts of Old Brack: A Pictorial History of the Brackenridge Park Golf Course*. San Antonio: Reid E. Meyers, 2003.

Morgan, Bobbie Whitten. "George W. Brackenridge and His Control of San Antonio's Water Supply, 1869–1905." Master's thesis, Trinity University, San Antonio, 1961.

Newcomb, J. P., II. "Some Notes on Brackenridge Park," 1962. Typescript in Texana Room of San Antonio Public Library.

Pfeiffer, Maria Watson, and Steve A. Tomka. "National Register of Historic Places Registration Form, Brackenridge Park." San Antonio Conservation Society, San Antonio, June 1, 2011.

Porter, Charles R., Jr. *Spanish Water, Anglo Water: Early Development in San Antonio*. College Station: Texas A&M University Press, 2009.

Ragsdale, Kenneth B. *The Year America Discovered Texas: Centennial '36*. College Station: Texas A&M University Press, 1987.

Reed, Doug, John Grove, Christina Sohn, Suzanne Turner, John Welch, Herpreet Singh, Ashley Braquet, and Michelle Bertelsen. *Brackenridge Park Cultural Landscape Report, San Antonio, Texas*. Prepared for Brackenridge Park Conservancy, San Antonio Parks and Recreation Department, and San Antonio River Authority by Reed Hilderbrand, LLC, Cambridge, MA, and Suzanne Turner Associates, Baton Rouge, LA, in collaboration with the University of Texas Lady Bird Johnson Wildflower Center, Austin, Texas. Cambridge, MA: Reed Hilderbrand, LLC, 2020.

Richter, William L. *Overreached on All Sides: The Freedmen's Bureau Administrators in Texas, 1865–1868*. College Station: Texas A&M University Press, 1991.

Ringenbach, Paul T. *USAA: A Tradition of Service*. Brookfield, MO: Donning, 1997.

Sibley, Marilyn McAdams. *George W. Brackenridge: Maverick Philanthropist*. Austin: University of Texas Press, 1973.

Steinfeldt, Cecelia. *Art for History's Sake: The Texas Collection of the Witte Museum*. Austin: Texas Historical Association for the Witte Museum, 1993.

Stubblefield, Joe, Steven Tillotson, and Daniel Hardy. "National Register of Historic Places Nomination Form, San Antonio Water Works Pump Station No. 2, Brackenridge Park." San Antonio, Joe Stubblefield Architect & Planner, July 9, 1981.

Texas: A Guide to the Lone Star State. American Guide Series. New York: Hastings House, 1940.

Walls, Thomas K. *Japanese Texans*. San Antonio: University of Texas Institute of Texan Cultures at San Antonio, 1987.

Wilson, Harold S. *Confederate Industry: Manufacturers and Quartermasters in the Civil War*. Jackson: University Press of Mississippi, 2002.

Wilson, William H. *The City Beautiful Movement*. Baltimore, MD: Johns Hopkins University Press, 1989.

Woolford, Bess Carroll, and Ellen Schulz Quillin. *The Story of the Witte Memorial Museum, 1922–1960*. San Antonio: San Antonio Museum Association, 1966.

Acknowledgments

Unearthing and synthesizing the twelve-thousand-year saga of Brackenridge Park has required not just one sleuth. In addition to the customary support group of institutional staffers, this project needed a phalanx of credentialed park enthusiasts willing to go on the hunt for answers to questions long unasked. I've had the benefit of just such a network.

It had taken the likes of Maria Watson Pfeiffer, in 2011, to overcome the city's chronic historical amnesia and shortage of records and figure out just what was in the century-old park and how it chanced to be there. Her heroic detective work with archeologist Steve Tomka culminated in a 114-page document that put Brackenridge Park in the National Register of Historic Places. It's been the go-to source for information on the park and its landmarks ever since.

For this book Maria graciously checked further as well as provided copies of her earlier research, which still held surprises. For one, she had preserved a 1960s park maintenance memo with a penciled note that gives the only clue as to the identity of perhaps the park's most curious feature ever: two rows of simulated gun barrels that once circled near the top of the landmark former cement kiln chimney.

Jay Louden, an architect who worked on the Japanese Tea Garden renovation and other park projects, was a quick study as he prepared first-ever professional explanatory maps of Brackenridge Park for this book and applied them to challenge the long-accepted official size of the park, however inconsistently it is defined.

The Indiana Jones of this project was Clinton McKenzie, an affable archeologist with the University of Texas at San Antonio's Center for Archaeological Research, always ready to square what we saw above ground with what he knew to be below. Gregg Eckhardt with the San Antonio Water System advised on the park's hydrology.

Tom Shelton, the peerless photo archivist at University of Texas at San Antonio Special Collections, enlisted the aid of his able associate Carlos Cortez and came up with important but yet-uncatalogued images.

Bill Pennell, landscape architect and assistant manager for planning with the city's Parks and Recreation Department, spent the better part of an afternoon with me sifting through surviving city records and a vast number of survey maps. Park stalwart Lynn Bobbitt and her assistant Doris Jewett at the Brackenridge Park Conservancy provided ready support, as well.

Andrew Brethauer, a specialist with the National Archives in Washington, gave key links to materials that became the basis in this book for the first account of the operations and fortunes of the Confederate army tannery, most of its remains now buried near the children's education center of the San Antonio Zoo. Maria McKelvey, a member of the Virginia-based National Society of Washington Family Descendants, came up with a series of clues that led to a photograph of the tannery's organizer and commander, Maj. Thornton A. Washington, a great-grandnephew of George Washington. Bill Lyons of Casa Rio restaurant fame produced a photo of the tannery's supervisor, Capt. William Lyons, his great-grandfather.

My wife, Mary, onetime English teacher and journalist, was always ready with a pencil to critique and improve, with remarkable patience, my numerous drafts. Our sons, William and Maverick, made their own thoughtful editorial contributions. Mary also offered insights on why multiple generations have cherished Brackenridge Park. She remembered her mother's tales of swimming at Lambert Beach and riding donkeys with her siblings. As a child Mary had ridden in a park concessionaire's canoe, on horseback along bridle trails, and atop elephants at the zoo, but not, she regrets, on Old Joe at the Alligator Garden, due to an overprotective grandmother. Our children and grandchildren are veterans of summertime zoo camps and museum camps in the park. More than ten years ago Mary began weekly walks through the park with friends, and has furnished memorable images she took on the treks.

Trinity University music historian Dr. Carl Leafstedt offered national and local background on the civic opera popularity that spurred construction of the Sunken Garden Theater. Jon Ott, chair of the International Sculpture Center and publisher of *Sculpture* magazine, provided background on sculptor Richard Hunt's notable work at the park's lower pump house, now known as the Borglum Studio. Everett Fly came up with material on segregation in the park. Cynde Zietlow at the Baumberger Endowment opened early files of the Alamo Cement Company.

A host of others searched for scarce images and information. Among them were Amy Fulkerson and Stephanie Pritchard at the Witte Museum, Alexandra Barrett Bynum and Ramon Smitherman at the San Antonio Zoo, Matt Dewaelsche at the San Antonio Public Library, Melissa Gohlke at UTSA Special Collections, Kimberley Wolf at RVK Architects, and, at the University of Texas at Austin, Linda Briscoe Myers at the Harry Ransom Center and Nancy Sparrow at the Alexander Architectural Library.

Charlotte Mitchell contributed several remarkable photographs she took in the park. Dr. Ricardo Romo offered a selection of his photos of Easter there. Dixie Watkins III found images from the Japanese Tea Garden renovation, Jeff Goodson lent an album with early photographs, and David Haynes made life easier with a large file of images already scanned.

Special thanks go to Trinity University Press director Tom Payton for his early encouragement; to editors Steffanie Stevens, Sarah Nawrocki, and Emily Schuster; and to the Semmes Foundation for funding this project.

Credits

Alamo City Golf Trails, 153 left
Baumberger Endowment, 36, 37, 38, 39, 82, 89
Charles A. Birnbaum, vi, viii
Brackenridge Park Conservancy, 21 right, 173 top, 179 top
Bill Fisher, 156, 159, 160, 161 top left
Bill Lyons, 23
Charlotte Mitchell, 147 top left, 161 bottom, 162 right, 166
City of San Antonio Municipal Archives and Records, 14, 18
City of San Antonio Parks & Recreation Department, 17, 74, 111 top right, 145 bottom right, 173 bottom
Denver Public Library, 47
Dixie Watkins III, 151 bottom left
Engineering News (June 15, 1916), 69 right
Goodson Collection, 28, 34, 57 bottom left, 57 bottom center
Heritage Group, 32
iStock/jodi4art/1189025083, i
iStock/redheadedhornet/920657440, vi
Jay Louden, 6, 21 left, 48, 94, 106, 119 top, 147 bottom right, 151 top left
Lewis F. Fisher, x, 3, 4, 35 bottom, 103 bottom, 113 right, 116, 120 left, 120 bottom right, 124 right, 147 top right, 147 bottom left, 148 right, 149, 151 top right, 151 bottom right, 152 right, 155 bottom right, 169, 170 left, 171, 172 top, 174, 176 left, 177, 179 bottom; collection, 25, 33, 35 top, 45, 46, 53, 56, 58, 60, 61, 63, 67 bottom, 70, 72, 73 top left, 73 top right, 73 center right, 75, 78, 80, 83 top, 83 center, 84, 85, 86, 87 top left, 88 right, 90 left, 91, 92, 95, 99 right, 100 top, 104, 111 center right, 111 bottom right, 112 left, 115 top right, 115 bottom right, 121 bottom, 125, 129, 130 bottom, 131 left, 132 right, 134 top right, 134 bottom right
Frontier Enterprises, 130 center
Hugh Hemphill, *San Antonio on Wheels*, 43
Library of Congress: 30 top left, 30 top right, 158 top
Martha Mood, 127
Mary M. Fisher, 135, 145 top, 145 bottom left, 146, 153 top right, 153 bottom right, 163 left, 164, 165, 168, 170 right, 172 bottom left, 172 bottom right, 175, 198
New York Public Library, 16
New York Times (May 14, 1914), 158 bottom
Notable St. Louisans (1900), 62
Pompeo Coppini, From Dawn to Sunset, 148 left
Popular Science Monthly (July 1892), 22
Ricardo Romo, 136
RVK Architects, 162 left, 163 right
San Antonio City Directory (1887–88), 26, 55
San Antonio Express-News/ZUMA Press Wire, 52, 130 top left, 133 left, 138, 140, 142, 143, 144, 150, 152 left
San Antonio Light, 42 bottom, 71, 83 bottom
San Antonio Museum of Art, 160
San Antonio Public Library Texana/Genealogy Collection, 54, 131 top right
San Antonio Water System, 69 left, 90 right, 101, 176 right
San Antonio Zoo, 73 bottom
Stillwell & Bierce Mfg. Co. Catalog (1882), 30 bottom left
Texas State Library, 114 left
University of Texas at Austin Harry Ransom Center Photography Collection, 12, 79 left, 134 left
University of Texas at San Antonio Special Collection, 29, 40, 41, 42 top, 50, 59, 64, 65, 66, 67 top, 76, 79 bottom, 87 top right, 87 bottom, 88 left, 97, 98, 99 left, 100 bottom, 103 left, 103 top right, 105 right, 110, 111 top left, 112 center, 112 right, 113 left, 114 right, 117, 118, 119 bottom, 120 top right, 121 top, 122, 124 left, 130 top right, 131 bottom, 132 left, 133 right, 137, 139, 161 top right
Vernon C. Helmke, 102 right
West Virginia University Libraries Regional History Center, 20
Witte Museum, San Antonio, 8, 11, 57 top, 57 bottom right, 79 top right, 102 left, 105 left, 108, 115 left, 126, 155 top, 155 bottom left
Worthington Pumping Engines Catalog (1883), 30 bottom right

Index

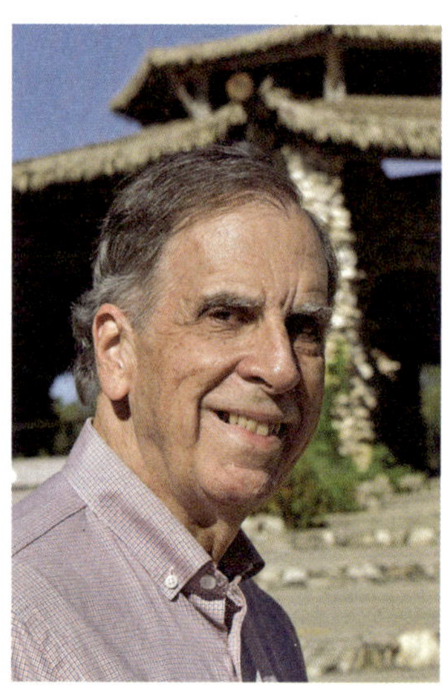

Lewis F. Fisher's books include *American Venice: The Epic Story of San Antonio's River*, *Saving San Antonio: The Preservation of a Heritage*, *Maverick: The American Name That Became a Legend*, and *Chili Queens, Hay Wagons and Fandangos: The Spanish Plazas in Frontier San Antonio*. He is a member of the board of the Brackenridge Park Conservancy.

Charles A. Birnbaum is the president and CEO of the Cultural Landscape Foundation and has been an adviser to the Brackenridge Park Conservancy since 2016.